JON E. LEWIS is a historian and regular author and editor of Mammoth titles for Constable & Robinson Ltd. He lives in Herefordshire with his wife and two children.

True War Stories

Edited by
Jon E. Lewis

Magpie Books, London

Constable & Robinson Ltd
3 The Lanchesters
162 Fulham Palace Road
London W6 9ER
www.constablerobinson.com

This edition published by Magpie Books,
an imprint of Constable & Robinson Ltd 2004

First published in the UK as *The Mammoth Book of War Diaries & Letters*
by Robinson Publishing Ltd 1998

Selection and introduction copyright © J. Lewis-Stempel 1998, 2004

A copy of the British Library Cataloguing in
Publication Data is available from the British Library

ISBN 1-84119-865-X

Printed and bound in the EU

1 3 5 7 9 10 8 6 4 2

CONTENTS

For Tristram and Freda Lewis-Stempel, in the hope that they only ever have to read about such things as ancient history.

"That is the infantry soldier's battle—very nasty—very tiring—very greasy—very hungry—very thirsty—everything very beastly. No glitter— no excitement—no nothing. Just bullet and dirt."

Lieutenant David Miller, 5 August 1901

"P.S. I am always thinking of you, lassie, night & day, you are never out of my thoughts, always remember darling that I love you dearly & don't worry too much about me, mind & write often . . ."

Private Jack Mackenzie, 3 July 1915

INTRODUCTION

Words about war come in many forms, from popular fiction to high minded scholarly histories. But for those who wish to know the reality of war, the truth is to be found in the words of those who have endured it on the frontline: the ordinary soldiers themselves.

This truth is less reliable in memoirs, written with the benefit of hindsight and plagued by the tricks of memory, than in the words of the time, written as letters and private journals. The soldier at war, at least with the rise of literacy in the eighteenth century, has been an almost compulsive penner of words as well as a wielder of swords. The letter home has sometimes been a duty, but usually a necessity—a means of maintaining personal contact, continuing the pre-war self, of communicating fears, hopes and experiences. As a result of this need to communicate, a staggering burden was put upon the postal forces of the past; in 1917 alone, the British Expeditionary Force sent 8,150,000 letters home.

Of course, mail is a two-way thing. For every letter a soldier sent, he expected at least one in return. 'Don't forget to write' is almost the standard sign-off of the soldier at war.

The blue pencil of the censor hardly inhibited the soldier-writer at all, certainly as wars wound their course. Family business, personal feelings, private thoughts were all expressed with little care to embarrassment. Not a few soldiers, wishing to give their family an accurate knowledge of their frontline position and condition resorted to code. Perhaps the most telling censorship was self-censorship, the desire to reassure loved ones that 'all's all right'. For their part military censors, usually junior officers, while always obliterating operational information let a surprising amount of critical detail through, and hardly touched battle accounts, no matter how badly their side had fared.

The keeping of private journals by soldiers has sometimes been banned by military authorities, but when this has happened soldiers have tended to honour the ban in the breach rather than the observance. The desire to record individual experience, the individual's part in history, has invariably triumphed over military rules. Understandably, given the constraints of service, most diarists have settled for a perfunctory record of things done and the state of the weather (an almost obligatory diary item for the soldier), but even such a terse list can be invaluable in conveying a picture of daily life. Other diarists have managed remarkably full descriptive journals, sometimes in the most difficult circumstances; Lieutenant E. Russell-Jones, of the British 30th Division Trench Mortar battery, composed an almost shell-by-shell account of the first day of the Battle of the Somme, which eventually ran to five closely written pages. Nor was he alone in this.

The letters and diaries in this book are taken from conflicts ranging from the American Revolutionary War (the American War of Independence, the first truly modern war) to the Persian Gulf, and thus all stem from the era of mass participation in war. This then is not a book about professional soldiers (who tend to be self-selected warriors), but a collection of the experiences of ordinary men in battle. And men rather than women, for female frontline soldiers in modern history have been almost non-existent, with such rare exceptions as the women's battalions of the Red Army and Israeli armed forces.

It is in the words of these 'ordinary' soldiers, written in pencil or ink, that the warfare of the last three hundred years is set, for us as it was for them. (In the interests of authenticity, spelling and grammatical mistakes have been left largely untouched). There is the pathos and suffering of love and homesickness, and shining moments of humanity and sacrifice. Equally, there are errors of fact, horrifying scenes, unpleasant or involuntary sentiments (racism, pleasure in the taking of life, and, to the confusion of sense, enjoyment of the thrill of battle), crudities of expression. But who can gainsay what they wrote, for they only described what they saw and felt?

This is war as soldiers have lived it.

And in their thousands died in it.

THE REVOLUTIONARY WAR [THE AMERICAN WAR OF INDEPENDENCE] 1775–83

Hostilities between the American colonialists and Britain broke out on 19 April 1775, with battles at Lexington and Concord. Although poorly equipped, the revolutionary army was able to withstand the drilled discipline of the British regulars, primarily because it was possessed by a double political imperative; it was fighting not only for a nation's independence, but the creation of a new, democratic society. (In warfare, at least, right sometimes beats might. Napoleon considered moral factors three times the worth of material ones). This political aspect also made the Revolutionary War—as it was known to the British; to Americans it is the War of Independence— the first war of the modern age. For it was largely fought without recourse to God. Unlike their soldierly predecessors, the combatants in the Revolutionary War—on both sides—did not see God's hand in every happening, and themselves as His divine instruments. They fought for rational, secular reasons, and were conscious of their mere humanity. They are consequently amongst the first soldiers to dwell, in their personal records, on their physical and psychological suffering.

There is another unmistakably modern element to the Revolutionary War; the American army, developed from the colonial anti-Indian militias, was an army of weapon-bearing citizens. No longer was military life restricted to the unfortunate few (usually poor) who were unable to resist the recruiting sergeant. The soldierly life instead became the lot of many.

Lieutenant James Waller, 1st Marine Battalion

Waller was the adjutant of the British 1st Marine Battalion. Below is his account of the battle at Bunker Hill, overlooking Boston harbour, on 17 June 1775, from a letter to his brother.

My dear Brother

Amidst the hurry and confusion of a camp hastily pitched in the field of battle, I am sat down to tell you I have escaped unhurt, where many, very many, have fallen. The public papers will inform you of the situation of the ground and the redoubt that we attacked on the heights of Charlestown. I can only say that it was a most desperate and daring attempt, and it was performed with as much gallantry and spirit as was ever shown by any troops in any age.

Two companies of the first battalion of Marines, and part of the 47th Regiment, were the first that mounted the breast-work: and you will not be displeased when I tell you that I was with those two companies, who drove their bayonets into all that opposed them. Nothing could be more shocking than the carnage that followed the storming this work. We tumbled over the dead to get at the living, who were crowding out of the gorge of the redoubt, in order to form under the defences which they had prepared to cover their retreat. In these breast-works they had artillery, which did so much mischief; but these they were obliged to abandon, being followed closely by the Light Infantry, who suffered exceedingly in the pursuit. The rebels had 5,000 to 7,000 men, covered by a redoubt, breast-works, walls, hedges, trees and the like; and the number of the corps under General Howe, (who performed this gallant business) did not amount to 1,500. We gained a complete victory, and entrenched ourselves that night, where we lay under arms, in the front of the field of battle. We lay the next night on the ground, and the following day encamped. The officers have not their marquees, but are obliged to lie in soldier's tents, they being more portable in case of our advancing.

We had of our corps one major, 2 captains, and 3 lieutenants killed; 4 captains and 3 lieutenants wounded; 2 serjeants and 21 rank and file killed, and 3 serjeants and 79 privates wounded; and I suppose, upon the whole, we lost, killed and wounded, from 800 to 1,000 men. We killed a number of the rebels, but the cover they fought under made their loss less considerable than it would otherwise have been. The army is in great spirits, and full of rage and ferocity at the rebellious rascals, who both poisoned and chewed the musket balls, in order to make them the more fatal. Many officers have died of their wounds, and others very ill: 'tis astonishing what a number of officers were hit on this occasion; but the officers were particularly aimed at.

Captain W. G. Evelyn, British 50th Foot

William Evelyn writes to a cousin, the Honourable Mrs Leveson Gower.

19 August 1775

Dear Madam,

The "Charming Nancy" [ship] returns once more to visit you, and carries with her Mrs Gage, and others of less note, whose curiosity as to the business of war is, I believe, sufficiently satisfied, and who begin to discover that a winter may be full as agreeable in London as in a town invested on all sides by thousands of armed men, cut off from all resources (I may almost say) by sea as well as by land, and threatened every day to be attacked with fire and sword. With you, who are so jealous of the honour of the British flag, I shall risk my credit, if I tell you what insults have been offered to it with impunity; but indeed they are too many to relate.

The Yankey fishermen in their whale-boats have repeatedly drove off the stock, and set fire to the houses on islands, under the guns of the fleet. They have killed a midshipman of the Admiral's (Brown), and destroyed the sloop he commanded. They have burned the lighthouse at the entrance of the harbour, killed Lieutenant Colthurst (who commanded thirty Marines), some of his men, and took the rest prisoners.

They have burned an armed sloop belonging to the "Rose" man-of-war, and we hear have taken another, called the "Diligence," belonging to the Admiral, and lastly have cut off nine-and-thirty of the "Falcon's" crew, and have taken all her boats except one; the Lieutenant has made his escape, much wounded. And to complete all, the Admiral has had a boxing-match in the streets, has got his eyes blackened, and his sword broke by a gentleman of the town, whom he had used very ill, and struck repeatedly, before he returned his blows.

A few nights ago General Clinton [British Commander] had laid the plan of giving the rebels a general *alerte*, which was to have begun at twelve o'clock, by surprising and attacking all their outposts at the same instant; and the Admiral was at the same time to have made a descent, and burned a small town on the coast. Our part succeeded as well as we could wish, indeed better, for with a few men of our regiment I had the honour of burning an advanced post of the rebels, which was more than was intended in the original plan. The Admiral's part miscarried, but for what reason I do not know. The truth is, there is no good understanding between him and the General, and he endeavours to counteract the General wherever he is concerned. Every man both in the army and navy wishes him recalled, as the service must always suffer where there is such disagreement betwixt the leaders.

Our situation has undergone very little change since the affair of the 17th of June, except the daily loss of men and officers in the hospitals. I suppose the accounts of that transaction did not meet with credit in England, and that it could not be believed that a thousand men and officers of the bravest troops in the world could in so short a time be cut off by irregulars. After two or three such instances, you good people of old England will find out that five or six thousand men are not sufficient to reduce a country of 1500 miles in extent, fortified by nature, and where every man from fifteen to fifty is either a volunteer, or compelled to carry arms; amongst whom the number of our countrymen is very great, and they are the most dangerous enemies we have to encounter. [The people of England] will find out that some other mode must be adopted than gaining every little hill at the expense of a thousand Englishmen; and if they mean to continue masters of this country, they will lay aside that false humanity towards these wretches which has hitherto been so destructive to us. They must lay aside the notion that hurting America is ruining Great Britain, and they must permit us to restore to them the dominion of the country by laying it waste, and almost extirpating the present rebellious race, and upon no other terms will they ever possess it in peace.

Major Bishop's state of health making it necessary for him to go home, I think I shall take the liberty of troubling him with this letter, though I believe he cannot get a passage in the "Charming Nancy," but goes in another which sails at the same time. I fancy George writes by him, and to his information I refer you for particulars as to us and our situation. I dare say this report of George will give you satisfaction. I shall only say in general, that he continues to improve. I dare say you are in some concern for us, from the idea of our being obliged to live upon salt pork and pease. Fresh provision is in general rather scarce, very dear, and not of the best kind; but we come in for a share now and then. We have had a good recruit within these few days; our transports having brought in upwards of two thousand sheep from some islands near New York, which is a very seasonable relief to our sick and wounded. George and I come in sometimes for a good dinner among the great people, and are particularly indebted to Lord

Percy and General Clinton. We have not the honour of an introduction to General Burgoyne.

I am strictly enjoined, whenever I write to you, not to omit presenting Adair's most respectful compliments to you and Captain Leveson. He is much taken notice of here, and in great repute from having been one of the first men who entered the enemy's works on the 17th of June. He is strongly recommended for a company, and I hope will get one, as there has been a great mortality among the Marine captains; five or six of them being already dead.

My best wishes attend you and Captain Leveson, and little family.

I am, dear Madam,

With the greatest esteem, Your faithful and obedient servant,

W. G. Evelyn

Evelyn was killed in action on 22 August 1776.

Abner Stocking, American Third Division

A young private from Connecticut, Abner Stocking was part of the American attack on British Quebec in the winter of 1775. An extract from his diary covering the "long and tedious march through the wilderness" to Quebec follows.

November 1st. Our fatigue and anxiety were so great that we were but little refreshed the last night by sleep. We started however very early, hungry and wet. Knowing that our lives depended on our speedy arrival to an inhabited country, we marched very briskly all day and even until late in the evening. We then encamped in a fine grove, but in a starving condition. Captain Goodrich's company had the good fortune to kill a large black dog, that providentially came to them at that time. They feasted on him heartily without either bread or salt. Our hunger was so great that many offered dollars for a single mouthful of bread. Such distress I never before felt, or witnessed. I anxiously turned my thoughts back to my native land, to a country flowing with milk and honey. I was surprised that I had so lightly esteemed all the good things which I there once enjoyed. Little, thought I, do we know of the value of the common blessings of Providence, until we are deprived of them. With such reflections I laid myself down on the cold, wet ground, hungry and fatigued.

November 2d. When we arose this morning many of the company were so weak that they could hardly stand on their legs. When we attempted to march, they reeled out like drunken men, having now been without provisions five days. As I proceeded I passed many sitting, wholly drowned in sorrow, wishfully placing their eyes on every one who passed by them, hoping for some relief. Such pity-asking countenances I never before beheld. My heart was ready to burst and my eyes to overflow with tears when I witnessed distress which I could not relieve. The circumstances of a young Dutchman, and his wife, who followed him through this fatiguing march, particularly excited my sensibility. They appeared to be much interested in each others welfare and unwilling to be separated, but the husband, exhausted with fatigue and hunger fell a victim to the king of terrors. His affectionate wife tarryed by him until he died, while the rest of the company proceeded on their way. Having no implements with which she could bury him she covered him with leaves, and then took his gun and other implements and left him with a heavy heart. After traveling 20 miles she came up with us.

Just at evening this day, we met cattle coming up the river, sent us for our relief. This was the most joyful sight our eyes ever beheld. The French people who drove them informed us that Colonel Arnold had arrived in their settlement two days before, with the advance party, and had purchased cattle as soon as possible and sent them on.

A cow was immediately killed and cut open in great haste; a small calf being found in her, it was divided up and eaten without further ceremony. I got a little piece of the flesh, which I eat raw with a little oat meal wet with cold water, and thought I feasted sumptuously.

November 3d. This day we proceeded on down the river about 20 miles, wading several small rivers, some of which were up to our middles. The water was terrible cold as the ground was at this time covered with snow and ice. At evening we came in sight of a house which was the first we had seen for the space of 31 days.

Our joy was inexpressible in breaking out of that dismal wilderness in which we had been so long buried, and once more beholding a country inhabited by human beings; it was like being brought from a dungeon to behold the clear light of the sun.

The French people received us with all the kindness we could wish, they treated our sick with much tenderness, and supplied us with every thing they could for our comfort. They seemed moved with pity for us and so greatly admire our patriotism and resolution, in encountering such hardships for the good of our country.

But they were too ignorant to put a just estimate on the value of freedom.

November 4. Last night we got a plenty of good beef and potatoes, but little bread could be procured. It snowed most of the night and the weather was cold. After marching down the river about 10 miles, we began to get such necessaries as we wanted; such as bread, milk, eggs, butter and most kinds of sauce. To be supplied with these articles, of which we had been so long deprived, was a great luxury.

Had we been in New-England among people of our own nation, we should not, I think, have been treated with more kindness. They readily supplied us with whatever they had to spare, and discovered much tenderness towards those of our company who were sick, or feeble. I last night lodged in a house, which I had not done before for 39 days.

Captain John Bowater, Royal Marines

Bowater writes to his patron, the Earl of Denbigh.

New York July 29th: 1777

My Lord

I begin to fear my letters are a very great Bore to your Lordship and its unfortunate at this distance, that its possible that I may persist in it for many Months before I can be Corrected at present I've a pretty decent hint, my last ten letters being as yet unanswer'd. I am tempted now by an old Acquaintance who has promised to put this in the Post Office, Capn. Parry, who is order'd home on the Recruiting service, tho I've some doubts of his taking a Nap & forgetting it. I think I inform'd your Lordship in my last of the Embarkation of the Troops, they sailed with Lord & Genl Howe the 22d Instant, and Yesterday a small Vessell Arrived from them Acquainting us that they was arrived at the Entrance of the Delaware. The Ships can go up as far as Newcastle which is but a very few miles from Philadelphia it will be an Easy conquest. I do not expect to hear of any Opposition as the Inhabitants of that Country have been long wishing for the Kings Troops. We have had in more Officers from Genl. Burgoyne with duplicates of the Account of his possessing himself of Ticonderoga the 6th: and of his being on his March towards Albany; his Army is Joyn'd by a Considerable Body of Canadians & Indians. I have also seen an Account publish'd by order of the

Congress, in which Genl Schuyler [Commander of American forces in upstate New York] Acknowledges that he Retreated with the Utmost precipitation leaving behind him all his Cannon. Baggage Stores &c. &c. he also informs them that he does not know what Route he shall take as he fears he may fall in with the Enemy. Major Hamilton with some Regular[s] & a body of Indians came Round by Oswego, & has destroy'd their grand Magazine near Carlisle. This is said to be a very Capital Bussiness. Sr. Heny. Clinton Commands at this place & at Kings bridge he has about 10 Thousand Men with him & is preparing to Enter Connecticut, so that we shall have three Considerable Armys in motion, & my next I hope will inform your Lordship of *Provinces Subdued*. Mr. Washington Remains at his strong Post at Morris Town with the long Range of blue Mountains in his Rear, it appears to me as if he means to Remain there on the defensive. We have had a great many deserters from him of late Chiefly from their light Horse a Reward of fifteen pounds has been given them with horse & Accoutrements, & five & twenty Shillings to their Infantry bringing in their Arms. I shall not be Surprized if they bring in their Generall, tho no price is as yet fixt upon him. We shall Certainly Come home this Winter, but my hopes are to Visit Boston first, the Retreat from that place sticks in my Stomach, (like Sr. John Falstaff, I hate to do any thing by Compultion). I thirst for Revenge on that place & nothing can pacify it but fire, the Harbour can be very easily destroy'd & the name should be Changed, it is said here that the presbiterian Clergy at Boston (after some pains have been taken with them) are to be made a present to the Managers of the Opera, the Reverend Colonels, Majors & Captains with their white Wiggs & Red Sashes over long black Coats will make a very pretty figure on the stage.

July 30th I am this Instant told that Lord Fielding is appointed a Lieutenant in ye Royal Fuziliers & that he is Coming to joyn his Regiment. If true I hope he will Arrive before I move from this place as I'm Acquainted with the Officers of that Corps & should do my Utmost by introducing him to the people worthy his Acquaintance & Endeavour to point out the line to him which has Recommended the most Amiable to preferment. We have been exceeding well Supply'd here with provisions and the moving off of near sixteen thousand Mouths during the last week to Pennsylvania, has lowered the price of Every Article. The beef is not half so good as in Old England & I'm glad of it, as the natives are ten times Worse, great plenty & Variety of Vegetables & fruits, but they do not Rejoyce in high flavour. Fish in Abundance, & good, &

we have been well supply'd with Turtle, & pine[apple]s, from the West Indies. The Water very bad but our Liquors are perfect. The Rebels having by stratagem, stole away General [Richard] Prescott, the Commandant at Rhode Island, has put our prisoner Mr. Lee, in high Spirrits thinking he should be Exchanged, but he has just now been told, that he is in a very different predicament & that no such thing will happen. The former is very much condemn'd for being at a lonely House four miles from his Camp with only one Centinal & a Corporals guard at a great distance. They took him & his aid de camp, [Lieutenant William] Barrington, out of their Beds with nothing but their shirts on, lapped them up in Blankets & Carried them to Providence. This happened at 12 oClock at Night & it was three in the Morning before it was discovered which prevented a pursuit. He was frequently told of the impropriety of his Situation, but despised Advice. He treated the Inhabitants with great severity & I shall not be Surprized to hear the Rebels have hanged him. We have had some small Men of War here lately from St. Augustine, the Rebels of Georgia & south Carolina have made two Attacks on that place & have been Repulsed with great loss the last time we let off the Creek Indians, who Kill'd & Scalpt one hundred & sixty of them, they do not expect another Visit. I've kept this letter unsealed to the last minute in hopes of getting some more Intelligence, but now I conclude in a hurry & Request your Lordship to make my best Respects to Lady Denbigh & Family. This will arrive, I expect at the time your Lordship is amusing your self with the destruction of the partridges, our Shooting is rather more serious. John Ladbrook [Denbigh's gamekeeper] wou'd be puzzled to bring in the game and I think your Lordship would not have so much Curiosity, if you was here.

Albigence Waldo, First Connecticut Infantry Regiment

Waldo joined the Connecticut Infantry Regiment in September 1777 as surgeon. Within three months he found himself in the midst of the agony of Valley Forge.

Journal: December 14, 1777—Prisoners & Deserters are continually coming in. The Army which has been surprisingly healthy hitherto, now begins to grow sickly from the continued fatigues they have suffered this Campaign. Yet they still show a spirit of Alacrity and Contentment not to be expected from so young

Troops. I am Sick-discontented and out of humor. Poor food hard lodging—cold weather—fatigue—Nasty Cloaths—Nasty Cookery—Vomit half my time—smoak'd out of my senses—the Devil's in't—I can't Endure it—Why are we sent here to starve and freeze—What sweet Felicities have I left at home; A charming Wife—pretty Children—Good Beds—good food—good Cookery—all agreeable—all harmonious. Here all Confusion—smoke and Cold—hunger and filthyness—A pox on my bad luck. There comes a bowl of beef soup—full of burnt leaves and dirt, sickish enough to make a Hector spue—away with it boys—I'll live like the Chameleon upon air. Poh! Poh! crys Patience within me—you talk like a fool. Your being sick Covers your mind with a Melanchollie Gloom, which makes everything about you appear gloomy. See the poor soldier, when in health—with what cheerfulness he meets his foes and encounters every hardship—if barefoot he labors thro' the Mud & every hardship—if barefoot he labors thro' the Mud & Cold with a song in his mouth extolling War & Washington—if his food be bad, he eats it notwithstanding with seeming content—blesses God for a good stomach and Whistles it into digestion. But harkee Patience, a moment—There comes a Soldier, his bare feet are seen thro' his worn out Shoes, his legs nearly naked from the tatter'd remains of an only pair of stockings, his Breeches not sufficient to cover his nakedness, his Shirt hanging in Strings, his hair disheveled, his face meager; his whole appearance pictures a person forsaken and discouraged. He comes, and crys with an air of wretchedness and despair, I am Sick, my feet lame, my legs are sore, my body cover'd with this tormenting Itch—my Cloaths are worn out, my Constitution is broken, my formed Activity is exhausted by fatigue, hunger and Cold, I fail fast. I shall soon be no more! and all the reward I shall get will be—"Poor Will is dead." People who live at home in Luxury and Ease, quietly possessing their habitation, Enjoying their Wives and Families in peace, have but a very faint idea of the unpleasing sensations, and continual Anxiety the man endures who is in a Camp, and is the husband and parent of an agreeable family. These same People are willing we should suffer every thing for their Benefit and advantage, and yet are the first to Condemn us for not doing more!!

December 15—Quit. Eat Pessimmens [persimmons], found myself better for their Lenient Operation. Went to a house, poor & small, but good food within—eat too much from being so long Abstemious, thro' want of palatables. Mankind are never truly thankfull for the Benefits of life, until they have experienced the want of them. The Man who has seen misery knows best how to enjoy good. He who is always at ease & has enough of the Blessings of common life is an Impotent Judge of the feelings of the unfortunate . . .

December 16—Cold Rainy Day, Baggage ordered over the Gulph of our Division, which were to march at Ten, but the baggage was order'd back and for the first time since we have been here the Tents were pitch'd, to keep the men more comfortable. Good morning Brother Soldier (says one to another) how are you? All wet I thank'e, hope you are so (says the other). The Enemy have been at Chestnut Hill Opposite to us near our last encampment the other side of Schuylkill, made some Ravages, kill'd two of our Horsemen, taken some prisoners. We have done the like by them . . .

December 18—Universal Thanksgiving—a roasted Pig at Night. God be thanked for my health which I have pretty well recovered. How much better should I feel, were I assured my family were in health. But the same good Being who graciously preserves me, is able to preserve them & bring me to the ardently wish'd for enjoyment of them again.

Our brethren who are unfortunately Prisoners in Philadelphia meet with the most savage and inhumane treatments that Barbarians are capable of inflicting. Our Enemies do not knock them in the head or burn them with torches to death, or flay them alive, or gradually dismember them till they die, which is customary among Savages and Barbarians. No, they are worse by far. They suffer them to starve, to linger out their lives in extreem hunger. One of these poor unhappy men, drove to the last extreem by the rage of hunger, eat his own fingers up to the first joint from the hand, before he died. Others eat the Clay, the Lime, the Stones of the Prison Walls. Several who died in the Yard had pieces of Bark, Wood, Clay and Stones in their mouths, which the ravings of hunger had caused them to take in for food the last Agonies of Life! "These are thy mercies, O Britain!"

December 21—[Valley Forge] Preparations made for huts. Provisions Scarce. Mr. Ellis went homeward—sent a Letter to my Wife. Heartily wish myself at home, my Skin & eyes are almost spoil'd with continual smoke. A general cry thro' the Camp this Evening among the Soldiers, "No Meat! No Meat!"—the Distant vales Echoed back the melancholy sound—"No Meat! No Meat!" Imitating the noise of Crows and Owls, also, made a part of the confused Musick. What have you for your Dinner Boys? "Nothing but Fire Cake and Water, Sir." At night, "Gentlemen the Supper is ready." What is your Supper Lads? "Fire Cake and Water, Sir." Very poor beef has been drawn in our Camp the greater part of this season. A Butcher bringing a Quarter of this kind of Beef into Camp one day who had white Buttons on the knees of his breeches, a soldier cries out—"There, there Tom is some sort of your fat Beef, by my soul I can see the Butcher's breeches buttons through it."

December 22—Lay excessive Cold and uncomfortable last Night—my eyes are started out from their Orbits like a Rabbit's eyes, occasion'd by a great Cold and Smoke. "What have you got for Breakfast, Lads? Fire Cake and Water, Sir." The Lord send our Commissary of Purchases may live [on] Fire Cake and water, 'till their glutted Gutts are turned to Pasteboard.

Our Division are under Marching Orders this morning. I am ashamed to say it, but I am tempted to steal Fowls if I could find them, or even a whole Hog, for I feel as if I could eat one, But the Impoverish'd Country about us, affords but little matter to employ a Thief, or keep a Clever Fellow in good humor. But why do I talk of hunger & hard usage, when so many in the World have not even Fire Cake & Water to eat.

The human mind is always poreing upon the gloomy side of Fortune, and while it inhabits this lump of Clay, will always be in any uneasy and fluctuating State produced by a thousand Incidents in common Life, which are deemed misfortunes, while the mind is taken off from the nobler pursuit of matters in Futurity. The sufferings of the Mind, and this Attention is more or less strong, in greater or lesser souls, althou' I believe that Ambition & a high Opinion of Fame, makes many People endure hardships and pains with that fortitude we after times Observe them to do. On the other hand, a despicable opinion of the enjoyments of this Life, by a continued series of Misfortunes, and a long acquaintance with Grief, induces others to bear afflictions with becoming serenity and Calmness.

It is not in the power of Philosophy however, to convince a man he may be happy and Contented if he will, with a Hungry Belly. Give me Food, Cloaths, Wife & Children, kind Heaven! and I'll be as contented as my Nature will permit me to be.

This Evening a Party with two field pieces were order'd out. At 12 of the Clock at Night, Providence sent us a little mutton, with which we immediately had some Broth made, and a fine Stomach for same. Ye who Eat Pumpkin Pie and Roast Turkies, and yet Curse fortune for using you ill, Curse her no more, least she reduce your Allowance of her favors to a bit of Fire Cake, & a draught of Cold Water, & in Cold Weather too.

December 25—Christmas—We are still in Tents—when we ought to be in huts—the poor sick, suffer much in Tents this cold weather. But now we treat them differently from what they used to be at home, under the inspection of Old Women and Doct. Bolus Linctus [Pill and Syrup]. We give them Mutton and Grogg and a Capital Medicine once in a while, to start the Disease from its foundation at once. We avoid Piddling Pills, Powders, Bolus's Linctus Cordials and all such insignificant matters whose powers are Only render'd important by causing the Patient to vomit up his money instead of his disease. But very few of the sick Men die.

December 26—The Enemy have been some Days the west Schuykill from Opposite the City to Derby. Their intentions not yet known. The City is at present pretty Clear of them. Why don't his Excellency [George Washington] rush in and retake the City, in which he will doubtless find much Plunder? Because he knows better than to leave his Post and be catch'd like a d————d fool cooped up in the City. He has always acted wisely hitherto. His conduct when closely scrutinised is uncensurable. Were his Inferior Generals as skillful as himself, we should have the Grandest Choir of Officers ever God made. Many Country Gentlemen in the interior parts of the States who get wrong information of the Affairs and State of our Camp, are very much Surprised at G Washington's delay to drive off the Enemy, being falsely inform'd that his Army, consists of double the Number of the Enemyies such wrong information serves not to keep up the spirit of the People, as they must be by and by undeceiv'd to their no small disappointment—it brings blame on his Excellency, who is deserving of the greatest encomiums; it brings disgrace on the Continental Troops, who have never evidenced the least backwardness in doing their duty, but on the contrary, have cheerfully endur'd a long and very fatiguing Campaign.

December 28—Yesterday upwards of fifty officers in Gen Greene's Division resigned their Commissions—Six or Seven of our Regiment are doing the hike to-day. All this is occasion'd by Officers Families being so much neglected at home on account of Provisions. Their Wages will not buy considerable, purchase a few trifling Comfortables here in camp, and maintain their families at home, while such extravagant prices are demanded for the common necessaries of Life—What then have they to purchase Cloaths and other necessaries with? It is a Melancholy reflection that what is of the most universal importance, is most universally neglected—I mean keeping up the Credit or Money. The present Circumstances of the Soldier is better by far than the Officers—for the family of the Soldier is provided for at the public expense if the Articles they want are above the common price—but the Officer's family are obliged not only to beg in the most humble manner for the necessaries of Life—but also to pay for them afterwards at the most exorbitant rates—and even in this manner, many of them who depend entirely on their Money, cannot procure half the material comforts that are wanted in a family—this produces continual letters of complaint from home.

When the Officer has been fatiguing thro wet and cold and returns to his tent where he finds a letter directed to him from his Wife, fill'd with the most heart aching tender Complaints, a Woman is capable of writing . . . What man is there—who has the least regard for his family—whose soul would not shrink within him? Who would not be disheartened?

December 29—Snow'd all day pretty briskly . . . So much talk about discharges among the officers—and so many are discharged—his Excellency lately expressed his fears of being left Alone with the Soldiers only. Strange that our Country will not exert themselves for his support, and save so good—so great a Man from entertaining the least anxious doubt of their Virtue and perseverance in supporting a Cause of such unparallel'd importance!

Lieutenant W. Hale, Grenadier Guards

The letter is addressed to Hale's parents.

Neversunk, 4th July 1778

General Clinton's dispatches will acquaint you of an action on the 28th June, of which our Battalion bore the principal part. Lee, acquainted with the temper of our present Commander, laid a snare which perfectly succeeded. The hook was undisguised with a bait, but the impetuosity of Clinton swallowed it . . . The Grenadiers were ordered to march to the heights of which the Rebels were already possessed; such a march I may never again experience. We proceeded five miles in a road composed of nothing but sand which scorched through our shoes with intolerable heat; the sun beating on our heads with a force scarcely to be conceived in Europe, and not a drop of water to assuage our parching thirst; a number of soldiers were unable to support the fatigue, and died on the spot. A Corporal who had by some means procured water, drank to such excess as to burst and expired in the utmost torments. Two became raving mad, and the whole road, strewed with miserable wretches wishing for death, exhibited the most shocking scene I ever saw.

At length we came within reach of the enemy who cannonaded us very briskly, and afterwards marching through a cornfield saw them drawn up behind a morass on a hill with a rail fence in front and a thick wood on their left filled with their light chosen troops. We rose on a small hill commanded by that on which they were posted in excellent order, when judge of my inexpressible surprise, General Clinton himself appeared and crying out "Charge, Grenadiers, never heed forming"; we rushed on amidst the heaviest fire I have yet felt. It was no longer a contest for bringing up our respective companies in the best order, but all officers as well as soldiers strove who could be foremost, to my shame I speak it. I had the fortune to find myself after crossing the swamp with three officers only, in the midst of a large body of Rebels who had been driven out of the wood by the 1st Battalion of Grenadiers, accompanied by not more than a dozen men who had been able to keep up with us; luckily the Rebels were too intent on their own safety to regard our destruction.

The column which we routed in this disorderly manner consisted of 4000, the force on our side not more than 800. In the mean time the pursuit of this column brought us on their main Army led by Washington, said by deserters to be 16,000. With some difficulty we were brought under the hill we had gained, and the most terrible cannonade ensued and lasted for above two hours, at the distance of 600 yards. The shattered remains of our Battalion being under cover of our hill suffered little, but from thirst and heat of which several died, except some who preferred the shade of some trees in the direct range of shot to the more horrid tortures of thirst . . .

Solomon Downe, American Navy

Diary: Tuesday 3 October, 1780
Sailed from Providence on board the Sloop *Hope*, mounting seven guns. Wind at N. E. drizzly, dirty weather. Outsailed Mr. John Brown in his famous boat. Put about for Capt. Munro, and take Mr. Brown and Capt. S. Smith on board, who dine with us. Some time after noon Capt. Munro comes on board, and a few glasses of good wishes founded on Hope having circled, Col. Nightingale, &c. depart, and we proceed on our course . . .

11 October 1780

Whilst at Dinner, a Sail cried. Immediately give chase, and discover another. One, a sloop which bears down upon us; the other a brig. Make every preparation for an engagement; but, on approaching and hailing the Sloop, she proved to be the *Randolph*, Capt. Fosdick from New London,—mounting 18 four pounders, 140 tons. The Brig, with only two guns, her prize from England, taken at 8 o'clock this morning.—Capt. Fosdick says her Cargo amounted to #20,000 Sterling. What good and ill fortune were consequent on that capture!—Hard for those poor fellows, their tedious Voyage being just accomplished, thus to have their brightening prospect clouded in a moment. If Virtue is the doing good to others, privateering cannot be justified upon the principles of Virtue;—though I know it is not repugnant to The Laws of Nations, but rather deemed policy amongst warring powers thus to distress each other, regardless of the suffering individual. But however agreeable to, and supportable by the rights of war; yet, when individuals come thus to despoil individuals of their property, 'tis hard:—the cruelty then appears, however, political.

12 October 1780

Early this morning two sail in sight, a Ship and Brig. Chase them chief of the day to no purpose. We conclude they sail well, and may be bound to Philadelphia.—Lat. 39°.6″. Soundings 19 fathoms. Lost sight of the *Randolph* by the chase.

13 October 1780

A foggy morning and Scotch mist. Clears away pleasant. Lat. 39°.31′. This Afternoon a Sloop discovered under the lee bow standing before the wind: All hands upon deck preparing for the chase:—but little wind so the oars are to be plied. I must go and see how we come on.—Night obliges us to give over the pursuit.

14 October 1780

A sail seen from Mast-head; proves a Ship. We chase. Catch a Herring-Hog, which makes us a fine Breakfast, and dinner for the whole crew. Another sail heaves in sight. Upon a nearer approach the Ship appears to be of the line. Several in sight. Towards evening signal guns heard. We take them to be men of War, standing in, N. W. by W. Longitude by reckoning 73°.30″. Lat. 39°.34″. 26 fathoms. A pleasant moon-light Evening. Spend it in walking the Quarter Deck.

15 October 1780

A pleasant day. See a Sail to windward; as she rather approaches us we lie a hull for her. I think it is more agreeable waiting for them, than rowing after them. Get a fishing line under way: catch a Hake and a few Dog-fish. It being Sunday, try the efficacy of a clean shirt, in order to be something like folks ashore. Give chase, as the vessel comes down rather slow On approaching discover her to be a Snow. She hauls her wind and stands from us;—sails very heavy, and Capt. Munro is sanguine in the belief we shall make a prize of her. Get everything in readiness to board her. There seems something awful in the preparation for an attack, and the immediate prospect of an action. She hauls up her courses and hoists English Colours. I take my station in the Cabin; where, remain not long before I hear the Huzza on deck in consequence of her striking. Send our boat for the Captain & his papers. She sailed from Kingston, Jamaica, upwards of 40 days since, in a fleet, and was bound to New York: Capt. William Small, Commander. She has ten men on board and four excellent four pounders. Her Cargo consists of 149 Puncheons, 23 Hogsheads, 3 Quarter Casks and 9 Barrels of Rum, and 20 Hogsheads Muscovado Sugar. Send two prize Masters and ten men on board, get the prisoners on board our Vessel, and taking the prize in tow, stand towards Egg Harbour. We hardly know what to do with the prize: the wind shifting a little we stand to the eastward.

16 October 1780

Keep an eastern course, to try to get her into our harbour if possible. Now we are terribly apprehensive of seeing a sail. About sunset a sail seen from mast-head, which excites no small anxiety. Cast off the Snow's hawser, &c.—however night coming on and seeing no more of said sail, pursue our course. Sound, 42 fathoms of water . . .

19 October 1780

The Snow in sight this morning; run along side and take her in tow again. . . Lat. 40°.30″. At this rate the West Indies will bring us up sooner than Martha's Vineyard or Nantucket. 49 fathoms. Have our Pistols hung up in the Cabin, to be in readiness for the prisoners, should they take it into their heads to rise upon the watch in the night . . .

Sunday, 22 October 1780
Very foggy. What wind there is, ahead. Weigh Anchor, and out
oars. A fair gentle breeze springs from the South. Pass through
Bristol Ferry way with hard tugging about the middle of the
afternoon: come to Anchor in the Bay, but where rendered uncertain by the fog having come up again . . .

23 October 1780
Early, after breakfast, we set off again in the boat, with the
Compass, being still surrounded with an excessive fog. Run ashore
to the Eastward of Nayat Point, and mistake it for Connimicut:
however, arrive at Providence about 11 o'clock, it having cleared
off very pleasant. Thus ends our short, but tedious cruise. At
sunset the Sloop and Snow arrive, firing 13 cannon each.

Lieutenant Benjamin Gilbert,
5th Massachusetts Regiment

Gilbert joined the Revolution as a teenage minuteman in 1775.
The letters below, written whilst Gilbert served as an infantry
subaltern, are from the decisive year in the war, 1781, when the
American cause—aided by the French army and fleet—went
from malaise to triumph.

Elk[ton, MD] 11th April 1781
Honoured Parents/
   I once more attempt to inform you of my situation, and
health . . .
   If I servive this Campain in this unhealthy country I shall not
Expect to see you under two or three years.
   Our situation is pecularly unhappy as the Troops that are with
us have not drawn one half of their winter Cloths and received but
one month pay for more than a year, and the People in this part of
the Continent are not given to acts of Hospitallity. Therefore I
think I shall be very unhappy in this Comand, and how I shall
furnish myself with Cloths I know not.
   Compliments etc.
Maubin Hills 18 July 1781
Honoured Parents
   Since writing my last, the Army under Marquis de la fayatte
moved towards James Town, where Cornwallis encamped his
Troops and on the 6th Instant, a small part of our army, Detached

as a front Guard, fell in with the Enemies Piquet, and drove them into their lines, on which their whole army formed for Action, began the attackt on our detachments. Our Army being at that time from Eight to fifteen miles from the field of action, no immediate support could be lent them, but they maintaining their groung with unexampled Braverey, kept the Enemy at such a distance, as gave time for six Hundred of Pensilvania line to come to their assistance. The Enemies front line at that time conssisted of 2100, our 700 often changing 4 or 5 shots of a side. The Enemy made a violent charge with Bayonetts, and being 3 to 1 they flanked our troops to that degree, that they gave way, and retreated with the loss of all their Dead and two field peices. Our killed, wounded, and missing is 111, some of which Deserted to the enemy in time of Action. The Enemies loss we are not able to assertain, but are informed it is very considerable. Next Day they crossed the river, leaving all our wounded that fell into their hands on the place of Action. After they had Crossed the River the foot marched toward Portsmouth, and the Horse thro the Center of the Country towards Carolina, where we are in Daily expectations of marching. But I dread the march, our men having not more than one pair of shoes or Hose to Eight men, and the sands are so hot in the middle of the Day that it continually raises Blisters on the mens feet.

Compliments etc.

To Lieutenant Park Holland

[August 1781]

Dear Park

I shall not attempt to give you any perticular account of the strength or situation of the Enemy. They ly at York[town] and in its Vicinity. Our army are lying in different parts of Kings County upwards of thirty miles from them, and are daily marching. Our Provision is very Indifferent but the duty is not hard. We are Ragged and destitute of Cash which prevents our makeing so great an aquaintence as we should do, were we other ways provided for. The Inhabitants are Exceeding polite and Hospitable which ennables us to make more acquaintance than could be expected with persons in our situation. The Ladies are exceeding Amouris but not So Beautifull as at the Northward, tho there is some rare Beauties amongst them. Amouris Intrigues and Gallantry are every where approved of in this State, and amongst the Vulgar any man that is given to concupcience may have his fill. The

Ladies are Exceeding fond of the Northern Gentleman, Esspecially those of the Army. Daily Invitations are given by the Inhabitints for our Gentleman to dine and dring grogg with them where they are generally entertained with musick and the conversation of the Ladies. Yet notwithstanding these diversions, my want of Clothes and Cash and the unwholesomeness of the Climent makes me anxious to return to Head Quarters where I shall Injoye the Company and agreable conversation of my old friends. Please to make my Compliments to the Gentleman of the 5th Especially Ensign Carlton. Captain Benson and Lieutenant Smith presents there Compliment to all the Gentleman.

To his father

Camp near Williamsburg
September 19th 1781

Honoured Sir,

Military affairs in this Quarter bears a more favourable Aspect than it has for some time passt. Count De Grass has arived from the West Indias with Twenty eight sail of the line and five Thousand two Hundred french Troops. His Excellency has Arived from Whites plains with Count Rochambeau and has Eight Thousand Troops French and Americans on their way for this place, some of which are arived, the others hourly Expected. Nine Ships of the line with six Hundred french Troops and a large Quantity of Artillerey have arived in the James River. What Troops Pensilvania Maryland and Virginia have Raised this sumer are with us so that a morderate computation makes our strength sixteen Thousand Regulars beside Artilerey Cavalry and Militia. The French fleet has shut Lord Cornwallis into York River and he is fortifying himself in york Town wheir we shall soon lay seige to him. If the French fleet continues long enough and the smile of Providence we shall give as good an account of him as we did of Burgoyine. Nothing but the warmest Expectations of capturing Cornwallis keeps my spirits hight, my Cloths being almost worne out, and no money to get new ones, having Received but 25 Dollars since March Eighty which passed six for one and no expectations of getting any sone.

The British under General Cornwallis surrendered at Yorktown on 19 October. It was the effective end of the Revolutionary War.

THE WARS WITH REVOLUTIONARY FRANCE & THE NAPOLEONIC WARS 1793–1815

In 1779, the French overthrew the ancien regime *of Louis XVI, to install in its place a radical democratic republic under the National Assembly. By desire the French Revolution was anti-militaristic; by the necessity of its own survival, however, it was obliged to arm itself with something more than the untrustworthy remnant of the regular army it inherited. Tens of thousands of citizens in the grip of revolutionary fervour rallied to the defence of the republic against its enemies from within and without, but when their numbers proved insufficient the* levee en masse— *conscription was introduced. Well-trained, freed from aristocratic hindrances—officers were promoted on merit not class or wealth— and fired up on a transcendent political ideology, the new model French army defeated all comers.*

Pre-eminent among the generals who brought victory, was the Corsican, Napoleon Bonaparte. As military success fell into Bona-parte's hands, so did political power. In the 1799 coup d'etat of 18th Brumaire, Bonaparte appointed himself First Consul of France. Five years later he crowned himself Emperor, before leading out the Grand Armee *on an epic decade of campaigning. If, in truth, the* Grand Armee *was not the idealistic Revolutionary Army of the 1790s, but an instrument of French aggrandizement, it still contained enough political spirit to achieve the seeming impossible. Half of Europe was conquered. Only in Spain, where the* Grand Armee *encountered a determined British expeditionary force under Wellington, did it suffer defeat. (Wellington's force was re-supplied by the Royal Navy, master of all it surveyed following its 1805 defeat of the French fleet at Trafalgar.)*

And then, in 1812, France invaded Russia. It would prove the turning point in the "Napoleonic Wars." Caught by the early onset of winter, the French army starved and froze to death. Those who escaped these fates were slaughtered by Cossack horsemen. Out of an invasion force of 450,000 only 10,000 survived. Pushed back into Germany, Napoleon was defeated at Leipzig by allies-turned-enemies, Austria and Prussia. Disgrace inevitably followed, and in 1814 Napoleon was forced to abdicate.

There was one more grasp at glory. Napoleon returned to power in 1815 to head the remnant of his armies against an Allied force under Wellington and the Prussian Blücher. The two sides met at a village in Belgium: Waterloo.

Corporal George Robertson, Royal Artillery

A regular soldier, Robertson was part of the British–Hanoverian army sent to mainland Europe to drive the French from the Netherlands. He participated in the storming of "Valencine" [Valenciennes], one of the expeditionary force's few victories.

Woolwich, February 26, 1793

Dear Mother

I have just received orders for Germeny under the command of the Duke of York, with 2,200 foot guards. We expect to embark tomorrow to go with His Royal Highness as a Bodyguard of British Heroes. We are to lead the Dutch Prushen and Hanover Troops into the field, as there is none equal to the British Army. We are chosen troops sent by His Majesty to show an example to the other Troops, to go in front, & lead the combined army against the French which consists of 150,000 able fighten men. You may judge if we shall have anything to dow. I had the pleasure to conquer the French last war; but God knows how it will be this war. I cannot expect to escape the Bullets of my enemies much longer, as non has ever entred my flesh as yet. To be plain with you and not dishearten you, I don't expect to come off so cleare as I did last war. But it is death or honour. I exspeck to be a Gentleman or a Cripel. But you shall never see me destress you. If I cannot help you, I never shall destress you.

Dear Mother, I take my family with me. Where I go, they most go. If I leave them, I should have no luck. My wife and two children is in good health, & in good spirits, fear not for us. I hope God will be on our side.

Valencine, August 1, 1793

I received your kind letter and am happy to find you are yet in the land of the Living and well. Dear Mother and Townsmen, I have great news for you. On the night of the 23rd, our British Troops stormed the Outworks of Valencine, and took them; killed and wounded 500 French; our lose about ten only. The Elements was like on fire with Bomb shell. Never did my eyes behold the like before; and on the 26th, we heard a horn blow in the Town for a parley, and a flag of Truce to come upon Terms, which was agreed on; on these terms, that the British Troops shall have possession of the Town & Garrison and no other. On the 1st day of August, we enter the Town with two 6-pounders and a silk Flag at the head of the British Grenadiers. This is over. Thank God. The number killed in that time in the town is 6,000, and a number of Women and Children. The British Artillery manned a Battery of eight 12-pounders which hurt them more than all the firing troops. I commanded one of those Guns one day on the Battry, when a 24-pound shot went thro' one of my men's shoulders & brock my Gun wheel. The blood and flesh of the man was all over my Cloas. The pipol in the Camp thought we was all gone. Mother, you cannot think how happy my wife and children was to see me return safe to my Tent. Every time I went to the Battery, I took leave of my wife & family. We staid 24 hours at a time; and when we returned, it was the same as new life to us both . . .

I will do more yet for my King and Country's saik. My country shall never be stained by me. After things is settled hear, we exspect to march for Dunkirk, to besiege that Town & Garrison. Then we shall winter, and rest till the Spring; and then I hope for Parris. Keep a good heart at home; we will conquer our enemies, and bring them down. May the British flag ever flourish over the world . . .

God bless you, Dear Mother, adu, adu, God bless you. I hope my Townsmen will drink sucksess to George Robertson.

Your ever loving Son,
Geo. Robertson

J. Wilkinson, HMS *Queen*, Royal Navy

Wilkinson describes the "Glorious First of June" naval action between the British and French fleets off Ushant in June 1794.

Spithead July 1794

Honourable Sir I make bold to write theas few lins to you hopeing thay will fiend you and your Farther Brothers and Sister all well as

thay leave me rather better thanks be to god for it—now Sir to leet
you know that I belong to H M Ship the Queen of 98 guns as
Steward to the Whard Roome and to leet you know Sir that I Have
bene to the Westindies in this ship and to leet you know that i was
in the action of the 29 and the first of June against the French fleet
consisting of 29 sail of the line and we ad but 26 sail of the line and
on the 29 in the morning a bought eight oclock we came to action
and we ingaged for Five howers successfull as hard as we cold fire
till at last the french run from us then we turnd two and prapaired
hower riging and masts

then on the First of June we came to action againe a bought eight
oclock in the morning and it lasted till two the sameday and to leet
you know that hower ship ad to run the gantlet twice throw the
french lins and we ad no less then three ships uppon us at one time
but by the help of god we made thiem strike to us and in the time of
action we sunk two of the french ships one of 80 guns one of 74
guns and a bought one thousend men sunk with the ships and in
one ship that we tooke we cild right houte five hundred men ded
and in hower ship we ad one hundred and thirtey eight cild and
wounded and to leet you know that at the gun that i was quarted at
we ad 4 shot Come in and cild two men and wounded five do witch
I was—wounded in my left harm and in my brest—but thanks be
to god im a grate deal better and to leet you know that hower
Captn. lost is leg and since dead and the Marster of the ship e was
cild right hout in the time of action

and to let you know that on the 28 of June sume of hower ships
ingaged a bought eight oclock at night but the best of hower fleet
cud not come to action as the french fleet was to windward of us
but we lay uppon the decks at hower guns all night for two nights
and three days as the french fleet still ceept in sight and to let you
know that before the action we tooke 10 ships that the french ad
taken from us and we sunk theiam all and one french brig of 14
guns we captured and a ship of 22 guns and a cutter of 14 guns and
we took all the french prisoeners houte and then sunk theain all

but to leet you know that we have brought 6 sail of the french
line of Battleships into portsmouth harbour whear the King and
Queen as bene to see theiam and lykewise to see hower shatterd
ships—Sir in the time of action you would of thort the ellement ad
been all on fire and the shot flying a bought hower eds 42pr and
case shot and dubbeleded shot it was all the same as a hale storme a
bought the ship

but to let you know that we are all ready for sea againe and I
believe that we shall go in 6 or eight days time from heare and to

leet you know that admiral gardner is hower Commander and i have bene this three years at sea and as but ad my foot on shore 5 times please to be so good as to give my best respects to Salley Borroues and to Cobbert Parsons familey and all that I know of you please at Kirby woodhous and to Mr.Mills if a live as e is some relation of mine I ad liked to of forgot im but i hope you will not forgat to spake of me and to leet theiam know whear I am but I hope this whar will not belong and then I meane to cum down to see you plas god to settel at home witch I make no doupt but what you wood be glad to see your old servant once more all tho it is so long since that i live with you as a boy you may of forgoot me but I lived with you when Mearcy seaman was your houscceeper

Jno. Wilkinson I am your mast on board H.M.ship obt and Homble sert the Queen of 90 guns Jno. Wilkinson Spithead portsmouth Mr. Jno. Clark Farmer in Kirkby woodhouse Near Cirkby Nottinghamshire.

Sam, Royal Navy

A letter to his father, written in the aftermath of the British naval victory at Trafalgar.

Royal Sovereign

Honoured Father,

This comes to tell you that I am alive and hearty except three fingers; but that's not much, it might have been my head. I told brother Tom I should like to see a greadly battle, and I have seen one, and we have peppered the Combined rarely; and for matter of that, they fought us pretty tightish for French and Spanish. Three of our mess are killed, and four more of us winged. But to tell you the truth of it, when the game began, I wished myself at Warnborough with my plough again; but when they had given us one duster, and I found myself snug and tight, I set to in good earnest, and thought no more about being killed than if I were at Murrell Green Fair; and I was presently as busy and as black as a collier. How my fingers got knocked overboard I don't know; but off they are, and I never missed them till I wanted them. You see, by my writing, it was my left hand, so I can write to you and fight for my King yet. We have taken a rare parcel of ships, but the wind is so rough we cannot bring them home, else I should roll in money, so we are busy smashing 'em, and blowing 'em up wholesale.

Our dear Admiral Nelson is killed! so we have paid pretty sharply for licking 'em. I never set eyes on him, for which I am both sorry and glad; for, to be sure, I should like to have seen him—but then, all the men in our ship who have seen him are such soft toads, they have done nothing but blast their eyes, and cry, ever since he was killed. God bless you! chaps that fought like the Devil, sit down and cry like a wench. I am still in the *Royal Sovereign*, but the Admiral [Collingwood] has left her, for she is like a horse without a bridle, so he is in a frigate that he may be here and there and everywhere, for he's as *cute* as here and there one, and as bold as a lion, for all he can cry!—I saw his tears with my own eyes, when the boat hailed and said my lord was dead . . .

Midshipman R.F. Roberts, Royal Navy

Roberts aboard *Victory* writes to his parents describing the Battle of Trafalgar.

> *Victory at sea off Trafalgar, 22 October 1805*

I have just time to tell you that we had a desperate engagement with the enemy, and, thank God, I have so far escaped unhurt. The Combined Fleet came out of Cadiz with a determination to engage and blow us up (as the prisoners say) out of the water, but they are much—very much—mistaken.

It was as hard an action, as allowed by all on board ship, as ever was fought. There were but three left alive on the Quarterdeck, the enemy fired so much grape and small shot from the rigging, there was one ship so close to us that we could not run out our guns their proper length. Only conceive how much we must have smashed her, every gun was trebly shotted for her. We have a great many killed and dangerously wounded—21 amputations.

This morning the enemy are out of sight and we have the prizes in tow, going for Gibraltar. The rascals have shot away our mizen mast, and we are much afraid of our main and fore-masts. The Royal Sovereign has not a stick standing—a total wreck. It was she that began the action in a noble manner, engaging four of them at the same time. Two of the enemy blew up and one sank. You can have no conception whatsoever what an action between two fleets is; it was a grand but an awful sight indeed; thank God we are all so well over it.

Admiral Nelson was shot early in the action by a musket ball from the enemy's top, which struck him a little below the shoulder, touched the rib and lodged near his heart. He lived about two and a half hours after; then died without a groan. Every ship that struck, our fellows ceased firing and gave three cheers like Noble Britons.

Adam Neale, British Army

An army surgeon, Neale writes home describing the winter retreat of 20,000 British troops, to Corunna in Portugal, pursued by 250,000 French.

Lugo, 5 January 1809

It was a sad sight to behold the wretched state of the troops. A degree of spirit approaching to mutiny was manifest among them, owing to the excessive fatigue which they had undergone, and the disgrace, as they deemed it, of running away from the enemy.

Early on the morning of the 3rd, we continued our march up to the mountain. The road is here cut through the rocks. On the summit which is the boundary of Gallicia we had to scramble through deep snows.

Broken waggons and carriages, money-carts, dead animals, and the bodies of human beings, who had perished from the inclemency of the weather during the night, strewed the way for miles. Never had I conceived, much less witnessed, so awful a scene. In one baggage-waggon, which had overturned, an unfortunate soldier's wife, with several children, were frozen to death. But why dwell on these horrors; the bare idea of which must make you shudder?

Corunna, 11 January 1809

On the morning of the 9th, amid a storm of wind, sleet, and rain, more severe than I can recollect ever to have experienced, we proceeded to Guitterez. Our poor soldiers, drenched to the skin, and covered with mud, lengthened out their line of march. I felt as if scalding drops of lead pelted my face. It was with the greatest difficulty I could keep my seat on horseback. Every human being fled, "the fenceless villages were all forsaken". Our soldiers absolutely lay down and died in the ditches without a struggle. Few women were now to be seen, the greater part had perished.

I halted for half an hour in the rain, but was so stiff, that, on attempting to remount I fell down, and could with difficulty get on my legs. Here the troops had some salt beef and rum issued. Not having any fires to cook the beef, much of it was thrown away; but the rum was drunk greedily, and the powers of their stomachs being almost gone, I saw them fall down, after drinking it, in a comatose state. Death, I have no doubt, followed in an hour or two.

at sea, 19 January 1809

A severe engagement has taken place on the heights above Corunna. Our sick, artillery, and dragoons commenced embarking. The enemy had got possession of the heights above St Lucia, from which he opened a spirited fire upon the ships in the inner harbour. Nothing was now to be seen but the most dreadful confusion. The transports slipped their cables, and put to sea instantly; many running foul of each other, and carrying away yards, bowsprits, and rigging. Four or five ships ran aground on the rocks, and bilged. A 74-gun ship immediately stood in towards the French batteries, and opened her guns upon them. Having put to sea, we saw, after it became dark, a considerable body of light streaming along the horizon.

I am myself a good deal indisposed, and not much the better for being shut up in a little, noisome, damp cabin, with six other officers. Four of them are extremely ill, and generally raving all night long. Their complaints are the consequence of over-exertion; and their distempered and horror-struck imaginations are perpetually pursuing some dreadful hallucination connected with the casualties of war, famine, and shipwreck. It blows so violent a gale that I can write no longer. Farewell.

Lieutenant G. Crompton, 66th Regiment

Crompton writes to his mother, describing the Battle of Albuera, Spain, on 16 May 1811, when an allied Spanish-Portuguese-British force was attacked by the French.

A few lines, my dearest Mother, I, in haste sit down and write, to say, that under the protection of Almighty God, I have escaped unhurt in one of the severest actions that ever was contested between France and England; to describe the Horrors that were witnessed on the ever memorable 16th of May would be impossible, but as the part the unfortunate 1st Brigade of the 2 Division took on that day might be a little interesting to you, I will relate it as far as I am able.

I think it was about 10 o'clock a.m. when the French menaced an attack on our left; we immediately moved to support it. It proved, however, to be a feint, and the Right of the Line was destined to be the spot (Oh, never to be effaced from my mind) where Britons were to be repulsed; 3 solid columns attacked our regiment alone. We fought them till we were hardly a Regiment. The Commanding Officer was shot dead, and the two Officers carrying the Colours close by my side received their mortal wounds. In this shattered state, our Brigade moved forward to charge. Madness alone would dictate such a thing, and at that critical period Cavalry appeared in our rear. It was then that our men began to waver, and for the first time (and God knows I hope the last) I saw the backs of English soldiers turned upon French. Our Regiment once rallied, but to what avail! we were independent of Infantry: out-numbered with Cavalry. I was taken prisoner, but re-taken by the Spanish Cavalry.

Oh, what a day was that. The worst of the story I have not related. Our Colours were taken. I told you before the 2 Ensigns were shot under them; 2 Sergeants shared the same fate. A Lieutenant seized a Musket to defend them, and he was shot to the heart; what could be done against Cavalry?

Adieu, my Dear Mother, for the present. Give my most affectionate and kindest love to my Father, Annie, William and all at home, and believe me to be your most affectionate Son.

[Signed] G. Crompton,
A miserable Lt. of the unfortunate 66th Regt.

P.S.—The Fuziler Brigade afterwards came on, also the other Brigades in the Division with some Spaniards and Portuguese beat back the French and gained a complete Victory.

Ensign John Mills, 1st Battalion, Coldstream Guards

Mills served in Wellington's army in the Iberian Peninsula from 1811 to 1814. Throughout he kept a detailed diary. The excerpt below records the siege of Burgos.

Diary: September 18th [1812]. We moved to within half a league of Burgos and after remaining a long time under our arms and trying forty men and three women by Court Martial for stealing onions, we bivouacked in a strong field and one of the coldest winds I ever felt. We were near the works which consist of an unfinished work, a strong redoubt and the Castle. The latter appears to be tremendously strong—ditch within ditch and palisaded. They have

thrown stones within the tower of the castle and have made it solid
so that shot cannot hurt it. They have several guns on it. They
were driven out of the town and there was a great deal of firing
with musketry on both sides. They command a great part of the
town and fire at people in the streets. Rain.

September 19th. We moved in the morning by a circuitous route to
avoid the fire of the forts to the other side of the town for the
pleasurable purpose of working. Major Cocks with the Light
companies of the Highland Brigade supported by General Pack's
Portuguese Brigade took possession of the unfinished work without French opposition. They retired into the redoubt and kept up a
heavy fire at our men. At eight o'clock the redoubt was ordered to
be stormed. The 42nd, as the strongest regiment in the Division,
was selected for the purpose, supported by the Light companies of
the Highland Brigade and General Pack's Portuguese Brigade. At
eight o'clock they advanced to storm but the Portuguese who
thought to raise their spirits by it began to shout at two hundred
yards distance and thereby drew the enemy's fire upon them. The
42nd advanced gallantly and planted their ladders which proved to
be too short and after persisting for some time they were beat back.
They returned again and with Major Cocks with his Light
Infantry companies got in first, his men scrambling over without
ladders. The French then gave way and after some little time the
fort was ours. The loss was about 250. We made 70 prisoners and
bayonetted a great many. There were 500 in the place, the
remainder of whom made their escape by the covered way into
the Castle. The working parties then began and dug some trenches
and suffered but little during the night.

September 20th. The works continue. They find it difficult to
throw their shells into the trenches, as we are working so near
them. They fire a great deal and do not do much execution. They
are not sparing of their ammunition. The garrison is said to consist
of two thousand men. The Governor is a General of Division who
volunteered his service. I rode into the town. Some parts of it are
unsafe as the Castle commands many of the streets. It appears to be
a very old town, the streets narrow. It appeared to have been a
good deal knocked about as the French had destroyed a vast
quantity of stores and had pillaged some of the houses. The
inhabitants looked sulky and Frenchified, as it never could till
lately have entered into their imagination that an English army
would have entered the town.

September 21st. At twelve I went into the trenches and remained there till six. They fired at us on going in and coming out, as in this place it is quite exposed. The moon is at the full and the nights are as bright as day. We worked at a communication and a one-gun battery. The news of today is that Caffarelli has joined Clausel with 7,000 men and the enemy have pushed on their advanced posts 1 league. The covering party is very much exposed and have lost a good many men today. General Hulse's horses etc., were sold today.

September 22nd. The works go on well; we have increased the fire and our musketry and in some degree silenced theirs. They fired from behind some oxen which graze on the outside of the Castle and our Riflemen were obliged to shoot them which otherwise would not have been fair. The 5th and 7th Divisions have advanced and the enemy retired again eight leagues up the Vittoria road. At twelve at night an attempt was made to storm the outer works of the castle. The Portuguese were to have attacked it in the flank, whilst four hundred men from this Division escaladed the wall in front. A party of 130 of the Brigade of Guards led the way with the ladders. The enemy opened a tremendous fire, on which the Germans filed off to the right and the Scotch followed them. Our men got the ladders up with some difficulty under a heavy fire from the top of the wall, but were unable to get to the top. Hall of the 3rd Regiment [3rd Foot Guards] who mounted first was knocked down. Frazer tried and was shot in the knee. During the whole of this time they kept up a constant fire from the top of the wall and threw down bags of gunpowder and large stones. At last, having been twenty-five minutes in the ditch and not seeing anything of the other parties they retired having lost half their numbers in killed and wounded. 3 officers were wounded. The Portuguese failed in their attempts. Thus ended the attack which was almost madness to attempt.

September 23rd. Lord Wellington sent in a flag of truce for the purpose of getting our wounded and dead. A cessation of operations was agreed upon for three hours. They brought the wounded up in stretchers half way up the hill, and lent our men the stretchers to carry them on, which were returned in like manner. They had treated our wounded in the kindest manner, giving them soup and things to eat and dressing their wounds. The body of Major Laurie who commanded the party was found and was the only one that was stripped. For an hour after the truce was at an end they did not fire a shot. They seemed confident about holding out the place till they were relieved which they looked upon as certain. At six at night I went to the trenches and continued till one. The moon did not rise till late which made it much more pleasant. The party was at work finishing a battery. I had but two of my party hit though they threw several shells into the very place they were at work. It appears we are undertaking this siege without sufficient means of any sort. There are but two regular engineers employed. We have but eighteen hundred round shot and everything else in proportion. They have discovered that one of the batteries is enfiladed as well as a communication. A party broke ground near the suburbs. It is to be carried on by sap, and the outer wall is to be blown in.

September 24th. Our batteries were to have opened this morning consisting of 3 eighteens and 2 howitzers to throw red hot shot into the convent, but the enemy had in the night mounted two fresh guns which enfiladed ours and it was necessary to make some alterations which will prevent their opening as soon as was expected. They seem to have slackened their fire, particularly during the night. I rode again into Burgos for the purpose of looking at the Cathedral, a perfect specimen of Florid Gothic. The steeples are particularly light and elegant. The interior is ornamented by some admirable carving in the highest state of perfection. The chapels were richly ornamented and finer than any I have seen. Upon the whole it stands next to Salamanca. I saw a group of Muleteers anxiously watching the proceedings of a large clock, and as it was nearly two o'clock I waited to see the result. Over the clock was the figure of a man dressed in red with large mustachios with a book in his hand. He struck the hour with it on a bell, each time making a hideous grimace which pleased the audience wonderfully. They fired three shells over the town at some mules but in general they are very quiet, only now and then firing musketry into the town. An officer of the 42nd was killed in the trenches this morning, and another dangerously wounded in carrying him off. An officer of the 42nd had his leg carried off by a shell. We are sapping and shall mine and blow up the wall that was attempted the other night and the report is, that our guns will not open till this is accomplished.

September 25th. One howitzer opened today but without effect— the wheel broke. The sapping goes on but slowly as they have but few who can work at it. The Engineers give a shilling a piece for all the large French shot that are brought and sixpence for the smaller. The men go out to look for them and stand watching the places where they hit, running the chance of being hit for the chance of getting a shilling or two. We are very well supplied here with the gross necessaries of life. Butter, bread, vegetables, country wine, etc. There is no claret to be got in Burgos now, as the Spaniards when they entered the town destroyed almost everything. The usual price of it is three and sixpence per bottle.

September 26th. The siege of this place promises fair to rival that of Troy in duration. Every day shows the deficiency of our means, the strength of the place, and the ingenuity of the garrison—in the refinements of war they far exceed us. We are stubbornly brave, they are gallant in spirit, but in all inventions and devices we must be content to copy, and the experience costs us dear. An acting Engineer was killed, an artillery officer wounded. The sap goes on well. They are so near that the garrison roll down live shells and throw hand grenades. We keep up a heavy fire of musketry which keeps their heads under. The 6th Division have a working party near the river, not connected with our works. I believe the object is to make a place for musketry.

September 27th. We are making a zig-zag to go close down to the wall for the purpose of putting musketry in. Our fire at the embrasures keeps theirs down. The working party at night broke ground at twenty yards from the wall.

September 28th. The mining goes on but slowly and as our chief hopes depend upon it, we think the siege doubtful. I went into the trenches at six in the evening and remained till twelve. We broke fresh ground nearer than on the preceding night but though they kept up a very heavy fire of musketry with occasional rounds of grape they did not hit a man. They threw two fireballs, one of which fell about ten yards from me and burned for twenty minutes. I wonder much that they do not throw more as during the time they are burning it is impossible for me to work.

September 29th. A number of people were collected on the hill at two o'clock to see the mine explode. The ceremony did not take place. Lord Wellington and suite rode too near the Castle and were fired at, one shell fell near. Our working party at six broke ground again, but the garrison kept up so hot a fire that after losing a good many men they were withdrawn. At twelve o'clock the mine exploded. The noise it made was very inconsiderable, so that it was scarcely heard by those in the trenches—it was a rumbling noise. It had the desired effect and made a very tolerable breach. A party of the 6th Division were awaiting the explosion to storm. Some confusion arose and a sergeant and six men only got up. Of course, they were soon beat down and the thing failed. The officer who commanded the party has been called upon for the reason of the failure in writing.

September 30th. Our howitzers opened today upon the breach, which is practicable though not very good. They fired with very great precision. The French were very hard at work endeavouring to cut off the communication between the breach and the other parts. At nine there was a heavy fire, so much so that I was persuaded they were storming. It turned out to be the garrison firing upon our men who were throwing up a battery at fifty yards. Captain Bouverie of the *Medusa* is arrived with dispatches from Sir Home Popham who has again been unsuccessful upon the coast. As a diversion it may be expedient to employ a Naval man but he should be much limited. Sir H. has first and last lost many a good man besides all his field artillery.

October 1st. A new battery was erected last night to bear upon the breach for three guns, which were drawn down during the night from one of the others. They opened in the morning and fired two or three rounds when they found they were commanded by two that the enemy had mounted during the night. They fired so much that our artillery men were driven out. I went up on the hill at four o'clock. They had not dismounted any, the distance being too near for round shot. They threw a vast number of shells and with the greatest accuracy, almost every one falling in the battery. Lord Wellington seems to have got into a scrape—his means are most perfectly inadequate and he has already lost 1,000 men. To shift the blame upon others he complains they do not work well. In short, during the whole of this campaign from the tone of his orders, it would appear that the conduct of the army had been mad. The few words he said after the Battle of Salamanca had more censure than praise. This is not the way to conciliate an army.

October 2nd. The enemy's fire yesterday destroyed one eighteen-pounder and damaged the carriage of another—the latter can be repaired. Lord Wellington persisted in making a battery close to the other. In the course of the night it was completed. Luckily the guns were not put in it as they shelled it in the same manner they

had done the other. There is an idea that the siege will be turned
into a blockade. There was a little skirmishing in front.

October 3rd. At one a.m. I went into the trenches and remained till
six. We finished the embrasure of a four howitzer battery. We have
now about eight times as many batteries as guns. A great deal of
rain fell during the night and the trenches were full of mud.

October 4th. Lord Wellington has given out orders wherein he tells
the two Divisions engaged in the siege that unless they work better
they will not obtain the same credit that other Divisions have done,
at the same time excepting the conduct of the Brigade of Guards
which has been as exemplary here as all other places. Our guns re-
opened in the morning upon the old breach which at two o'clock
appeared to be very practicable. It was then determined that the
outer wall should be stormed at daylight, the other attempts at
night having failed. The 24th Regiment supported by two hundred
men of the Division were to go up the old breach. The signal for
the attack was to be the explosion of the mine. The 6th Division
were to mount the breach which the mine was to make. At four
o'clock the hill was covered with spectators. I took post in front of
the breach and about half a mile from it. At half past five the mine
exploded and made an excellent breach. The troops rushed forward from the place where they were concealed. A Grenadier
officer of the 24th led that regiment in the most gallant style. He
was first on the breach but when near the top appeared to find
great difficulty in getting up, the ground slipping from under
his feet. Just at this moment about ten Frenchmen appeared;
they seemed quite confounded and not to know what was going
on. Two or three ran to the old breach, one fired close to the
officer but missed him, the men then peered over and the
French ran off as fast as they could into the fort. The 24th
advanced and hid themselves behind a pile of shot from whence
they commenced firing. Thus far the French seemed taken quite
unawares. The explosion of the mine and the storming were so
instantaneous that they had not time to do anything before the
men were in and then it was too late. The 6th Division got in at
their breach without any sort of difficulty. The French now
opened a most tremendous fire from every part of their works—
musketry, shells, round shot and grape. Every musket and gun
seemed to be at work. Our men returned the fire, and as it was
getting dusk the sight was truly magnificent. As it got dark the
fire slackened.

I reckon myself fortunate in having had so good an opportunity of seeing it—it is a chance if ever I may have another. As soon as it was dark the working commenced, and in the course of the night a trench was dug parallel to the breach, to afford cover to the men. At twelve o'clock the garrison made a sally but were repulsed. At first they drove our men back, but the tables were soon turned. It was accompanied by a very heavy firing and loud and repeated cheers.

October 5th. It is thought that a hundred will cover yesterday's loss. The men are well covered, and an incessant fire of musketry is kept up on both sides. It is said that the French officers could not get their men on in the sortie. The enemy is manoeuvring in our front with a view to drawing us off. We are now too far engaged to be drawn off. Colonel Jones of the Engineers, an able officer, was wounded yesterday. He was to give Lord Wellington the signal that the mine was ready and for that purpose got out of the trenches and stood in the open, and was of course immediately hit. At five o'clock our musketry slackened from want of ammunition. The garrison made a very spirited sortie with a view to regaining what they had lost. Our men were taken by surprise and driven from the breach. For some time the French had possession of the whole wall excepting a small space at each end. After destroying all our work and carrying off the tools, they retired. Our loss is from two to three hundred. Clitheroe was wounded whilst leading his men up the breach.

October 6th. It would seem impossible to maintain ourselves where we are as we cannot put men in front of our working party and whenever they choose to sortie they can destroy all our works. It rained incessantly the whole day and it would seem that the rainy season has set in. The covering party is now to be found by entire regiments to furnish 450 men to be relieved every twelve hours. Our party marched off at seven but the rains had made the trenches so bad, that the party did not get to the breach till ten o'clock. I was sent with twenty men as an advance party to give alarm on a sortie. My post was under the pile of shot; on any appearance of a sortie I was to advance, charge, and keep them off till the tools could be got away or in other words to be a dead man for the sake of a few pickaxes. On taking my post I discovered that our firing parties fired just over my head and several times hit the shot I was under. I sent several times to order them to level higher but I confess I was very glad on being withdrawn at daylight. Had a sortie been made I should have been between two fires, and between one and the other stood but a bad chance. The enemy threw a vast number of fireballs during the night for the double purpose of seeing where we were, and setting the gabions on fire. The distance is now so very short that a great many men are lost and almost killed every day.

October 7th. It rained incessantly during the day and night. They dismounted another eighteen pounder this morning so that there is now but one left and yet the siege is continued though the chance of success must be very remote. At three in the morning the garrison made another sortie. They advanced under favour of a very heavy rain and got up to the breach without being perceived, and drove our men from every part of the wall. The Germans were on the covering party. After some time the Germans succeeded in regaining the wall after a most obstinate defensive, being so closely engaged that they knocked each other about with their butt ends. Major Cocks, of the 79th, the Field Officer in the trenches, was killed at the beginning of the business. His loss is irreparable. He was of the greatest promise and during the three years he had been in the country had greatly distinguished himself. Every officer present was either killed or wounded, and the loss in men is about a hundred and fifty. They levelled all our works and buried some of the sappers alive. Two officers and 50 men were in my post behind the shot. They [the French] got into their rear—the officers were killed and hardly a man escaped. I cannot help thinking myself very fortunate in having escaped.

October 8th. The disasters of last night have depressed everyone. We are just where we were three days ago and whenever the garrison chooses the sortie they can drive us out. The weather too conspires against us, and our resources so inadequate at first, and since so much reduced, give us no hopes of success—it must end in a blockade. The French stole out so quietly last night that they came upon the trench before the men at work had the least idea of their approach. The first intimation was finding the earth sho- velled down upon their heads. One of the sappers finding it impossible to escape allowed himself to be buried, and came out when they retired. Another followed his example but was struck twice with a pick-axe, at which he said he would be damned if he stood that and ran off. The man who was buried said that a French officer of Engineers who stood over his men directing them, was shot. The rain continues.

October 9th. We fired red hot shot at the convent but with no success. They have dismounted our only sound eighteen pounder, and a howitzer, and knocked one of the batteries to pieces. It is almost impossible for us to keep a gun at work more than an hour. They fire with such accuracy that they are sure of dismounting. At seven in the evening the Coldstream again went on covering party. I remained in the upper part of the works. The men were put close up to the wall and the new breach. At about eight the garrison attempted a sortie. They no sooner showed themselves than they were driven back by our men in the most gallant style. Buckeridge was killed as well as some men. Our parties maintained themselves during the whole of the night. We had two sentries on our side of the sally port. They opened it once and our men fired down. They think they hit a good many men as there was a great cry. This covering party is become quite a perilous service, we are so near that many men must be hit.

October 10th. The conduct of the Guards last night is the general topic of conversation here and is universally praised. A drum major deserted from the fort yesterday. Two others from the party were shot in the attempt. The drum major says that many would desert but that they are too strictly watched. He says they have lost 500 men, and that there is a fever in the place. The rain which is incessant has made the trenches almost impassable.

October 11th. General Paget arrived from England this morning to act as second in command in the room of Sir Thomas Graham. The round shot is entirely expended and "Thunder" the only eighteen-pounder, "Nelson" being in the mud and "Lightning" ditched. Rain.

October 12th. The rain is quite incessant. We are trying to accomplish the remainder of our work by mining. The French have countermined, but are much alarmed by our mines. The whole of their force is bivouacked. Their sick and wounded were in the fort but our hot shot forced them to move and they share the rain with the others. They are very ill off for wood and are obliged to burn their palisades. Our cavalry dove in the enemy's outpost this morning which had advanced.

October 13th. The mine now runs forty yards—fifty will bring it under the enemy and then it will explode. The enemy attacked our outposts this morning and Colonel Ponsonby was wounded in the thigh. We had one man killed and three wounded this morning going near the town for wood.

October 14th. His Lordship had been strongly advised to give up all the idea of taking the place but he is still obstinate. I believe he is determined to wait for the mines which may perhaps frighten them into a surrender.

October 15th. Our regiment formed the covering party and I went on at half past one in the morning and remained on till five. My post was to observe the gate of the Castle and I had forty men. At twelve o'clock our batteries made another attempt but they no sooner opened than twelve guns were brought to bear upon our three. In half an hour the battery was knocked to pieces and the men driven from the guns. I take this to be our last dying speech. They throw during the day a vast number of shells and as the day was dark I could see them in the air which I never remember to have done before. The splinters came back into their own works and troubled us as though under cover we were not more than twenty yards from the Castle wall. A man sitting round the fire was hit. Two Frenchmen jumped out from behind a bank and shot two sentries who were posted in advance. Upon this two officers went out to see whether there was any better place to post them and whilst looking another Frenchman jumped out from the same place, levelled and pulled at them but luckily his piece missed fire. The French army advanced a little, but did not drive in our outposts. Rain in the evening.

October 16th. Sir Edward Paget was to have seen our Brigade out this morning but the rain prevented it. The enemy made a reconnaissance in front and it is thought that Massena was present. Some movement has been made by our troops and the 6th Division had orders to hold themselves in readiness. There was but little firing either upon the fort or us during the day.

October 17th. Notwithstanding a rainy morning, Sir Edward Paget inspected us. Our battery opened early and the embrasures having been altered it was enabled to play for the greatest part of the day. The 3rd Regiment was on covering party at night and a mine exploded that was intended to blow up some palisades. It succeeded but ill, and the men were unable to force their way through. Two officers were wounded and about twelve men.

October 18th. The Coldstream formed the covering party in the morning. Harvey was killed whilst visiting his party. The battery continued firing upon the breach and succeeded in making it very good. At three o'clock it was communicated to us that the place was to be stormed at 4 o'clock. The signal was the explosion of the mine, on which a flag was to be held up on the hill. The mine exploded—the explosion was attended with so little noise that though we were anxiously expecting it, we could hear no noise. The earth shook a little, we looked to the hill and saw the flag. The 300 Germans stormed the breach and got well up it. They then attempted the third line, by a place in the wall which was broken down. It ended in their being beat out of the whole with the loss of 7 officers and a great many men. Our party was to escalade the wall in front. Burgess ran forward with 30 men, Walpole and myself followed with fifty each and ladders. Burgess got up without much difficulty, Walpole and myself followed. The place we stood on was a ledge in the wall about three feet from the top. A most tremendous fire opened upon us from every part which took us in front and rear. They poured down fresh men and ours kept falling down into the ditch, dragging and knocking down others. We were so close that they fairly put their muskets into our faces, and we pulled one of their men through an embrasure. Burgess was killed and Walpole severely wounded. We had hardly any men left on the top and at last we gave way. How we got over the palisades I know not. They increased their fire as we retreated, and we came off with the loss of more than half our party and all the badly wounded were left in the ditch. Burgess behaved nobly—he was the first up the ladder and waved his hat on the top. I found him lying there wounded. He begged me to get my men up and in the act of speaking a stone hit him, he fell on the ledge and was shot dead. The time we were on the wall was not more than six minutes. The fire was tremendous, shot, shells, grape, musketry, large stones, hand grenades and every missile weapon was used against us. I reckon my escape particularly fortunate. A party of sixty men attempted to escalade on our right. They were met by a very superior force and were immediately driven back but with very little loss. The mine destroyed a small church on the right. Colonel Brown with some Portuguese got possession of it. It completes our possession of the whole of the first line which was before incomplete. The failure of this is to be ascribed entirely to our want of men. Had we but double the number we could have maintained ourselves but they dropped off so fast and none coming to supply their place, we failed from sheer weakness. Crofton was slightly wounded in the arm whilst waiting with the support. Walpole had his arm shattered with a grape shot, which struck him likewise in the side, but the shot most providentially glanced, striking and tearing Ninon de l'Enclos, which he happened to have in a side pocket at the time, otherwise it must have killed him. Thus finished this trying day. I was slightly wounded in the arm by a stone, but not the least hurt.

October 19th. In the storm of yesterday we had 60 of the 130 killed or wounded. A great number never got up and many were pushed down without being wounded. The Germans lost seven out of nine officers—the men in the same proportion as ourselves. Notwithstanding the failure we are still going on. They attempted in the night to regain the church but were after some sharp work driven back. We began to mine from near the church. A party of French came out, took one miner who was on the outside, and shut the others into the mine. They were rescued from their perilous situation by a party of Caçadores [Portuguese]. Lord Wellington expressed himself perfectly satisfied with our attempt, and the impossibility of remaining any longer than we did.

October 20th. Our Division marched at daylight to the strong position in front of Burgos leaving the 58th and some Portuguese to live in the trenches till our return. The French army appeared on a range of hills opposite. In the evening some cavalry and three divisions of infantry moved into the plain below us, apparently with the intention of attacking us in the morning. The 5th Division on our flank moved down to attack them. They stood their ground so long that I thought we were in for a good thing. Our artillery fired upon them, they went to the right about and we returned to our old ground. General Souham commands in the room of Clausel. Caffarelli has joined with 5,000 of the Imperial Guard. The remainder are either conscripts or the debris of Marmont's army. Their cavalry are remarkably good, some of them just joined. The 7th Division and some Spanish had a brush on the right and both behaved very well according to what I can collect. The enemy have about 35,000 infantry and 5,000 cavalry. We have about 14,000 infantry and 1,300 cavalry—the Spaniards nearly the same. Bivouacked.

October 21st. Everything was quiet in the morning. The men were ordered to hut. At two the baggage was ordered to retreat. In the evening preparations were made for a retreat. At dusk we stole off quietly and what is most extraordinary, at the very same moment the French did the same. We halted for some time at Villa Irin. I went with Colonel Macdonald into a house to warm ourselves as it was a cold night. We found General Alava and General Longa, the celebrated partisan. We talked with them for half an hour. They then returned to their beds and their place was most ably supplied by some guerrilla servants to the above mentioned chieftains. We were hungry and desired them to get us some supper. They knocked the Patrone about, who immediately produced some bread, wine and salad. They furnished us with some boiled beef of their own, and some eggs destined for the breakfast of their masters. Fortified by our good cheer we sallied forth, prepared for the dangers of the night. Our Division was ordered by way of expedition to pass through the town and over the bridge of Burgos, on which two of the Castle guns bore and about a hundred yards from it. The moon shone clear. Luckily we got over without the loss of a man. They did not see us which was almost a miracle. We marched all night and halted for a short time during the morning then moved again and halted at Celada del Camino.

Private William Wheeler, 51st Regiment

Camp Near Pampluna [Spain]
1 July 1813

. . . On the 20th June we encamped near Vittoria. In the afternoon Major Roberts, as he was wont to do, came round our camp to take a peep at the camp kettles. I with some of my comrades were smoking a pipe in our tent when the Major peeped in saying very good humouredly "Well my boys have you any bread to give away." We answered "we had no bread but if old Bob, meaning his favourite horse, wanted corn we could supply him with plenty." He smiling replied "Never mind my lads there is plenty of bread there" pointing with his stump towards Vittoria. "And by this time tomorrow we shall have plenty." The Major's prophesy proved true. In twenty four hours after the soldiers of the "Great Nation", Napoleon's Invincibles, were totally defeated with loss of all their cannon, ammunition, baggage, money and stores of every description by a half starved army of British and Portugueses . . .

On the morning of the 21st. June we advanced. We had not proceeded far when the company to which I belonged to was ordered out to scour a wood on our right flank. We extended and marched through without falling in with the enemy, but we fell in with plenty of cattle, sheep and goats. We haversacked a few sheep and ran against an old shepherd, we soon relieved him of all he had, viz a four pound loaf, some cheese and about a quart of wine. The poor old fellow cried. It was no use, we had not seen a bit of bread these eleven days. The old man was not far from home and could get more.

The battle had now began on the right of our army. We got clear of the wood and saw our Division crossing a river by a stone bridge, but they had got a long start of us and it was some time as they continued to advance, before we could get up. In passing through a village we found many wounded men, several belonged to our Corps, from these men we learned the Regiment had been engaged and had taken fourteen guns. After this we soon joined. The Brigade were in column, in front of a strong position occupied by the enemy. After sustaining their fire some time we dashed forward, drove them from their position in such a hurry that they left ten guns behind. This charge was executed so sudden that altho they sent us a shower of balls and bullets very few done any harm. Soon after this the entire of the French army broke up, and so precipitate was their flight that they left all their material of war on the field. We continued the pursuit till near dark, passed the city of Vittoria some distance on our right, then halted for the night. Here was a scene of confusion, we were surrounded with guns, waggons, horses, mules and baggage. The dead and dying lay scattered all around us.

As soon as we halted my comrade, a famous hand to look out, proposed to go and see if he could get some money, as several men had come into camp loaded with money. In case we should move I was to carry his firelock and pack. He had not been gone long before I grew impatient so I started after him. I had not proceeded far when I met one of the 68th. Regt with a handkerchief full of dollars. He was followed by about a dozen Portuguese soldiers, one of these fellows ran in and cut the handkerchief and down went the dollars, a general scramble followed. As the Portuguese were down on their hands and knees picking up the money, we paid them off in stile with the sockets of our bayonetts. After this fracas was over I proceeded on until my ear caught the welcome sound of Brown's voice, he was singing his favourite song "When wild war's deadly blast was blown." I knew there was luck, for he never sang this song but when he was elevated with the juice of the grape or he had met with good luck. I soon found him, he had been in a flour cask and was as white as a miller. As soon as he saw me he shouted "my dear fellow come back to camp, I have enough to last us both as long as we live." I soon learned that the extent of his treasure was two canteens of brandy, three loaves, two haversacks of flour, one ham and two dollars and a half. I took a good swig of brandy and half a loaf. Brown went home to make dumplings and I started off in the direction I heard most noise, soon came to the place where the money was. After much difficulty I secured a small box of dollars, and was fortunate enough to get back safe to camp.

Camp, Heights of Eschellar, 17 July 1813

When I returned to camp, how was I surprised at the great change that had taken place during the short time I had been absent. When I left no fires had been lit, now the place was all in a blaze. I knew of nothing to compare it to but an Arab camp after a successful attack on some rich caravan. Wearing apparal of all sorts and description lying about in heaps or trampled under foot, boxes broken to pieces for fuel. Every one was in motion, some bringing in loads of different descriptions on their shoulders, others leading or driving horses and mules loaded with baggage, provisions and liquors and something of everything that forms the baggage of an army. Dame Fortune had distributed her gifts in her usual way, to some money, others bread, hams, cherries, tobacco etc. This of necessity soon established a market. Now the camp represented a great fair and the money and goods soon became more equally distributed. "Who will give fifty dollars for this pipe." "Here is a portrait of Napoleon for one hundred dollars." Then a General's coat would fetch more dollars than it cost francs. Wine and brandy would fetch a high price. Cognac from forty to fifty dollars per bottle. The market soon changed into a grand maskerade. British soldiers were soon to be seen in French General's and other officer's uniform covered with stars and military orders, others had attired themselves in female dresses, richly embroidered in gold and silver.

In the midst of all this hurly burly, frolic and fun, the belley was not forgotten. An hundred fires were occupied in preparing food, all our campkettles were in requisition and loads of cooking utentials that had been taken from the enemy. The cooking reminds me of seeing one of our men walk into camp having a large table cloth tied by the four corners, it contained dishes, tureens, plates, knives and silver forks. He found it ready laid. The guests were not there so he bundled it up together and walked away with it. While we were regaling ourselves Major Roberts paid us a visit, he said "Now my lads you see I am no false prophet, did I not tell you yesterday we should have plenty." He told us to make ourselves merry, but above all things to keep sober, for the moment was not known but we might move.

What a contrast between this night and the last. Twenty four hours before we had not enough in the regiment to bait a mouse trap, this night we could scarce move without trampling on all kinds of provisions. Suffice it to say that after eating and drinking, singing and smoking we dropped off asleep, marched the next morning loaded like donkeys, leaving as much provisions in the camp that would serve for a month.

General Hospital Fontarabia, 14th June 1814

. . . It is now nearly two months since I wrote last. I have had a severe time of it. Banish your fears about my safety, I am fast recovering. It was in the afternoon of the 3rd. May that I felt a beating in my wound as if any one was tapping the place with their finger, in the night the beating increased attended with pain, the next morning when the doctor opened it, it was declared to be sluffed. I was then ordered upstairs to what we call the incurable ward, none of the other patients in the hospital are allowed to enter this ward as the sluff is infectious, so that it is a kind of senetar. My wound continued to get worse, I had every attendance that could possibly be given and all the remedies applied to prevent morti-fication, at length my leg and thigh was reduced so small that I could span it with my hand, but the wounded part and foot were swollen to an enormous size, and the wound was as large over as a tea saucer. It was at length agreed to amputate my leg, this I joyfully agreed to being heartily tired of such a frightful trouble-some member. Twice were I removed to the surgery to undergo the operation, but each time the little Spanish Doctor, who had charge of me, overruled it and I was taken back to my bed, I understood my Doctor wished to try something else, then if that failed the leg was to come off. He brought from his home a small bottle filled with some thing like pepper and salt mixed, with this he covered the wound on` which he put lint, bandaged it up, crossed himself, muttered something to himself and left me. Several times that day he visited me and my answers to his questions seemed to perplex him much. The next morning my answers seemed to please him, he took off the bandage in good spirits—when all the sluff excepting two spots, one about the size of a sixpence, the other smaller, came off with the lint. My wound now was changed from a nasty sickly whitebrown colour to a bright read. He capered about like a mad fellow, called the other doctors who all seemed surprised, he put some more stuff out of the bottle on the spots and the next morning I was removed down stairs. This was on the 9th. inst. Since then my wound improves surprisingly . . .

The ward I had left upstairs was one continued scene of misery and woe, the dreadful sufferings of the patients is beyond description. During the five weeks I was in it, what numbers have I seen die under the most writhing torture, and their places filled again by others, who only come to pass a few days in misery, and then to be taken to their last home. The bed next mine were occupied by six different soldiers, five died, the sixth I left in a hopeless state. One of those men I knew, he was a Serjeant of the 82nd. Regiment, his wife was nurse to the ward, she pricked her finger with a pin left in one of the bandages, caught the infection, her finger was first amputated, then her hand, the sluff appeared again in the stump, she refused to undergo another operation, the consequence was she soon died. In this house of misery how many fine brave young fellows have died without the assistance of a friend, mother, sister or wife to soothe their agony in their last moment. No minister of religion to cheer the dying sinner.

The people of England little think how her soldiers are neglected respecting spiritual aid, or I believe it would not be so. If they could but hear or see the agony of the dying, their prayers, their despair and the horrid oaths uttered by some in their exit from this world, I am sure this most of wants would be attended to. It is true there are chaplains with the army who sometimes perform divine service, but of what use are they, the service they perform has no effect, for their mode of living do not agree with the doctrine they preach. I have often heard the remark "That a Chaplain is of no more use to the army than a town pump without a handle." If these Reverend Gentlemen were stationed at the sick depots and made to attend to the hospitals, they would be much more usefully employed than following the army with their brace of dogs and gun, running down hares and shooting partridges etc. In winter quarters these men once on a Sunday (weather permitting), perform divine service, but when the campaign opens, it is seldome or ever an opportunity offers, every day then is the same, few trouble themselves about days or anything else. It is only on the eve of a battle that any enquiry is made, what day is it.

Trooper Charles Stanley, Kings Dragoon Guards

Stanley writes to his cousin, Christopher Alvey, three days before the Allied armies and Napoleon engaged at Waterloo.

Brusels, Flemish Flanders May 15th [1815]

Dear Cusson I take this Oppetunety of Riting to you hoping this will find you all In gud helth as it leves me at Pressent I Thank God for It I have ad a Verry Ruf march Since i sow you at Booton we am onley 15 miles From Mr. Boney Part Harmey wish we Expect To have a Rap at him Exerry Day We have the Most Cavilrey of the English that Ever was None at One time and in Gud Condishon and Gud sperrits we have lost a few horses by hour Marshing I have the Plesure to say my horse Is Better Everry Day Wish i think im to be the Best frend i have at Pressant there is no dout Of us Beting the Confounded Rascald it ma Cost Me my Life and a meaney more that will onley Be the forting of War my Life i set ne store By at all this is the finest Cuntrey Exer i So far before England the peepal is so Sivel thare land Coltevated so well most of them as a littel land and they Havit as Clen as a Jentelmas Garden tha are Sadley a frad of Boneys Harmey Comming a gane he Distrest them so before we have sum Littel trubel to make them Understand us not noing thare Languige we do a grate del By makin moshins We have one gud thing Cheap that is Tobaco and Everrything a-Cordnley Tobaco is 4d Per lb Gin is 1s 8d Per Galland that is 2½ Per Quart and Everrything In Perposion hour alounse Per Day is One Pound of Beef a Pound and half of Bred half a Pint o Gin But the worst of all we dont get it Regeler and If we dont get it the Day it is due we Luse it wish It is ofton the Case i asure you My Dear Lad I hop Wot Ever may Comacros your mind to trobel You wish i hope nothing will I hope you never will think Of Being a Soldier I Asure you it is a Verry Ruf Consarn I have Rote to my Sister Ann and I ham afraid She thinks the trubel to mush to answer my Letter wen Over at Woodhous she semed Verry Desires of mi Ritting to her out of site ou of mind I have not ad the Pleasure of Ling in a Bed sinco In the Cuntrey thank God the Weather is fine Wish is in hour faver we Get no Pay at all onley hour Bed and mete and Gin we have 10d Per Day soped from us wish we shal Reseive wen six months is Expiered I thank God i have a frend with me wish i Find verry yousfol to me i asure you (I have not any Time to say any) I hope you will Excuse my Bad Inditing and Spelling my Love to Aunt and Cussons Mrs Darby Cusson Joseph and family

at Edwinsto and all that Thinks well to ask after me my Duty to
Mother wen you see her.

If you think well to answer my Letter wish I should Be Verry
gad You would I Should be Verry Glad To here from you all Plese
to Derect to me

To Charles Stanley the fost or Kings Dragun Guards Kings
Troop Brstels, Flanders or Elswere

Hour Rigment is Brgaded with the Two Rigments of Life
Guards and the Oxferd Bluse So no more at Prssant from your
Ever wel wisher C. Stanly God Bles you all

Be so gud as to Pay a Penny with your Letter and see it marked
Post Pade

Private Stanley was killed in the Battle of Waterloo.

Trooper John Marshall, 10th Hussars

Marshall describes the Battle of Waterloo in a letter to his family.

Pildute, near Paris, 11 July 1815

I have availed myself of this opportunity, to give you as much
information as comes within my knowledge, though you no doubt
are well acquainted with what has transpired during that short, but
ever-glorious Campaign: but as the scribbler of a newspaper can
say what he pleases, I shall take the liberty of saying what I know to
be true—and so to the subject. On the 16th of June, our troops
were in motion. At day-break in the morning, the British were
advancing with all possible speed towards the Enemy, who was
waiting our approach, and had already made an attack upon some
Hanoverian troops, and on that account we had a forced march.
The brigade to which I belong, marched a distance of about fifty
miles, taking their posts the same evening about seven o'clock; and
being the first cavalry that arrived, we remained under arms all
night, during which time several brigades of cavalry, and most of
our infantry, arrived. But the enemy was so strongly posted, that it
was thought prudent not to attack them in their works, but to fall
back. The infantry, therefore, about ten in the morning of the
17th, began to withdraw, leaving us to cover their retreat. The
French, perceiving this, did not remain long inactive, but soon
brought up their Lancers to attack us; but we were not to bring
them to action, but retreat, which was accordingly done. General
Vivian, who commands our brigade, conducted the retreat; in a

most able and skilful manner did he complete it, covering the
retreat with our brigade of the whole army, that fell back on this
point. The enemy, seeing us retreat, were quite delighted, and
followed us with all speed, cheering and hallooing at us, thinking
to alarm and frighten: but in this they were disappointed, for we
did not lose a man, although they attempted to charge us several
times; but our skirmishers kept them back, in spite of all their
boasted bravery. Thus was our retreat completed, after having
fallen back about eight miles: thus far then they were to come, but
no further. But we were much hurt by a thunderstorm, which
brought with it the most heavy torrents of rain that I ever beheld,
nor did it abate during the night, nor till about nine the next
morning; and we were exposed to it all the time, for we took up our
abode in a wood all night, so that we were like drowned men, more
than soldiers: but as many of us have long been enured to hardships and privations of all descriptions, it went off cheerfully, and
none seemed to repine; for when the motives of the mind are strong
for exertion, all things are set aside to gain the wished-for purpose.
This it is that makes us think light of misfortunes, and bear
deprivations beyond conception to those who never trod this
thorny path; yet, with us, they are borne without a murmur.
But I am wandering from my subject. About nine on the morning
of the 18th, the clouds dispersed, and it gave over raining, and the
enemy drew up in order of battle, and our line had been formed all
night, so we were quite ready for them. Our troops were posted
upon a chain of rising heights, which commands the plain before it,
whilst those of the French were posted upon a rising ground, in a
parallel line with ours; and their position was covered by a long
chain of woods, which favoured, and hid many of their movements, so that we had no advantage of them, for we had the plain
before us, and they the same. Thus all were ready, and about
twelve the onset commenced, by a brisk fire from the sharpshooters, and soon after a very heavy cannonading ensued; and
by two the action became general, and most desperate did it rage;
for both sides seemed determined to keep their ground; but the
enemy showed us, that they did not only mean to have their own
ground, but our also. With this seeming determination, did they
bring up a strong force of cavalry and infantry, and pushed with all
their might upon the centre of our line, thinking to break it; but in
this they were disappointed, for our cavalry met them, and drove
them back, as fast as they advanced. Finding, therefore, that they
could not move our centre, they then endeavoured to turn our left
flank, by pressing upon it in the same manner. Upon this point our

brigade was posted; but they met with the same reception as before: so, finding that we stood firm at this place also, they took up their own ground, and soon after endeavoured to advance at all points; but their attention was then arrested by a large body of Prussians, who came point blank upon their right flank, and opened a very heavy fire of artillery upon them. This for a little time put them in a consternation; but even this they recovered, and, altering their lines, seemed to suffer but little from this our new reinforcement. This was about five in the evening, and victory was still doubtful. The enemy then made one more attempt to vanquish us, by bringing the most of his force at our right flank, trying to force it, and to gain the high road for Brussels, which if he had succeeded, our defeat would have been complete; and here it was that our Commander the Duke of Wellington was put to the test; for they advanced with a vast and numerous body of cavalry, supported by infantry, and covered by artillery, and seemed determined to have this road. The chief of our artillery was then brought to this point, and theirs parallel with ours; such a tremendous peal of thunder did they ring one against the other, as I never knew since my name was Marshall. The whole of the cavalry belonging to the British was also brought to the right of our line, and charged them in brigades; and ours also left its post, where it had been all day on the left, and came to the right, and, having the greatest distance to come, we of course was the last, and the whole of our cavalry nearly had charged them. This stopped their progress in advancing in a great measure. Our brigade was then formed into line, and then we stood showing them that we would have the ground, or perish in the attempt; but they did not much like our sturdy front. They had some brigades of Imperial Guards to confront us, and at a small distance off, but would not charge us; but we stood under a most galling and destructive fire from infantry and artillery for near an hour: but this could not move us; but firm as a rock we stood, except those poor fellows who fell victims to their bravery. It was now eight in the evening, and still the battle raged with redoubled fury, and still was much to be done, and but little time to do it in, for night was fast approaching; therefore, no time was to be lost. Our brigade was then formed into three lines, each regiment comprising its own line, which was the 10th, 18th, and a regiment of the German Legion Hussars, my own regiment forming the first line. The General then came in front of the line, and spoke in the following manner: "Tenth," he said, "you know what you are going to do, and you also know what is expected of you, and I am well assured it will be done; I therefore shall say no more, only wish you success"; and with that, he gave orders for us to advance. I am not ashamed to say, that, well knowing what we were going to do, I offered up a prayer to the Almight, that for the sake of my children, and the partner of my bosom, he would protect me, and give me strength and courage to overcome all that might oppose me, and with a firm mind I went, leaving all that was dear to me to the mercy of that great Ruler, who has so often in the midst of peril and danger protected me. After advancing about one hundred yards, we struck into a charge, as fast as our horses could go, keeping up a loud and continual cheering, and soon we were amongst the Imperial Guards of France. The 18th Hussars also charging, as soon as we got amongst them, which so galled them, that we slew and overthrew them like so many children, although they rode in armour, and carried lances ten foot long; but so briskly did our lads lay the English steel about them, that they threw off their armour and pikes, and those that could get away flew in all directions. But still we had not done, for there were two great solid squares of infantry, who had hurt us much, whilst we were advancing, with their fire, and still continued to do so, whilst we were forming again: in short they were all around us. We therefore formed as well as we could, and at them we went, in spite of their fixed bayonets. We got into their columns, and like birds they fell to the ground. Thus they were thrown into confusion, for it seemed like wild-fire amongst their troops, that the Guards were beaten, and, panic-struck, they flew in all directions. But we had done our part, and left those to pursue, who had seen the onset. We took sixteen guns at our charge, and many prisoners: but it was so dark, we could not see any longer, and at length we assembled what few men we had got left of the regiment, and the General of Brigade formed us in close columns, so that we might all hear him, and he addressed us in the following manner: "Now, Tenth," he said, "you have not disappointed me, you were just what I thought you were. You was the first regiment that broke their lines, and to you it is, that we are indebted for turning the fate of the day; and depend upon it that your Prince shall know it; for nothing but the bravery and good discipline of the regiment could have completed such a work." We then gave him three cheers, and since that he has given us at great length, in our orderly books, his thanks and praise for our conduct. You may perhaps think, because I have spoke of this, that it shows my vanity; but my motive for having done so, is because I saw in an English newspaper, that the Life Guards were the only cavalry that had been of any service. It therefore did not much please me nor my regiment, that we should not have a little of the credit. The Guards certainly made a very brilliant charge; it ought to be spoken of. You will, however, see, by what I have here stated, that the regiment did its duty, and that is all we wish to be understood of us. I am sorry that we have to lament the loss of a most brave and gallant officer, Major Howard, who led on the squadron that I belong to; and most nobly did he show himself formed, to let them know that he was an Englishman; but when we charged the infantry, one of them shot him dead, just as we got within bayonet length of them. We had two officers killed, wounded three captains, and two lieutenants wounded. But how many privates we have lost, I do not know: but not so many as might be expected; for the French fired so high, that when we were at close quarters with them, half their shots did not tell, or they might have killed every man of us. But Providence is ever on the watch, and orders every thing as it pleases; and I can never return too many thanks to the Almighty, for preserving me through that day's peril and danger: for never did I behold such a day's slaughter as that. Never did British troops try more for victory, and never were they nearer being beat. But, thanks be to heaven, the work was at last completed, for the Prussian troops finished what we had begun, pursuing and driving them all night, the darkness of which helped to add to their horror-struck minds. Thus was the proud and destroying Tyrant once more beaten, and compelled to fly to his Capital for shelter, leaving his troops to their destructive fate. This proves him to be a coward, for he abandoned them in the hour of danger: and he, like the fretful porcupine, can no where find rest; his fate, and that of all Europe, depended upon that day; but the evening's clouds saw him a wretched fugitive, not daring to stop, nor yet to go on. We took from them two hundred and ten pieces of cannon, and stores of all descriptions, and many prisoners. He had during the action, in several places of his line, the black flag flying, which signifies "no quarter." No, if he had beat us, I dare say they would have showed us none; and myself am eye-witness to it, that many of them were laid to the ground, which would not have been, but for that he had covered his cavalry with armour to secure them; but we wanted no steel covering, for our hearts proved to be already steeled, and we let them know it. We have followed them to the gates of Paris, which place gave up to us on the 6th of this month.

Lieutenant William Turner, 13th Light Dragoons

VILLEPEUT near PARIS, 3rd July 1815

My Dear Busby,—I assure you it is with the greatest pleasure I can find time to inform you I am perfectly sound and in good health and spirits.

We marched into this village last night from near Louvres, and are only nine miles from Paris and can distinctly hear the firing, which takes place at Paris, between the Prussian advanced posts and the French. This war cannot possibly last long, for every town and village is completely ransacked, and pillaged by the Prussians and neither wine, spirits, or bread are to be found. The whole country from the frontier to Paris has been laid waste by the march of troops, and the crops nearly destroyed, we are waiting for the Prussians when that infernal City Paris will be attacked and no doubt pillaged, for it is a debt we owe to the whole of Europe, all the inhabitants for leagues round here have taken themselves and their effects into Paris, so that it will be worth taking if we lose 20,000 men.

You have no idea of the enthusiasm of the troops and their determination to carry before them everything in their way, the Prussians are also determined soldiers and I expect in one week Paris will be completely sacked and perhaps burned.

Our Rocket Brigade went to the front yesterday, and Blucher is much exasperated because they have detained the flags of truce.

I will as shortly as possible give you some particulars of what I have seen since I wrote to you at Ghent, three days after I joined the Regiment at Castes near Grammont, where we were quartered for some days and had a review by Lord Uxbridge with the other Cavalry Regiments.

On 15th June I rode to see the City of Brussels 16 miles distant, it is a handsome and pleasant place, returned in the evening home (very fortunately); at 7 next morning 16th instant was rousted out of my bed by a Sergeant to say we were to march immediately, soon turned out but owing to the Regiment being so distributed about the country we were not able to march before 11 a.m., we then marched by Eughien, Brainale, Cante and Nivelle and arrived on the field of battle near Genappe about 10 p.m. just as the battle ended, (nothing to eat all day), bivouacked all night in corn, at 3 a.m. turned out, had . . . at 10 a.m. rode over the field of battle which was covered with dead, went to the front when I was near being shot by four Frenchmen, whom I took for Belgians, they all fired but luckily missed me . . . and the officer who was with me retired, and soon after began the retreat.

The Cavalry in the rear went slowly, the French followed the Hussars and Life Guards on one road, we and the 15th on the other were about 300 yards distant when the 7th charged and the Life Guards charged in support. We then continued retiring and one of the heaviest showers I ever felt made us wet to the skin, we halted close to the village of Mont St Jean with the whole Army.

It was a dreadful rainy night, every man in the Cavalry wet to the skin and nearly all the Infantry as bad; nothing to eat all day, being without rations and our baggage at Brussels. At 4 A.M. on the memorable 18th June turned out and formed on the field of battle in wet corn and a cold morning without anything to eat, nothing but some gin, which I purchased from a German woman, saved and enabled me and three other officers to stand the fatigues of the day.

About 10 A.M. the French began to move large columns of troops in our front, and about half-past eleven the Battle began, we were put with the 15th and commanded by General Grant, we were on the right of the great road and nearly the right of our line, we covered the Artillery of Captain Macdonald's troop who behaved well, before two o'clock we had three officers and several men killed by Cannon Balls and Shells, we were then put close to some Belgian Artillery, to keep them to their guns and there we suffered from musketry and roundshot; we then moved to the right of the line to charge the French Lancers but they retired.

We then came back to our place close to the Artillery which the French Imperial Guard a Cheval and Cuirassiers had taken, we immediately formed up in line with the 15th, gave three cheers, and went at them full speed, they retired immediately and we charged after them all down their position up to their Infantry, when we were ordered to retire, which we did but in confusion, we formed and told off again having lost a good many men; I shot one Frenchman with my pistol but did not use my sword, (I had the misfortune to break the double barrelled one in marching up the country or else I should have shot two); at 4 P.M. the French Cavalry came up again but on our trotting to meet them they immediately retired, we then came back on our side of the hill beyond our guns; the Battle was now most dreadful and the field covered with dead and dying in all directions.

Lord Wellington repeatedly passed us, when we Huzzared him; the French Cavalry advanced again to the muzzle of our guns, the Gunners were ordered to retire and we charged them again in the grandest style between our masses of Infantry; they retreated and we charged them close to their Infantry, who were formed in

Squares the same as ours; in this charge I am sorry to say the black mare I purchased from Paddock got two musket balls in her close to my lee just behind the shoulder joint, it was with difficulty I got her to the rear of the Artillery when I dismounted and sent her to the rear by a Dragoon, whose horse I mounted as he was.

We still continued retiring on guns when the havoc amongst us was dreadful, one cannon-ball killed General Grant's horse, Col. Dalrymple's horse and took off his leg, it then passed between Wallace and me, we remained here still exposed, every minute some man or horse falling, Captain Goulburg at whose side I was, had just mounted a trooper after having had his horse wounded, when he was knocked off by a spent ball but fortunately without injury, about half-past six we charged again down the hill and then retreated to our guns; again about 8 P.M. the great attack was made when the French were repulsed, we were immediately ordered to charge as our Infantry were . . . General Hill came in our front and called out "now 13th come on" he took off his hat with several other Generals we immediately Huzzared with the whole of the Infantry and charged, the French retired in the greatest confusion, our Infantry advancing kept us at a trot for three miles when we with the whole of the Cavalry pursued them about three miles further when darkness, at 9 P.M. put an end to the slaughter, the last charge was literally riding over men and horses, who lay in heaps.

Such is the account of the battle I myself saw and can vouch for the general particulars you have in the despatches and news-papers I assure you our Regiment had been without rations since Thursday, and it was not till Monday evening June 19th that we got our meat, I luckily had one fowl and some mouldy bread in four days. We bivouacked for the night and next day advanced and have continued to do so (except one day) ever since we crossed the frontier on the 21st June, the Cavalry have advanced here chiefly by cross country roads through the fields as it is not enclosed as in England.

I have heard since of the Black mare and find she is in Brussels and hope she will recover but have no great hopes, she is an excellent charger. Our loss in Officers is Captain Gubbins killed, ditto Pym, ditto Gale, the two former by cannon-balls, two Lieutenants severely wounded and five slightly, seven or eight Officers had their horses shot and wounded under them, and General Grant had five horses shot under him.

When the Regiment mustered after the action at 10 P.M., that night we had only 65 men left out of 260 who went into the field in the morning, the rest were either killed, wounded, or missing, the 15th have also suffered most dreadfully as well as the whole of the Cavalry, and yet notwithstanding such losses we are as ripe and anxious to try our fortune once more at Paris and settle the peace of Europe. You may expect and depend upon everything from the English and Prussians who will go hand and heart together as brothers. I must finish for the Bugle sounds . . . but I hope not to march this day.

THE WAR OF 1812
1812–15

During the Napoleonic Wars, both the French and British fleets routinely violated the maritime rights of the United States, seizing nearly 1100 American vessels between 1803 and 1812. Eventually the French were persuaded to repeal their blockade of American ports; the British, however refused to do so and in June 1812 the United States Congress declared war on Great Britain.

For both sides the war was an inglorious affair. British forces, in alliance with northwestern Native Americans, seized Detroit, occupied northeastern Maine and burned Washington DC, whilst the Royal Navy blockaded most of the East Coast. Yet, in turn, the British lost Detroit, and were defeated at Lake Champlain and Baltimore. After a year and a half of stalemate, the warring nations headed for the diplomatic table, signing the Peace of Ghent in December 1814. But before the treaty was ratified, General Andrew Jackson's volunteers defeated the British at New Orleans on 8 January 1815, with 3500 assorted Americans—including Kentucky and Tennessee militiamen, Negroes, and Creoles—withstanding a charge by 6000 British regulars, battle-seasoned veterans of the campaign against Napoleon. This victory, in the very moment of the war's official end, retrospectively cast the 1812 conflict, for Americans at least, as a second War of Independence, a decisive victory for the American character ("untutored courage" as Jackson defined it) and the American way of war. If this has truth, so has the myth of the unflinching British infantryman. The British at New Orleans continued the assault until nearly all officers had been shot down, and 2000 men had been killed or captured. American losses were eight dead.

Major James Miller, 4th US Infantry Regiment

Upper Canada, August 27th 1812

My Dearest Ruth,
    When I last wrote you my feelings were very different from what

they now are. I then thought that things appeared prosperous and flattering. I considered we had a sufficient force to bear down all opposition and I still think had we done as we ought we could [have] carried conquest to a very considerable extent, but alas times are now altered we are all Prisoners of War. Sunday on the 9th, I was on a march from Detroit to the river Reason with the 4th Regt. and a Detachment of Ohio Militia consisting of six hundred in the whole in order to guard some provisions which was coming on for our Army. About sixteen miles from Detroit at a place called Maguago near an Indian town or rather betwixt two Indian towns, I was attacked in a thick wood by a superior number of British and Indians. They made the first attack a very heavy fire upon us then the most hideous yell by the Indians. The woods appeared to be full of them. I had all my men formed to the best advantage the moment we saw their fire. I ordered a general charge which was instantly obeyed by every officer and soldier. We visited closer on them then made a general fire upon them and put them to flight. We drove them through the woods firing and charging them without a halt for more than two miles completely defeated them and drove them every devil across Detroit River home to their own Fort except those who we took prisoners and killed, which was a considerable part of them. My killed and wounded amounted to seventy five, sixteen of whom were killed dead on the ground. They took no prisoners from me. I secured the body of every man I had killed or wounded. We took five prisoners, but made no Indian prisoners. We gave them no quarters. They carried off their wounded generally from the number of the enemy found dead. Their loss of killed and wounded must have been nearly double to ours. We wounded the famous Tecumich in the neck, but not sufficiently to kill him. Lieut. Larrabee has lost his left arm in consequence of a wound in the action. No officer was killed, but five wounded. Lieut. Larrabee the worst.

Only one week after I with six hundred men completely conquered almost their whole force which they then had. They come and took Fort Detroit and made nearly two thousand of us Prisoners on Sunday the 16th. Thus being no operations going on against them below us gave them an opportunity to reinforce. The number they brot against us is yet unknown, but my humble opinion is we could have defeated them without a doubt had we attempted it, but General Hull thot differently and surrendered without making any termes of capitulation. Col. Brush and I made the best termes we could after the surrender which was but poor. The Militia they let return home by agreeing not to bare arms against his Majesty or his subjects during the War or until exchanged. All the Regulars are kept except a few Subaltirn Officers who are allowed to go home on "parole of honor" whether ever I shall get away from them, God only knows. I have been sick with the fever Ague for a long time. It takes me every other day, the intermediate day I feel very well.

I have petitioned repeatedly for leave to be paroled, but to no affect. We are now apposite Niagara on our way to Montreal. I intend to repeat my request I had thot they would let me return until I had recovered my health, but they appear to think that of little consequence to them by this capture. I have lost two horses, two saddles and two bridles. One horse was a very fine one which I gave one hundred and forty five dollars for with the saddle and bridle. The other was a low priced horse which I got for a pack horse on the march from Nineennes. I petitioned repeatedly for my clothing which was taken, my cloak I wanted very much, but they utterly refused. Well as God would have it Sgt. Gooding was there a Prisoner and my chest got wet on the passage and several others so they were delivered to Gooding to dry. Sergent[s] Furbush Tracy and Jenisong took my things to dry which took them a long time. while they were doing it, they smuggled my cloak and eight of my best shirts, my stockings, vests, pantaloons, small clothes and in fact almost every thing worth any thing and fixed them up nice when we were brot from Detroit they were brot from Malden and brot my cloaths with them and delivered them safe to me so I shall do very well for cloaths. I am sorry to inform you of the death of Doctor Foster. He died at Detroit on the 8th. Mr. Bacon is waiting the officers are hurrying him. I must leave the rest for them to tell you in Jenson Prisoners are not treated with so much indulgence I must close. You must not mention my remarks respecting our surrender to Mrs. Bacon as she will tell it to every one being all honey with G. Hull. Please to give my love to all friends, tell them I love to see them, but uncertain when. That God may bless and protect you all is the most ardent prayer my dearest Ruth of your ever affectionate and most devoted

James Miller

Fort Erie, July 28th 1814

My beloved Ruth,

I have great reason to thank God for his continued mercies and protection. On the 25th inst., at the Falls of Niagara, we met the enemy, and had, I believe, one of the most desperately fought actions ever experienced in America. It continued for three hours, stubbornly on both sides, when about ten o'clock at night we succeeded in driving them from their strong position. Our loss was very severe in killed and wounded. I have lost from my regiment, in killed and wounded and missing, one-hundred-and-twenty-six. The enemy had got their artillery posted on a height, in a very commanding position, where they could rake our columns in any part of the field, and prevented their advancing. Maj. McRee, the chief engineer, told Gen. Brown he could do no good until that height was carried and those cannon taken or driven from their position. It was then night but moonlight.

Gen. Brown turned to me and said, "Col. Miller, take your regiment, and storm that work and take it." I had short of three hundred men with me, as my regiment had been much weakened by the numerous details made from it during the day. I, however, immediately obeyed the order. We could see all their slow matches and port-fires burning and ready. I did not know what side of the work was most favourable to approach, but happened to hit upon a very favorable place, notwithstanding we advanced upon the mouths of their cannon. It happened that there was an old rail-fence on the side where we approached, with a small growth of shrubbery by the fence and within less than two rods of the cannon's mouth, undiscovered by the enemy. I then very cautiously ordered my men to rest across the fence, take good aim, fire, and rush, which was done in style. Not one man at the cannon was left to put fire to them. We got into the centre of their park before they had time to oppose us. A British line was formed, and lying in a strong position to protect their artillery. The moment we got to the centre, they opened a most destructive flank fire on us, killed a great many, and attempted to charge with their bayonets. We returned the fire so warmly they were compelled to stand; we fought hand to hand for some time, so close that the blaze of our guns crossed each other; but we compelled them to abandon their whole artillery, ammunition-wagons and all, amounting to seven pieces of elegant brass cannon, one of which was a twenty-four-pounder, with eight horses and harness, though some of the horses were killed. The British made two more attempts to charge us at close quarters, both of which we repulsed before I was reinforced, after which the 1st and 23rd Regs. came to my relief. And even after that, the British charged with their whole line there several times, and after getting within half pistol-shot of us were compelled to give way. I took, with my regiment, between thirty and forty prisoners, while taking and defending the artillery. After Generals Brown, Scott, and others were wounded, we were ordered to return back to our camp; about three miles, and pre-

parations had not been made for taking off the cannon, as it was
impossible for me to defend them and make preparations for that
too, and they were all left on the ground except one beautiful six-
pounder, which was presented to my regiment in testimony of
their distinguished gallantry. The officers of this army all say, who
saw it, that it was one of the most desperate and gallant acts ever
known; the British officers whom we have prisoners say it was the
most desperate thing they ever saw or heard of. Gen. Brown told
me, the moment he saw me, that I had immortalized myself.
"But," said he, "my dear fellow, my heart ached for you when
I gave you the order, but I knew that it was the only thing that
would save us." We wounded Major Gen. Druininon, took Major
Gen. Null Prisoner, with betwint twenty or thirty other officers.
How many non com officers, and Privates I have not yet learnt as
they were sent hastily across the River, but a very considerable
number. I should like to fill up the paper but time will not permit.
Tell Mrs Noar ——— is well was not in the fight as I had sent him
back to Buffalow on business. You may direct to me at Buffalow. I
hope I shall hear from you soon, if you could only be sensible how
much comfort your letters afford me you would even let the
children try to get time to write. I have not been well for a week
or ten days, but am better, I hope you are all well. May God
continue his blessings and protection to us all and return me safe to
the bosom of my adored Ruth. Please to give my love sincerely to
all, particularly to Catharene and the children. Tell them I want to
kiss them but you must do it.
    Until.

Ensign Thomas Warner, Baltimore Voluneers

A Maryland silversmith, Thomas Warner enlisted for service on
September 8 1812. The letters below, written on a tour of duty
which took him into British Canada, are to his wife, Mary Ann.

                    Carlile [Pennsylvania], *October 7 1812*

Dear Mary
    We arrived here after fatiguing a march to some of our men on
Saturday evening, very good weather until the last day when it
rained the whole day. The water ran down the mountains in
torrents, however our men were in the highest spirits singing
and joking each other all the way. Will have not a man on the sick
list. For my own part I never was healthier in my life. in high

spirits. The citizens of Carlile have treated us with the greatest hospitality. They would not suffer us to pitch our tents until Sunday. They came forward and offered their houses beds and provisions for our accommodation gratis. On yesterday they presented the whole corps with an ellegant dinner and plenty of wine to drink their healths with which was done with enthusiasm. In truth their hospitality is beyond anything I ever experienced. Please to inform Mr. Barckley I saw his Brother Robert who was well. I met here a great number of old acquaintances Brother officers who treated me with the most marked attention. Should you be acquainted with any of those particular Ladies of the seventh ward who presented us our stand of colours you will please inform them they were so much admired we were obliged to display them.

My dear wife you will please inform my mother, my brothers and sisters and my friends also of my health etc. tell them I would write them but the extreme difficulty an officer is under of getting paper, time and other necessarys totally incapassitate me. Therefore they must wait with patience.

Do be pleased to write me how my dear children are and yourself as you and them are the only thing that prey on my mind I hope you will excuse me for not calling to bid you adieu as the trial would have been too great for me to bear At the same time remember you are a soldiers wife—and one who loves you dearly give them one kiss and tell them their father puts up a prayer to heaven for their welfare—Mr. Nolan, Our waggoner will be in town on Saturday and if you or any of my friends will write he will bring them direct to me. He will be found at Mr. Leypolds. Afterwards then letters must be directed to Niagara. Be pleased to tell Mr. Barckley to give my respects to Mr. Richardson, Mr. Sollers, Haslet, Taylor, Barry, Myers & all enquiring friends.

Buffaloe November 27, 1812

My Dear Wife,

It is with a degree of satisfaction I inform you of my health and the greatest part of the Company. Tomorrow at 7 o'clock we embark for Canada—consequently it will be liberty or death—You must excuse me for not writing you more as I am officer of the day and guard both, therefore, I am obliged through necessity to wright at 12 o'clock to night. My love to my parents and relations and tell them the next they hear from me I shall be in Canada— remember me to my Children tell them my soldiers love, and that nothing but death shall ever part us—You will please remember me to Mssrs. Graof, Barkley, Sollers, Richardson, Taylor, Haslet, Barry and all enquiring friends—

except my dear wife my
sincere love and esteem
Mrs. Mary Ann Warner
Thomas Warner Ensign B. V.

N.B. direct your letters to Thomas Warner Ensign, B.V. care of Major Noon at Buffalo or elsewhere Yours, T. W.

N.B. intended to wright my Brother Andrew but it is impossible at present therefore please show him this letter and with it he will receive for himself and wife, family my faithful boys etc. etc.

Sackets Harbour April 19, 1813

My Dear Wife,

I arrived here on Saturday last after a disagreeable journey blocked by ice, snow, etc. We are preparing to move off from here but to where I do not know. Under the circumstances I cannot tell you where to direct your letters which is truly mortifying to me. If I should be spared when I possibly can I will write you. I am rather unwell at present. I hope it will not continue long. Remember me to my children. Tell them I have not forgot them. You please inform my Brother and all those who may enquire after me that I would write them but it is with the greatest difficulty I have time to write this to you, therefore tell them that our regiment is divided and our Company and the Albany Greens are attached to general Pikes Brigade and are to embark abroad of the fleet for some secret expedition which they shall hear of as soon as the nature of it has transpired. Tell them our Company has reduced to 65 effective men out of all those brave fellows we started with. That their decipline far exceeded any regulars I ever saw, that the British call us the Baltimore Blood hounds. If we should meet with any of them we shall give a good account of them. The beauty of our little fleet surpasses anything I ever saw, I think they can flog twice their number without any difficulty. One of them, called the growler, has gone out as a spie to see whether the coast is clear or not etc. etc. Give my love to my father and mother sisters, brothers & to old seventisixer and tell him I have not forgot what he suffered for my liberties. Neither will I part with them until I suffer full as much. Being hurried I must close.

except for yourself and children My Dear Wife a father and Husbands love and esteem
Mrs. May Ann Warner
Thomas Warner Ensign

B.U.T. Vtrs.

N. B. my sincere respects to Mr. Taylor, Froly, Barkley Majors Haslett, Richardson, Soller etc. etc. etc.

Yours T. W.

York [Upper Canada] *April 29th–1813—*

My Dear Wife,

It is with sincere satisfaction that I inform you of my being well after a pretty severe engagement. Our Captain has lost his leg, Lester Irvine is badly wounded and poor Hazeltine. They will I expect recover, at least I hope so. I did-intend to have resigned after the engagement but now it is impossible in consequence of the wounded officers. For more particulars I refer you to the letter I write my Brother Andrew which I have directed him to show you if you wish to see it. My love to my dear children and be particular with my boy. Love to all enquiring friends, Henry Groff in particular who I shall never forgett————[one line missing]

My love to the boys. I shall probably write you again in about 8 or 10 days. Our brave general Pike was killed in the engagement—

Accept for yourself and Children my sincere love and esteem

Mrs Mary Ann Warner

Thomas Warner

Ensign Balt. Volt.

Corporal Samuel Stubbs, Kentucky Militia

Stubbs joined the United States' army at the age of sixty-three, fighting at Queenstown, Lundy's Lane, Fort Erie and New Orleans.

Brother Ephram,

I just write you to enform you that I'm still alive and in tolerable helth and choice spirits—altho as well as my brother *officers*, I have had some hair bredth escapes. Sposing that you would like to know something about my military life since I quit home, I'll give you the whole story.

When the express first came into our neighborhood, calling upon us all to turn out and march against the Canadians, I was like another [Israel] Putnam, ploughing in my field—but I immediately unharnest the old daples, swung my napsack, shouldered my old gun that had killed me forty-five deer the three months past, and marched away for head quarters.

In four days time I joined the army with a dozen more of my neighbors, near Queenstown. The brave Col. Van Rensselare was our commander in chief, under whose command we the next day (which being the 13th day of October 1812) in boats crossed over to Canada—But, ah, in the end it liked to have proved rather a bad job for us, for the opposite shore was lined with redcoats as thick as bees upon a sugar maple—but after exchanging a few shots our brave Colonel buzzed in among them, while I and the rest followed close to his heels, and drove them all up a steep bank. We now got a fair footing and stuck up the American colours in Canada! We did not obtain this much however without some loss on our part, and what was unfortunate for us all, our Colonel was severely wounded—but he was still able to keep upon his legs and with great courage ordered us to push forward and storm their fort, and that we did, and made them one and all scamper off into the woods.

But we were now in our turn unfortunate, for one half of our army was yet on the other side of the river, nor would the cowardly dogs come over to assist us when they saw the d———d redcoats cutting us up like slain venison! The enemy now doubled their numbers while every shot diminished ours; in truth they got the better of us, and again got possession of their batteries, altho we let fly showers of ball and buck shot into their very teeth and eyes! Ah! the poor Yankee lads, this was a sorry moment for ye! They dropped my brave companions like wild pigeons, while their balls whistled like a northwest wind through a dry cane break! Our Commander ordered a retrete, but nature never formed any of our family you know for runners, so I wadled along as well as I could behind; but the redcoat villains over-haul'd me, and took me prisoner! But not until I had a fare shot at their head commander General Brock, who galloping his horse after my retreting comrads, bellowed out to 'um like a wounded buffalo to surrender; but I leveled my old fatheful Bess, which never disappointed me in so fare a mark, and I heard no more of his croaking afterwards.

Oh one thousand which crossed over, but a few escaped biting the dust! As for poor me, I expected they'd kill and scalp me, but after stareing at me as if I had been born with two heads, and enquiring of what nation I was, and from what part of the world I came, their Colonel ordered me liberated, who said to me, "Old daddy, your age and odd appearance induces me now to set you at liberty; return home to your family and think no more of invading us!" This I promised him I would do, but I didn't mean so, for I was determined I wouldn't give up the chase so, but at 'um again.

So I hastened off and joined General Deerbon's army; and on the 27th day of April [1813] we took Little York, which is the chief town of the Upper Province. We went in boats, and the redcoats peppered a good many of us before we reeched the shore. But when we got footing, they fled before us like an affrighted flock of redwinged boblinkons. We drove 'um, from their battery, and then in a powerful body of pursuing 'um, when on a sudden, as if the whole earth was paring asunder and discharging from its bowels huge rocks and stones, a dreadful exploshon took place from the maggazeen, which the arch dogs had fixed for the purpose! And a serious exploshon it proved for us, I tell ye, for it killed one hundred of our men, including our brave commander General Pike. For my own part, I scaped with just my life as you may say, for a stone as big as your fist struck me on the head, and nocked off a piece of my scalp as broad as your hand! But, faith, this I didn't mind much, but waddled on with the rest, over dead bodies as thick as cowslops, and soon got posesshon of the town. The cowerdly British chief, General Sheaff, had thought it best to scamper off with his soldiers and Indians before we entered the town, so that I got but one fare shot at one of their copper-colour'd sanups, whose heels I soon made too light for his head, and would have scalped the dog, but my captin would'nt allow it.

As all the work appeared now to be done in this quarter, I marched off. And on the 20th June [1814] joined General Browne's army, which amounting to about three thousand brave boys of us, on the 3d day of July, crossed the Niagara. General Scott commanded the first brigade, Gen. Ripley the second, Gen. Porter the militia, and Farmers' Brother the Indians, who were painted as red as maple blosums. Fort Eree surrendered to us that very day, and on the next we marched to Chippewa, driving the enemy before us like so many fire-frightened antelopes!

On the 5th, the enemy's commander, General Riall, came out upon Chippewa plain, with two thousand two hundred regelers, while my militia boys and the Indians on both sides were engaged in the woods. For my own part, I climed a sturdy oak, where I assure you I did not suffer my old Bess to grow cold, for whenever I saw an Indian creeping like an allegator upon his belly, I gave him the contents in full, and made him hug the ground to sum purpose. I'm sure I killed fifteen of 'um in fifteen minnits, and shood have been glad to have fleeced them; but the New England men don't approve of scalping. At this time our brave troops under Gen. Scott was hotly engaged with Gen. Riall's redcoats, who after an hour's hard fighting, they turn'd tail to and run in all directions, and saved their pork by gaining their works at Chippewa. We killed about five hundred of them, while our loss was three hundred twenty-nine killed wounded and prisoners. And thus ended this engagement.

On the 25th, I agin marched with Gen. Scott, who advanced with his brigade, betwixt eight and nine hundred, about a mile in the Queenstown road, where we found the enemies, and engaged 'um about sunset. The enemies were guessed to be four thousand stout, and were cummanded by Gen. Drummond. The tussel lasted til about leven a'clock, when, gad! I believe both parties were willing to quit the field. We took twenty pieces of artilary from 'um; one of 'um I took, faith, myself alone with charg'd bagnut [bayonet]! The loss on both sides was about nine hundred; the redcoats commander, Gen. Riall, and about twenty officers were taken prisoners. Our Gen. Brown and Gen. Scott were wounded. The next day, we return'd to Fort Eree, under command of Gen. Ripley.

August 15th, Gen. Drummond ordered an assalt upon our fort in three columns, consisting of the bestest men of his army, to the amount of three thousand. There was about one thousand five hundred of us, under Gen. Gaines, who took cummand of us about the first of August. We repulsed the redcoats with great loss. We killed, mangled and made prisoners of about one thousand five hundred of 'um. They lay as thick as slartered mutton around. Ha, brother Ephe, a fine picking for skelpers! Our loss was sixty killed and wounded.

I continued with the American troops until they were about to go into winter quarters, when with the thanks of my General, like another Cincinnaty, I started home, to exchange my rifle and bagnut for the ploughshare and pruning hook. But I did not get half way when I was summoned to repair to New Orlenes, where the redcoats had landed and were thretening to over run the whole country! Accordingly, I right-about-face, and with quick step steered my course for New Orlenes, where by land and water tacks I arrived in seven days.

I found the whole place in alarm. They had had some skermishing with the redcoats, but the desisive battle was yet to be fought, as you shall here. I joined capt. Copp's company, a nice man, who gladly receiv'd me, and in three days promoted me to the office of a CORPORAL! As I never held any office before, you know, it made me feel kinder queer at first; but I soon learnt my duty, and the grate responsibility attached to my office.

On the morning of the 8th, before day-light, the enemy silently drew out a large force to storm our lines, where we were entrenched up to our chins. There was a great fog, and their columns advanced unperceived to within about half a mile of our camp, and drove in our piquet [picket] guard. About the break of day, they as bold as hunger wolves advanced to our entrenchments, led on by their foolish officers up to the very muzels of our guns. I could have dropped them as easy as a flock of benumb'd wild turkeys in a frosty morning. But I picked for those who had frog paws upon their shoulders, and the most lace upon their frocks. Aye, the Corporal did his duty that day I'll warrant ye. Some of the foolish redcoats penetrated into our lines, where they were soon baganuted or taken prisoners; many fell mounting the brest works; others upon the works themselves. The roar of artillery from our lines was insessant, while an unremitted rolling fire was kept up from our muskets. Ah, *my men* performed wonders. For an hour and a quarter the enemy obstinately continued the assault; nor did they faulter until almost all their officers had fallen. They then retreted, leaving from one thousand five hundred to two thousand in killed mangled and prisoners. On our side the loss was confined to about twenty men—but I lost but one out of my company!

So I remain, yours, &c.

Corporal Samuel Stubbs

THE WAR WITH MEXICO 1846–8

The Mexican War was caused by the USA's annexation in 1845 of Texas, an American-settled province of Mexico. Resentful of the loss, and fearful of further American expansionism, Mexico launched an attack on US forces under Captain Thornton at Brownsville, Texas, in April 1846. A month later, Congress passed the War Bill and two short but bitter years of conflict ensued. There was considerable opposition within America to the war—New England dissenters viewed it as an immoral, imperial landgrab—but its successful prosecution did much to further the mythical self-image of Americans as naturally able citizen-warriors. (This despite the fact that much of the fighting, especially in the early days, was done by regulars). By the war's end California, Arizona, New Mexico, and parts of Utah and Colorado had been brought into the boundaries of the USA.

Lieutenant Napoleon Dana, Seventh Cavalry

The son of a professional soldier, Napoleon Jackson Tecumseh Dana graduated from the US Military Academy with the class of 1842. The letters extracted below are written to his wife, Sue, and begin when Dana was stationed on the Mexican border in readiness for war.

On the Nueces. September 1, 1845

. . . The skin, dear wife, [is] off of two places on me, it is burned off of my face by the hot sun and rubbed off of my tail by a hard-trotting horse. You did not know that I am a mounted officer, though, and I belong to the regimental staff. Yesterday I was appointed quartermaster to the regiment by Major Brown, under an order from General Taylor. It has nothing to do with the company, but quartermaster alone. So that I have charge and conduction of all the transportation, mules, horses, oxen wagons, baggage train, etc. of the regiment. It is a high compliment paid me by the major when there are so many officers senior to me. The task is very arduous and responsible and will keep me riding about pretty near all the time. I have a good horse and saddle and have used him a good deal already. This will give me back the sixteen dollars a month which I lost by leaving Fort Pike. How long I shall keep the appointment I cannot tell, because there are three quartermasters ordered out here from Washington, and one of them may be required to perform the duties for this regiment. Should I retain it and we commence our marches, all my energies will be called out, every one of them in full play. The office, if faithfully fulfilled, is no sinecure.

Besides being a mounted officer, I have also mounted my bed. Until last night I have slept on the ground, but the reptiles were so abundant I could stand it no longer, so I made Evans cut me four crooked forks and plant them at the four corners of my bed. Across these I laid two crooked poles and again across these I laid some flour-barrel staves. This is my bedstead. It broke down this afternoon and I rolled out of the tent, to the great amusement of Britton and all hands. When I rolled out, the horse kicked and Bascomb barked and everybody laughed.

But the snakes are really bad here and are the only bedfellows we have. Yesterday morning Whiting found a huge rattlesnake coiled up at the foot of his bed. He woke all around him with his nine rattles. They killed him and Whiting has his skin. A Lieutenant Smith had one crawl over his bare legs one night and he laid still until His Snakeship crawled off. We all get used to the varmints here and you must not be surprised if I bring home a few pets of the kind.

October 11, 1845

When I come home . . . I shall want to kiss you all over, and won't you let me do it? I know you will, for you told me on the steamboat you would do everything I want. May I kiss you over and over again on your lips, titties, belly, legs, and between them too? Yes, I must. Tell me, dear one, if I may.

You don't know how anxious I am lest you are in a delicate situation. Tell me all about it, Sue. It is possible that nursing may make your courses irregular, and they may come yet, but it was after the time when you last wrote me? I really hope you are not so. It appears too much to lose. You will have all the pain and trouble, without our having all the enjoyment. If you are so, we are losing a deal of fun in bed.

Say, darling, don't you like for me to talk to you in this way? Do you ever think of me in that way? So you have not put my miniature in my place yet? Are you not going to do it? I am just as big a rascal as ever, am I not? It is my love for you which prompts it all, dearest one. I never think of anyone else in that way and when I used to talk to you of others it was only to laugh at you. A brute beast will lick the dirt from its own young but will only bite those of another. So with me, darling wife. Your parts inspire me with love and excite my desires. Other women would disgust me. Conversations which, before I was married, I would sit and listen to and join in now fill me with the deepest disgust. Will you really send me the measure of your leg right high up?

Well, no paymaster came by the *Alabama* and I am sure you will want money. Captain Sanders of the engineers very kindly volunteered to lend me a check, which he has, and I will get that and send it to you. It is not a large one but it will do for you until I can send you more. You shall have just as much as you want, and I want you to tell me always how much you stand in need of. I would send you a pay account of seventy-five dollars but I owe these men so much that I am anxious to keep by me all you have not use for.

Fort Brown, Texas, Monday night, May 11, 1846
My own dearly beloved wife:
I am now, after the labors of the day, after tattoo has sounded, and the men are all sleeping under the starry canopy on the cold ground, going to devote my first leisure and chance that I have had for the last ten days to commencing one of my regular letters. I cannot describe, my darling, all my feelings of delight at being able once more to pour my words into your ears and to tell you how dear, how doubly dear, you are to me during all my troubles, labors and occupations. Danger and death for a time no longer before me, I see with deep, deep love the guiding star which cheers me on in trying hours, and to its influence I can attribute a great share of my courage, at the same time nearly all, my dearest Sue, when the swift-winged messengers of destruction were passing in this direction, my thoughts were with you and our little one and my prayer to God was that all this day of happiness might be in store for us—and when from a sound sleep the midnight alarm would call me from my couch, to repel assaulting columns and destructions, my first thoughts were always of my chosen one and my child and my second that I would not make them ashamed of me. God has spared me, has spared us all, in many cases most miraculously, and the most skeptical can but acknowledge that He is fighting for us and that His shield covers us.

The enemy has hardly believed it true that we have escaped so well, and I am not blaming them for their doubts, for unless we had seen we would not have believed. Shells are well known to be the most deadly weapons of war, and although their batteries threw 800 of them at us, besides 2,000 shot, although they fell in our very midst at the very feet of men and burst there, but two were hurt. It is no chance but it is an overruling Providence. I wrote you, my dearest wife, on the 4th, which was the day after they had commenced bombarding us. Well they continued their games night and day for seven successive days. The third day they commenced and bombarded very hotly. Indeed, very many shells burst inside the fort. They were evidently trying their hardest then.

In the forenoon of that day a howitzer shell mounted the parapet and before he could escape took off the leg of Major Brown below the knee. An amputation was immediately performed, and he would have done well but that there was no safe place to put him in but in a magazine, where it was too hot. It was so hot he could scarcely breathe. Of course his fevers raged and he died day before yesterday, even whilst we heard the general's cannon pouring death among the enemy whilst marching to our relief. We buried the gallant major yesterday under the flag; he is a very serious loss to our regiment: one which we will not be able to replace. He was a perfect bulldog for the fight.

Well, on the third day after they had tried their best, and as they thought they had killed a great many of our men, who, by the way, they thought had got out of provisions, in the afternoon they stopped their firing and sent in to us four officers with a white flag. Soon as we heard their trumpet sound the "parley" we knew what was coming. They brought a letter from General [Mariano] Arista summoning our garrison to surrender as prisoners of war. He told us that he had a large and well appointed army between us and our supplies, that the success we were expecting could not reach us, that he had large forces in reserve, that we were reduced to the last extremity, could not possibly hold out much longer, and that circumstances of humanity dictated that we should save our men from sacrifice. He gave us an hour to consider. Captain Hawkins who was left in command immediately convened a council, who unanimously agreed that as the enemy had not hurt us and probably could not the very idea of a surrender was absurd. An answer was returned to General Arista that we begged politely to decline his invitation.

Well, that night we expected that as a matter of course we would be stormed. Our men were delighted, in the highest spirits, and highly incensed at the idea of a surrender to those "niggerly rascals". They swore they would not do it if they had a load of powder left. All made up their minds to shoot as many Mexicans as each man could. If they had only brought us their assaulting columns they would have been cut all to pieces, but they knew better than that. Mexicans cannot yet be found who will assault a work garrisoned by our troops.

Tuesday morning, May 12

A tremendous thunderstorm came up last night, my own dear wife, and I was obliged to stop writing. Everything got wet, my candle blew out, and I put things away and went to sleep. Nothing new of consequence this morning, dearest, so I will commence where I left off.

The fourth day of the bombardment was made still hotter and the shells were thrown better than on any day previous. They fell everywhere amongst us and burst in all direction in crowds of men, and still no one was hurt; a kind Providence kept us safe. A shell fell at the feet of Corporal Van Voorhies, another rolled over a man's back, and another between a man's legs whilst he was eating dinner, and although they all burst, they hurt no one. A shot went through Captain Hawkins' tent just over his head when he was eating breakfast. Two through Mr. Page's tent, two through Major Brown's. A shell fell in the chest where the band instruments were packed, burst there, and smashed every one of them. One of the shells went through three horses.

On the fifth day a man's arm and another man's leg were broken. The sixth and seventh days were kept up by the enemy as usual with just as little injury to us.

We all the time husbanded our ammunition for the assault, and only now and then threw a few 18-pound shot where we saw men, and we killed and wounded at least twenty of them. One of our shot passed through a house in the town and killed two poor women. They ought to have been out of the way. Twice a couple hundred rancheros were sent up to open musketry on our men, but they did not care to approach near enough to see any advantage and all their bullets fell short. We placed a few rifles on the parapet and killed a couple of those fellows, and they went off satisfied.

Last Friday about three o'clock in the afternoon we heard cannonading about eight miles [away], and immediately knew that the general was on the move and had met the enemy. The cannonade lasted until sundown, which showed us that the enemy had made a tolerably good stand.

Next day we heard nothing at all for so long a time that we began to be somewhat disheartened, thinking that the general had met an overpowering force and had been obliged to retire. If this had been the case, we would indeed been in a bad way. We saw columns of the enemy in the distance passing down to reinforce their army, which had been attacked. However, about three o'clock in the afternoon we again heard the cannon and musketry within four miles of us; we then knew that the enemy had retreated to a new position and that the general had advanced. We saw the retreating columns of the enemy hurrying from the field of action towards west, a perfect rout, horse and foot had thrown their arms and would plunge in [the Rio Grande River] to swim over. Many were drowned. Panic and consternation had spread through them. They were wild with fright. They knew not what to do and only sought to fly as swiftly as possible to save themselves from the terrible effect of the fire of our troops, and close upon their heels with shouts appalling to their ears came our dragoons and light artillery, dealing death around them and cutting off from many the last hopes of flight. Our fellows were perfect devils. The heat and excitement of the battle and the flush of one of the most astounding and brilliant victories on record had made them terrible in wreaking vengeance on these savage peoples. All who did not throw down their arms and ask for quarter were cut down without any hesitation.

Soon some of our dragoons came toward the fort; they swung their hats over their heads to tell of their victory. They were the first friends we had seen for eight days. Five hundred of our brave fellows mounted the parapets, threw their caps in the air, and gave them such cheers as made [the city of] Matamoros ring from the faubourg [suburb] to the square. You might have heard the cheers two miles. Those shouts told the enemy what had happened on this side. The effect was instantaneous. Their guns immediately ceased to fire upon us, and disheartened, disgusted, and appalled, they slunked from their batteries into the town to bear the terrible tidings of their disasters, not knowing what to think was the reason why their fire was not more hurtful to us.

Since then they have been perfectly quiet, doubtless dreading that at any moment we would open our batteries to take the town. We will allow them but two or three days of quiet. We will then be perfectly ready, plenty of guns and plenty of ammunition. Matamoros will then be summoned to surrender and if she refuses, which we do not anticipate, she will be forced to do so. I do not think that the Mexicans after having been so terribly cut up as they have been will be induced again to make a stand for some time to come.

May 13

I have been hard at work all before noon, my own darling Sue, and now, after dinner, I will see if I cannot get this letter ready to go by the first chance: I have to perform the duties of ordnance officer at the fort and I have been handling powder, arms, and all kinds of things which have been captured from our unfortunate and fallen enemy: I am mighty well and hardy, my beloved one, and enjoy the best spirits and you have no idea how much happier it makes me feel to hear that you are getting on so well and [in the mail] I received five letters from you. The first I had received for so long a time, and you may rest assured that I await on every word contained in them. I am delighted that you are so comfortably fixed and right proud that you are going on smoothly on your own hooks. God grant that we may not long have to live this life of separation, but that we may soon again be brought together to renew our happy life.

But—I finished telling you yesterday of the cannonade and bombardment of this fort and now I must communicate and give you some descriptions of the two battles and the most brilliant victory which has happened since the Battle of [New] Orleans.

You recollect, my darling one, that General Taylor left here on the first of the month with all the army except this garrison, to escort up the train of the army loaded with provisions, ammunition, and other miscellany. He had a double object in view in taking all the troops he had as an escort. He knew that the enemy were on this side of the river in force superior to his own. Their object was to recapture the train and attempt Point Isabel. He was to protect his train and, if he found them in his way, to give them a fair fight, if they were double his numbers, but he little knew that they were more than three to one.

He arrived at Point Isabel on the second and the first thing he heard on the morning of the third was the cannonade of our batteries. This put him in a fever at once and he wanted to start right off to return and fight the enemy if he could find them and compel them to raise the siege of this fort. Reflection, however, and advice taught him that it was useless to return, and worse than useless, without a fresh supply of provisions, arms, ammunition, and ordnance; and it was also advisable to get reinforcements if possible. He had the highest confidence in this garrison, and knew that it would hold out to the last and repel any attack which the Mexicans were able to make upon it. So he contented himself with sending to us an express of a half a dozen rangers of Texas to get information of our condition, and went to work leisurely to load up his train, and refresh his troops for the coming storm, when the Texan company returned with news of our wonderful good condition. The greatest excitement prevailed at Point Isabel and lots of champagne was wasted in health to the gallant command which so firmly held Fort Brown, our stronghold on the Mexican frontier. All the army felt the extreme of anxiety to hasten up to our relief, and they felt confidence in us and as long as they heard the firing they knew we held out.

Well, the general remained at Point Isabel until the morning of the eighth. Then, at a very line of march from this place, he marched all day until about one o'clock when evident signs of the vicinity of the enemy were seen and it was a certainty from the signs that they were in large force, with a very numerous cavalry and plenty of artillery. Soon the two opposing forces came in sight of each other.

The enemy had chosen a position which at once proved the well known ability of their General Arista. They were very cunning and tried to get our columns within short range, by a kind of stratagem—their cannon were concealed. They held a position on the edge of the prairie at the skirts of a thick growth of chaparral, almost impassable. In this more than half their troops and nearly all their cannon were masked, and drawn up in beautiful order in battle array. Where the remainder of their battalions giving a very inviting chance as it would seem for a fair pitched battle in an open plain. They expected that we would advance heedlessly to defeat what troops they had laid out as a bait, and then they expected to astonish us by a fire from their masked batteries and a sortie from their concealed column. But the general was not in such a hurry. He meant to have his fight and as they were, in numbers, three to his one, he advanced very carefully and cautiously. Their left flank rested on the chaparral, whilst their right extended out into the plain. Our general also went to the chaparral, rested his right on it, and threw out his left into the prairie, at the same time holding it back from the enemy. The enemy were so much more numerous than ourselves that in this position they outflanked us a good deal, but Lieutenant Duncan's light battery was thrown some way out, which obviated the sum.

When all was ready, the movement commenced by the army, swinging around on the right as a pivot and throwing the left wing in advance to meet the enemy. When within long shot the enemy opened fire from his heavy cannon, which he thought much superior to ours. Since he had not heard of our having field guns heavier than sixes, whilst his were nines, you may imagine his astonishment then when two huge eighteens drawn up by six yoke of oxen each (which the general was bringing up to put in the fort) were advanced and thundered to him. Although the effect of this could not be seen, it was ascertained afterward to be terrible. The fighting continued hotly for a short time, doing some damage among our troops, but a great deal among the Mexicans. Under cover of the eighteens Lieutenant Duncan's right battery on one flank, and Major Ringold's on the other, advanced, guarded by the different regiments of infantry, to take the enemy on the flanks, or as you would call it, raking. Their effect was terrible. The enemy felt it immediately. The rancheros which composed the Mexican volunteers were not able to stand it, and 1,500 of them were put to shameful flight. The enemy's cavalry then saw that to maintain themselves at all they must charge those regiments of infantry which supported the artillery. They must charge. Eight hundred lancers formed to charge the Fifth Regiment. On they came, with the speed of the wind. Quicker than thoughts the regiment formed in square, and with bayonets awaited the charge. Our fire dashed the cavalry of the Mexicans, [who advanced] as if they would ride right over the front of the square attacked; [the regiment] poured in its volley of buckshot, and balls and horses, officers and men of the lancers were brought to the ground. Many more reeled in their saddles, wounded. Some were thrown, and the rest in confusion galloped back to their own side of the field.

The same game was tried on Colonel Childs' battalion, with pretty much the same effect.

The enemy's cavalry then made two demonstrations to charge the batteries, but all the exertions of their officers, who were beating them with their sabers, could not induce them to do it.

In the meantime our guns had been pouring in a terrific fire. The enemy fired equally fast from an equal number of pieces, and fired well too, but there as well as here a kind Providence protected us. Not so with the enemy though. The sun went down on the fight and it was supposed that both armies could sleep on their arms and renew the battle in the morning. Our fellows made the proper dispositions and went to rest. Little did they dream of the immense damage they had done the enemy in comparison to what they had received. Little did they dream of the horrible sights which were on the opposite side of the field. Little did they think that their victory was complete, and that whilst they were taking their rest, the enemy, leaving a great part of their wounded, dead, and baggage on the field, were retreating to a new and stronger position. Seven thousand men before 2,000 of our little regular army! That night more than 400 wounded were carried into Matamoros.

Next morning our army arose bright and early, ready to continue the battle, and expecting to find the enemy in the same position he had occupied the evening before, but when our fellows looked about nothing was to be seen of a foe. It was taken for granted that they were secreted in the chaparral in order to catch our men as they came on. But on reconnoitering it was discovered that the Mexicans had evidently left their position in the greatest haste during the night, having on the field a cannon which had been broken down by our shot, all their dead, unburied, a great many wounded, and considerable baggage. The battle was a horrid spectacle, corpses mangled most horribly lying where they had fallen. Our grape and canister shot had literally mowed them down. They strewed the plain, and the wounded crying for assistance and interspersed here and there among the dead. Some were cut nearly in two by large shot, some had their heads off, some had lost arms, some legs, and so forth. Many officers were among them. One officer of lancers had a daguerreotype likeness of his sister on him, another had three letters in his cap to his father, sister, and wife, in which he said that some of the regiments had suffered much for food, that on some days past a number of them had nothing but salt meat.

The general waited in the field to bury the dead of both parties, and to give attention to the wounded. None of our officers were killed in the battle of the eighth. Major Ringold, Lieutenant Blake, Captain Page, and Lieutenant Luther were wounded. The two first are since dead. There is but little hope for the third, but the last is doing well.

After the men had breakfasted the general left his train in park with a guard and continued to move on, expecting to find that the enemy had taken up a very strong position in the chaparral. Their whereabouts was found about three o'clock in the afternoon. They had chosen one of the strongest positions possible in chaparral and in a ravine. Their battery of eight guns was placed with the intention of cutting our columns all to pieces as they advanced, but they did not know then that the American soldiers would charge right up the cannon's mouth. The two light batteries were ordered forward to the attack, with the dragoons Fourth, Fifth, and Eighth infantry, the Third and Colonel Child's battalion in reserve, our men spread in the chaparral and advanced on the enemy's lines.

The determination today was to go the whole hog and charge at once, without standing off at shooting distance. As our troops advanced their fire was terrible. Our shot and ball told with wonderful effect and the grape and canister scattered death in all directions. So swift was the advance that the enemy had only time to fire two rounds from his batteries before our troops with yells and shouts charged in amongst them. Captain May's squadron of dragoons and the Fifth and Eighth infantry charged right up to the batteries. The Mexicans stood their ground for some minutes like men, fighting hand-to-hand with sword and bayonet. Now was their last chance. If they gave ground now they were lost, and they knew it. One regiment, the Garda Costa from Tampico, would not give an inch and were entirely cut to pieces. Our fellows fought like devils. The enemy was brought down on all sides. They were forced back from their guns. The determined courage and valor of our men disheartened them. A panic seized them, and throwing down their arms they broke and fled in all directions.

A total rout followed. Each fled for life. Mounted and foot sought the nearest point. Huddled together, with our dragoons at their heels, many of them plunged into the river. Some were drowned. A great portion were dispersed among the chaparral, and many of them gave themselves up as prisoners of war. They left nearly everything they had behind them. Everything fell into our hands: nine pieces of brass cannon, a large quantity of ammunition, 500 pack mules with their saddles and equipments, 500 muskets, a great deal of baggage, some wagons; all of Arista's private baggage, plate, public and private correspondence, military papers and so forth, several hundred dollars in specie, horses and saddles, and so forth, General LaVega, and twelve or fourteen officers [as] prisoners besides about 300 or 400 men. This is one of the most remarkable and brilliant victories on record. A well-appointed and well-disciplined army of 7,000 men in their own chosen positions, with eight pieces of cannon, utterly routed, with the loss of all they had, by 2,000 men, and look at the immense difference in the loss of the two armies. Our loss was about 150 men in both engagements in killed, wounded, and missing, whilst theirs was in killed, wounded, and prisoners not less than 1,400. All their rancheros dispersed to their homes, and their infantry broken up. Out of 3,600 infantry which left Matamoros, only 300 have returned as yet. Their killed alone was upwards of 500, whilst ours was only about 65.

The Mexicans don't know what to make of it. They can scarcely realize their misfortune and cannot account for the best army which ever left Mexico being thus cut up by a handful of men, and they will not believe that they did us so little danger by the bombardment.

But you don't know, my darling Sue, how much we rejoice that all this has happened before the volunteers arrived. The country will see that it is the regulars which can do their business, and had the volunteers been here they probably would have gotten all the credit for our hard fighting.

General LaVega is quite a dashing-looking fellow. I believe he is going to Washington on parole. Captain May took him from his guns. All of his men ran: he stood there and was taken a prisoner. He is astounded and he says that all Mexico will be. He says he cannot account for the decided superiority of our soldiery. He has fought Spaniards, Frenchmen, Mexicans, Texans, and Indians, but cannot understand where we can find men who will charge right up to the muzzles of a battery. He says that it is of no use to bring numbers to whip us. It can only be done by the hardest kind of courageous fighting.

In the action of the ninth, our officers suffered much more severely. Lieutenant Inge of dragoons and Lieutenant Cochrane of the Fourth and Lieutenant Chadbourne of the Eighth were killed. Colonels McIntosh and Payne, Captain Howe, and Lieutenants Seeden, Indan, Gates, Maclay, and Burbank wounded. A kind Providence has certainly protected us; when we look over the field of battle and see the large number of the enemy slain, and the number of wounded prisoners we have joined to the 670 which are in the hospital at Matamoros, and then look at our own suffering, we have abundant reason to be grateful to God for his goodness. Some officers who were badly wounded, after giving them the best medical attendance here we have sent over to Matamoros. An equal number of officers and men have been exchanged for Captains Thornton and Hardie and Lieutenant Kane and the dragoons who were captured a short time since, and they are all with us again. The former is under arrest and will be tried for the affair.

And now, my own sweet little Sue, I will bid you good night, and tomorrow if I do not have to close my letter to you of what happens here nowadays, I can get a chance to talk about other things, I've got to tell you yet all about your letters and how much

I am longing to see you and everything else. I hope I shall get a chance tomorrow. It is now very late and I must go to sleep. So now good night, my dear Sue, and may Heaven forever keep you and our little one.

May 16, 1846

I do not think, my darling Sue, that our war will last much longer. The people of Mexico will not stand it to be whipped so badly as they have been. Old Paredes, I expect, will soon be supplanted by someone else, perhaps Santa Anna, who will urge a peace and accept pecuniary compensation for whatever Mexico may imagine herself to be despoiled of.

We hooked all their boats from them the other night. Fifty men with muskets went down to the river bank as a guard to the swimmers, whilst six dragoons stripped and swam across to cut loose their boats. It was a daring thing, but no sooner had these naked men got on the other side than the Mexican sentinel, without even firing his musket, ran off as fast as his legs would carry him, and our fellows took the boats . . .

It will not be long before the Texas rifles get here, a couple of thousand of them, and they are a perfect terror to the enemy. They spare none of them. They merely bring in prisoners enough to keep up appearances and kill all the rest. We can hardly blame them, for they get no quarter from Mexicans. It is a war of extermination between them, and there is scarcely a Texan who does not thirst for Mexican blood. A party of forty-five rancheros met fifteen Texans at the Colorado not many days since, cut the throats of all of them, and threw them into the river. Miraculously, two of them survived and are here now and will take ample vengeance, they say, for the whole gang . . .

God knows that after this feud is over, if He sees fit to spare me, I would most gladly and joyfully lay aside the sword and seek in a more peaceful walk of life an asylum from the noise and busy bustle of the outer world. The sight of ghastly wounds, the agony of death, its look in every shape, the groans of the expiring and the cries of excruciating pain, the smell of blood and putrid human flesh and the polluted atmosphere, and a woman on the field of battle, with a babe in her lap, unable to weep but wringing her hands and combing the hair of her mangled husband's corpse and kissing his bloody lips, are all sights unsuited to my tastes and shocking to my feelings. The latter case is a real occurrence. A sergeant of the Eighth Infantry who was killed had his wife in the train of wagons coming on from Point Isabel. I did not see her on the field myself, but Dr. Porter told me that he did. I, however, saw her the next morning sitting with a child in her arms, her face buried in its sleeping form, sitting beside a group of dead.

But never had a people [more] cause to be grateful to a kind Providence for warding off dangers than have we. We have heard that poor old Captain Page is dead. Poor fellow, it perhaps is for the best. He could never have spoke or have known a pleasant moment again. The whole lower part of his face—lower jaw, mouth, teeth, tongue, and all—were carried away by a cannonball in the Battle of Palo Alto on the eighth. Colonel McIntosh, it is thought, will recover. He was shot through the body with a musket ball and had a bayonet run through his cheek near his mouth out the back of his neck. You see, our fellows came hand to hand with the yellow rascals and fought them like devils. Lieutenant Jordan of the Eighth got into a crowd of them all alone by some accident. They knocked him down after shooting him in the side, and three of them got on him with bayonets. Lieutenant Lincoln came up and killed two of them with his sword. The third one ran his bayonet through Jordan's shoulder. He is doing very well and will recover. It is well that these things happened, for the Mexicans say that we are not men in a fight but diablos.

Private Carr White

An infantry soldier from Ohio, White participated in the battle for Monterrey, which is the "great fight" mentioned below in the letter to his sister.

n.d.

Dear Sister:
You would laugh if you could see how we soldiers live here. every felow has his knife fork Tin cup and plate. we do our own cooking. we have got a great big Bak Oven. we bake 20 Big loves at a time. we boil our victuals in a great big kettle, and every fellow gows and gets his tin full of Coffee his plat full of Meat & soop. we sprad a Blanket down on the ground and every felow is like a Hungry Hog. we have fine times, all we have to do is to keep our guns and swords clean, and I tell you the way they shine is a show; we muster two hours each day, and then sweep up our quarters we then go and swing or play Ball or lay down in our tents and read. we have lots of fun. Oh! it is the prettiest sight you ever saw to see about two thousand soldiers all dressed alike with Bright and

shining guns, swords, & belts white as snow, if you could see them marching and hear their music. we have some of the Best swings you ever saw. we have ropes fixed to the tops of trees so that we can swing 20 feet into the air. we have a circus show here too. they are performing in the camp now. there are some little felows like Gip that can stand on their feet and ride as fast as their Horses can run. we have some little felows here not much larger than Gip that can beat the drum and play the fife as good as any body.

I have got a fine silk sash to sent to you. I was gowing to send by Capt. Johnston but he had his saddle Bags so full that he could not take it. I will send it by Adam who is gowing home in the course of a week or two, it is about four yards long and a half yard wide. I gave four dollars and a half for it in the city of montarey. when you get it take good care of it. keep it as a relick of the great fight we had here. I have a fine silver mounted Bowie knife that I found on the Battle field the day of the fight. I picked up a fine sword on the Battle field which I still keep and ware every evening on dress parade. I could have picked up a dozen swords that were laying around without scabords, but I had enough to do to handle the gun and sword I had. I shot eleven times at the Mexicans that day as deliberately as I ever shot at a squirel They shot at us all the time with their Big Canons and muskets, one poor felow by the name of Pierson was shot right by my side[.] the Ball went clar through him and within an inch of his heart. he felt as though he were dead but lived. I steped over the Bodies of a[t] least 20 men who were either dead or wounded, I would not let myself sympathize with them for fear it would tend to intimidate. If I saw anything horible I would turn my eys away but after while I got so I could look at a dead man and feel no more sympathy than I would to see a dead dog. It was a terible time the Bulets whized arond us like so many Humin Birds. But I guess we whipe them at last.

You must write to me as soon as you get this. you must study hard. I will get some good Book for you as I go home. Tell Gip that he must study hard. Lem must study too. I want him to be as great a man as his namesake. he can if he will. Tell Gip and Lem they must keep good fires for Mother & little Liz—this winter & not lit them get cold. Gip and Lem are big enough to feed the cows & horses & they ought to do it. I am going to bring a wife home with me when I come.

Yours

Broth Carr

Captain Edmund B. Alexander, 3rd Infantry

To his wife

San Angel, New Mexico
August 27, 1847

My dear beloved Pet

It is again my happy lot my dearest to be permitted to give you an account of two hard fought battles which took place on the 20th Inst & in each of which my regiment bore a conspicuous part & well did it sustain itself, as usual your husband was among the foremost, now it is all over, I cannot see or account for my miraculous escape & I most sincerely offer up my thanks to the ruler of all for the protection which he has extended to me. And I know there is no one on earth who will more sincerely do the same than my beloved wife—I do assure you we had an overwhelming force opposed to us but right appeared to be on our side—and the day was ours—the enemy were sanguine and relied on superiority of numbers of both men & cannon—I will now dear give you the incidents connected with our approach to the City of Mexico. The army was halted at Ayotla distant from the city of about 12 or 15 miles for the purpose of Reconnaissance which was immediately commenced 7 or 8 miles ahead. I was sent with my Reg't to protect the engineers to El Pinzon the most advanced work of the enemy & some 6 or 7 miles from the city. This was found to be so strongly fortified & manned as to determine the Gen'l to select a different route—the first division of regulars being in rear was immediately put in motion—it being in the rear and we had to make a partial countermarch. This put our Division (Twiggs) in rear and we did not leave until the next morning[.W]e had not gone far when large force principally lancers were discovered on our left, preparations were immediately made to attack them, when a few shots from a piece of artillery dispersed the crowd, killing 5 or 6 horses & probably as many men. We encamped this night at ———— about 8 miles from Ayotla. The next morning we had not proceeded far on route towards San Augustine when we heard many discharges of cannon, which proved to be at Worth's division—we arrived at this latter town about 9 o'ck and were ordered to leave our baggage train so as to turn the position toward San Antonio before which place Worth's division was then lying & which proved to be strongly fortified—we left all we had with the wagons save a blanket and two days rations—we had not proceeded over 2½

miles on our route when a large force was seen immediately in our
front, and to the left of a small town Contreras and immediately a
heavy fire of cannon was opened upon us which did considerable
execution. I ordered the reg't behind a ledge of rocks in doing
which a ball passed so near my horse as to cause him to wheel
immediately around & so alarmed him that he became unmanage-
able, in fact I did not know for some time whether the ball had
passed through him or not or whether I was shot myself. I
immediately abandoned him & gave him to an orderly who had
my pack mule containing all my provision, blanket etc. here the
Reg't marched to the right to gain a road leading from Contreras to
San Angel—the ground over which we had to pass (there being no
road) except directly in front of the enemys cannon was impassible
for any but foot men. Consequently I left my horse & mule & all I
had—provisions Blanket etc. waided a stream gained the road
above mentioned & formed my regm't in line of battle immediately
on the left of the rifle Reg't[.H]ere a large force variously estimated
at 14 thousand and upwards under Santa Anna in person was
found directly in our front and intended to reinforce Valencia then
in command of about 7000 Troops in Contraros—This was near
sundown, arrangements were immediately made to attack them.
We were about 600 yards apart when the enemy commenced a
cheering Viva etc and blowing their trumpets & playing all sorts of
instruments. To all of this our Division were quiet listening and
finally the enemy not contented with these demonstrations of
hostilities fired two or 3 cannon shots directly at my Reg't but
without effect—Night coming on put a stop to the strife for this
day the 19th. I was ordered to move my Reg't in the Town of
Contreros to a church the yard of which we occupied for the
night—it commenced about dark and rained hard all night many of
the men had early in the day thrown away their blankets and
suffered much for the want of covering—As for myself I had not
eaten a mouthful since early daylight. Fortunately I met Dr.
Randall who gave me ½ a cracker & a small piece of raw pork
or bacon which I ate raw, I next went into the church & was about
disposing of myself at full length on the bricks feet wet & cold
when Dr. Cuyler came and offered to share his blanket—which I
readily accepted & thought myself fortunate in having even this
protection from the rain, my pillow was one of the Drs boots.
From the excessive fatigue of the day I soon fell asleep but was
woke by the Dr. saying he was very cold and told me to hug him—
which I did. We had not laid long in this way when I told him I was
cold & that he must hug me, we were shifting in this way the

remainder of the night—until about 3 o'ck when the reg't was formed. It still raining hard and quite dark & the road over which we had to march being narrow & muddy caused much delay in getting our position which we gained about daylight[.] I took advantage in the delays on the march to have the loads drawn & the guns wiped out—we had not been long in our position when a charge was ordered which resulted in one of the most brilliant affairs of the war, or in modern warfare—this charge was in Contreros where we kill upwards of 700[,] wounding thousands & putting the whole army to flight, taking upwards of 20 pieces of large cannon with much ammunition, etc. etc. and munitions of war were taken—This was the most complete route and slaughter I had ever seen—and did not exceed over ½ an hour after the charge was ordered—this was termed the battle of Contreros and took place immediately after sunrise on the morning of the 20th of Aug'st—I soon reformed my Reg't and rec'd orders to march in the direction of San Angel about 3 miles—where we halted and rested. This was about 12 m. Here for the first time since last night I got a cracker and two small slices of bacon given me by Mr. Throgmerton from Louisville. We talked much about home what he would tell my friends about me etc—here I had some talk with Butler Masons fortunate friend—who in a short time after received two wounds one in the leg and the other through the head which ended his existance—here a party of lancers made their appearance directly in our front as a decoy to lead us to Churubusco a strongly fortified work having many cannon and a very large force at least 16 thousand men & probably more—the Reg't was immediately formed and marched in the direction of Churubusco 2½ miles when a heavy fire of cannon & musketry was opened upon us as we halted in a road parallel to the works and again, I directed the men to lye down behind some maquay plants to protect them from the fire where we laid some considerable time, without being able to fire a shot. When the regm'nt was ordered by me to move forward and gain a position nearer the works I immediately rushed forward leading and gained a mud house some 60 or 70 yards from the enemys strongest position under the greatest fire you can imagine. Here my reg't opened a most destructive fire upon the enemy and in a short time compelled them to surrender when my Reg't had the good fortune to be the first to enter the works and raise their collers. I was detailed some little time with Lt. Buell a gallant officer who rec'd a severe wound but a short distance from the works—I found many officers of————Gen'l Rincon who by the by resembles Genl Taylor so much that I & several other

officers told him so which pleased him much. I immediately raised
the flag of the 3d Infy where those officers were, saying to Genl
Rincon the seignior in the excitement of the moment, that the
tattered flag which I then unfurled had fought in all the battles
from Palo Alto to this place—and which that day had recd two
additional holes—Placed it on the walls and ordered the Regt to
give it 3 cheers which they did most heartily—here the strife ended
for the day, and we could then have marched in the city without
the least interruption it being about 2 miles distant, in fact some
did enter the gates. Capt Kearny of the Drags. who lost his left arm
by so doing—Genl Scott determined to wait here and receive
propositions from Santa Anna who is most anxious to come to
terms—a white flag was sent out and an armistice was entered into
for the purpose of giving them time to appoint commissioners to
make peace[.H]ad we marched in Santa Anna with his army would
have fled to some other part of the country & we should have been
compelled to follow him, as it is he has the power and I think will
be glad to come to terms, and now for the first time do I feel as
though I should get out of the country soon[.S]hould they prove
false, we have taken cannon and ammunition enough with what we
had of our own to batter the city down—or to fire at least 1 month,
without interruption. The 3d have been in so many battles that
they know how to fight, and when to lay low. If I do not get a
Brevet for each of the 2 last fights I think I will quit—for no one
ever fought harder & with greater presence of mind than myself,
though I say it—I find the men have great confidence in me, I will
relate a little familiar conversation I had with a soldier as I rode
through the ranks after the battle at Contreros on the morning of
the 20—this in presence of 2 or 3 officers & many soldiers—it was
immediately after a victory when great latitude was given to the
men[.H]e began by saying well captain I am willing to follow you
anywhere, Why so? was the reply from me[.] I watched you closely
during the whole of the fight & I will fight for you as long as I live
& will go anywhere with you, and many other such remarks
[.W]hen I ordered a charge at Churubusco which I led I had to
pass a wide road about 150 yards from the enemys ranks, I soon
saw that a shower of musketry & grape was poured down this road
at the crossing & that there was a slight intermission[.] I took
advantage of this and made the men run across immediately after
each fire by which means many escaped, when about ½ were over I
found the remainder a little backward in crossing I ordered the rest
to follow & rushed ahead. The poor fellow who was close to me was
wounded—I visited the wounded today they were pleased to see

me & their being near me etc. I find if I cant get near a man in
action & he does not act right I am sure to throw a stone at him[.] I
did this in the hottest of the last when the individual thought he
was struck with a cannon ball—though I am strict with both
officers & men and they accuse me of having a temper—still they
have great respect for me, and obey with promptness any order I
give—and well they may for I am just in all matters and they know
I am ready to lead them into action & in the hottest of the fight—I
have given you all the incidents connected with the 2 battles as
near as I can recollect them, all blunders you must excuse as I have
written in a court room being one of 13 members sitting for the
trial of deserters from our army found in the Mexican ranks
fighting against us at Churubusco—you can readily imagine that
the interruptions were frequent—you know I am not at liberty to
tell you the sentences though you will hear them in due time, you
can readily imagine they will not be very light—for it is thought
their duty was to pick off the officers—we took near 100 of them,
they had formed themselves into a corps called the legion of
strangers—I refer you to the papers where you will see the reports,
many of which are much exaggerated and in some facts are related
which did not occur, and many are lauded to the skies who are not
deserving it, and those who are deserving are—I do not know
whether any mention will be a made of me or not but I do assure
you dear wife there is no one more deserving—or who risked
more—but a captain is small fry compared with those of higher
rank who are trying to take all praise to themselves & their
favorites[.] I gave you in my last which I wrote on the night after
the battle an account of your poor brother's death—for fear it may
not reach you I will now say he recd his death by a cannon ball
striking him sidewise under the chin taking off the entire throat
but injuring the neck bone[.H]is death was instantaneous he was a
brave little fellow and had advanced near the enemys works greatly
ahead of his Co. and shown himself behind a mud house which was
no protection against cannon—I learn these facts from an officer
who was with him, he appeared anxious to gain distinction—I sent
a lock of his hair for you to send to his poor mother to whom I fear
it will be a severe shock. I send in this a lock for yourself & shall
keep some to bring with me. I saw in his bag of clothes your
mothers likeness which I took out to bring to you, but William told
me he wanted it. If he insists on it, I will give it to him—I can
sympathize with you sincerely my dear Pet for his loss. I had seen a
great deal of him & liked him much & he became quite attached to
me—I have seen William, Penrose & Capt Alex'r they are all well

& escaped unhurt. Johnson poor fellow of the 6th looks miserable he has not recovered his eyesight, has no pain but is compelled to were specks & a handkerchief tied around it—I pity him much— tell Cass she would have a severe time with him—my love to her when you write—I hope to get back soon thus far all negotiations I hear are progressing smoothly—rumor says the Gen'l says all the army will be at Vera Cruz by the last of October—if so the passage from there to those I so dearly love is but short—tell dear ———— she will have no trouble in feeding me, as I have learned to eat everything & have a good appetite—a big slice anywhere I like best—now that prospects of peace are near at hand I am so restless & homesick I do not know what to do with myself—I would be willing to start to-m and walk all the way to Vera Cruz—tell Bettie her pa is anxious to see—permitted to do so—if we reach Vera Cruz by the last of Oct. I shall give up the comd of the regt probably to Maj. Clark who I am told has transferred with Jewett and will only stay long enough to dress myself up a little—Give my love to Ma your Mother, the boys sister E. and all tell them I am anxious to see them I think so much of home that I am dreaming of my dear Pet all the time. Kiss little Eddy & often for his Pa and [d]o take thousands for yourself from your heart husband.

Edm

God bless you again & again your devoted

E

THE AMERICAN CIVIL WAR
1861–5

On April 12, 1861, Confederate forces began the bombardment of the Federal arsenal at Fort Sumter, South Carolina. Four years later, almost to the day, on April 9 1865, in the silence of Appomattox Courthouse, the Confederate army of General Lee surrendered. In between times, over 600,000 soldiers had died of wounds and disease, and much of America, from Virginia to Arkansas, had been reduced to a battlefield.

Even when compared to the Napoleonic and Crimean Wars, the American Civil War was a peculiarly bloody conflict. In Pickett's charge at Gettysburg, 8000 (60 per cent) of the participants died in one single attack. In part this bloodiness was caused by the high passions involved; in part it was because of the advanced technologies available: mass-produced rifled artillery and firearms, iron battleships, even machine guns. The American Civil War was the first industrialised slaughter. As such, the Unionist anti-slavery North was always likely to win, since it had more and bigger factories, and a more extensive rail network. It also had the larger population, 20 million whites against 6 million in the Confederate South. To load its chances even more, the North began the recruitment of black soldiers in 1862. At its peak, the Union army was one million strong; the most the Confederacy ever put in grey at one time was 500,000 men.

Many of those who fought, aware that they lived in historic days, had an urge to record their experiences. They were able to do so, for the soldiers of the American Civil War were the most literate in history thus far. Perhaps as many as 180,000 letters passed to and from Union soldiers each day of the war; the troops of the Confederate States of America were no less productive with the pen.

William A. Montgomery, Company A, 33rd Virginia Volunteer Infantry, CSA

June 18, 1861

Dear Brother John,

In great haste I take my pencil in hand to drop you a few lines. I have nothing to write on but the head of the drum. Though a soldiers life is a hard life to live yet I am happy to say to you that I am in better health than I have been for 4 months. I can just eat anything that comes to hand and drink as much coffee as anybody. I will also say that if any of you writes to me that you need not direct your letters to me as Commissary of the company but as Second Sergeant of said company. The boys are all well but all homesick. You ought to see Wm. A. Daily. He is as quiet as a mouse. I believe he is satisfied soldiering. I can not say when I will be home to see you all again but I think I will be home this week but I do not know where we will but I think we will march to Romney today or march in the direction of Martinsburg to meet Col. Johnston's regiment. As for today, I was detailed as officer of the day over the guard of both company. I will not be relieved for 24 hours. Do not forget to have our knapsacks made as soon as possible and send them to us and tell Shonse to send that sword on as soon as he can do so. If we come to Romney I will send you word and I want you to come to see us. I must now close by hoping that these few lines will find you all well and in good spirits. I do not hear anything that is going on in the country here. I seen all the troops that came up on Sunday. So farewell friends at present. May the god of battles preserve and bless you all is my peace.

Your affectionate brother,

Wm Montgomery

John H. Ervine, Company 1, 1st Virginia Cavalry, CSA

To his wife

Berkeley County
June 18, 1861

Dear Ellen:

As we are not marching today I have another chance of writing, I shall write again. I have not heard from home yet except by Andrews letter which was dated the 9th. I know you have written several times but I have no chance of getting them. Yesterday was an exciting time with us as the enemy was at our old camp (Camp [Clover]) & we expected a fight but they did not come, they retreated it is said to Maryland. We were marched to Martinsburg early yesterday morning & taken in a corn field over a hill from the road & was kept waiting for 7 or 8 hours dismounted with our guns in hand ready to mount at the [word] & two companys sent out to meet the northern men & get them to advance on us but they had not the spunk. There is now 8 cavalry company in this regiment all well mounted on the very best of horses & about 16 or 18 thousand infantry within a few miles at a little town called Bunker Hill. Since I wrote to you at Winchester we have been marching all the time. I will try & give you the routes.

About ½ hour after I finished my last letter to you we left that place to cover the retreat of some troops from Sheperdstown. Then to Charlestown to cover the retreat of the troops from Harpers Ferry. We got to Charlestown early in the morning & stayed there for several hours, while we were there the road near filled with soldier from the ferry as full as you ever seen a road filled with stock cattle. I do not know how many thousand this I can say the road near full for about 12 or 15 miles one regiment after another as close as they could march for the baggage wagons. After they got past we left that place & come about three or four miles & stopped until about ten o'clock when we left & marched about 30 miles taking a back road to a point back of Martinsburg about 2 miles where we had to sleep on the ground with out our tents so as not to be easily seen. Now we are about 3 miles from Mburg on the Winchester road. There was three companys left here this morning to go down to see after the enemy & join Whites that was out in that part as a scout. I expect there will be a skirmish today if they can find the boys. News come to camp several times today that they had been plundering houses stealing negroes & stock of all kinds. Several family have moved by here today & a great many persons passing in vehicles of all kinds fleeing from the fiends.

I heard that the R-ham Regiment had gone to Romney but do not know it to be certain. I told Capt Yancey today if there was any more men detached from his company for express riders I wished to be one as my chance for getting letters would be better as I would go as often to Winchester as any other point. We are treated with all the kindness that any one could wish by citizens. Everyone has water and provisions ready for soldiers which is either sent to camp or handed out as we pass. I have no idea which way we will go from here no more than you do & can't tell until we get out on the road which way we will go so secret are the moves kept. I have been quite well since I left home & did not find it so hard to sleep on the ground as some did. I suppose the rest of the family think I ought to write to them but I can't get the time to do so & they must not complain for I will not write to anyone unless I can write to you oftener than I have done. I don't want you to imagine so many things about me as you have done especially that I will be hurt in a fight for I do not have any fears of being hurt if we do get in a fight. I have not thought that anyone [would] be hurt after hearing from those fights where two men at Romney [could] keep back several hundred. It is a bad show for hard fighting with abolitionists is said & believe to be true that 2 men in a bridge there with several negroes to [hold] for them made several hundred retreat.

We had our horses valued today & at big figures as well as I can guess the average must have been at $175. My horse was valued at $175 and saddle & bridle at 18. It is said by everyone that we have the best lot of horses in the regiment. Col Stuart said about 40 of our men are the best mounted men he ever seen as good the [—star] company is [here] the one other said who had such fine horses. There was some 20 of our horses went to & over $190. The highest was 225, only one as low as a hundred.

I wish you could see us getting meals. You used to think that we was dirty but if you was to see the beef strewn about on the ground & men cooking off it you would think we did not care for dirt. Our fare is nought nothing but beef or bacon & wheat bread. The bread is baked. Coffee we have to toast & grind ourselves. We have had sugar all the time until a few days ago the supply gave out.

Tell grandmother I will write to her soon & will try to give her all the news in camp. Tell Maggie & May for me the dear little things Pappa will come back some day & bring them candy & will tell them so many pretty story about little girls giving Pappa bread & butter & pies. Tell Father I want him to get me some goods for pants as my pants is getting somewhat worn and will not last me very long. Line the legs below with something strong as they soon cut through with the stirrups [tethers] & send me ten dollars by someone for I may want more money if I should get a chance to go home. I can't go on horseback as they will not let a horse go out of camp unless on duty. Though I will not come back without [Percey] unless he is killed or shot or I lose him some other way. You must not try to send any provisions to me for I can't get it. There is a number of boxes there now for our company in Winchester. When you go home to your Ma's I want you to take Ginnie with you & ride her as much as you wish to do & take good care of the colt. Tell me if Henry Applegate will stay in our house until I get back & when you expect to leave & how everything looks.

All the ladies or most of them are leaving. I seen Miss Sue Pitman last Friday. She said she would leave for Shenandoah the next day also said she was going to write to Mary H. in a few days. She come to the gate & cheered the soldiers as they passed & gave some of them water while two or three servants did the same & Mrs. Arch Pitman.

I want you to give every soldier you see something to eat as I should hate to have it said that you refused a soldier food when I have been fed by everyone almost. I will stop. Tell Sister I will write to her soon. I want to hear from Howard & Sam when you write again. I will perhaps get some of your letters tomorrow as Dr. M[—] will send his servant to Winchester for the mail for our company. If I should fail to get one I will be badly disappointed worse than I ever have been before. I will now close this. Give my love to all of the folks at Fathers. Tell Father if I don't write to him not to think I don't want to do so as our chance for writing is bad and mailing worse. I want you to kiss the children once a day for me until I get home. Then I will get to take the job off your hands. Good bye,

from your husband
John H. Ervine

Major Sullivan Ballou, 2nd Rhode Island Volunteers

Major Ballou writes to his wife in Smithfield.

July 14, 1861
Camp Clark

My very dear Sarah:

The indications are very strong that we shall move in a few days—perhaps tomorrow. Lest I should not be able to write you again, I feel impelled to write lines that may fall under your eye when I shall be no more.

Our movement may be one of a few days duration and full of pleasure—and it may be one of severe conflict and death to me. Not my will, but thine O God, be done. If it is necessary that I should fall on the battlefield for my country, I am ready. I have no misgivings about, or lack of confidence in, the cause in which I am engaged, and my courage does not halt or falter. I know how strongly American Civilization now leans upon the triumph of the Government, and how great a debt we owe to those who went before us through the blood and suffering of the Revolution. And I am willing—perfectly willing—to lay down all my joys in this life, to help maintain this Government, and to pay that debt.

But, my dear wife, when I know that with my own joys I lay down nearly all of yours, and replace them in this life with cares and sorrows—when, after having eaten for long years the bitter fruit of orphanage myself, I must offer it as their only sustenance to my dear little children—is it weak or dishonorable, while the banner of my purpose floats calmly and proudly in the breeze, that my unbounded love for you, my darling wife and children, should struggle in fierce, though useless, contest with my love of country?

I cannot describe to you my feelings on this calm summer night, when two thousand men are sleeping around me, many of them enjoying the last, perhaps, before that of death—and I, suspicious that Death is creeping behind me with his fatal dart, am communing with God, my country, and thee.

I have sought most closely and diligently, and often in my breast, for a wrong motive in thus hazarding the happiness of those I loved and I could not find one. A pure love of my country and of the principles have often advocated before the people and "the name of honor that I love more than I fear death" have called upon me, and I have obeyed.

Sarah, my love for you is deathless, it seems to bind me to you with mighty cables that nothing but Omnipotence could break; and yet my love of Country comes over me like a strong wind and bears me irresistibly on with all these chains to the battlefield.

The memories of the blissful moments I have spent with you come creeping over me, and I feel most gratified to God and to you that I have enjoyed them so long. And hard it is for me to give them up and burn to ashes the hopes of future years, when God willing, we might still have lived and loved together and seen our sons grow up to honorable manhood around us. I have, I know, but few and small claims upon Divine Providence, but something whispers to me—perhaps it is the wafted prayer of my little Edgar—that I shall return to my loved ones unharmed. If I do not, my dear Sarah, never forget how much I love you, and when my last breath escapes me on the battlefield, it will whisper your name.

Forgive my many faults, and the many pains I have caused you. How thoughtless and foolish I have oftentimes been! How gladly would I wash out with my tears every little spot upon your happiness, and struggle with all the misfortune of this world, to shield you and my children from harm. But I cannot. I must watch you from the spirit land and hover near you, while you buffet the storms with your precious little freight, and wait with sad patience till we meet to part no more.

But, O Sarah! If the dead can come back to this earth and flit unseen around those they loved, I shall always be near you; in the garish day and in the darkest night—amidst your happiest scenes and gloomiest hours—always, always; and if there be a soft breeze upon your cheek, it shall be my breath; or the cool air fans your throbbing temple, it shall be my spirit passing by.

Sarah, do not mourn me dead; think I am gone and wait for thee, for we shall meet again.

As for my little boys, they will grow as I have done, and never know a father's love and care. Little Willie is too young to remember me long, and my blue-eyed Edgar will keep my frolics with him among the dimmest memories of his childhood. Sarah, I have unlimited confidence in your maternal care and your development of their characters. Tell my two mothers his and hers I call God's blessing upon them. O Sarah, I wait for you there! Come to me, and lead thither my children.

Sullivan

Sullivan Ballou was killed a week later at the first battle of Bull Run.

George H. Sargent, Company C, 2nd New Hampshire Volunteer Regiment.

The "hardest Battle" referred to by Sargent below was the first battle of Bull Run on July 21 1861.

Washington, D.C.
July 28, 1861

Dear Brother:

Yours of the 18th is at hand. I was verry glad to here from you. In my last I told you we were to go father South. We have been and got back one week ago today. Today is Sunday. We had the hardest Battle ever fought in this Country. We started for the south. We went to Fairfax Court House as soon as we got there. It was evacuated and our Brigade was encamped the nearest the Court House. We were encamped in the yard.

The rebels left in such hast that they left there blankts and a few other small things which we boys soon found use for. Took all we could cary with ease but we had to throw them away when to the field of Battle. When we got there we had a tough time of it. Went to fighting at 11 o'clock in the forenoon and fought till 4 in the afternoon when we had to retrete. I will tell you how it was.

We were the first to go onto the field and the last to leave it. We had to fight hard. We were drawn up in line of Battle when a masked Battery began to play on us with great loss on our side. In a short time the Rifemen opened on us and we fell like hail. Soon other masked Batteries began to play on us, then our cannon began and we had tough and tight, but after 4 or 5 hours we gained an advantage and we kept it. We drove them from one of their Batteries at the point of the Bayonet. When they were reinforced by about 30 thousand fresh men and we had to retrete in hast. Our orderly of our Company and five others with about 30 of other Regmts. went through or part way through some woods, we went through when we were on the way to Battle. We had got part through on our way back when we surrounded by 200 hundred Rebels when we broke away and ran for life. I got home the first one of our camp and on the whole I went over sixty miles and fought over six hours in 30 hours. I call that a good days work, dont you. I guess that would have given out if you had been me. Some of the men were taken prisoners. Thurl Emerson is one, so I guess he will not write you very soon.

If you have not enlisted, dont you do it. If you do, you will wish you had not. Now don't you do it and if you have enlisted, get out of it as soon as you can. I shall come at the first opitunity. It is not the Cannon Ball or the Bomb Shells of which I come for, although we had a plenty of them. It not them but don't you enlist in a company. We had one Ball took the legs of three boys at one time. They marched right behind me.

As for Mother, I must see here. I think she is sick. Write me all about her. I want to see you all, that wood of the old house.

Sargent was wounded at Gettysburg on July 2, 1863. He was mustered out of the Union army in the following year.

Isaac Austin Brooks, 2nd Division,
Third Army Corps, Army of the Potomac

Camp Caldwell
October 13, 1861

My Dear Children,

As there are so many of you in the nest at home, I cannot write to each one, and therefore send this to you all. I think you will be glad to hear from me, in a letter to you all, as well as to hear of me through Mothers letters, for I never forget you, even if I do not write to you. Mothers accounts of you are very gratifying to me, for I think you are all trying to be good children, to give Mother as little trouble as you can, & to improve yourselves. My life here, is not very pleasant, but I submit to it because I think it is for the best and it is the duty of us all, to do what we can for our country and to preserve its integrity even to the sacrifice of our lives, if that is necessary. It is a glorious country, and *must* be preserved to our children. It was given to *us entire*, and *we* must give it to you, entire and *you* must give it as you receive it, to those who come after you. Remember your *country* is next to your God, in love, and never see it injured, or disgraced, if you have a hand, or a mind, to put forth in its defense. I hope to return to you in due time, safe and well, and find *you* are well and happy, but should it be so ordered that we do not meet again on earth, remember to love, and serve your country in whatever way it may be your lot to do so. To do this, many things are needed, which you will all learn in due time, but one of the *foundations* will be, to be sober, honest, and industrious.

So be good children all of you, & remember I *think* of you all, *daily*, even if I can not see you.

Your Affectionate Father

Charles Woodward Hutson,
Washington Light Infantry, CSA

A college graduate, Hutson served in the Washington Light Infantry before joining the Beauford Artillery. Below he describes his experiences in the Confederate victory at the first battle of Bull Run.

22d July, 1861, Monday
University at Charlottesville

Dear Father & Mother

I have been in a great & bloody battle & am wounded. Do not be at all alarmed. It is only a flesh wound in the head; and as the ball grazed the skull & glanced, there can be no danger. It is only through the Lord's great mercy, that we were not cut to pieces to a man, so fearful were the odds opposed to our division. Friday night the six infantry companies of Hampton's Legion took the train for Manassas. So slowly did we travel, that it was Sunday morning before we reached that point. Our breakfast was not cooked, when we heard the booming of artillery in the direction of Bull's Run. Orders presently came, that we should hasten to the field, as soon as we had eaten something. In fifteen minutes more we commenced our march for the field of battle. We were taken around to the left of the place where the engagement began, in order that we might secure against a surprise of the Camp at Manassas. This was evidently the game of the enemy. They played us a ruse: the heavy cannonading near Bull's Run was intended to deceive Beauregard into meeting them at that point with his whole force. Meanwhile an immense body of their troops advanced on the left with the intention of outflanking our main army, getting into our rear & seizing our fortified camp. They were held in check, however, by a few battalions, including our own & two Georgia regiments & perhaps one or two more. The whole battle was fought not far from the base of mountains, & the ground was very hilly; so that they were unable to perceive the immense disparity between their numbers & ours. Had they known how few were the forces between them & Camp Manassas; they would doubtless have advanced more confidently; & every man of us would have fallen upon the field. As it was, their movements were irresolute; they advanced & retreated alternately, & I suppose later in the day Beauregard must have come up with his main force to the assistance of our shattered columns; & then commenced the rout of the enemy. Terribly disproportioned as was our force, we held them in check for at least three hours. Nor was the disparity in numbers alone; the enemy were armed with the six-shooting revolving rifle, & their fire was incessant. Never have I conceived of such a continuous, rushing hailstorm of shot, shell & musketry as fell around & among us for hours together. We, who escaped, are constantly wondering how we could possibly have come out of the action alive. The words I used just now; "we, who escaped", have a sad, sad sound to us; for we know not yet who are to be included in that category, & are filled with terrible anxieties as to the fate of dear friends. I must trace now to you my own course through the action, which I can or ought to do clearly enough, since, I was cool & confident from first to last, knowing where my trust was placed, that no real harm could befall me & that there was a duty before me which I must perform at every hazard. All of our men behaved gallantly, though few were free from excitement. After being marched & countermarched for some time almost within reach of the enemy's missles, we were thrown, by order of Gen. Bee who commanded us to that part of the field, to the left of a corps of Flying artillery [house artillery] (I think the "Washington" of New Orleans), under shelter of a fence. Here we were first exposed to the hissing balls of the enemy; but the men took aim deliberately & stood fire beautifully. The artillery having then withdrawn from our side, we marched down the hill, unfortunately in disorder; we were halted halfway down in a hollow place, where we had the protection of a few trees & bushes. Here, seeing that our men hesitated to fire upon the force below, became doubtful whether they were not friends. I entreated the Captain to let me advance alone near enough to the ranks of those who were firing upon us to ascertain whether they were Federals or Confederate. But the Captain would not consent, & wished to go himself; this, however, Col. Hampton would not permit. Seeing, I could do nothing there, I attempted to persuade our men not to dodge, satisfied that we could never keep orderly ranks as long as the men persisted in dodging. But all my efforts in this line were unavailing; the men were fearless, & advanced undauntedly enough; but, I suppose, they thought dodging was a "help", anyhow, to escape from the balls. Iredell Jones, & the officers kept erect; & neither they nor I were any the worse for it. Our next advance was to a fence in the valley at the bottom of the hill. Here we made a stand, & here our company fought absolutely alone, the other Legionary companies having retreated to a yard at the top of the hill, where houses gave them shelter. Here they reformed. Meanwhile our men were subjected to a raking fire. I was the first who fell. I had put on my spectacles, taken good aim & fired my first shot. As I was in the act of re-loading, a rifle-ball struck me in the head, a little above the forehead; & the violence of the concussion felled me to the earth immediately. I drew off my spectacles & flung them aside; & not believing my wound a bad one, as it was not painful, I attempted to reload. But the blood was gushing over my face & blinding my eyes; & I found it impossible to do so. I knew pretty well the extent of my wound, as I had probed it with my finger as I fell; & as the gash seemed to be a deep one, I feared faintness would ensue from loss of blood, especially as there was a large puddle of it where I first lay. So, I put aside my gun for a while, & put my white handkerchief inside my hat upon the wound & tied my silk one around the hat. By the time I had

finished these precautions, the company were in retreat; & with
Jones & a few others I made my way to the clump of trees, whence
we had advanced. Here protected by the trees & squatted down,
these few detached from the company continued the fire. Jones
having given me some water from his canteen, & my eye being by
this time wiped pretty dry of the blood, I again attempted to reload. But before I could do so, a ball from the enemy shattered my
rifle to pieces. I now made the best of my way to the shelter of the
house on the hill, the shell & shot of the enemy ploughing up the
ground at every step I took, & the musketry rattling like hail
around me. I lay behind the house quite exhausted, & much pained
by the sight of some of my comrades badly wounded. Dr. Taylor
examined my wound here, & charged me to use all my strength to
reach the Hospital. While I lay here the body of Lieut. Col.
Johnson was brought into the yard & stretched at my side. He
had been shot dead a few moments before, while riding fearlessly
up & down the field. I remained at this place, until the companies
there began to retreat yet farther back; when, seizing my smashed
gun I hurried along by the gullies & other protecting places to a
field beyond the line of the missles, which before flew so thick &
fast around me. At the extremity of this field was a house used as a
temporary hospital. This place I reached, & after resting awhile,
walked to the wagons in the yard used to convey the wounded to
the Camp. The ride in was a long & tedious one, & I very soon
became aware that had I ventured to remain longer on the field, I
should soon have dropped & been only a burden to retreating
friends, or else have run the risk of falling into the enemy's hands,
a risk which I would have resolved, if possible, by forcing them to
cut me down. When I reached the Camp, I found many wounded
comrades there, who were under treatment. As the Hospital was
crowded with groaning men, some undergoing the agonies of
amputation, I very gladly accepted the kind attention of a gentleman named Lamotte, who soon proved that he understood well the
art of dressing wounds. He trimmed closely the hair around mine,
washed out the clotted blood, bathed the wound, ascertained that
there was no split in the portion of skull exposed, & bound up my
head nicely for me, strengthening me also with a glass of excellent
whiskey. I felt much more comfortable, when this was done, & the
encrusted blood, which stuck like a black mask to my face, was
washed. Much of my hair is still clotted with blood. After getting a
little supper & having deliberated on what would be our wisest
course, most of us wounded who were safe in camp concluded,
that, as no tents were pitched & we could not be cared for properly

there, it would be best to go down on the evening train to Culpepper C.H. where the hospitals are. The cars were crowded with the wounded. At Culpepper we found that accommodations could not be had for all; & some of us came on to Charlottesville, where we already perceive that we shall not want for gentle tending. I am writing now on a marble table in the hall of the University, where the wounded are lodged. Two of my company, Atkinson & Gardner, are with me, the former wounded like myself in the head, the latter in the wrist & side. Before we left Camp we heard, that the enemy had suffered heavy loss, were in full retreat, & that Beauregard was in hot pursuit. Many regiments lost almost all their staff-officers; two Georgia ones lost all. Col. Hampton was, by one report, dangerously wounded; by another, dead. Our adjutant, Barker, was also said to be dead. The Legionary infantry was certainly much cut to pieces. Our cavalry & artillery were not in the action, not having arrived yet. All the forces, on both sides, must have been engaged; & if the enemy have met with a serious defeat, I imagine it will be the last general engagement. Patterson was taken & Col. Scott killed. Many prisoners were taken. Before we left, fifty eight were brought into the camp at Manassas. The battle lasted all day, & was very bloody. Early as it was when I was forced to retire, I met few, who were not hurt.

I brought off my knapsack with me, & will be quite comfortable. We are very uneasy about our friends yet unheard from. Many, I fear, whom I care greatly for, are now mangled or dead. At the last accounts, Conner was leading our shattered Legion & perhaps other officerless battalions, & pressing on the rear of the enemy within two miles of Centreville. I trust he yet survives. I long to hear how the Carolina regiments fare. Kershaw's was in the battle; & you know I have many friends among them.

As soon as my wound permits, I intend returning to Manassas & making every effort to rejoin the army, wherever it may be. I hope to be able to bear arms again, before we enter Washington. You will see, by my writing so long a letter that I am in no danger from my wound. My head feels heavy, & the place throbs, that is all. I hope you are not too much troubled. My love to sisters & all the dear kinsfolk & friends.

Your Ever Loving Son

C. Woodward Hutson

How we ought continually to thank God for the mercies which he does so inceasingly show us! The Dr. here has just dressed my wound, says it is an inch & a half long & would have gone deeper had it not struck the bone, says I am a very hard-headed fellow. He is a kindly, merry gentleman, & I like him much. He asked me if I was not related to Willy Wigg, knowing him well & knowing his middle name.

Wilbur Fisk, 2nd Vermont Regiment

Letter to his family.

> *From the Second Vermont Regiment*
> *Camp Griffin*
> *Fairfax County, Va*
> *Dec. 11, 1861*

By way of preface I ought to say that my rank here is that of a private, and privates are expected to know just enough to obey orders. Many of us have yet to learn even this. As for the plans our superiors are laying out for us to execute we know as little as a horse knows of the plans of his driver. The answer we are obliged to give to all inquirers, is one that would be perfectly familiar to those who belonged to a certain secret political organization noted chiefly for its hostility to foreigners.

This regiment would relish a fight now extremely well. When that event takes place you may be assured the Vermont Second will do their share to wipe out the stigma upon our arms, which they have coveted the privilege of doing ever since the Bull Run disaster.

Since the boys here have received their new clothes, they have been able to keep themselves tolerably comfortable. Before this they had just cause for complaint. I cannot very highly recommend some of the clothing they have given us. I have seen some of these blue pants after a fortnight's service, so far gone as to be actually indecent to wear. Some of the boys have no rubber blanket, nor bed-tick, nothing but the ground to lie on. These articles are very necessary,—almost indispensable. Many of the soldiers would gladly accept an extra woolen blanket these cold nights. In other respects we are as comfortably provided for as our circumstances will allow. You must bear in mind, however, that I lay no claim to any extended observation.

Most of the large tents have small stoves in them made especially for this business. The boys procured them on their own hook. They are bound to keep warm if possible. The tent I occupy is the smallest-sized army tent. To call these tents *contemptible* is using the mildest term that will apply to them. I don't know their exact dimensions in feet and inches, but a man any above the medium height, lying down, can touch the opposite sides of one of these tents with his head and feet at the same time, and the united breadth of five ordinary men will cover its entire length. Three others with myself make one of these our temporary home. When we are all in the tent, together with our bed blankets, overcoats, knapsacks, haversacks, canteens, guns and equipments, besides having a fire-place and generally as much as a half cord of wood on hand seasoning for use you may imagine that there is but little room to spare. This is no Gulliver tale. We contrived to make so much of so little room by digging down and settling the floor (i.e. the ground) of our tent about two feet and then building up around this excavation with logs in regular Tippecanoe style about two feet more and over the whole placing our cloth tent. This basement protects us securely from the wind, is quite warm, and affords us a chance to stand erect anywhere within our circumscribed limits while before we could do so only along the middle of the tent. We made a sort of platform for a bed on each end of the tent which gives us room, underneath for our wood, &c. On one side we excavated a fire-place with an opening to the surface of the ground outside the tent around which we built a chimney. The soil here is of a peculiar kind of clay indigenous to this locality and when heated by fire it becomes firm as a rock. Two of our number sleep on the ground with their feet in pretty close proximity to this fire-place. Neglecting to place a big stone before it one night to protect them nearly cost us our lives. A woolen blanket took fire, and before we awoke we were nearly suffocated with smoke.

The Vermont M.C.'s made us a visit last Saturday, and out of curiosity peeped into this tent. They admired our ingenuity, but were apprehensive that living below the surface of the ground was prejudicial to health. Our experience however fails to corroborate this view. To our anxious friends at home, I beg leave to say that the fire in our rude fire-place *draws* remarkably well, and we find no difficulty in keeping ourselves warm by it this cold weather. There are other tents fitted up in a manner similar to ours, and some of the boys have built regular log huts.

But my letter is swelling far beyond the dimensions intended. That we may prove ourselves worthy sons of Vermont, and inherit the title of Green Mountain Boys, with all its historic luster, is the firm determination of every brave heart, and their number is not few.

Austin Perkins, Company B,
4th Regiment, Rhode Island Volunteers

Perkins writes to his wife, Sarah Maria Newton Perkins.

Headquarters 4 RI
Co. B Camp California, 1861
December the 19

Dear Wife,

I thought I would write you a few lines to let you know how I am getting along. Our regiment has been out on picket duty and we have been very nigh the rebel picket. We took two cows and one horse and a load of corn. The Jersey regiment that was with us lost one man killed and two taken by the rebel but we never lost a man. There is about three hundred dollars lost in this regiment sending their money home. I want you to let me know when you get that money. I shall send my next money home by express and they will have to pay for it if they lose it. They will pay up the last of this month. I know you think hard of me because you did not get that money, but I can't help it Maria. I want to hear from you Maria the worst kind. Kiss George for me. Good bye Maria.

I dreamed of George last night and I hope I shall be with you and him once more. If I had known as much about how they was going to use us, the Union might go to the devil before I would come out here again. The hogs has better quarters than we do. Good bye Maria.

Hatteras Inlet
January the 19, 1862

Dear Wife,

I thought I would write you a few lines but I don't know whether you ever will get it or not. We left Annapolis the 7th. Arrived at fortress morning of the 9th. Had very foggy weather. Left the next night and arrived the next night off Cape Hatteras. Lay low all that night. It cleared. And most all of them was sea sick but you know that I wasn't. One large steamer was lost on the bar and some men has been lost. I don't know how many. Her name was the New York [?]eitty and there is three more vessel sunk in the side but we got in safely. We have nothing but hard bread and salt meat once a day and they didn't give us water enough til we took the water away from the guards and helped ourselves. Where we go now I can't write till we get there. I want to hear from you the worst kind. I dreamed of home last night. I saw you set by the west winder up to mother's and you was looking out of the winder with George in your lap. And I come in and you did not see me till I put my arms around you and we arose together and mother was in the other room and she lay on the bed and signal gun waked me up and I made ben [??]ering. I expect 'ere another sun shall not set we shall be in deadly conflict with the rebel and if I fall take good care of George. Bring him up to be good like yourself. I spose you have heard that William Kane is dead. Yes he is dead. When we left VA he was very sick and we could not bring him away and he died all alone with nothing but strangers around him. His body will be sent home when it can be attended to.

Direct your letters to: 4 Regiment R.I. Com B

Parks Brigade Burnside expedition

Good bye Maria, Good bye George, Good bye Mother

I want to know whether you got that money or not.

Francis William Kimble, Company B, 14th Iowa Infantry

Camp Heron, Davenport, Iowa
February 24, 1862

Miss E.E. Kimble

I take this present opportunity of writing you a few lines to let you know that I am well at present and hope that those few lines may find you enjoying the same blessing. Well, Eliza we do have some of the greatest times in camp. Some of the boys has a violin which affords us sufficient music for our company for dancing. We have a dance most every night. For our ladies several boys with his hat off. That is the way we tell the ladies from the gentlemen. We publish a paper every week which is read every Saturday evening. Liza it looks very odd to see 100 men a setting listening to the paper read. It makes me think that they ought to be in their homes. I have sat and wondered if this war is close or not. Well Liza there has been two of our company out of the army. They ran away and enlisted and their fathers came after them a few days since and took them out of the army. We have not got our pay yet. Some of the boys that enlisted since I did got their bounty and are now on a furlough. We expect our pay in a few days and a furlough of a few days. I want to know what regt. S. Nelson is in. Liza I think you and Mother write very short letters. I was to church Sunday evening. There was about one hundred and fifty soldiers there. I have had one letter from Mary Louis some time since. Well I think that I have wrote all the news so good bye for the present. I must go to my supper. I bought this book for a present.

Camp in the Orchard
Columbus, Ky
Sept. 18th, 1863

Dear Mother

I set myself to inform that I am well at present. Mother I just received your letter of the 13th which is much pleasure to me for I expected it sooner than now. Well Mother it is cool enough this morning to wear an overcoat but it will be pleasanter in a day or two. I would rather have cool weather that to have it so warm for it is much pleasanter for the sick and I think it is healthier to be a little cool. Mother we have left the Fort. We are now camped about one mile east of town in an old apple orchard on the picket line. The health of our regt is much better since we moved from the fort. Mother 3 weeks ago today there was 3 male negroes hanged. They was executed for murdering a man and his family. I believe that 3 of the family was little children. The negroes was soldiers. They was hired to do the deed by a white man. There was about 2500 people at the execution. I was an eye witness to it. When the scaffold fell there was several of the wenches fainted. Mother, one week from today will hardly find the 14th at Columbus for we are under marching orders all ready but our destination we know not. It is rumored that we will go back to Cairo, but I think it doubtful. It is my opinion that we will go to Union City in Tenn which place is about 35 miles east of Columbus. Some thinks we will go down the river. Two of our boys started home yesterday on sick furloughs. Mother I am utterly fleshly for I weigh one hundred and 42 pds. Littlefield and his wife are both sick. She will go to Iowa since she is better. Tell Dad to never vote for a copperhead candidate for governor of Ia. The soldiers feels for Gen Tuttle but we can't reach him where he stands. Mother when you say abolish think of the soldiers, just think of the soldiers. I expressed a little box to Sarah the 3rd of Sept I brought with me from Memphis. I don't know whether she has got it or not. She has quit writing to me. Tell Dad that Col. Stone is the man for us. We hate Cops [Copperheads] I think this will do for the present. My respects to all so no more. F. W. Kimble to M.A. Kimble

Eliza I guess E.R.C. has played off since she has got my miniature for I haven't heard from her since I got the letter with yours in it. She had better write soon or I will find a Ky. gal. I was out in the country last Sabbath and I was as good as I was when I went a sparking. I think that I will have to go again. Give my compliments to Dad. I think Jimmy don't break so many drum heads as I do. I haven't nary one in my drum and haven't had for some time. No more.

Lieutenant Dana Green, Federal Navy

Green writes to his family describing the naval battle at Hampton Roads between 8–9 March 1862, the first clash in history between "ironclad" warships. He served aboard the USS *Monitor*. The Confederate opponent was the *Merrimac*.

n.d [March 1862]

At daylight we discovered the Merrimac at anchor with several vessels under Sewell's Point. We immediately made every preparation for battle. At 8 a.m. on Sunday the Merrimac got underweigh accompanied by several steamers and steered direct for the Minnesota (a wooden battleship). When a mile distant she fired two guns at the Minnesota. By this time our anchor was up, the men at quarters, the guns loaded, and everything ready for action. As the Merrimac came close the Captain passed the word to commence firing. I triced up the port, ran the gun out and fired the first gun and thus commenced the great battle between the Monitor and the Merrimac.

Now mark the condition our men were in. Since Friday morning, 40 hours, they had had no rest and very little food, as we could not conveniently cook. They had been hard at work all night, had nothing to eat for breakfast except hard bread, and were thoroughly worn out. As for myself, I had not slept a wink for 51 hours, and had been on my feet almost constantly. But, after the first gun was fired we forgot all fatigue, hard work and everything else, and went to work fighting as hard as men ever fought.

We loaded and fired as fast as we could . . . Our tower was struck several times, and though the noise was pretty loud it did not affect us any. At about 11:30 the Captain sent for me.

I went forward, and there stood as noble a man as lives at the foot of the ladder of the Pilot House. His face was perfectly black with powder and iron and he was apparently perfectly blind. He said a shot had struck the Pilot House and blinded him. He told me to take charge of the ship and use my own discretion. I led him to his room and laid him on the sofa and then took his position. We still continued firing, the tower being under the direction of Stimers. We were now between two fires, the Minnesota on one side, and the Merrimac on the other. The latter was retreating to Sewell's Point.

The fight was over now and we were victorious. My men and myself were perfectly black, and my person in the same condition . . . Batsy, my old roommate was on board the Merrimac. Little did we ever think at the Academy we should be firing 150 lb. balls at each other. But, so goes the world.

Anon Soldier, 1st Battalion, US Infantry

An account of the battle of Shiloh by a Union private, possibly W.W. Worthington.

Field of Shiloh, Tennessee, April 14th, 1862
Dear King:—I commence writing you a letter, which, I know, you will be glad to get; for I mean to tell you what our battalion did on the 6th and 7th inst., whilst the great battle at this place was progressing. . . . Leaving Columbia, we took up the line of march for Savannah, a distance of eighty-two miles through a country almost uninhabited and barren to the last degree. On Saturday night we encamped at a place seventeen miles from the latter town. Starting again the next morning, we had proceeded but a little way when the noise of the battle of that disastrous day broke upon our ears. As we advanced the cannonading became each moment more distinct. It was plain that a desperate fight was going on some-where: but not one of our number dreamed that Grant had been attacked and was at that instant slowly losing ground before the enemy. Indeed the general belief was created by reports brought from the front that our gunboats were attacking some batteries at a place called Hamburg. About noon, however, we began to think it possible that in some way or other our aid might be needed; for we were halted in an old cotton field, our arms were inspected, and rations and ammunition were issued. Still we were ignorant of the terrible conflict then going on, though by this time the ground fairly trembled under our feet with the rapid discharge of artillery. Again pushing on, sweltering in the hot southern sun, travelling over roads almost impassable and fording several streams, about dark we halted for a few hours at a creek three miles inland from Savannah. There we learned for the first time, that instead of a gunboat bombardment, that day had been fought at Pittsburg

Landing, the bloodiest battle in which American troops were ever engaged. The accounts of the conflict were most cheering. They represented that Grant had that morning attacked the immense army under Albert Sidney Johnston and Beauregard, completely defeating and routing it after a desperate fight of fifteen hours duration. The cannon we continued to hear at intervals were said to be those hurried forward in pursuit of the flying enemy. You may be sure we were jubilant at this news; although we declaimed somewhat against the selfishness that precipitated the engagement and won the victory before Buell's column had an opportunity to take a part. Little did we dream that so far from having gained a triumph, Grant's force was then defeated and panic-stricken, with an insolent foe occupying most of his camps, and that the morrow would introduce us to scenes of carnage the mere imagination of which sickens the heart.

It was quite dark, though still early in the night, when we moved on again. The men were in the best of spirits, rude witticisms, laughter and snatches of song ran along the whole line. Here and there some fellow boasted of the gallant deeds he would have performed had he been in the day's engagement. The officers, on the other hand, were more quiet than usual. They marched in silence or gathered in little knots and conversed in whispers. At length, the town of Savannah was entered. Every house in the place seemed to be illuminated; for each had been converted into an hospital and was packed from attic to basement with the dying and wounded who had been conveyed thither by the steamer.

Groans and cries of pain saluted our ears from all the buildings we passed. Through the windows, the sash of which were removed to give air to the injured, we could see the surgeons plying their horrid profession. The atmosphere was that of a vast dissecting room. The streets were crowded with ambulances, baggage trains, parties bearing the victims of the fight on stretchers, on rails, on rude litters of muskets and on their shoulders, and with batteries of artillery and long lines of infantry waiting to be taken to the scene of the struggle. The confusion everywhere visible, the shouting, cursing, quarrelling, beggars descriptions. Teams of mules, abandoned by their drivers, ran away trampling down every thing in their course. Quartermasters rode about at furious pace trying to extricate their transportation from the general mass. Doctors, one hand full of instruments, the other of bandages, and covered with blood, wildly rushed through the immense crowd in search of additional subjects of their art. Still, from all that could be gathered, the idea appeared to be that we had achieved a great victory. No one could exactly tell the events of the day; but the fact of our decisive triumph was unquestioned. The falsity of this common opinion every reader of the newspapers already knows.

Getting on board the "Hiawatha," by midnight we were ploughing the turbid Tennessee river *en route* for Pittsburg Landing, by water a distance of fourteen miles. From the officers of the steamer we got other accounts of the battle, which we afterwards ascertained to be correct. Their statements were, that Johnston and Beauregard, hoping to destroy Grant before he was joined by Buell, then close at hand, made a furious attack upon him, in great strength, that Sunday morning immediately after daylight. There is some dispute whether or not we had outposts; those who maintain we had, admit that they were playing cards at the time of the assault. At all events our troops were completely and criminally surprised. Unable to form to resist the onslaught, hundreds of them were mercilessly shot down in their tents and company streets. Those who escaped fled in the greatest terror through the camps in their rear, spreading the panic and closely followed by the successful foe. At least two miles of the ground occupied by our forces was thus abandoned before the regiments near the river could be brought to present a front to the rebels. A temporary check was then given to the enemy's impetuous advance, but being strongly reinforced they pushed our army slowly and surely towards the landing. During the whole day the battle raged with violence. Several corps of our volunteers behaved with great gallantry; but others ran at the first fire, and with those surprised in the morning (at least 10,000 men) could not again be brought into action. But the Secessionists steadily gained upon us. Seven batteries of our light artillery and a large number of our soldiers fell into their hands, as well as thousands of tents, and immense quantities of Commissary and Quartermaster's stores. When night closed upon the struggle we were driven within three hundred yards of the river, and would have been pushed into it had not the spiteful little gunboats then been enabled to come to our relief. Our loss in the engagement was terrible; but it was not all we suffered. At times when the fortune of war was most decidedly against us, the skulkers under the bluff, would rush in crowds to reach the steamers moored in the Tennessee, and by jostling and pushing each other into and struggling together in the water, hundreds of them were drowned. Little pity is felt for their fate, of course; but still these help to swell the casualties of that disastrous day.

Regaled, as we were, during the entire passage from Savannah to Pittsburg Landing, with stories of defeat and forebodings of what would occur the next day, you may be certain that we were not as comfortable as if we were in the old barracks. It was plain to the dullest comprehension that McCook's, Nelson's and Crittenden's divisions of Buell's army, then arrived at the scene of action, would have work enough to do early in the morning, and that too against an enemy flushed with recent victory. It seemed like folly to hope for success; for our strength did not exceed thirty thousand. From Grant's badly beaten and demoralized force we expected nothing, unless it was a mere show of numbers. On the other hand, the rebels were estimated at from 60,000 to 80,000. These consideration did not do much to inspirit, whilst throughout the night our anxiety was kept alive and our consciousness of the immediate presence of the foe not permitted to slumber by the regular firing from the gunboats upon the camps of the enemy close beside those of our own.

At daybreak on Monday the 7th inst. our battalion was disembarked. Forcing its way with difficulty through the vast crowd of fugitives from the previous day's fight gathered on the river bank, we scrambled up the bluff in the best way we could and formed in the camp of the Missouri Artillery. Here there were more refugees, their officers riding among them and urging them to rally, but without the least success. I never witnessed such abject fear as these fellows exhibited. Without a single avenue of escape in the event of defeat, they were unable, even, to muster up the desperation of cornered cowards. It is said that several in high command set them the example of pusillanimity. As we moved among them they inquired "what regiment is that?" "15th Regulars," replied some of our men. "Well, you'll catch regular hell to-day," was their rejoinder. Others said "Boys, it's of no use; we were beaten yesterday and you'll be beaten now." But still our men got into line well, and were marched by the right flank a few hundred yards to the place where the action of the previous day had ended. Here Capt. Swaine and Major King joined us, knapsacks were unslung, and we made the final preparations for the conflict we knew to be imminent. Being informed that we were the reserve of Rousseau's Brigade, we were slowly moved forward in column at half distance, through camps our troops had abandoned in the fight of the 6th inst. Other corps, all the while, were passing us on either side, and disappearing from view in a dip of ground in front, but as yet the engagement had not begun.

Let me try, at this point, to give you as good an idea of the field of battle as I am able. The Tennessee river at Pittsburg Landing describes a considerable curve; in the neck formed by this bend and some distance outside of it were the camps of Gen. Grant's command. On the morning of the 7th, the rebels were posted some distance inside of the ground formerly occupied by us, so that the line of conflict was pretty nearly straight between the two points of the semi-circle. Nelson's division was on our extreme left, resting on the river; Crittenden was next to him on his right, then came McCook in the centre, and joined to him was McClernand, who had other of Grant's generals beyond him. This order continued unbroken until the struggle was over.

Nelson and Crittenden's commands having passed the left flank of our battalion speedily became engaged. A few scattering shots were heard from their direction, which were soon followed by such a heavy firing of small arms that it was plain our men had found the enemy. The field artillery also broke in with its thunder, increasing the din already so great that it was difficult to hear one's self speak. As further evidence that the battle had begun in earnest, a mounted officer dashed by, crying, "bring on the ambulances," and those vehicles were at once taken to the front, to return in a few minutes laden with mangled freight. Other wounded men, some on foot, others carried by their comrades, likewise now came to the rear. From these we learned that Nelson and Crittenden, although suffering severely, were steadily pushing the rebels back, a story attested by the frequent cheers that arose from their gallant fellows.

A sharp firing that now took place almost immediately in our front, showed that the left and centre of our (McCook's) division had got into action, and that the battle was rapidly becoming general. Our battalion was instantly deployed into line to receive the foe should the troops in advance give way. While in this position, Generals Buell and Rousseau rode up, ordered us to proceed to the right of the brigade, which was the right of the division, and be ready for any emergency, and to send out at the same time a company of skirmishers to provoke an attack. This converted us from a reserve into an assaulting party.

Forming in column by division on the first, we marched by the right flank to the position we were to occupy, Captain Haughey with his command, being thrown forward to feel the enemy. (I will state here that battalions of the 16th and 19th regiments U. S. Infantry, the whole under Major John H. King, were with us and shared in all our operations.) At this place we again deployed, then moved by the right of companies to the front, until a little hill between us and the rebels was surmounted, when we were again brought into line. Rapid discharges of small arms forward of our left flank, now showed that our skirmishers were successful in their search. Again we were advanced, until having gained some distance, we were ordered to lie close to the ground. Immediately we were exposed to a cannonade and fire of musketry, whose severity defies description. From three batteries and their strong support of infantry just before us, masked by the underbrush, came a shower of grape, canister, spherical case, rifle balls, &c., that would have swept every one of us away had we been standing on our feet. An examination I have since made of the ground exhibits the fact that every tree and sapling bears the marks of shot. Protecting ourselves as we did, our loss was still severe. Among the injured were Capt. Acker of the 16th, killed, and Capt. Peterson of the 15th, wounded in the head. As yet, as I have said before, the foe was concealed in the thick woods so that we could not see them; but now emboldened, perhaps, by what they supposed their irresistible attack, they emerged from their cover. Never did they commit a more fatal mistake. Our men, restrained by their officers, had not discharged a piece up to this time. But now each coolly marked his man; and when Capt. Swaine, in a voice that could be heard along the whole line, gave the command to fire, our Springfield rifles dealt a destruction that was awful. After pelting the rebels a little while longer, we again moved forward to the sound of the bugle, taking to the earth once more when the enemy opened upon us. Here Lieut. Mitchell of the 16th was killed, and Lieut. Lyster of the 19th, and 1st Sergeants Williams and Kiggins of the 15th dangerously wounded. Halting a few moments to reply, we moved down upon the traitors a third time, subjected the while to a fearful storm of missiles, by which Capt. Curtiss and Lieut. Wykoff of the 15th were very severely hurt, and 1st Sergeant Killink of the same corps instantly killed. But at length the artillery of the enemy, that had been playing upon us so long, came in sight. Hastily fixing bayonets, we charged upon it at a double-quick. Capt. Keteltas of the 15th being then shot through the body. Unable to withstand our desperate assault, the rebel cannoneers abandoned their guns, and with the infantry supports fled across an open space into the woods beyond. An opportunity offered at this point to ascertain the havoc we had done. Every horse in each piece and caisson lay dead in his harness, and the ground was covered with the killed and dying. Among the latter was the Chief of the Artillery. As we came up he said, "You have slain all my men

and cattle, and you may take the battery and be damned." But we
had not leisure to stop and talk with him or any other person; for
we were already being fired upon from the new covert of the foe.
Pushing forward amid great danger across the field, we gained the
edge of the timber and continued the fight in which we had then
been engaged for more than five hours.

The foregoing was the state of affairs at high noon. Let us pause
a moment to see what was the condition of the battle field at that
hour. There was no fighting on the right of the centre; indeed it
had not been severe in that quarter during the day. On the left,
Nelson and Crittenden having repulsed the enemy, were resting on
their arms; for the foe in their front had mysteriously disappeared.
Our three battalions were our only troops then hotly engaged. You
inquire, "where were the rest of the rebels?" That is just what I
propose telling you. Leaving only enough of men before the other
divisions to mask their purpose, they were engaged massing their
troops, those that had been engaged as well as their reserves, for an
overwhelming onslaught upon the right of our centre, where we
had contested all morning without support. I think it possible that
Gen. Rousseau suspected their scheme; for whilst we strove in the
edge of the timber, two regiments of volunteers took position on
our right, and a section of a battery quietly unlimbered on our left.
Scarcely were these dispositions completed, when down upon us
came the enemy, pouring in a withering, staggering fire, that
compelled the regiments just mentioned to break and fly, in such
confusion that they could not be rallied again. This panic not only
left us alone to sustain the dreaded onset, but in addition, put us in
extraordinary peril by the total exposure of our left flank. The
occasion was indeed critical. But before the enemy could take any
advantage of the condition of things, Capt. Swaine averted the
danger by causing our battalion to charge front, thus giving the
15th, 16th and 19th the form of two sides of a triangle. Here we
fought for a time that seemed interminable, holding the rebel force
in check, until Col. Gibson's brigade, hastily brought up to our
relief, assisted by a flanking attack from Nelson and Crittenden's
divisions started the foe in the retreat, that shortly became a rout.
Falling back, then, only long enough to replenish our ammunition,
we joined in the pursuit, keeping it up, notwithstanding our
exhausted condition, until we got beyond the line of the camps
captured from our troops the day before.

I do not undertake to say what body of troops engaged in the
battle of Shiloh, is entitled to the most honor. But I unhesitatingly
assert that the 1st Battalion of the 15th U. S. Infantry did its whole

duty. For seven hours it fought without ceasing, that, too, after it had marched seventeen miles the day before, and been deprived of sleep the night previous. And when the dreadful attack upon our centre was made, which caused Willich's German veterans to scatter like cattle upon a thousand hills, it still stood up to its work as though there was no such word as defeat in its lexicon. Throughout the struggle, Major King, Capt. Swaine and the company officers conducted themselves with great gallantry. In our company, nine men are killed and wounded. The loss of the command is sixty-three. Curtenius escaped without a scratch.

Dr. Parry informs me that our loss in killed and wounded, will not fall short of nine thousand men, and may exceed that number. From what I have seen myself, I give the fullest credence to his statement. On the evening of the engagement, the dead were everywhere. There never has been such carnage on this continent. I trust I may never again see anything of the kind.

The battle was fought in the woods, which were as serviceable to the enemy as fortifications. You may travel for a day around here and you will scarcely find a tree, sapling or twig, that has not been struck by a bullet. How any of us escaped is more than I can imagine.

W.

Sergeant Edward N. Boots, 101st Pennsylvania Veteran Volunteer Infantry

A former schoolteacher, Boots enlisted on 4 October 1861. He was promoted to Quarter Master Sergeant a year later.

> *Camp on the Chickahominy river on the road to Fort Darling*
> *June 9th* [1862]

Dear Mother

I embrace an opportunity, which I now have of sending a note to you by esqr J. Wilson, who has come to remove the body of the Col to Penna. The excitement of the battle has passed away & the wounded have been sent to Northern Hospitals. Cannonading is frequent, but there has been no regular fight since the end of the three day's battle on Monday 2nd but I expect that there will be a terrible battle, before Richmond, some of these days. Our Pickets are close enough to Richmond now to see the spires of buildings in the city & the frequent balloon ascensions of Prof Lowe gives to Gen McClelland all the necessary information about the whereabouts of the rebel army. We often see the balloon when up, it is generally just before sunset & it look grand to see it floating in mid air while the tops of the vast pine forest are made glorious by the rays of the setting sun. Ed & George have both been unwell, but both are getting better & will soon be well. I think that you might as well quit sending papers for they never come to me. The reason is; I suppose, because you try to make one cent pay the postage on two papers & the result is that the Post office department throws them under the table as the law commands. Papers are continually arriving for others from our Neighborhood, but none come for me. I send home ten dollars $10.00 in this letter, you will put it on interest as I directed before. Our labors here are not so heavy as they were, when we occupied the Richmond road, but still we have enough to do. I think that we shall stay here a few days, until we get rested from the effects of the fight & then we shall occupy the Richmond road again. I hear that they are enlisting fresh men in Penna. Tell the boys to be sure & not enlist, but to stay where they are, for they could not stand the climate of Va. if they were sent into it at this time of the year. send me a few postage stamps both one & three cent, but do not send many at once for the letter may get lost. give my love to all Write soon

ever your Son

E N Boots

Camp near the White Oak Swamp
June 15th [1862]

Dear Mother

The long hours lengthen into days & the days drag slowly into weeks, & still no letters come from home & I wait & wait until the heart is tired of waiting. some weeks ago; your letters complained, that you got no letters from me. Well I have no doubt but such was the case. But, nevertheless, through all those weeks, it mattered not how hard the labor was, nor how much I was exposed; I still wrote a letter for home every week & sometimes oftener. I did not wait for letters to come, but I wrote as often as possible & I feel sure that you have better chances for writing at home, than I can have among the swamps of Virginia. I wrote a long letter to you on the 3rd, though I had received no letter from home. last week I sent a letter home by J. Wilson, esqr (the Col's Brother). In the letter I also sent ten dollars, which I wish you to take care of for me. We are laying in a rather pleasant camp for Va., that is; we have pretty good water & there is no swamp nearer, than twenty rods. We are in the woods, among tall Pine Timber. We occupy the road, leading across the White Oak Swamp & the Chickahominy at long Bridge to Fort Darling on the James river.

We are stationed here to prevent the rebels, from making a flank movement from James river, as a natural consequence we have frequent alarms. On the night before last Com. A. was sent out at midnight to guard a ford & at 3 o'clock in the morning, the whole Division was ordered out under the expectation of an attack, but the rebels did not come & after awhile the troops were allowed to return & get their breakfast. Yesterday; we were ordered to pull down our tents and clean all the rubbish off from the ground (a thing that we have done three or four times already in the last two weeks). soon we were busy picking, scraping & burning, causing our camp to look like a vast smoke house, for as all the brush is of the Pitch Pine kind, the smoke is of a very dark character, but by noon; we had it all cleaned off & our tents pitched in fine style & to-morrow we may be ordered to march ten miles & leave all our work behind us, but such ever is camp life. The weather is very warm & we do nothing in the middle of the day, unless we are forced to it. We think that the dry season has began, for we have had three days without rain. Ed is with me his health is much improved, George Coleman is also pretty well. I wish that you would send me a few postage stamps, both one & three cent, do not send many at a time, for they may never come. We cannot get them here. Do write. my love to all.

　　your son etc
　　E N Boots

Boots was captured in the Battle of Plymouth, 17–20 April 1864. He died at Andersonville whilst a prisoner of war.

Lieutenant-Colonel William M. Bentley, 24th Virginia Infantry Regiment, CSA

Bentley graduated from the Virginia Military Institute in the Class of 1860.

Camp near Richmond
June the 13th, 1862

My Dear Mother

Your affectionate letter of the 7th inst was received on the 9th (last Monday) whilst I was at Mr. Robertson's. I had written to Lucie the day before or I should have answered your dear letter sooner. I came out to camp day before yesterday (Wednesday the 11th). I never fared better from home anywhere than I did at Mr. Robertson's. He & Mrs. Robertson were very kind & attentive & they both protested very much against my coming out so soon. I am in some better health than I was sometime before I got unable to attend to duty but I am still unable to stand much fatigue which is incident to our hard life.

Oh that God would in His infinite goodness bring about a speedy peace. My prayers are earnest & oft repeated to Him who ruleth for support & deliverance in these troublous & turbulent times. The clouds seem to thicken & grow darker & friends & comrades in arms are going to their long homes. May God make me thankful that I am still spared when so many have fallen. Oh! My Dear Mother you do not know how my *heart aches & how sad* I feel when I think that I may never see you all again on earth, & that my body may not rest under the sod of my own dear home but may be left to moulder on the field probably with the bodies of the wicked invaders.

The mortality in this division has been very great in the late engagements, particularly among the officers. Everything is managed so badly when going into battle. At the battle of Williamsburg poor Willie Radford & myself stemmed the torrent of misles [missiles] with not more than eight or ten of our company & some time we were not supported by any company in the Regt. I will endeavor to do my duty & may it be the will of Almighty God to spare me to see the independence of my country achieved. I derive great comfort from the precious promises of Our Lord & Saviour. May God give me faith to sustain me under every trial & to feel full assurance of His Favor in this life & in the world to come . . . Genl Jackson has been very successful in the valley in spite of the Yankee combinations to catch him. He is the Christian Patriot. In all his official dispatches the attributes his success to the blessing of God.

The weather for the last day or two has been exceedingly warm. We are now encamped three or four miles from the city with our bivouac nearly in the bogs & swamps. We are held in a constant state of readiness to meet or attack the invader. The men have orders to sleep on their arms. Provisions are very scarce and very indifferent. I get a little coffee by paying two dollars a pound & sixty five cents a pound for bacon. I fared well (after I got so that I could eat something) at Mr. Robertson's. I never drank better coffee anywhere. Mr. Christian advised me to not even offer him pay—that it might offend him. He made me promise to come back if I got sick again & said I must come to see him whenever I could get out of camp.

I must close hoping that I can write you often until I can return in peace to my dear home. God grant that it may be so. Give much love to my dear sisters & my dear brother whom I trust is with you. Remember me kindly to Miss Vic. Do not allow yourself to feel too much anxiety for me my Dear Mother. I have committed myself to the keeping of my God & I pray earnestly that I may be held up under all circumstances by His omnipotent arm. May the blessing of God rest upon us all & bring us together in health is the daily & earnest prayer of your devoted & affectionate son,

Wm. W. Bentley

William Colley, Connecticut Volunteers

Hilton Head
June 22d. 1862

Dear Parents.

I will try to write a few lines to let you know how & where I am although you may know all about it by this time through the Papers.

Well I was in the fight on the 16th & got slightly wounded in the Right Arm just below the Shoulder. there was five wounded in my Com[pany] & our Capt. was killed poor fellow. how we miss him he was a brave & good man It was a hard fight. Bull Run was not a comparison to it. the Enemy had very Strong Batteries & Rifle Pits & we had to march right up in front of them. the charges of Grape & Canister from the Rebels raked us down in scores. it was a regular Slaughter Pen to march us up in the way they did but our Boys stood it nobly & Bravely every man had a fixed will & determination to drive the Rebels out of their Entrenchments but they were to strong for us It was a regular Hornets Nest & I never expected to come out of it alive. but as luck would have it I came away field of Battle with an honest & honorable wound just enough to give me a very unpleasant recollection of the field of Strife & who we were contending with.

We done all we could do with our small force to whip them out. but entrenched & fortified as they were it was an utter impossibility to do it. So we retreated in good order.

We are now erecting a Battery of nine Guns directly in front of the Rebel Batteries we have to work under cover of the night & when we get that done I guess we can Shell them out All of our wounded is here at the General Hospital at Hilton Head. my wound will soon get Better & then I shall return to my Regt. to give the Rebs annother brush. Your Son, Henry

Marshall Philips, Fifth Maine Volunteer Regiment

Phillips writes to his wife, Diana, in North Auburn, Maine.

Harrison's Landing, Virginia
July 25, 1862

Dear Wife

I received a letter from you this morning mailed the 21 was very happy to hear from you but am very sorry to hear that the babies health is so poor if he has got the direar try evry thing you can think of take all the care of him that you can my health is improveing but I have got so tired of war and am so anxious to get home once more that I cant feel contented and cant enjoy myself at all but if I am well must stop until I am discharged the papers call the health of the potomac army good but we call the health of the army in this vicinity very poor more sickly than it has been since we have been in the survice there is one or two burials in this regt and in the brigade evry day mostly of tyfoid feaver and direar one of co E men is to be buried to day of this regt I see that Auburn and Lewiston has offerd a big bounty for volinteers I am glad to have them volinteer instead of being drafted I think I have done about my part should like it if they could come out and let me come home but if I am well must stand my chance with the rest keep up good courage it will do no good to worry although it is hard to keep from doing it. when I lay down I think of you and the family I feel some times as if I done wrong by inlisting and leaveing you with a family of small children I want you to take good care of your self and family you dont write anything about how Florances ear gets along of late, I hope the next time I hear from you to here that Lincoln is better [Florance and Lincoln were Phillips' children] do all you can for him give my respect to all Diana I never was in any place before but what I could come [home] if I had a mind to and hope if ever I get out of this that I never shall be again I have been here so long and our living the same thing day after day very poor and at that this with evry thing else to think of makes me sick of war

from your anxious husband
M.S. Phillips
write often

William Augustus Willoughby, Company A,
10th Connecticut Volunteer Regiment

August 1862

Dear Wif

I have not time to notice your letter of July 15th in all its details in be in time for the mail for I am just informed that the mail closes in half an hour. You speak of the probabilities of my return home I do not expect to come home under one year from now. I made another effort to get a furlough for 30 Days after Col Perdee returned to the Regt he said he would use what influence he could for me but he says its impossable to obtain more than two furloughs at a time from one company and there C[on]valesents enough to occupy and fill the chance for gitting home

You make some allusion in this and in your letter of the 11th to soome persons who seem to gather satisfaction from our seeming defeat. Whatever satisfaction they take they have got to take now for the time is not far away in which all their hope will be swept away like a fog before the Sun And I wish it distinctly understood that whoever says I want the war because I was out of work or that I was from necessity obliged to go falsifies the truth and I do not thank them for such an Apology no matter who they are and what is still more if when my three years is up I will prove their courage by another (if the war is not closed) three years enlistment and they may enlist with seseshs and they may prove their courage and loyalty at the same time. I was always a law abiding citizen and joined the Army to sustain the Govermunt and Laws under which I was willing to live and obey. And if nessesary will join for 3 Years more to fight any rebel "north" or "south" who seeks to break down either. One word more and I must close for now and that is this

You seem to fear that I may become hardened by being in the army, and while passing the trying scenes of a Soldiers life. I think to many and perhaps to most such will prove true. Yet so far as I am concerned I am in hopes to turn these scenes to some good account and return a better man than when I left home. As to what is said in your letters respecting mother I shall leave in till I come home. I have no time to notice Celias letter for the want of time and room now. I send her my kindest regards and will try to say more in answer to her in my next. I send her my kindest for now and Remember me to all others relatives and friends. Tell Father when I get my mind a little settled I shall write him a letter. Write me how he is situated: And now Nancy accept my warmest love for yourself and dear little Raymond and answer this as soon as you can, while I remain Your true and Affectionate Husband

W. A. Willoughby

It is almost impossable for one to write about any thing for some is dancing some playing cards others reading loud enough to be heard ¼ of a mile So you must excuse all mistakes William

Lieutenant Edwin I. Kursheedt, Washington Artillery, CSA

Kursheedt writes to Sarah Levi, a neighbourhood friend.

Battle Field near Gainesville Va.
August 25, 1862

My Dear Miss Sarah,

This is the first opportunity I have had since my last to you from Gordonsville about two weeks ago. Since our departure from Richmond we have not remained 24 hours in the same place & have been in two engagements—Last Saturday the 3rd Compy and our Battery together with others, engaged the Enemy at Rappahannock Station & after a hard fight of 4 hours drove the enemy from his position occupying his camp in the evening. The loss in our two companies was very heavy. 23 killed & wounded—one man of my piece was killed instantly & two wounded. A statement of our loss was sent to the "Whig."

The little *Battle Flag* is pretty well cut up by the shells of the enemy & we are all very proud of it. One of our guns (nigger baby) burst mortally wounding one of our men. We lost 25 horses—This was the hottest place we have been in. Yesterday we went into another artillery duel severe engaged for two hours & had 3 men wounded in the 3rd co. none in ours. The tables have been turned & we are now pressing the enemy to the wall.

We are looking for an engagement tomorrow & should the same take place I fancy it will be quite heavy—the relative positions of the armies are on a portion of the Battle Field of Manassas—we are but 10 miles from Centreville—a great many prisoners are passing on the road & the enemy are shelling the woods about 1800 yards from us but hurting no one.

By the Protection of a kind Providence I am again spared after having had some very narrow escapes. I write today for the purpose of informing you of my safety as I suppose the accounts of these engagements have been published. Henry Florance is quite well & begs to be remembered. All of our wounded boys were taken to Culpepper C.H. where the ladies are attending to them.

There is no telling when we shall see Richmond as we might march into the Enemy's country, but I shall certainly try to come down for the Holy days.

Remember me to Mrs. Davis & family say to her Eugene Levy & brother are both well—we fought side by side in both engagements.

I hope ere long we will have regular mail communication with Richmond. I must close in haste—a heavy engagement has just opened on our left. Give my love to all the family.

Yours very affectionately,
Edwin

Should you see Mr. Everett tell him to go to Mr. Gardeners & inquire for letters for things to bring us up 10 lbs. Sugar & some Confederate coffee. We have plenty of eggs & butter at 12½ cents per doz. Send my white flannel over shirt & socks by him.

Dennis Ford, Company H, 28th Massachusetts Volunteers

Ford, a labourer, enlisted on 17 December 1861, at the age of 38.

Washington, September 6th, 1862

Dear wife and neighbors. I am living still, thank God. I been in four battles since I left Newport News. We had two severe ones. We lost half our regiment. The last fight, my clothes were riddled with balls. I was grazed in the right arm. It knocked my arm dead, though thank God I have not seen one drop of blood as yet. The rubber blanket I had on my back was riddled. A ball struck me on the shoe. They fell around me like hail. James Phillips is shot dead. The rest of the boys are safe. John Maher was wounded. Peter King got something like a wound, it is nothing. John Fenning was wounded. Con Roach came out safe. Maurice and the Donnellys are safe. We lost in the last fight 130 men out of our regiment.

It would be too tedious for me to tell what I went through—the long marching for the last 26 days. Half hungry, some would kill cows and skin a part of them, cut off a piece and waste it, and never open them. Some would shoot pigs and sheep, and would never open them, only cut a piece and roast it and leave the rest behind. Some would carry their coffee in their hand and march in the ranks and drink it, some would spill it. Sometimes, the dinner and breakfast would be cooking, they would get word to march, they would have to spill it and throw it away and march. The rebels fare worse than we do.

Let me know how are the children. Let me know about the note. I did not receive an answer to the last letter I wrote you from Newport News. Write as soon as you receive this, as we don't know the hour we will be on the march.

The war is raging in every direction the rebels fight in the woods. So I must conclude. Give my best love and respects to all the friends and neighbors. Let me know how times are in Haverhill. We received no pay for the last two months. When you write, let me know all the particulars. Our priest can't stand the hardship, we fear he will leave though he is a smart young man. They treat him very bad.

So I must conclude. Do pray for us, we look shabby and thin, though we were called a clean regiment. I saw a great deal shot and wounded. Balls drove through their [lines]. The 28th Mass. suffered [along with] the 79th New York. Our regiment stood the severest fire that was witnessed. During the war, when we got into the woods, we ran through what we did not shoot. We bayoneted them. One man begged and got no mercy, a yankee ran him through. Thank God it was not an Irishman did it.

So I must conclude. I remain your humble husband Dennis Ford until death. I am in hopes I will see Haverhill once more before I die with the help of God. Direct to Washington, to me, Company H, 28 Regiment Mass. Vol. Tell Mrs. McCormick her friend Thomas Cline is well. There was one James Short from Lawrence [who] fell in the last battle.

Ford was captured at Charles City Cross Roads, Virginia, on 16 August 1864. He was exchanged 3 months later, and served out the remainder of his 3-year enlistment, being discharged on 19 December 1864.

Private Oliver Giberson, 14th New Jersey Volunteers

Giberson was mustered into the Union Army on 15 August 1862.

Camp Hooker Oct 27/62

Dear Cousin,

It is with the greatest pleasure that I take my pen in hand to write you a few lines to inform you that I am well at present, hoping these few lines may find you the same. I am encamped at Frederick Junction, Monocacy Bridge, Maryland guarding the government stores and railroad bridge which was blown up by the rebels just after we left there and went to Elyaville. They done quite a good deal of damage in coming through here, for the railroad bridge cost eighty thousand dollars. It was a double track bridge, it being the central railroad from Philadelphia to Ohio, and the main road from here to Harper's Ferry and Washington. It hurt us a good deal putting our troops and supplies through to the main army. The rebels didn't make much by going through for they got most an awful hammering at Harper's Ferry. We had one thousand of the prisoners here. They was a pretty rough customer, I tell you—half naked, lousy and barefooted. It would have made you shudder to look at them and think how will they stick and fight. I should think they would give up and come under the laws of the United States and not fight any longer, but I don't believe they ever will until they are whipped in and I hope they will be before long.

I have been in the service very nigh three months and haint had a shot at the rebels yet. It is quite hard to go so far from home a gunning and not find any game to shoot. It's a worse place than Jersey for game—all but the rebels.

Tell Grandfather and Grandmother that I am in Dixieland trying to fulfill my country's duty and bear up that starry flag which our forefathers fought and bled under to gain us the most glorious country and government that ever existed and I thought it my duty to come and fight for my country, my parents, and the rest of my family was well when I heard from them. If you can tell me what regiment James is and what company and name of his captain, I will try and send him a letter, for I would like to hear from him and let him know where I am now. You think because I am a soldier I am like a brute, but theres not a day that passes over my head but what I think of my folks and believe me to ever be your affectionate cousin, Oliver C. Giberson.

Giberson died of typhoid fever at Fairfax Seminary Hospital on 1 September 1863.

Sergeant Ambrose Doss, Company C, 19th Alabama Infantry Regiment, CSA

Camp Near Knoxville Tenn
this October the 29th 1862

Mrs Sarrah Doss

Dear Wife and Children I am permited through kind providence one time more to drop you A few lines Which leaves me Well and hope that this Will Reach you and find all Well————I have Not Seem No Knews from home Sence the letter Hix Brought me I am thairfore Anxious to hear from home————I can Say the I do Knot think thair has Bin much made By our Kentucky Trip it Seemed that our Generals could Knot Be kept from Running All tho the officers and men Was Anxious to fight Brag Will knot fight if he can find any Ground to Run on————many of our Soldiers has and Will die from hard Marching and Suffering We Went 3 days A time or two Without any provision only What parched corn We Could git which was A Small Amount you can Amagin our Suffering————We was Skirmising and in line of Battle for many days and Nights With Nothing like half Rations None of the time————Thomas C. Hudelston of our com(pany) died the day after We Reached hear of pueinomia feavor and Many of the Boys is unwell and A few of them Very Sick————Bud Fields of the 28 Regt is dead he died Some time Back————as to Clothing I Need two Colered Coten Shirts and two Janes par of pants and 2 par of drawers and 2 par of Socks if you can get them for me By frist passing Send me my necklace I Need A par of Good Strong Shoes if you can Get them made if knot try to Send me A Good par of letters I will Close this yours tell death Ambrose Doss to Sarrah Doss and Children

Doss fought in the battles of Murfreesboro and Chickamauga, before being killed in action alongside the Chattahoochee River in July 1864. Below is the notification to Sarah Doss of her husband's death.

At Chattahoochee River West bank at fortifications
July the 6th 1864

Mrs Sarah Doss

Much Respected friend, it(s) with sad heart that I this Morning take up my pen to Anounce to you the most painful Intelagence that could posable Be pened to you your husband is No more on Eath forever Ambrose is gone to the spirit World he Was Killed yesterday About 1 oclock A Cannon Shot it Struck him in the Right side Nearly Even With the Right Breast and passed Intirely through his Body and through his left Arm Killing him Instantly We had Been ordered to the left to suport that Wing of the Army We had to pass some Distance Along the lines under A terific Cannonade and hence the Above Named Causality. he has Been Sargt of the Infirmery Corps Ever Since the Commencement of this move and Was at the time of his Death marching in Rear of the Regt at post as usual I was in front But When I learned that he Was killed I Got leave from the Col and myself and James G. and John F Rogers and Geoge Eaton and . C. hix Went Back and got the Body of our fallen Brother and Intered it With as much Decency as the Nature of the Case Would admit it Was Knot Done in as Nice a maner As We Would have perfered But fare better then is common with us Soldiers————he is Buried in 1 hundred yards of the chattahoochee River on the West Side in or Near the Edg(e) of the River Botum A pine sapling grows at Both hed and foot of his grave on the Bank of the 1 growing at the head of the grave his Rank Name Co and Regt is cut the plantation Where his Remains Rests is owned by A man By Name of Turner it is About 4 Miles Below the Rail Road Bridg(e) leading from Marietta to Atlanta ga in Fulton County Well Dear madam I Would in this letter Which is pened under the loud Roar of Artilery and Bursting shells Nearly in all Directions offer you Words of Consolation Knowing that consoling Words is Seldom of But little comfort to the Deeply Wounded heart yet I Do from from my heart Symphathize With you in this your greatest and most heart rending trial of life While I can not feel the Irreparable loss in all its painful and heartrending power yet I feel my loss in my Departed Brother in Arms But While I mourn A Noble and Dear friend I am free to Acknowl-edge(e) that you mourn the loss of A Devated and Dear husband Ambrose has Been my Constant friend for years But 3 years in the face of the Enimys our Country hand in in hand Battleing for the Rights of posterity has Double Indeared him to me I have looked on that Calm Soldiers face in Battle my last time he has Done his Duty Noblely and the thread of life has Never yet Been but of A Braver man Brave and yet cool and composed in the hottest conflicts that it has Ever yet Been his lot to Engage in Which conflicts has been common in 3 years War life his conduct As A Soldier is unimpeachable in his life he had the confidence and Esteem of Both officers and men of his Intire Acquaintance Which Was Very Extensive for Such Soldiers as ambrose Doss is not common in No Army hence his Aquantance Was Saught By all

good men—Dear Niebher I Will Speak of your husband in Regard
to his morality and christain Deportment While the heart Seckens
and grows sad at the Loss of Loved ones and the Cruelitys of War
and Bloodeshed We looke fare Away Beyond this Veil of tears and
sorows and then consider the christain conduct that marked the
life of our galant Brother in arms We are bound to Exclaim With
Joy after all our Grief that our loss is his Eternal gain he is gone
from this World Mortality has put on Immortality But Rejoice yet
his comrades in Battle for his last hard Battle has Been fought and
he is more then Victor the Battle Cry Will No more Reach his Ear
no more Will the hoarse sound of Martial music Salute him the
Clash of Arms to him has ceased his spirit has took its flight
from this World of troubles and sorows his Bosom has heaved
it(s) last sigh Concerning loved ones at Home his spirit Rests
Beyond this World of Strife Wigh God Who gave it Where his
happeness is compleete Liveng and Reigning With holy Angels
and Spirits of Just ones made perfect Being heir of God and
Joint heir of Jesus Christ then grieve Knot Dear Mother Altho
the cross is heavy Indeed yet your husband has only gone Before
and A few more tears and sighs A few more fleeting months or
years and you go hame to meet him Where parting is at a End
your husband has only changed this mortal Body for Immortality he cannot come to you But yet A little While and you can
go to him So press Back the tear and Stop the upheaving Boson
as much as Nature Will admit and Rejoice in God Who arders
all things Well James and John Rogers is trying to keep all of his
things they can to send to you When they have A oppertunity if
thair is Anything that I have not wrote that you Wish to no
write to me and your letters Will Be promptly Awnsered if I am
no life let my folks no I am Well first chance your friend J.W.
Rouse to Sarah Doss

Sergeant Charles Wickesberg, Company H, 26th Infantry, Wisconsin Volunteers

Wickesberg writes to his parents in Shebuygan County, Wisconsin.

Washington, October 16, 1862

Dear Parents Brothers and Sisters,
    Finally, I found the time to let you know what happened to us up
to now.

We left Milwaukee at noon on the 7th of October, came to Chicago In the evening, then went to Toledo and Cleveland, and from there to Almeier through Donkirk. Harrisburg and Baltimore, we went to Washington. We arrived in Washington on Saturday and stayed there till Monday. Then we packed our belongings and marched to Fairfax Courthouse. Now we are stationed one mile away from there. We had to walk 20 miles in all.

Fortunately, our knapsacks were driven for us. Now we got settled here as well as we could again.

Yesterday, the 15th, Carl Schurz came to visit us. He talked to our officers, Then he left again, together with his staff.

Today, we had the honor to see our General, Franz Sigel. We paraded be-fore him, he made a speech and told us how things would be here, then we gave him three hurrahs, after which he left. So we live here happy and healthy all day long. The worst is, we do not have any girls here. But we get along without girls too.

It is not as warm here as you might believe. I had thought it would be very warm here. Dear Parents, otherwise I do not have much news to write about. We are 20 miles away from Washington and do not get to see much. So far all of us are still happy and healthy. Have to close now. Give my best regards to all relatives and friends.

Respectfully yours, Your Son

Charles Wickesberg

I have here a few postage stamps that I cannot use. Please send me some new ones instead, and pardon me.

Stafforts Courthouse December 25, 1862

Dear Parents, Brothers and Sisters,

I take my pen this Christmas morning to let you know how we are.

We have had a pretty hard time lately, because we had to march to Fredericksburg which was an eight day walk. But we were too late to take part in the battle. And we were satisfied with that, because the people were slaughtered for nothing.

Dear Parents, I hope you can celebrate Christmas better than I. As I and another four men from our company have to leave today and work on the telegraph. I do not know how long that is going to take. The others have to do outpost duty. That is how we celebrate Christmas. I hope I will be in your midst next year.

Now a word to you Fritz and Mina. Please do not forget me. Keep are in your heart until I come home. And you should write to me sometimes and tell me how you are. My dear parents, I did not get any answer to my last letter. If the letter was lost or something else happened to it, I do not know.

I do not have much news to write about. I wish all of you a very Happy New Year. I hope this war will soon be over. I think the New Year will bring peace.

I have to stop writing now. And I hope these few lines reach you in good health as they leave me.

Stafforts Courthouse
January 1, 1863

Dear Parents, Brothers and Sisters,

I take the pen on this New Years Day to write you a few lines.

We had a pretty amusing evening yesterday because our Brigade General Krzyzanowski had given our regiment a barrel of whisky and many a soldier was a little tipsy. Especially the officers. Our Captain came around at 1 O'Clock and wished all of us a Happy New Year, and said we should keep ourselves prepared because the Southern Cavalry was going to launch a surprize attack on us.

Last Sunday afternoon we had to go, too, to have an encounter with the enemy. About 15 miles from here the enemy cavalry had attacked a small town, and we were supposed to help them. When we were 6 miles away, we heard the news that the enemy was beaten. And we went back home, where we arrived at 9 O'Clock in the evening.

Dear Parents, this morning we received flour and molasses. And because I, the sergeant, and the corporal are in the same tent, I always get a little bit more than the others. So we baked some pancakes. That was the first time I had any as long as I am soldier. It is true the eggs were missing, but they still tasted very good.

Private Newton Scott, Company A, 36th Infantry, Iowa Volunteers

Scott writes to his neighbourhood friend, Hannah Cone, in Albia, Monroe County, Iowa.

Camp Lincoln Keokuk Iowa
October the 24th 1862

Dear Miss

I will Inform you that I am well at this time & that our Co. is all well Except two or three Persons our Mess is all well at the Present & I hope that when this Reaches you that it may find you &

Friends well. Yours of the 19 inst is Rec. I was Glad to Hear from you & that you was well But I Had about given up getting any answer from you But Better Late than Never for Indeed Miss Han. I do love to get News from Home for it looks as if that is all the consolation that us Soldiers Have for we are away from Home & We Have to do as Best we can it is & Has Bin verry cold & Disagreeable to Day We cook & Eat out Doors & we Run to the Table & Eat But nearly Freeze our Fingers While Eating We Have one Stove in our Barracks Which Does a great Deal of good But one stove is a small make Shift for 80 or 90 men it is verry cold Standing guard Especially of nights But If we are Spared to get through the war & Return to our Homes all will be well

My Self & H.W.Reitzel & J.M. Osborn will Be on guard Sunday & Sunday night I hope that we will leave for a warmer climate Soon. We Have not recd our clothes yet But our Major tells us that we will get them the first of the next week. I hope that we will get them Soon You stated in your letter that Sister Amanda looked for me Home She was verry much mistaken for Indeed it is verry Doubtful Whether I come Home Before we leave Here: If we should Stay Here 5 or 6 weeks yet I would likely come Home But I think that we will leave Here in 2 or 3 weeks our Major tells us that we will leave in 15 days The 30th Regiment Has 3 days Rations cooked & Every thing Ready & will leave to morrow for St. Louis they Have Recd there guns & Success to them I Hope that we will follow Soon I would Inform you that one of Capt Nobles men Died last night His name is Taylor Four of Nobles men & four of our men Starts Home with his Remains in the morning Indeed Dear Miss there is thousands of Poor Soldiers that will see Home & Friends no more in this World If you was in Keokuk & See the number of Sick & Disabled Soldiers it would make your Heart Ache. they are Dieing [illegible] Every Day. But anough of the Hard Side of a Soldiers Life I would tell you the good Side If I know it But don't think that I am Home Sick or Disheartend for such is not the case for I am only telling you a few simple Facts of a Soldiers campaign Indeed I wish never to Return Home Permantly until this Wicked & God Forsaken Rebellion is Destroyed—If we had our choices of course we would Be at Home for we are not in the army for fun nor money & Furthermore we wish never to fill a cowards grave & Dear Miss we Have no Fears But that we will Ever Have the good will of those Kind Friends Left at Home. Success to the union Armys & Ere Long may we all Be permitted to Return to our Homes & Live a quiet & Peaceably Lives

Give my love & Respects to all Friends & Reserve a Share for
yourself Please write Soon & tell all to Remember & write to the
Soldiers for it gives them great Pleasure to hear from Home
   In Friendship
   Love & Truth
   I am Truly yours

Helena Arks April the 9th/63

Dear Miss Han. M. Cone
   I will Inform you with Pleasure that I am well at the present & I
hope that when this Reaches you that it may find you well I Have
Recd. no letter from you Since the about the 1st of March I wrote
you an answer on the 9th of March & Rec. no *Ans* yet & I Have
concluded to write one letter for Spite Well Han. I dont know that
I have much of Interest to write at the Present But I will write
alittle & tell you How the Boys are getting along Since I wrote you
last we Have Had considerable Sickness in our Co. E. F. Knight
Has Bin verry sick But is Getting well now. Dorsey Makin is verry
Sick at the Present He took Sick on or about the 15th March & Has
Bin Gradualy Sinking Ever Since He is not Exspected to live I
Have Bin waiting on Him Ever Since the 24th March We carried
Him from the Boat yesterday Evening to His Relatives Here & I &
Will P. is Staying with Him I think that He can not last But afew
Days longer. the Rest of acquaintances are Generaly well I Beleive
at this time—
   Well Han, Since I last Wrote to you I Have Heard Rebel Bullets
Sing But we Have Had no General Fight we was Fired on Several
times By Gurillas Fired on us & Slightly Wounded 2 of our Co.
Sergt. D.P. Bay was Shot in the Shoulder But not Seriously also
Thomas Nichol was Shot on the cheek the Bullet was taken out But
it will Soon Be well again
   We left Ft Greenwood on the 4th & arrived Here on yesterday
We Will go into camp Here But I know not How long we will
Remain Here I think it Doubtful Whether we stay Here verry long
I Have not Room to tell you any thing about our Expedition for it
Would take about 20 Sheets of Paper to tell all But Suffice it to say
that we Had apretty Hard time & Sufferd considerable with
Sickness & Done But little Damage only in the Destruction of
Cotton & Property I Have See a great many large Buildings &
Fencing Burned and any Amount of other Property taken We got
Several messes of Good chicken While we was gone we Respected
Rebel Property But little & where Ever they Fired on our Boats
We landed & Burnt Every thing that would Burn

But enough to this for the Present Well Han. I must tell you that I & the old Lady liveing at this Home Had a Big chat last night She Has two verry nice girls they are Sociable & Friendly & good looking But they are Secesh they Have Sent there only Grown Brother to Join the Rebel Army He left Here on the 9th of March they are verry Good to Dorsey they will give Him any thing that he will Eat If they are Secesh they are in favor of Peace on any terms they are verry tired of the war But they hear that the war will last Some time & I think my Self that it will Be some time yet Before the war closes.

But I will Have to close for I Have my sheet Filled & nothing writen Will is Sitting By me writing to David Cone Please write all Particulars & write Soon give my Respects to all

Respectfully yours Newton Scott

Scott survived the war, and was mustered out of the Union Army in the autumn of 1865. A year later he married Hannah Cone.

Corporal Adam Muenzenberger, Company C, 26th Regiment, Wisconsin Volunteers

Muenzenberger writes to his wife. The 26th Wisconsin was a "German Regiment" raised almost exclusively from German-speaking immigrants.

Gainsville, November 12, 1862

Dearest Barbara

Having no duties to perform today—I was on sentry duty yesterday while our company was on picket duty—I felt that I should write to you. Adam and I are well and happy and we hope that these lines may find you the same.

The day after my last letter we marched with the Hills of Bull Run on the one side and the fields on the other and occupied the main street of the town where two days before the enemies pickets had been posted. They had been driven in by our cavalry under General Stahl. We left our camp at eight o'clock in the morning and arrived in full equipment at one P. M. We were given immediate orders to set up our tents. We have barely finished with this when the younger soldiers of the regiment went out foraging and brought in pigs, chickens, duck, turkeys and geese in large number. We roasted and cooked them. We are staying at a place called New Baltimore. The other day thirty thousand men of

General McClellans's command passed on with orders to march double time toward the enemy. A couple of days ago we were ordered to break camp and to march east towards Gainsville which is a railroad station from which we draw supplies. Ten days ago this town was still in the hands of the rebels. It lies between Centerville and Manassas Junction and was destroyed by them before their retreat. The rebels are in constant flight and are being followed by our companies, particularly by General Stahl's brigade. We are still held in reserve. We have seen no rebels but here and there the wives and children who have been left behind stare at us—sometimes sadly, sometimes hatefully. Occasionally we come across a farmer who says that he has rented his farm and would gladly go north if he could only secure his possession safely. These men are sent north immediately. No horse or cow is safe from the old regiment. The soldiers take everything along on the plea that they wish to pay the rebels for the treatment at the last battle of Bull Run.

We hear that our wives have received no assistance from the government and a lot of other idle talk. Please write and tell me how everything is at home, [?] Walsh paid the constable's expenses, and what is happening. You write me that you have heard it prophesied that we can be home by spring. Let me know whether we can believe this or not. Please tell me who the prophet was and where he gets his prophecies and whether we can believe them or not. Please tell me what the teacup gives as truth. I'd rather believe that then any other thing.

We haven't received any pay as yet and haven't heard when we will be paid. If you haven't sent me any post stamps as yet, send me some—but all new ones—and I will write you one or, even two letters every week. Stamps cannot be obtained here. Write me also whether you received the power of attorney and let me know how many letters Adam wrote to Christina and especially how that last trouble with Wallace turned out on account of that window peeking. Please greet all my acquaintances, relatives and friends, especially you mother, your sisters and brothers, my brother-in-law, sister and brother, my father and grandmother, my godfather and family, and Lehr and his family in Milwaukee. Many thousand greetings to you and your children.

Your faithful husband,

Adam Muenzenberger.

We just received the news that we march tomorrow. Whether we don't know. Kiss the children for me. I hope to a speedy return. Answer soon.

Gainsville, November 16, 1862

Precious Barbara, My Dear Wife:

As soon as I received your long expected letter, I felt the urge to sit down and answer it immediately. I don't know what to think of the fact that you didn't receive an answer for so long. Your letters arrived as we lay in our tents and you can't imagine how happy their arrival made me. News again from my dear ones! I had been very much depressed because I had heard that you were seriously ill. Fritz had received a letter from his parents in which they mentioned your illness. Now as I hear your sweet voice again in your letter, I find peace again—but this only through prayer.

I do everything as I promised you—everything with which so long as we are together I could please you. I am very happy to hear that our children are so diligent in study and especially in penmanship, which as you know was always my greatest pleasure.

Since the 30th of October I have written you two letters besides this one. I take pleasure from that fact that the Walters and Hirach families were so helpful to you in your sickness. I am indeed very grateful to them. I thank your mother as well and all those who stood by your during your distress because it shows that I and my family still have good friends and brothers.

My clothing is still in good shape. I wash my blue shirts and my underwear every week in spite of a lack of women to do it. Only the soles of my boots are worn through. My shoes and the new grey shirts which I received from the government are like new. We have received no money as yet nor do I know when we will receive any but as soon as we are paid I will write and send you some. Report has it that we will march again tomorrow or the day after. They say that we will go back to Fredericksburg, Maryland. I was just invited to a sausage lunch by Jacob Michel, Louis Mechel, and Nicholas Frederick. We live as well here as we can. The food is good and the Crackers taste—or rather must taste—good to us. We have fresh meat almost every day.

Don't give up hope, old lady, trust in the Lord. In the wish that these lines find you in the best of health as they leave me I salute you all heartily. Send my best wishes to all that ask for me and to all the relatives.

Your Ever Loving,

Adam Muenzenberger.

Answer soon. Farewell. Kiss the children for me. I am sending you 39c for stamps. Now you can send me many letters. It must be nice to hear little Adam talk. You can't imagine the pleasure I get from looking at your picture.

Centerville, November 19, 1862

Precious Barbara:

Troubled with lonesomeness and with my thoughts forever with the loved ones at home I take my pen in hand to write you a short letter. We are, God be praised, in the best of health and hope that this letter finds you the same. We enjoy happy times here in the encampment at Centerville. We take long walks and pass our time in the easiest fashion. From time to time we have to take picket duty or night watches. Several rebels are captured every day. They are taken as spies. Seeman is provost marshal and sends the captives to Washington where they must stay until they are exchanged.

We have target practice today, twenty men being selected from each company. Adam is with the twenty men today but not I and on that account I have a chance to write a letter and to give the children a little pleasure.

Today several of the officers of our regiment were shipped back to Milwaukee for good, some for being incapable and others for being opposed to commander Jacobs. The commander is still down with the chills and fever. This week as corporal I had the watch before his room. In the morning he treated us with a bottle of brandy. He is in all respects the best officer in the regiment. He is not naughty like Hehman and Major Horwitz. General Schurz is a good man to his division. All of his men have great respect for him. He cares for them like a father. Every two days we get good wheat bread; the other days we have crackers. We likewise have fresh beef every two days. On the other days we have salt pork and bean soup.

We have receive no money as yet and don't know when we will receive any but as soon as I do get some I will write to you. The weather here is about the same as it is in October at home. It freezes just a little at night and there is a light frost. We are camped here in our cotton tents, quite well satisfied and filled with the hope that the war will be over in spring. Report has it that there has been drafting in Wisconsin and great resultant scandal. We have had a great laugh at the simpletons who laughed at us because we volunteered. Please let me know who was drafted if you can find out so that I can laugh at their lot the way they laughed at mine.

I find happiness in the thought of a loving wife and children who still remember their father in the north and the more I think of you the more I count on seeing you soon again if God wills. Therefore be comforted. As I have found out here a protecting hand is over us. I send my greetings to all my friends and acquaintances, all my society brothers, to all who ask for me, to my sister and brother-in-law, your mother and family, to Adam Muehl and grandma and family, and to George Michel and his wife. Many greetings to you and to the children, and I remain, true soul.

Your loving husband
Adam Muenzenberger.
Farewell. A speedy return. Answer soon.

Muenzenberger was captured at the battle of Gettysburg. He died a prisoner of war in November 1863.

William H. Jackson, Company F, 53rd Pennsylvania Infantry Regiment

Head Quarters
Nov 26 1862
Falmouth Va

Dear Brothers
I now Sit me down for a (few) momentes to converse with you. Feeling myself very much indebted to you. I rec'd your letter the 24 and was much pleased to hear from you I feel very happy to Know that you arived at home Safe once more Well Hear we are on the bank of the Rapahanock I reg't has the honor of guarding the town. We are situated in a church on an elivated Spot favoring us with a very good sight at the Rebs we can see their guns their pickets and considerable of their force, it is the grandest Sight at them we have ever had but the more I see of them the more I hate them. Well we came here by way of the Valey Came through several towns, (not worth mensioning) except Warintown, we came below the Junction about three miles. The weather is qiute wet and cold and has been for some time, I presume you have heard of the removal of McClellan and the promotion of Burnside.

Well I dont expect now that we Will see winter Quarters in a month if at all, if I can judg I think we will moove Shortly

I am honored with the position of comisary Sargent so you see I am free from guard duty & c I have been drawing today and they bother me so I can hardly write We have not seen the Paymaster in Five months and the thing loocks just as dark as ever you Know how it is, no money no stamps & c. I will have to Send my letters without Stamps for their is no use trying to get any thing from home we have had but one mail in three weeks. and no way of Sending any out but I will try you need not expect us to write very often unless something happens but you must write as often as possible for you know how much good it does a Soldier to hear from home but out mail rout is rather unhandy at preasant for the Rebs are in our Rear. O How I would like to See you I wish I could come home and See Pa and Ma and the rest of the folks for I am geting so tiared of this war that I am geting Some what homesick, but I am so glad you are home and more wheir you can get attended to and I hope soone to hear that you are well as ever, Then I shall expect to see you hear or wheirever We may chance to be tell Father to save them Chestnuts for me untill I send for them. then send me the price and I will send the money for them.

You can hardly read my scribbling for I have been in so much of a hurry the candle is very dim. Their is three Companys in the church and it is a perfect thunder all the time I cant hear myself think so I will close for the preasant

Give my love to all inquiring friends With these few lines I close hoping they may find you as they leave me Well Write soone From your Most affectionate Brother Will. A soldier of the 53rd reg't Comp. F.
No more

n.d.

Some one called for Supper and I must close for a few moments I thought I would write some more of the perticulars We have the first detailes of the fight if there is any others we have not heard them so I will tell the first, Handcocks Divison went on the field with 6600 and came out with 1800 So you may by this see whether their was any thing like fighting done or not fifteen thousand is the reported lost of our Side————Now I will tell you what I think of Burnsides first move I think he Sat a time to bucher and he made a good Job of it. If [?] alimon hall had been in comand I should not have thought so much of it and I think the sooner Burnside is kicked out the better it will be for us you said in adds letter you thought I was getting discouraged yes I am more and eavery day I am Sick of this war and the loss of my only friend makes me more so than eaver. I dont believe it will eaver amount to a pinch of Sh—t and its nothing anyway but the acurssed Nigger, its all fudge and I am **mad**.

You was saying in your letter that I said nothing about your Coat or [?] in the Q M hands Well our coats are not charged to us and all that wanted any drawed them but they was charged us so I thought I wou not draw one for you for I could not send it to you Now for the money. I went to the Q.M. with Quatermaster Rice

and Laffingwell said he didnt [oew scratched out] owe you a red
Sent but that you owed him $15 and he would streighten it up
someday. That was all the Satisfaction he gave me you must See to
that yourself for I dont know much about the matter Well I must
close But their is that butter if you can get a good price for it you
had better Sell it and not run the risk but if I had it I could Sell it
for 56 cts lbs and the chestnuts I will send for when I get money
Please tell my friends that I escaped with a whole hide much more
than I expected I will close with sending my love from your affet
and loving Brother Will to J.C. Jackson Carverton Luz. Co Penna

P.S. Excuse me I will give you the directiones all you want is the
Divison and Corps
"Hancocks Divison
"Couches Corps
excuse haste & mistakes
I recieved those stamps

Captain Michael Shuler, Company H, 33rd Virginia Voluntary Infantry, CSA

The below are excerpts from Shuler's diary, kept from June to
December 1862.

Diary: July 30 Wednes—Nothing of interest everything quiet. We
now have been drilling and cleaning up camp as though we were
going in regular encampment. Wm Purdam came back the 31st. I
wrote a letter home, the second. I find everything is beautiful this
morning have had but little rain since we have been at camp. Had a
very heavy rain this evening.

Aug 7 Thurs—Had orders to cook two days rations about 12 M, we
marched about 4 P.M. in the direction of Orange C.H. of which
place we encamped about 4 miles, distance 6 miles.

Aug 8—We marched by day light this morning by Orange C.H.
took the Culpepper road. It is exceedingly hot. Encamped about a
mile below the Madison Mills. The Yankees scouted very close to
our camp in the night but were met by some of the 3rd Brigade.

Aug 9—We were in line this morning before day, thought we
would have the enemy upon us, it was nothing but their scout.
Marched by sun up in direction of Culpepper C.H. It is very hot
here today the men suffer a great deal by the heat. When we
arrived within about 8 miles of C.C.H. rested and found our
artillery getting in position. Cannonading commenced about 12

M. We were soon advancing from the hill we could see the Yank line. Our batteries soon advanced from the hill. Ewell's division on the right, Hill's in the center, ours on the left. We lay under a very heavy fire of shell before going in the fight. Not more than 10 minutes after the musketry commenced upon our right we were ordered to advance. Col. Reynolds in advance of the brigade (he having command after Gen. Winder fell). We had not gone far before he came galloping back to say, "1st Brigade, prepare for a charge bayonets". The brigade charged with a sirabile yell the Yanks fled the men fought well. I had but wounded. Captured a great many prisoners. The enemy were driven from the field leaving their killed and wounded and a great amt of arms. We encamped on the battle field.

Aug 11th Thurs—This day has been set apart by order of Gen. Jackson for prayer and thanksgiving for the late victory at Cedar Run. I have for the first time the duties of field officer of the day to perform. Robert Aleshire, Jn. S Wilson and Reub Comer came in to duty.

Aug 18th Monday—Everything quiet this morning. Expect to move today. Orders to cook two days ration and put in haversacks by sun set. Expect to move early in the morning.

Aug 19th Tues—Slept on my gum cloth did not rise until after sun up no move yet as expected. I witnessed the execution of 3 men this evening one from the 5th Reg, 2 from 10th Regt. Both the 1st and 3rd Brigades were drawn in to witness the execution. Orders to keep cooked rations on hand, 3 days rations in haversack and canteens ready filled. We have been disappointed as to moving but expect to move early in the morning.

Aug 20th Wednes—Reville at 1 this morning but is after sun up now and we have not moved yet. Yanks are moving on down the road. Took up march about 9 A.M. Crossed the Rapidan River. Tis very warm and dusty. The Yanks are retreating. Had a cavalry fight this evening drove the enemy to the Rappahannock. We encamped below Stephensburg. Marched about 12 miles today.

Aug 22nd Friday—Ewell's division was marching by us to the ford very early this morning and we expected would cross the river but the enemy's batteries were still in position and opened a heavy fire upon the wood we lay, shelling continued until about 9 P.M. when we left our position. Following Hill and Ewell's division, we marched up the river and about 5 P.M. crossed the south fork of the Rappahannock. Our advance was engaged with a brigade of the enemy and we lay in line of battle all night. The heavens looked terrible as a heavy rain might be approaching. Firey streaks of lightning was quickly followed by sharp peals of thunder.

Aug 23rd—After the threatening passed we had but little rain last night. We were exposed again for about 2 hours this morning to the shelling. We changed positions about 9 A.M. Marched about 8 miles up the River to Jim Jacksons at Lee Springs. It was extremely hot. Our rations ran out last evening and our wagons have not been able to get to us. We are getting very hungry. Bob Cubbage came to the Company yesterday, Daniel Abbot came to the Company to day.

Aug 24th Sunday—We are all suffering in fact for something to eat, got beef and had to boil it no bread. Drew a days ration of hard bread and bacon about 12 M, cannonading coming about 10 A.M. Our forces fell back from the other side of the river. Cannonading is kept up pretty lively. I have not heard with what results. Ruben Somers and Jno. Printz just came to camp. Cannonading kept up until dark. Drew and cooked 2 days rations.

Aug 27th Wednesday—Marched by daylight our brigade in front. Had a slight skirmish across the creek to the left of Bristoe then marched to Manassas found the Yankees had retired but a short distance. Got rations then took the breast-works and waited for the enemy to advance which they did. There was but one brigade of the enemy they were soon routed. Started from Manassas after night. burnt all the cars and stores that were there, marched in direction of the old battlefield we marched all night.

Aug 28 Thursday—We rested a little north of the old battlefield of Manassas, shifted positions often during the day and had nearly given out the idea of a fight as the sun was fast sinking in the west. About an hour by sun we heard distant cannonading in the direction of Thoroughfare Gap. We were ordered forward to the right of Grafton lay in the woods a short time advanced just as sun set and fought about an hour and a half the severest infantry fighting I ever saw. Drove the enemy back lay upon the battlefield at night. I went to see my wounded, I had one killed and 8 wounded in my Co. viz. killed Jno. I Wilson wounded Serg Menifie, Privates Webster, Ambrose Huffman, David Hite, Geo. Kite, Jos. L Cullers, Silar A Somers, A.P. Printz, none I think dangerously.

Aug 30th Saturday—Got with the Regt about 10 A.M., we lay in line of battle until 3 P.M. when the greatest battle of the war commenced in earnest. Regular skirmishing had been kept up all day. The battle opened right in our front. We were ordered immediately forward. We met a desperate fire but pushed forward until we gained the old rail road. Soon got the Yanks in full retreat. Longstreet closed in from the right and did some desperate fighting finally got them to running. We followed in pursuit about an hour after dark, encamped the night near Stone Bridge. We had two days fight the following wounded . . . I am now left with not over 15 men present in my Company.

Aug 31st Sunday—Wrote a letter home this morning made a detail to bury the dead. Knapsacks, blankets, and oil cloths are strewn in all directions. Cooked some rations and took up the march in the direction of Leesburg . . .

Sept 16th Tuesday—Reville about 12 in the night, marched at 1 A.M. passed through Shepardstown a little after sun up. Waded the Potomac again and are again in Maryland. Cannonading commenced in our front very early this morning. Marched to a woods but a short distance from the cannonading and rested. Marched to the left of Longstreets line of battle took position in line about sunset. The Yankees opened a very heavy fire of shell upon us. Infantry skirmishing to our right, marched 15 miles.

Sept 17th Wednes—We lay on our arms all night in line of battle. Skirmishing keeps up all night to our right, day light heavy firing commenced. The enemy advanced upon our line about sun up. The fighting was terrible, we have possession of the battlefield. The fight has been general today and very hotly contested. I am feeling very ill this evening went to the rear.

Sept 18th Thursday—Got with our wagons today, found Lieut Kite with them, cooked rations no fighting today. Our division moved out of line about 12 in the night.

Sept 19th Friday—Got to the Potomac about sun rise, found the whole army was massing in Va. We crossed and marched through Shepardstown took the Martinsburg Road. Encamped about 4 miles from town. I took command of the Regiment this morning, marched about 11 miles didn't get any sleep last night.

Sept 27th Saturday—Marched out of camp at 8 A.M. and lay in a road near by awaiting the movement of other troops until about 3 P.M. when we marched through Martinsburg and took the road to Winchester. Marched very slow stopped very often. Encamped in a field near Bunker Hill about 2 in the morning. Marched the greater part of the night. Marched 11 miles.

Sept 29th Monday—In camp today. Drill, a morning report required. Philip Long came to camp. Tuesday in hunt of God. Nothing of importance, everything quiet in camp. Father came down Wednesday and left for home Friday. Commissary brought something to eat for us. Have had regular drills.

Oct 16th—Reville at 3 this morning. Cooked breakfast and marched out of camp by day light through Smithfield to the Shepardstown Road and marched to the Baltimore and Ohio Railroad at Kerneysville. Commenced to tear up the Railroad but were soon interrupted by Yankees after a slight skirmish we [?] back the enemy, did not pursue, marched back some two miles after dark through the rain and encamped in a large mill.

Nov 29 Sat—Marched out of camp by sun up, passed through Orange and encamped about 7 miles below. Marched about 12 miles . . .

Nov 30th Sund—Marched out of camp at 8 this morning, William Purdam was detailed as wagoner. Encamped for the night in a woods about 16 miles of Fredericksburg. Marched about 12 miles today.

December 1st Monday—Marched by 8 A.M. Encamped in a woods about 6 miles and to the right of Fredricksburg. Marched about 12 miles today.

Dec 2nd—Marched by 7 A.M. to the Fredricksburg and Richmond Road, the road leading to Guinea Station. Encamped in a woods to left of road about 2 miles of Station. Marched about 10 miles today. I was ordered under arrest by Genl Lee for shooting my pistol at a squirrel when we stopped this evening.

Dec 2nd + 4th—We lay in camp quietly, was relieved of arrest the evening of the 4th, Jesse Rily and D B Abbott came in the 3rd Dec, 5th Friday moved camp about ½ mile at 9 A.M. to where wood was more plentiful, commenced snowing this evening.

Dec 6th Sat—Tis pretty cold snowed some last evening. Capt Hensley and I went hunting today caught an opossum everything quiet very cold this evening. Remained very quiet in camp until *Thurs 11th Dec* when we were awakened very early by heavy cannonading in direction of Fredricksburg. We were ordered to cook and keep 2 days rations on hand. Orders to move by 6 in the morning.

Friday Dec 12th—Marched out of camp

Shuler's diary ends abruptly after this entry. The Battle of Fredericksburg commenced that same day.

Galutia York, Company G, 11th New York State Volunteer Infantry

A farm boy, York was mustered into the Union Army in the Summer of 1862.

1862
Chessapique hospital Dec 11

Dear father and mother

it is with much pleasure inded that I once more seat myself to write you a few lines to let you know whats the matter well I have got the measles or rather have had them but I haint got well yet but I am gaining good I shall get along now if I dont take a cold I am so hoarse that I cant talk a bit I haint spoke in 4 days but I shall be so that I can talk in a day or so I hope this will find you all well and enjoiing good health I received your most welcomed letter last Friday and you dont know how glad I was to hear from home again I had allmost given up getting anymore I had not had one in so long I have not had a letter from Henry yet yes I got the last letter you directed to Baltimore I would get them if you should direct them all to Baltimore I got Lucys letter I shall have to answer it some day I wrote 2 letters home in answer to the last one I got before this did you get both of them————and I sent a check of $10 I was took with the measles and brought to the hospital last Tuesday I was sick 3 days before I was taken to a hospital Dave Loomis————Judson Palmer Hinman and one other fellow was taken to the hospital out of *Co G* the same day that I was all with the measles we have good care taken of us plent to eat and drink I suppose Dan and Uncle Stephen has wrote all of the news they told me they had both written to you about me that is one reason that I did not answer your letter before and another reason was because I was not well enough to write but I will write just as often as I can Pa what is the reason that you dont write any to me do you have so much to do or what how much did the old sow weigh have you killed your beef if did she weigh and how much did you make on her I want you to remember and haing that peice up to dry for me has warren sold his hops yet how much of your wood have you drawn of how mutch coal are you a burning I should like to be there and help you this winter help drink up that barrell of cider any weigh and eat some of the apples we have to pay 3 cents a peice for aples down hear and they are pretty poor at that no dont send me anything for mebby I shall get them and mebby should not or the socks them you mite send and I dont know but I should get the mittens it is not cold enough to nead mittens now but how cold it will be is more than I know well I have wrote about all that I feall well enough to so I must close write as soon as you get this write all of the news dont be afraid of writing to much this from your most affectionate son Galutia York

There is one thing more I forgot ma you wanted to know if I use tobacco no I dont use it is any way whatever that was as much news to me as it was to you I should like to know what put that in her head I believe she is the biggest sap head I ever saw I wonder how long it takes her to write a letter to dan it takes dan 3 or 4 days to write to her I guess he haint wrote one in less than 3 days and there was one that I know he was over 8 days Henry Chesebro is alive and enjoiing good health he has not been shot yet as I know of I than you verry much for them postage stamp you sent me I got them all I have got over a dollars worth now they will last me some I guess I must go to bed now for I have so up now longer than I had ought yes ma that was a nice kis I think considerable of it I will send you all one if they will be exceptible direct to Chesapeake General Hospital Virginia dont put on the Co nor reg

Quarantine, Feb. 14th, 1863

Dear Father & Mother

It is with a verry great degree of pleasure that I once more seat myself to write you a few lines to let you know how I get along I am not verry well I have been quite down to heel for the past 2 or 3 days but I am some better now I have had the diarrhoeah I have got a verry bad cough and it has settled on my longues. but I hope this will find you all well and injoiing your selves. I received your verry prescious letter of Jan. 12th this morning and you cant imagine with what joy I received it. for I found out that I had not got so far from home but what I could hear from there once in a while and I hop that you can get my letters so you can hear from me once in a while I hope and pray that you have got the 2 letters that I wrote before since I have been hear so you wont worry about me We are on land now each man does his own cooking or cook by squads of 8. we are having as good a time as can be expected consiterating the place we are in we are in hopes we shant have to stay hear much longer our reg. is calculating to go into battle before long they have got so near the rebbels that there haint nuthing but a bay between them they are all in good health & spirits. Nathan Sampson got a letter from Uncle Steve this morning he and Dan both sent their best respects to me they have never wrote to me Jud is verry sick he has got the mumps he took cold and they settled he is having a tough time. There was a

man died hear with the small pox last night it was a man by the
name of Beckwith he was from Podunck perhaps uncle John knows
him. I got a letter this morning that you wrote to me Nov 22d. it
went to the reg. and they sent it to me from there I got a letter from
Stephen Coon this morning so that made 3. they are the first I have
received in 5 weeks. I should think the young folks was having a
gay old time up there this winter well let them cut around if they
want to my turn will come by and by I hope. I wish that I had a
fishline and some fishhooks hear now for there is a first rate good
place to fish down hear in the Mississippi and then I could have
some fish to eat we cant get any milk down hear oisters is worth $1
abushel oringes 50 cents a hundread whiskey is worth $2.50 a galon
and tobacco $2. a pound. so come————I wish I had the old gun
down hear I would shoot black birds enough for one good stew
they are firstrate cooked. we haint heard a word from Dave Loomis
since he left I guess he will be to home before you get this. I heard
that Ambrose Sandurs come down to see frank and the old doctor
would not let him see him. Capt. Tucker haint dead our [?] is dead
his name was Nickles. how did Elder Todd make out to his
donation who for gods sake was S.H. Yorks lady and who was
H.G. Coons lady I would like to know. I should think it was a
pretty place to play play to a donation what did Henry Emily and
Irene have a good time down there. I have got so far away from
home that I haint going to write to any one only home/ over 2,000
miles away well I will finish on this I guess I lent my jack knife the
other day and he broke the blade into in the middle he said he
would pay me for it when he got his money so I am without a knife
now. take it among a lot of souldiers it is the worst place to beg and
borough that there is in the world always some one wanting
something. Tell aunt Amanda that she dont know the whole of
it. if you should send the whole of your letters to Chesapeake
General hospital they would send them all on to me for they would
be olbiliged to direct to Galutia H York Co. G. 114. reg. N.Y.S.V.
Washington D C Care Capt Charles Tucker and it will come to me
any where in the U.S. that is if I am with the reg

my clothes wear good they are all whole yet I haint had to do any
patching yet. peach trees are in bloom hear and they hang full of
oringes to they are ripe allmost the year round there haint many
lemons down round right hear I haint seen but a few. well I have
wrote about all I can think of this time so I must close I dont
believe you can mak out what this is for it is a mixed up mess. I
wish that I had a book so that I could keep a diary but I cant get
one hear. I shall write to Henry in a few days I am expecting a

letter from him before long. well write as soon as you get this wrall of the news write a long letter for I want to know what you are all a doing. this from your ever loveing and most affectionate son Galutia H York to Zebulon T and Lucy F York good by for this time.

York died of disease on 20 May 1863.

Private Isaac Howard, CSA

Camp near Fredericksburg
Christmas morning [1862]

My dear Father

I received your letter of the 22nd. [torn] today I was very glad indeed to [torn] home once more as it was the first h[torn] I had heard from home in nearly 4 mon[torn] I was very much releived to hear that all were well at home. I was sorry to hear that Tom was ill all of the time that he was at home. I suppose you will have heard of the great battle of Fredericksburg before this letter reaches you. The Yankees sustained the most utter and terrible defeat, probably that they have experienced during the war. It was the most glorious victory we have ever gained, our loss is trifling in comparison with the enemy, according to Gen. Lee's report of the battle our loss was 1800 killed wounded and missing, while that of the enemy according to their own statement was 15,500, and many of their papers place it as high as 20,000. Not more than one half of our forces were engaged [torn]r brigade didn't fire a gun. Gen Lee [torn]d that we had suffered so severely [torn] Gaines farm, Manassas No 2 and Sharps—[torn]rg, and that he had called upon us so [torn]ften in tight places, that we should be held in reserve. Our regt had 5 or 6 men wounded by shell, no one was killed. I think that we will go into winter quarters soon, as the yankees seem to be disgusted with their ill success of this winters campaign, & they are said to be going back to the Potomac, to go into winter quarters.

The yankee scoundrels almost completely destroyed Fredericksburg, they vented their malice & spleen in the most wanton manner, Breaking up and destroying whatever they could not remove. Nothing was too pure or sacred for their unbridled lust. The very churches were pillaged of of whatever of value or ornament they contained. The retribution they received for their iniquitous proceedings was sudden and terrible. The town was literally choked with [torn] dead. There was 5,000 dead bodies of [*torn*]kee soldiers lying stiffening on that [*torn*]d field the day after the fight. And [*torn*]he fight had been general throughout the whole line, the yankee army would have been nearly annihilated, as it was their army was completely demoralized and recrossed the river more like a rabble rout than the grandest army the world ever saw as the yankees were so fond of terming it. The weather for the last few days has been admirable and to day it is as mild and beautiful as any Christmas I ever remember having seen in Texas.

Tell Ma not to be the least uneasy about my personal comfort. I have plenty of good clothes and blankets and have been in excellent health ever since the fall set in.

There is'nt much preparation for Christmas in camp, the boys are in excellent spirits however, not much doing in the egg-nog line, but with butter, molasses, sugar, confederated c[*torn*] and apples, from the sutler's, and peas[*torn*] roast-beef and hot biscuit from our own [torn] we managed to make out a pretty good [*torn*] dinner. I wish I could send some apples, nice red rosy cheeked fellows to Nellie and Susie, bless their little hearts. I am going down to see Conway sometime during the C.X. who is camped about 8 miles below here near Port Royal. I got a letter from Aunt Ellen a few days ago, all were well. I send this letter by private conveyance and will send some papers with it.

Good bye my dear father, God bless and preserve you all from every danger. Give my best love to all, and to Charlie and Tom whenever you write.

your affectionate boy

Isaac Howard died at Gettysburg.

David Humphrey Blair, Company D, 45th Ohio Volunteers

A farmer from Logan Country, Ohio, was mustered in on 19 August 1861.

Mt. Sterling Ky
Feb 19th 1864

My Dear Sister

and friends at home (that is if I have such a thing as friends at home) I have not heard from you for so long that I cannot imagine what has become of you I have not had any word from you that I remember since before the siege of Knoxville I presume you have certainly written often since that but perhaps not as often as I have or I certainly would have gotten one letter for we had mail a few times. We have now got to within 38 miles of Ohio and I guess this is as close as we need to come until we know if there are any folks still living there these times.

We started from Cumberland Gap on the 8th of this month and arrived here last evening. The distance the way we came is about 150 miles the roads are very bad but we had fine weather to march in and we took our time to it. We are to get horses again in a few days. Wolfords whole division has come back here. The rebs are coming down into this state again from western Va. and we are sent down here to attend to them At least the program of the war is going to be changed again. The boys of the company are all well and in fine spirits It is like getting out of prison to get back out of Tennessee. There we would not get anything scarcely to eat only what we could wax out of the citizens and then had to pay three or four prices. E.G. corn meal $1.75 per bushel bacon 25 cts per pound Apples $1.50 to $2.00 per bushel and that is all we could get. Salt is very scarce in Tennessee and can scarcely be had for any amount of money. Our money went off there like hot biscut until most of the boys are out but we don't need it much here as we can get plenty of rations. We had quite a feast of "hard tack" old bacon and coffee when we got back to this state where we could get them. We used to think we had hard times in this state but it was nothing compared with what we have seen since the siege the two armies together soon laid East Tennessee wast and desolate with what desolation was there before. There are a great many poor soldiers laying back there now living on less then half rations. Still there is scarcely a word of complaint uttered. They know that it must be done and think the war cannot last long. I suppose you have heard before this that Newt Bennett has been promoted to orderly sargeant of this company in place of Wm Wallace.

But I must close
please write and direct to Co D 45th OVI
Loves Brigade
Wolfords Division
centrel Ky
D.H. Blair

Mt. Sterling Ky
April 4th 1864

My Dear Sister
Your kind letter of March 30th came to hand this evening and I haste to reply. I am still enjoying myself as usual and the health

here is generally very good I believe there is no sickness of any consequence in the reg't.

I believe I wrote a letter some time ago that you did not receive at least I sent your likeness home and you did not say any thing about it and I have been looking for the other one you promised me You mentioned geting a likeness in a little round case but you did not tell how you got it or who it was please tell me all about it in your next also if you got your own picture that I sent and send me the other if you can.

You wrote that Morrow had some notion of enlisting tell him that I would advise him not to. But I do not pretend to dictate for him. he can use his own will But I think he has a very good excuse for not coming and as he has that he would regret a thousand times of ever enlisting. I know if I had had as good an excuse as he has I would have regreted ever coming but as it is I am very well contented. But if he will wait till my time is out I will agree to stay and let him go or perhaps Sam will stay in Morrows place when his time is out I have often thought when I had to sleep in the mud & snow or stand in or march through the rain snow and mud almost dead with fatigue and no place to rest but in the mud. and nothing to eat or wear but what I had on my back carrying or when the bullets and shells were whizing around like hail. I say I have often thought to myself "Dont I wish I could have had some good excuse for not being here". Morrow can use his own pleasure for my part but if he comes with me I will do the best I can for him But he may expect to stay his three years or at least prepare for it and may prepare to endure what he would not now think he could endure at all. Infantry is the hardest there is and I think heavy artilery is the easiest. It is what I would go in if ever I have to go again. But I guess I have written enough on this subject. Lizzie I think that was a very good story you sent me especially the last one. You did not tell me anything about Newt Bennett what he is doing now or how he is geting along and where he is staying or what he has to say for himself or others. We are still lying here taking times easy But Pete Evert the old reb is coming down this way over the mountains from Virginia and we are ordered to sleep on arms and be ready to march at a minuts warning. We have no horses yet and Col. Runkle said today that we were not going to get any but would have to go either to the potomack or down to Paduca or Bowling green. I do not like the idea of having to leave here. I would rather fight here every day for a month than go back to East Tennessee or to the potomack and starve and march and wallow round in the mud and water and fight and everything else that is disagreeable.

But who cares. It is all for the sake of the union. We have done it once and can do it again. We are used to everything but hanging and that has no terror for us. What men have done men can do. "There is no use trying to kill a soldier" is a common expression among us.

I have been on provost duty in town for about a month We have very easy times. We have nothing at all to do but stand on the corners of the streets four hours a piece each day and see that the soldiers do not loaf around town without leave or passes from their regiment, and to keep order in the town. We are kind of police men. If the soldiers do not behave right or if they come to town without proper permission, or pass, we arrest them and take them to the provost martial and have a trial, and perhaps send him to the guard house.

There has just came a dispatch that old Evert is still coming. and it is the talk in town that we have a skirmish line out ready for them. well all I can say is let him come. I think he knows better than to try to come in at night and it is now 8 oclock.

We provost guards are ordered to sleep tonight up stairs in a college near headquarters I guess it is make headquarters safe But I think they are worse scared than hurt. I think I have seen much better prospects for a fight. and still no one was hurt At all events I am going to finish this letter if I can unless they get to shooting at me. I think it is only done for an April fool. But it may be that I am that fool.

I had a letter from Sam a few evenings since he was well and still had no notion of reenlisting I believe I shall not reenlist if I do get the chance There is so very much immorality in the army that three years is as long as I care about living among it. and then I would not go in infantry anyway. There is but little or no respect at all paid in the army to the sabbath. And of all the swearing steeling drinking gambling cheating quarreling and blasphemy it is awful. You can have no idea of the vices of camp life. If they would live up to the army regulations it would be pleasant soldiering; but as it is, it is hard enough sure I should like to see this war settled soon for if it is not, our government is as near destroyed as any one ever was and recovered. Still I believe we shall win for I think our cause is right if our army is wicked.

But I guess I have written enough for tonight my head appears to be dislocated thinking about old Everett coming but he has not come yet. But pleas write soon and oblige

Your devoted brother

D. H. Blair

I send you Gen Burnside photograph He looks as natural as ever This is a very true picture

John Garibaldi, Company C,
27th Regiment, Virginia Volunteers, CSA

Camp Winder
January 4, 1863

Dear Wife:

With these few lines I hope to let you know that I am well and hope that when these few lines will come to hand will find you enjoying the same blessing. I received three letters from you since I have been with the company and have been awaiting the fourth one but I haven't seen it yet. I hastened therefore to write this present one and to tell you to send me one and don't care whether you either write it or buy me one and send it to me so I may get a letter from you.

I have send you sixty seven dollars since I have been in the Company and would like to know whether you received it or not. I have more to send you but would like to know if you got that I send you before I send you any more. I send fifty dollars enclosed in a letter to Mr. Pursinger by Mr. Lamby just few days before Christmas which I hope you shall have received before this time. You now can buy yourself a cow if you see one that suits you and if Mother is going to sell that little colt you can buy it too provide you can keep him.

I do not know when I shall get chance to come home. It may be that I'll be able to come home but I think it very doubtful. There is no chance for any furlow at present and I don't know when there will be any. There is a heap talk of peace now in the north, but I wouldn't put no dependence in them. But after while I think they'll get tire to get whipt and they will then give us up for a bad joke but that may not be for a good while.

I have not much to tell you at this time. I wrote to you day before Christmas and told you all the news I knew then about the battle. I have written to MackPherson, to old man [A—] and to Pursinger several times since the battle. [*illegible*] soon have another pay day. Dear you must write to me as often as you can and beg to take good care for yourself until I come home and stay with you and I hope that we shall never forget the hour in which we were joined together but that bless the day on which you and I were joined together with the ties of Matrimony. I shall quit writing by just remind you to write to me and wish you all the good that the world can afford you and remain your affectionate husband untill death,

John Garibaldi

To Mrs. Sarah A. V. Garibaldi

Camp Winder
March 29, 1863

Dear Wife:

As we are on the eave of a march and the commencement of the spring campaign I thought it better to write you this letter in order to let you know that I am yet in this camp and well, but every indication seems that we are on the verge of move as we had order to pack up all our extra bagages that we can not carry on our shoulder and send it away to Richmond. The days are getting long and the weather dryer and it shall soon pleasant enough to admit of active movement. I might not have time to write to you as regular as I have done, but you must write to me steadier, and not await to write to me untill you get a letter from me, but just write to me as often as it will be convenient to you. It has been long time since I haven't received a letter from you by mail, don't be too stinger in saving writing paper. This is leaving me well at present except a bad cold and hope that when these few lines will come to hand they may find you enjoying the same good health that you was enjoying when I last saw you.

Although there is a heap of talk about fighting, I think that there wouldn't be as much fighting this summer as there was last summer. There may be a fight or two here and if we whip them I think they give it up provide we don't go to Maryland. But if we go there I think we shall have some tall fighting to do. This winter they intended to do active operations with there navy but they have been idle all the winter. The biggest navy ever was witnessed went to threaten Charleston but having arrived to the place of operation they paused and hesitated before the harbor as if they was afraid of attacking it and they have been never attacked Charleston yet, and if they don't make an attack within two or three weeks from now I doubt very much whether it ever will be attacked or not, the reason of this is that they have been whipped so often that they are afraid to be whipped again.

The furloughs have been suspended for the present and it is very likely that there will not be any more granted untill next winter, but I hope that by that time we shall have peace and that we shall all come home to stay with our families never to be divided any more unless by death. Dear you must tell me whether you have received the money that I send you or not. I send you 50 dollars by Lieutenant Clark and when he come home on furlough, and twenty dollars by Mr. McCordy afterward of which I haven't heard anything of it. Dear, if there is anybody administering on Captain Holloway's Estate, you must give that account that I left you to Pursinger and let him make the best of it and get the money if he can.

Dear whenever I come home I will try to fetch you something but I don't know what it will be. If you want anything particular you must write to me about, and if my purse shall contain enough to buy it with I shall be happy to please you, but every thing is so high now that it almost take fortune to buy any thing. At the same time if you may make use of the money that I have send you if you see anything worth buying, and make use of it.

Give my respects to Mrs. Sarah Johnson and to all the neighbors around you. To Mr. Pursinger also and keep a [*illegible*] for yourself, mother Russia and George if this shall come to hand before he shall have gone back to the army and I'll remain your affectionate husband untill death John Garibaldi

Still direct you letters as you allways did. So Good by.

May 9, 1863

Dear Wife:

I take this blessed oppurtunity to drop you these few lines in order to let you know that I am well at present and hope that when these few lines will come to hands they may find you enjoying the same blessing. I have written you a letter the last day of April with a pencil because I had no other way to write it and I hope that you have received it and will write to me every time you get chance.

Dear I must tell you that we have been engaged in a hot battle since [Chancellorsville] I last wrote to you and with the help of God I came out safe but out of about forty of our company that went in to the fight last Sunday there was only about thirty came out safe.

Dear I must tell you that Lee A.B. Terry got wounded in wrist. There was six hundred and fifty odd killed out of our brigade and wounded. Our brigade went into battle twice, and the second time charged over the yankee brest works and ran the yankees away from there. Men fell on both side of me and if it had not been that God was with me I believe I'd fell too. I saw a man at my left hand who was shot in the face and when he fell he grabbed me by the legs and I got loose from him by jurking away from him. I expect he wanted me to help him out of the battle field but it was against my order to do it because there was men detailed for that purpose. In that fight I got me a portfolio full of writing paper and envelops which I needed badly and an oil cloth coat, our boys are now well supplied of oil cloths.

We got in the rear of the yankees saturday and we were fighting nearly all night saturday and all Sunday. We got thirty pieces of artillery. I can't tell you how many small arms but we have got any number of them. There was yankee knapsacks enough left on the ground to supply our whole army. The blankets were laying there in piles and were trampelled over by our men in the mudd. I never saw so much waste of property in my life. The enemy was laying behind their breastworks sunday morning with their knapsacks off and blankets and when they saw us coming they ran away leaving every thing behind them.

We are now encamped in the wood here close to Fredericksburg but we don't know how long we shall remain here. It is believed by good many that we shall have another battle before long, but I hope that we shall have some rest now for a while for we have been laying out in battlefields and without tents for nearly ten days and during that time we haven't had a whole night of sleep and been laying all the time under arms. The enemy is now across the river and I don't know how long he shall remain there.

I have giving you some account of the sunday battle but I expect you shall have heard of it before this [letter] will come to hands and perhaps you shall have heard some fuller accounts than I have given you because them around the battle field not actually ingaged generally knows more about the battle than them that were engaged in it. If my head was right for wrighting you some thing about the battle I might perhaps tell you something more but as I don't [feel] enclined on account of their being such noise in it as I heard in the battle field. But if as soon as I get chance I shall write you again and tell you something more about the battle.

Dear I must tell you that [I saw] George Poor before and after the battle and he was well and he came out safe of the battle, and he sends you all his best respects. I hadn't time to speak to him long. I saw him Friday evening before the battle and only had time to shake hands with him. Then I saw him again tuesday after the battle and hadn't time to speak to him long then as we were ordered off again immediately, but he told me he was well, and came out safe of the battle field and he sends you all his best respects. You must write to me soon and direct your letter as you did before.

Mr. John Garibaldi, care of Captain C.L. Haynes
Company C 27th Va. Infantry
Stonewall Brigade
Near Fredericksburg

John R. Hepler sends you all his best respects and he is well. I
shall finish off writing by giving you to mother and Russia my best
respects and remain your affectionate husband untill death.

John Garibaldi.

Samuel S. Dunton, 111th New York Infantry

*May 5th 1863—In camp, near New
Iberia, formily called Newton, La.*

Dear Parents, Brothers and Sisters,

It has been a long time since I wrote to you and now don't know
as I can write any news, but what you have heard by way of Rosa.
But having a little time this morning and knowing that it would be
a satisfaction to you to get a letter direct, I will try to write a short
one to you.

Well to commence with, I have been in one small battle and
some not so very small either and came out alright, but pretty well
tired out. I will give some of the particulars as near as I can
recollect. The first day, we commenced our march about noon. We
went seven miles that afternoon. Our calvry skirmishing with the
enemy, most of the way. The next day we went about three miles,
when the engagement became general. We formed into line of
battle, little before noon. Our brigade in front and the right wing in
advance. Five companies were ordered forward as skirmishers.
One company of the 8th Vermont on the extreme right, one
company of the 75th New York, Company D of the 114th New
York next, which was center, then Company G. 114th N.Y.S. next
and the 12th Conneticut on the extreme left. The guide was in the
center and Co. D took the least. We marched forward with the
brigade about forty rods behind us for about two miles, over corn
hills, ditches, hedge fences, briers etc. Then the enemy opened on
us from the gun boat and two guns from the fort. When we saw the
smoke from their guns we dropped to the ground, then up and on
again. We made four such advances, before we were ordered to
halt. Then our folks commenced cannoning. Then we were
ordered into the ditches, up we got and forward into the next
ditch. We went, the cannon balls flying thick and shells bursting
all around us. We lay there till after dark, when our enemy fell back
and we were ordered to retreat. We fell back about fifty rods and
remained there all night, with occasionally skirmishing. I never
was so near melted down in my life, as I was at the time. I went into
the ditch and there was no air there, so it was not so cold, as

standing up. One William Roberts, in our company, laid little below me in the ditch. He was hit in the forehead with a shell and died four days afterward. That you may know something of the battle, I will say that the reporters who were there, near as they could keep count the reports of the cannon from both sides, were at the rate of five hundred rounds every fifteen minutes. You see, it was something of a battle. When we fell back at night, the enemy supposing where we were whispered, hollered and cheered with all their might. We could hear their corp band play two or three tunes. The next morning, soon as light, we were ordered forward without anything to eat. Before we gained the old ground, they opened on us again and the engagement became general. We advanced little, occasionally they direct a number of their guns at us, skirmishes, in order to drive us back. At 10 o'clock, we were relieved and fell back to the rear and allowed two hours rest. We then joined the regiment and were immediately sent out to skirmish again in the afternoon. Our regiment and the 75th and the 1st Conn. men were sent into the woods to drive off the sharpshooters, who were picking off our gunners. We came very near getting into bad fire then, but finally got out of it. We had to hug the ground close, then get up, fire, down again and so on. The bullets falling around us like hailstone. Well, to some this matter all up, we fought till 9 o'clock at night and lay on the field till morning. As soon as light, without any breakfast, we started in pursuit of the enemy, who were retreating all night. We soon came up to their rear and then kept a running fight, killing, wounding, and taking prisoners. We went two miles. The next morning, we started at four o'clock, so as not to give them any rest. Well, we followed them day after day to Opolousas. We rested there one day and then we shot back to [*unreadable in original*] country and drive in all the cattle, horses, mules, sheep, etc. Well, were on the march almost three weeks, fighting every day, on our way up, taking over two thousand prisoners killing as near as can be estimated about five hundred and wounding as many more. We have taken twelve cannon, wagon loads of small arms. Our estimate, over thirty millions worth of properity. I heard it estimated how many bales of cotton we have taken, but have forgotten, but it is a number of thousand. We got fifteen hundred hogsheds of sugar at one plantation. It was two years crop. Such sights of sugar, lotta molasses, [?] and so on. I never ran in my life. We lost in our regiment in battle, only two killed, and perhaps twenty or less wounded. Of the killed, one was from company H, and the other was Roberts from Company D, who died four days after. One, in one company, had his thumb shot off. There were a great many narrow escapes. One of our boys, when he opened his blanket, found a grapeshot that had gone through his rubber blanket and one thickness of his woolen one. Another, had the button of his cartridge box shot off. I can name a great many more, but it is taking up time and paper.

We staid at Brashear two days and again ordered out and have no idea where we are going or what to do, no faster than it comes along. Sunday, it was assigned for two of our company to go over to Vermillion Bayou and take a rebel transport than, but they got the start by burning it themselves, the night before. General Banks and Weitzel said they never saw troops in battle for the first time do as well as we did. Not a man flinched that I knew of. I knew of some of our boys who would stop every little while and pick berries, as though there was nothing going on. I believe they would have walked up to the cannon mouth, if they had not been ordered to halt. Well I have seen all the fighting I want to, but expect to see lots more of it yet. If I should live, you see we were under the fire of both armies. The shells of our own guns bursting all around us, as well as those of the enemy. I don't know how many were lost in killed and wounded, but not one quarter as many as those of the enemy. When we lay there under fire, I didn't think it possible for one third of our regiment to come out alive, but it proved a lucky day for us. I am proud to say that we think that we have done as good fighting, greater marching and followed up the enemy closer and taken stuff for the government, according to our numbers, than has been by any expedition since the war commenced. When we got them whipped, we did not wait and let them fortify somewhere else, but hugged them close, till we have completely routed them. In less than three weeks, we marched over three hundred miles, fighting most of the way, conquering as we went. We flatter ourselves that this expedition will be of more benefit the United States than any since the war began. You will probably see more details in the papers, than I have time to write. All I have to say is that I hope I shall never have to witness another scene, such as the one on our backward march. We saw where some of the enemy were buried, with an arm or leg sticking out of the ground and maggots crawling in and out. They left in such a hurry, they threw their dead in between corn rows and shoveled dirt from each way on them. One shot from one of our large guns killed eight of their horses at once.

Well here I am, well, hearty and tough as a bear. Never felt so well or better in my life and never wanted to see my wife, child, parents, brothers, sisters and family so much in my life as at the present time, but don't see any prospect of so doing at present. I have received letters from you all and want you all to accept this as a good answer to all. I would like to write to you all separately, but if you knew all the duties of a soldier, you will not expect it. We have our own messing, washing and cooking and everything else. So there is not much time and where there is time, there is everything going on, that keeps one confused all the time. Charlie Smith is in the hospital at Franklin. I went in and saw him as we come up this time. He is better, but all broke down. The other Sherburne boys that are here, I believe are all well. M. Bake, Srgt. Deitz and Allen Hawley. Rosa has sent me a boxe, which I hear is at New Orleans. Will probably get it in a few days.

Flour in this county sold from one hundred and fifty to two hundred dollars. We have a government store at Franklin that sells, to those who have taken the oath, for twenty two dollars.

I must bring this to a close. I want you to all write as often as you can. It does me more good to get letters from home and friends than you think. Direct as usual. If our armies' generals were doing as much as we are, I think this war would soon end. Oh how I wish this unnatural war was over. Excuse this hasty letter.

From your affectionate son and brother,
S. S. Dunton

J.C. Morris, 21st Texas Cavalry, CSA

Camp near Lanjer, Ark.
May 10th, 1863

My Dear Amanda,

It has been a long time since I had an opportunity of writing to you, and I gladly avail myself of the present opportunity. I am not certain that I will have a chance of sending this but I will write a few lines any how and try and get it off to let you know that I am among the living.

We have been on a raid into Ms. but I have not time to give you the particulars of our trip. I will write in a few days if I can get a chance to send it and write you a long one. I just came off of picket and found the boys all writing to send by a man that has been discharged who is going to start home this morning. I was quite sick three or four days while in Mo. but have entirely recovered. We captured a good many prisoners while in Mo. and killed a good many. We went up as high as Jackson 8 or 10 miles above Cape

Girardeau. We fought them nearly all day at the Cape on Sunday two weeks ago today. The yanks boasted that we would never get back to Ark but they were badly mistaken, for we are back again and have sustained but very light loss, we never lost a man out of our company and only one or two out of the regt. I wish I had time to give you a full description of our trip. It would be very interesting to you I know; but you will have to put up with this little scrawl for the present. I am in hopes that I will get a whole package of letters from you in a few days. I never wanted to see you half as bad in all my life as I do now. I would give anything in the world to see you and the children. I have no idea when I will have that pleasure. We can't get any news here—do not know what is going on in the outside world. The boys will all write as soon as they get a chance to send them off.

We will remain in this vicinity, I expect for some time to recruit our horses. Our horses are sadly worsted. We found plenty to eat and to feed our horses on in Mo but hardly even had time to feed or eat as we traveled almost insesantly night and day. We could get any amount of bacon of the very best kind at 10 cts and every thing else in proportion.

I must close for fear I do not get to send my letter off. Write offten I will get them some time. I will write every chance, do not be uneasy when you do not get letters, for when we are scouting around as we have been it is impossible to write or to send them off if we did write. Give my love to the old Lady and all the friends. My love and a thousand kisses to my own sweet Amanda and our little boys. How my heart yearns for thou that are so near and dear to me. Goodbye my own sweet wife, for the present. Direct to Little Rock as—.

As ever your devoted and loving Husband, J.C. Morris.

Samuel Cormany,
2nd Cavalry Brigade, 2nd Division, Union Army

Diary: June 30, 1863
Tuesday. We moved out early to within a few miles of Westminster and drew up in line for battle—our advance moved on—and the Reg't supported—met little resistance in taking the City—Took 8 prisoners.

The Regiment halted close to the City—We got some eatables—The people were ecstatic to see our troops driving out and following up the "Johnies." They did all in their power for us—The Rebs had acted awful meanly—Took everything like hats, boots, shoes, clothing &c—The streets and fence corners were strewn with their discarded old ones. Some of them, yes many, were almost able to join in the march, being so full of lice— We struck Hanover at dark. Found N.C.R.R. badly torn up—We lay on arms in a field for the night—we were well fed, but awfully tired and sleepy—A shower of rain failed to awaken me—I was lying in a furrow, an old furrow. I partially awakened in the night feeling coolish on my lower side—but didn't fully awake. In the morning I discovered that water had run down the furrow—and I had "dam'd" it somewhat and so was pretty wet from below, while my poncho had kept me dry from the top—

July 2, 1863
Thursday. More or less Picket firing all night—We were aroused early, and inspection showed a lot of our horses too lame and used up for good action—So first, our good mounts were formed for moving out, and were soon off—with the Brigade and took Reb. Genl. Steward by surprise on the Deardorf Farm—on right and rear of the army line—where Steward was expected to at least annoy the rear of Genl Mead—But our boys charged him—and after severe fighting dealt him an inglorious defeat and later in the day came in and lay on arms in the rear of Meads right— While our mounted men were paying attention to Genl Steward, we fellows had our horses cared for and were marched down to the right of the main line—to occupy a gap and do Sharpshoot- ing—at long range, with our Carbines—we soon attracted atten- tion, and later an occasional shell fell conspicuously close—but far enough to the rear of us so we suffered no serious harm. Towards noon firing became more general and in almost all directions—and we were ordered to our horses—and joined our returned heroes, and lay in readiness for any emergency— The general battle increased in energy—and occasional fier- cenes—and by 2 P.M. the canonading was most terrific and continued til 5 P.M. and was interspersed with musketry—and Charge-yells and everything that goes to making up the inde- scribable battle of the best men on Earth, seemingly in the Fight to the Finish—At dark, our Cav Brig—2nd Brig 2" Div—was moved to the left—many wounded came in—Taken as a whole from all one can see from one point—it seems as tho our men— The Union Army—is rather overpowered and worsted—Lay on arms to rest—Little chance to feed and eat.

July 3, 1863
Friday. Canonading commenced early—and battle was on again in full intensity at 10 ock we were ordered to the Front and Center, but immediately removed to the right of the Center—had some skirmishing. Pretty lively—Our squadron almost ran into a Rebel Battery with a Brigade of Cavalry maneuvering in the woods. They didn't want to see us, but moved left-ward and we held the woods all P.M.—All seemed rather quiet for several hours—From 1 til 4P.M.—there was the heaviest canonading I ever have heard—One constant roar with rising and falling inflections—Our Boys opened 54 guns at the same time on the Rebel lines and works from a little conical hill, Cemetary Ridge. We were picketing in the rear and on the right of it—Many shells came our way—some really quite near—But it is wonderful how few really made our acquaintance.

July 4, 1863
Saturday. The great battle closed and quieted with the closing day—Some firing at various points—

Our Regt layed on arms with Pickets out—on the ground where we had put in most of the day—Rather expecting attack momentarily—Rained furiously during the night—We had fed, eaten, and were standing "to horse" when about 6 ock *NEWS CAME*— "The Rebs are falling back!" and "Our Forces are following them" and our Regt went out towards Hunterstown reconnoitering. We found some confederates who had straggled, or were foraging, not knowing yet what had happened and was taking place—Of course, our Boys took them in—Making a little detour I captured two. Sergt Major J.T. Richardson and Private Cox 9th Va Cav—disarming them and bringing them in—I guarded them—while the Regt gathered in some others—P.M. Captain Hughes came along and paroled them—and we were ordered to camp near Hanover—where we first lay on arriving near Gettysburg—Evening awfully muddy and disagreeable—I saw much of the destructiveness of the Johnies today—

July 5, 1863
Sunday. Rained awfully during the night. I got very wet—

Early we took up the march for Chambersburg—Crossing the battlefield—Cemitary Hill—The Great Wheat Field Farm, Seminary ridge—and other places where dead men, horses, smashed artillery, were strewn in utter confusion, the Blue and The Grey mixed—Their bodies so bloated—distorted—discolored on account of decomposition having set in—that they were utterly unrecognizable, save by clothing, or things in their pockets—The scene simply beggars description—Reaching the west side of the Field of Carnage—we virtually charged most of the way for 10 miles—to Cashtown—Frequently in sight of the Rebel rear guard—taking in prisoners—in bunches—We captured some 1,500 wounded men, and 300 stragglers—we went as far as Goodyears Springs, where we rested for the night. (I had to guard a Reb all night.)

July 6, 1863
Monday. Had a good breakfast. Turned my prisoner over to others We took up the march—via Fayeteville for Quincy—I told Corp. Metz I intended going on—To Chambersburg—To see wife and Baby—and would report in the morning again. He understood and I slipped away—and was soon making time for home—I got a fine "10 oclock piece" at Heintzelmans—on approaching Chambersburg I was assured there were still squads of rebs about town—Near town I was met by town folk inquiring about the battle. I was the first "blue coat" they had seen—and the first to bring direct news of the Enemy's defeat—as communications had been cut. As I struck the edge of town, I was told "The Rebel rear-guard had just left the Diamond." So I ventured out 2nd Street and ventured to strike Main near where Darling and Pussy lodged—and behold They were at the door—had been watching the Reb Rear leaving town—and Oh! The surprise and delight thus to meet after the awful battle they had been listening to for passing days—My horse was very soon stabled. My Cavalry outfit covered with hay—and myself in my citazens clothes—So should any final "rear" come along, I would not be discovered—To attempt to describe my joy and feelings at meeting and greeting my dear little family must prove a failure—We spent the P.M and evening very sweetly and pleasantly, but only we had a few too many inquiring callers.

Corporal George Bolton, Company B,
77th Regiment, New York Infantry

Born in England, Bolton was mustered into the United States
Army on 1 October 1861.

Camp near Birlin, MD
July 18, 1863

Dear Wife:

I snatch this opportunity of answering your letter of the 1st. I
received it on the 12th about 10 o'clock at night after I had a hard
days march. We had just got to bed and was going to sleep when
the mail came in. You had better believe I was glad when I learned
that I had a letter. I was happy to learn that you are all well as I am
at the present, thank God. Dear Lib. you say that I must try to
have two letters on the way all of the time. I assure you that I have
done the best I could to write as often as possible since I got back.
This will be the third on the way that I've received no answer
from, the chances of writing now adays are few and far between so
you must excuse the poor writing bad spelling and short letters.
You know you said that I must write if it was only a line or two so I
take you at your word. You don't need to think that I ever could
ever forget you or forget to write when there is any chance. You say
that you cannot write as I wish you because you have nothing to
write about. Well I won't ask you no more. Do as you please, only
answere me all my letters, if they are as short as mine. I should
have wrote you yesterday, but I was on duty all day. Dear Lib, we
are kept on the go most all of the time since I got back to the Regt.
We are marching night and day, it comes pretty hard I tell you. I
wrote you a letter when we was on picket at Antietam Creek about
7 days ago. We left there that night and have been marching ever
since with the exception of yesterday. We are expecting to move
every hour now. The next move will be back to So. Virginia again.
My dear, I am in great hopes of the war coming to close soon.
What do you think? We have given Gen. Lee a good licking here.
Look at Vicksburg and Port Hudson the prospect is good now
anyway.

I am glad that Diantha is going to school but I hope she is not
going amongst such a set as before. You keep a good lookout and
tell me how she gets along. It pleases me to think that the baby
don't forget me. I hope I shall get back then she never will as long
as she lives. Do you think she will? Give my respects to Isaish & his
wife. Tell them I am in hopes of seeing them soon if I am spared to

get through. If we do meet we shall certainly make that old Building totter won't we. It will be different to what my furlough can do. I never met with a stranger and formed acquaintance so quick and I am sure I never saw anyone that I thought so much of as I do them, and I hope you are the same. Our Regt. was paid when I was to home but I think that we shall get our pay again pretty soon, but I am not sure. I rather dread this payday coming for I have got to pay out so much but you are aware of it. I shall send all I hopefully can but I don't want to disappoint you. I saw Dick three nights ago, he looks first rate. He had a very near escape when in the Battle. There was a ball passed through between the sole of his shoe & his toes. he was lamed a little and was taken prisoner of war but was recaptured again. He is all right and on duty again. He was very fortunate indeed. There is only about one hundred and 20 of them left in their Regt. I don't blame him about not writing much for there is very little time now adays. He says that he writes more to Cal than to his own folks. He wants I should send his love to all of you. Tell Cal Deek says if I don't write much it is not because he is forgetting anyone. I believe him. He has not had a letter from Charlie in over 2 months. What is Charlie doing now adays? Tell Cal to give that Clark the sack if she interests to have deek. I was in hopes that I should get a answer to the letter that I wrote you when we was near Manchester, before we leave this place but I shall be disappointed of course it is 18 days since I sent it. If I get time I can write on another piece of paper about our marching.

Give my love to all and accept the same yourself from yours the same.

Geo. Bolton

George Bolton was killed at Cold Harbor, Virginia, on 4 June 1864.

Private Edmond Hardy Jones, Company F, 64th Georgia Volunteers, CSA

The below are letters from Jones to his wife, Susan.

October 21st, 1863
Camp Randolph near Tallahassa, Fla.

My dear wife

yours of the 11th came safe to hand. It gave me the extream pleasure of hearing that you was all wel. This leaves me in good health at present hoping this may find you all enjoying the same blessing. We have a grate del of sickness here in camp mostly chills and fever. Mr. Peddy is better than he was when I wrote you last. I receved the stamps that you sent me in your letter. The reason I hav been franking my letters to you is that I had no stamps and could get none here. The soldiers all say that letters go through safer without paying the postage here. I have not got anything of importance to write to you. We get no news only camp rumors and they almost all ways prove to be false. We get no war news only through the officers as there are no privates in hour company that takes any newspaper. We will start out on picket about next Saturday to be gone 15 days. We will go to Newport down near the coast which is abowt 10 miles from here. We are living in hour winter quarters now which we have about completed. When you answer this, direct as you have been doing and if we are gone the letters will go on to the company. I will look for a letter from you this week as I writ to you last Sunday which you had not recd it when you writ your last. I recd a letter from George a day or 2 go which stated they were all wel and that he was improving himself. Write as soon as you receive this. You dount no the pleasure it gives me to hear from you and the children. I want to see you vary bad indeed but I try to bear it the best I can and you must bear it the best you can. I cant think this war can last six months longer. If you happen to get dangerously sick write to me and send your doctors citifiket and I would stand a chance come home to se you. Without something of that sort should turn up there will be no chance for me to come before next spring or summer. Kiss all the children for me and tell them Pa will come home sum time to se them. Give my love to all enquiring friend and shear a large portion yourself. I remain your affectionate husband til death. E.H. Jones

> *December 20th 1863*
> *Camp Randolph near*
> *Tallahassa, Fla.*

My Dear Wife

Yours of the 14 Inst has come safe to hand. It gave me much pleasure to hear from you and hear that you was all well and doing well. I am sorry to hav to state to you that I have been a little sick but nothin serious. I hav had vary severe pains in my head and jaws produced from the affects of cold. I am better off than I hav been for the last 8 Or 10 day. At preasant now dount understand me to say that I hav been vary sick for I hav been doing duty all the time when ever called on. It is vary cold here today plenty of ice this morning and the ground frozen stiff.

From the way you writen your last letter you had not reced my last letter which was writen abowt the 12 of this month as well as I recollect. I writ to you in that letter for you to send me paper anowgh in your letters for me to write on. This you can do by writing say half a sheet yourself and send me the other half. Paper is vary scarce and the price high.

You writ that you was kniting me a cumforter which I was vary glad to hear for I knead sumething of that sort vary much at times but there will be no chance for me to get it soon as furlowghs has been discontinwed by a order from old Boora-gard. I recon however they will be granted again after Christmas. When they get to granting furlowghs again Mr. Peddy will be at home vary soon thare after and I will write to you and you can try and send it down and he will bring it to me. I was glad to hear that you had engaged you some corn. I do not know what you will do for meal it is so high that those that downt raise it will hav to do without. I recon, or at least they will hav to make out on short rations. I do hope however you and my children may never hav this to do. We hav to by a little pork here occasionally and pay from 75 to a dollar per pownd. We by potatoes and pay $3.00 per bushel. You write to me if you hav ever got my money from the court yet. If you hav not drew anything yet you hardly will before toward spring.

I hav not heard from the old settlement since I hav been here only what I hear through you. I wonder if Martha Weever has got shet of her cold yet. I promise to write to Hannah when we started to move and I never have done it but I think I will soon. I hear of no prospect of this cruel war coming to a close soon, in fact I hav come to the conclusion that it will not end before next March at which time old Abe's term of office expires. All most any termes of peace would be accepted by the men this part of the survice for the men is all sick and tired of the survice and wants to go home and quit the war as it is.

Give my love to all enquiring friends and accept a large portion yourself. Kiss the children for me.

Edmund H. Jones

Private John F. Brobst, 25th Infantry Regiment, Wisconsin Volunteers

Camp Near Vicksburg
February the 7th/64

Dear Friend Mary,

I have just received your welcome letter and I was more than glad to hear from you and to hear that you are well. I am well and all right yet.

I am writing to you by the light of a camp fire out of doors because I have been so busy ever since we got back that I have not had time to write.

We only got back yesterday. We have had a long and hard march, since I last wrote you. We have gone through the state of Mississippi. You have undoubtedly heard of General Sherman's great ride. We were in it. We left every town that we passed through in ashes. The first place was Jackson, the next Morton, Brandon, Hillsboro, Meridian, and Marion. That was as far as we went out that way.

At Meridian we captured ten thousand stands of small arms, three trains of cars and burned them all up and destroyed about 50 miles of railroad. We stopped at Marion 4 days, then we started back to another route and came to Canton. There we stopped 3 days. There we captured 28 railroad engines, destroyed them with several miles of the track, and a lot of us boys had some fun on one of the engines. We carried water all day to fill the boiler of one of them to have a ride. We got it all steamed up, blew the whistle and started up the road. After we got tired of that fun we moved the track [from] where it was about 30 feet down onto level ground and let the steam out and let it go and it struck head first and blew up. That was fun for us.

We burned up 11 towns, captured 10,000 mules and horses and the Lord knows how many darkies for I don't, but everything looks black with them. We did not have much fighting to do, for the rebs ran so that we could not catch them. The woods were full of trunks and boxes filled up with dresses, bed clothes, and all manner of stuff that they thought they had hid from us, but hide from a Yankee soldier if you can. We had some very hard times and some very good times. As long as there was plenty to eat in the country, we had plenty, and when that ran out our rations ran out and we had to live on parched corn for twelve days. Then was the hard times. March twenty miles a day and nothing but parched corn to eat, then you can hear the boys say, "Oh, if I was home I never would enlist again." But now we have plenty again and feel all right, but we are preparing for another tramp. The orders came today to fit out in new clothes and be ready to march in two days. Where we are going I cannot tell. Up the river I think.

Well, I wish old Jeff and all his gang were in the regions of the low lands where sinners go, and I was Commander in Chief. I would take them through a course of tactics that has not been heard of in modern times.

We were 25 thousand strong on this raid and the rebs say 42 [thousand]. Now you can see by that how near they came to it. They acknowledged they had 23 thousand but did not have enough to risk a battle with us. Oh, the poor Godforsaken cowards. I am ashamed of them, if they are not ashamed of themselves.

I wish this war would end and let us go home, but I don't believe it will end in two years yet. Well, I have got my time more than half out now and the last half goes faster than the first half. At least, it seems so.

The Army of the Potomac has never done anything and never will. If they had done half as much as the western army, this war would have been rubbed out before this time. This army will have to go down there and take Richmond for them, poor fellows.

My learning to sing and play on the violin has played out, for just as I got the note books, we had to start. All I learned was a few letters of the notes.

Well, Mary, I do wish you would get your picture taken and send it to me. I should be more than glad to get it. Please send it as soon as you can. If you do not believe that my youngest sister does not look like you, when you are over to Mr. Allen's, just have Mrs. Allen show you the picture that I sent home that has two ladies in one frame—they are both my sisters—and see for yourself.

Thomas Stewart enlisted for three years unless sooner discharged. The same way with myself, and I think I shall have to stay the three years out and so will all the boys that went when I did, for this war is a long way from being played out yet.

We have got a lot of new recruits. They are green as we were when we first came out. They make real nice playthings for us. We have our own fun with them, and call them four hundred dollar men. They do not like it very well, but it can't be helped. We do not want them. We wanted to be consolidated with an old regiment and let the new recruits go in a regiment by themselves.

I heard that you had grown so that I would not know you if I was to see you. Now, Mary, I tell you what, if you grow out of my remembrance, I shall have to punish you severely when I get back.

I wish I could have been up there to go to the dance the 22nd, but we were tramping along two hundred miles back in this state playing all kinds of tunes, colors flying, for it was Washington's birthday and we let the rebs know that his old flag should fly yet.

Well, Mary, you will not believe that Elsie has soured on me. Now I am sorry, for you know what becomes of the unbeliever. I would exhort you to repentance if I was up there so that I could, but for me to write it, why it would all get cold before it reached you. Now, Mary, if you believe it or not, it is true.

It is very warm here. Peach trees are all out in bloom. In thirty days we marched four hundred miles. You must not think strange if your letters are not all answered promptly, for I will answer them as soon as I get them. We will have to be marching around so that I can't get them, but I hope you will write often. I shall answer them all as fast as I get them. I love to get letters from friends when I come in after such a march.

I shall have to close for the present. Direct as usual, write soon. My respects to all. Good-by. Yours truly, a true friend,

John F. Brobst

P.S. Excuse poor penmanship for I have a very poor chance to write.

Anon, 6TH United States Colored Infantry

A black private, signing himself "Bought and Sold", writes to the Afro-American newspaper, *Christian Recorder*.

Yorktown, Virginia
February 8, 1864

I am a soldier, or at least that is what I was drafted for in the 6th USCT; have been in the service since Aug., last. I could not afford to get a substitute, or I would not be here now and my poor wife at home almost starving. When I was at home I could make a living for her and my two little ones; but now that I am a soldier they must do the best they can or starve. It almost tempts me to desert and run a chance of getting shot, when I read her letters, hoping that I would come to her relief. But what am I to do? It is a shame the way they treat us; our officers tell me now that we are not soldiers; that if we were we would get the same pay as the white men; that the government just called us out to dig and drudge, that we are to get but $7.00 per month. Really I thought I was a soldier, and it made me feel somewhat proud to think that I had a right to fight for Uncle Sam. When I was at Chelton Hill I felt very patriotic; but my wife's letters have brought my patriotism down to the freezing point, and I don't think it will ever rise again; and it is the case all through the regiment. Men having families at home, and they looking to them for support, and they not being able to send them one penny . . .

Private Bingham Findley Junkin, 100th Pennsylvania Volunteer Infantry

Junkin was mustered in to the Union Army at North Liberty, Pennsylvania, on 8 March 1864.

Diary: Friday, March 11, 1864
Took french leave and went into Pittsburgh on the morning train; ran around some to see sights awhile. Called at Mr. Wightmans and took dinner, spent an hour or two there and returned to camp.

Saturday, March 12th
Nothing of worth notice.

Sunday, March 13th
Sabbath heard a short sermon by Chaplain [Robert] Dickson. Got the banner from him and read it and spent the day as much as circumstances would permit in reading my Bible and thinking upon it's many precious promises. The only wonder is that our armies are as successful as they are owing to the great wickedness that prevails.

Monday, March 14th
Was turned over to the regiment which puts us under the control [of] our Regimental and Company Officers

Tuesday, March 16th
Nothing of importance.

Wednesday, March 17th
Went into city to Wightmans, had a bath and dinner.

Thursday, March 18th

Received a letter from home which states that the children were sick, got a pass, started home, took sick on the way, got home on the 18th and remained home until the 22nd.

Tuesday, March 22nd

Started back to camp, stayed at Mr. Wightmans at night.

Wednesday, March 23

Went out to camp, drew three days rations, and started for Annapolis. Got to Johnstown about dark. Saw Harrisburg across the Susquehanna. We ran down the right bank, got to Little York about noon of the 24th, out of Baltimore about five o'clock. Baltimore a nice city.

Friday, March 25th

Got aboard of a transport and had a very pleasant ride down the bay to Annapolis. Marched out about three miles to camp which gave us a good appetite for our hard tack. After supper some of the boys got to dancing and seemed to enjoy themselves right well. I step into a cookhouse and sit down by the stove and endeavored to cast my thoughts on God, ask him to take care of my dear ones at home, keep me and preserve me from evil. Oh, how much grace the Christian soldier needs and how comforting the thought that God reigns everywhere.

Saturday, March 26th

Nothing worthy of note.

Sunday, March 27th

Sabbath—Spent the day pleasantly reading and having God's word. Attended Bible class in Chapel in camp parole near Annapolis at 11 o'clock. Heard Chaplin Dixon at 2 o'clock and a Rev. Moore of the Christian Communion at seven—he's from Massachusetts. Oh, how pleasant when separated from the endearment of home to enjoy such privileges. How good God is to thus provide for the instruction and comfort of his people under every circumstance.

Monday, March 28th

Left the barracks at camp parole and went into tents nearer town. I think I can enjoy life better now being messed off; one can have a better opportunity to read and meditate. This has been a very pleasant day.

Tuesday, March 29th

Slept very comfortably that night. How good is the Lord to all those that put their trust in him. He is never night to them that calls upon him.

Wednesday, March 30

A cold, damp day, very unpleasant for camp life. Time passed heavily away but we had no reason to complain. Our lot might have been worse.

Thursday, March 31

Much more pleasant; commence drilling today.

Friday, April 1

Very pleasant day, yet a little cool.

Saturday, April 2

It commenced raining last night, was snowing this morning. Snowed and rained alternately all day. Took breakfast, no roll call or drill today. Had to lie, sit, stand in tents just as we fancied or go out and get wet. About three minutes was long enough to be out at one time. Read the White Rover, a tale of the early settlement of New Orleans. Worth reading

Sunday, April 3

Slept very little last night, although it continued to rain. Woke about daylight, took up my Bible and read awhile before I got up. I make it a rule to read a portion of scripture every day, although I cannot have any set time; have to be guided by circumstances in a great measure, but always try if possible to read a chapter just before going to sleep. It would be very hard indeed to endure the separation from those that are dear were it not for the consciousness of being in the line of duty, and that God Rules; and that he doeth all things well. Oh how comforting the thought that we have such a God to go to; and make all our wants known onto him. At 10 o'clock went to church; that is we gathered in a group in the grove nearby; and heard an excellent sermon from Chaplain Dickson. Text, 1st Timothy, 4th chapter, 8th verse. "Godliness is profitable onto all things having the life that now is and that which is to come." Had prayer meeting at six, a very pleasant meeting. Mr. Dixon made some very appropriate and touching remarks. It was good to be there.

Monday, April 4
Nothing worthy of note. commenced raining about five.

Tuesday April 5
Still raining and cold. Got our breakfast, lay down and rested, then sat up awhile, stood up awhile, then sat down and read awhile, then lay awhile, and so on. But we have no reason to complain for we might be in much worse condition. Received a letter from home.

Wednesday, April 6
Rained until daylight this morning, it it now appears as though it would clear off pleasantly. I hope it will. Answered a letter which was received from home on the 5th. This day decided the question of emancipation in the state of Maryland. I hope it will decide in favor of emancipation. Was on dress parade for the first time this evening. The sunset clear and beautiful this evening.

Thursday, April 7
This has been a beautiful spring day. Makes one feel like ploughing and making garden. Had prayer meeting in the evening.

Friday, April 8
Another beautiful day. Dressed up our steed and drilled considerably. Two negro regiments left for some parts, but unknown to me.

Saturday, April 9
Apparance of rain this morning. Drilled some in the manual of arms for the first. About ten o'clock the 3rd Regiment of New Jersey passed, the first I had seen. Rather a nice sight. Just as we had sat down to dinner there was some great cheering by some regiments nearer town. Presently General Burnside [commander of the Ninth Corps by this point in the war] hove into sight. Dinner was suspended for the time being and cheer after cheer rent the air and caps were thrown up by the scores. The boys all seemed glad to see him. He passed through the different encampments and we could hear their cheers as he passed the different regiments. I would say he was about 45 years of age. It is now raining. We will have to remain in our dinner houses or get wet.

Sunday, April 10
Sabbath—it rained about daylight, cleared warm and pleasant.

Had a good sermon by Mr. Dickson from Isa. 55–7. Had prayer meeting in the evening. We had dress parade at five o'clock, 30 minutes, something I think is entirely out of place, to thus desecrate the Sabbath. It is a practice which is entirely unecccessary and should be discountenanced by all good men. I have and will continue to speak against, for I think it is very wrong to ask God's blessing on our army and then wilfully disobey him is a mockery. Can we expect a blessing?

Monday, April 11
Threatened rain in the morn but cleared off and was pleasant. Nothing of note transpired, I think.

Tuesday, April 12
A beautiful day, clear and warm. Wrote home. Usual drill.

Wednesday, April 13
Lieut. Gen. Grant reviewed the 9th Corps [the 100th PVI was in the Ninth Corps] by regiments. Each regiment gave him three lusty cheers. He was accompanied by General Burnsides [sic] and other field officers. He is a plain man of medium size, a little stoop shouldered. Does not make so fine an appearance as Burnside. Received a letter from Lydia today.

Thursday, April 14
A beautiful day, clear. Nothing transpired of consequence. Wrote A. B. Moore.

Friday, April 15
Another beautiful day. Spring seems to have set in. Wrote Lydia today.

Saturday, April 16
A wet day—no drill today. Wrote a letter to sister Mary. Looked very anxiously for a letter from home but was disappointed. Must wait longer. Hope it will come soon.

Sunday, April 17
Sabbath—had preaching at eleven o'clock and prayer meeting at seven. No dress parade today. This is as it should be, there is not the least shadow of excuse for our armies parading on the Sabbath, when lying in camp.

Monday, April 18
Clear but cool, the usual drill. A Negro regiment from Pennsylvania passed our camp.

Wednesday, April 20
Received a letter from home and answered it. Had our first regimental drill.

Thursday, April 21
Received orders to turn over our A tents, prepare to move out at 4 o'clock AM on the 23rd which created quite a stir in camp. Wrote to Mother.

Friday, April 22
Made preparation for to march. Expressed my overcoat home. Drew five days rations.

Saturday, April 23
Left Annapolis for Alexandria. Marched 15 miles.

Sunday, April 24
Sabbath—started about 8 o'clock. Marched 16 miles. Stopped about dark. It rained in the night.

Monday, April 25
Started at 6 o'clock and marched 16 miles. Waded a considerable of a stream. Passed through Washington and camped near Alexandria.

Tuesday, April 26
Day in camp all day but under marching orders. Wrote home.

Wednesday, April 27
Left camp and marched to Fairfax courthouse. Distance 15 miles. Very desolate looking country.

Thursday, April 28
Continue our march. Passed through the old Bull Run battleground and also passed—Manassas Junction and camped at Bristol station. I was also called out about 11 o'clock to guard an ammunition train.

Friday, April 29
Got permission from the Capt. to go ahead of the Regiment to call at the Bucktails a short distance ahead [Bingham's brother, George Q. Junkin, was a member of the 13th Pennsylvania Regiment Reserves. the "Bucktails"]. Met with Capt. McNaughten and Lieut. Hall Passed where 155 were encamped. Saw some of the boys but did not see Mr. Mateer.

Saturday, April 30
Marched about five miles and encamped. Other regiments, other troops left for the front as we came, and we are to take their place.

Sunday, May 1
Sabbath—After breakfast got orders to pack up. We moved about 150 rods. Our objective was to support a battery. We collected some of our stuff for our tents. Then the order came to move so we made a move back about 50 rods. Was ordered to put up our tents. We did. Thus the Sabbath was spent in noise and confusion. I want to say the move was unnecessary but maybe it was. We had prayer meeting in the evening. We are now at Bealton station. May probably lay here for months and may lie only a few days. Time can only tell.

Monday, May 2
Nothing of note. Some of the boys were sent out on picket. I was out target shooting.

Tuesday, May 3
Lay around camp all day. Got ordered to march. Drew 6 days rations. I have to go on guard duty tonight.

Wednesday, May 4
Marched about nine miles and took dinner and lay at Brandy Station until about four and marched about 13 miles further. Got our coffee and lay down about 12 o'clock. Slept well. God has thus far given me strength to perform the labours required for which I hope I feel truly thankful.

Thursday, May 5
Arose, took breakfast, commenced a letter to Mary [Junkin's wife] but had to march. Crossed the Rapidan. Are now lying just across it. Hear some canonading on the front—noon. Our brigade was sent out on picket at night.

Friday, May 6 [Battle of the Wilderness]
Did a good deal of marching. Made one reconnaissance through thick wood. Scared the rebs but did not hurt them. Were then marched back to the rear and lay there in the woods till 4 o'clock; then the rebs made a charge on our lines in front of us [manned by General Hancock's II Corps]. The first line withstood the charge a short time and then broke and came rushing back over our breast-works, saying for us to run but we had no notion of that; so we gave them a few rounds and then rushed forward to the front line of our works which our men had deserted and drove the Rebs back clean and clear. Without doubt our brigade saved the day at that point. Through the goodness of God I was spared for which I feel thankful.

Saturday, May 7
Moved a short distance to the right and remained in the woods as a reserve, but there was no attack made on our part of the lines. Slept on our arms again.

Sunday, May 8
Sabbath. Started about three in the morning. Kept moving along steady in the direction of Fredericksburg [?] in the pine wood. About three o'clock in the afternoon passed through the Chancellorsville battle ground. Had a good sermon in the evening.

Monday, May 9
Started about three in the morning. Marched several different directions, I suppose 10 miles in all. Formed line of battle about 2 o'clock. Again slept on our arms but were not disturbed. Had a good sleep which we needed very much.

Tuesday, May 10
Arose at three and had our coffee by daylight. Are still lying in our rifle pits (noon). Were ordered to advance about one hour before sundown. Advanced during the night about one-and-one-half miles and had a breast work thrown up by daybreak.

Wednesday, May 11
Lay in our ditches till about three o'clock. Then retreated across the Ny Branch of the Mattaponi river. Returned to our pits a little after dark and was on guard a part of the night. It rained and we had to sleep on our arms again.

Thursday, May 12
Had coffee and started off for the line of battle [Spotsylvania]. Kept up a skirmished fight through the woods during which Joseph [Bingham's brother, the Union Chaplain of 11 PVI, Company E] and Paree killed. About 2 o'clock we were forced to fall back with heavy loss to our regiment. Company E lost in wounded and killed 22 during the day. Killed: Paree, Stewart Hunt, James S. Gill, Milton C. Campbell, W.H. Rodgers, Wounded: Sergeant McKune, Sgt. John W. Bentley, George Maxwell, Corp. Samuel Moore, David H. Stevenson, Privates Rounds, Daniel Shaner, [?], [?], James J. Book, John S. Barber, Abraham & Alexander Hannah, William H. Brown, P. Cook, John H. Martin [and] Tomkin. We fell back a short distance and lay on our arms all night. Had our skirmishes and ordered not to sleep for fear of a surprise. Rained on us all day and night.

Friday, May 13
Threw up our entrenchments and again had to put in a sleepless night. Are still holding our position. Have to keep a sharp lookout day and night.

Saturday, May 14
Still laying in the woods in our pits and still sleep on our arms, what little sleep we get, and that is but little.

Sunday, May 15
Sabbath generally quiet along the line except some picket firing. We have been in here five days, raining most of the time, more or less, but notwithstanding the exposure and danger to which we are exposed, *"The Lord has been very gracious to me in preserving my health and sparing my life."*

Monday, May 16
Nothing of note occurred. We still hold our pits and keep out our skirmishers. I did hear that Joseph had died of his wound, but am not certain of the truth of it yet.

Tuesday, May 17
Lay on the watch as usual. Nothing occurred along the line worthy of note. Met with Hugh Means in the evening, who informed me that a Mr. Dickson told him that Joseph had died. How true *"that in the midst of life we are in death."*

Wednesday, May 18
I got permission to go back to the hospital this morning provided all was quiet to learn any particulars I could of Joseph, but our men made an attack on the right early this morning and was continued more or less all day on different parts of the line. Shells flew over us quite briskly at times and we were expecting an attack so I could not leave. Perhaps I may go back tomorrow. Things are quiet now along the line except some firing along the skirmish line.

Thursday, May 19
Started before daylight and changed our position some three miles to the left and made some advance and commenced to throw up rifle pits. Received a letter from sister Mary dated April 28 and one for Joseph from Mary and Josephine Joseph's wife. Wrote to her of Joseph's death.

Friday, May 20
Still lying in our entrenchments. Had an opportunity of sending a letter out. Wrote to Father and Mother and sister Mary in the morning. In the afternoon I got a pass and went back to the hospitals of our corps. Found them all together but could learn nothing more of Joseph or any of his things. Only learned that Chaplain Jones of the 20th Michigan had charge of the burial of the dead the day Joseph should have been buried. Did not see him as he had gone to Fredericksburg. Got back and ate my supper and was sent out to the front picket line to remain 24 hours.

Saturday, May 21
Was relieved about three o'clock and returned to the line. Received a letter from Lydia and one for Joseph from sister Mary. Took early supper and started on to [?]. Marched all night and until about 11 o'clock, and then rested a short time to take breakfast. Then marched on and stopped about 4 o'clock. Had our meeting on the 22nd and rested until the morning of the 23rd. I did justice to the sleeping having been on picket line the night of the 21st and then marched the night of the 22nd.

Monday, May 23
Moved out about 8 A.M. Still bearing toward Richmond but marched on a very crooked road, going during the day to almost every point on the compass. Got within hearing of very heavy cannonading, our musketry firing, it being on the North Anna

river, branch of the Pamunkey. Crossed the Polecat river just after dinner. Slept on the hill this side of the North Anna.

Tuesday, May 24

Lay still awhile and then made a short move, remained on North Anna hill until near dark, rained at supper, then waded across the river and lay on the bank till morning. There was heavy cannonading over our heads all day at intervals.

Wednesday, May 25

Were sent out on the front skirmish line. Shot at and was shot at by the Rebs but by the infinite mercy of God my life was spared, altho the bullets frequently came near me, but in God alone is our help to be found.

Thursday, May 26

Received a letter from home and one from Mother. Wrote to sister Mary and to Samantha. Made several moves in the woods. Met with the 10th R.P. Saw Gerome [?] and W. Patton. Recrossed the river about dark and went up to another fording and took our position as a son guard of the 5 [?]

Friday, May 27

Remained in our pits untill 11 o'clock and left in the direction of the White House. Marched until 12 o'clock. Was sent out on picket.

Saturday, May 28

Came in off picket. Got my coffee, lay around awhile and started on the march keeping down the Pamunkey on the left bank some distance from the river. Marched all night and crossed the river at daybreak.

Sunday, May 29

Sabbath—After crossing the river, resting and getting our coffee, we moved forward about two miles. A large portion of the army are lying here. Met Will McClellan while moving in the evening. I visited Cooper's battery—saw Capt. and George McGinnis. We got sleeping all night, the first undisturbed night's rest we have had since the night of the 3rd, and have frequently lost all night. It is trying on men, but all seem to be in good heart.

Monday, May 30
We marched about 5 miles and are about six miles across the
Pamunkey and within 12 miles of Richmond and our army is still
advancing very slowly. I trust that God will still enable us to
advance until the enemy is vanquished and peace be restored to
our country. May he guide us.

Tuesday, May 31
We remained in our pits all day. There was considerable skirmishing but no engagement. I paid a short visit to the 155 R V. but did
not see Mr. Mateer. He had gone back to the R.V. hospital but I
made my acquaintance with Lieut. Allen of Co. H.

Wednesday, June 1
Still in our pits. Wrote to Lydia. Just finishing it as Mr. Mateer
and Lieut. Allen came stepping along. I was very glad to see him.
In the evening the Rebs made an attack on our left and a heavy [?]
line was thrown on our front but they were repulsed. Lieut.
Gilfillen of Co. F was killed and Golon of Co. E slightly wounded.
I picked up part of a bible that was printed in 1813. It is complete
as far as [?].

Thursday, June 2 [Battle of Cold Harbor]
Lay in our pits till about three o'clock. We're the rear guard. Had
gone but about one-and-one-half miles when we were attacked by
the Rebs and a pretty sharp time of it for about two hours when we
retired to the rear of another line of battle but not before we had
checked the Rebs. Just before we were attacked there was a very
heavy rain. Co. E had 7 wounded, F. Brest, Lieu. James Offutt,
[Lieut.] William H. Corbin, O. McGee, Benoni McConnel, James
A. McCommon, Wilson E. Reed, none thought to be dangerous.
Capt. Oliver and Sergeant Oliver of Co. [?] were both wounded,
thought not dangerous.

Friday, June 3
Made a short move at 3 o'clock in the morning and threw up rifle
pits. There was heavy fighting both on right and left of us but we
had no engagement. We were shelled some. One came through our
pit right over our Capt.'s shoulder. I was sitting right next to him.
It did not burst and therefore did no harm, only covered us pretty
well with dirt. The Lord alone can protect and preserve life and
may be enable us all to be thankful for his care over us.

Saturday, June 4

We lay in our pits until about 6 o'clock when we moved about one-and-one-half miles toward the front. I received another letter for Joseph from his family. I wrote a few lines and returned three that I had received. Commenced raining in the evening and rained all night.

Sunday, June 5

Continued to rain awhile but quit about 10 o'clock and was a very pleasant day. So far as we were concerned it was quiet as could be expected until 5 o'clock. We moved about 1 mile and threw up pits. Worked until about 12 o'clock. Just after dark the Rebs made a desperate charge on the line of the 5th and 18th Corps but were repulsed, with what loss I have not heard. Was generally quiet the rest of the night. I wrote a letter home.

Monday, June 6

Pleasant day. Washed both my shirts and socks. A few shell and grape came over our regiment and scared some butchers off that were back in the woods a short distance. The beeves were just skinned ready, so our Corps, some 2 or 3 of each company made for the beef, so we got an extra ration of meat. The butchers soon came back but their beeves had taken legs and gone. I took my post on picket at 6 o'clock for a 24 hour term.

Tuesday, June 7

A very pleasant day. Remained on picket till 5 o'clock. Nothing of note transpired on our part of the line. We hear no news from the other parts that is reliable. Can't say what is going on.

Wednesday, June 8

Pleasant day. At 4 o'clock in the evening our bridge was taken out of the front picket line. Were placed in squads. Most of the boys in our company would fall asleep part of the time, but the Capt., orderly Sergeant, and I kept our eyes open all night.

Thursday, June 9

Pleasant day. Remained on picket duty all day and kept watch until 12 o'clock that night. Then lay down to sleep. I also received a letter from sister Mary. No one I think can appreciate the reception of letters as the soldier can and how it cheers him.

Friday, June 10
Pleasant day. Was relieved of picket about 5 o'clock. Fell back [?] as reserve. Mr. Mateer made a short visit.

Saturday, June 11
Started to visit the 155th but on the way learned that they had moved. Came back and wrote home and to sister Mary.

Sunday, June 12
A very pleasant day. Had preaching. Spent the day as quietly as could be expected. Had orders to move at 6 o'clock but did not start until about dark. We started and got to the White House about daylight of the 13th, the distance 12 miles.

Monday, June 13
Pleasant day. Remained near the White House until after dinner and then started across the country to the James River. Nothing of particular interest occurred. Stopped at 10 P.M.

Tuesday, June 14
Continued the march, crossed the Chickahominy and camped near the James.

Wednesday, June 15
Lay in camp until 10 o'clock, then started. Crossed the James river, marched until 10. Stopped for coffee. Marched on and about sundown took a position in the rear [?] lines near Petersburg. Threw up rifle pits.

Friday, June 17
Advanced and lay in pits till 4 o'clock and the 9th Corps prepared for a charge. Our regiment was to act as skirmishers for our division. We advanced, then fell back when we discovered the enemies position. We were soon ordered again to advance. Again we did—a short distance we were to fall down and the lines of battle to pass over us. Just after they passed I was wounded. The fire of the Rebs was terrible. I figured our men could not drive them, but they did but with heavy loss.

Junkin's thigh was shattered by gunshot. He was honourably discharged from service on 8 July 1865.

Lewis Warlick, CSA

Warlick writes to his wife.

Spotsylvania C.H. Va.,
May 19th 1864

My dearest Corrie,

As there is an opportunity or soon will be of sending a letter I will write to you again.

I wrote two or three days since but being aware that you will be very anxious to hear from me frequently during these fighting times I will endeavor to write as often as an opportunity affords.

We had a mail to-day, the first in nearly two weeks, none from you. Our command has not been engaged since I last wrote but expecting every night and day to be attacked: the enemies line of battle is in full view, about a thousand yards in our front but I think it very probable he will never attack us in our strong position, if he should be will be repulsed as heretofore. We were under a terrific shelling yesterday for two hours with very little damage. Ewell repulsed the enemy yesterday three times making great slaughter in his (the enemy) ranks. To-day so far everything is quiet the skirmishers dont even fire at each other but seem to be quite friendly, meet each other and exchange papers and have a talk over the times; one came and met Capt Brown of the 44th and after having a chat he, the Yankee, told Brown that Lee had destroyed half their army; there has no doubt been an awful slaughter in their ranks as, men who have fought over many bloody fields in Va. say they never saw dead Yankees lie so thick on the ground as they do in front of the works where they charged. Their dead lie unburied from the Wilderness down here, the enemy went off and left them and we did the same. I see from Northern papers they claim a great victory at the Wilderness, well I wish they could all the time have such victories I consider when an army is driven back leaving their dead and wounded both in the field and hospitals that they have been badly whiped, dont you? That is the kind of a victory they gained at the Wilderness for I was there and know it to be so, we remained on the field till Sunday evening of the 8th and not an enemy could be found in front by our scouts.

We have to mourn the loss of many good officers and soldiers since the fight began. From all quarters we have good news, every where our arms have been victorious—Butler driven back Grant checked, Steele captured with his command and many other places

we have been successful for which we ought to give God the praise.
In my last I wrote to you of the death of brother Logan I also wrote
to his wife. Bill McGimsy had an attack of cramp yesterday is
nearly well to-day. Aus P. has been a little unwell but improving.
Pink and I are very well. I am very thankful that we have come out
through so many dangers as well as we have, nothing but the hand
of an Allwise providence has protected us thus far, for which we
ought to be very humble and give him all the praise for his
goodness. My wound is not well but does not hurt me. I saw
Sam Tate when we were coming down here—haven't seen or
heard from him since. We have had a hard time since we left camp,
have been marching, lying in line of battle and fighting all the time,
are now in the works [and] not allowed to leave any distance as
Grant is a sly fellow and has to be watched closely.

Grant is twice as badly whiped now as was Burnside or Hooker
but he is so determined he will not acknowledge it, but I think
before he gets through with Lee he will have to own up.

I haven't had any clean cloths since I left camps the wagons are
in the rear and we can not leave to go where they are to get our
cloths, all the officers are in the same fix, so you may well suppose
we are somewhat dirty.

Give my love to uncle John, Puss and
Sue. Do you get your papers?
Your devoted
Lewis

Warlick did not survive the war.

Corporal Edwin Horton,
Company C, 4th Vermont Regiment

Letter to his wife.

Chesnut Hill Hospital, Philadelphia, Pennsylvania
July 7, 1864

Dearest Ellen

It is almost to weeks since we parted and the time has seemed
real long to me I never have had time seem so long as it has since I
came back I havent heard from you yet but I am in hopes to hear
from you tonight if I dont I shall think you have given up the
notion of writing to me any more this is the third letter I have
written to you and I cannot think of writing any more until I get
one from you my finger is getting along first rate I presume they

will send me to the regiment next week and I dont care if they do it is so lonesome here. I wouldent be lonesome here or any where else if you was only with me but I suppose it will be too long years before we shall be allowed to meet again I hope Nell this will find you enjoying yourself first rate My God Nell I never felt half so bad about anything as I did to leave you that morning dident you notice I dident bid you good bye it was because I couldent speak I dont never want to come home again until I come home for good the war news is so bad now I guess their is no doubt but what I shall have to serve my time out but I am going to apply to go to the regiment right away if I have to serve my time I am going to serve it in the field time dont seem as long there as it does here well Nell I must close . , . please write soon give my respects to the old folks this from your true and loving Husband

Edwin Horton

dont show this foolish letter to any one

Frank S. Morley, Union Army

Morley writes to a Miss M.L. Lynn of Washington Co, Pa.

Bermuda Hundred, Va
July 12, 1864

Miss Maggie:

Doubtless you will be somewhat surprised at the reception of this note and wonder in your mind who it is that has had the impudence to thus address you.

However I hope after you have kindly considered the matter you will hold me guiltless.

In the first place consider our position, hundreds of miles from home and friends in an enemy country: here we are constantly exposed to the deadly missles from the enemy hurled into our midst and more than this the many diseases that ever follow camp life are to be dreaded by the soldiers.

In hours of affliction is the time a soldier feels most the want of that dear mother, kind sister, or fond brother. But as we cannot be blessed with the society of our friends while we are in the army why can I not have some good letters from the Patriotic and Union loving ladies of the North? I think I may. I think you will write me at least one. Nothing is better adapted to promote the happiness of a soldier while in the field than plenty of good letters. Camp life becomes loathsome and monotonous after we have staid in one place untill I could point out every particular spot of ground or perhaps point to every leave of vegetation growing on it. I must acknowledge we have not wanted for excitement here though, most expecially that of the field of battle.

This is a very mild and beautiful evening. The sunlight has fallen from the leaves of the forest and lingers no longer on the summits of the Western hills. Every thing so calm, the air so pure and a gentle zephyr playing by me, it makes me long for to be at home again that I might take a walk on some of those fine evenings with some of my lady friends.

I heard from you a short time since; an Officer from our regiment was passing up the River on the Boat and he saw you standing in the door of your dwelling. He waved his hand-kerchief. he did not know whether you recognized him or not. He was not close enough to speak to you. He is an old acquaintance of yours. I was at Millsboro last fall when I was on furlough but I did not see you. Is Amanda Evans teaching school this summer? If so, where at?

I shall not trouble with a long letter this time but if you condescend to answer this imperfect note I will be most happy to entertain you the next time with something more interesting. And as I know generosity and benevolence to be two prominent features of character, I have no fears but you will answer it and write me a long letter. 'Tis under this impression that I bid you adieu. Truly your friend, Frank S. Morley

To Maggie Lynn
Address:
Frank S Morley

Lieutenant William F. Testerman, Company C, 8th Tennessee Cavalry, CSA

Gallotin, Tenn.
July 25, 1864

Dear Miss,

I again take the opportunity of Droping you a few lines in answer to your kind letters which I recieved a few days ago one bearing date June "23" the other June the "24" it was a pleasure to me to have the honor to recieve a letter from as charming a young girl as the one whos name was asscirbed at the bottom of each of them I was glad to hear that you was well but I was more glad to hear you express your mind as fully as what you did this note leaves me well and I truly hope that this will find you in good health I can't say anything to you by letter more than what you have heard from my letters before + Jane I hope the time will soon come when I can get to see you again I can write many things to you but if I could see you I could tell you more in one minute than I can rite in a week The letters that you wrote to me has proved verry satisfactory to me if you will stand up to what you told me in your letters I will be satisfied which I have no reasons to Doubt but what you will but if you was to fail it would almost break my heart for you are the girl that I am Depending upon and if it was not for you I would not be riting by my candle to night as you wrote to me that many miles separated us in person if my heart was like yours we would be united in heart you kneed not to Dout Though we are fare apart at present my heart is with you every moment for I often think of you when you are asleep when Travailing the lonesom roads in middle Tenn The thought of your sweet smiles is all the company I have I trust that you are cinsere in what you have wrote to me. Your sparkling blue eys and rosey red cheeks has gaind my whole efections I hope for the time to come when we shall meet again then if you are in the notion that I am we can pass off the time in plesure My time has come for sleep and I must soon close I want you to rite to me as soon as you can for I will be glad to hear from you any time. Direct your letters as before and dont forget your best friend so I will end my few lines but my love to you has no End remember me as ever your love and friend. Excuse bad riting.

William F. Testerman to Miss Jane Davis

Private Frederick C. Buerstatte, 26th Regiment Wisconsin Volunteers

Not yet eighteen, Buerstatte enlisted in the Union Army in February 1864, and kept a diary until his discharge in October 1865. The extract here, from enlistment to the winter of 1864, includes his participation in Sherman's historic march on Georgia.

Diary of Frederick Charles Buerstatte.
All your life keep God before you and in your heart and beware that you do not linger in any form of sin but always follow God's command.

Tobias: Chapt. 4 Verse 6

1864

12th February—Tonight I volunteered for duty with the 26th Regiment Wis. Infantry Volunteers for 3 years or duration of the war.

6th March—I received a physical examination by the doctor at Camp Randall and was declared fit.

15th March—We were mustered into the service of the U.S.

18th April—We left Camp Randall and were sent to the regiment.

23rd April—We arrived at the regiment at Lookout Valley, Tennessee.

27th April—We finally received *rifles*.

2nd May—We left on march from Lookout Valley this morning. We are now 15 miles from Georgia. We came to Missionary Ridge battlefield on the way. The roadside was full of graves and the cannonballs and rifle balls were buried in the trees.

5th May—Today in Georgia it is [?] day. We marched here yesterday. The Rebs are not far from here. Weather is beautiful and the air warm.

7th May—The entire army is on the move. We marched farther south yesterday and today. The area is hilly. We see few men but often women and children.

8th May—We marched to Tunnel Hill where the Rebs were. In the afternoon we had an encounter with the Rebs in which they were driven from their first position. We lost 2 dead and some wounded.

11th May—We marched in the direction of Rome. We drove the enemy before us and we heard General Grant had beaten the Rebs in Virginia. The soldiers hope to see the war come to an end this year. So do the enemy prisoners, some of whom look quite bewildered.

14th May—Since yesterday and today a lively skirmish has been occurring in front of us. We are lying here in a battle line. The enemy is resisting heavily and we will soon get into the fire because our advance troops are already in it. The Adjutant had acquired a detachment from the Army of the Potomac with which General Grant had beaten the Rebs after a 4 day battle. He captured 30 cannons and an entire division. We hear loud gunfire to the left and in front of us and it seems the enemy is being driven back.

15th May—Today is Pentecost day. The battle lasted yesterday into the night and this morning it continues again. We were relieved last night. Our entire division is on the march to try to surround the enemy. We marched until noon and set up a battle line and moved out. Our brigade attacked the enemy defenses but we were thrown back. We regrouped and attacked again. Our regiment moved ahead in good formation, but the other regiments broke up and we had to retreat again. We attacked again but did not succeed. We received reinforcements and took the defenses. This was a horrible fight. Dead and wounded lay everywhere. We were taken to the rear and spent a quiet night we are considerably disappointed since our regiment lost 70 men of 370 total.

16th May—The enemy was beaten this morning. We have the last stragglers of the Rebs behind us. We captured more material and ammunition. The guns they left behind are all destroyed. The road is scattered full of dead, horses, pieces of clothing, weapons. cartridge containers, etc. These are the tracks of an army in flight.

17th May—Last night we marched until 1:00 o'clock. Our cavalry is following the enemy. We are finding while marching many dead and wounded left behind by the enemy.

18th May—In the evening we got to the enemy area and built breastworks overnight. Enemy cavalry is in front of us. We are extremely exhausted from the long march.

19th May—At noon we engaged the enemy and the battle started. In spite of this, our regiment did not get into it. Good news from Virginia.

21st May—Rest day.

22nd May—One does not realize it, but today is Sunday. Tomorrow we march again. The heat is terrible and we are all almost "finished".

23rd May—Our company was assigned to train guard duty.

27th May—We were relieved of train guard duty and at midnight returned to our regiment encamped at Burnt Hickory.

28th May—The Rebs greeted us with cannon fire this morning. We relieved the 1st Brigade which was positioned behind breastworks. The entire area is thickly wooded.

30th May—The Rebs attacked last night but were driven off.

31st May—We were relieved last night and lay in reserve today.

2nd June—We marched on the right flank today. It rained a great deal. We are all wet through and through and there is an awful lot of mud! mud!

5th June—Today is Sunday, a beautiful day at home, but here we must keep our thoughts together, otherwise one does not know it is Sunday. The weather is finally clearing up after a long period of rain. Rations are becoming scarce.

7th June—Today we are encamped on a hill. We had to build breastworks deep into last night and are learning what the word hunger means.

8th June—Rest day.

16th June—We marched out at 2:00 o clock and met the Rebs at 6:00 o clock at Big Shanty. We laid for 2 hours through cannon and rifle fire on the ground and dared not get up. Two men were wounded from our regiment.

17th June—Last night we had to lay at night with rifles in our arms and then we built breastworks.

19th June—We advanced 2 miles. The Rebs left their defenses, strong defenses, which were built a long time ago.

20th June—We got into a skirmish yesterday in which we lost a lot of men.

22nd June—Today was again another bloody day near Marietta.

We had to attack the well-entrenched enemy at noon. We ran across a wide open field with shouts and into the next woods where we came upon the enemy outpost defenses and got to within 300 yards of their main defenses. Our regiment lost 45 dead and wounded.

23rd June—We were relieved last night and marched farther to the right where today we built breastworks in view of the enemy who provided us with cannonball music.

3rd July—While we were on the march, the Rebs gave up their forward defenses and retreated with us at their heels.

4th July—Today we stood watch and returned at noon. All day long a terrible cannonade has been going on in front and to the left of us. Toward evening we marched about 3 miles and built breast-works.

6th July—Today we are positioned on a hill about 2 miles from the Chattahoochie River. The Rebs are in retreat. We marched here yesterday in the greatest heat in which many of our men collapsed from exhaustion.

9th July—We established our camp here. Weather is beautiful.

16th July—We stood general inspection today.

17th July—Today is Sunday. We had to clean up the camp after which we received orders to march.

18th July—Yesterday evening we crossed the river on pontoons and marched back and forth in the woods.

19th July—We rested today.

20th July—Today we are engaged in a terrible battle with the Rebs at Peach Tree Creek. At 2:00 o'clock PM. our brigade which was at the left Rank of the corps, joined the 4th Corps in battle line. The enemy attacked at which time we advanced. Our regiment was as always in the forward battle line. We advanced over a small hill and into a valley in which a small creek flowed. Then the Rebs came toward us down the hill in front of us. Now the firing really began. The gunfire exceeded anything I had ever heard before. We loaded and fired as fast as possible. The Rebs came to within 10 paces of us, at which time our musket balls became too thick for them. They turned to the right and retreated up the hill with us behind them. This was a sight which I had never seen before and hope never to see again. The entire field was scattered with dead, wounded and dying. The wounded moaned so much that I could hardly watch. However, we had no time and had to advance up the hill. There stood a fence behind which we petitioned ourselves. The Rebs tried to advance again but did not succeed, because a battery was placed on the hill behind us which greeted the enemy terribly with cannonballs. After 4 hours of firing, we were finally relieved and went to the second battle line. The firing lasted into the night. At night I helped carry more wounded from the field. We also captured a flag from the 33rd Mississippi Regiment.

21st July—This morning our regiment, after a sleepless night, had to bury the dead Rebs which laid before our regiment. They were all from the 33rd Mississippi Regiment. Our regiment lost 9 dead and 36 wounded. We buried over 50 Rebs, among them Colonel Drake and most of the officers of the 33rd Miss. Regiment. Now we had to clean our guns.

22nd July—Today we marched toward Atlanta and built breast-works. Toward evening the Rebs greeted us with cannon fire. Four cannons are positioned between our regiment. One can see the towers of Atlanta.

23rd July—We changed our position again. We marched further to the right near the First Division and lay behind "Dulgars Battery". Now the bombardment of Atlanta has begun. Heavy defenses rise before us.

29th July—A bloody battle occurred yesterday to our right and in front of us at the 15th Corps.

21st August—Today is Sunday. One almost doesn't realize it because the bombardment continues without letup. We received a little whiskey today. The Rebs bothered us very much. They lobbed 64-pounders at us.

27th August—Last night we quietly left our breastworks and retreated to the Chattahoochie River where we burnt breastworks today.

28th August—Today is Sunday. Yesterday the Rebel cavalry attacked our outposts and took several prisoners. Our Corps is stationed at the river as bridge guard.

2nd Sept.—This morning we left our quarters at the river at 5:00 o'clock and filed through wood and field over hill and dale toward Atlanta. We came to the city at 10:00 o'clock. The city immediately surrendered. We drove 30 Reb cavalry before us through the city. Several stores were broken into and tobacco was taken from them. Many Germans live here.

6th Sept.—We have established summer encampment on the south side of Atlanta.

8th Sept.—The Army finally returned with 6000 prisoners.

11th Sept.—Today is Sunday. The bells in the city are ringing but one cannot go to church no matter how hard one tries because one must "stay home" and clean rifles.

19th Sept.—We signed our pay lists.

26th Sept.—Today our division stood review before Major General Slocum. Our regiment was highly praised.

1st Oct.—Our tie with the North was again cut by the Reb General Wheeler with his cavalry.

5th Oct.—Hood's Army is to our rear and our whole army including our Corps chased him. We were paid today.

8th Oct.—Our regiment marched away from Atlanta to the river to a position at the railroad bridge.

19th Oct.—This morning we took 3 days ration and patrolled and foraged toward Roswell.

21st Oct.—We returned today at noon. Yesterday we camped 1 mile on this side of Roswell overnight. Yesterday the wagons were loaded with corn. At noon we marched toward Marietta and today we marched 16 miles in 6 hours.

9th Nov.—Today we heard loud cannon and musket fire near Atlanta.

10th Nov.—We heard that yesterday 2 Reb infantry regiments and 1 Reb cavalry regiment were seen near the city but retreated quickly.

14th Nov.—This morning we burned our camp and marched to Atlanta to our brigade. We received more whiskey last night.

15th Nov.—This morning the entire Army of the HAC. 15 A.C. 19 A.C. and the 20th Army Corps [A.C.] was on the move toward Atlanta.

19th Nov.—Tonight we are about 45 miles from Atlanta. We began to live from that which we found on the plantations such as potatoes, pigs, chickens, sheep and cornmeal.

20th Nov.—Today is Sunday but just the same we are marching in rainy weather and mud. We came through the little town of Madison.

21st–22nd Nov.—Rain and mud.

23rd Nov.—It cleared up today. We had strong winds. During last 3 days of marching through rain and mud, we crowded ourselves quite close together. We passed through Milledgeville which was the governor's residence. He fled 3 days ago; it is the capital city of Georgia.

26th Nov.—Tonight we came upon Andersonville.

27th Nov.—This morning we had inspection of rifles cartridges and cartridge cases. We moved on at 10:00 o clock.

29th Nov.—Today we marched through the considerably larger town of Louisville.

30th Nov.—We had a well-deserved rest day today.

4th Dec.—Today is Sunday but we had to march anyhow. The entire area around Andersonville is swampy and roads are bad.

7th Dec.—We marched among ruins and mud. It is still 25 miles to Savannah.

9th Dec.—We hear cannon fire to our left in front of us near the 14th Army Corps.

10th Dec.—Before us and near us we hear cannon fire near the 14th Corps and 17 A.C. The 14th is to our left and 17 A.C. is to our right and in front of us. We were formed into a battle line at noon.

11th Dec.—The bombing continues without stopping near us. Our rations are now short and one discovers what hunger feels like.

12th Dec.—All the trains which we encountered from Atlanta to Savannah were destroyed.

14th Dec.—The bombing still continues vigorously. This morning the 2nd Div. of the 15th Army Corps attacked Fort McEllister and captured it on the first advance. They captured 26 cannons and 1500 men which was the entire complement of the fort. Our food line should now be open again. We now have too little to live on and too many dying. We have only a small amount of rice and an ounce of meat per day.

16th Dec.—One hears that a 15 ton food supply for this army is on the way which should arrive in about 2 days.

17th Dec.—Another food supply arrived which made us very happy.

19th Dec.—We received ½ rations again.

21st Dec.—This morning the order came to advance. The Rebs have left and we had to pack in 5 minutes and march toward Savannah, where we set up quarters 1 mile west of the city. We now have as much rice as we want. The Rebs have fled to South Carolina. We captured much rice, cannons and munitions which the enemy left behind. We also captured many prisoners.

24th Dec.—We cleaned our quarters. Each person planted a Christmas tree in front of his tent.

25th Dec.—Christmas morning inspection. We received a ½ unit crackers, rice and meat.

26th Dec.—We received orders to march tomorrow across the Savannah River.

27th Dec.—The march orders were rescinded. Good news from Tennessee. General Hood's army is completely demoralized.

30th Dec.—Today the entire 20th Army Corps was reviewed by General Sherman in Savannah in beautiful weather. We received orders to march tonight.

31st Dec.—We marched in the rain 2 miles east of the city. It was cold and returned to our old quarters for the first time since November 14th. We received sugar and full cracker rations. Cold wind.

End of 1864.

Sergeant James H. Harden,
43rd United States Colored Infantry

A Quartermaster Sergeant from Philadelphia, Harden writes to the black American newspaper, *Christian Recorder*.

> *Near Richmond and Petersburg, Virginia*
> *December 3, 1864*

. . . We are constantly under the fire of the enemy, who shell our camp nearly every day. There has been some few wounded in our regiment since we have been here, but no one killed as far as I can ascertain.

There is one poor fellow soldier, belonging to the 23rd regiment, which is in our brigade, struck in the head by a bullet which caused his death.

The next morning, I saw some four or five men of his company digging a grave, and I inquired after him, and was told that he was dead, and that he was to be buried there. After the grave was finished, his body was borne by some of his comrades to its resting place, and laid in the grave. His clothing formed his shroud, and his blanket the coffin.

The chaplain then made some few remarks, and prayed over the grave where the remains were laid, after which he was covered with earth by some of his comrades.

The same day, another man of the same regiment was struck by a shell, which shattered his thigh to pieces. Another man was struck with a shell which cut him in two.

How will their families and friends feel when they receive the sad tidings of their husbands, fathers, brothers, or sons, or whatever relation they may be, who have fallen in behalf of our glorious Union, and their fellow comrades in the South?

I had a very narrow escape myself, the other day. Commissary Sergeant John C. Brock and myself were standing together, and had just finished issuing rations, when a shell came hissing over us and bursted. We started and ran a few yards, and I fell to the ground, and the pieces flew all around us. One piece struck an old log, which was lying on the ground where we were standing, and glanced off and out through the cook's tent, striking a glass bottle, smashing it, and then struck the upright pole that holds the tent up, which stopped its progress.

I thank God that he has spared my life so far, and still hope to see the city of brotherly love once more.

We have a very nice and attentive chaplain in our regiment. He attends to and furnishes nourishment for the sick and wounded. I do not think that there could be a better one found, for he studies our interests, and tries to supply our wants.

I will now close my letter, for there is neither pen, paper, ink, nor pencil that can describe the desolation of war.

Private John Milton Pierce, Company B, 15th Regiment, Iowa Volunteers

Pierce enlisted at Waterloo, Iowa, on 21st October, 1864.

Savanah, Georgia
December 22, 1864

Dear Wife and Children,

I take my pen in hand to write you a few lines to let you know that I am well and I am in Savanah. We took Savanah or rather marched in Savanah yesterday, the Rebs left night before last. They shelled us very strong day before yesterday until after dark and they quit shooting and fled. I dogged a great many shells yesterday as my company was on picket. We laid in the ditches all day and thought that when we got out to cook our grub they would pour the shells in on us, but providence smiled on us and not one of us were hit, but they throwed their shells near us often times.

There are over One Hundred Thousand soldiers in Savanah today. It is quite a business place at this time as they are going to and fro. Where we will go next I can't say but I should like to be at home if the war was over, I should like the war to be over and we could all come home to our families. This has been the coldest day that I have seen even in Southern Iowa. The wind has blown very cold last night and today altho it has not frozen up yet. Down here everything looks green, here there is plenty of green corn that has lately come up on the commons, nice and green oats and everything looks green. The tall cedars wave in Georgia as the greater part of the timber is pine. Here there is a timber they call live oak that is a beautiful tree, has green leaves on at this time. Savanah and the country around here is very level and swampy and I suppose it is very sickley in the summer season. We have had plenty to eat since we have got to town, we have plenty of rice and sugar, coffee, beef, hardtack, turkeys and chickens. The water is good tasting, but very warm. There are more niggars here that you could shake a stick at in a month. There are all kind of negroes here, both black and white. There are some white women here, but I think they are not the right stripe as far as I have seen of them. I think we will take Christmas in Savanah, we will kill the rebels by eating their food and burning their property. As it is getting late I shall have to close by saying write often and don't forget to pray for me as I stand in need of your prayers as wickedness doth abound in abundance.

Take good care of yourself, send me some stamps in the next letter as I am out of stamps and there is none here.

This is the 23rd and we have been out drilling this morning. There was some frost this morning and there was some ice as thick as window glass. The weather is a little more moderate this morning. We marched around thru town. We saw General Pulaskas monument—it is a splendid thing, it is about the height of a five story house. We were marched thru the park this was a beautiful sight. This is a large town, some fine buildings in it altho it is going to rack pretty fast. At this time we are in camp, we have built us quite a shanty so we can live comfortable. There are some of them unwell this morning—I think it is on account of them eating and drinking too much. I still remain yours in the Lord. I still remain your affectionate husband until death directs us before.

J.M. Pierce
Port Royal, South Carolina
Jan 12, 1865

Dear Wife and Children,

I take my pen in hand to write you a few lines to let you know I am well at this time and hope that these lines will find you all well and enjoying yourselves very well. I am enjoying good health and am enjoying myself pretty well as I am a great ways from home. I received a letter from you yesterday dated Dec. 22nd. I was very glad to hear from you. I should be glad to hear from you every week at least. I have written some two or three letters every week since we have had communication and sent several papers also. We are camped in a pine grove, but we are under marching orders to be ready to march tomorrow morning, where I can't say but I suppose it is somewhere to fight the rebels for that is what we are down here for. What amount of fighting we will have to do is more than I can say but I am in hopes it won't be much. The less fighting we have to do the better I like it.

I think you sold our hogs well. You did not say whether you sold them alive or slaughtered them. I should like to know what you have done with old Dave. You must not feed your stock too high for fear your feed runs out before spring. If you have not heard from Charley Shersburg, I think you had better write again to him as I don't think I shall be home in time to put in a crop. I know you can't put in much of the place yourself. I may have a chance to hire a substitute down here as there are a great many soldiers time out, but the most of them want to go home. I should be glad to get some papers from you. I have got a few papers since I have been here. Jane, I am out of money as we have not drawed any pay yet and we have had to buy a great many things and they came very high and that took money very fast, and I wish you send me some so I will have enough to last me until we draw our pay from Uncle Sam.

Sarah Jane, if you have not got your county, you had better try and get it as soon as you can. You had better settle up your taxes as it is on big interest and you had better stop the interest. Should have liked it if you could have had a school there this winter but so it is. You must try and learn the children as much as you can. I should like to know in your letter if you got my clothes or not, and what about that box fast that went to Marshalltown.

By the help of God I intend to hold fast to the faith of our Lord and Saviour Jesus Christ. I intend to live so that if I should fall on the battle field, I will be prepared to meet my God and that I may have it said of me "Come up higher it is enough of you" for you have kept My Commandments, may the Lord bless us all and finally save us all in the Portals above where there is no more War nor sinning of any kind, and won't that be a happy place to meet to part no more. Parents and children there can meet to part no more.

Children, I want you to be good children and obey your Mother for she can give you good advise and she will give you good instructions, be of good cheer for I think your papa will get home again. Dear wife, pray for me that I may not go astray, yours in the Lord, I still remain your affectionate Husband until death and after death I hope to meet you in Heaven.

J.M. Pierce

Pierce died shortly after writing this letter, at the age of 34. The Surgeon General recorded his death as being due to acute diarrhoea. Pierce left a wife and seven children.

I. Shoger, United States Army

Raleigh April 16th. N.C./65

Dear Wife

When I wrote you last I told yoou we were agoing some where we mached the next morning for Raleigh 50 miles it took us three days we went through Smithfield which is a very fine city at this place we got the news of Lees capture you had aught to have seen the excitement. the dispatch was redd by Genl. Sherman in front of the Court house. our band was at the head of the collume we playd all the National airs the soldiers threw up thair hats and chreed with all thair might. they got a negro on a blanket and threw him ten feet. we then marched for Raleigh. this also a very fine city. all the frrce we have to contend with now is Johnson comand wich left the city as we entered it beign surrenderd by the mayor and council. negoations are now going on while I am writeing for the surrender of his command (Johnson) this will close up the whole concern what we shall do next I do not know but untill then I remain yours as ever from the beginning to the end

yours. I. Shoger

N.B.—

we expect to have a mail to day

Abram Fulkerson, CSA

Fulkerson writes to his wife, Selina.

Field Officers Barracks May 7, 1865

My dear wife—

I have not heard directly from you since the 4th of Feb. Your letter was directed to Ft. Pulaski. I received on my way here at

Hilton Head S.C. Since that time we have passed through the most eventful period of the war. The closing scenes are being enacted, and with hearts overwhelmed with grief & sadness we bow in deep humiliation in their contemplation. The present, thank God, is only the "beginning of the end." The military power of the South is broken, the spirit is not. The ball has been put in motion by the people of the South, an impetus has been given it, which will eventually result in the destruction of the U.S. Government and if not in the independence of the South, certainly in the disenthrallment of her people. Ten years will see us under the protecting wing of a foreign power, or independent.

I expect to meet you soon, not crowned with the laurels of victory but with the oath crammed down my throat, a quiescent citizen of the United States. I have the sweet consolation of being conscious of having served the cause faithfully. I sacrificed everything but life, and hazarded that, many times & in many ways, in behalf of my country. I have not the slightest fear that any man can ever point at me the finger of scorn and say "you done it." I have performed my duty and now abandon the cause as (at present) hopeless, without in the least having changed my opinion as to the justness of that cause. I go now to share with the people of the south the deep humiliation which will be dictated by yankee vindictiveness.

I have heard from you thr'o your father up to March 1st. Receive letters from him often. Says he will send you money & c thr'o Mr. Armstrong. Hope you may have no difficulty in getting along. I cannot tell when I will be released, but probably soon. My love to Kate. Tell the boy, I'll be home soon. Your affect. husband. A. Fulkerson P.W.

US–INDIAN WARS 1865–1890

With the Civil War won, the Union Army turned its attention
from the South to the West: the final winning of the Great Plains
from the Indians. The soldier charged with the pacification of the
1.5 million square miles of the West under the control of the hostile
tribes was Major-General William Tecumseh Sherman. A believer in total war, Sherman determined to take the conflict to the
enemy. The Plains Indians, however, proved elusive, stubborn and
underestimated. They were fine horse soldiers, making up for their
generally low firepower by dazzling feats of equestrianship. A
punitive expedition mounted against the Southern Plains tribes
(notably the Cheyenne and the Comanche) in 1867 only managed
to kill a handful of warriors. Meanwhile, the Plains tribes of the
North, headed by the Tencton Sioux, found in Red Cloud a
master strategist, one who forced America to abandon its forts
on the Bozeman Trail and designate the Powder River country
"unceded Indian Territory". It was the United States' first
defeat in warfare.

In the autumn of 1868, Sherman called Lieutenant-Colonel
George Custer into service as the one field commander he believed
possessed the determination to crush the Indians. All through the
winter of 1868, Custer and the 7th Cavalry pursued the Southern
tribes in a campaign which saw the beginning of the end of their
resistance. At Washita, Custer and the cavalry attacked an Indian
village believing itself under the protection of the Treaty of Medicine
Lodge, massacring 200. For good measure, the cavalry also slaughtered the camp's entire livestock. Five years later Custer headed into
the Northern Plains as escort to surveyors of the Northern Pacific
Railroad. For three weeks in the summer of 1873 the 7th Cavalry
skirmished with Sioux under Crazy Horse and Sitting Bull along
the Yellowstone, until the expedition withdrew (principally because
Northern Pacific Railroad had collapsed in the Great Panic of that
year). In 1874 Custer again ventured into Sioux country, this time
at the head of a gold-prospecting expedition. When gold was discovered in the "unceded" Black Hills of the Sioux, the US government tried to buy the Hills for $6 million. The Sioux refused to sell,

so the US government turned the matter over to the War Department. A punitive expedition was accordingly dispatched.

On 26 June 1876, Custer and the 611 officers and men of the 7th discovered a hostile Sioux–Cheyenne–Arapaho village in the valley of the Little Big Horn. Fatally dividing his force into three, Custer led one battalion of 225 men in a direct attack on the village. They were repelled by 1500 warriors. As they retreated up a ridge, they were outflanked by Crazy Horse and 1000 braves. Every man in Custer's command was killed.

Although the Indians had won a famous battle, they would not win the war. Retribution was swift. Congress passed a law compelling them to sell their remaining land and move onto reservations. US forces under Colonel Nelson Miles and General Crook harassed them until they did. Starving (not least because of the white man's slaughter of the buffalo), dying of disease and exposure, bands of Indians surrendered until by 1881 all the Sioux were on reservations. The last battle in the Indian wars came at Wounded Knee, South Dakota, on 29 December 1890, when 300 mostly unarmed Sioux Ghost Dancers were shot by US forces, including the 7th Cavalry. So indiscriminate was the firing that the soldiers killed twenty five of their own ranks by mistake.

Captain Albert Barnitz, 7th Cavalry

Barnitz was part of the 1868 expedition against the Indians of the Southern Plains. He writes to his wife, Jennie.

Camp near Fort Dodge, Kan., Oct. 28, 1868

Day before yesterday a party of Indians made a dash upon some animals lariated in the vicinity of Fort Dodge, and succeeded in stampeding and driving off a few horses and ponies, besides doing some other damage, whereupon General Sully wrote a personal letter to Genl. Custer telling him that they *"didn't feel safe* at the Post, without some cavalry" and requested that a Troop should be sent up "to protect them!" It is really amusing, isn't it?—when you reflect that there are *seven companies* of Infantry here, armed with the finest guns in the world, and having in their possession, in addition to their ordinary arms, 3 or 4 pieces of Artillery, with men detailed to operate them! General Custer says that he is going to hold onto the letter, to show, if there is any dispute about it, i.e. that the cavalry was wanted here to *"protect"* the Infantry! Well, I was sent up yesterday with my Troop, to protect them, and here I am, encamped about $\frac{3}{4}$ of a mile below the Post. It has been arranged with General Sully that I am not to report to either the commanding officer of the Post, Major Douglass (3d Infantry) nor to the commanding officer of the Infantry camp near the Post, Brevet Major Page, 3d Inf. but am to be entirely independent, and use my own judgment in all cases. I expect to be stationed here until the expedition starts, and will then accompany it, in command of a squadron composed of "G" & "L" Troops—"L" Troop is soon to arrive here from Puebla. It is Col. Sheridan's Troop. A change was recently made in the composition of the squadrons, so that "I" Troop was put into another squadron. Today it is very windy, and I have seen no Indians yet, and suppose that they will hardly make their appearance until the wind subsides, as they cannot shoot their arrows with much accuracy except when the air is comparatively still.

The Indians who approached nearest the Post the other day were all *little boys*—only 8 or 10 years of age it appears!—A large band of warriors, however, was collected in the hills, in rear of the Post, watching them, and ready to make a descent if they had been closely pursued. One of the boys, a son of "Big Mouth" a noted chief, was wounded by "Romeo" a half-breed Arapahoe boy who is acting as guide and scout, and who recognized many of the Indians in the attacking party. Romeo's horse was wounded—in the encounter, and he himself made a narrow escape, as his horse fell just as he reached a point from which he was covered by the fire of the Infantry . . .

Genl. Gibbs is expected here from Harker with a detachment of 150 recruits for the 7th Cavalry in a few days. I become very much exasperated occasionally, when I think of the old gentleman, and wish him all manner of unhappiness! . . .

. . . Concerning all the other columns of cooperation there may be some doubt, but there appears to be no doubt whatever that *we* are to go down at the appointed time, and spend the winter in harrassing the Indians, and in operations calculated to wear down their ponies, so that in the spring—say in March, when their ponies are poorest, we can easily overtake them, and their "villages" and teach them such lesson as they will not be likely to forget soon! However the President of the society for the prevention of cruelty to animals might regard the matter, I do not think that any mercy will be shown to the Indians when we overtake them! If we fall into their hands, we expect to be tortured to death, and any that fall into our hands may expect to die very speedily . . .

I suppose you are anxious to know who are at the Post. Well,
there is Lieut. Stouch, 3d Inf. & A.A.Q.M., and wife—Major
Douglass, Lieut. "Tommy" Wallace, Capt. [William] Mitchell, all
of the 3d Infantry, and also [Bvt.] Maj. [and Capt. William M.]
Beebe [38th Infantry] and several others whom you do not know.
Lieut. Wallingford & family, and Capt. Gillette & family are also
here, Wallingford and Gillette having received permission to
come up here and remain because their families are here. So
much for being stationed at a little western Post! Lieut. Wallingford's babe died day before yesterday, and was buried yesterday. Capt. Gillette and Major Beebe are confirmed inebriates,
and the same may be said of Col. Keogh—they are seldom sober.
The same is true of Col. West. He was drunk all the time that we
were on the late expedition, and had to be hauled in an ambulance. He has been drunk for a week past, and having become sick
in consequence, was sent up here, by the surgeon for medical
treatment! I might name a good many others who are addicted to
intemperance!—Sam Robbins and "Salty" Smith are not always
duly sober, and Captain Hamilton winks with unusual rapidity at
times!—I cannot say that I ever know him to be more seriously
affected by liquor. Brevet Major Asbury 3d Inf. who is here, is
drunk nearly all the time! The fact is Jennie, there appears to be a
premium offered for drunkenness in the army! Almost *all* the old
officers drink a great deal. Indeed I do not know any one except
General Hoffman who does not, more or less, and a man is not
regarded as sociable who does not keep a sort of open house and
have something for his friends to drink, and he has a very small
chance of becoming popular with the drinking class, unless he
indulges a little himself—in fact, they are rather inclined to
regard him with some distrust, I think, as one who may be
intolerant of their vices!—At all events, I have observed that
about nine out of every ten of those who are selected for staff duty
are of the drinking class, and as a consequence are most sociable
with those who drink and are always ready to lend their influence
to have good companionable fellows selected to fill any position
that may become vacant on the staff! What I deduce from all this
is, that I am never likely to be selected for any staff duty, but will
have the pleasure of riding about on these plains so long as there
is an Indian left to cause a feeling of uneasiness along the borders.
If that is any consolation, dear, why you may as well avail
yourself of it!

I can not conceal from you that I do become dreadfully discouraged. Not because of the hardships which I endure, and

dangers which I undergo, but because of the necessity of being forever separated from you. I dare not tell you how unhappy I am at times, when I think of the dreary prospect. All my philosophy is of no avail, and my only relief is in tears. The companionship of those about me is irksome to me, and I long, oh, with an *unutterable* longing for the society of my own, dear wife! So wretched do I become, at times, in spite of all efforts to prevent it, that I could wish to die, if it were not a selfish wish.

The following letter was dictated by Barnitz. The battle he describes was the Washita on 23 November 1868.

When the appointed moment had arrived, the Regimental Band struck up "Gari Owen," and the squadrons moved forward with a rush, and all was activity; the Indians were completely taken by surprize. Yet they were instantly up and around. The fighting was severe but I am unable to say how many were killed. The bodies of one hundred and three warriors were found in and around the village, but many more must have been killed whose bodies were carried off by their friends. It was surprizing to see how soon, when once the action had commenced, how all the hills were alive with mounted warriors, armed and equipped with their shields, and war bonnets. These as it was afterwards ascertained had come from other villages in the valley, having heard the firing. Shortly after the firing commenced I observed a large body of Indians running off towards the left. I at once dashed in among them, passing through a large drove of Squaws and children who were screaming and very much frightened. I came upon the warriors who were ahead and striking out as hard as they could run for their ponies. Riding up close along side of the first I shot him through the heart. He threw up his arms, by the same movement drawing his bow from the scabbard let fly an arrow at me. This was the last act of his existence. I passed on to the second and shot him in the same manner. There was yet another close to me. He was armed with a large Lancaster rifle given to him by the peace commission. He took aim, while I was closing upon him and about to fire, but was several times disconcerted by my acting as if I were about to fire upon him myself, until finally I had some doubt if his rifle was loaded. When however I got quite close to him to fire, he returned my fire at the same instant, both shots taking effect. Mine I believe must have passed through his heart, as he threw up his hands frantically and as I was told by others of my company died almost immediately.

I rode back toward the village, being now unable to manage my horse, and the pain of my wound being almost unbearable. I dismounted and lay down in such a way that I would not bleed internally. As soon as the fight was nearly decided I was placed upon a buffalo robe and carried down the hills a few hundred yards further, where I was allowed to rest in a place of comparative security until Doctors Lippincott and [William H.] Renicke arrived. Both were so blind, from the effects of snow, that they with difficulty could attend to the wounded, and pronounced my case truly hopeless, but made every effort for my comfort for the short time it was supposed I had to live. All the officers gathered about me, as the progress of the fight permitted, and endeavored to cheer me with their condolences; in the meantime the Indian village was burned together with a quantity of stores, supplies, gun powder, &c—and all the ponies that could be gathered together, were driven in. Two were selected for each of the Squaws, who were captured, and two for each officer; the remainder, some eight or nine hundred, were shot to prevent them falling into the hands of the Indians. We now awaited the arrival of our ambulances, which were toiling towards us through the intricate labyrinths where our horses could hardly proceed by file. When at length these arrived the wounded were loaded in, and we commenced our return march towards this point.

Second Lieutenant Charles W. Larned, 7th Cavalry

Larned writes to his mother whilst on an expedition into Sioux country. The expedition was to establish the route of the Northern Pacific Railroad between Bismarck and Bozeman.

Camp at Yankton, Apr 12, 1873

You will not blame me, I am sure, for having allowed a day to slip by since my last without a letter, when I tell you that my desk with my furniture has been boxed all day awaiting our change of camp. I told you that the five companies under [Major] Tilford had arrived while I was writing. The same day I mailed the letter [Lieutenant Colonel George A.] Custer came with the remaining four troops. His arrival was the signal for an entire change of location, so that ever since, the whole command has been hard at work taking down tents and moving bag and baggage to the new site—about half a mile from our temporary location.

We are now regularly encamped—ten companies in all, and the regular routine of military discipline established. My tent is an admirable one and a model of comfort and neatness. Bed on one side, chest at the end, table and desk in the corner, washstand at foot of bed, trunk opposite and a bit of carpet on the ground to complete the picture of luxury. As I write the wind, which, it seems, never ceases here, shakes my habitation to its "foundations," and flares the candle in a highly unsatisfactory manner; but all its efforts to distort my equanimity are fruitless, on the principle that familiarity breeds contempt. The climate is fast making an aboriginal of me, both as regards complexion and health, so that I am not disposed to be captious with its eccentricities however annoying . . .

Camp Sturgis, Yankton, DA
May 6th, 1873

. . . The order was . . . sent around today for a start at 12 m. tomorrow. Our allowance of baggage is quite comfortable, much better than we had anticipated. Each officer is allowed to carry one medium trunk. This will give me ample room for all the necessaries and many comforts. I have packed my trunk with all my substantials and transferred all the superfluities to the chest. I am provided with everything I can think of necessary for my physical well being and with a small dictionary and my Shakespeare in the bottom of my trunk shall not suffer mentally. Dick rides in Capt. Yates' wagon and takes charge of the lunch together with my valise. There is a steamboat provided to carry forage, following on the river our march by land, and meeting us at different points whenever practicable. The ladies go on this boat together with the sick. Our first stopping place available for mail will be Fort Randall—four days' march. The condition of the roads between may however delay us several days.

Fort Rice DA
June 11, 1873

We arrived here the day before yesterday, eleven days from [Fort] Sully—and no mail between. The last week's marching had been fine and enjoyable—pleasant camps and short tramps. We met two Indian camps on the road, one at Grand River Agency, and another some forty or fifty miles from here, comprised of nearly a hundred lodges under Two Bears, a Yankton Sioux. We have had no trouble with any of these gentlemen but have had our fill of their society. Tawdry cavalcades of the rascals, mounted on their little ponies, decked in comical assortments of skins and rags, tin plates, feathers, neckties, beads, earrings, and stove pipe hats, have thronged our camp semi occasionally affording gratification to a mutual but quickly satisfied curiosity.

The Court Martial at Sully was the source of endless annoyance and trouble to all concerned. Custer undertook to bully and insult that body at the start, and, finding that his efforts at control were powerless, did everything in his power to hector and annoy its members. The court has made an indignant protest against his assumption, the which as recorder I have written out and will forward to Dept. Hqrs. On our arrival here we found all of the infantry already in camp and waiting. Stanley [was here] with his staff, and [so was] all our baggage which had been left behind at Yankton for shipment . . .

The infantry officers I have met have not impressed me favorably. They appear to belong to a very inferior class of society. There will be, however, very little necessity for association as the two corps will be quite isolated . . . The scientific corps has not arrived yet, but are expected tomorrow. They say Stanley has received more orders in regard to them than for all the rest of the expedition. Stanley seems to be very much liked and impressed me very favorably when I met him. Large, handsome and dignified. Since the establishment of the depot at the mouth of Powder River, by means of steamboat communication, our facilities for mail will be very much increased. Boats will make several trips from there in all probability—backwards and forwards and in addition, trains with scouts will be sent back occasionally.

The appearance of things here would seem to indicate a picnic on a grand scale. Three large steamboats lay at the wharf, soldiers, officers, Indians, scouts and guides throng about the post and keep up quite a metropolitan bustle and excitement. Two young English lords are to accompany us and have bought a wagon and team bodily to take them and their effects . . .

Your wishes in regard to accompanying the ladies up would speedily change into congratulations at having escaped their experience. Only today Mrs. Yates and others were saying that you had acted so wisely in remaining. They have all been more or less sick, cooped up in the small cabin of a rear wheeled boat, living on the most atrocious of boat fare for 34 days. During that time they have succeeded in discovering each other's failings with astonishing distinctness, and, from all I hear, have made the atmosphere pretty warm. Add to this the difficulty of officers communicating with the boat after a hard day's march—forced to go sometimes two or three miles to where she lay, through the woods, and returned late in the dark—losing thereby the best part of a much needed night's sleep, and there is but little remaining to make the trip desirable. Here the ladies are all adrift with the prospect of the command leaving in a few days. I never saw such confusion and uncertainty. No two of them think alike or seem to have any definite plan. They were all obliged to hustle off of the boat on its arrival, and seek accommodations on another whose stay is almost as uncertain as the first. Some talk of going back to Yankton and Sioux City, to St. Paul, to Indiana, and even to Canada . . .

Camp on Heart River DA
June 25th, 1873

Here we are sixty miles from Rice in a delightful camp with a day's rest before us. We have had a pleasant and interesting march out with a fair proportion of rain and storm, but still altogether delightful. We make an imposing show on these rolling prairies—1500 men, 250 teamsters, 40 scouts, 250 wagons, 800 horses, 600 head of cattle and 1500 mules; too imposing, in fact, for the Indians who have not as yet put in an appearance. The marches have been short and somewhat tedious, on account of the difficulty of moving so large and heavy a train. The average will not exceed 8 miles a day, although some days we have exceeded it largely and on others fallen very much below that mark. The weather, as I have said, has not been uniformly pleasant but then the storms, although terrible and severe while they last, are only of hours instead of days duration. The thunder and lightning I have never seen equalled for intensity and grandeur. Fortunately, we have been in camp, with one exception, before their commencement . . .

We find the country a perfect wilderness. Grass is the only vegetation with a few scattered trees along the creek and river bottoms. The prairie is broken by ravines and barren stony bluffs which cross and cut it in every direction. We have passed through hundreds of antelope that follow the column and trot curiously along its flanks. Hunters are out every day and keep our mess supplied with their meat which has become quite a drug on the market. The dogs catch the young and afford many an exciting chase. A very pretty young fawn came into my hands through their agency, which I brought into camp with the intention of raising. By evening, it was quite tame and docile, but the difficulties of finding proper nourishment and the want of means for its transportation induced me to let it go.

Camp on Yellowstone
July 21st, 1873

. . . We left Lincoln with 53 wagons heavily loaded and have been exactly twelve days in making the journey here—250 miles. Every morning saw us up at 3 o'clock and on the march by 5. Have averaged eleven hours in the saddle. Sometimes marched twelve and once it was fifteen. Our object was to reach Stanley as soon as possible and to accomplish this it was necessary to double up on his marches with a train as heavily loaded as his own. Continuous rains for the first week filled the creeks and ravines and rendered bridging and filling necessary every few miles. We expected to find Stanley encamped on the Little Missouri 140 miles from Lincoln waiting our arrival in case we did not reach him before. On the fourth day we rejoined [the] camp where we had left Custer and came suddenly on a small war party of 11 Sioux quite ignorant of our proximity. They were not long in the neighborhood, some business of a pressing and unexpected nature requiring their attention "over the hills and far away." This was on a small stream called the "Little Muddy" perhaps on your map. On the seventh day we began to approach what are called the "Mauvises Terres" or Bad Lands. We found a note on the trail left by Adjutant General informing us that Stanley had pushed on to the Yellowstone but had left a body of 100 infantry on the right bank of the Heart river near its source to await our arrival. This was good news as we had but ten days rations. The next day we crossed to the right bank of the Heart and began to keep a lookout for reinforcement. We marched all that day, however, without striking them and went into camp in a ravine by some rain pools. We had made about 24 miles and had ridden eleven hours and were well fatigued. Two hours before sunset four men were sent forward to find the infantry, if possible. They were to return, if unsuccessful, after ten or twelve miles. At dusk our pickets and one of the scouts reported a number of Indians on the horizon. This news made us anxious for the safety of the party sent forward to reconnoitre and I was accordingly ordered out with a detachment of 25 men to follow their trail and bring them back. This I did with some difficulty as the tremendous storm rendered it a very difficult task for two hours at a very rapid gait. I lost the trail several times and only recovered it again by the aid of the vivid and incessant lightning . . .

[Camp on the Musselshell River
August 19, 1873]

Dr. John Hensinger, veterinary surgeon, Seventh Cavalry, and Mr. Balaran, sutler, were [on August 4] the two victims to a want of caution that our long immunity from attack had engendered. They had left the train during the halt for the purpose of watering their horses, and on their way back skirting the foot of the bluffs in order to meet the column in its descent, quite unconscious of danger and the horrible fate awaiting them, were suddenly surprised by a party of three Sioux, who had secreted themselves in a ravine, and shot from behind with arrows.

General Custer in the morning had taken a squadron, A and B troops of the Seventh Cavalry, and moved rapidly ahead of the main body about four miles beyond the point at which this tragedy occurred. There, in a belt of woods, his escort had unsaddled, picketed their horses and were lying under the trees awaiting the arrival of the main body, when a shot from the pickets and their sudden appearance brought everyone to his feet. Quickly and quietly the horses were brought in and saddled, a dismounted detachment thrown out as skirmishers, while the remainder of the command moved in the direction of the attack. But three or four Indians were to be seen, galloping and gesticulating wildly in front of the column, which moved quickly forward at a trot. Hardly, however, had the flank arrived opposite a second belt of dense woods before a long line of Indians suddenly moved in regular orders from their midst straight to the attack. They were all in full war costume, mounted on stalwart little ponies, and armed, as are all we have seen, with the best of Henry rifles. As rapidly as possible the command was dismounted and formed in skirmish line in front of the horses, but not a moment too soon, as the enemy came whooping and screeching down upon it. A square volley in their teeth cooled their ardor, and sent them flying back to a respectful distance. For three hours the fight was kept up, the Indians maintaining a perfect skirmish line throughout, and evincing for them a very extraordinary control and discipline. After this desultory fighting had become tiresome, the cavalry mounted suddenly and dashed forward at a charge, scattering their wary antagonists, who were not prepared for such a demonstration, in every direction. Our casualties were one man and three horses wounded. The loss of the enemy, estimated from those seen to fall, must have been something in the vicinity of ten in all, and five ponies.

For the next three days nothing was seen of our friendly neighbors in person, but abundant evidence of their camps, and

the heavy trail of a retreating village, numbering, as our Indian
scouts told us, in the neighborhood of eighty lodges. Each day
General Custer, with two squadrons of cavalry, pushed on in
advance, following rapidly on the trail.

It was not, however, until the evening of August 8 that he
received orders from General Stanley to push on with the whole of
the available cavalry force, make forced night marches, and overtake the village, if possible . . .

At early dawn on the 10th our efforts to cross [the Tongue
River] commenced, and it was not until 4 in the afternoon that they
were reluctantly relinquished, after every expedient had been
resorted to in vain. The current was too swift and fierce for our
heavy cavalry. We therefore went into bivouac close to the river
bank to await the arrival of the main body, and slept that night as
only men in such condition can sleep. We hardly anticipated the
lively awakening that awaited us. Just at daylight our slumbers
were broken by a sharp volley of musketry from the opposite bank,
accompanied by shouts and yells that brought us all to our feet in
an instant. As far up the river as we could see, clouds of dust
announced the approach of our slippery foes, while the rattling
volleys from the opposite woods, and the "zip," "zip" of the balls
about our ears told us that there were a few evil disposed persons
close by.

For half an hour, while the balls flew high, we lay still without
replying, but when the occasional quiver of a wounded horse told
that the range was being acquired by them, the horses and men
were moved back from the river edge to the foot of the bluffs, and
there drawn up in line of battle to await developments. A detachment of sharpshooters was concealed in the woods, and soon sent
back a sharp reply to the thickening compliments from the other
side. Our scouts and the Indians were soon exchanging chaste
complimentary remarks in choice Sioux—such as: "We're coming
over to give you h—I;" "You'll see more Indians than you ever
saw before in your life," and "Shoot, you son of a dog" from ours.
Sure enough, over they came, as good as their word, above and
below us, and in twenty minutes our scouts came tumbling down
the bluffs head over heels, screeching; "Heap Indian come." Just at
this moment General Custer rode up to the line, followed by a
bright guidon, and made rapid disposition for the defense. Glad
were we that the moment of action had arrived, and that we were to
stand no longer quietly and grimly in line of battle to be shot at.
One platoon of the first squadron on the left was moved rapidly up
the bluffs, and thrown out in skirmish line on the summit, to hold

the extreme left. The remainder of the squadron followed as quickly as it could be deployed, together with one troop of the Fourth Squadron.

On they came as before, 500 or 600 in number, screaming and yelling as usual, right onto the line before they saw it. At the same moment the regimental band, which had been stationed in a ravine just in rear, struck up "Garry Owen." The men set up a responsive shout, and a rattling volley swept the whole line.

The fight was short and sharp just here, the Indians rolling back after the first fire and shooting from a safer distance. In twenty minutes the squadrons were mounted and ordered to charge. Our evil-disposed friends tarried no longer, but fled incontinently before the pursuing squadrons. We chased them eight miles and over the river, only returning when the last Indian had gotten beyond our reach.

No less than a thousand warriors had surrounded us, and we could see on the opposite bluffs the scattered remnants galloping wildly to and fro. Just at the conclusion of the fight the infantry came up, and two shells from the Rodman guns completed the discomfiture of our demoralized foes. Our loss was one killed, Private Tuttle, E Troop, Seventh Cavalry, and three wounded. Among the latter, Lieutenant [Charles] Braden, Seventh Cavalry, while gallantly holding the extreme left, the hottest portion of the line, was shot through the thigh, crushing the bone badly. Four horses were killed and eight or ten wounded, and deserve honorable mention, although noncombatants. Official estimates place the Indian loss at forty killed and wounded, and a large number of ponies.

BRITISH COLONIAL WARS
1839–1902

*The nineteenth century belonged to Britain. At home it was the
"workshop of the world"; abroad it built the greatest empire in
history. If it was a Victorian truth that "coloured" races needed
colonisation by Britain for their own benefit (making them, in
Kipling's words, "the white man's burden"), it was a Victorian
necessity that lands be conquered by Britain as markets for its goods.
Inevitably Britain's imperial plans did not accord with the wishes of
all "natives", while emerging powers resented British monopolies.
Consequently, Queen Victoria's reign, from 1838 to 1901, saw
Britain fight a string of wars in foreign lands: The Afghan Wars
(1839–42 and 1879); the Sikh Wars (1845–9); The Crimean War
(1854–6); The Indian Mutiny (1857); The War in China (1857–
60); The Zulu War (1879); The War in Burma (1885); the Boer
War (1899–1901). Militarily, the hallmark of these wars was their
tendency to initial blunder, their excessive cruelty, and their tendency to rely on the determination and courage of the British
footsoldier for their ultimate victory.*

Lieutenant T.W.E. Holdsworth, Queen's Regiment

Holdsworth writes home detailing his experiences in the British
storming of Kelat during the 1839–42 Afghan War.

Kotree, December 8th, 1839
. . . About three miles and a half from Kelat the fortress appeared
before us, frowning defiance. The sun had just burst out, and was
lighting the half-cultivated valley beneath us, interspersed with
fields, gardens, ruinous mosques; while Kelat was still in the shade
and seemed to maintain a dark and gloomy reserve; nor was the
effect diminished when a thin cloud of smoke was seen spouting
forth and curling over its battlements, followed, in a short interval,
by the report of a large gun, which came booming over the hills

towards us. "Hurrah! They have fired the first shot", was the exclamation of some of us, "and Kelat is prize-money!" . . .

We could only see the citadel, which was more commanding and difficult of access than that of Ghuzni. Nearer the fort we could observe the body of cavalry drawn up, under cover of the redoubts of the hills. Gen. Willshire now ordered one of the guns to open on the horsemen, to cover the movements of the advance companies, who were driving the enemy's matchlock-men before them. The third shot went slap in among them . . . The whole affair was the most exciting thing I ever experienced. We moved steadily on, the guns from the redoubts blazing at us as fast as they could load them, but only two shots struck near us. When our artillery unshipped one of their guns they exploded their powder, and retired in the greatest disorder . . .

Capt. Outram here rode up to us, and cried out: "On men, and take the gate before they can all get in." This acted like magic on the men. All order was lost, and we rushed madly down the hill on the flying enemy, more like hounds with the chase in view than disciplined soldiers. The consequence was, we were exposed to a most galling fire from the ramparts . . . The fugitives were too quick for us, and suddenly the cry was raised by our leading men, "The gate is shut". Unluckily a rush was made by the greatest part of the regiment who were so closely jammed that they could not move, exposed to the fire which the matchlock-men kept pouring in with utmost impunity. Had the artillery been less expedient in knocking down the gate, the greatest part of them would have been annihilated . . . Our men gave the general hurrah; and Gen. Willshire came up to us at his best pace, waving his hat, "Forward, Queen's", he sung out, "or the 17th will be in before you." On we rushed again for the gate as hard as we could . . .

However, on entering, we found matters not so easy as we expected. The streets were very narrow and so intricate that they formed a perfect labyrinth. The men, therefore, soon got scattered about and some, I am afraid, thought of loot more than of endeavouring to find a way to the citadel . . . In a short time we found ourselves in a large courtyard with Beloochees right under the windows of the citadel. These men cried out for "mercy"; but the soldiers recollecting the treachery that had been practised at Ghuzni were going to shoot the whole kit of them, when I suddenly received a shock, which made me think at the moment I was smashed to bits, by a ball from a ginjall, or native wallpiece. I was knocked senseless to the ground . . . When I came to myself I found myself coughing up globules of clotted blood at a great pace. I made a desperate effort, got on my legs, and soon found some of our men, who supported me until a dooly could be brought and I was soon on my way to the doctor.

In the meantime, there had been sharp fighting in the citadel. One party reached the place where Mehrab Khan, at the head of his chiefs who had joined his standard, was sitting with his sword drawn. The others seemed inclined to surrender, and raised the cry of "Aman!" but the Khan, springing on his feet, cried, "Aman, nag!" equivalent to "Mercy be d—d" and blew his match; but all in vain, as he immediately received about three shots . . . So fell Mehrab Khan, and died game, with his sword in his hand, in his own citadel . . .

At length a few survivors, being driven to their last stronghold at the very top of the citadel, surrendered; then one loud and general "hurrah!" proclaimed around that Kelat was ours . . . The loss was 140, about one in seven. My wounds continued doing very well; I caught a low fever and I have continued to grow better ever since.

Anon Officer, Coldstream Guards

The writer relates the Battle of Alma in the Crimean War.

Bivouac, River Alma, 21 September 1854

I hasten to write a few lines to tell you I am safe and sound, knowing how anxious you will be, after hearing that we have had an action with the Russians.

Accounts of the battle you will see in the papers, much better describing it than any I could give, as I could see nothing beyond what was going on in my own brigade. That you will see was in the thickest of it, as the returns of our casualties will prove, our loss being very severe. The march from Kamischli to Baljanik, where we bivouacked on the night of the 19th, and again from Baljanik to Alma, was the grandest spectacle I ever saw. The whole Army, French, English, and Turkish, advanced in battle array for that distance over a plain as smooth almost as a lawn, and with just sufficient undulation to shew one at times the whole force at a coup d'oeil. My division was on the left, and we were about three miles from the sea; the fleet, coasting along abreast of us, completed the picture.

At about 12 o'clock on the 20th, on crowning a ridge, we came all at once in sight of the Russian army, in an entrenched camp beyond the Alma, distant about three miles. Immediately we appeared they set fire to a village between us and them so as to mask their force by the smoke.

We continued advancing steadily, halting occasionally to rest the men, till half-past one, when the first shot was fired, and soon after the rattle of musketry told us that our rifle skirmishers were engaged. Our division then deployed into line, and we stood so for about twenty minutes, an occasional round shot rolling up to us, but so spent that one was able to step aside from it. Wounded men from the front soon began to be carried through our lines to the rear, and loose and wounded horses began to gallop about.

At last we were ordered to advance, which we did for about 300 yards nearer the batteries, and halted, and the men lay down. We were now well within range, and the round shot fell tolerably thick, an occasional shell bursting over our heads.

After standing steady for about twenty minutes, the light division (who were in line in front of us) advanced again, and we followed.

The Russians had put posts to mark the ranges, which they had got with great accuracy. We now advanced to within 200 yards of the river and 700 from the batteries, and halted under a low wall for five minutes, till we saw the light division over the river, when we continued our advance in support of them. On crossing the wall we came into vineyards, and here the cannonade was most terrific, the grape and canister falling around us like hail—the flash of each gun being instantly followed by the splash of grape among the tilled ground like a handful of gravel thrown into a pool.

On reaching the river, the fire from a large body of riflemen was added, but the men dashed through, up to their middle in water, and halted on the opposite side to reform their ranks, under shelter of a high bank. At this moment the light division had gained the intrenchment, and the British colour was planted in the fort; but, ammunition failing them, they were forced back.

The Scots Fusiliers were hurried on to support them before they had time to reform themselves, and the 23rd, retiring in some confusion upon them, threw them for a few minutes into utter disorder. The Russians, perceiving this, dashed out of the fort upon them, and a frightful struggle took place which ended in their total discomfiture.

For a minute or two the Scots Fusilier colours stood alone in the front, while General Bentinck rallied the men to them, their officers leading them on gallantly.

At this moment I rode off to the Coldstream, through whose ranks the light division had retired, leaving them the front line. They advanced up the hill splendidly, with the Highlanders on their left, and not a shot did they fire till within 150 or 200 yards from the intrenchments. A battery of 18 and 24 pounders was in position in our front, and a swarm of riflemen behind them. Fortunately the enemy's fire was much too high, passing close over our heads, the men who were killed being all hit on the crown of the head, and the Coldstream actually lost none. When we got about fifty yards from the intrenchment, the enemy turned tail, leaving us masters of the battery and the day.

As they retired they took all their guns except two, and a great many of their wounded. In spite of this the ground was covered with dead and dying, lying in heaps in every direction on what might be called the glacis, and inside the intrenchments they were so thick that one could hardly avoid riding over them; but the excitement of the victory stifled for the time all feeling of horror for such a scene, and it was not till this morning when I visited the battle-field, that I could at all realise the horrors which must be the price of such a day. Most fervently did I thank God, who had preserved me amidst such dangers. How I escaped seems to me the more marvellous the more I think of it. Though on horseback (on my old charger), my cocked-hat and clothes were sprinkled all over with blood.

The loss of the Brigade of Guards is very severe but the proportion of deaths to wounded is extraordinarily small. On calling the roll after the action, 312 rank and file and fifteen officers were discovered to be killed and wounded.

Besides there was my poor friend Horace Cust, who was struck by a round shot in crossing the river. He was aide-de-camp to General Bentinck, and we were watering our horses at the time when the shot struck his horse in the shoulder and smashed poor Cust's thigh. He died soon after the leg was amputated. Charles Baring, who has lost his arm (taken out of the socket) is the only other Coldstream officer hit. They only went into action with sixteen officers, less than half their complement.

We have been occupied the whole day in burying the dead. About 1000 were laid in the ditch of the fort, and the earthen parapet was then thrown back upon them. We find that the whole garrison of Sebastopol were before us, under Mentschikoff in person. His carriage has fallen into our hands, and in it a letter stating that Sebastopol could hold out a long time against us, but that there was a position at Alma which could hold out three weeks. We took it in three hours.

So convinced were they of the impossibility of our taking it that ladies were actually there as spectators, little expecting the review they were destined to be spectators of. We expect now to find no resistance whatever at the Katcha river, the whole Russian force having retired into Sebastopol. We always turn out at four o'clock in the morning, an hour before daybreak.

Lieutenant Richard Temple Godman,
5th Dragoon Guards

Temple Godman writes to his father, describing the charge of the British Heavy and Light Brigades against Russian cavalry at the Battle of Balaclava, during the Crimean War.

October 26, 1854

Yesterday the attack came off, and here I am, Thank God, safe and sound, though the loss of cavalry we have sustained is very severe . . . When we got the order to advance, the Greys and Inniskillings went first, then we came in support, the charge sounded and at them went the first line; Scarlett well in front. The enemy seemed quite astonished and drew into a walk and then a halt; as soon as they met, all I saw was swords in the air in every direction, the pistols going off, and everyone hacking away right and left. In a moment the Greys were surrounded and hemmed completely in; there they were fighting back to back in the middle, the great bearskin caps high above the enemy.

This was the work of a moment; as soon as we saw it, the 5th advanced and in they charged, yelling and shouting as hard as they could split, the row was tremendous, and for about five minutes neither would give way, and their column was so deep we could not cut through it. At length they turned and the whole ran as hard as they could pelt back up the hill, our men after them and cutting them down right and left. We pursued about 300 yards, and then called off with much difficulty, the gunners then opened on them, and gave them a fine peppering . . . The ground was covered with dead and dying men and horses, strewn with swords, broken and whole, trumpets, helmets, carbines . . . Lord Raglan who was looking down from a hill close by sent an A.D.C. to say "Well done the Heavy Brigade" . . .

Owing to a mistake in an order from Lord Raglan, the Light Cavalry then charged down the valley, under fire on each side, and a battery of, I believe, 20 guns in front. They drove all before them; took the guns, cut down the gunners and then retired but were perfectly annihilated by the cross-fire . . . It was a terrible sight to see them walking back one by one and the valley strewn with them—all for nothing . . .

Sergeant John Hopkins, Grenadier Company, 97th Regiment

Hopkins writes to his family during the siege of Sebastopol in the Crimean War.

Camp before Sebastopol
Christmas Day, 1854

My Dear Brother,
I am almost too vexed to write to you; for since I came from England I have had but two letters from you, and I think I have wrote about a dozen to you; but something tells me you are not to blame, so I am not vexed at all; but I hope this will find you in good health, in which I am sorry to say it does not leave me, for since I came to the Crimea I have been ill. I was attacked with diarrhoea almost as soon as I landed here. I continued to do my duty til I was a mere skeleton. We have trench duty, which, to a sick man, was indeed trying. I did not like to give in till forced to do so by weakness. The trenches are full three miles from our camp, and we have had continual rain every day. In going to the trenches we have to cross two ravines, which, in wet weather, are complete rivers. About three weeks ago I was for what is called the advanced works, in the day. It is situated about 200 yards from the Russian lines – a very dangerous post. We crossed the ravines; it was more than knee deep in water. It rained heavily all day, till about 4 o'clock in the evening. It was too deep in mud in the trenches to walk about. We had, therefore, to stand in the wet, with stones under our feet, leaning against the breastwork. I tried to amuse myself, firing at every moving object I could see in the Russian lines; but as evening came, I was beat up. I was not able to stand or walk; but, my dear Bob, I had many kind friends, and, amongst them is an officer. He

joined our company in Pentelouis; his name is Mr Dawes, a native of Bolton. He has shown a decided liking for me since he first knew me. Upon the day in question he was on duty with me; in the morning he gave me his arm to help me along. In the evening, I told him it would be midnight before I got to camp; he took my rifle from me, slung it on his back, and told me to do my best. The rain was succeeded by a heavy fog. I lost my way home, and it was midnight before I got to camp. I was wet through. I had eaten nothing for 24 hours; all I took was my grog, a gill of rum. I laid down in my tent and the next morning was carried to hospital, more dead than alive. Every officer in the regiment came to see me, for on coming here I was as strong a man as stood in the regiment, and now I was like a child; the once stout and firm limbs were gone; my big broad face was completely hid in the hair which grows on it, for I have not shaved this six months, to speak the truth. I was a fright. I was in hospital only four days; the diarrhoea was gone, and weakness only remained. The doctors and all about me showed me the greatest kindness. I was discharged from hospital, but was to do no duty till strong. The officer, Mr Dawes, took me to his tent; he supplied me with every luxury that a well-filled purse could supply, and told me to make free with anything that was in his tent. We are served out with coffee in its green state, and we have to roast and grind it, that is, to pound it in a bag between two mallets. When done, it is bad. The officer, therefore, gave me what tea I could use, a glass of whiskey punch twice per day, cheese, rice, fresh bread, and, if I could get anything for money, he would give me his purse to satisfy myself. My dear brother, what would I not face by the side of such an officer? Would I shrink from death? Perish the idea! I am now recovering fast, and should this arm recover its former strength before the attack on Sebastopol, should he want its aid, how freely shall it be extended towards him. I had many presents from other officers, and soon, my dear Bob, shall the light and merry song of happy Jack be heard in camp again. My dear brother, the duty is very hard; we are in the trenches every other night; sometimes two or three nights after one another. I have exchanged many shots with the Russians, though I have not been exactly in an engagement, and scarcely a day passes but we have someone wounded. The day I mentioned before, we had one shot dead and three wounded. At night we find sentries in advance of those works. I was on one night, very moonlight. All the sentries have a wall to cover them; but forgetting myself, I walked from my cover, when about a dozen of what they call needle-balls whizzed past my ear. I soon returned to my cover, nor left it again until relieved. In rear of those works we have what they call the Cow Horn Battery, also a Lancaster Battery, in fact we have batteries surrounding this part of the town; and if you were to walk from our camp to Balaclava you would think there were English and French troops enough to eat Sebastopol if it were pudding. On this most remarkable of all pudding-eating days, there is little of it here; but I hope you did not forget my health in brown stout, for I drank yours in muddy water, for it was all I could get, and little of that, for I have not washed my shirt since I came here, and never had my clothes off except for an hour during the day, for a rather disgusting purpose, which you may easily guess, when I have been more than a month with my clothes on; but it is common here even with officers. The reason we do not attack Sebastopol is, we are making a battery to destroy shipping which, when finished, I think will be the signal for attack. My dear Bob, I have no more paper, and to obtain more I should have to walk seven miles and pay 6d for a sheet and envelope, and 6d is what I have not seen since my arrival here. I enclose a note for James. We have lost half the draft they sent us, also a great number of old hands. Give my kind love to all at home. Wishing soon to hear from you, I remain my dear brother, yours ever, with my usual prayer of God bless you all.

Camp before Sebastopol
16 September, 1855

My Dear Brother

Most likely before this reaches you you have heard both of the downfall of Sebastopol and of my safety, as I wrote to mother two days after the action, and I desired her to send the letter to you after reading it; but I merely stated in that that I had come off all right, so I dare say a few particulars will be welcome. Our regiment has suffered very much. You must know it was one of those regiments that had never been engaged since it was re-organised in 1822; but still it was a regiment that was always praised for appearance, steadiness, and cleanliness by all generals who ever saw us; and as we always thought ourselves second to none, we were determined, if ever an opportunity occurred, to prove it. On the morning of the 8th we paraded, as we thought to see if we were ready – that is, with two days rations, &c. we thought it was only a parade; but alas, my dear brother, it was the last for many. Volunteers for the first storming, or ladder party, were ordered to the front. I need not to tell you, I suppose, that I was amongst

the those. So well was the secret kept, we knew not of the attack till
then. We were marched to the trenches, and our party occupied a
sap leading in an oblique direction from our advanced trench to the
Russian battery known as Redan. The regiment was to storm along
with the 3rd, 90th and 41st, all of which occupied the advanced
trench. In fact all the army was in position by nine o'clock; nor did
the enemy appear to know or suspect anything extra; I suppose he
thought we should not have the audacity to attack his strongholds
in the noonday. But no sooner had the sun reached the meridian
than the tricoloured flag of France appeared over the Mamelon,
and with a cheer the French began to pour into the mightly
Malakoff, an overwhelming force taking the Russians completely
by surprise; and in less time than I have taken to relate it the eagle
was planted on the parapet which was the signal for our attack. Its
appearance was enough. The word 'Forward' was indeed given,
but not needed. But the attack of the French had put the Russians
on the alert, and no sooner did we show ourselves than they began
to pour on us their deadly charges of grape; in fact it was a
complete storm. However, we carried our ladders in spite of all,
and planted them in the ditch, which was about 14 feet deep on our
side; but on the Russian side it could not be less than 20, as it ran
up to the parapet. The side was composed of a sandy sort of
substance, and it was with difficulty we could keep our feet, even
when we had gained it; but soon we made an entrance, and then
came the work. For a considerable time it was bayonet work on
both sides and the Russians being more than treble our number, it
was for a time doubtful which side would carry it. At last, with a
cheer and a rush we made them give way; and then came a battle of
musketry. In this they had the advantage, for the works of the
Redan afforded them every shelter, and the force from the
Malakhoff joining those in the Redan, likewise troops from the
town, made it impossible for us to keep it. We were not supported
as we ought to have been, or we should not have lost so many. We
kept our ground, and as we were first in we were the last to leave,
and when we did we had not half the number of the 97th left
uninjured. But now to myself. As I was a volunteer I kept my place
amongst the foremost, and on leaving the battery I turned round
on the parapet, with the butt of a broken firelock, my only weapon
having had it smashed in my hand, the blood of a slight wound in
the forehead trickling down my face. I did my best, but I got
knocked off my position, backwards, and fell stunned into the
ditch, and it was miracle how I escaped falling upon a dozen of our
bayonets, belonging to men who had got in, and for want of a good

spirit could not get out; but, however, I got out, and without the aid of a scaling ladder, after two hours' hard fighting against a superior force. Shortly after we gained the trench. The conduct of the regiment was the admiration of everyone, particularly the general of the division and his staff. It is impossible for me to convey to you my feeling upon being ordered home – I mean to camp – to find we had lost the flower of the regiment. As for myself, I was not much hurt, though I have not been able to do any duty since. In the action we had our colonel, major, volunteer for the ladder party, and adjutant killed; one captain killed, three captains wounded, four lieutenants wounded; but tell the number of non-commissioned officers and privates I cannot. However, it is more than those who escaped can do to attend upon the wounded. A few nights before this we were attacked by a large force of the enemy's picket, and had one officer killed, two wounded and 18 non-commissioned officers and privates killed and wounded; but we won a rifle pit from them; so you see, my dear brother, we are but a mere skeleton. During the night of the 8th the Russians blew up, burnt and destroyed all they could, sank the ships, and fled to the north side, where they have taken up position. Active measures are in preparation for them, but what we are to do is doubtful. Strange reports are current that we are to winter in England (our regiment), and others at Malta; but it is my opinion we shall winter in Sebastopol. I have had the pleasure of being in town since it was taken, but found it the ruins of a once grand city. I have not been able to get much of a trophy, through not being able to move about for a few days after its downfall; but anyhow the trophy I am anxious to bring you is my own head, and I have not the least doubt that will please you best. In Sebastopol there was a large bell, that often brought us in fancy to the days of childhood. Now, the shipping was an eyesore – the bell was an eyesore. Some time ago, whilst in the trenches, I wrote some lines on this bell, which I send you, though I do not think them finished, as the downfall of Sebastopol interrupted it. However, I have got a piece of the said bell, which was brought down by a shot from our battery. I could get firelocks and swords, but if we took the field I could not carry them.

THE SEBASTOPOL BELL

When night's cloudy mantle around us is spread,
And the bright silver moon its radiance shed
We have watched, we have wept for comrades that fell
Whilst listening to the sound of the Sebastopol bell;

And often with limbs all benumb'd with the cold,
And fainting with hunger the moments have told,
Whilst thinking each sound was our own death knell,
As 'twas borne on the breeze from Sebastopol bell.
Again, when the rain in torrents did pour,
And darkness hid us from each rampart and tower,
We have heard from our foe a fearful yell,
Mingling strangely with the sounds of Sebastopol bell.
The column after column of Russians advance,
But are met by the warriors of England and France;
Whilst the honour of their homes makes each bosom swell,
As they fight mid the sounds of Sebastopol bell.
Then back to the batteries the Russians fly,
And leave their wounded men to die;
And whilst their rage they try to quell,
There's a dismal sound from Sebastopol bell.
But the winter it passed and summer came,
And still the bell tolled on the same,
As Russians swore they would dearly sell,
The spot where tolled that dismal bell.
But on we toiled, with pick and spade,
And miles of sap and trenches made;
Through rock, ravine and mossy dell,
We slowly neared Sebastopol bell.

My dear brother, if you like you may finish this; but give me love
to all at home. God bless you.

Lieutenant Coghill, British Army

Coghill writes home describing his part in the siege of Delhi, held
by sepoy rebels during the 1857 Indian Mutiny against British
rule.

. . . I took a bit of pistol bullet in my mouth and with a devil's yell
rushed from under cover, knowing that the quicker the rush the
nearer the enemy and the earlier the revenge. The musketry and
jingalls poured in like rain and men kept falling on every side of
me, but I thought my life charmed and they could not touch me.
The groans and execrations of the wounded and dying, cursing

their fate at being left outside and not being able to revenge themselves, was pitiable in the extreme. They rolled and writhed in agony . . . I felt like a drunken man. I just remember putting my sword back and seizing the ladders and throwing them down the ditch. They were over 8 ft. long and the ditch we found 20 ft. deep. In the excitement we just dropped down and then rushed up. The brutes fought till we regularly cut and hacked our way through them with sword and bayonet. Unfortunately the first thing my sword struck in was the body of a colour sergeant of mine who was shot and fell onto it. But the next moment I was skivering through the Pandy and then another. All orders and formation was over and we cut and hacked wherever we could. I never thought of drawing my pistol but poked, thrust and hacked till my arm was tired.

Richard Stevens, Natal Mounted Police

Formerly of the 10th Essex Rifles, Stevens left England to join the Natal Mounted Police. He was one of four members of the unit to survive the 20,000-strong Zulu attack on British forces (numbering 1600) at Isandhlwana, on 22 January, in the 1879 Zulu War.

Helpmakaar, 27 January 1879

I am almost afraid to tell you all the dreadful news I know, but I think it is better to let you know all. I will commence from the day of our entrance into Zululand. It took two or three days for all of our column to cross over the river. There was not a Zulu to be seen for some distance. Patrolling parties were sent out, and they came back with a lot of cattle, and said there were not any niggers to be seen. We pitched camp over the river, and stayed there some time. On Sunday, 12 January the outposts reported the enemy in great force at the back of the hill in the distance. We all turned out, and went to the hill, but could only see a few of them. We saw them following us. We did not think they meant to do anything, so we went right close to them, and when we were about 100 yards off they fired on us. We all dismounted, and let them have it. They hid away in the stones; we turned them out and killed most of them. That's the greater part of that affair.

I must go on to the most dreadful case. We were ordered to move the camp further up into the country, so we went ten or twelve miles and pitched camp again. The next day patrolling parties—in fact, the greater part of the camp—went out. I could not go; my horse was sick. A message came in that they had seen the enemy, and were going to be out all night, so we sent biscuits and great-coats out to them. The next morning our camp outposts came and reported the enemy in sight again. We had only about 600 men in camp altogether. Well, we all formed up ready for action, and at that time seven or eight Zulus came in and gave up their arms, and the Colonel let them go, and soon after that we saw the hill black with them coming on in swarms. They were estimated at 20,000.

We went out and held a ditch as long as possible, until we were outnumbered. The order was given to get into camp. We got there, and I went all over the place looking for a gun, but could not get one; my revolver was broken. I stopped in camp as long as possible, and saw one of the most horrid sights that I ever wish to see. The Zulus were in the camp ripping our men up, and also the tents and everything they came across, with their assegais. They were not content with killing, but were ripping the men up afterwards. Never has such a disaster happened to the English Army. There were no means of sending to the General, who was out of the camp. Well now, about myself. I got out of camp somehow, I don't know how, and went through awful places to get to the Drift, where my horse was taken away from under me, and I was as nearly drowned as could be. I just happened to catch hold of another horse's tail, which pulled me through. Thus we came on to this place and threw up a fortification, and here I am, thanks to the Almighty, all safe as yet, and I hope to see you all again. I have not told you all of it, as I have not time or paper. I will write again the first opportunity. I do not think the people of Natal will let us cross the border again. There were 537 of the 24th Regiment killed in camp, and twenty-six of us, and several others, so you can imagine what it was. The Zulus have all our waggons, with stores and ammunition. There will be an awful row at home about this.

Private William Meredith, 24th Regiment

Meredith writes to his brother and sister in Pontypool, Wales, in the aftermath of Isandhlwana.

n.d.

I write you these few lines in hopes that you are in good health, as it leaves me at present, thank God, considering we had our second fight, in which we got defeated. At our first fight we gained the day, and took a good many head of cattle. But we are properly defeated now; so we cannot go any further now till we get more troops from England, we lost so many men at the last battle. We lost 500 men from the 1st Battalion and 184 from the 2nd. The second is the regiment that I am in, so don't make a mistake. These are Pontypool boys that got killed at the battle, Alf Farr, Dick Treverton, and Charley Long. I expect you will see more of it in the papers, but they generally print them wrong out here, and so they will at home. I could describe the battlefield to you, but the sooner I get it off my mind the better. It was a pity to see about 800 white men lying on the field cut up to pieces and stripped naked. Even the little boys that we had in the band, they were hung up on hooks and opened like sheep. It was a pitiful sight. We had to retire, and make the best of our way to where we could get ammunition. Please let me know, have you sent more than one letter?

Private Henry Moses, 24th Regiment

Moses writes to his family about Isandhlwana.

I take the pleasure of writing these few lines to you, hoping to find you well, as I am, so far. I know what soldiering is now. We have marched 200 miles and haven't had a night's sleep this month. We are in fear every night, and have had to fight the Zulus, who came on us and killed 800 of our men. I wish I was back in England again, for I should never leave. It is sad times here, and we are on the watch every night with our belts buckled on and our rifles by our side. It is nothing but mountains here; all biscuits to eat. Dear father, and sisters, and brothers, goodbye. We may never meet again. I repent the day that I took the shilling. I have not seen a bed since I left England. We have only one blanket, and are out every night in the rain—no shelter. Would send you a letter before but have had no time; and now, you that are at home stay at home. Good-bye, if we never meet again, and may God be with you. Give my kind love to all friends; and how is Billy and Tim?

Trooper Harry Lugg, Natal Mounted Police

Lugg writes home recounting the battle of Rorke's Drift, when 150 soldiers and patients at the hospital there were besieged by

4000 Zulus. The battle took place on the same day as the massacre at Isandhlwana.

January 1879

I know you were surprised to hear from Fred that I had been at Rorke's Drift. I should have written you the same morning I wrote to Fred, but I could only find an old envelope and a small piece of paper, and then only a piece of pencil to write with. I shall not profess to give you an exact account of the fight, but will give just the heads. It must have been about two forty p.m. when a carbineer rode into the little yard, without boots, tunic, or arms, and leading a spare horse. All we could glean from his excited remarks was, "Everyone killed in camp, and 4,000 Kaffirs on their way to take the mission station" (or rather, hospital)—not pleasant tidings for a hundred men, you may be sure. When he came to himself a bit he said, "You will all be murdered and cut to pieces," and the only answer he received was, "We will fight for it, and if we have to die we will die like Britishers."

All those who were able began to throw up sacks and knock loop-holes out with pickaxes, and otherwise make preparations to receive them. We had some 2,000 Native Contingent there on a mountain, and occupying the krantzes and caves. Noble savages! As soon as they heard the Zulus were to attack us they made a great noise, had a big dance, clashing their assegais against their shields, and otherwise showed their war-like spirit. Now I must describe the fort. It consisted of two small houses, one used as a store and the other as a hospital and mission station. These houses were about 40 yards apart, and our ramparts were composed of mealies three sacks high, and running from the corners of one house to the corners of the other, but the one great danger being thatched roofs to both. There were two missionaries (Swedish) living in the hospital. They were absent for some twenty minutes, out for a ride, and no one could help laughing at their gesticulations when they came back on seeing the best parlour paper being pulled down and loop-holes being knocked out, while splendid furniture was scattered about the rooms. His first question was, in broken English, "Vot is dish?" Someone replied that the Zulus were almost on us, upon which he bolted, saying, "Mein Gott, mein wife and mein children at Umsinga! Oh, mein Gott!"

In the meantime a mounted infantryman and two of our men, Shannon and Doig, came in excited and breathless. Upon my asking, "What is it, is it true?" Doig replied, "You will all be murdered," and rode off with his comrade. Consolatory, certainly, but nothing remains but to fight, and that we will do to the bitter end. A man named Hall, of Natal Mounted Police, rode out to see if he could see anything of them, and on going about 1,000 yards out he could see them just a mile off, as he described it, "as black as hell and as thick as grass". "Stay operations and fall in!" My carbine was broken, or rather the stock bent. I found a piece of rein, tied it up, and fell in with the soldiers. I thought, if I can get somewhere to sit down and pop away I shall be all right, because my knees were much swollen. I was told off in my turn to take a loop-hole, and defend the roof from fire. At about three thirty they came on, first in sections of fours, then opened out in skirmishing order. Up came their reserve, and then they were on us. The place seemed alive with them. No orders were given, every man to act as he thought proper. I had the satisfaction of seeing the first I fired at roll over at 350, and then my nerves were as steady as a rock. I made sure almost before I pulled the trigger. There was some of the best shooting at 450 yards that I have ever seen.

Just before dark we had beaten them off with great losses, and only a few casualties on our side, two killed, and one wounded. One of our fellows named Hunter, also ill with rheumatism, was assegaied in the kidneys and five wounds in the chest. Before it got really dark the fiends lit the hospital thatch, which being very closely packed did not burn well. At about ten they came on in tremendous force, sweeping the fellows before them and causing them to retreat to the store. But Providence favoured us. The thatch roof burst out in flames, and made it as light as day, and before they had time to retreat we were pouring bullets into them like hail. We could see them falling in scores. Then you could hear suppressed British cheers. They kept up the attack all night with no better luck. We knocked them down as fast as they came. At five a.m., 23 January, the last shot was fired, and the last nigger killed; he had a torch tied on his assegai and was in the act of throwing it into the storehouse thatch, but he was "sold". The column came to our relief about five thirty and real British cheers went up, I can tell you. When the major [Dartnell] saw me he said, "I never thought of seeing you alive again, my boy." The tears were standing in his eyes. He said, "We saw the fire last night, and thought you were all murdered." Thank God, it is not so, I have sustained no damage beyond the loss of everything (except letters) and a little weakness of the eyes, I suppose from peering out of the loop-hole all night, and the constant straining of the eyesight.

Private Ellis Edwards, 24th Regiment

Edwards writes to his family in Wales about the British victory at Ulundi, the final battle of the 1879 Zulu War.

I received your kind letter and the *Genedl*, with much joy, and was very glad to know that you were all quite well, as I am at present, thanks be to God. I must tell you that you need not put a sixpenny stamp on my letters, as a penny one will do. I wish to express my opinion of the great battle which we had on the 4th day of July whilst taking the capital of Zululand. The scene was horrible. The fight lasted for one hour and ten minutes and was extremely hard. The strength of the enemy was 25,000 whilst our strength was only 4,500. After hard fighting we repulsed the enemy with the loss of 3,000 killed and 500 wounded; our loss was ten killed and forty wounded. I can assure you that the Zulus are a lot of fearless men. They poured upon us like a number of lions. The burning of Ulundi—their main support—was the greatest fire I ever saw. It continued burning for four days. I am very much pleased to tell you that I really think the war is close at an end now. We captured 800 head of cattle. I am very sorry to tell you that it is rumoured in this camp that we are going to India after this affair is settled. At the same time I hope it is wrong as we have had plenty of foreign climates.

I can assure you that the hardships which I have gone through are beyond measure. I have got to wash all my clothes and bake the bread which we eat. We have to march fourteen miles a day and, after arriving in a strange camp, we have to dig trenches before we get any food. If this regiment does not go to India I shall be at home by Christmas. Dear father, I hope that you will send me a newspaper, and send me all the particular news about home. I am very sorry to tell you of the sad misfortune which befell the young Prince Napoleon whilst scouting out in the wilds of Zululand. After the Zulus had killed him they stabbed him in fourteen different places. I was one of the men who removed his body in the van in order to send it home to England. It is a dreadful sight to see a lot of naked savages pouring down in such masses as they come in. I have plenty of news to send you, but I haven't got any time at present. It is very hard to get any paper or stamps in this part of the world. I have been forced to steal out of the way every time I want to write, because we haven't got one moment as we can call our own. I have very much pleasure to tell you that we have a divine service every Sunday out on the wild mountains of Africa.

Should I be killed in this place, my friend will write home and let
you know. I gave him my address in case of something should
happen to me, so that you can claim my money. He will give you
the full description how to get them. At the same time, I trust my
Almighty Maker will protect me. Wood is very scarce here at
present. We cook our food with dried cow dung. Please give my
address to my sister Jane, and also my best respect to all enquiring
friends and accept the same yourself. Don't forget to remember me
to Esther and Sarah Roberts, and my cousins from Abernant.
Hefyd cofiwch fi at Edwin fy mrawd am bewythr Evan.

Percy Marling, Mounted Infantry

Marling writes to his father describing the campaign against
Madhist forces in the Sudan.

On board steamer on the Nile near Gubat, 8 miles the Khartoum side
of Shendy, 90 miles from Khartoum January 28, 1885,
Tuesday, 11 a.m

My dearest Father,
I hope the two letters I sent off three days ago to tell you of my
safety will have reached you. I also sent you a telegram but as it had
to go nearly 200 miles by camel first, the odds are rather against
your getting it. We had an awful week of it, three fights in five
days, the first two desperate ones, the last quite nasty enough for
the most bloodthirsty amongst us. Out of a total of 1,700 that left
Gakdul we have lost 305 killed and wounded. as I told you we got
near Abu Klea wells about 1 p.m. on Friday, January 16th and
found the niggers in force about 56 miles the Gakdul side of the
wells. We made a *zareba* and encamped for that night, and were
shot at the whole night through, so with that and constant alarm
and having to stand to our arms for two hours before dawn you
may imagine we get precious little sleep; three men, some horses
and several were hit.
    Just as we were trying to get a little breakfast the order came to
move off, poor Gough our CO was hit in the head, fortunately by a
spent bullet. We advanced for about 1½ miles in square, the enemy
slowly retreating in front of us with a lot of flags, and we could see
another large force move to our left but out of shot. All the hills
round were lined with their sharpshooters who gave us a lot of
trouble. A message came in from our scouts to say that the niggers

had all gone, we could only see their flags sticking as we thought in the ground, when suddenly as though out of the ground about 3,000 niggers jumped up and rushed on the square. Our skirmishers prevented us firing at first, and they only got back to the square about 250 yards in front of the niggers, who came on to the left front where the MI [Mounted Infantry] were, but we gave them such a warm reception that they wheeled off to where the heavy cavalry stood. These were very unsteady and fired wildly, and when the niggers came close up they gave, and the niggers broke into the square, right on to the rear rank of the front face.

I had to turn my rear rank about, so that our men were fighting back to back, shooting in front and sticking behind. For about 10 minutes it was touch and go, but we beat them off and every nigger who got inside was killed. Our loss was very heavy, 9 officers and 66 men killed, 9 officers and 72 men wounded. I was all but shot by one of our sergeants who put his rifle over my shoulder and fired bang off close to my right ear. By the time we got the square reformed it was 3 p.m., when we advanced. I was sent out in front in command of the skirmishers. Poor old Moses, my pony, was shot dead under the general at the very beginning.

We pushed on another four miles and got to the wells of Abu Klea just as sunset. They were just a collection of about 20 holes (some of them choked up) in the sand, from about 8 to 20 feet deep, with about a foot of the dirtiest, filthiest water at the bottom. I should think I drank a bucket of it all the same. One's work for the day was not over yet, as at 8 p.m. I had to start back with 300 men to bring up our 8,000 camels, stores, wounded, etc., from the *zerba* six miles back. I don't think I ever felt so dead beat, we had had nothing to eat all day, and next to no sleep the night before. We got back to the *zareba* about midnight and I got a mouthful of grub and cup of tea, and started to load up. The men were at it all night and we started back for the wells about 7 a.m., each man leading three camels behind his own, and the native drivers about 10 each, besides this we had some wounded.

The column was about a mile long with an advance guard the same, if only 100 niggers had come they would have played Old Harry with the lot of us. I never knew such a long 6 miles. We repassed the battlefield on our right, where our dead were still lying unburied, and came across a lot of wounded niggers whom we shot at once. I got some breakfast and lunch, and all started again at 3.30 p.m for the Nile, leaving 100 of the 35th Regiment to hold the wells and protect our wounded. We had to leave all our dead on the field, amongst them old Burnaby, who was killed trying to rally the heavies. Some of the wounds were ghastly, men literally nearly cut to ribbons. We marched the whole night without intermission till 9 a.m. the following morning, one of the worst nights I ever had, I was continually falling asleep on my camel. Everything got mixed up, commissariat, mounted infantry, artillery, Guards and Marines, and the whole time of the rearguard was occupied in picking up men who had fallen off their camels asleep. One man in the Guards was lost altogether and strayed into Metemmeh and was killed.

Our way was through a lot of dense scrub which made it worse. I should think that night march we lost nearly 800 camels. Morning found us about five miles from the river, with dense masses of the enemy all along our front and flanks, and our supply of water running short. We made a laager with all the camels tied down in the centre, and a small parapet of the saddles and biscuit boxes outside. The niggers started shooting at once and hit no end of our men. I had three of my own men hit in a very short time, one a Lance-Corporal, Howard by name, almost as I was speaking to him, and the other two (one is since dead) just in front of me. Poor Herbert Stewart, the General, was badly wounded in the groin about midday, I went up to say good-bye to him and he shook hands and wished me luck, but he evidently thought it was nearly all up. Poor Sankey Herbert, his private secretary, was shot dead too, also Cameron the correspondent.

However I was so utterly tired out that in spite of the firing I lay down behind a camel and fell fast asleep for nearly an hour. About 2 p.m. we got the welcome order to form up outside in square to force our way to the water. It was a regular forlorn hope but our only chance. We moved off, some 1,300 men with about 20 camels in the centre. We marched oh so slowly, constantly moving to the right or left to get open ground and stopping altogether to keep the square together. I should think we took two hours to do as many miles. All this time the niggers were potting at us as hard as ever. The Guards, and Marines formed the front force, and the Mounted Infantry the left. Every minute the firing was getting hotter and hotter, and our men were falling fast every second. Hore and I were together in the left-front corner when a bullet came right between us and hit a marine in front of us in the head, killing him dead.

At last, just as it was getting sunset, the niggers charged in two columns. I don't think I ever felt so glad as when I saw their flags appear over the crest of the hill, bearing down on us. They came straight on to our left face and left front, but not one of them got within 40 yards of the square. It was now we began to feel the want of a general, as Sir Charles Wilson, RE, who was the senior officer, knows nothing of drill and is besides an awful old woman, and Boscawen, a Lieut.-Colonel in the Guards, though a very good fellow has very little experience and was utterly unfit to take the command, in what really was a most difficult and dangerous position. After we had repulsed the niggers he actually wanted to march the front face of the square away to water in the river two miles off, and the other three sides to go back to the *zareba*, although the enemy's cavalry were threatening us some 500 yards to the rear. The front face had actually marched off 100 yards from the remainder, but everyone shouted 'Halt', and Johnny Campbell went and expostulated with old Wilson, and used such awful language that it was stopped and we all went on together.

I shall never forget when we got to the top of a slight rise and saw the Nile glistening below us in the dim moonlight, we reached it about 8 o'clock. I had such a drink of muddy water, ate a small piece of bully and biscuit, and as soon as the square sentries were arranged fell asleep. Our wounded had an awfully bad time of it, most of them lying on the ground without any covering at all. The doctors did all the could, but of course they had next to no appliances with them. I woke about 1 a.m. when there was a bit of an alarm, bitterly cold with my teeth chattering so I could hardly speak. Sewell, our adjutant, most kindly lent me one of his blankets, and three of us (Hore, Payne, and myself) all got under it and crouched close up to one another for warmth.

Up at daybreak and occupied a village on high ground about 4 miles from Metemmeh, there we left our wounded and 100 men of the Sussex Regiment, and started back to the *zareba* to fetch the rest of our wounded and all the camels; on our way we saw a lot of niggers above Metemmeh, and had a good deal of shooting at them. We got to the *zareba*, about noon and found to our great relief that it was alright. Poor fellows, they gave us such a cheer when we arrived. We started back in square with the general and Hon Crutchley of the Guards on stretchers in the centre, and all the camels in a bunch on our right rear. However the enemy did not venture to attack us and we got back to our village just before dark, and started to water the camels at once. They had been 8 days without water and nearly 4 without food, and in that time had marched close on 80 miles carrying heavy loads.

That night we got our first square meal for I don't know how long, and I had a bit of a wash, the first time I had touche water since we left Gakdul nearly a week before, except when four of us sponged our faces over at Abu Klea, out of the lid of my canteen, which I gave to my camel to drink afterwards. Reveille at 4 a.m. and paraded in the dark to attack Metemmeh but found it too strong, all the houses loopholed and full of sharpshoters and two big guns. The whole business too was disgracefully mismanaged, so we had to give it up with a loss on our side of one killed and 11 wounded. We have only three small guns with us and next to no ammunition for them, and one Gatling which is of course no good for bombarding.

Whilst we were in front of Metemmeh four of Gordon's steamers appeared most opportunely, they had been waiting near an island some little way off for five months, expecting us, and hearing the firing came down. We got back to our village and moved down here to be close to the water. That night I was on outlying picquet so had a pretty wakeful night of it, it was bitterly cold too. Next day we were occupied in entrenching ourselves, and in the evening I had a bathe, not at all before I wanted it, and shaved off my nine days' beard. You would scarely have recognized me, I was such a dirty-looking scarecrow. Next day I was on fatigue from 6 a.m. till one, but was so seedy I had to lie down about noon. At dark we sent back a convoy to Gakdul of 1,000 camels, with about 300 men, with which I was to have gone but the doctor said I was to remain here; I could hardly stand, I had such frightful pains in my stomach, our medic said I had probably got a lot of mud and sand in my tum-tum caused by the bad water, and dosed me accordingly. However I am quite fit again now.

We have heard nothing of the convoy since it left over a week ago, and in fact have not had any communications with the outer world since we left Korti three weeks ago. As to what is going on four miles anywhere away from this we are as ignorant as unborn babes, our last newspaper is nearly two months old, I think December 3rd is the last one we have. At present we are sitting watching the niggers in Metemmeh just like two cats. Two of Gordon's steamers have gone back to Metemmeh and Sir Charles Wilson with them and 20 men of the Sussex Regiment. Now that poor Stewart is wounded we want a lead badly, I only wish Wolseley or Buller were up here. Don't imagine this has been written all at once, I began two days ago and go on with it at odd times whenever I have a moment to spare.

At present I am writing by moonlight; you can easily read print by it, it is so clear. There will be very few things soon I shan't have turned my hadn to, I am in charge of one of Gordon's steamers and eight boats we have captured from the niggers, besides 150 of

Gordon's troops, Bashibazouks, Turks and Egyptians, about the most finished collection of scoundrels I have seen. I'm going to bed now, save the mark, on the ground five yards from the water, *sub Jove frigido*, so good night, I can hear the tom-toms still going in Metemmeh.

Lieutenant Frank Isherwood, British Army

Isherwood served with General Sir Redvers Buller in the attack on Colenso (held by Boer commandos) during the Boer War, 1899–1902. He writes to his fiancée Kathleen.

Venter's Spruit, January 22nd 1900

A letter written actually under fire . . . We had a terribly long morning of waiting, from 3.30 a.m. to about 2 o'clock, under a burning sun and then we moved forward and got it pretty hot, 77 killed and wounded. You will of course want to know, was one frightened; personally as long as I was moving and under the excitement of getting the men together, I wasn't in the very least. One had a most "supporting feeling", as you say, of heroism, but since then we moved on to this valley where we have sat for two days doing nothing and every now and then having shells pitched into us. You can't imagine anything so demoralizing. The awful sinking at one's stomach pit when you hear the nasty buzz, followed by a plomp and burst. Then there are nasty pieces of shell which wander about and are quite capable of taking one's head off. "I feel dreadfully sorry for the men, having to lie out doing nothing under fire" is the polite and proper way of putting it, but one's sorrow is mostly for oneself, *really* . . .

I wish you could see us cooking such nasty messes as we make on our little fires, and then we all lie down together as close as we can to keep warm and forget our sorrows and discomforts and see that we haven't had our boots and puttees off for a week. You see, I'm piling it on to give you that comfortable feeling you like so much.

The views of the mountains have been lovely. Extraordinary great precipices and pointed peaks all tumbled together, and the most varied lights. Sometimes they are a filmy blue, sometimes a dark mysterious purplish colour, just like the "old master" mountain in fact, both in shape and colour. Saint Jerome would be quite in his proper background against them. This morning just at daybreak there was a rich orange ring in the sky just above them, fading away to primrose, to dark blue and then, far up above one, the southern cross shining faintly. I think the stars at daybreak are so comforting. As the day begins again and the fusillade starts and everything seems so unpleasant, they seem to say "God's in his heaven, all's right with the world" . . .

Gunner Osman F. Green,
J Battery, Royal Horse Artillery

Osman served in the Boer War from October 1900 to June 1902. During this time his unit was converted from gunnery to cavalry as part of the new Royal Horse Artillery Mounted Rifles (RHAMR). He writes to his parents in England.

Bloemfontein, October 1900

The weather is fine but very hot in the daytime and cold at night. There are quite a lot of men down with dysentery caused with drinking bad water. Our menu up to now has been bully beef and biscuits . . .

Bloemfontein, October 1900

. . . Our camp at Bloemfontein is on a sandy strip a few miles in length and a couple of miles wide. There are about 15,000 troops camped here in rows and rows of tents. Soldiers are going and coming all day in both large and small parties. We have had another sand storm. It is like a little cyclone and often carries tents and everything away if they are not securely fastened down. The sand rises up in great clouds and smothers everything. The heat is pretty bad now and makes one very thirsty and cracks your lips and makes them very sore and painful.

Pretoria, February 1901

My pay out here is one shilling and seven pence a day.

The death of Queen Victoria came as a great surprise to us as we had not heard of her illness. We heard a gun fire and, on enquiring what it was all about, were told it was for the death of the Queen.

[In the field] February 1901

I have a rather unpleasant experience to relate . . . We were acting as advance party and chased the Boers 6 or 7 miles as hard as we could go. But, on getting orders that the main body of the force was retiring, we became the rearguard. Immediately the Boers came back in force and tried to cut us off from the main body as we were holding a small hill. My horse had shown signs of being "done up" and I was told by my sergeant to try to get along to the main body whilst they were holding the hill. I got my horse about a mile further when he refused to go a step further. There I was between the rear guard and the main body. I began to see I was going to be in a queer position as the rearguard was withdrawing with the Boers hot on their heels. I had just managed to get my horse started again. I was leading it along when the boys came galloping past as hard as they could go about 30 yards to my right. My Battery being furthest away on my right. The Boers were about 800 yards away and commenced firing at me. Things were desperate now so I made no more ado and took my rifle and shot my horse dead and, picking up my cloak, I made a run for it on foot. I had gone about 200 yards or so when I heard a shout behind me of "Hands up!". When I looked round a group of Boers were not 50 yards away. One had halted his horse and was covering me with his rifle whilst the others galloped around me. I realised in a flash that I had no chance, so I threw down my rifle and put up my hands.

Well there I was, a prisoner, and feeling anything but happy. One Boer took my rifle and bandolier whilst the others made me run in front of them until we got out of range of our rearguard, who were firing on them.

After getting over the rise they made me take off everything but my helmet and drawers. However after they had talked for a while one old Boer made one of the young men give me back my shirt, which he did very reluctantly. They also gave me an old pair of boots made from cow hide. Then one of the Boers took me to a kaffir kraal a few 100 yards away. After stopping for a couple of minutes he took me across an open space to another kraal where their Commandant was. Our rearguard had evidently been watching that kraal from a distance and directly the Boer and I commenced walking across they poured such a terrible fire at us that God only knows how I escaped. The bullets passed so close to my face and body that I could feel the rush of air they caused. It was like a small hail of lead, and bullets seemed to rip up the ground for yards around . . . the I have never experienced anything like it before and hope I shan't again. I seemed to have a charm over me. I expected a bullet every second but am thankful God spared me for I got across without a scratch. I was taken before the Commandant and was questioned by my guard who could speak English. I could give them no information as I told them I was only a "Tommy" and that I did not know anything about the size of the force, and that ordinary soldiers were not told anything about such things. They simply got orders and had to follow them out. They told me I could go. Then the Boer, who had been my guard, took me [out] . . .

I asked him to see me over the skyline as I was unarmed and there were parties of young Boers who might easily put me out. He pointed me the way to Frankfort and told me to follow the telegraph wires. So I left him and made my way as best I could.

The heat was terrible and my saliva dried up until my tongue seemed nearly too big for my mouth. I went off the track to a pool I came across and got an old tin can full of water after having had a good drink. I carried the tin full of water and kept dipping in a piece I had torn off my pants to moisten my tongue with, to stop it sticking to the roof of my mouth. I found gun wheel tracks and followed these until I reached the outskirts of Frankfort, after walking about 14 miles. I found the Battery camped outside Frankfort where I arrived at 5pm, properly footsore and done up.

[In the field] *February 1901*

. . . Our job [on 23rd February] was to break through the Boer lines and drive them to the Kelrkdorp-Lichtenburg blockhouse line. We kept up a quiet trot. The moon shone upon rain clouds producing a beautiful lunar rainbow. At about 3am we made for a nick in the Kopjes. As we made a dash through the defile one shot was fired. Evidently the Boer sentry giving the signal, as there were no more. The Boers on the hillside jumped on their ponies and rode for dear life, in many cases leaving their saddles behind.

When we got through the hills we spread out and joined up with a line of mounted men on each side and drove back. From dawn to 7.30pm we moved incessantly, sometimes at the gallop. Unfortunately a gap developed during the night through which a number of Boers escaped. The General said afterwards that the drive was a success and yielded 178 Boer prisoners and 2 pompom guns. The R.H.A.M.R.s covered no less than 100 miles in 24 hr. Just prior to reaching camp we were overtaken by a terrific hailstorm and got soaked to the skin. Ten of our men got detached in the darkness and lost themselves in the mimosa bush, which abounds in these parts . . .

[In the field, South Africa] *April 1901*

. . . At dawn a convoy, escorted by about 500 Boers, was sighted and pursued. The Canadians formed the rearguard to protect the light baggage which followed behind. We of the R.H.A.M.R.s were on the left galloping steadily in three lines. After about 7 miles we were brought to a standstill by heavy fire from the Boers who had turned. Damant's Horse lost about a dozen men in the first few volleys. We got the baggages in, after some delay, but suddenly large bodies of Boers gathered around our flanks. We got the waggons in as quickly as possible. The Boers then opened fire, with the guns he had, and dropped three shells in the middle of the laager. Everyone was full of excitement as it all happened so suddenly. Our General soon got the troops in fighting order, but by this time the Boers had encircled our position. They appeared to be firing three 15lb guns and a pompom. They did their best to try and rush us and charged on three successive occasions. Each time they were repulsed under heavy fire from our men. In the last charge the Boers made they got within about 200 yards of our guns. (. . . we were acting as escort to the guns and lay out in the open to their right). We were lucky as, although the Boers were particularly anxious to get our guns, most of their bullets flew over our heads. We were able to stand up when the Boers made their final charge and, as their horses turned as they could not face our fire, we let them have it as fast as we could fire. They then galloped off, glad to get out of our range. Our casualties were light as we only have four wounded, one gunner mortally so . . .

We are now on half rations which consist of two biscuits a day, half a pint of coffee without sugar or milk, and half a pint of tea. We get plenty of meat though as we have captured cattle and sheep. But too much meat is not good in this hot climate.

Lieutenant David Miller, British Army

Miller writes to his mother about the Boer War.

5 August 1901

There is so little to describe. The infantry soldier sees nothing except the men on either side of them and the enemy in front. He hears the crackle of the enemy's fire somewhere—he does not know where—and he hears the whit! whit! of the bullets, and every now and then he knows vaguely some one near him is hit—he feels the smell of the powder (cordite) and the hot oily smell of the rifle. He fires at the range given, and at the given direction, and every now and then he hears "Advance!" and he gets up and goes on and wonders why he is not hit as he stands up. That is all. Then the bullets cease to come and the action is over . . . He marches to the chosen camping ground and perhaps goes on picket—very tired and dirty—and he does it all again next day. That is the infantry soldier's battle—very nasty—very tiring—very greasy—very hungry—very thirsty—everything very beastly. No glitter—no excitement—no nothing. Just bullet and dirt.

THE FIRST WORLD WAR
1914–1918

The Great War began in Summer 1914, when the heir to the Austro-Hungarian throne was assassinated by a Serbian fanatic in the Bosnian town of Sarajevo. The incident was obscure, but as a pretext for war in a Europe long riven with nationalist rivalry it served. The Austrian government—with the enthusiastic backing of its ally Germany—declared war on Serbia. Russia mobilized to defend Serbia, Germany declared war on Russia, then on Russia's ally France. When Germany invaded "poor little Belgium" on 4 August Britain joined the fray on the side of France and Russia. Europe and its colonies were at war.

Few imagined it would last more than a few months. All over Europe millions of men were cheered on their way to the frontlines. Yet within three months, the principal armies on the Western Front had settled down to a double line of muddy entrenchments that stretched from the English channel to Switzerland. For four years, the combatants hurled shells and bullets across the dividing yards of No Man's Land, each in an effort to budge the other, the numerical inferiority of the Kaiser's army offset by the simple fact that it held the high ground along the front.

Into this infernal maelstrom men poured by the million—most of them to die. Before it petered out, the battle of the Somme (1916) claimed 418,000 British casualties alone. In efforts to break the deadlock, infernal weapons were developed such as gas, tanks, and the conversion of aircraft into fighters and bombers—but none to any decisive effect. At sea, Germany tried to starve the Allies by sinking their merchantmen. Meanwhile, the more casualties the armies sustained, the more men were recruited to fill their places. Unsurprisingly, when the flush of patriotic fervour chilled on the reality of mass war, voluntary recruitment broke down. In 1915 forced enlistment was introduced in Britain. The men who died on the frontline were from every rank of society, every village, every family. By this date, the whole of the economy and society of the participating nations was devoted to the war effort. It was total war on a scale not even envisaged by Napoleon.

Exhausted, Germany and her allies finally surrendered in 1918. Perhaps the decisive contribution to her defeat was the entry of the USA into the war in 1917. When the Allied final push came in 1918, it contained 42 double-sized American divisions. The odds had simply become impossible for Germany. Behind them the belligerents left 10 million dead. An entire generation of men.

Walter Limmer, German Army

Limmer writes to his family.

Leipzig (still, I'm sorry to say)
August 3rd, 1914

HURRAH! at last I have got my orders: to report at a place here at eleven o'clock to-morrow. I have been hanging about here, waiting, from hour to hour. This morning I met a young lady I know, and I was almost ashamed to let her see me in civilian clothes. You too, my good Parents, you will agree that I am right in saying that I don't belong in this peaceful Leipzig any more. Dear Mother, please, please, try to keep constantly before your mind what I have realized, in the midst of conflicting emotions, since I said good-bye to you yesterday, namely that if at this time we think of ourselves and those who belong to us, we shall be petty and weak. We must have a broad outlook and think of our nation, our Fatherland, of God—then we shall be brave and strong.

Leipzig, August 7th, 1914

After all, I am glad that we have stopped here a few days longer. It has given me time to put my thoughts in order and get them thoroughly under control again. Every soldier must, to start with, be, as I was a week ago, oppressed by the first mental picture of horrors which are no longer mere possibilities, but actually approaching realities; and on the day of the first battle the feeling of dread is bound to try and get possession of one's heart again, but now it won't find us shaky or unprepared. I personally have entirely regained my self-possession. I have thought out my position as if I had already done with this world—as if I were certain of not coming home again; and that gives me peace and security. Dear Father, good Mother, beloved Brothers and Sisters, please, please don't think me cruel for saying this, but it would be a good thing if already you too would, with brave hearts and firm self-control, get accustomed to the idea that you will not see me or any of my brothers again. Then if bad news does come, you will be able to receive it much more calmly. But if we all do come back, then we can accept that joy as an unexpected and all the more gracious and glorious gift of God. You will believe that I really mean this. The matter is much too sacred to me for me to be capable of merely making phrases in what I have just said.

In any case I mean to go into this business "like Blücher". That is the simple duty of every one of us. And this feeling is universal among the soldiers, especially since the night when England's declaration of war was announced in the barracks. We none of us got to sleep till three o'clock in the morning, we were so full of excitement, fury, and enthusiasm. It is a joy to go to the Front with such comrades. We are bound to be victorious! Nothing else is possible in the face of such determination to win. My dear ones, be proud that you live in such times and in such a nation, and that you too have the privilege of sending several of those you love into this glorious struggle.

In the train

Our march to the station was a gripping and uplifting experience! Such a march is hallowed by its background of significance and danger. Both those who were leaving and those who remained behind were beset by the same thoughts and feelings. It seemed as if one lived through as much in that hour as ordinarily in months and years. Such enthusiasm!—the whole battalion with helmets and tunics decked with flowers—handkerchiefs waving untiringly—cheers on every side—and over and over again the ever-fresh and wonderful reassurance from the soldiers: "*fest stetht und treu die Wacht am Rhein!*" This hour is one such as seldom strikes in the life of a nation, and it is so marvellous and moving as to be in itself sufficient compensation for many sufferings and sacrifices.

South of Chalons, September 9th, 1914

This ghastly battle is still raging for the fourth day! Up till now, like most battles in this war, it has consisted almost entirely of an appalling artillery duel. I am writing this letter in a sort of gravelike hole which I dug for myself in the firing-line. The shells are falling so thick to-day, both before and behind us, that one may regard it as only thanks to the special mercy of God if one comes out of it safe and sound.

Attigny, September 20th, 1914

MY DEAR, GOOD PARENTS AND BROTHERS AND SIS-
TERS,—

Yes, I can hardly believe it myself, but it's true: I am on my way
to you and home. Oh, how happy I am to see a brighter world
again, instead of that world of horror! At last I am free from that
secret dread which always haunted me, that I should never see you
and your world again, for Fate has presented me with the hope
that, unless some unforeseen obstacle should arise, I shall look into
your dear eyes once more.

Limmer died of tetanus on September 24th, 1914, at the Military
Hospital in Luxemburg.

Sergeant B.J. Fielder, Royal Marines Light Infantry

Fielder writes to his wife, Nell, in Kent.

17th August, 1914

. . . If I go away you must not worry if you don't get my letters,
because you must understand it is all for the Good of England, and
the English Soldier is not only fighting for his country but to save
his own *home* from destruction and being ruled over by the Germans. My dear Nell, you ask me if our people have started fighting
yet, yes it was officially announced in the papers last week that the
British force were working with the Belgians at the town of Liege.
A telegram stuck up in the PO last night said there had been more
fighting but no British killed or wounded, these Germans are
getting an awful licking according to accounts. I cannot tell you
how long it will last but Lord Kitchener says it will be a long war
and is making preparations for one . . .

1 October, 1914

. . . I am sending this from a little place called Cassell about 25
miles from Dunkirk and 75 miles from the scene of the actual
fighting so that you can see that I am safe as houses. The only thing
I don't like to think is that you are all needlessly worrying yourself
about me, I only wish you would believe me that they will not send
us to the Front we are being kept to look after Commander
Sampson's aeroplanes, there is nothing in the least to worry about.
I am in the very best of health, this life evidently suits me to a T.
I am writing this sitting out on a verandah of a small school where
we are billeted, it is a lovely sunny afternoon and this place is on

top of a high hill and some lovely country is to be seen whichever way you look . . . PS please don't cry so much when you write next, as it makes them in an awful mess.

RND Base, Alexandria, Egypt
21 July, 1915

. . . I think I may be able to keep here a few weeks yet, anyhow I've got hopes of staying until the Dardanelles job [Gallipoli landings] is over . . . You ask me when the war is going to be over. Well, I will just tell you, only keep it secret. *In October*. You say we don't seem to be getting on very well out here; My Word if you only knew what a job we've got before us, just try to imagine a hill called Achi Baba, just fancy yourself at the bottom of a big hill with trenches and trenches piled on top of one another, made of concrete with thousands of Turks and machine-guns, five of these trenches we took one morning one after the other, but before we got to the first trench we left a good many of our chums behind, but it's no good stopping and the faster you can run the better chance you have of getting through the rain of bullets, and our boys went mad.

I have thought just lately what a lot of savages war turns us into, we see the most horrible sights of bloodshed and simply laugh at it. It seems to be nothing but blood, blood everywhere you go and on everything you touch, and you are walking amongst dead bodies all day and all night, human life seems to be of no value at all—you are joking with a chap one minute and the next minute you go to the back of the trench to do a job for yourself and then you see a little mound of earth with a little rough wooden cross on it with the name of the man you had been joking with a short time before. My dear Scrumps, I don't know whether I'm right in telling you this, because you worry so but I would not mention it only for the reason that I don't think I shall have any more of it, but I certainly *do* thank the One Above and you for your prayers at night together with our Boy for keeping me safe throughout it all.

Always you are both in my thoughts, I think of you both in that little kitchen by yourselves and know that you are thinking of me and wondering perhaps if you will ever see me come back again, every night at nine o'clock out here which is seven o'clock in England, I think that it is the Boy's bedtime and I always can picture him kneeling in his cot saying his prayers after Mummy. But "Cheer up", my Scrumps, this will all end soon and we shall be together again and carry on the old life once more.

My dear Scrumps, I wonder if the Boy still thinks of the gun I promised to bring him home, I got hold of two Turks' guns to bring home and after keeping them for about two weeks, I got wounded and then of course I lost them as I did everything else. I might also say that the Deal Battalion have all lost their bags again, they were coming from the ship in a barge and a Turk shell hit the barge, so they sank to the bottom of the Dardanelles. The Naval Division is pretty well cut up, especially the Marines, they can only make 3 btns out of 4 even after the last lot came out from England. I think there is some move on to withdraw the Marines and Naval Division from the Dardanelles also the other troops which were in the first part of the fighting as they are in a bad state and I expect we'll get a quiet job as garrison for some place. I expect by this time you have got General Hamilton's report of the fighting here, my dear Scrumps I think I will wind up now as I've just looked at the watch and its a quarter to eleven. I've been writing ever since nine o'clock, so Night Night and God Bless you . . .

Fielder was killed in action on 29 October 1916 on the Western Front.

Private Henry Gibson, London Scottish Regiment

> *I don't know where I am*
> *Somewhere in France*
> *Thursday*
> [17 Sept 1914]

My Dearest Father and Mother,

Our regiment is quartered in a spacious engine shed in a little suburban looking French town. We came here from Le Havre this morning travelling all the way in fairly comfy cattle trucks. At about 10 o'clock today I caught sight of the Eifel Tower and for a long way we went along the strategic railway encircling Paris; but how far we have got to the N.S.E. or W. of Paris only God knows—as far as I am concerned. This place seems to be rather an important base, for the glorious wounded pass out from the trains in intermittent streams borne very steadily and slow. I have seen three wounded German officers, pale and somewhat bearded on the face. Some of the wounded look happy, some very sad as if they didn't know the meaning of it all. The Scots wounded are magnificent. One poor fellow with a blood stained bandage over his head and blood besotten wad on his left eye shouted to us not to get downhearted but to go in and win—he was a Gordon. A Cameron Highlander, wounded and delirious, passed from the train into the hospital shouting, "Give me my pipes." He evidently was a piper. But this I am giving you is only the more ghastly and glorious side of war. All the way along right from Watford through Havre and all the nameless excited little places we passed through on our way here we had a grand reception. Every station all through the night at which we stopped had prepared for us coffee or wine and bread. "Vive l'Angleterre" was shouted incessantly. At Le Havre we had good fun singing all the good old Scottish songs—"The Banks of Bonnie Doon", "Kind, kind and gentle was she" and some of our chaps gave us Highland dances accompanied by the pipes. French ladies decorated our pipes with tricolour ribbon and I have a little piece pinned under my Scottish badge. We have no paper news but a presentiment haunts us all that things are well and that soon the Germans will be in a vice. The tales I hear from the wounded and from men who return from the front (I had a conversation with three men of the 12th Lancers who rode in the charge with the Scots Greys at Mons) are too detestable to mention. At any rate we are proud of our nationality, our officers and our cause and if it is fated that we enter the firing line I am sure we will do our duty. Scotland for Ever! Do write me [*Deleted by Censor*] British Expeditionary Force.

Ever Your Loving Son.

Henry
Love to all x

Gibson was killed in action on 31 October 1914.

Fritz Meese, German Army

November, 1914

. . . For the last week in a trench which is a mere ruin through which water flows in wet weather—stiff with clay and filth, and thereby supposed to protect us from the awful shell-fire. A feeble human defence against powerful forces. I am still alive and unwounded though my pack and my clothes are torn to rags by bullets. I can't say that I am enjoying myself, but I have not lost my sense of humour. Pray for fine weather and food for me, for wet and hunger are the worst enemies. You simply can have no idea what it is like, to be in the trenches for days and weeks on end under enemy fire. Never again shall I be able to shout a thoughtless "hurrah" in a café at the news of a victory—oh the poor patriots!

I have been on sentry-duty for five hours and shall probably be awake all night, but, anyhow, to sleep standing up or half sitting on the wet clay is a very doubtful pleasure. My letter has of course been written like this: five words and then a long look at the enemy, now and then up with the "cannon" and a shot.

Boys, you don't realize how well off we were in Berlin! Truly and honestly, if I ever felt inclined to moralize about my past life, every such thought has vanished now. I am quite convinced that everybody who gets home safe and sound will be a totally different fellow in every way. He will certainly be more considerate towards other people, especially in the matter of exploiting them for his own ends. The habit of comradeship necessitated by the war will have that result.

Life here isn't worth a damn, one thinks nothing of losing it. To-day, for instance, I walked for half an hour through violent rifle-fire just to have a wash and because I hoped to get one or two cigarettes . . .

December, 1914

. . . Had a few pleasant hours in billets to-day at coffee-time. Some comrades got a big parcel. There was singing. Thoughts of home. One becomes a child again here in the war. At one moment under the most terrific fire, at the next innocently gay. Happy the man who knows how to live in the mood of the present moment, paying no heed to the next. One learns to do that. Outside the enemy thunder growls, and inside it is like home—almost!

Boys, how one gets to love one's home when one has learnt to bear what one would otherwise never have imagined possible! One can never tell what are the little things that weigh most upon different individuals, nor can one, on the other hand, explain what are the things which are shaping us and chiselling such deep impressions on our characters. Anybody who can send home high-flown accounts of life at the Front has had no real experience of it. If one could describe actual facts! But one can never write about things as they really are, and, thank God, the next minute brings relief. One would have to write at the actual moment, and that's not possible, thank God. Therefore nobody will ever know how despairing one sometimes feels and yet how, in the midst of that depression, one is revived by a mixture of duty, necessity and ambition. So it must go on . . .

My dear friend Ernst is missing. There it stands, short and plain, and yet I felt a lump in my throat when I read it. Poor dear

chap—Missing! that is a terrible word to anybody who under-
stands what it means. It brings old pictures to my mind. I am lying
before Dixmuide, in the evening of October 21st. We have been
repulsed, nobody knows how. In front of us is a farm and on the
right the road, as far as which we had advanced as gaily confident
of victory as if on the parade-ground. Forward we went, step by
step, upright too, too proud to duck before the continuous whistle
of bullets. Then suddenly we were lying in the front line with our
machine-gun. Our Corporal was killed beside me. On my right J.
was shot in the arm and I got a bullet through my mess-tin. So we
lay, behind a hedge; were supposed to fire, but could see no enemy.
Then came the order: "Up, march, march into the farm!" There a
metallic song was whistling and singing among the branches, the
house was burning, and behind what was left of the wall where
Jaegers and the 201st, while machine-gun fire was crumbling the
wall, stone by stone. I tied up first N. and then R. with the Field
Service dressing which could only with difficulty be compressed
(he is running round Berlin to-day hardly realizing that I saved his
life with that bandage). We went farther on, getting into complete
disorder, no officers left and comrades falling in rows. Still we
went on (for nobody dreamt in those days that we could possibly
not be winning), till suddenly—tick—tack—our own machine-
guns firing at our backs, and that finished us. Back, bitterly
disappointed, grinding our teeth. And then, from behind the last
straw-stack, we heard the cries of badly wounded comrades lying
still under heavy fire. Two comrades and I crawled out in spite of
the fire but couldn't get them in. Then we went back a bit farther
and dug ourselves in where we were, still waiting for the enemy to
be repulsed. And between us and the enemy, under fire from both,
lay the wounded . . . Weeks later, when we had advanced again, I
came upon them, on patrol, and had to crawl over them—rows of
dead bodies.

Meese was killed in May 1915, at Loretto Hill.

Werner Liebert, German Army

Morning of December 4th, 1914
My dear, dear parents—
   Your letter of the 26th brought me the sad certainty that my dear
brother had died a hero's death for Germany's victory. The post
came early this morning.

My pain is inexpressible. I am not to be comforted. I can't yet realize that I shall not see Hans or hear his voice again. The thought that the dear fellow, who went off so full of joy and hope, will never again see that home and those dear ones for whom he was no doubt longing just as I am, is intolerable. Of you and your sorrow I cannot think without tears.

Only one thing comforts me a little: since I have known that my dear brother is no more, a wonderful change has taken place in me. I suddenly believe in immortality and in a meeting again in the other world. Those conceptions were empty words to me before. Since the day before yesterday they are objects of firm faith. For it cannot be that death should part one for ever from those one loves. What would be the use of all love and affection, which are the most beautiful flowers in human life, if they were to be destroyed for ever in an instant? This is certainly but a small consolation for the fact that the poor fellow has been deprived of all his life's happiness. How beautiful life is one only realizes out here, where one has constantly to risk losing it. It was the clearest, most beautiful night we have had for a long time, just as still and pure as Christmas ought to be. It was freezing too, which put an end to the mud and filth. I thought much about home and was sorry you were not having a Christmas tree, because I wasn't able to picture what you were doing.

It was delightful to see the men all standing together while the names were read out and the parcels handed out over their heads. They were all real "Christmas children" as they knelt before the packages and burrowed into them—by a manager in a cow-house, as on the first "Holy Night".

In the evening we had our real Christmas celebration. There were two big trees, standing all lit up on big tables. We got everything we could possibly wish for: knitted comforts, tobacco, cake, chocolate, sausages—all "Love-Gifts".—What Germany has done for us! Then the Colonel and the Divisional Chaplain came in, the Bible story of Christmas was read and the dear old hymns were sung.

January 3rd, 1915

I have lit a pipe and settled myself at the table in our cow-house in order to write home, where they are certainly looking for news again. The pipe tastes good and the old soldier is also otherwise all right.

New Year's Eve was very queer here. An English officer came across with a white flag and asked for a truce from 11 o'clock till 3 to bury the dead (just before Christmas there were some fearful enemy attacks here in which the English lost many in killed and prisoners). The truce was granted. It is good not to see the corpses lying out in front of us any more. The truce was moreover extended. The English came out of their trenches into no-man's-land and exchanged cigarettes, tinned-meat and photographs with our men, and said they didn't want to shoot any more. So there is an extraordinary hush, which seems quite uncanny. Our men and theirs are standing up on the parapet above the trenches . . .

That couldn't go on indefinitely, so we sent across to say that they must get back into their trenches as we were going to start firing. The officers answered that they were sorry, but their men wouldn't obey orders. They didn't want to go on. The soldiers said they had had enough of lying in wet trenches, and that France was done for.

They really are much dirtier than we are, have more water in their trenches and more sick. Of course they are only mercenaries, and so they are simply going on strike. Naturally we didn't shoot either, for our communication trench leading from the village to the firing-line is always full of water, so we are very glad to be able to walk on the top without any risk. Suppose the whole English army strikes, and forces the gentlemen in London to chuck the whole business! Our lieutenants went over and wrote their names in an album belonging to the English officers.

Then one day an English officer came across and said that the Higher Command had given orders to fire on our trench and that our men must take cover, and the (French) artillery began to fire, certainly with great violence but without inflicting any casualties.

On New Year's Eve we called across to tell each other the time and agreed to fire a salvo at 12. It was a cold night. We sang songs, and they clapped (we were only 60–70 yards apart); we played the mouth-organ and they sang and we clapped. Then I asked if they hadn't got any musical instruments, and they produced some bagpipes (they are the Scots Guards, with the short petticoats and bare legs) and they played some of their beautiful elegies on them, and sang, too. Then at 12 we all fired salvos *into the air*! Then there were a few shots from our guns (I don't know what they were firing at) and the usually so dangerous Verey lights crackled like fireworks, and we waved torches and cheered. We had brewed some grog and drank the toast of the Kaiser and the New Year. It was a real good "Silvester", just like peace-time!

Between Lille and La Bassée, January 10th, 1915

The trenches are full of mud and water: water from below and rain from above. We slave day and night shovelling earth and dipping and pumping out water. And it is all fruitless and in vain: the water remains. And the rain still goes on falling in heavy showers. And in addition there is the depressing effect of pitch darkness, as any light would give us away! Things are unspeakably gloomy, when perfect darkness gathers, in the pouring rain!

I must admit that I often feel perfectly sick of life in this mud and filth and everlasting, bitterly cold, perfectly futile work. Nobody would ever put up with such hardships for any ordinary cause in time of peace. Only one thing comforts me a little, which is that one's strength seems to increase with the demands on it. I feel conscious of an amount of patience and endurance such as I never knew before and should never have believed myself capable of. And it is splendid how the men put up with it all, how nobody gives in to exhaustion or despair, even when the dug-out has fallen in and one has to work all night making a fresh one. It is a joy to see how fundamentally religious the general frame of mind is and how, if one regards religion as the connecting link, one can feel the respect and awe inspired by perfect serenity. One hardly ever hears frivolous remarks now. They all seem imbued with a new life. This tragically late, awkward development into maturity and calm is delicious! Some of the old Folk Songs move men to tears, men from whom one would never expect such a thing, who seemed just what one used to call proletarians. They sing songs of the Fatherland, soldier-songs and hymns quite naturally. One nearly always hears hymns from the sentries at night. There was a fellow with whom I was on sentry-duty in the trench only yesterday: he sang a hymn and then one of these old, slow, rather melancholy soldier-songs; in spite of all he had gone through, he was still just a cheery peasant. A few hours later he lay dead, with his face in the mud. This chance of coming into direct contact with a rich vein in the life of our people is very valuable to me, especially as it is certainly a new development.

Liebert was killed on 10 May 1915.

Private Montague S. Goodbar,
4th Battalion Cameron Highlanders

Diary: Wednesday, March 10 [1915]
The battle of Neuve Chapelle commences. At 4 a.m. our Artillery
commences to bombard the German trenches until 7 a.m. when
their guns were elevated they continued to bombard the rear for
the remainder of the day. During the 3 hours from 4 to 7 a.m. were
had orders to pour rapid fire in to the 'Allemands' who were
retreating from their trench to [?] safer quarters. With the constant
rapid fire my rifle steamed like a boiling kettle and became so hot
that I could scarcely hold it. During this time I think we managed
to bag a good few of the enemy between us. Their parapet was so
badly damaged by our high explosives that they stuffed the gaps up
with their dead . . .

Thursday, March 11
After a fairly quiet night the bombardment was again opened this
morning. During the night however they have brought some
artillery up and started giving us a few back. About 11o/c it gets
too hot for them and up go 'white flags' (shirts etc on their rifles).
We get the order to cease fire and our captain tells them to come
over to us which they do after a little hesitation, each holding his
hands high above his head. We took about 300 prisoners, a great
many of them wounded. We now take possession of their trenches.

Friday, March 12
We have to change our position temporarily, a little further south.
In order to do so the men have to wade through trenches waist
deep in water, which is like syrup and as cold as ice. We are
however not a bit worried by our personal discomfort as the
excitement is so great – this is our first glimpse of real warfare.
What a sight! I cannot describe it . . . At about 4 o/c we return to
our old position, things now having quietened down a bit. Hungry,
wet and smothered in mud. At 7, 7-30 p.m. we get the order to agin
leave our trench in order to make a bayonet charge. We proceed to
cross the field which was behind the original German trench.
What a gruesome sight! Dead and wounded are strewn everywhere, the latter groaning and moaning in a most heartbreaking
manner, there are British and Germans mixed up lying side by
side, rifles and equipment everywhere. We eventually get the order
to lie down and await orders, the 'Warwicks' are already in position
on our left and the 'Grenadiers' in our rear in reserve. We are

about 100 yards in front of the new German position, it is pitch dark and we are lying in a field of rotten turnips. We are un-opposed by the Germans and intend taking them by surprise. After waiting about ½ an hour we are discovered and for reasons I am unable to to find out we get the order to get back on the road as quick as we can, the road is about ½ mile in our rear. As soon as the Hun discovered us they opened a terrific fire of machine guns, rifles, artillery, cries of chaps getting hit go up on all sides. Eventually myself and three pals get clear but find we have lost touch with our Battalion and are mixed up with lots of 'Warwicks'. We decide we had better make for headquarters which we find after a great deal of tramping and arrive there at 5.30 a.m. Saturday . . . . absolutely done up. All day long chaps keep turning up which had got lost in a similar manner to ourselves.

Monday, July 12
Shelling going on, nothing very great. 7.30 p.m. I clicked. I stopped about 20 pieces of a rifle grenade with my leg. Am bandaged up and taken to see advanced dressing station, where I arrive about 8.30. There I am re-dressed, taken to the dressing station at Vielle Chapelle by Motor Ambulance. Here I am examined by Doctor, dressed again. Spend the night here on a stretcher in a Barn.

Tuesday, 13
Left here 11 a.m. and taken by Motor Ambulance to No 7 Clearing Station, Merville. Dressed again. I remain on stretcher for rest of day.

Wednesday, 14
Left here at 8o/c and taken to Merville station, put aboard a Red X Train and taken to Rouen at 8.45 a.m. we made our way to the latter place at a very slow place and eventually arrived there on

Thursday, 15
On arrival I was taken by Ambulance to No 12 Stationary Hopsi-tal, which is situated on the Race Course. I was put in Surgical Hut No 2 where I was put to BED with sheets and everything complete. I was dressed again and at 11.30 a.m. taken to the operating theatre and operated upon, several pieces of shrapnel being removed from my leg and hand.

Friday, 16
Feeling a lot better, slept a good geal.

Saturday 17
X Rays, and several more pieces of shrapnel were located.

Sunday, 18
Again X Rayed.

Monday, 19
Underwent another operation to have the remaining pieces of shrapnel removed from leg.

Wednesday, 21
Happens I dream night and day of 'Blighty'. I wondered if my luck will be in. The suspense is awful, am I to be sent home or not.

Thursday, 22
Doc came round and put a 'B' on my board, which I find stands for 'Boat'—not Blighty although it's the same thing. Well of course my spirits rose to boiling point. At 2.40 a.m. leave here and I am put on the RX train to Le Havre . . . we remain on the train all night in a siding, and were taken on the Hospital ship 'Carisbrick Castle' of the Union Castle Line at 8 am on

Friday, 23
Was put in a nice little cot down in the saloon and had my leg dressed. Then we were each given ¼lb of tobacco and 20 cigarettes and books to read and a Gramaphone player. We sailed at 8.30 a.m. and arrived at Southampton at 3p.m. On arrival I was taken by Ambulance to Highfields Hll Red X Hos, S'hampton and again put to bed.

Saturday, 24
Am excited at being home again.

Sunday, 25
Surprise visit from Mother and Father. First time I have seen them for 6 months.

Goodbar recovered and later transferred to the RFC. He was killed in action in 1917.

Sergeant S.V. Britten, 13th Battalion, The Royal Highlanders of Canada

As a member of the Canadian Division at Ypres, Britten was witness to the first use of poison gas in World War I.

Diary: 17 April 1915
Rose at 8.30, went down to Ypres with Capt. Morrisey & Rae, & spent day there, saw over the ruins of the Cathedral & Cloth Hall etc. Stopped all the afternoon, bought a handkerchief of Flemish Lace (& sending it to Vera as a souvenir), brought back a quantity of stuff for ourselves, including two bottles of wine. Witnessed an exciting battle between a British & a German biplane. The latter was brought down about 7 p.m. Terrific artillery fire started about 6 p.m., & lasted all night.

22 April
Left at 6.30 p.m. for reserve trenches and reached our reserve dugouts via St Julien. Just rat holes! One hell of accommodation! Got to the trenches as a fatigue party with stake & sandbags, and thought they were reserve trenches, they were so rotten. No trenches at all in parts, just isolated mounds. Found German's feet sticking up through the ground. The Gurkhas had actually used human bodies instead of sandbags.

Right beside the stream where we were working were the bodies of two dead, since November last, one face downwards in full marching order, with his kit on his back. He died game! Stench something awful and dead all round. Water rats had made a home of their decomposed bodies. Visited the barbed wire with Rae—ordinary wire strung across. Quit about 1 a.m., came back to our dugouts and found them on fire. Had to march out to St Julien, & put up in a roofless house—not a roof left on anything in the whole place. Found our sack of food had been stolen and we were famished. Certainly a most unlucky day, for I lost my cherished pipe in the evening also. Bed at 4 a.m.

23 April
Up about noon and had no breakfast. Had a good view of the village of the dead, everything in a most heartbreaking state. We found a piano and had music. Furious shelling started about 4.30 p.m., and we took to the dugouts. Almost suffocated by the poisonous fumes! Got into marching order (without packs) & lined for action outside the village. Got to No. 7 station & found

Captain Morrisey there, almost suffocated. Brought Lieutenant Molson out to St Jean, & we came to St Julien, getting a lift in an ambulance. Village a mess of dead horses, limbers and men. Went on ration fatigue & tried to get up to the trenches but failed. Scouted the road, waited under heavy shell fire for about two hours, then moved off, & made a circumference up to the trenches via 48th communication trench. Getting there at almost daybreak.

23 April
Terrible day, no food or water, dead & dying all around.

24 April
Dug ourselves in with entrenching tools on left flank approaching St Julien. Just got finished about 3 p.m. (4½ feet deep and a little later the artillery opened fire). At 7.30, trench blown to hell, and we were terribly cut up. Rae & I got separated from the rest, and I helped Gardiner (wounded) who got wounded again, and finally reaching reserve trench found Captain Ross and Sergeant-Major Jeffries there. At 8.10, took message with Rae to Colonel through artillery fire, entered St Julien, and found him transferred to a farmhouse outside. Brought him, and Sergeant Claridge, Colonel Batemare and four others up to trenches with all the ammunition we could. No casualties. Reached trenches, our left flank broke, and orders to fire on them. Captain Kenway killed on the road. Then went with the Colonel to relay message for him. Met Colonel Currie on way. Left Rae at farm, and went on to General Head Quarters (General Turner) with the Colonel, then back to local Head Quarters, and back again to General Head Quarters, with the Germans already in village of St Julien. Brought back General Retirement order from General Head Quarters, and gave same to Major Buchanan, and finally to the Colonel. Left the Colonel with Rae, to advise everyone in front of us. Then on the way back to General Head Quarters, met Irish Rifles extended, ready to attack village of St Julien. Shell fire most awful—never such known before. Knee gave way through a cut by shrapnel, so lay down and rested.

26 April
In canvas rest Camp Hospital at Etaples, in bed next to Fred. Many Canadians here. Division pretty nearly wiped out.

Private W. Parker, 12th (S) Battalion, The York and Lancaster Regiment

France.
24 June, 1916

Dear Blanche,

Just a line to say Reg and myself are all right. I am a little over a mile away from our Reg in a barn, so you see I have a soft bed to sleep on, but everything has some drawback and this billet has, every night as soon as the light goes out, the rats start their nightly manoeuvres, they are just like young cats running over you, the other night we were awakened by one of the fellows swearing as hard as he could. A rat had knocked a tin of bully beef down and it caught him just under the eye, it made a nice eye for him. I think I would rather have the bugle to wake me up than a tin of bully. Our Spot would have a birthday if he was here. I often think about him. There is a little terrier on the farm but he doesn't understand good English.

Some chaps came in the billet last night out of the trenches and brought a dog with them. It came over from the German trenches into ours. The men have christened it "Boche".

Will you send me ten shillings as I have only drawn five francs since I came to France. Our Reg and myself went in a café (just a cottage), he ordered two coffees and four buns. He gave her a five franc note and she charged ninepence. (1d. under one franc), then I ordered the same and offered her a five franc note. She reckoned she hadn't change—she knew our Reg has some small change. So I put the note in my pocket. We finished our coffees and was walking down the yard innocent like and the old girl came rushing out screaming "*Café, café*". I asked our Reg what was the matter. He said she wants paying so I gave our Reg my five franc note to pay her and she snatched it out of his hand. So we started having our money's worth. We had two bottles of wine, box of buns and chocolate. She gave us the note back when we got as far as this. All the French people think about is getting as much as they can out of the English soldier.

Remember me to Harry and all at home.

I remain
Your affectionate brother
Willie.

Private Horace Bruckshaw, Royal Marine Light Infantry

Bruckshaw volunteered in August 1914, enlisting in the Royal Marines. The excerpt below from his diary details some of his experiences at Gallipoli, Churchill's doomed attempt to force the Dardanelles in the Mediterranean, held by Germany's ally, Turkey.

Diary: Sunday, 9 May 1915. Spent a rotten night of it. This is a terrible place simply infested with snipers. Nine of us went out with Capt. Andrews hunting them during the morning. Could find nothing however although we were sniped at every step we took. Luckily we all got safely back to our trench. Chapman wounded in chest this morning just as he got up to go to the assistance of another wounded man. It made us a wee bit nervous as he was sitting against me. After dark we went over the back of the trench to a point about a mile back to fetch rations up. We had just returned when the Turks greeted us with a fusillade of rapid fire. This they kept up all night.

Monday, 10 May. Things went quieter by breakfast time but the snipers kept very busy. We laid pretty low all day. We have lost nearly all our officers with these blessed snipers. Captain Tetley is the latest victim having been hit in both legs while leading a party sniper hunting. Very few of them got back again. Heavy firing commenced at dusk and continued all night.

Tuesday, 11 May. Getting our full share of casualties. Poor Capt. Andrews killed by a sniper just after dinner. We have lost our best friend. We have only about five officers left. We are to be relieved today sometime. Left the trenches after dark and made our way back to some open ground about a mile and a half back. We had to doss down in the open. To make things worse it started raining.

Wednesday, 12 May. It poured with rain all night but we were tired out and slept through it all. We got some breakfast and then made ourselves as comfortable as we could in some vacated trenches waiting for further orders. We buried Captain Andrews this morning together with Lieut. Barnes. The Colonel read the service and was very much cut up. The poor Captain's men felt it very much, most of us turning away before the service was finished. A mound, a small wooden cross and a few pebbles alone mark the last resting place of as brave a gentleman as ever walked. In the afternoon we moved further back and dug rest trenches for ourselves. Sir Ian Hamilton paid us a visit and complimented Col. Matthews on the work he and his men had done.

Thursday, 13 May. Enjoyed a good, long nights sleep for we were very tired. Our artillery has been bombarding since yesterday afternoon. We dug a hole in the ground first thing and put a waterproof sheet in it, which we filled with water. Stripping ourselves we then enjoyed a much needed bath. Soon after we had completed our rough and ready toilet a big shell dropped right in amongst us knocking out seven or eight. Pollard and Madden were two victims out of our section. Duckworth, the man who did such good work in the landing was blown to atoms. It gave us a terrible shaking up. We got shelled all the afternoon so were obliged to remain in the trenches. It went quieter towards evening however. The Turks very rarely fire the big guns after dark, thank goodness, so that we can get a bit of peace at night.

Friday, 14 May. Got shells for breakfast and got the meal crouching down in the trench. Some of the shells, which were for the most part shrapnel, did not burst, but buried themselves. Went trench digging elsewhere in the afternoon. At tea time the enemy started putting some big shells into us. We were bobbing in and out of the trench all tea time. In the evening they shifted their range to the aeroplane base at the back of us. It was a lively evening but we were consoled with a quiet night.

Saturday, 15 May. Turks seem to be attacking this morning. Very heavy firing is going on. We are getting our fair share of shells in our camp. We spent the morning cleaning our ammunition. Went to W. Beach in the afternoon gathering big stones for road making etc. In the evening heavy firing recommenced and the artillery started on both sides. Our chaplain arranged an open air concert to take place after dark. It was the most weird concert I have ever attended. It went very dark and lightning was playing in the sky. The artillery were roaring a solo with a chorus of rifle fire, stray bullets even reaching the spot where we were. Every now and then Veras Lights were shot up from the French and our own lines, bursting into a shower of stars when in the air. All the while our fellows were in turn singing comic, secular and sacred songs. The limit however was reached when Gilbert Wilson, a chum of mine, and who is a professional sang Will o' th' Wisp. He sang it splendidly but the effect was almost unearthly. We piped down about 10 p.m. to dream of Turks, Germans, goblins and goodness knows what.

Sunday, 16 May. We are commencing the week well with the usual shelling. They kept it up nearly all the morning. We had an early dinner today and spent the afternoon making a new road. The rough and ready way of making a new road employed here is to dig a trench having sloping sides on either boundary. These trenches are about three feet wide and eighteen inches deep. All the earth is taken from these trenches and utilized to make a camber on the roadway. We got back for tea about 5 p.m. and were quite ready for it.

Seeing that it is Sunday and that I have now had time to look round I cannot do better than give a few of my impressions of the peninsula of Gallipoli.

The ideas I had formed of the peninsula were altogether wrong in most respects. I had always imagined a rocky, barren land, but instead I found it quite fertile, cultivated, in many parts with orchards, vineyards and fields sprouting up with good crops of barley. There is plenty of good sandy soil. The uncultivated portions are covered with heather and wild sage for the most part, the latter giving off an odour which reminds one of last Christmas dinner.

The place lends itself naturally to defensive purposes. On all sides there are very steep cliffs right from the edge of the sea. From the southern end of the peninsula to Achi Baba is a stretch of plain or plateau extending four or five miles. Achi Baba rises here, not to a very great height, but extends itself across the peninsula in such a way that it effectively bars the way to an intruder. It has barred it to us anyway. The ground is broken up by deep ravines and gullies most of them having a stream running in the bed. These gullies abound with frogs which make the nights lively indeed with their continual and loud croaking. Lizards of the common variety are to be plentifully found. I have seen snakes as big as four feet in length and as thick as my wrist. I am no naturalist but should take them to be the ordinary grass snake.

The only two towns on this, the southern side of Achi Baba, are Sedd-el-Bahr and Krithia. Sedd-el-Bahr is on the mouth of the Straits and was the Turkish fortress. Our ships soon laid that base. Krithia is a small town on the slopes of Achi Baba and looks very quaint and picturesque from our front line of trenches. I have not yet had the privilege of seeing it from a nearer point owing to the strenuous resistance of the Turks.

Tuesday, 13 July. We spent the remainder of the night in our old spot on the gully after aimlessly wandering about half the night as usual. At dawn we moved from here, which now were the supports and went into the new fire position which was taken from the Turks yesterday. We just had to go into a Turkish communication trench which now formed part of our supports. This was in a terrible state, simply full of dead bodies and filth of all kinds. Up to dinner time all our time was taken in burying the dead and cleaning up. Where some of the dead had already been half buried was a sight awful to witness and the stench was terrific. Heads, arms and legs were sticking up from the ground and out of the parapets. It was terrible and a sight I can never forget. In addition to cleaning all this mess up we had to make this trench possible for a fire trench should it be necessary.

Bruckshaw was later transferred to the Western Front. He was killed during the battle of Arleux in 1917.

Second-Lieutenant A.D. Gillespie, Argyll and Sutherland Highlanders

Gillespie writes to his parents.

12 May, 1915
From the trenches

I have just been looking at a full-page photo in an illustrated weekly with the stirring title, "How three encountered fifty and prevailed", and a footnote describing their gallant deeds in detail. The dauntless three belong to this regiment, but we were a little puzzled, because we have never been at La Bassée, where their exploit took place. A close inspection showed that the trees were in full leaf, and that the men were wearing spats and hose-tops, which we have long since abandoned for general use. Finally, someone recognized the sergeant as our shoemaker sergeant, and his companions as two men from our second line transport. They are usually at least three miles from the trenches, and the whole story is a lie from beginning to end, without a shadow of truth in it. It makes one distrust all newspapers more than ever, to catch them out like that. The photo must have been taken somewhere on the retreat [from Mons] last year . . .

24 September, 1915
Trenches

My dear Daddy,—This is your birthday, I think, but this trench has not provided me with a present.

We had an eight-mile march down last night, an extraordinary hot night, hotter than any I remember this summer. There was a lot of R.E. material—timber and so on—to carry up, and just as we reached the end of our mile-long communication trench, down came the rain. Of course in five minutes every one was wet through and up to the eyes in mud, and it was terrible work to carry these heavy timbers up in slippery darkness, with only the flashes of lightning to help. The thunder drowned the sound of the guns, which is saying a lot, for they have never ceased night and day lately, and there is a tremendous bombardment of the German trenches going on as I write.

We got everything up in the end and we are beginning to dry now . . . unfortunately, the men can light no fires in these trenches, it's too near the Germans, but they had a ration of rum this morning to cheer them up. Before long I think we shall be in the thick of it, for if we do attack, my company will be one of those in front, and I am likely to lead it; not because I have been specially chosen for that, but because someone must lead, and I have been with the company longest. I have no forebodings, for I feel that so many of my friends will charge by my side, and if a man's spirit may wander back at all, especially to the places where he is needed most, then Tom himself [his brother, killed in action] will be here to help me, and give me courage and resource and that cool head which will be needed most of all to make the attack a success. For I know it is just as bad to run into danger uselessly as to hang back when we should be pushing on. It will be a great fight, and even when I think of you, I would not wish to be out of this. You remember Wordsworth's "Happy Warrior":

Who if he be called upon to face
Some awful moment to which heaven has joined
Great issues, good or bad, for human kind,
Is happy as a lover, and is attired
With sudden brightness like a man inspired.

Well, I never could be all that a happy warrior should be, but it will please you to know that I am very happy, and whatever happens, you will remember that.

Well, anything one writes at a time like this seems futile, because the tongue of man can't say all that he feels—but I thought I would send this scribble with my love to you and Mother.

Always your loving
Bey.

Gillespie was killed in the Battle of Loos on 25 September 1915.

Second-Lieutenant Graham Greenwell, 4th Battalion, Oxfordshire and Buckinghamshire Light Infantry

Greenwell writes to his mother.

24 May, 1915
[Ploegsteert Wood, Belgium]

I am now at last among all my friends and have seen them all, including dear Hermon: I am supremely happy and have had the most interesting day of my life. I can't believe it is true. At 11 o'clock our *horses* came round and Alan Gibson [Alan K. Gibson, Transport Officer] and I mounted in the most divine sunshine to *ride* up to the trenches! I felt most contented and told him that I could scarcely believe we were so near the war. Our horses shied at all the steam trolleys and motor-vans, and otherwise were good: it was a glorious ride. In a few minutes we came to the village and then I first saw what war meant. It was shelled to pieces and almost every house had a hole in it, although the women and children, poor wretches, were still there! We were riding along gaily enough when we met dear old Hugh Deacon who had come in to buy wine. We pulled up and chatted with him until Gibson laughed and said, "Well, I am not going to stand just here much longer"—we were at a cross-roads, just the place for shells. Ten minutes later, the Germans put their daily quota of five or six big shells into the little village, and Deacon told us later that he was just buying some *vin ordinaire* when a shell burst just outside the shop and the poor woman bolted for her life downstairs and absolutely refused to reappear, even to take his money. Of course we heard the shells going overhead, but the horses didn't mind a bit. We dismounted just behind the wood in which our regiment is, and walked through it along specially raised wooden platforms made by the Engineers which intersect it. They all have names: the main road through to the trenches is called Regent Street. Hyde Park Corner, the Strand and Piccadilly are all official names, so I feel quite at home. I lunched with Hermon and his Company officers—six of them—in a beautiful wooden cabin: we had fresh meat, peas and fried potatoes, then tinned fruits and cheese and coffee. Hermon was very glad to see me again and everyone is very nice.

Conny took me round this afternoon and I went through all our trenches with him: they are most weird and quite different from what one expects, not a long continuous line, but all zigzagged anywhere and very bad ones. I looked through all the periscopes and peepholes, and had a quick look at the German trenches round a corner; they are only 40 yards away and it was most interesting and amusing. I kept meeting all my old friends round different corners. We had tea in a little dug-out with six other officers in the trenches, cakes galore and jam: very pleasant. Conny had three or four pot-shots with a rifle through a peephole. Our Company is having its four days' rest in the reserve trenches, so I was free to go round with him; but there are lots of fatigue parties for the men which make life very unpleasant I believe.

At night the reserve companies—two out of four—man their trenches and sleep in them. We may not take off our clothes or boots at all. Luckily there is a ruined cottage in the middle of our line which is our Company Headquarters and Mess. I have just had an excellent dinner in it, a beautifully cooked beefsteak pudding and rhubarb tart with cream; your present of a ham arrived to our great joy.

I get up at six tomorrow to serve out a *rum* ration to my platoon . . . This is a very quiet part of the line at present, though the guns go on day and night. The shells start with a heavy dull bang and then come through the air in the most extraordinary way just like a railway train. The anti-aircraft guns are great fun and very pretty to watch: first a deep plomp like a rocket and then a little cloud of white smoke in the air with an aeroplane gaily circling above it, always quite safe.

I have had a most ripping day. I can't remember ever having had so much pleasure and excitement, seeing so many old friends and experiencing such new sensations. I can see that one must be resigned to keeping one's clothes on all day and night for weeks at a time and to getting sleep always in the open and only for an hour or two; but it is all so delightfully fresh after England that the unpleasant side of it does not strike me, though all my friends have been trying to instil into me the gospel of "frightfulness".

I have been made Mess President by Conny and he says that as long as things are packed *very securely* all is well. Good cheeses of the small Dutch variety and chocolates are welcome but Harrods will make suggestions. In Hermon's Company they have a hamper from Harrods weekly—but I need not tell you what I want because you always know best and anticipate me.

We have great fun inviting people to lunch and other meals and are quite a gay party.

27 August, 1915
[Hebuterne]

I am so hot that I can scarcely control my pencil.

I have just been having a tremendous fight against Conny and Freddie Grisewood, armed with long sticks and apples. It is much more fun than real war.

The weather is glorious; I was out again last night under a full moon, putting up barbed wire defences; but there was such a glorious moon that I quite enjoyed it.

August 3rd, 1915
[Hebuterne Trenches]

You would never believe the state your beloved first-born is in.

Yesterday the Germans left us fairly quiet, and only put over a dozen shells, which hit no one; but at about 4 o'clock we had a terrific thunderstorm; the artillery was silenced by the clamour of the thunder and in two minutes our beautiful little trench was a revolting quagmire. By a most fortunate chance I had borrowed a pair of top-boots from a friend who was not in the trenches. I was on duty last night from eight till midnight, and when the time for me to wake Conny up arrived I was plastered in mud from head to foot and the water had got in over the tops of my boots, which is fatal.

However, I went to bed till 3 o'clock in the morning, when the weather seemed to have cheered up a bit. It was a beastly night and has made a hopeless mess of the dug-outs, though mine is pretty clean and I am now burning "ruban de Bruges" furiously to take away the smell of the mud, which is caked all over my boots and up to my middle. I don't know how we shall clean up, but I am glad to say that we are being relieved very soon and shall not return to the front trenches till the middle of August.

I had a great piece of luck yesterday and saw some Germans quite plainly for the first time since I have been out here. I was using a good telescope and saw a typical German calmly walking along in the open behind their second line of trenches, laying a telephone wire, I think: he was joined by two others in grey uniforms. I watched them for about half an hour, but of course they were far too great a distance away to fire at—nearly three miles I should think.

The French are convinced that the Germans are going to attack here and constantly send us warnings, so we have to keep a careful look-out at night. Last night another subaltern, Rose, and I, with a few men, were going out on a patrol in front of the trenches, but Conny wouldn't allow me to go as only one officer should go at a time. However, I saw Rose at twelve o'clock after he came in and asked him if he had come across any Germans. He hadn't met anyone but had a most singular experience. Having posted his four men in a line quite close together and told them to listen, he went off himself with his cap reversed so that it shouldn't blow off, or for some such reason. Apparently he went along to talk to one of his men called Saunders, and he (Saunders), mistaking him for a German, leapt at him. Rose thought that Saunders had been killed by a German and that his party of four men had been surrounded by a larger one. However, he fought like the deuce, rolling over in the mud; fortunately he couldn't use his revolver. He finally managed to overcome Saunders after nearly strangling him. He asked him to surrender and come back quietly to the trenches with him. Saunders surrendered and they then discovered their mistake. Meanwhile, of course, the three other men had been standing round ready to bayonet Saunders, whom they also didn't recognise, and of course as they had kicked up the devil's own row, the Germans started firing at them. They got back home very quietly and that was the end of that patrol. But it really might have been a most tragic affair if the man had stabbed Rose with his bayonet and then been killed by his own pals. It illustrates rather well the extraordinary confusion arising in the dark even with two or three men who all know each other. Otherwise it might have been rather comic.

October 1st, 1915
[Courcelles]

Alan Gibson and I bicycled over last night to see the "Follies," an entertainment run by our neighbours, the 4th Division. When we got there the cupboard was bare, as the theatre had been closed and removed to another village somewhat nearer the front. I shall go and see it some other time.

This morning we had a grand apple fight in the orchard where the Transport is, and the men were regaled with the sight of six officers all pelting each other.

October 19th, 1915
[Hebuterne Trenches]

Thank God, in two or three hours' time I shall have left these trenches for billets.

Since I wrote to you yesterday we have had a ghastly time. The German bombardment, for so it became after lunch, grew extremely violent; they were using some of their largest shells, which shook the earth and sent splinters flying hundreds of yards away.

At 4.30 p.m. a white-faced officer, one of our subalterns, came up to my trench from somewhere behind and told me that the front line trenches were completely wrecked: the officer in charge buried and killed in the signallers' dug-out, all the telephone wires were cut, and that I, in fact, was virtually the front line. This news was certainly depressing and I gave up Conny for lost as he had gone up there a few minutes before.

About a quarter of an hour later the Colonel came up, called me out and ordered me to take my Platoon down to the front line as quickly as possible, as it had been reported that the German front line and saps were full of men; they might be in our trench now for all he knew. I hastily turned them out and rushed down the communication trench with only about two men at my heels, hearing appalling explosions ahead of me.

The trench was blocked in one place by a stretcher with a wounded or dead signaller on it, and this delayed us until I got him removed. Finally, when I reached the front trench the most terrible scene of destruction confronted me; it was impossible to see the old trench line. Then Conny came running up very dishevelled and shouted to me to take my men down one of the front trenches at once and stand to, ready to be attacked. As it was impossible to get to this trench except overland—the communication trench being filled in—it was a nasty job. The Huns had turned on to the spot which we had to pass their most appalling of all engines—the meinenwerfer or mine-thrower. As I was about to go across I saw a blinding flash in front of me and a great column of flame and earth rose into the sky: the concussion hurled me backwards into a deep German dug-out. I felt shaken to pieces: it was a most horrible feeling of being absolutely dazed and helpless just at the wrong moment. A corporal who was with me pulled me up and we went back to get the rest of my men up, as they were straggling behind and getting lost in the confusion. As we were waiting about a few minutes later Conny saved our lives by yelling out "Look out for the meinenwerfer!" He had just heard the faint sound of its discharge. There was a rush backwards and everyone flung themselves face downwards under any sort of protection that offered. There was another terrific explosion and we were covered with filthy smoke and falling mud and earth. However, after this I ran the gauntlet and got safe into the trench, which I found quite intact, thank Heaven, though it was cut off at the end. It was now mercifully too dark for the shelling to continue, so we had the meinenwerfer instead. About three fell in it, all of which, by some extraordinary chance, did no damage to life. I felt most frightfully shaken and pretty rotten, but after about half an hour it passed off.

Two other Platoons had by this time reinforced the front line; the enemy had ceased every kind of fire and there was dead quiet. We posted sentries all the way along and the rest had to work like niggers to try to rebuild the trenches before daylight—luckily we got plenty of sand-bags. A large party of R.E.s came up and a few Gloucesters. The men worked splendidly. We were on duty all night without a stop, building up to the front line, renewing the wire in front, and clearing the entrances to the trench so that we could get out when it became light.

The wreckage was awful, dug-outs completely smashed in and everything pitched up all over the shop. It is a miracle how few the casualties were. Captain Treble, who was taking charge of our Platoon in the front line, as we had an officer away, was killed sitting by the telephone in the signallers' dug-out. The shell scored a direct hit on it and his head was smashed in by the timbers. The signaller was, I think, mortally wounded and one bomber broke down. There were no other casualties.

During the worst part of the show I saw a young subaltern of the Seaforths, the battalion on our right, who had actually come round to have a look. They had had it as badly as we had, but had only three casualties. He seemed pretty cool and was wearing a squash hat—a Homburg. We fraternised over the wreckage and voted the Huns rotten beasts.

Twenty minutes later

I thought this letter would end abruptly at "beasts." For just after I had written that word I heard to my horror one of those awful explosions which made yesterday so hideous, followed by two or three others. They were again firing, away to the right this time. I telephoned back to Conny to ask him where the shells were actually falling, and he said that it was a good way over to the right on the next Division. It turns out that they were not the heavy guns as I had thought, but only that formidable meinen-werfer firing from the German front trench. Our heavy guns then put shells into their front trench with wonderful accuracy; the ground shook, huge clouds of yellow smoke arose and some of the fragments flew back to our trench. Since then we have had peace; it looks like raining and I pray that it will pour. We have only another two hours here and then freedom.

The row these things make is incredible and I can hear nothing but the low whistle of heavy shells; every puff of the wind startles me and I feel as nervous as a cat. It is the sitting still throughout a solid day listening the whole time to shells and wondering if the next will be on the dug-out or not which is so unnerving. I cannot understand what sort of men they are who can stand three or four days of continued bombardment. Of course, at the end the ones who are alive are absolutely demoralised.

Major Oliver Hogue,
14th Australian Light Horse Regiment

A former journalist, Hogue joined the 14th Australian Light Horse as trooper before being commissioned. The letter below was written during the Gallipoli campaign.

3 August, 1915
Ryrie's Post, Anzac

My Bonnie Jean,
You'll be sorry to hear that poor Harry Robson is dead, killed on 24 July by a shrapnel shell. He was one of the patriots, well off, with a wife and family, automobile and everything that makes life worth living. Yet when Britain stepped in to defend Belgium and when Australia offered 20,000 men, Lieutenant Robson heard the Empire call and buckled on his sword. (By the bye, Australia will have sent nearly 250,000 men to the war soon.)

Robson was all over South Africa with Colonel Cox during the South African War and was a splendid transport officer. He could do anything with horses and cattle. On various occasions when the columns were stuck up and bogged in the drifts he managed to improvise some scheme for getting the wagons through. He was a great swordsman and won several prizes at the big tournaments when he went to London with the New South Wales Lancers. We put up a cross with crossed swords over the little shallow grave on Shell Green. May poor old Robbo rest in peace!

Tresilian has gone—top-sergeant Tresilian, whom you met at the camp. He was reckoned quite the best of all the non-coms in our regiment and was generally looked upon as certain for a commission. He was game as a pebble, a regular dare-devil, and he never knew what fear was. He came from down Wagga way originally, but of late had been a station manager in the north-west of New South Wales. He got a bullet in his brain, when looking over the parapet on Holly Ridge, and died without a sound.

Did I tell you about Major Midgley? He is one of the very best officers in our brigade, got the D.S.O. in the Zulu War, went through the South African War, and is a regular little fire-eater. He is in charge of Chatham's Post and is always pulling the Turks' leg. He conceives the most wonderful ruses and tricks to worry the Turks and draw their fire. He sends out fiery arrows and rockets and flares, and by simulating preparations for attack at all times, he has the Turks in the Gaba Tepe zone worried to death.

The other night, however, one of his patrols nearly got cut off. They went out under Lieutenant Bolingbroke to try and snare a prisoner, but as they went south along the beach a strong Turkish patrol tried to sneak in behind them and cut them off from our lines. Our lads streaked back like startled wallabies. The men on the post could not give covering fire for fear of hitting our patrol. However, they all got back safely, and the moment they were in, Chatham's Post opened a hot fire and sent the venturesome patrol about their business. They must have thought that the Post was only lightly held, for some time after midnight a couple of hundred Turks made a dash at the Beach Post. They gave us warning by accidentally kicking the tins we had scattered in the grass. Our chaps were ready and the first Turkish shot was answered by a veritable fusillade from our lines, and after a half-hour's hot firing the enemy drew off.

We have come to the conclusion here that only about 10 per cent of the Turks are good shots and snipers, while about 90 per cent of the Light Horsemen are crack marksmen. This being so, we are able to keep their snipers well in subjection. Lately in front of Ryrie's Post and Chatham's, the Turks cannot show a periscope without having it smashed, and our lads now are actually shooting them through their loopholes and smashing the mud bricks with which the Turks surround their fire recesses.

Several of our snipers are putting up fine records in the matter of bagging Turks. But the champion sniper of them all is Trooper Sing of the 5th Light Horse. He is a champion shot, terrible quick on the up-take (as your mither would say), has keen eyesight, and abundant patience. He has now shot over one hundred Turks; and every one is vouched for by an officer or the sergeant on duty, who sits by Sing all day with a telescope and never gives him credit for a kill unless he actually sees the Turk fall. Some of the infantry on our left are rather inclined to be sceptical as to Sing's performances, but there is not the slightest doubt about it. Major Midgley reckons that Sing must have killed at least one hundred and twenty and wounded thirty more, but he only gives credit for those the observer sees actually fall. But Sing never shoots at a stretcher-bearer. He will wait for hours for a sniper. "There is always tomorrow," he says.

Our sharpshooters always get a bag when a batch of Turkish reinforcements arrive. The newcomers don't know the ropes.

They are always very inquisitive, and will go poking their heads up over the parapets, or round sandbags. They don't know that while they may not be visible in front they are "wide open" from either flank, and with trenches rather zigzagging here and there, well, as Sing says, "It's a shame to take the money." One old Turk yesterday was fixing his overhead cover, when one of the Fifth smashed a brick and the thing toppled down on top of him. He lay quite exposed, kicking and yelling and waving his arms frantically. Sing exclaimed, "I'll put the poor cuss out of his agony", and promptly put a bullet through his brain.

Doesn't all this sound shockingly cruel and callous, my darling? But you made me promise to tell you everything; anyhow I have broken my promise time and time again. I simply can't tell you about the aftermath of battle—the shockingly mangled bodies and the comrades maimed and crippled, and the agonies of those poor wounded fellows left between the two firing lines. Yet we are all erring mortals, when we try to gloss over the horrors of war. It's only when the women of the world realize all war's wickedness and misery that there will be even a faint chance of turning our swords into ploughshares . . . Yet I remember when poor Belgium was trodden beneath the iron heel of the Hun, her shrines desecrated, her citizens butchered and her women outraged, it was the women of Great Britain that gladly sent their men to avenge the wrongs of the plucky little kingdom. And when the Empire called, the women of Australia gladly bade their sons and brothers "Go and God-speed". You, too, are not blameless in this regard, my angel, for if you had lifted your little finger to hold me back, I would have been numbered amongst the shirkers . . .

When will it all end, I wonder? How long, O Lord, how long?

Yet I know we cannot sheathe the sword till the Hun is humbled
and the spirit of Prussian Militarism quenched for good and all. As
for the poor turbaned and malignant Turk, he's merely the unhappy dupe of the German intriguers. Our Australians don't hate
the Turk like they do the Hun. The Turkish prisoners have taken
quite a liking to the Australians—but they all voice their fear of the
Australian bayonets. They call us the "White Gurkhas".

I'm getting long-winded today. Au revoir.

Yours ever,
J.B.

Hogue survived the war only to die in March 1919 in the
influenza pandemic which swept the world.

Captain Norman C.S. Down,
14th Battalion, Gordon Highlanders

To his fiancée.

SAME PLACE,
June 12th 1915

Cherie (French)

Still here, and no word of being relieved. That's only nineteen
days that we've been in the front line without a relief, and we
haven't lost more than two hundred men during the time, so we
aren't doing so badly.

All the same, life's hardly worth living. From dewy dawn till
the stars begin to peep the Hun shells us, shell after shell the
whole day long, and we just have to sit and look pleasant. Our
own artillery do their best, but all they can do is to polish their
guns and think how nice it would be to have something to fire out
of them. If only we could have the man here who said that there
was no shortage of shells.

I'm not being very cheerful, am I, but at present I'm suffering
rather badly from lack of sleep. This morning after "stand to" I
told my servant to make me a cup of cocoa. Before it was ready I
had fallen asleep and he had to wake me. I took the cocoa from him
and tried to drink it, but it was too hot, and so I sat down and
waited for it to cool. I must have fallen off again directly, as I woke
up with a start to find scalding liquid tickling down my kilt and on
to my bare knees. I didn't want to let my man see what a fool I had

made of myself, so I raked up an old Tommy's Cooker and put a dixie of water on it. My dug-out was on fire when I woke up again, and I had to use all my remaining water to put it out. After this I gave up all idea of a hot drink and went to sleep on the sopping floor of the dug-out. Five or six hours later a small earthquake roused me to the fact that all around me was dark. This was astonishing for midday in June. A shell had closed up the dug-out door, an ungentlemanly thing to do, but better perhaps than coming in through the door. When my men dug me out they told me that this sort of thing had been going on for over an hour, and that they had retired to the far end of the trench, and had wondered why I didn't do likewise . . .

Later.—I've been hit, Phyllis, and am feeling a regular wounded 'ero. I was walking along the trench when there was a bang, and I was thrown forward on to my face. "You're hit, sir, hit in the back," said one of my men, and with a breathless haste my tunic and shirt was torn off, to disclose a shrapnel ball clinging lovingly to my spine in the midst of a huge bruise. The skin had just been scratched. Oh, I was sick, I had fully expected a nice cushy one, and a month down the line, with perhaps a fortnight's sick leave in England to top up with, and then to find it was the merest scratch. Oh, it was cruel. However, the news got round, and I had a message from battalion H.Q. asking whether they should send along a stretcher! And when I went down to the dressing station to get some iodine put on the wound the M.O. turned round to the orderly and said, "Just put some iodine on this officer's wound, will you. You'll find it if you look long enough". That put the lid on it. No more wounds for me.

Till next time.
Your wounded hero.
THOMAS

Captain Rowland Fielding,
3rd Battalion, Coldstream Guards

Fielding writes to his wife.

Bethune
7 August, 1915

On my return from leave, on the 5th, I found the battalion just finishing a tour in the trenches in front of Cambrin, immediately south of the La Bassée road.

The trenches which the battalion was holding were new to us, and were very lively; and the contrast between the peaceful life I was leading with you and the children last Wednesday and my occupation the following day and night could scarcely have been greater. Nowhere along the whole front are the Germans and ourselves more close together than there. Twelve to fifteen yards was all that separated us in the advanced portions of the trench, and the ground between was a shapeless waste—a mass of mine-craters, including two so large that they are known officially as Etna and Vesuvius.

The ragged aspect of this advanced trench I cannot picture to you. The hundreds of bombs which explode in and around it each day and night have reduced it to a state of wild dilapidation that is indescribable. There is not a sandbag that is not torn to shreds, and the trench itself is half filled by the earth and debris that have dribbled down. So shallow and emaciated has this bit of trench now become that you have to stoop low or your head and shoulders poke above the parapet, and so near are you to the enemy that you have to move in perfect silence. The slightest visible movement brings a hail of bullets from the snipers, and the slightest sound a storm of hand-grenades.

The conditions are such that you cannot repair the damages as they should be repaired. You just have to do the best you can, with the result that when the tide of war has passed beyond these blood-soaked lines they will soon become obliterated and lost among the wilderness of craters. The tripper who will follow will pass them by, and will no doubt pour out his sentiment on the more arresting concrete dug-outs and the well-planned earthworks of the reserve lines well behind.

I did a bit of bombing myself during the thirty hours I was there—a rather different occupation to our tea-party in the grotto at Rainhill! Who would have imagined, two years ago, that I should actually so soon be throwing bombs like an anarchist?

Tommy Robartes's Company has a band, and, the night before my arrival, being the anniversary of the declaration of war, he tried a "ruse de guerre". The band was posted in a sap [a type of trench] leading from the fire-trench, and, at six minutes to midnight, opened with "Die Wacht am Rhein". It continued with "God Save the King" and "Rule Britannia", each tune being played for two minutes. Then, as the last note sounded, every bomber in the battalion, having been previously posted on the fire-step, and the grenade-firing rifles, trench-mortars, and bomb-throwing machine, all having registered during the day, let fly simultaneously into the German trench; and, as this happened, the enemy, who had very readily swallowed the bait, were clapping their hands and loudly shouting "Encore!".

"English treachery!" I feel sure they are saying, but it is only a leaf out of their own book, after all.

On the evening of my arrival I tried to get into conversation with them, as they had been very talkative the previous day, but they were disinclined to be drawn. The experience of the night had evidently upset them, and we had also given them a severe strafing [artillery bombardment] during the day, which did not help matters. And at 10 p.m. No. 2 Company band once more gave a recital. But there were no "encores" this time, and no applause. When the band had exhausted their stock of tunes they sang, but all was unavailing; their efforts were ignored.

Even Chapman—one of the Company wits—failed to get a reply. I tried a London Scottish machine-gunner who spoke German, and he could get no answer till he asked whether they had orders from their officers not to speak to us; then someone answered in a coy kind of way so that we could not hear what he said. My impression was that he had been promptly silenced from behind.

In these conversations the soldiers on both sides address one another familiarly, as "Kamerad", or "Tommy" or "Fritz". On the whole, the remarks made to men of my Company during the three days they were in these trenches were vacuous but rather amusing. Once the Germans called out "Coldstream form fours": so they apparently knew who was opposed to them. Another time one of our men called, "Do you know a man called Cooper?" It was just one of the catch sentences you so often hear out here, but the reply came: "Yes, he's here". One of our men asked: "Aren't you sick of it, Fritz?" and got the answer: "Yes, aren't you?" Another man shouted: "Wouldn't you like to have peace?" to which the reply was: "We aren't ready for peace, but let's have it tonight!"

Then they asked if we had lost a corporal who had been born at [?] This was a corporal of the Scots Guards who had crawled to the edge of one of the craters the night before we relieved his battalion, and had been bombed and killed at a range of two or three yards. His Captain, Harold Cuthbert, who is a very gallant fellow, had subsequently crawled out and collected some of his private belongings. Drury Lowe, of the same regiment, told me today he had heard that the Germans had put up a notice saying that they had buried this man properly. I cannot vouch for this, but the body had disappeared by the time I arrived from the very prominent position it had occupied on the lip of the crater.

And they also put up a notice-board, which I saw, saying "Warschau is our" [sic]: [The Germans entered Warsaw 5 August, 1915]—which, I am afraid, is true. The men tried to shoot this down, and eventually, the rain washed it off.

I enclose some weed which I got among the ruins of Cambrin. I picked it yesterday as I came out of the communication trench, after being relieved. It is "Flos Crucis", or the flower of the Cross, so Egerton has told me. The legend is that it grew beneath the Cross, and the black spots are supposed to represent the stains of the Lord's blood.

Fielding was now the CO of the 6th Battalion Connaught Rangers.

Near Ervillers
8 October, 1917

. . . The section of front line which I hold is, as I have told you, more or less of a graveyard. Many soldiers lie buried in the parapet, and in some cases their feet project into the trench. The positions are marked, where known. We come across others, unmarked, as we dig. On such occasions the men put up little notices, some of which combine with the tragedy of it all a certain amount of pathetic and unintended humour. As you may imagine, the names of the dead are generally undiscoverable. On one board is written: "In loving memory of an *unknown* British soldier." On another—in this case the man's paybook was found on his body and therefore his name is known—the following words appear in chalk: "Sleep on, Beloved Brother; take thy Gentle Rest." In another case somebody has contented himself by just writing piously in chalk on the sole of a projecting foot: "R.I.P." Over another grave a bas-relief of the Head of Christ has been carved with a jack-knife on a piece of the chalk through which the trench is dug. It is embellished with hair and a fine halo drawn in purple indelible pencil.

If you saw it all you wouldn't know whether to laugh or cry.

Front Line, Lempire.
10 January, 1918

A few minutes before four-o'clock this morning the enemy tried to raid one of my Lewis gun posts which is placed well out in No man's Land, about 150 yards in front of the fire-trench, in a sunken road which crosses both lines of trenches. The raiders came across the snow in the dark, camouflaged in white overalls.

In parenthesis, I may explain that while I have been away there have been two unfortunate cases of sentries mistaking wiring parties of the Divisional pioneer battalion for the enemy;— whether owing to the failure of the wiring parties to report properly before going out, or to over-eagerness on the part of the sentries, I do not profess to know. No one was hurt on either occasion, but a good deal of fuss was made about it, our new Brigadier blaming the men who did the shooting—his own men— and saying so pretty forcibly.

When I first heard of this I thought that a mistake had been made—if for no other reason than that there would for a time at any rate be a disinclination on the part of sentries to shoot promptly, which might prove dangerous;—and that is what happened this morning.

The double sentries on duty in the sunken road heard, but in the darkness did not see, a movement in front of them. Hesitating to shoot, they challenged. The immediate reply was a volley of hand-grenades. Private Mayne, who had charge of the Lewis gun, was hit "all over" in many parts, including the stomach. His left arm was reduced to pulp. Nevertheless, he struggled up, and leaning against the parapet, with his uninjured hand discharged a full magazine [forty-seven rounds] into the enemy, who broke, not a man reaching our trench. Then he collapsed and fell insensible across his gun.

The second sentry's foot was so badly shattered that it had to be amputated in the trench. The doctor has just told me that he performed this operation without chloroform, which was unnecessary owing to the man's numbed condition, and that while he did it the man himself looked on, smoking a cigarette, and with true Irish courtesy thanked him for his kindness when it was over.

Words cannot express my feelings of admiration for Private Mayne's magnificent act of gallantry, which I consider well worthy of the V.C. It is, however, improbable that he will live to enjoy any decoration that may be conferred upon him.

Private Mayne died soon after; to Fielding's anger, Mayne was only awarded a posthumous mention in dispatches, the lowest posthumous award.

GH Cecil Thomas, Shropshire Yeomanry

A schoolmaster's son from Abbeydore, England, Thomas volunteered in the summer of 1914 serving first with the Shropshire Yeomanry, before receiving a commission in the Royal Flying Corps as an Observer with 144 Squadron. He writes to a friend, Dorothy, later to be his wife.

> *Shropshire Yeomanry Camp*
> *Benacre Park, Wrentham*
> *August 31, 1915*

Dear Dorothy,

Very many thanks for photos received this morning – they are splendid: The one of the 'Country Lad' is a treat and I have looked at it quite twenty times today . . . We have not had any more visits from the Zeps lately. Did I tell you that we had a free hand in colouring our tents, so that they would not show up so plainly in case of a raid by hostile aircraft? Well the tents were wonderful things to behold when we had finished them. All that were not done by Saturday were finished by the defaulters, who probably feeling that they had been unjustly dealt with, wrote some hard, plain truths on the remaining tents. On Sunday the officers brought their cousins, sisters and aunts round the camp. We have to do them all over again now.

I got back here on Thursday and Ted went home on the following day. He wasn't half bucked up at the prospect as he did not think he had an earthly and had only sent his name as a matter of form. You see Ted and I always keep our names well to the fore on the list of applicants for leave; one of the first things I did when I got back was to apply for 14 days leave for the corn harvest, the last leave I had was my hay harvest leave. Have just had another look at the photos; I rather think the one in which Clarrie and Bert were holding hands is the best.

Of course if Clarrie still persists that they were not holding hands and you cannot bully or cajole her into telling the truth, we must dismiss the charge and very reluctantly given them the benefit of the doubt.

Well Dorothy 'last post' has gone and I must knock off. Thanking you again for the photos which I shall take care of as they are so nice to have as a reminder of a pleasant holiday.

1740 Motor Cycle Section
Shropshire Yeo
4th Dismounted Brigade
E.E.R [Egypt]
30/5/16

Dear Dorothy

We had a mail in last night and I can assure you that we were really pleased to get a line from you.

It's really kind of you to sympathise with us having to 'stick it' in a show like this; although it is *hot* here sometimes, I am not hurting. Just at present am writing this seated in the back of the General's car, at rest under a (or rather) *the* tree. You see it is essential that motor cars should be kept as much as possible out of the sun—at least that is the plea that was put forward the Brigade car drivers. Of course the same applies to motor cycles and although we cannot exactly turn a tree into a lock up garage still we manage to get a fairly good time in the shade. There are three cars and two bikes crowded underneath and it's quite a home from home. Gals drives the Generals 'Sunbeam' and of course whenever he is not actually using it, we make it our headquarters.

We have got a job on here that will last for a few weeks yet, but we hope that when it is finished we may get a move out of the land of Egypt.

Am affraid that is not much use applying for harvest leave this year. Hope they will be able to manage somehow at home. There is rather a cheerful rumor flying about here at present, to the effect that Lloyd George said in some speech that the war would last another three years. Well if it is true I suppose we can manage to last it out, although if I had known it was to have lasted all that time I think I should have tried to squeeze into group 45.

Still, I suppose the first four years will be the worst!

Have just been chucked out of the Sunbeam and transferred to the Ford. They are jolly good cars (the former I mean) at least there is good glass in the screen—it's a wonder my boot did not break it when they were transferring me . . .

If you take any photos when you are down home we should very much like one or two, if you would please spare them. It seems ages since you took those on the (Skirrid)? . . . I'd give something to be up there for a breath of fresh air, up on that old hill, after riding through some of these native villages . . .

Have you had the Zeps at B'ham again? You must envy us out here, as we are well out of their visiting zone.

Have to go out in half an hours time so must knock off.

5.5.18 [Cairo]

Dear Dorothy

Am afraid that the letter I wrote soon after Christmas thanking you all for your splendid parcel went to feed the fishes. At present we are miles away from any fighting—plenty of food to eat, and a fair share of comfort but when that parcel came we were just outside Jerusalem, feeding on bully and biscuits and having a pretty miserable time, and I can assure you that we did appreciate that cake. We had had about five days heavy rain when we heard that there was a parcel mail down at the rail-head—about 12 miles away. We went down and used what we could. It had just been dumped out in a heap, not covered up, and as I have told you it *had* been raining. There were tons of parcels, just like a pulp. We were four motor cyclists, and we managed to find about 8 parcels between us, but your parcel was the only one that was really dry out of the 8. So once again please let me thank you all not only for the cake, but for packing it in such a sensible way. I wonder what the people who had sent those parcels out would have thought if they had seen that dump. One poor chap had a turkey (at least he informed us that it had been mixed up with cigarettes and chocolates. We packed it up again and addressed it to a sergeant who had been kind to him. A few weeks later I came down to Cairo to the Cadet Wing and met ted. We had just been sent down the line for a course in bayonet fighting, so if you did not hear from him, it must have been because he was away when his parcel arrived and following a time-honoured custom, his mates must have opened it for him. Expect that Ted is going to France. Hope he will be able to get leave from there and I bet that he will have a try. We get very little war news here but it seems that the German offensive is a tremendous affair and the old war doesn't look as though it's going to be over for a while yet. I suppose though that when they stop for a breather it will be our turn to start. I had a letter from Bert last week he tells me that everything is going well at home. I should love to drop in and see them all again at home. Egypt in the Spring looks the same as any other old time of year, nothing but sand except right in the Nile Valley, and there it is all cultivated ground, grass won't grow anywhere at any price . . . . Am still trying to fly and have got to the stage where I take the old bus up on my own and flip around like an old hen. I rather think that I have broken my instructors heart (if any); it's ages since I saw him smile. Well Dorothy I must dry up.

Jack Mackenzie, Cameron Highlanders

3/7/15 [France]

My Own Darling Wife,

Your dear letters all safely to hand. I am please to see you are keeping so well. Your parcel also arrived last night and I am just delighted with the contents many thanks for it Minnie but I really can't thank you enough here and will do better when we meet, the cake is just delightful darling, just like a wedding cake, the boys enjoyed it so well, and the papers were nearly fought for, you will be please to know that your shirt and socks just arrived in the very nick of time as the visitors [lice] had just arrived. You know we have been in the trenches for nearly a week now and under fire the whole time, the shells are flying round thick now and I am writing this in my dug out, so you will have to excuse the dirty paper sweetheart. There are three of us in the same dug out and we are so closely packed that we cant turn. We relieved our fourth battalion in here, these are the trench which they lost so many men in capturing, & is just one vast deadhouse, the stench in some places is something awfull, the first thing we had to do was dig the trenches deeper & otherwise repair them & we came across bodies all over the place, you know the Germans occupied these trenches nearly the whole winter and have been losing heavily & has had to bury their killed in the trenches, there were legs and arms sticking out all over the place when we arrived but we have buried the most of them properly now. The ground behind us us [sic] is covered yet by dead Camerons and Germans who fell on the seventeenth of May & we go out at night & bury them, it is a rotten job as they are very decomposed, but it has to be done . . . and we think it only right to their relatives at home, to put their poor bodies under the ground properly. The smell is a lot better now & we hope to have all the dirty work finished by tomorrow night. Our chaps are just grand sweetheart, it is an honour to be amongst such a crowd, they are all cheery and always in good humour, & always willing to help each other. We have only had about eight casualties so far that is a very light bill. We are going to be relieved on Monday night & are going down to a rest camp, so will write to you better from there. One good thing darling we get our letters delivered to us & can get writing home, so that is great consulation isnt it. did you get the pc [postcard] view I sent you Min, it was of a village which had been shelled, all the villages round here are like that, it is awfull darling the damage done to innocent people, & it makes me feel ten times more proud that I enlisted when I did. The arrangements in the trenches are good & we are as comfortable as it is to be under the circumstances, we are very well looked after & not allowed to take any unnecessary risks or anything, the only thing is it is always bully beef & sea biscuits & one gets very tired of that, could you send me a tin of cocoa in your next parcel, & a candle, candles & sugar are the things we are most short of, & when you send anything sweetheart could you put it in a tin box, as the trenches are swarming with big blue bottles, which one sees in thousands on the dead bodies & then they come crawling over the food. Our officers are just grand & every one of us would do anything for them, especially Mr Ellice our junior officer, he is always smiling & has a kind word for everyone. We[ll] dear heart it is not half so bad being under fire as some people say at least I did not feel so jumpy as expected to be, dont you fret about me dear heart it is not half so dangerous in the trenches as one would expect, the worst danger is the snipers. This is the first time I have ever wished I was a wee chap, I feel as if I am going to get a kink in my back. Well Minnie sweetheart the pants will do alright but would have been beter if they had been dark, even black, as the white shows the dirt up so much, but many thanks dearest for sending them they will do fine.

P.S. I am always thinking of you lassie night & day, you are never out of my thoughts, always remember darling that I love you dearly & don't worry too much about me, mind & write to me often. Give my love to Father & Mother & all the rest, tell father that I got his letter. I am addressing this to Straiton, you might let me know when to adress them to our wee home. Mind & enjoy yourself, remember me to all; write often to me, with best love and kisses, hoping this finds you well. So ta ta just now & God bless you darling.
Your ever loving sweetheart
Jack.

Mackenzie was killed in action in 1916.

Hugo Muller, Germany Army

A former law student, Muller writes to his family.

At Agny, near Arras,
17 October, 1915

I am enclosing a French field-postcard, which I want you to put with my war-souvenirs. It came out of the letter-case of a dead

French soldier. It has been extremely interesting to study the contents of the letter-cases of French killed and prisoners. The question frequently recurs, just as it does with us: "When will it all end?"

To my astonishment I practically never found any expression of hatred or abuse of Germany or German soldiers. On the other hand, many letters from relations revealed an absolute conviction of the justice of their cause, and sometimes also of confidence in victory. In every letter mother, fiancée, children, friends, whose photographs were often enclosed, spoke of a joyful return and a speedy meeting—and now they are all lying dead and hardly even buried between the trenches, while over them bullets and shells sing their gruesome dirge.

Muller was killed in October 1916 in the Ancre Valley.

Athanse Poirier, 26th Battalion, 2nd Canadian Division, Canadian Expeditionary Force

In the trenches, Belgium
9 December, 1915

My dear parents,

. . . I was face to face with several enemy and although they are supposedly good soldiers I—poor little Canadian recruit who, only a few months ago knew nothing but forest and farm—I came out the victor. Several times. The first one I met looked like a lion, his eyes on fire and his face red with rage. He came at me muttering in his language something I took to be oaths. Truly I believed I had eaten my last supper. But, gathering all my strength and courage, I gripped my gun more firmly and thrust my bayonet into his heart. I felt the steel go through the flesh and bone which hid his wicked heart. It was horrible. With a cry of pain and rage he fell to the ground, stained red with his blood. I, without losing a moment, turned on a second and a third, when a whistle announced the end of the combat. So there are a few more [Germans] who will eat no more bully beef and hard tack . . .

Your affectionate son,
Athanse

Captain Bill Bland, 22nd Battalion, The Manchester Regiment (7th Manchester Pals)

Bland, a former university lecturer, writes to his wife Lettie.

18 February 1916
[France]

Darling, I can't bear you to be unhappy about me. Don't be grey and old, my darling. Think of the *cause*, the cause. It is England, England, England, always and all the time. The individual counts as nothing, the common cause everything. Have faith, my dear. If only you will have faith in the ultimate victory of the good, the true and the beautiful, you will not be unhappy even if I never return to you. Dear, if one's number is up, one will go under. I am here, and I shall either survive or not survive. In the meantime, I have never been truly happier.

P. S. Hardship be damned! It's all one long blaze of glory.

Bland was killed in action on the first day of the battle of the Somme, 1 July 1916.

Lance Corporal Thomas Part, 6th Infantry Battalion, 2nd Division, Australian Imperial Forces

Part arrived in France on 26 March 1916, reaching the frontline a fortnight later.

Diary: Apr. 7 Passed through AIRE & on to HAVERSVILLE where we stayed the night.

8 Moved off at 8AM & after a 14 mile march over flagstones we brought up at STEENWERCK [?] All the troops were absolutely buggered on a/c of the long march with full packs, etc. over the cobblestones nearly everyone had sore feet.

9 Last night had a bath in the creek the water was icy cold, but I felt OK afterwards. This morning Bde. had a foot inspection. Over 100 shrapnel shells were fired at an enemy aeroplane which was very high in the air but she escaped. We move off tomorrow for the trenches Fleurbaix & Armentieres.

10 Arrived at FLEURBAIX at 12.30p.m. & took over phone at 3PM from 4th Bn. Royal Scots, the 15th & 16 Bn. R. Scots work together in the line. Fritz this afternoon shelled the township & some of the building suffered. Things were very lively for a time. The French people still continue to transact business & the shops are well stocked.

Apr. 11 Had a walk around the town, houses & churches everywhere were knocked rotten, some roofless others with walls knocked bandy & others just a heap of debris. This morning fritz shelled a farm dwelling & set alight to it & this afternoon the whole place is completely gutted. The inhabitants of the dwelling only moved out yesterday which appears suspicious, although a battery is alongside which may have been the cause of the shelling suspecting it to be a FOP. From 8AM to 1PM drizzling rain, now clearing up. Yesterday Br. HQRS (trench) was bombarded & signal office was set alight. 23rd Bn. who had dumped their equipment in the office, lost everything, altogether 90 shells fell around HQRS (FORAY FARM).

14 Weather absolutely rotten, a cold biting wind is blowing a drizzling rain & sleet is falling. 23rd report 3 men shot by snipers. This is the 8th casualty (by snipers) since being here.

16 Yesterday Fritz shelled our domicile & another building 10 chains away, first they gave us about 100 shells of lidite & then peppered us.

Apr. 16 with shrapnel & 77s, the other building was knocked bandy & it collapsed within 2 hrs. & We, well, we still exist.

23 Grand exhibition of aeroplane shooting. Thousands of pounds worth of shells spent yesterday & today firing on enemy aeroplanes. This afternoon we brought 1 enemy TAUBE & they brought down one of ours.

24 Easter Monday, first fine day for a week. 20 aeroplanes are flying directly overhead.

25 Anniversary of the starting at ANZAC. Div [?] order that each Bde. sends 6 men from Bde. on 8 days leave, . . . dated from when they embark at BOULOGNE. Snowy Verity left . . .

26 A real bonzer day, yesterday we went to ERQUINHEIM for a hot water bath & it was OK. We stripped in one compartment then went into a room where large vats (old brewery) filled with hot water constituted our bath, after which we were supplied with clean u/clothes in exchange for our filthy ones. French girls (who wash the clothes) constantly pass to & fro, when we strip, but custom is everything & it is merely the mental attitude which concerns the question of moral or immoral.

Apr. 28 Urgent signals & gas alarm gongs (STRUMBUS horns) going. "Stand to" ordered. I had just in & couldn't find my pants for a while. Ordered by CO to lay line at once from HQ to sap. After struggling about amongst barb wire entanglements we had just finished laying line when "CARRY ON" was given. The gas attack turned out to be gas arising from exploding shells. B. Coy rushed from supports to the firing line (across country).

29 This morning our Artillery opened up on Fritz & kept the bombard up for 3 hrs. & things sounded very lively while it lasted. Left FLEURBAIX at 5PM arrived at L. HALLOBEAU at 6.30PM & took over from 7th Bde. sigs. at 6.45.

May 1 Rode on cycle to Bde. HQRS this afternoon to ERQUIN-HEIM thence on to ARMENTIERES.

2 Today shells fell amongst 27th Bn. as they were being billeted & 1 man was blown to pieces & 3 others injured.
May 2 Hobo Hughes returns from Bde & we have a Champagne night 1 Doz. bottles @ 6 Francs.

11 Went to baths & had a decent change. Visit by Gen. Birdwood today.

17 Went to concert at ERQUINHAM.

20 to LA MENEGATE & had first test of helmets under gas & tear bombs.

22 Capt. McKenzie who demonstrated at LA MENEGATE gas school was today killed at ERQUINHEIM by shell, 3 little kiddies also killed same time.

23 Steady showers falling.

28 Battalion to move off to ROLANDERIE FARM tomorrow at 9AM.

29 At ROLANDERIE in wooden huts.

June 1 This afternoon Fritz shelled a battery ½ mile from here, they landed 40 shells all around it. One anti-aircraft shell landed 10 yds from one hut but no damage done.

2 This morning a balloon at LA HALLABEAU broke adrift from the moorings & rose rapidly before the observers were aware of it. They alighted by Parachutes.

June 4 Slight showers & thundery, cold wind, orders to hand in final blanket.

5 A heavy bombardment of Fritz line; was to have taken place this morning, but owing to heavy rain it was postponed.

8 Bs. birthday.

12 Left ROLANDERIE at 3.30PM arrived at our billets in ARMENTIERES. On arrival discussion arose between 24th & 25th Bns. as to the HQRS sigs & orderly billets. We have swapped twice & still things are unsettled.

13 Raining all day. 12 midnight, water has just broken through roof & swamped our posseys? We move into a good billet tomorrow.

16 The 7th Bde. were this morning inspected by Gen. LEGGE after the inspection they travelled to STEENWERCK thence by Rail to YPRES.

22 Left for trenches at Bars GRENIER, in advance of Bn. then on a/c of heavy bombardment Bn. didn't come into trenches so we returned to old place at Rue MARLE.

June 23 In the trenches again, deadly bombardment. Fatigue work on stores for HQ.

24 During the day visited the supports & firing line & inspected site for lamp station, site previously selected too open to shrapnel fire ordered it to be thickly sandbagged. While in firing line enemy opened heavy bombardment. This evening our artillery opened fire on enemy supports & firing line.

25 Fine weather, slightly cloudy, our aeroplane fleet attacked support & firing line of enemy. They also dropped incendiary bombs on enemy balloon & it was a very fascinating sight.

27 At 12PM began a heavy bombardment of enemy trenches opposite our Bde. position. The N.Zs on our left are having a raid tonight hence the bombardment opposite our possy to distract the enemy from the raiding position.

29 At 12PM began a severe bombardment of enemy trenches, first on firing line thence in a semi-circle around the objectives to be raided by the 6th Bde. This is our 1st raid 200 taking part, the 24th were the first to reach enemy trenches & were the first back with prisoners (5).

29 The other Bns. could not bring back any prisoners on a/c of the heavy opposition. The result of raid was—between 80 & 100 of the enemy killed by the raiders, whilst our losses were 7 killed & 15 wounded & 2 missing. The raiders brought back many trophies viz. swords helmets rifles etc. This raid was all the more successful on a/c of the fact that the barb wire was not completely cut & that according to a prisoner, the enemy were aware of our raid on a/c of a N.Z. (stretcher bearer) deserter giving them information.

30 The 4th Div. are taking over the battery & infantry position from us in 6 days time.

July 3 Relieved by the N.Z. Rifle brigade, the 4th Bn. taking over our position in trenches at CHAPELLE ARMENTIERES. Relief completed at 11.40PM 2/7/16.

All very quiet. Raining all the time during relief & after a 10 mile march through water & slush we finally landed at LA CRECHE at 5AM.

4 Visited BAILIEUL a large town & had a good time.

July 8 Left "LA CRECHE" at 1.30PM & arrived at "MERRIS" (a small village of "PRADELLE") at 7PM.

9 Left "PRADELLE" at 11AM & arrived at "EBBLINGHEM" & put up at the Mayor's residence.

10 Left "EBBLINGHEM" at 10AM for "WARDRECQUES".

11 Left "WARDRECQUES" at 7.15AM with transports (in charge of panniers) & arrived at "ARQUES" at 9AM to entrain.

12 Left "ARQUES" at 11.30AM by train passed through ST. OMER thence through BOLOGNE, past ETAPLES (the Aust. training camp) thence through St.ELOI. The railway practically follows the RIVER SOMME all the way. We finally arrived at ARMIENS where we dis-entrained. The scenery of the country was unsurpassed & the trip one to be always remembered. It was like the MARSEILLE–PARIS–AIRE trip. We arrived at AR-MIENS at 8PM & untrucked transports etc. From the railway siding the whole body marched through the main streets of ARMIENS. The French people especially the girls were hilarious with joy, they threw kisses & pressed wine etc. upon us. "VOO-LAY VOU MOMBRASSAY" was what most girls asked, hand shakes & souvenirs collectors in galore. This was the first occasion of Australian troops passing through their City. We marched past nearly 4 miles of buildings & splendid avenues. It was a never-to-be-forgotten sight & experience. We had a spell about 3½ miles out & had tea & then proceeded on to "St. SAVAEUR".

13 We are now billeted at ST. SAVAEUR. This is a fair sized village & 3 of our Bns. are camped here.

16 Bn. moved this morning at 10.30AM for RAINNEVILLE 8¼ miles march, arrived at 2.40PM.

17 This morning lined up & inspected by a French woman who was trying to identify some suspected individual who stole 400 Francs from her shop. This village has rather a forlorn & dela-pidated appearance.

18 Left RAINVILLE at 11AM & rested by roadside for lunch, some cows even close by & some of our chaps milked them. Gen. BIRDWOOD has just passed us.

19 Arrived at TOUTENCOURT at 4PM yesterday light showers falling.

July 19 Sleeping in huts, no sleep last night on a/c of extreme cold so got up & promenaded for a spell.

21 Left TOUTENCOURT at 9AM & arrived at VARANNES at 1PM & then went for a walk to German prisoners camp.

27 Left VARANNES at 5AM & arrived at ALBERT at 8AM Our Bde. takes over firing line tonight; we in supports. We are busy cleaning rifles & having tin diamond discs put on our backs.

28 Arrived at destination last night 5½ miles from "Albert" & have taken over trenches. Lost & wandering in No Mans land. Shrapnel & H.Es is simply hellish sigs acting as runners & guides. Sigs are in deep German dugout 20 ft.deep electric lights were used here, fittings still remain. In large hand painted letters over the mess room are the words "GOTT, STRAFF ANGLAIS".

29 6th & 7th Bdes charged & endeavoured to take 2 lines of trenches. There was a bollocks up, 7th Bde. failed to take their position & 23 Bn. had to fall back one trench on a/c of their Right flank not being covered.

July 29 Our Bn. casualties up to now today 168. Both yesterday & today it was a perfect "HELL". This evening while returning to "SAUSAGE VALLEY" (after having guided a party in) BILLY HILL was shot through the heart by machine gun bullet. Bn. now camped in saps at SAUSAGE VALLEY near the "CRATER" on the Albert-Bapaume Rd.

30 Last night I had the first nights sleep for 4 nights. I slept only 10 yds from guns of battery which were going all night. We've had plenty to eat since being here. An aeroplane left FRANCE & flew to BERLIN & dropped "PAMPHLETS" thence on to RUSSIA & when over AUSTRIA had to descend on a/c of dirty sparkling plugs & he was captured. He did 850 miles in one lap. At POZIERES, one could take a 1000 acre patch & you wouldn't a piece of ground not turned up, on which you could place a threepenny piece, so heavy are the bombardments in this area. A chap feels like shaking hands with himself when he gets out. Today the weather is very hot. Our casualties in this area to date approx 250.

Aug. 3 The 1st & 2nd of month the enemy fire was normal. Last night we bombarded Fritz severly—The Anniversary of the

French declaration of War on the "Huns". Tonight we hop the parapets. My "Kingdom" for a Blighty says many.

Aug. 4 Left SAUSAGE VALLEY at 6PM for trenches got mixed up with the 22nd Bn. & kept with MAJOR McKIE (since killed in charge this evening). We were blocked in sap by 7th Bde & others whilst in "DINKUM ALLEY". Fritz kept up a deadly barrage & gave us "HELL" one shell landing near top of sap buried 3 of us, got out alright. From "DINKUM ALLEY" hopped sap & did a dash along road for "KAY" got blocked there, so made back for CONCRETE HOUSE (on GIBRAL-TER) thence struck out along old sunken road for "CEME-TARY" HQRS.

Machine gun bullets, 77s & HEs in abundance. Earth torn up everywhere, our chaps scattered about. We were walking over scores of our own dead & wounded in the semi-darkness.

Aug. This evening it was "HELL" with a vengeance we passed a 22nd Bn. C.S.M. who had gone mad. We 9 sigs who had started off together found ourselves scattered 3 of us were together at front line & were on our way back—while charge was on—looking for HQRS near the cemetary, when Vic Hughes got his Blighty, Alex Munro & Arthur Kayburn? also wounded—3 sigs at a time. 3 other sigs stopped in dugout near "GIBRALTER" and wouldn't venture out & come up. I found HQRS, the first sig to report & straight away I had to run out a line to Cement house (3/4 mile) got tear shelled while running out line, fixed everything up but the line had been chewed up while running it out. I was absolutely "buggared" having been buried 3 times & gassed within two hours, so I took a good pull at the "Demijohn" (Rhum) & had an hours spell at Bde. before returning.

Aug 5 Returned to HQ at 4AM & found that 5 other sigs had just turned up, so they ran out wire, which was cut to pieces they ran out 2 more & they lasted 5 minutes. In the afternoon Bde. ran out 2 wires which never worked. So 5 of us sigs acted as runners, 3 evacuated wounded, 1 shell shock, & 3 others who wouldn't venture out of their warren. Heavy fire was kept up all day, in the evening Fritz put up a heavy barrage & completely demolished "KAY SAP", & a pitiful sight it was, as I cut across it, from Cemetery H.Q to Bde. HQ with a message at 4.30AM—scores & scores of our men buried & ½ buried, about

50 were lying about severly wounded, nothing but shell holes & dead & wounded was left to mark what was once "KAY SAP". No stretcher bearers were available to carry away the wounded for a while.

6 We moved out of trenches to "TARA" HILL. 4th Div. relieved us, & just as we were preparing to go to sleep Fritz lobbed shells around & one went into the deserted gun pit where COL. R. WATSON, Mjr. MANNING, CAPT. TATNALL, CAPT. PLANT & Lt. CARVISK? were asleep. Only COL. WATSON escaped with severe shell shock, the others were killed, 4 of our best officers gone in a second.

7 Moved out this morning & billeted at WARLOY-BAILLON.

Part continued writing his diary until April 1917 and his first leave. He was killed in France on 25 April 1918, the first anniversary of Anzac Day.

George Cracknell, Royal Navy

Cracknell writes to his mother, describing the Battle of Jutland on 31 May—1 June 1916.

4 June, HMS *Champion*

My Dearest Mums,

Now that the papers have published it I can tell you all about the scrap. When I wrote you the other day I thought you would have already known about it, hence my telling you I was safe and well; but they didn't publish it until after we had returned. Well it was an exciting episode in one's life. I don't want to go through it every day in the week. We were with the battle cruisers and were the first to sight the enemy in their battle cruisers and battlefleet. They were engaged at once and shells soon started falling round us like hail our lot were taking on the whole German fleet and fought them for about three hours when the Grand Fleet arrived and put a different appearance on things. The Huns immediately altered course South and made for home and lager but they got a fine hammering from our battlefleet first for some time. I was on the deck most of the time and saw mostly all of it—it was providence which saved us from being blown out of the water—shells, 12 inch etc. fairly rained round us. Saw the Queen Mary—about 440 yards from us go up in a puff of smoke and flame afterwards there was nothing more to see only 6 or 7 saved. It was all a magnificent sight. Especially after our battlefleet engaged them. But the night was very thrilling the sky was lit up with flame and intermittent actions were going on all round us. Saw two or three ships on fire and one Hun dreadnought blown up by a torpedo. We had a narrow squeak, ran into some German big ship who turned their searchlights on us and blazed away but did not touch us, although bits of shell were picked up on deck next day. I was up all night— you can imagine I wasn't disposed to turning in. Next morning we had the devil's luck, a torpedo passed within a yard of the stern and another passed under us! We should now be little fishes if there wasn't some one keeping an eye on us. I hope he will continue to do so. There's no need to be depressed—the Huns got a good hammering and lost more than you yet realise—if we cop them a little further from Berlin next time they'll be lucky to get their lager again in this life. I wonder if any of Huths late employees were with the Huns. I hope they got it in the neck if they were. We passed a german ship sinking—though most of the crew seemed to have gone down. Next day on our return we passed through masses of corpses. Reminded me of the "Aboukir" days—rescued several lots on rafts and in small boats but they had been adrift for hours and many died from exposure. It was a horrible sight. Doesn't it seem funny that Tuesday afternoon I was playing golf and 24 hours afterwards wondering when my time was coming—its a funny world. I'm enclosing you a few snaps taken a few days before the battle—although you might not think it to look at them, I'm not the C in C. I'm sending Dad some in my next, so you can keep these yourself. Well I wished you many happy returns today over a "Martini"—I'm afraid leave is now more distant than ever, but it will come some day. I could do with only a weekend. Saw my late ship during the battle and my late Captain was giving them it hot in a ship just ahead of us. Which must be nameless. All our losses have been officially stated, theirs haven't yet! so don't worry. Thanks for Collens and when you feel like making another cake there are plenty to do it justice. Much love. Wish you could come here for a few days—

Ever yr affec son,

N

Lieutenant Henri Desagneaux,
French 2nd Infantry Regiment

Diary: Saturday, 10 June [1916]
At one in the morning, order for departure at 4 a.m. We are to march in the direction of Verdun. That gives us an extra day of life! We are billeted at Rosières near Bar.

Monday, 12 June
Issoncourt, Last stage before Verdun. There is not much room as car-load upon car-load of supplies and munitions speed past us.

Tuesday, 13 June
Reveille at 2 a.m. At 5, we travel by car and are put down at Nixéville, 6 kilometres from Verdun. We bivouac in a wood in a lake of mud. The guns fire angrily, it's pouring down. At 3 p.m. we are ordered to stand by to leave. We don't, however. We spend the night and the day of the 14th waiting, in torrential rain with mud up to our ankles. Our teeth chatter with cold, we are very uncomfortable. Although the troops have been stopping here for the last four months to go to and from verdun, there is not one single hut or shelter. We camp in individual tents in thick mud. You should hear what the men say about it!

At 5 p.m., order for departure at 6.30. We are going to be quartered in the Citadel of Verdun. Faces are grave. The guns are thundering over there. It's a real furnace. Everyone realizes that perhaps tomorrow death will come. Numerous rumours are circulating; we are going to 'Mort-Homme' which has been captured by the Boches; or to the Fort at Vaux . . . What is certain, nothing good lies in store for us.

We arrive at the Citadel at 10 p.m. after a difficult march through the mud.

Thursday, 15 June
We spend the day in the Citadel waiting. The guns fire ceaselessly. Huge shells (380s–420s) crash down on Verdun causing serious damage. I walk as far as the town; it's in ruins and deserted. One can't stay outside for long as shells are dropping everywhere.

The Citadel is a real underground town, with narrow-gauge railway, dormitories, and rooms of every type; it's safe here, but very gloomy.

At 9 in the evening, we leave, not knowing our destination. We advance slowly through the night. At every moment huge shells come and explode on Verdun, at the crossroads, and in the direction of our gun-batteries which are stationed on all sides. We march in silence, everyone conscious of the seriousness of the moment.

At 1 a.m. we arrive at the Bras-Ravin Quarries, where we remain in reserve. No shelter, nothing, we are in the open fields at the mercy of the first shell.

Friday, 16 June

Superb weather, but not far from us, it's a furnace of artillery fire. The Boches pump their shells at us, and our guns reply. What a racket! 150s and 210s scour the land on all sides and there is nothing anyone can do but wait. The battalion is massed in the ravine without any shelter, if their shelling was not at random it would be dreadful for us. The German observation balloons scan the horizon. Up in the sky, their planes search for us; we curl up in a hole when a shell bursts near us and it's like this until evening when orders arrive.

At 6 p.m. my company and another (the 24th) receive the order to advance with a view to reinforcing the 5th Battalion which is to attack on the following day. We leave, not knowing exactly where we are going; and no one has a map. We have a vague idea where the command posts are; guides are rare in this area where death stalks at every step. With difficulty, we move along crumbling trenches, cross a ridge to take up our position in the Ravin des Dames. The shells rain down, still no shelter.

We haven't eaten for twenty-four hours and don't know if supplies can arrive tonight.

Saturday, 17 June

The attack is due at 9 a.m. The 106th is in charge with the 5th Battalion of the 359th as support. We have to recapture a trench at the top of the ravine that the Boches took from us the day before. We spend the night in the Bras-Ravin; hurriedly we dig a trench to give our men some shelter. Just beside us there is a cemetery where the dead are being brought at every moment. The guns fire furiously, from 3 o'clock it's hell. One cannot imagine what the simple phrase of an official statement like 'We have recaptured a trench' really means! The attack is prepared from 4 to 9 o'clock; all guns firing together. The Germans fire non-stop, ammunition dumps blow up, it's deadly. There are so many explosions around us that the air reeks of powder and earth; we can't see clearly any more. We wait anxiously without knowing whether we shall be alive an hour later.

At 9, the gunners' range lengthens. We can't see anything up in front any more. The planes fly low, signalling all the time.

At 11, after a relative pause, the cannonade starts up again. At 2 p.m. it's worse still, it's enough to drive you mad; the Boches are only firing their 210s and 150s, shrapnel explodes above us, we have no idea of what is happening or of the result. We are infested by huge black flies. You don't know where to put yourself.

At 6 p.m. I receive the order to reconnoitre the gun emplacements in the front line, as our battalion is relieving tonight. The shell-bursts are so continuously heavy that we cannot advance before nightfall and it is impossible to cross the ridge.

The wounded from this morning's attack are beginning to arrive, we learn what happened: our artillery fired too short and demolished our front line trench (evacuated for the attack), instead of firing on the Boches. When we attacked the Germans let us advance to 15 metres and then caught us in a hail of machine-gunfire. We succeeded in capturing several parts of the trench but couldn't hold them; at the moment our troops are scattered here and there in shell-craters. During the attack, the German planes bombed our men ceaselessly. Our losses are enormous: the 106th already has 350–400 men out of action, two captains killed and a large number of officers wounded. The 5th Battalion of the 359th. which was advancing in support was caught by gunfire and suffered heavily. The 19th Company hasn't got one officer left, in the 18th, three are missing. We have 32 Boches as prisoners. The positions are the same as before the attack—with our troops only being able to maintain the front-line position which they had previously evacuated.

At nightfall, the dead arrive on stretchers at the cemetery. In this, the Ravine of Death, they lay there, lined up, waiting to be put into the holes that are being hastily dug for them: Major Payen, his head red with blood; Major Cormouls, black with smoke, still others unrecognizable and often in pieces. A sad spectacle, which is repeated here every day.

Sunday, 18 June
We have had to leave to occupy our new positions before our food arrived. It's the second day without food. We eat what little we've got amid huge black flies.

We are now stuck at the top of the ridge in a half-collapsed trench, without any shelter. The whole night there is terrible shelling; we lie flat and pray for any hole to shelter in. At every moment we are sprayed with clouds of earth and stone splinters. There must be an attack on the right, as one can hear the chatter of machine-guns! How many men are afraid! How many 'Croixes de Guerre' are weak at the knees!

The 210s make the ground quake, it's hellish, and explains the dazed looks of those who return from such a sector.

It's Sunday! day breaks amid bursts of gunfire. We await orders. One can't think of washing or sleeping. No news: neither papers, nor letters. It's a void, we are no longer in a civilized world. One suffers, and says nothing; the night has been cold; lying on the damp earth one just shivers, not being able to breathe properly because of the smell.

The afternoon doesn't pass too badly. It's an artillery duel, where the infantry is not spared.

At 8 p.m. I receive the order to relieve in the front line a company of the 106th.

At 9 p.m. this order is countermanded, I am to relieve a company of the 5th Battalion of the 359th in the ravine, at the 'Boyau-Marie', near the 'Trois Cornes' wood where there are attacks every day . . .

Orders and counter-orders follow each other; no-one has a map, or even a sketch. We don't know where the Boches are, but there is some fear that they will attack us on our right.

My company is all in a line in this trench which collapsed yesterday under the bombardment following our attack. A squad of machine-gunners of the 5th Battalion is buried in it; the following day at dawn we will discover all along the trench, corpses, then legs and arms protruding out of the ground.

Scarcely are we in position when the shelling restarts; the only shelter is small crannies in which one must curl up. We are being shelled from the front and from the flank. What fire! The ground trembles, the air is unbreathable; by midnight I have already eight wounded in my company.

Monday, 19 June

We are expecting an attack at any moment. There is talk of recapturing the trenches with grenades. But what are our leaders doing? Ah, we don't see them here. We are left to ourselves, they won't come and bother us.

We try and make ourselves as comfortable as possible but the more we dig, the more bodies we find. We give up and go elsewhere, but we just leave one graveyard for another. At dawn we have to stop as the German planes are up above spying on us. They signal and the guns start up again, more furiously than before.

No sleep, no water, impossible to move out of one's hole, to even show your head above the trench. We are filthy dirty and have only cold tinned food to eat. We are not receiving supplies any more and have only been here for four days!

The afternoon and the evening are dreadful, it's an inferno of fire. The Germans are attacking our front line, we expect at any instant to be summoned to help. The machine-guns sputter; the ground trembles, the air is full of dust and smoke which scorch the throat. This lasts until 10 p.m. The fatigue party has to leave under a hail of fire to go and fetch our food just outside Verdun – 6 kilometres there and 6 more back. The men go without saying a word!

Tuesday, 20 June
The food supplies only arrive with great difficulty at 2 this morning. Still no water. When one has exhausted one's ration of coffee and wine, you have to go thirsty. By day, the heat is overpowering, we are surrounded by flies and corpses which give off a nauseating smell.

On the alert the whole night. Our position is critical. The Boches harass us. On our right the ravine cannot be occupied because of the shelling. The Thiaumont and the Vaux works are being bombarded continuously. On the left, too, Bras and Mort-Homme are being shelled.

Yesterday my company had 2 men killed and 10 wounded.

The morning is calmer, but at 1 p.m. the firing starts up again. It's a battle of extermination – Man against the Cannon.

8 p.m. Night falls; time doesn't go fast enough – we would like it to be tomorrow already.

10 p.m. Great commotion, red and white flares, chatter of machine-guns, thunder of artillery. 400 metres from us, a new attack is unleashed upon our lines. Every man is at his post waiting, the whole night through. Will the Boches rush us from the top of the ridge? Shells explode only metres from us and all around men fall wounded. We are blinded by the shells and by the earth they throw up, it's an inferno, one could write about such a day minute by minute.

Meanwhile, orders to stand by arrive. Ready we are, but those who are sending these orders, without knowing what is happening, would do better to come here to see the position we are in.

Today again, 1 killed and 9 wounded in my company.

Wednesday, 21 June

Impossible to sleep, even an hour, the deluge of shells continues and the whole night frantic orders follow each other: you may be attacked, be ready! We have been ready for three days.

The night passes in an inferno of fire. Near Mort-Homme, calm has returned, the Boches are concentrating on Hill 321 and Vaux – it's hell out there – you wonder how anyone will come out alive. The shells, the shrapnel, the 210s fall like hail for twenty-four hours non-stop, only to start again; everything trembles, one's nerves as well as the ground. We feel at the end of our tether.

And what a responsibility! The chiefs tell us: keep watch, but no-one can give you any indication about the terrain; on our right, there's the ravine of Hill 321, but we don't even know the positions occupied by our troops and by the Boches. Our artillery itself, is firing without knowing our positions.

8 p.m. We have been bombarded by 210s for exactly twenty-four hours. The Germans have been attacking on our right since 6 p.m. My company at every moment receives the order to stand by to advance. It's a state of perpetual anguish, not a moment's respite.

We crouch there, with our packs on our backs, waiting, scanning the top of the ridge to see what is happening and this lasts until nightfall. We are haggard, dazed, hungry, and feverishly thirsty, but there is no water. In some companies there have been cases of madness. How much longer are we going to stay in this situation?

Night comes and the guns still fire; our trenches have collapsed, it's a tangle of equipment and guns left by the wounded, there's nothing human about it. Why don't they send the deputies, senators, and generals here?

9 p.m. 210s still, our nerves can't take much more. Can't move or sleep. There are no more shelters, one just clings to the wall of the trench. We wait. At 9.15 the bombardment starts again: the front line troops are so fatigued and jumpy that at every moment they believe they are being attacked and ask for artillery support. Red flares follow, our artillery does its best, it's hellish.

Thursday, 22 June

At last in the evening I receive the order to relieve the 24th Company in the front line. The whole afternoon there has been a deluge of shells on the ravine, perhaps we will be calmer in the front line? But where to go to relieve? A reconnaissance is impossible, no one has an idea where the troops are exactly.

At 9 p.m. an avalanche of fire bursts on the ridge, the relief has to be delayed, it would be impossible to pass. Is it an attack? There is gas as well as shells, we can't breathe and are forced to put on our masks.

At 11 p.m. we leave. What a relief! Not knowing our front line positions we advance haphazardly and over the top we find our men crouching in shell holes.

My company is placed in one line, without any trench, in shell craters.

It's a plateau, swept continously by machine-gunfire and flares. Every ten steps one has to fall flat on the ground so as not to be seen. The terrain is littered with corpses! What an advance! It's dark, one feels something soft beneath one's feet, it's a stomach. One falls down flat and it's a corpse. It's awful; we start again with only one desire – to get there.

My company occupies a broken line. Impossible to move around in daylight. To the left, no communication with the neighbouring company; just a hole 100 metres long; we don't know if the Boches are there. In the centre, the same hole – occupied or not? I have a squad which is completely isolated and stay with it.

The captain I am relieving (Symian) tries to show me the terrain. He doesn't know it himself, dazed by four days spent up front amid dead and wounded.

In a nightmare advance, we stumble forwards falling in shell-craters, walking on corpses, flinging ourselves repeatedly to the ground.

Ground where there lie forever men of the 106th, of the 359th still others of regiments who preceded us. It's a graveyard, a glimpse of hell.

Friday, 23 June

5 a.m. The bombardment starts up again fiercely. I get a shell splinter in my lip. Nothing serious fortunately, as the wounded have to wait until evening to get their wounds dressed. One cannot leave the shell-hole even by crawling on one's stomach.

7 a.m. Alert. Commotion. The Boches attack. They are driven back by our return of fire. In the direction of Hill 321 huge attack which lasts three hours with wave upon wave of them.

The heat is oppressive. Around us the stench of the corpses is nauseating. We have to live, eat, and wait in it. Do or die! It's six days now since we had a moment's rest or sleep. The attacks follow each other. The Boches have succeeded in advancing towards Hill

321 and in occupying a part of the ravine behind us, where our reinforcements are.

The shelling has completely destroyed the trench where we were yesterday; the dead and the wounded are too numerous to count.

Saturday, 24 June

Big German offensive on the right bank of the Meuse. This news arrived during the night. There is no question of our being relieved. Everything is silent and behind us, on Fleury ridge, the Boches continue infiltrating. We have been turned! There is no longer any doubt, as we can see enemy columns invading the terrain and their machine-guns are attacking us from behind while our artillery has had to move back.

Now something worse: my men, who have been suffering all sorts of hardships for the last seven days, are becoming demoralized. The word 'prisoner' is being whispered. For many this would seem salvation. We must fight against this notion, raise morale. But how? We can't move around, and only those near us can hear. They are all good chaps, devoted, who won't leave us and will form a bodyguard.

What are we waiting for? We don't know. Yet we can only wait for it: perhaps the attack which will kill us, or the bombardment to bury us, or exile even. We spend some anxious hours, without knowing how long this will last.

At 11 a.m. artillery is heard. Our batteries have taken up new positions and are opening fire, the Boches reply.

Impossible to eat, our nerves can't stand it. If we have a call of nature to satisfy, we have to do it in a tin or on a shovel and throw it over the top of our shell-hole. It's like this every day.

Sunday, 25 June

Terrible day and night.

At 3 a.m, without warning, our own troops attack us from behind in order to recapture the terrain lost the day before on our right. These troops, without precise orders, without maps, without even knowing where our lines are, ventured off. They fell upon us, believing they had found the Boches. But the Boches were 100 metres in front, lying in wait and bursts of machine-gunfire cut them down in our trench. We thus have another heap of corpses and wounded crying out, but whom we are powerless to help. Trench! – well almost every evening we bury the dead on the spot and it's they who form the parapets!

At 6 a.m., the guns fire furiously and to add to our plight, our 75s fire at us. Terrible panic; six wounded at one go from a shell-burst, everyone wants to run for it. Agnel and I have to force these poor devils back by drawing our revolvers.

Major David is killed in turn by our 75s. Our green flares ask for the range to be lengthened, but with all the dust our artillery can't see a thing. We don't know where to put ourselves, we are powerless. Isolated from everything with no means of communication. There's blood everywhere; the wounded have sought refuge with us, thinking that we could help them; the blood flows, the heat is atrocious, the corpses stink, the flies buzz – it's enough to drive one mad. Two men of the 24th Company commit suicide.

At 2 p.m., our 75s start firing on us again. our situation is critical. It is only improved when I send a loyal man at full speed with a report to the Colonel. Luckily he gets through.

Monday, 26 June
Our 220 mortars bombard Thiaumont: we must recapture some terrain to give ourselves some room and to drive the enemy back in its advance on Fleury. We attack incessantly. It's four days since we have been in the front line and the relieving troops have been annihilated this morning during the attacks.

Rain replaces the sun; filthy mud. We can't sit down any more. We are covered in slime and yet we have to lie flat. I haven't washed for ten days, my beard is growing. I am unrecognizable, frighteningly dirty.

Tuesday, 27 June
The guns thunder the whole night: the men who left to fetch the food at 10 last night haven't come back. Still longer without food or drink.

4.30 a.m., first attack on Thiaumont and Hill 321.

9 a.m., second attack. All around us, men are falling: there are some only 5 metres from us in shell-holes, yet we can't help them. If you show your head, you get a burst of machine-gun bullets.

The whole day, incessant firing: the Boches counter-attack; we drive them back by our rifle fire and with grenades.

My company is rapidly diminishing, we are about sixty left now, with this small number we still have to hold our position. In the evening, when the men go to fetch supplies we are really at the mercy of an attack. Still no relief.

Wednesday, 28 June
Hardest day to endure. The Boches begin to pound our positions, we take cover; some try to flee, we have to get our revolvers out

310 THE FIRST WORLD WAR 1914-1918

again and stand in their way. It's hard, our nerves are frayed and it's difficult to make them see reason.

At midday, while we are trying to eat a bit of chocolate, Agnel's orderly has his back broken beside us; the poor chap is groaning, there is nothing we can do except to wait for nightfall, and then, take him to the first-aid post, and will we be able to? The wounded are so numerous and we have so few men left that those who can't walk sometimes have to wait for forty-eight hours before being taken away. The stretcher-bearers are frightened and don't like coming to us. Furthermore, the nights are so short, that they can only make one trip. One trip: four men to take one wounded on a stretcher!

1 p.m., it's an inferno: the Boches undoubtedly are preparing to attack us. Shells scream down on every side: a new panic to be checked. At 6 p.m. when we are dazed and numb, the firing range lengthens and suddenly everyone is on his feet, shouting, the Boches are coming. They attack in massed formation, in columns of eight!

These troops who, moments ago were in despair, are at their posts in a twinkling; we hold our grenades until the Boches are at 15 metres, then let them have it. Guns bark, and a machine-gun which survived the avalanche of shells is wreaking havoc.

The Boches are cut down; amid the smoke, we see dozens of dead and wounded, and the rest retreating back to their trenches. Our commanding officer, thinking that we are hard-pressed, sends welcome reinforcements. They will be useful for supplies and taking the wounded away.

Only around 9 p.m is it quieter. We help the wounded who are waiting to be taken away. Our shell-holes are lakes of mud. It is raining and we don't know where to put ourselves: our rifles don't work any more, and we can only rely upon our grenades which are in short supply.

This evening, still no relief; another twenty-four hours to get through. It gets colder at night, we lie down in the mud and wait.

Thursday, 29 June
Our fourteenth day in this sector. The bombardment continues, our nerves make us tremble, we can't eat any more, we are exhausted.

Yet still no relief.

Friday, 30 June

Attacks and counter-attacks. Frightful day – the shelling and the fatigue are becoming harder to bear. At 10 a.m., French attack on Thiaumont; the artillery fires 12,000 rounds of 255s, 550 of 220s, and the 75s fire at will.

The din began at 6 this morning; the Boches reply furiously. It's hell, we are getting hit more and more often, as our position is the favourite enemy target. The majority of the shells fall on or around us. The shelling will last ten hours! And during this time we expect an attack at any moment. To make it worse, my own company is hard hit. A 210 falls directly on a group of men sheltering in a hole: 3 killed and 2 seriously wounded who drag themselves up to me to plead for help. A minute later, a second shell sends a machine-gun flying, killing 2 more men and wounding a third. It's panic stations – the men run, and under a hail of gunfire, I have to force them back again with a revolver in my hand. Everyone goes back to his post, we set up another machine-gun and keep watch.

At 10 a.m. and 2 p.m. first and second French attacks on Thiaumont. The Boche harass us with their fire. Our heads are buzzing, we have had enough. Myself, Agnel, and my orderly are squashed in a hole, protecting ourselves from splinters with our packs. Numb and dazed, without saying a word, and with our hearts pounding, we await the shell that will destroy us. The wounded are increasing in numbers around us. These poor devils not knowing where to go come to us, believing that they will be helped. What can we do? There are clouds of smoke, the air is unbreathable. There's death everywhere. At our feet, the wounded groan in a pool of blood; two of them, more seriously hit are breathing their last. One, a machine-gunner, has been blinded, with one eye hanging out of its socket and the other torn out: in addition he has lost a leg. The second has no face, an arm blown off, and a horrible wound in the stomach. Moaning and suffering atrociously one begs me, 'Lieutenant, don't let me die. Lieutenant, I'm suffering, help me.' The other, perhaps more gravely wounded and nearer to death, implores me to kill him with these words, 'Lieutenant, if you don't want to, give me your revolver!' Frightful, terrible moments, while the cannons harry us and we are splattered with mud and earth by the shells. For hours, these groans and supplications continue until, at 6 p.m., they die before our eyes without anyone being able to help them.

At this moment, the hurricane of fire ceases, we prepare to receive an attack, but fortunately nothing happens.

We look at one another, our eyes haggard, trembling all over, half-crazy. Is it going to start all over again?

At last, at 8 p.m., an order: we are to be relieved. What a cry of joy from those of us left. We wait anxiously and it's 2 a.m. before the replacements arrive. Our information is quickly passed on. Soon it will be dawn and we have to cross the zone before sunrise. Tiredness disappears, and our limbs regain enough strength to escape from these plains where at every step the guns have done their work; corpses of men, carcasses of horses, overturned vehicles, it's a horrific graveyard all the way to Verdun. We halt, the guns are rumbling in the distance, we can breathe at last; we call the roll, how many are missing when their names are called!

Our time at Verdun has been awful. Our faces have nothing human about them. For sixteen days we have neither washed nor slept. Life has been spent amongst dead and dying, hardships of every sort and incessant anguish. Our cheeks are hollow, beards long and our clothes thick with mud. And, above all, we have a vision of these horrific days, the memory of a comrade fallen in action; each one of us thinks of those who have not returned. Despite our joy at being alive, our eyes reveal the crazy horror of it all.

During the struggle, whole regiments have melted away. The 129th Division doesn't exist any more. The 359th has lost 33 officers and 1,100 men. My company, with the 22nd, had the heaviest pressure to bear. Both resisted all the German attacks. They prevented their descent into the ravine and therefore the complete encirclement of the area.

Saturday, 1 July
After being relieved, we are quartered at Bois-la-Villee, in the same camp where we stopped on the way here. We arrive at 2 p.m., exhausted. We fall into bed and sleep like brutes.

Sunday, 2 July
At 8 a.m., we pile into cars, glad to leave this ill-fated region far behind. We get out at Ligny-en-Barrois at 2 p.m. We spend the evening at ablutions.

Wednesday, 5 July
Promoted captain.

Lieutenant E. Russell-Jones,
30th Division Trench Mortar Battery

A diary account of the first day of the Battle of the Somme.

Diary: 1st July 1916

Am just going to try and write a few impressions of my first big engagement, for we're within a very few minutes of what is to be the beginning of the end of German culture.

For seven whole days our guns have been pounding the enemy's line, and now on the early morning of the eighth day, the attack is about to take place.

Our little battery has done its share in preparing the way for the infantry. Most days we have fired with excellent results, though I'm sorry to say not without casualties to ourselves.

We were up at 2 a.m. this morning and at 3.45 a.m. set off for our positions. Dawn was just breaking and a heavy mist hung over everywhere, shutting out any view of the lines. As we came up communication trenches there were hundreds of infantrymen lying about in all kinds of old corners, some even stretched out on the bare trench boards, sound asleep and sublimely unconscious to the sounds of war, which even at that early hour were making themselves heard. Just a few salvos from an 18 pndr battery, then some of our big guns, their shells sounding for all the world like an express train rounding a curve at top speed, now a battery of those wonderful French guns the 75s opens fire and drowns everything in their uproar. We'd got close up to the trenches proper by this time and distant objects were coming into view. Right ahead could be seen the tall trees surrounding the village which we are to take today. An aeroplane could be heard buzzing away in the distance. Fritz tries several shots at him but they were all far away from their mark.

I'm sitting in a tiny little dugout which is just about splinter-proof but no more, surrounded by dozens of our bombs and ammunition boxes, waiting for the next 35 minutes to pass as quickly as it can, for at the end of that time we open fire and keep it up for 65 minutes, just to put the wind up Fritz before the assault.

War is a curious business, and very well for those who like it, but I must say I am no lover of the game. At the moment I feel pretty rotten and hate myself for it, for when one has such splendid fellows under one as I have, one feels one's deficiencies very much, but here we are and we've all got to see it through now, so all there is to do is to stick it to the end as well as possible.

[9.15 am]

We got our rounds away quite nicely, heaps of stuff all around us but just seemed to miss each time. Our troops going over was a magnificent sight. At the given signal they were all out of their trenches, lined up as if on parade, and set off for Berlin. The front line presented little difficulty having been almost levelled or rather filled in by the artillery fire, but of course their curtain of fire did a heap of damage and many poor fellows only got outside the trench to be knocked in again. We're sitting now in an underground dugout, which if it were only propped decently would be a decent place, but the props we have are none too strong, and as a shell falls within yards of us every few minutes, I don't like it, but there are at the moment thousands of men out in the open without the slightest cover, so we ought to be thankful for what we have got.

There are three poor fellows lying in here with us, one a sergeant has had his left foot blown off, and the other two are pretty badly messed up. It is useless to try and get them away at present, we're waiting to see if things will cool down a little. I can't write any more yet a bit.

[2 pm]

Am back in Maricourt writing this; after writing my last we endured perfect Hell for a couple of hours, shells landing within a few feet of us every few seconds. Then three men came across from the opposite dugout to say it had been blown in and ten men lying buried in it. Not the slightest use trying to dig them out. It would be a day or more's job and they're already dead. One of the men who came across was Davidson, my old servant in England and sometime servant to Watson. He has caught it very badly. He cannot see and has a piece of shell in his chest which apparently has entered his lungs for he cannot breathe properly poor lad I very much doubt if he will get over it, and I'm afraid two other of my very best boys are dead in that other dugout.

Both my guns were out of action and there was no use in keeping the men up there, so off I went to get medical aid for the many wounded that we'd taken in and to ask the HQRA [Headquarters Royal Artillery] if I might get the men away. Coming down the trenches I was chased by shells all the way, and the wounded passed on the way, too horribly mangled for words. What a ghastly business this whole affair is, but on the other hand what a success it has all been. The Boches are simply giving themselves up in hundreds. We've captured Montauban, on our left they've got Mametz and on our right the French have taken Hardecourt. Let us hope we are in sight of the finish. All the Allies are advancing and behind the dark clouds there is just a little ray of sunshine which we trust will mean peace for ourselves, our children, our children's children, aye and even Peace for ever and a day.

Private Sidney Williamson, 1/8th Battalion, Royal Warwickshire Regiment

Diary; 1 July 1916 [on the Somme]
It was a lovely bright morning, but the feelings of the men were tense. We had breakfast at 5.0 a.m., afterwards the officers were going round to see all the men and have a talk with us. The shelling was terrific and the Germans started to shell our lines. At 7.20 a mine was exploded under the German trenches. An officer detailed me and another soldier standing by me to carry forward with us a box containing a signalling lamp. At 7.30 a.m. whistles were blown and the attack started. What did I see! To the left as far as Gommecourt and to the right as far as Beaumont Hamel, lines of soldiers going forward as though on parade in line formation. Just "over the top" the soldier helping me with the box stopped and fell dead. I had to go on but without the box. Lt Jones was the next officer I saw to fall, then CSM Haines was calling for me, he had been wounded. I reached the first German line and dropped into it where there were many German dead. The battlefield was nothing but shell holes and barbed wire, but now I noticed many dead and dying, and the lines of soldiers was not to be seen. With no officers or NCO near I felt alone and still went forward from shell hole to shell hole. Later Cpl Beard joined me and he asked me to hold down a ground signalling sheet so that he could get a message to the observing aeroplane flying overhead. He asked for "MORE BOMBS" and the Pilot of the aeroplane asked "Code please". This was flashed back and the aeroplane flew away.

Things were now getting disorganised and at this point we could not go any further. The machine-gun fire was deadly. And our bombs had all been used up. The Colonel of the Seaforths came up and took charge of all the odd groups of men belonging to various Regiments. He told us to dig ourselves in and eventually there must have been 50 or 60 men at this spot, and it all started from the one small shell hole Cpl Beard and myself were first in.

Now there was a lull in the fighting till 3.0 p.m. At one time a shout went up that we were surrounded by Germans, but they were Germans running from the dugouts in the first line and giving themselves up. I do not think they made it.

With Cpl Beard we started to get back to our lines shell hole by shell hole, but we soon got parted. I managed to reach the British lines at 7.30 p.m., but the sight that met my eyes was terrible. Hundreds of dead soldiers were everywhere, and the Germans kept up their heavy shelling. Met Sam and Bob Patterson in the trench, the only two of my own Battalion. Stayed in the British trench all night.

Private Arthur Hubbard, 4th Battalion, the London Regiment (London Scottish)

5 July 1916
[The Somme]

Dear Mother and All

No doubt you have been worrying about me very much, but now you can rest assured I am quite all right, [though] suffering from slight Shell Shock.

Went over and took the Huns 4th line of trenches on Saturday morning at 7.30 a.m. and held same until 3.30 in the afternoon when by that time their artillery had completely wiped our battalion out, and what was left of us had to crawl back to our own trenches, but the bounders mowed us down with machinegun fire as we were returning. I managed to get back safely after a long and weary struggle over 300 yards of rough ground. I got buried over in their second line by a shell but managed to work my way out. My steel helmet saved my life, a piece of shell knocked it off my head without the slightest injury. I shall be quite myself in a week or two, as you will notice by my writing, only my nerves are shook up, severe headache now and again when my mind is on the affair.

Poor Isaacs must have gone under as I did not see him when we got back to our own trenches.

Adolf Sturmer, German Army

A former law student, Sturmer served on the Eastern Front.

Not far from Povorce, August 9th, 1916

Yesterday I volunteered for the patrol that was to blow up the bridge which the Russians had thrown across the S. I knew the terrain from various wanderings. When there are so many of you, you can't swim over, because that would make too much noise, so we had to manage with a raft. We lit a small fire beforehand so as to see from which direction most of the bullets came, and immediately realized that we couldn't get through on the right. So we started off to the left, where we got across the river and surprised the nearest Russian post.

It was funny how startled the chaps were! One great big bearded Hun especially; Kramer was going for him and he hastily made the sign of the cross and then put up his hands. Then they were all full of joy; kissed our hands and coats; tore the cockades out of their caps, and threw down their arms. They fell rather than walked from one shell-hole to another while they were being taken back to our lines.

However, we had made rather too much noise, and as we advanced we were fired on. We threw ourselves down and stuck our heads into the earth, but we managed to reach the long bridge. The Austrian sappers put the dynamite in position and then: "Back! Quick march!" An explosion scattered earth in all directions, and again we took cover. One Austrian got a splinter in the head and bled like a pig. As we were tying him up I saw a patrol coming after us. Immediately: "Right turn! March!" and we found ourselves on a branch of the S. The ones in front tried to cross, but comrade Kramer sank up to his waist, and another man went in up to the neck in the bog and shouted: "Halt! I can't swim!" With some difficulty we pulled him out, and then proceeded along the bank.

At this point Senhöfer, a perfect comrade, promoted Corporal only to-day, was shot. He had been four years with the regiment. The bullet went in through his mouth and came out through the back of his head. I remained remarkably calm and cool; one has got so accustomed to the thought of death; one is on familiar terms with fate; one must be hard—remorselessly hard; but later on I felt it very much, for I was very fond of this comrade. I must admit though that I couldn't bear to look long at the dead man, with his face now so set, pale and covered with blood, when only that morning we had sat together, chatting and laughing . . .

To-day I have had a rest. I went for a walk through the forest and across the dunes. On the way I stuck a bit of heather in my cap, and picked a whole bunch of it to send to my dear good mother at home.

When it began to get dark, I sat down under the birch-trees on the edge of the forest. From the neighbouring trenches comes the murmur of soldiers" voices: some telling long yarns; some arguing about politics. Then everything becomes quiet. From the Austrians beyond comes the sound of singing: a single, beautiful voice rings out into the night. The dark forms of the trees loom above me like the shadows of giants and in the night-sky stars again stand so bright and near over my head. Suddenly I feel so buoyant and free from all earthly trammels that I could almost fly away up and down among the stars. And then I said a very earnest evening prayer.

August 28th, 1916.

I often think about Strassburg now. I got really to appreciate and love it for the first time during my last leave at home, in June. I realized for the first time what a beautiful city it is, and felt that it really was my home. I can't understand now how I have managed to ignore its beauties so long. I only knew the Cathedral and the old Kammerzell House. But this time I only needed to walk through the streets or along the Ill Straden to notice wonderful groups of houses, some timbered and covered with ancient carving, and some Gothic, with pointed arches, little towers, stepped gables, and steep roofs like those in Schwind's picture-books. The old black towers past which the Ill flows stand like a row of rugged giants, guarding the city. And then the splendid buildings of the French period! One could hardly keep count of the beautiful houses, as one after another appeared. The buildings in few towns of Germany can be richer in interesting associations, among which shine the names of Gottfried of Strassburg, Tauler and Fischart, Gutenberg, Master Erwin, and Goethe. Strassburg bears witness to the time of Germany's greatest and most beautiful productivity. Why is all that dead and forgotten? Directly we realize it, it seems to revive, and one's home, which was almost unknown before, appears beautiful and lovable. That is what I often dream of nowadays when I am on guard in the trenches or lying, as at this moment, in the camp under the birch-trees.

Sturmer was killed on 23 October 1916.

Friedrich Steinbrecher, German Army

Steinbrecher writes to his family.

August 12th 1916

Somme. The whole history of the world cannot contain a more ghastly word! All the things I am now once more enjoying—bed, coffee, rest at night, water—seem unnatural and as if I had no right to them. And yet I was only there a week.

At the beginning of the month we left our old position. During the lorry and train journey we were still quite cheery. We knew what we were wanted for. Then came bivouacs, an "alarm", and we were rushed up through shell-shattered villages and barrage into the turmoil of war. The enemy was firing with 12-inch guns. There was a perfect torrent of shells. Sooner than we expected we were in the thick of it. First in the artillery position. Columns were tearing hither and thither as if possessed. The gunners could no longer see or hear. Very lights were going up along the whole Front, and there was a deafening noise: the cries of wounded, orders, reports.

At noon the gun-fire became even more intense, and then came the order: "The French have broken through. Counter-attack!"

We advanced through the shattered wood in a hail of shells. I don't know how I found the right way. Then across an expanse of shell craters, on and on. Falling down and getting up again. Machine-guns were firing. I had to cut across our own barrage and the enemy's. I am untouched.

At last we reach the front line. Frenchmen are forcing their way in. The tide of battle ebbs and flows. Then things get quieter. We have not fallen back a foot. Now one's eyes begin to see things. I want to keep running on—to stand still and look is horrible. "A wall of dead and wounded!" How often have I read that phrase! Now I know what it means.

I have witnessed scenes of heroism and of weakness. Men who can endure every privation. Being brave is not only a matter of will, it also requires strong nerves, though the will can do a great deal. A Divisional Commander dubbed us the "Iron Brigade" and said he had never seen anything like it. I wish it had all been only a dream, a bad dream. And yet it was a joy to see such heroes stand and fall. The bloody work cost us 177 men. We shall never forget Chaulmes and Vermandovillers.

Steinbrecher was killed in action in 1917.

Helmut Zschuppe, German Army

No. 11 Field Hospital, October 25th, 1916
It doesn't do one any good to spend one's time between going on
guard every fifth and sixth hour and sleeping in a mud-hole or a
half-finished dug-out at the far end of which the air is so bad
that a candle won't burn. And after an attack in a trench with
bombs and flame-throwers one's very soul is seared. By the time
I was wounded my nerves were in such a state that I had to
make a great effort to control myself even though it didn't hurt.
"There's no need to get in such a fuss, you silly ass!" the staff-
doctor said, and no doubt he was quite right. One must keep
perfectly calm in body and mind. Therefore instead of sym-
pathizing with the sufferings of others, I have become as one of
them—looking on death with indifference because I myself may
die at any moment, and no longer sickening at the sight of
wounds and of dark-red blood on pale, yellowish skin. Pity must
be left to the angels.

We moved up at night, under shell-fire, into the front line. The
next day there was drum-fire for eight hours. I lay in a so-called
"rabbit-hole"—a burrow under the firing-step—there were only
four dug-outs for the whole Company. Thank God I was quite
calm. The air was rent with bullets and shells. There was a wild
medley of a thousand different whizzing, whistling noises, buzzing
like bumblebees all around us. When the fire is most intense it is
impossible to distinguish between the crashes. The shapes of the
splinters too varies in a fantastic manner such as no power on earth
could devise. During the attack I looked round for my rifle—the
smooth, shining barrel, which was lying close to me had been torn
open without my noticing, and was hanging in jagged strips. One
heard a dull, metallic hammering noise, like that made by central-
heating. Our shells were flying one above the other like flocks of
birds. As the shells pitched nearer, one could calculate the chances
of being covered with earth. I kept wonderfully cool. I suddenly
remembered the words, "God and myself", thought how fitting
they were, and smiled. How wonderfully were the saints protected—the stake fell and the fire was quenched!

Military Hospital, Cologne, November 13th, 1916
. . . The Cathedral. Great halls of stone. In a dim corner gleams
the little red light; worshippers kneel before it. The gold of the
open Shrine begins to glimmer through the dusk, only the red in
the garments of the figures depicted on it is visible—dimmed by

age and veneration. There is a dark brown organ in an alcove. Perhaps a note is sounded. The painted windows are dark and confused. Suddenly one colour comes into its own, and shines out as the nimbus round the head of a saint; the wintry sun throws a yellow-and-red patch upon the stone; a long ray pierces the mist of dust and dreams. Dividing grilles become visible. Pillars renew their youth; they lean towards one another but never fall; theirs is no dead, stiff, erect, encompassing of space . . .

The Holy Ghost is captive in the Cathedral. In the form of a dove. He must hang, with outstretched wings, above the nave. Far below stray a few human beings—lost in the vastness.

One should never stand still to look at the outside of the Cathedral, but should walk round as one gazes; then one realizes how one harmony melts into another. Gargoyles jut out in their primitive isolation and inaccessibility into the air.

September 5th, 1917
I rejoice in the beauties of Nature; in this summer-like Renoir autumn of the canal and the Aisne; in the ever-shimmering, ever-rustling avenue of elms. The hedge-bordered meadows take on a bluish tinge from the rising mist on the brink of the water, and a faint, blue-green reflection is mirrored below. This green, flourishing wilderness is woven in summer's threads of autumn-tinted, soft-toned wools. One can hardly look into the dazzling blue sky. In the tangled grass blooms—an exquisite miracle—the autumn crocus. Long, slender, pale-lilac flowers, with their wonderfully varied length of petal, and the pistil, thickly coated with scented yellow pollen, shining through the frail calyx. Their delicate stems are snow-white. The ruins of the town are pastel-white in the heat. Sometimes one sees here the "classic" landscape of Poussin or Böcklin. I realize how art is determined by landscape. I have drunk all that my eyelashes could encircle of the world's golden superabundance.

Military Hospital, Rethel, September 10th, 1917
I have reported fit for service. I am restless. I hate the kitchen-table at which I am writing. I lose patience over a book. I should like to push the landscape aside as if it irritated me. I must get to the Front. I must again hear the shells roaring up into the sky and the desolate valley echoing the sound. I must get back to my Company. They are all now very much reduced in strength; and, worn out and over-tired, have to be on guard the whole time in the Front line. I must get back into touch with the enemy. I know far

too well what the danger is, but I must live once more in the realm of death.

September 14th, 1917

Yesterday the Iron Cross of the Second Class was sent to me. The pleasure this gave me was some small compensation. To-morrow I start back to the Company. To-day I am in the Convalescent Section getting ready. Well, and what now? When one thing is over one begins to ask, what next? I wait for what fate may bring; am low-spirited, pale, and love the dusk. It seems as if many sleepless nights had made one ultra-sensitive. When I was left alone for a few minutes with the Cross, I had quite different thoughts from those that were in my mind before. It seemed as if the Cross were made of shell-splinters—black blood congealed on a yellowish dead face with open mouth—bandages encrusted with pus—the strangled cries of hoarse voices—flaccid, gangrened flesh on the stump of a leg. But all that shall not make me hold back! And I am comforted by the thought of your prayers and your love.

Zschuppe was killed on 18 September 18 1917, on the Western Front.

Lieutenant Brian Lawrence, 1st Battalion, Grenadier Guards

Lawrence writes to his family.

November 1916

On the day we went up into the trenches, most of the morning and early afternoon in that Trones Wood camp, were spent in inspecting the men's arms, ammunition, gas helmets, rations, etc. We were due to march off about 4pm and at 2.30 pm all the officers and men had to rub "whale oil" into their feet to keep them warm, and to prevent frostbite.

All the officers' food for the trenches had to be packed up in sandbags, and our trench kit rolled in oil sheets, and. our servants left with it about 1.30pm. The remainder of our food and the balance of our kit was given in charge of the waiters who were not going into the line, and they departed in a waggon for our rest camp.

From 1.30pm till 4pm we had nothing much to do, all our kit, food, and servants had departed, so we just sat and shivered and talked in the tin hut. I don't think anyone likes the last hour or two before you leave for the trenches; there is nothing to do, one is left without any creature comforts, and there is an unpleasant feeling of anticipation. A trench relief is always a little difficult, and perhaps the most dangerous part of the tour of duty, for except in very quiet lines you nearly always have some casualties. The object of the enemy artillery is at all times, and especially at night, to make the approach to the front line trenches unpleasant.

There were no communication trenches up to the line we were relieving, but there was what is known as a duck-board track up to the support line. This is a narrow wooden track just wide enough for one man to walk along. We were to go as far as Waterlot Farm on our own, and there we were to pick up guides from the battalion we were relieving, who would take each company into its proper trench. The duck-boards started close to our camp, and there was a signboard pointing along the track saying "To the Support Line and Needle Dump." Our journey to the farm was uneventful and uphill, the country was the same as we were leaving behind us, and from time to time we met a few gunners, RE officers, etc. wandering about. Waterlot Farm was just a collection of dugouts, and a dump of RE material. After a short delay we collected our guides and moved on.

After leaving the Waterlot Farm we got on to a sort of plateau, and in spite of the failing light we could see a good distance. We could distinguish the mound that *was* Guillemont, on our right and close on our left a few stumps of trees marked the sight of Ginchy. After about 500 yards we got on to ground that must have been under continuous shell fire for at least three months, for we were in the locality of Ginchy Valley where the bulk of our artillery was placed during the latter stages of the attack in September. Shells were pitching round about us every now and then, evidently the Boche gunners were searching the battery positions, many of which were just ahead of us.

There was a winter ground mist that made distance look big, and in the twilight the scene was extraordinarily weird. The duckboard track seemed to go forwards to eternity and looking back it disappeared into the mist, the ground on each side of us was nothing but recently churned up earth, and amongst the millions of shell holes, you could have hardly found a flat piece of ground big enough to stand on. There was no sign of a tree, bush, ditch, road or building, no sign of life or anything living, an extraordinary stillness, broken only by the noise of a shell passing overhead or the crack of an adjacent 60lb gun. It was uncanny to a degree, one felt one had stepped into the underworld, and the sound of one's own voice seemed to echo away into the mist in strange contradiction's to one's surroundings. Compared with this our camp in Trones Wood seemed like civilisation. As soon as it was quite dark I had to concentrate all my attention on keeping on the duck-boards, for a careless step would be likely to lead to a twisted ankle or worse.

At about 6.30 we arrived at the support trench, and everything there seemed such confusion, and there was such a congestion of men in what appeared to be a very small and narrow trench, that I could only stand at the entrance and wait to see what happened. I tried to make my bearings, but the trench seemed to run in all directions, men were facing all ways, and I felt that I could hardly say for certain which was our front.

In an extraordinary short space of time the men seemed to sort themselves out, and the company we were relieving began to file out, and there was room for me to move about and find out our position. The darkness is very deceptive, and what at first had appeared a sort of Hampton Court maze, resolved itself into a short curly bit of trench about 250 yards long with a shallow control trench (to enable people to walk along the line without having to push by the man in the fire trench) behind it. I then investigated the officers' dugout, which was small but deep, with a levelling half way down for the signallers and orderlies. In the main chamber there were two shelves of wire matting with shavings on them which acted as beds, a small flap table and a broken chair. I found out in daylight that it was a Boche dugout built for their gunners who had a battery on the site of our trench a few months before.

As soon as things had settled down a bit I went round the trench with the captain of my company, and we decided what work was to be done. For one has to be always working on a trench, either improving it, or repairing the damage done by shell fire and weather conditions. When we had seen the men started on their work, and the reliefs of sentries and working parties told off, we went down to our dugouts for some dinner, This was quite a wonderful performance consisting of soup, stew with vegetables, stewed fruit and sardines on toast, and drinks and coffee. It is quite amazing how well, and what a quantity of courses, our servants manage to cook on a coke brazier, in a dugout in which there is hardly room to turn around.

The rest of the night I spent in the trench, watching the work, talking to the men, and trying to keep warm. A few shells dropped near us, mostly about ten yards in front of us, but things were pretty quiet. An officer came up with a working party to dig a communication trench forward to the front line, but he had been at work on it for two nights and it must have been seen by Boche airmen, for he got so badly shelled he had to give it up. The commanding officer also came round and had a look at us, but he did not stay long, for he was bent chiefly on seeing the front line.

The hour for "stand-to" (one hour before dawn) came at last, and I was so cold I felt quite wide awake and I went up and down the line seeing that all the men were standing up on the fire step. When all the excitement was over, I began to feel so sleepy, I had to be constantly moving about or I think I should have slept where I stood.

As soon as it was nearly light, we got the order to "carry on", and I retired to my dugout, and after a hasty breakfast, slept soundly till lunch, and then again till tea. Directly after tea, we had to "stand-to" again till it was dark, then dinner, then a repetition of the former night. When the commanding officer came round that night, he told us, the Battalion was to stay another day in the line, and that we were to relieve one of the front line companies the next evening.

"Stand-to" the next morning was more unpleasant than ever, as it had begun to snow in the early morning, the trench was getting very muddy, and the cold was intense.

The dugout seemed most warm and comfortable after the cold and wet of the trench, though we began to notice a sort of stale musty smell about it, due probably to the dirty, black, sticky mud we kept on bringing down with us on our boots and clothes. Soon after I woke up, about lunch time, a scared looking Corporal came rushing into the dugout to say the Company Sergeant Major had been killed, and one man wounded. I went up to investigate and saw one of the most terrible sights which shook me up, and gave me a healthy respect for shells. It seems the CSM and several men were sitting in a little shelter, made under the parapet, and a dud shell had come right through the roof, straight on to the unfortunate man's head. It had split his head open and doubled him up in a heap breaking both his legs. None of the other men, some of whom were touching him at the time, and to whom he was talking, were hurt in the least. It was strange, as the CSM had been out ever since August 1914 and had never had a scratch.

The shelling was now fairly heavy and it seems a splinter had hit one man on the head, cutting right through his tin helmet, which must have saved his life.

There was a sunken road about 400 yards in front of our trench and a steep hill the other side of it, full of dugouts and disused trenches. The Boche must have thought we had guns about that spot, for they kept a continual barrage on the sunken road and kept searching all over the side of the hill. This was all right as there was nothing there, but it was unpleasant to think that our route to the front line lay across that road and up the hill.

It has now been raining for about 12 hours, the mud is beginning to get troublesome and the sides of the trench to slip down. What with the mud and the rain and the constant shelling just in front of us, I don't think I have ever seen a more hopeless aspect. When it was dark, we all got into the trench and lined up in the order we were to lead into the front line. Each platoon had its own guide, who was to lead them into their own section of the trench. The water and rations for the extra day were very late in coming up, so that we had no time to let the men fill their water bottles but just gave them a petrol can to each section, which they had to take in turns to carry.

You may not know that all the water you get in the trenches is carried up in petrol cans, real petrol cans still tasting of that precious spirit. It is extraordinary how flavour clings to those cans, literally for weeks and months, and the result is that tea, coffee and cocoa, have a flavour peculiar to themselves in the trenches.

Well, when we did eventually start, we had a quiet passage as far as the sunken road, though the mud was slippery and treacherous, crossing the road the road was unpleasant, but I am glad to say the shells dropped mostly right and left of us. Half way up the hill there was a halt for some strange reason and I who was in the rear of the company was left just on the edge of the road. A big shell fell on the road just behind me and covered me with a shower of mud and stones, and I was just contemplating which way to go when the cavalcade moved on. We halted again very shortly and we all squatted down in a sort of ditch to get as much shelter as possible. They put three small shells as close to us as I think was possible without being actually on us. After the second shell, I had the sort of feeling, "Well, this is rather beyond a joke, it's all very well to have shells close to you as an experience, but enough of experience; I believe I shall have a little more than experience." At the third shell, I felt, "It's true, I'm not likely to get out of this alive." At the same time I experienced a fierce anger against the rest of the British Army and in particular our gunners, born of a feeling of one's own helplessness and powerlessness to defend oneself. One felt, here are all our wonderful artillery behind us, and yet they can do nothing to help us or stop this sort of thing. Behind us we have brilliant Generals and staffs and they know nothing of this and do nothing to help or protect us. It was a funny state of mind.

After we got up the hill we came to a sort of plain very deep in mud, owing to the way it had been shelled, and the ring of evening "Very" lights seemed to close us in on both sides. The men, exhausted by their toil up the hill, began to straggle, and getting a few yards to right or left lost touch, and then the wholesale dropping of the heavy water tins began. The zip of a few machine-gun bullets finished many of the inexperienced, who simply dropped in a heap and said, "me 'eart's broke," and refused to move. When we were close up to the front line we seemed to be clear of shells and with infinite trouble and great delay we collected the stragglers. My platoon was taken by its guide to the wrong piece of line, so we had to scramble along asking which was No. 4 platoon (the one we had to relieve). We found it at last, in a very narrow and absolutely straight piece of trench about 150 yards to 200 long, with a dugout at one end. We were completely cut off from the rest of the company, and our line had of course to be very thinly held.

On going round the line I found both our Lewis guns had jammed, several of the men were absolutely exhausted, one badly hit in the stomach and what was worse no one had any water at all. I found my bottle was also empty, and the only drink I had was raw brandy. Further, many of the men had dropped their rations, and I found I only had some bread and cheese, in fact the only thing that had arrived intact was the rum ration, this of course for thirsty and hungry men was so strong that it went straight to their heads and made them drowsy. Nothing much happened that night except that I had an unpleasant ten minutes from a "whizz-bang" battery. Crossing a gap in the parapet with an NCO and a man, I think I must have been seen, for they started on that spot as I was crossing it. Now a "whizz-bang" is a high velocity low trajectory gun, and is fired straight at the top of the parapet. We lay flattening our noses in the mud for exactly ten minutes (I timed it), while they shot over us, bursting the shell behind the trench. Beyond the suffocating smell of fireworks, no one was any the worse.

The dugout was beastly, and smelt most terrible; it had the stale smell of filthy mud, peculiar to all dugouts, and a little something extra special as well. I don't know for certain what it was, but as half a stale Boche fell out of the wall during the night, I might guess.

The prospect next day was more encouraging, the rain had stopped, the shelling had decreased, and one was able to have a look at the surrounding country. We were in front of, and to the right of Guedecourt, (but could not see it) and looked right on to Le Trausloy which was in a hollow below and to the right of us. It had been much damaged by shell fire, but the houses were still standing, though many of them were roofless. The enemy line seemed to be about 500 yards from us and midway between us and Trausloy. In "no man's land" about 300 yards from our trench, there was an English aeroplane which had been shot down a few days before. In the middle of the day I noticed a party of Boches walking from the aeroplane towards our lines, probably to surrender, and our men did not shoot. I told the Lewis gunners to open fire, which they did, and I don't think many of the Boches returned to tell the tale.

By that night we were all worn out with hunger and thirst and trusted the relief would arrive early. The relief were Australians, and I don't think they could have done a relief worse. Their men ran all over the place like frightened rabbits, and none of the officers or NCOs seemed to have any control over themselves, or their men. We marched back by platoons as soon as we were relieved, each platoon having its own guide, as before.

All went well till we got to the top of the hill, with the sunken road below us, then the shelling began. Our guide took us a bit off the track, slipped, and fell into a shell hole full of half liquid mud. The more he struggled, the deeper he became embedded, and when we tried to help him we only began to sink ourselves and could do no good. I was afraid any moment a shell might settle the majority of us, I was not sure of the way back, and could not leave our guide stranded. I have rarely felt so desperate and helpless. The only thing to do, seemed to be to leave an NCO and two men with spades and rope to try and get the guide out, and for the rest of us to find our own way back. We had little difficulty till after we crossed the sunken road, and then they started to put shells all over the area between the road and our support trench. Seeing the entrance to the communication trench that the officer had tried to dig to the front line a few nights before, I dived into it and I am very glad I did. Just as I got into the trench a shell burst right on the path we should have been walking, and knocked down a lot of earth and sandbags, burying me and pinning me to the bottom of the trench. I had the feeling that the end had come, and seemed to feel quite annoyed when the men proceeded to shovel away the earth and lift off the sandbags. When at last I got up, none the worse except for a headache, I felt somehow I had been cheated.

We passed on after this into our old support trench, and then passed out into the duck board track we had come by, a few days before. By this time I felt so utterly weary from lack of sleep, lack of food and drink, and anxiety and fright, that I did not much care what happened. The men also, especially those who had been carrying Lewis gun drums, etc. began to straggle. It was not long before two men fell off the duck boards into a shell hole. One had fainted with fatigue, and the other was delirious and talked incessantly about a Xmas party with wine and nuts and crackers. By the time we got near to Waterlot Farm our party had dwindled considerably, and I know that one had to keep one's eyes glued to the duck boards in order to keep on the track and these boards seemed to dance and zigzag about, while one was oppressed by the feeling that one had done nothing else for about 5 years but walk along duck boards as if they were a kind of endless treadmill. We met a man who had a water bottle full of cold tea and he gave it to me, and I think this just brought the men into Waterlot Farm, where there was a soup kitchen.

We halted at the farm for about half an hour and drank hot tea and soup and ate biscuits till we felt new men. There were several officers and NCOs at the farm, who had not been up to the line and who were to act as guides to take us back to our rest camp at Montauban.

It was much further than any of us thought to our camp, in fact if the men had known how far they had to go, I think more of them would have fallen out. There was no track for the first part of the way, we stumbled along through the mud on the site of the old railway, through Guillemont station and then on to a road of sorts running with muddy water. Well, like all things, our journey eventually came to an end, and we noticed an iron gate by the side of the road, and here and there a few piles of odd bricks and a bit of a wall, so we knew we were in a village, and when we came upon a large notice saying "Montauban", we felt sure we had arrived.

In a sort of mud morass, just off the road, there were a dozen newly erected Nissen huts, which constituted our camp. As we turned into the camp, I was greeted by my Company Quartermaster Sergeant, who took charge of my men, showed them their hut, and served out food and drink to them. I then repaired to the Officers' Mess and partook of stew, champagne and tinned fruit.

It was a funny sight to see a small hut destitute of furniture except for a table groaning under stew and champagne bottles, a small stove, with a collection of officers who had not washed or shaved for five days, sitting round on odd boxes discussing their recent experiences.

When I repaired to bed, I found our sleeping quarters consisted of a Nissen hut without doors, or windows, the floor of which was consequently damp and dirty. We had no sort of kit except what we brought out of the trenches, which in my case comprised, a wet and muddy blanket and a waterproof sheet. There was nothing for it but to put the oil sheet on the floor, wrap the wet blanket round me and try to sleep. I don't know when I have spent a colder, more uncomfortable or more sleepless night.

Luckily we had to leave camp at 8.30 am and as we did not get to bed till the small hours of the morning, the night was not too long. After a hurried breakfast and still unwashed and unshaven, for we could not get any clean water, we marched out of camp en route for Méaulte, where we went to rest for ten days.

Second-Lieutenant Norman Collins, 1/6th Seaforth Highlanders

Collins writes to his family describing his experiences in the Battle of Ancre, the end of the Somme campaign.

25 November 1916
[France]

Dear All

It is with great thankfulness that I have so far come through the Battle of the Ancre without a scratch.

The last fortnight has been absolute Hell.

On the 13th at dawn the Battalion went over the 'bags' and after a few hours hard fighting captured four lines of trench and *the* village en route, that the Boche has held for over 2 years.

It was a magnificent success and our division has made a name for itself.

On July 1st the Regulars attempted the feat and failed. I suppose you will know all about it from the papers.

We were relieved on the Wednesday following and after two days rest to be reorganised went in the trenches again in support.

This morning we came out again much to my relief.

I have had my first wash and shave for a week!

I needed it badly.

There are only 2 officers of my company left now and I am one of them.

For 3 days I have been O.C. party collecting the dead and it was the most loathsome job I've ever had.

We were shelled heavily all the time as of course we were working in the open in full view of the Boche. He used to spot us from his observation balloons and aeroplanes and send over "crumps" and shrapnel.

I had a few of my party knocked out and had some miraculous escapes.

A 6″ [shell] on one occasion burst 10 yards away but I was only covered with mud.

We are back a few miles for a short rest.

Yesterday I had tea with the Brig. General as he was so pleased with the work done.

His dugout was a splendid place.

My word, you should have seen and heard the barrage. Every minute four shells burst on every *yard* of the ground.

The trenches were just wiped out and it was only by the mouth of the dugouts that one could tell that there had been a trench.

Of the village all that is left is a few heaps of bricks.

I expect that we will get a rest soon, for a month, at any rate we will not be going over the "bags" again for some time so don't worry.

Well, there is no more news, so ta! ta!

Best Love
Norman

P.S. My poor servant was "nah-poohed" and I haven't found the body.

In a second letter on the 28th he continued in similar vein:

You will have received a letter written after the big battle, I should think.

I've had enough of 'pushes' for a long time.

Been busy writing to the different homes in Elgin and Glasgow etc of the "B" Coy men, knocked out.

I found my old servant. I'm very sorry about him as he did look after me well.

I wrote home to his mother.

He has a brother in this battalion also.

I was reading a paper on the 'push' and it gave the Naval Division a lot of credit for work we did.

Well, cheero.

Corporal Francis James Mack, 29th Battalion, Australian Infantry

ENGLAND
27th January, 1917

Dear Mother and Father,

Just back from leave in London. I had a real roaring time. The time (4 days) was rather short. I managed to see most of the old ancient and historical sights. I was somehow disappointed in London after reading so much about it—really expected to see something more impressive than it is. Mind you, we see London now at its worst for everything is in darkness at 5pm in the afternoon so the days were terribly short. I went to see the Tower of London, Buckingham Palace, Whitehall, The War Office, Westminster Abbey, St. Paul's Cathedral, Trafalgar Square, Leicester Square, Piccadilly Circus, Bond Street and other places too numerous to mention. These sights are grand—there are no two ways about that but the rest, the business houses and eating places are only commonplace. The big difference between Sydney and London is the trams. London has no trams through the streets—they all run underground and are all privately owned. There are two classes of trams—the Tube and the Electric Line. The Tube is a way—it Billy O down—say 5 or 600 feet down while the Electric is only about 50 feet. They are very cheap and extra fast. On the streets run O'Buses (Motor) after the style of the trams. There are thousands—you can see them everywhere and these were very attractive to see. You wonder why. Well, firstly you can see London better from an omnibus than anything else and secondly but none the least important is that the conductor is a Girl. That's a thing which struck us as peculiar, girls doing all sorts of jobs, walk down the street and you see a window cleaner. I had seen photos of them in papers but had I not seen them I would not have believed it. But never the less they were there dressed in men's clothes of oilskin. Go a bit further and you see a girl page, girl done up in livery to put it plainly, girls are doing everything . . .

I'll answer all letters I receive so if anyone wants to hear from me direct, it's up to them to write now and again. I am not too bad. I have had, and in fact I still have a very bad cold and terribly sore feet from walking over the hard frozen ground. Otherwise I am splendid. Well mother must close. Am sending you some views of London and the places I have visited together with some English papers. Well goodbye mother and father, sisters and brothers. Fondest love to you all.

I remain yours, am luckily your loving son, Frank.

France
May 19th, 1918

Dear Mother & Father,

No doubt you have been surprised to have had no news from me lately but we have been having a rough passage—been in front line for over a month now and still no relief to hand—can't get anything here, for example look at the paper—it has been "souvenired" from the little shell riddled village we are holding—tis on the nearest front to Fritz's first objective A————. We have suffered pretty heavily, over 40 in our company casualties but since taking over we have advanced over 1000 yds and are now in a fairly good position. Received all your last mail OK. Am glad to hear Keith passed his 25 test OK—hope he brings the other part off. Auntie May's letter arrived this mail too but I will have to wait till we come out to square up all letters I owe. Please tell all other relatives the cause of no mail—tis hard to get a green envelope and the officers can't censor letters in the line so delay cannot be avoided. We are getting ideal weather—lovely long days, not dark till after 10pm and stand down at 4am. Naturally there is great aerial activity—have seen dozens of planes come down this trip in— some from terrible heights—tis great but awful sight to see the manouverings in an air fight. Artillery also is pretty warm. Am enclosing a shoulder strap of the Fritz Battalion we pushed out when we advanced the line. We have plenty of sniping and shooting—good sport. One morning Fritz attacked on our left and after digging in the Fritz kept coming in "Kamerading" right up to midday. Have heard plenty of talk about Fritz coming over and giving himself up but tis the first time I have seen it. T'was funny, also pitiful. They started across No Mans Land hands right up then their own machine guns at them and then some of our "fools" started potting at them and they did the Chinese trot in with hands up—did look comical for we were in a position to enjoy it. The weather has been glorious Dinkum Australian. No doubt this letter is a ragtime but it is never the less a dinkum one straight from the busiest part of France. We are only about 300 yds from the canal and river ————. Well mother I think this is all this time—would very much sooner be getting ready for the theatre than getting ready for my job now. Tis a fighting patrol. We met eight Fritzies last night. Well fondest love to all. Hope they are all well and in the best of health. I am in the best of health and spirits. I remain,

Your loving son,
Frank.

P.S. Mother please post enclosed letters for me as can't secure and envelopes
1 to Linda
1 to Auntie Tilly
1 to Florrie
You may get extra news from the first 2 but just post the 3rd on to Ivy Cottage, Menangle.
Thank you.

Mack died of wounds on 29 July 1918.

Lieutenant Eric Marchant,
7th Battalion, London Regiment

Marchant enlisted in November 1914 as a private soldier, later being commissioned from the ranks.

Calais, 4 February 1917

Dear Mother
. . . This morning I spent the whole time censoring letters. This is the first time I have had this job and though it is rather irksome after an hour or two I found the letters of absorbing interest.

I suppose there is no better way of getting an idea of the spirit of the men and I won't deny that I was surprised at the tone of practically all the letters. The percentage that showed a realisation of religious truths and faith in God, was tremendously bigger than ever I suspected, and such phrases as "we must go on trusting in God" were in dozens of the letters I read. In particular I noticed one letter from a young fellow to his brother who was in the trenches and had evidently been out here some months and was getting badly "fed-up". The letter was worth printing if it had not been so sacred. The spelling was execrable and the writing almost illegible in parts but, strange to say, there was very little that could be called ungrammatical, and I am sure that the recipient will be cheered and helped beyond all measure when he gets it. In practically all the letters came the request "Write as often as you can" and nobody can doubt that the letters and parcels from 'Blighty" keep up the spirits of the men as nothing else can.

You must remember that the men in this camp are of a very different class to the 7th London. There were not more than two or three letters in the whole bag addressed to London and the majority were going to little unheard of villages in Cambridgeshire and Suffolk. you would laugh at in the quaint spelling. Quite a number always spelt "here" as "hear" and one man spelt "used" as "Youst"! All express their firm conviction that the war was "nearly over" and one breezy optimist said that he thought "pece terms was already ben (being) arranged and shud (should) wake up one morning and find ourselfs (ourselves) orf to Blighty agen".

Altogether I found the duties of a Censor Officer most entertaining.

This afternoon it was too bitterly cold and slippery underfoot to go out so I stayed by the fire in the mess tent and read an extraordinary yarn by Max Pemberton called "Pro Patria" which I found more amusing than edifying. This evening I hope to go to a camp service if there is one. Everyone in the Mess seems to be contracting a "churchyarder cough" but so far I have kept clear of that and similar ills. The weather still continues extremely cold but dry and sunny, and I hope it will continue so, but the wind seems to be veering round to the west this afternoon so I suppose we must not be surprised if the rain comes into its own again, with its attending evils.

Well, I have no more news of interest at present so will close, give my love to all. Hoping to hear from someone shortly.

Your loving son, Eric.

Marchant died on active service on 20 November 1917.

Captain John Coull, 23rd Battalion, Royal Fusiliers

France 2.4. 17 1 pm

My dear boy Fred,

This is a letter you will never see unless your daddy falls in the field. It is his farewell words to you in case anything happens. My boy I love you dearly and would have greatly liked to get leave for a few days to kiss you and shake hands again, after a few months separation, but as this seems at the present moment unlikely, I drop you this few lines to say "God bless you" and keep you in the true brave manly upright course which I would like to see you follow.

You will understand better as you get older that your daddy came out to France for your sakes and for our Empire's sake. If he died it was in a good cause and all I would ask of you dear boy, is that you will keep this note in memory of me, and throughout your life may all that is good attend you and influence you. May you be strong to withstand the temptations of life and when you come to the evening of your days may you be able to say with St Paul "I have fought the good fight".

Goodbye dear boy and if it is that we are not to meet again in this life, may it be certain that we shall meet in another life to come, which faith I trust you will hold on to and live up to.

I remain ever
Your loving Daddy
J.F. Coull

John Coull was killed on the Western Front on 30 September 1918.

Rudolf Kruger, German Army

April 23rd, 1917, near Rheims

Yesterday, that is to say on April 22nd, I received my baptism of fire from enemy Artillery. We had to occupy a Reserve Position again, but this time we had to go up over open ground. It was not long before the enemy guns spotted us and scattered some very heavy crumbs for our benefit! Just at this spot four of our Company were killed by direct hits. I did not wink an eyelash and was not in the least uneasy or upset, though the beastly things often landed quite close to me, but all the same thanked God in the evening when we were out of it.

Here we are living in an absolutely uncivilized fashion—no houses or beds, and no means of washing or shaving, and look like wild men of the woods. My own sweet face is adorned with a yellowish-red beard, the colour of pickled-cabbage, a yard long. In the morning one cleans one's eyes with 'spit' and then spits on one's handkerchief to do the rest of one's "washing". The whole business is beautifully simple and accomplished in a few movements of the hand. And yet how I long to get back to decent conditions, where one could also get the rags off one's body and a proper night's rest oftener than once a week!

A mail has just come in after a long interval and I have got letters. I am glad to hear that you have seen the *Evangelimann* at the Opera. I once took part in it as a supernumerary, and ran from left to right across the stage carrying a long pole as a fireman during the burning of the church. I still remember distinctly how beautifully the rising of the moon was represented. Oh, what a glorious *motif* that is: "Blessed are they who are persecuted for righteousness' sake."

What wouldn't I give to be able to do a theatre once again, or— what would be simply ideal—to spend a few days with you! I simply long to make my 'cello sing for joy during a trio-evening. But brace up! All will yet be well! Besides, Papa has taken immense trouble in copying out a whole lot of beautiful well-known musical themes for me. By that means one can listen, if only with one's mind's ear, to the glorious old melodies which have so often thrilled us.

Kruger was killed on 3 May 1917.

Second Lieutenant H.G. Downing, Royal Flying Corps

To his family.

Castle Bromwich
Near Birmingham
July 24 1917

Dearest All,

I suppose I am exceeding the speed limit in letter writing, but daresay an extra letter will meet with your approval. I have been leading a most strenuous existence lately, and put in a tremendous amount of flying. Of course, unfortunately perhaps, it means going out to France sooner than expected but suppose pilots are wanted fairly badly.

I went on a cross country to a neighbouring aerodrome about 30 miles away this evening and had tea there. On my return journey I ran into a rain storm and got lost. When I came out I found I had wandered in a circle and was back at my original starting place. I thought I had just enough petrol, so continued my journey. When about 4 miles from this aerodrome, the engine started to misfire and finally stopped. I was a fair height up, about 1000 feet and just managed to make the aerodrome, missing some telegraph wires by a few inches, and finally stopping right in front of our mess door, without breaking anything. As you may guess it caused great excitement and everybody seems to think it is a good effort.

Ah! Well we don't get much money, but we do see life. I shall be going to Turnberry in Scotland for a aerial course on the 1st of August, for a fortnight. After that I shall be able to put up my wings if I do alright. In the meanwhile I had a very nice time last Saturday. Two charming members of the fair sex helped to look after this bashful young man and have now an invitation to the house, which I might say is *some* place. Oh! it is quite alright. I went and stunted over their house yesterday, and was pretty bucked to see an answering flutter of cambrio from the ground. Quite romantic. What! Well I suppose that is about all the news. Cheer oh! everybody.

BEF [France]
October 20, 1917

My dearest all,
I have been hoping for a letter, but so far the weekly budget has not turned up. I expect it takes some time nowadays.

Well, I am still in the land of the living and am enjoying myself no end. It is quite like old times. I had an exciting experience a day or two ago. You know how misty the weather is nowadays. Well we were flying about over the line, when a fellow and myself lost the rest of the patrol in a fog and we had not a bit of an idea where we were, so we came down to a few hundred feet from the ground. Presently we came to a large Town, which puzzled me immensely, and I circled round quite comically trying to locate it on the map. I thought, and so did the other fellow, that we were on our side of the lines. Imagine my amazement when I discovered it to be about 12 miles in Hun land. We were soon greeted with shells and machine gun fire. So of course we frightened everything we met on the roads, diving quite close to the ground and on to motor lorries etc and I bet we scared Huns out of their lives. When we eventually came home we noticed all the roads quite clear of men and lorries etc . . . so we were immensely bucked with ourselves and enjoyed a jolly good breakfast . . . Tonight I am dining with another squadron. I know a few fellows there and expect to have quite a cheery evening. Oh! Yes! I shall be quite good.

By the way I unfortunately smashed a machine the other day. I landed on my nose by mistake in the middle of the aerodrome. I didn't hurt myself though and my CO only laughed and suggested mildly that I should land on my wheels another time.

It was very funny because four more did exactly the same thing five minutes later. Well cheery oh! everybody.

George Downing went missing in action in November 1917.

George W. Lee, American Expeditionary Force

Lee writes to his mother in Greensboro, North Carolina.

[France, 1917]

Dear Mama,

I am well and feeling good as I have just been to dinner, and had all I wanted to eat, and you know that is what pleases me. Just give me plenty to eat and I will take care of the rest.

It is quite different here about buying things to eat. Candy is hard to get! No oranges or peaches at all; eggs about 15 francs a dozen. The people over here think we Americans are all millionaires, and we have to pay high for things.

I wish I could see you all, I could tell you many things I am not allowed to write. All our letters are blue penciled. I am not allowed to tell you where I am, and whatever my duty is, that shall I do to the fullest extent.

If you want to do something for us, please boost the Y.M.C.A.—also the Red Cross. They are both wonderful organizations. The Y.M.C.A. is our only home and the Red Cross girls our mothers. Believe me, I can never do enough for them. If the folks at home do their share, we will sure do ours for you, and do it willingly.

Gee! I often think of the time when I was at home. Mama, you know I believe that one day I will come back to you and the loved ones I left behind. Wouldn't you be glad to have your soldier boy with you again? My prayer to God is that we will have peace with all the nations and we boys get back home with our dear ones.

Private George Barlow, JR.
American Expeditionary Force

Barlow writes to his father in New Jersey.

[France, August 1917]

Your welcomed letter of July 5 received and I was very glad to hear from you. I was also glad you received the card stating I arrived safely overseas. I suppose it made you feel better after the U-Boat scare.

I cannot tell you what part of the country I am in, but I have seen a whole lot of it, and most of it was by walking.

I have been up in the trenches. It was pretty quiet while I was there. When we were in the support they used to shell us. One day they kept sending shells over for about a half an hour and they were landing right around us. We were pretty lucky we didn't lose a man.

We have had quite a little rain over here but it is better now. It rained every day for over a week. A soldier's life is all right in France as long as the weather stays clear but when it rains it is a rotten life. I hate to think of winter coming. It will be a cold job in the trenches, but we still have to take the bitter with the sweet.

I have seen quite a few air fights. Some nights they fly over the towns all night, but don't seem to do much damage.

I saw General Pershing today he came around to inspect our division. He certainly is a fine looking man. He said the men were in good shape, and seemed to be pleased with us. I suppose he will have us shipped up to the front again. I only wish you could see the rats in the trenches. I believe they are as big as cats.

We lost our last old officer Lt. Jemson, they sent him back to the States for an instructor. But we still have a good set of officers.

Well, I guess I have told you all the censor will let me so I will close hoping this letter finds you all in the best of health. Tell mother I hope to get back soon and eat a good square meal with her.

As ever, Geo.

Lieutenant Lambert Wood,
American Expeditionary Force

[France] 7 December, 1917

Dearest folks,

Well, Monday was a happy day for the officers [at a school Wood was attending]. We got a sack of mail—the first for three weeks.

I got ten letters, nine from home and one from my girl. Do you know, I really must be in love, for I opened her letter first. I am very, very happy that you folks are all so well and working so hard. I laughed when you wondered if the big harvest moon was looking down on me. It probably was, but I had somewhat the feeling of the man in one of Bairnsfather's cartoons.

I am very happy in my work. My captain and myself are great friends . . . Let me tell you this, we can beat the Boche to a frazzle if we go into this with heart and soul. If you ever hear of any calamity howlers, squelch them for being traitors. We can beat the Boche only by fighting, and we are better fighters and better killers than the Boche. There is no pessimism in the American Army over here but we must have the support, moral and material, of the folks at home! Our killing spirit must be aroused but it is rising and Lord! I hope I am in the drive when it comes—when the Americans bloody their bayonets! . . . But just keep in mind the people who are shouting calamity are pro-German and traitors . . . Prepare for years more and do things thoroughly. We are fighting a nation that is as bad as its individual soldiers, who sham death and then shoot the soldiers in the stomachs who pass over them. Try to spread the gospel among your friends. I believe it is the truth, as I have done all in my power to find out the situation. I always was an inquisitive cuss.

Oh yes, I guess I am in love with M——————S————, my first real affair. She seems to care for me, thank the Lord! and some day, if I live, I will ask her to marry me. I am very happy and hope she loves me—but don't know. She may just feel sorry for me and I am no object of pity.

Rifleman B.F. Eccles,
7th (S) Battalion, The Rifle Brigade

France,
28 December 1917

Dearest Mother, Dad and kids,
This letter will be posted by a chap on leave so here goes:
Before I begin. I am quite well, alive and kicking, happy and 'grateful for life'. So by that you can bet I have had the most exciting run of my existence. Christmas on the Passchendaele Ridge. Yes, and take it from me it is not a nice place to spend one's Christmas Vacation. Fortunately winter had come and everything was icebound which banished the mud.

I was on a bombing post with six others in a shell hole about eight yards long. We were out of touch with the rest, but Fritz did not know exactly where we were. We were so near him we could hear him talking and coughing. It was trying work as we had to be so vigilant. On the night of the 24th I was warned to report to a pillbox (Company Headquarters) as guide. The snow was thick and being moonlight I had several times to throw myself down to avoid the machine-gun bullets, for as you know there are no trenches. Five of us had to find the track to Battalion HQ, which was not too easy seeing the snow had obliterated many landmarks. On our return we were rewarded by a decent tot of rum. On Xmas night, we five had again to set out and report to a place known as 'so-and-so' farm and stay till Boxing night to guide up our relief, a battalion of the Worcesters.

We were not sorry to get out of it for a day, although the journey is so risky. For the cold was pretty keen, and jolly hard to bear especially in a shell hole, where to stand up by day means a bullet through the napper.

More snow on Boxing Day and a brilliant moon. How we cursed that moon.

Consider it. A full moon on a vast waste of snow six inches to a foot deep. And to take a battalion of men over open country in full sight of the enemy. All went well until we had gone two kilos, and appeared on the last ridge, within 600 yards of what is left of Passchendaele. Then we were spotted by Fritz and he opened on us with machine-guns on three sides (the salient is like a horse-shoe). We carried on until it became too hot and fellows were drooping over too thickly. Two of my platoon (I mean the platoon I was guiding) were knocked over besides others, so we dropped on the track, and rolled into shell holes. Bullets were whizzing over us a hundred to the minute. We tried to move forward again from shell hole to shell hole, when the platoon behind shouted they had lost their guide. I cried to them to follow me. We were so massed that Fritz properly got the breeze up. He fully thought that we were extending to make an attack, so up went his SOS signal. It was what I had dreaded, for immediately his artillery opened a terrific barrage. Talk about a big slice of Hell! I yelled to the chaps to get flat. I went forward on my hands and knees in the snow and dropped into a shell hole with Ravenhill my fellow Guide, and for fully half an hour we lay with our faces in the snow, while shells did everything but hit us, even though they seemed to burst on the edge of the shell holes. It was the worst half hour I have ever spent. Casualties were heavy and many were the cries of wounded men. In one place no less than four men had their heads blown off.

Then—thank the Lord—our artillery got the wire and they put up such an avalanche of shells on Jerry's lines that he closed up like a wet sack. Then came a respite and a bit of mist arose. I went forward to our lines and we made the relief as well as possible although so many were missing. I met an officer, told him we had got the men up, and he said, "Grease out of it", which I did. I closed up with some of my old platoon, and we did that three miles out of the danger zone in double quick time.

We had one more narrow escape after, being nearly gassed when a shell hit the track within a few yards of us.

Then at last we reached a zone of safety. Exhausted after living on biscuits, bully etc. for four days, but happy as lords, for after twenty–four days in the Ypres sector our Division had been relieved. We were met by Brigade Officers near St Jean, and a Canteen by the roadside provided hot tea and rum, biscuits and cigs. Then to a camp under canvas until morning. On the 27th, we arose and got the thickest of five days beard off. Then a train journey to our present place sixty miles behind the line near St Omer.

The snow is thick and the frosts are keen, but what matters is we are away from it all again. So we can sing and shout once more.

I may be wrong in telling you all this, but the reason I do is that it is some record of exciting adventure which I never dreamed of.

But here I am, I am not worrying so you need not. I am in the pink, barring being a bit stiff and bruised.

But believe me anything is preferable to that Hell upon earth, Passchendaele Ridge.

So dear people you can play the piano when you read this, and make your minds easy for a bit.

The weather is severe, but we get hardened. We are having our Xmas feed on Sunday, a big pay day. I have plenty of fags, and a fine pipe so I am très bon.

Meanwhile we are nearer the end of the war. I have seen no paper lately but shall get my chance now. I will write Emilla as soon as possible. Tell her she is a dear for sending me such a jolly fine pipe. Meanwhile, the best of wishes for 1918.

May next Christmas be quieter for me. Bank Holidays seem to be Helldays. So Cheero Mother, darling, I enjoyed the Butterscotch within forty yards of Fritz. The socks and gloves reached me just in time.

Fondest love,
Burton.

Second Lieutenant Arthur J. Robinson,
55 Squadron, RAF

Thursday, 15 August '18

Dear Kath,

Hope well, I am. I have been on my first 'show'. It was jolly
decent; perhaps, or rather doubtless, there will be an account of it
in the papers. In spite of every resistance we got to where we
wanted to be and dropped our bombs.

It was all very interesting but not very exciting. The German
'Archy' is much more accurate than ours, but it is not very
formidable. As all our 'pills' went right into the town and railway
sidings I have least got some of my own back and some of yours too
in return for when the Huns disturbed your nights sleep at Hetton.

The Huns are cheeky little beggars they [sic] way they try to
prevent us getting to our targets. Four or five went down in
consequence but we don't know whether they crashed or not.
They paint their buses all [?] colours, mainly red, blue, and yellow.

My 'bus' went somewhat 'dud' after dropping my 'pills' and we
were left behind about 300 yards for about 10 minutes and several
Huns took a fancy to bringing us down, but by the Grace of God
and skill of my Observer with his guns we got back. We were jolly
lucky and only got bullets . . . just above my head, another
through the Observer's map, and another through my main petrol
tank . . .

Yours (nervously)
Arthur

Arthur Robinson was killed in action on 15 September 1918.

Lieutenant Phelps Harding, 306th Infantry Regiment,
77th Division, American Expeditionary Force

10 September 1918

Dear Christine,

The last time I wrote you I was in Paris, having received my
Commission and about ready to start for my new Division. Since
then I have covered a lot of territory, both in lorries and on foot,
and I have passed over a battlefield that has but recently been the
scene of some mighty hard fighting—some that my new Division
and people of New York will long remember.

My orders took me first to Château Thierry. You have probably read about the fighting in that city. The place is pretty badly banged up from shell fire, but not as badly as most of the smaller villages beyond it. The Huns tore things up in great shape—statues, ornaments and pictures in homes were broken and cut up as if by a band of plundering outlaws. From Château Thierry my trail led toward the Ourcq River, which our men had to cross under heavy machine-gun fire and artillery shelling. Beyond was open country. You will see what a tough proposition it was when you read the casualty list for the few days when the Boche were retreating. They retreated, but they put up a stiff resistance with machine-guns, artillery and planes—and taking machine-gun nests is a real man's job.

I found my Division by the Ourcq, having been relieved, and spent three days in camp with it. The men were pretty tired, and of course they felt the loss of their comrades. I realized this latter point best when censoring their letters. It is mighty hard for a boy to write home to his mother and tell her that his brother has been killed. I read two such letters in the first batch I censored. Each writer tried to tell how painless the death was, and how bravely the brother met it—but in each case I imagine the mother will think only of her loss, and not of the fact that her boy died a true American.

22 September, 1918

Dear Christine,

My last letter was written just before we commenced the St Mihiel offensive, which began September 12th. I am writing this letter in what was then German occupied territory, sixteen kilometers from our original front line.

When the Division left the Chateau Thierry front we thought we were bound for a rest camp, for the organisation was badly in need of both rest and replacements. Then the order came to move. We marched by night and slept in the daytime, arriving at our position back of the front line after several nights of pretty hard going—hard because the rain fell almost continuously, the roads were bad, the traffic heavy. Our stopping places at the end of each march were thick woods. It is no fun moving into thick, wet woods in the dark, and trying to find places to sleep.

The last night the rain and wind were fierce—I had to be careful not to lose my platoon, the night was so dark and the marching conditions so bad. We moved to within about a kilometre of our line, my battalion being in support of the regiment, and took cover in an old drainage ditch. Wet? Rather!

At exactly 1 a.m., the artillery cut loose. It seemed as if all the artillery in France had suddenly opened up. The sky was red with big flashes, the air seemed full of Empire State Expresses, and the explosion of the heavier shells made the ground tremble. It was a wonderful and awe-inspiring sight.

At 5 a.m., the assault troops went over the top. We followed in the third wave. First we passed batteries that had been shoved right up to our lines—75s firing like six-shooters. Ahead of us French tanks were ploughing along like big bugs, standing on their beam ends at times as they crossed the trenches or unusually bad ground. Our first line went too fast for them, but they did a lot of good work in breaking up machine-gun nests and in taking villages. Our boys in front just couldn't wait for them, even to smash the wire.

Before we had gone far prisoners began to come in first by twos and threes, then by platoons and companies. We took 13,000 Boche that day. We passed dead men of both armies, but many more Boche than Americans. I was surprised at the indifference I felt toward dead Americans—they seemed a perfectly natural thing to come across, and I felt absolutely no shudder go down my back as I would have had I seen the same thing a year ago.

We kept on going forward until we reached the crest of a hill, and here the shelling became so heavy that we made ourselves as small as possible in ditches and holes. Shells were striking all around us, and too close for comfort. A big "dud"—a shell that failed to explode—landed in the middle of my platoon and hit a man from the Engineers on the thigh, practically taking his leg off and tearing him up pretty badly. He died in a short time. The company at our right had sixteen casualties from this shell fire, but we, apparently being better duckers, came out without a scratch except for the Engineer who had happened to take cover with us.

After taking the shelling for possibly twenty minutes our artillery spotted the Boche batteries, which were either destroyed or withdrew, permitting us to move forward again. After this the Boche did not make much of a stand. His artillery was apparently too busy moving homeward to bother about fighting.

The first day we covered nearly sixteen kilometres, reaching our objective on scheduled time. It was pretty hard work, for the going was often bad, even after leaving the front line area. It was up and down hill, and at a fairly fast pace. That night we slept on a hillside, and since then we have been moving around slightly, digging in each time, and acting as a reserve for the troops ahead who, with Engineers, are making a line of trenches and putting up wire, placing machine-guns and doing everything necessary to give the Boche a warm reception if he attempts a counter-attack.

In this recent drive, our artillery moved almost as rapidly as our Infantry—sometimes faster than our kitchens and wagon trains—and a Boche battery would hardly open up before a plane would go over it, signal the battery location, and presto! American shells would drop on it. The Boche may not have had much respect for the American Army a few months ago, but from what prisoners say now, we are about as welcome as the proverbial skunk at a lawn party!

Just one more item before I end this letter and go to inspect my platoon. We had expected to be relieved before now, but yesterday news arrived that changed all our plans. Probably my battalion will go into the new line in a day or so, possibly to stay there for a fairly long period. We may even move forward again—no one knows definitely. Anyway, you may not hear from me for a couple of weeks or so—longer, if we push on toward Berlin.

Rudolph Bowman, Headquarters Troop, 89th Division, American Expeditionary Force

Bowman writes to his wife, Gertrude, and children.

[In German envelope]
France, September 20th 18

My Darling Wife and Loved Ones:

Has it been ten years since I wrote? Ten years have passed for me. This letter will sound like I am drunk, but I'm not—just tired. This is the synopsis of a long long story.

On Sept 10th I was sent to a village ½ Kilometre behind the front line, for final instructions in enemy observation. Our O.P. (observation post) was shelled that night because an ammunition truck had gotten stuck near it. (Now, all thru this everything seemed natural and I thought nothing of it.) Shrapnel struck our building (the only one with a roof on it in town) but we got no direct hit. The next day we (three other observers & I) went up to the front line trench to take over an advance O.P. Rain–Rain–Rain–Mud-Mud-Mud-Wet to the skin. Well—two of us were on our post at 1:00 A.M. Thurs. Sept 12th when all our big guns broke loose at once.

I can't describe it—it was awful—and wonderful—glorious—hideous—hellish, to think what one shell will do—then to think what 6000 to 8000 guns will do all firing as fast as they can, all sizes—well we stayed on till 3:00 and our relief came—went back to dug out for a last rest, for we had decided to go "Over the Top" with the doughboys ("God Bless Them") on the big drive.

Well we went over in the second wave, its all confused to me—I saw many dead men (mostly Boche) many of our boys wounded, men fell all around us, we were shot at by snipers, machine guns, Boche avions, and went thru our own barrage twice—those guns kept up that fire till about 9:30, then the light artillery tried to move up with us but could not keep up, all I could shoot at was mach. gun nests (I can only hope I got *one* Boche for I got no fair shot) but I saw boys throw grenades in dugouts full of Huns, and was glad,—we advanced all day, first with one company & another, everybody was lost; late in the afternoon we reached our objective, but we could not find where we were to stay, we kept going till 4:30 A.M. Fri, then we came back to this village—and I dropped on the floor with my saddle pockets (I hung on to them) over my shoulder and slept—and my pal could not wake me to make me eat. We'd had no sleep since Sun. night, except an hour at a time.

So we established an O.P. about a Kilometre behind the present line, we can see all the action for six Kilometres, there's not much doing except artillery fire, constantly from both sides, I've been under shell fire almost constantly for ten days—the closest one came within twenty feet, I wouldn't tell this now, but I'm going to send a wire home as soon as we are relieved, which will be soon. I got enough souvinirs too. Expect to get a chance to go to Paris for a week now. I want to come home, but this will be over soon I think. I got six letters from you sweetheart and about six from home yesterday. I'll answer them all when I can. Phone Mother when you get this. I can only write one letter now. I'll have some tales to tell Dear, but the one I want to tell most is the story of my love for my wonderful little wife. You & Mother and the rest must not worry about me, I'll be relieved long before you get this. Now I can come home satisfied to *stay* and *love*. Your Own Loving

Soldier Boy X X

R.M. Bowman

Hq. Troop, 89th Division

American E.F., A.P.O. 761

(I pray always before I sleep, for my wonderful Mother & Wife and the rest, and for our early reunion.)

Heard from Johnnie

Private Charles Bottomley,
Heavy Artillery, Canadian Corps

Bottomley joined the Canadian army in 1914. This extract from his diary covers the last days of the war.

Diary: November 1, 1918 [France]—Our guns were firing heavy in the morning. On the right of Hasnon, the Imperial made an attack and advanced four miles. In the afternoon, several prisoners came through the village.

November 2, 1918—Working around guns in the morning. Taking life pretty easy. Had the afternoon off.

November 3, 1918—Reveille 6 a.m. Only stable parades during the day. We heard that hostilities were going to cease by the end of this week. Had a walk around Hasnon. Saw the canal and railway bridge that had been blown up by the Hun.

November 4, 1918—Working around guns and horse lines all day.

November 5, 1918—Working around guns and limbers. Raining all day. Got orders to get everything ready to pull out next morning.

November 6, 1918—Pulled out at 9 a.m. Before leaving, the O.C. inspected the battery. Our sub section got the prize for cleanest gun and limbers. Left the town of Grand Bray passing through Raismes and we billeted in a big town called Anzin in a big house. Piano, up to date furniture, everything O.K. Had a good feed of spuds. Met Captain Hinds, also the 16th Battalion. We had a nice little concert. At night, slept on the carpet floor.

November 7, 1918—Left Anzin about 9 a.m., passing through Valeberas over the River Shelat. This place has certainly been destroyed. The station and bridges all blew up. Met Harry Ring, also saw Captain Hinds leading the 116th on their way to Mons. Slept in a big house on the Mons Road in St. Saulve.

November 8, 1918—Left St. Saulve about 9 a.m. and went along the Mons Road to a place called Quaropible. Along the Mons Road, dead horses and Fritz guns and limbers were laying. They had been caught in our barrage. We slept in a house on the Mons

Road. The civilians were coming back to their homes and it would make your heart bleed to see them trudging along with their loads.

November 9, 1918—We stayed in Quaropible all day. Our traffic had been passing continually for two days following up the Hun troops, guns of all sizes, trucks and all kinds of army material. It was a sight worth seeing. Civilians were passing back to their homes with their workday belongings in a two-wheeled rig. Pretty near all the houses had been shelled by the Hun.

November 10, 1918—Resting in Quaropible during the day. Troops, guns, motor trucks and war material were passing in one continuous stream for the last two days. Civilians were pouring back with their push carts the other way. A French man dropped a message from a plane. We were putting in a good time.

November 11, 1918—We got the good news that hostilities had ceased. It was too good to believe. During the afternoon, Percy Boyce and me had a walk across to the Belgium border on the Mons Road. Went into the cathedral. Coming back we helped a couple of civilians back with their load. Traffic still pouring ahead.

November 12, 1918—Still resting around Quaropible having a good time. We were cleaning up guns, limbers and harness before starting to march into Germany [as an occupation force]. Refugees still going past the house to their respective town looking tuckered out and hungry.

November 13, 1918—Still resting around the same town. Refugees still going past. Some thousands must have gone past. Nothing but a continuous procession of guns and troops going towards the German boundary.

THE SPANISH CIVIL WAR 1936–9

In July 1936, the Spanish army launched a coup against the country's elected Republican Government, seizing control of much of the north as well as major cities in the south. Initially the revolt was led by General Sanjurjo, but when he was killed in a plane crash, General Franco (Europe's youngest general since Napoleon) became the caudillo *of the Nationalist forces. Franco received considerable material support from the regimes of Nazi Germany and Fascist Italy, the latter dispatching 50,000 troops alone. The Republican Government, in turn, was supplied with arms from the Soviet Union, but lacked a regular, trained army to use them. The brunt of the fighting against the Nationalists was borne initially by workers' militia and leftist political organizations, until a Republican conscript army was raised. Its numbers were swelled by thousands of anti-fascist volunteers from Britain, America and France, who formed an International Brigade to fight alongside the Republican Army.*

Battlelines were almost static until 1938, when Republicans began a sustained offensive on the River Ebro. This, however, was undone by political divisions in the Republican side between Communists and more radical elements. The Nationalist army, spearheaded by Moroccan troops and battalions of the Spanish Foreign Legion, pushed government forces back, breaking through on the Catalan front at the end of the year. Barcelona fell to Franco in January 1939, and Valencia, the temporary capital, fell in March. Madrid surrendered on the last day of March 1939, thus ending the Civil War. Around 600,000 Spaniards perished in combat, from political executions, and from starvation during its course.

Will Lloyd, International Brigade

Lloyd writes to his mother in Wales.

[Spain, mid-January 1937]

Dear Ma
    Again I can find time to drop you a line or two. Well we have had

our first test and came through all right, I'm glad to say. We are
now having our first rest since we arrived here. You should see
both of us now. We are in the barber's shop waiting for a shave.
We've got three weeks' growth on, and we resemble what some
people think Bolsheviks look like.

What sort of Christmas did you have? Hope you enjoyed
yourselves. Give my regards to all [Communist] Party members
and all my pals. So long now; enjoy yourself and don't worry about
me. Salud

From YOUR LOVING SON

PS Try and send some Wodbines if you can. I'm dying for a smoke
of a REAL fag.

Jim Brewer, International Brigade

Brewer writes to a former tutor in Britain.

20 June 1937

Dear Friend
   I am writing this from the front "somewhere in Spain" . . .
   These days are among the happiest in my life, since I'm doing
what I think is most worth doing in all the world at the moment;
the driving of these Fascist bastards from Spain and eventually I
think from the face of the earth. Its Sunday today I believe and this
morning our artillery observed it by sending a few dozen rounds
into the enemy lines. All's quiet at the moment it being afternoon
and siesta time. Silent but for the hum of unnumerable flies, a
grasshopper or two and a few larks and occasionally the vicious
crack of an explosive bullet. I have never heard a more uplifting
sound than the whine of our 60 lb'ers as they go overhead. Or
anything more devastating than to have one land nearby. The
fascist artillery men are either secretly communists or damned
rotten marksmen since, on this front at least, they rarely get near
their objective. The flies are much more accurate. There was a
time when one took pains to kill them but since they outnumbered
us by a thousand to one its a waste of time.
   Last night we had an alarm. The enemy were well oiled with
wine and under its influence appeared to start an attack on one of
our flanks. Then hell was let loose. My job only takes me up the
line at daytime but I found a pretext for going up a few minutes
after the shindy started. Its funny how quickly one loses fear of

bullets and what not. That I think is because ours is the first army since the Crusades which knows what its fighting for and is utterly confident of success.

I was lucky enough to be put in a detachment which is trained to use any and every weapon which we love with a love surpassing that of man for woman. I don't think any of us knew such pride before. We have very good officers, one an artist and a Scotsman. Our second in command is also a Scotsman, a miner from the Kentish Coalfield sound men. We are three Welshmen, above five Englishmen and all the rest Scots. I'm almost becoming a Scot myself since all in the group to which I am attached are Scots. True comrades all. We have in our ranks miners, factory workers, building trade workers, an industrial chemist, a chartered accountant, a public schoolmaster and a few students. A motley crowd. Tom ought to invite us all to Harlech someday, when the war is over. I'm sure we'd exert a good influence on the boys there. Discipline and all that, I can assure you that we are well disciplined, but its self-discipline. Here there is a minimum of discipline imposed from above. We had a chat with our general the other day. Who ever heard of that in any other army, certainly in any capitalist army?

There is so much manyana in Spain that I think I shall be a very efficient fighter when I come home. I don't think I've been less lazy since those early days at Harlech when I was really keen. A temperate climate would work wonders again. I have learned for instance that a man doesn't need more than 5 to 6 hours sleep and can keep an active mind for the other 14, provided he's on the right job.

As ever,
Jim Brewer

Bosco Jones, International Brigade

Jones writes to a friend in Britain.

Socorro Rojo
Plaza del Altazone
Albacete
SPAIN
5.8.37

Dear Tom

Am taking the chance of writing now. I am resting in hospital in [illegible] and am expecting to leave here at any moment as I am now feeling very fit, although I have got very thin these last few months. Well, I was very lucky as usual. In our last attack Cyril got rather a nasty one in the cobbelers but writes and ensures me he will be ok . . . I said I was lucky. I guess I am. I was strolling along with a mule packed with food for the boys when I see many planes flying over. I soon got to know they were not ours as the anti-aircraft opened up on them. I tied the mule to a tree and dived into the nearest dug out and began to write my will. I left you my pipe. I tried to imagine I was at Hendon air display but was no use. Down they swooped. They seemed to bomb every place but mine. Anyway they blew the mule up in the air and something crashed on my tin hat and the fumes got down my throat. I then reported to the doctor as I could not see and was afraid I was going blind. He then sent me to hospital.

For my first meal I received eggs and bacon. I then thought I was delirious when I saw it was real. My eyes soon got better . . .

Your pal
Bosco

Socorro Rojo
Plaza del Altazone
Albacete
SPAIN

7 September 1938

Dear Tom

Am writing to you from the front line after some really terrific battles as we have been advancing for nearly two weeks capturing village after village. In the last two towns we have captured over 2000 prisoners. This is no story as we had to escort 800 down. We had surrounded the town and after three days they surrendered having to bayonet their officers who had been forcing them to fight on. The Fascist air force fly over us three times a day. We often have to hold our breath as they bomb in circles around us. The government planes have brought down 10 withing [sic] the last two days. There was a funny incident last night. We had surrounded a town cutting off completely any food supplies. The Fascists decided to drop food into the town by plane. When they circled over head one of the Spanish comrades noticed a torch being flashed in the sky. He did the same. To our surprise the planes started dropping objects. We then took cover thinking they might be bombs. But it was food, mostly tinned stuff marked plainly in Italian. I have not received any letters now for about two months, as it is very difficult to get mail into the front line. I have heard no news of Charlie Spiller although I have made thorough enquiries. Am feeling very anxious. Can [only] hope for the best . . . Saw our friend Tomlinson of the Party. He is with the Anti-tank gun and they have been doing some great work. He had been having a rough time and I had to smile when I [. . . saw how] different he looked [from] in Finsbury, as he had a beard about four inches along . . . If my luck holds out I hope to see you this side of Xmas.

Your pal
Bosco

Jim Strangward, International Brigade

Strangward was a Welsh miner, and volunteer with the International Brigade. He writes to his brother.

[Spain]
12 July 1938

Dear Comrade Brother,

Thanks for your letter for the 5th of July and was ever so pleased to hear some News from Home. Your letter was the first letter for me to have except the Note and fags from Johnny. I'm glad you like the photos I sent and did you receive the Book of the International Brigade that I sent the Party as you did not mention it in your letter.

Tell Johnny that I have not received any of the parcels yet but may receive them later on but I want you to thank Mrs. Francis and Dal for sending me a parcel but I have not received it yet and that I'll write to them later.

Well we had a delegation of students from England here yesterday and they spoke well and promised to do all they possible can for the Spanish Govt. when they get back to London. Tell Ior Evans that the sooner victory is ours I'll he Home. Try and send some fags next time you write if its only a 2d pkt of woodbine. Its best to send them in the letters. Well must draw to a close hoping you'll do all you can to help "Spain" and when the time comes I'll do my share here.

With revolutionary Greetings.
Jim. "Salud".

P.S. send some envelopes and paper in a big envelope and write often in turns say 2 a week.

Strangward was killed in the Ebro offensive in August 1938.

Edwin Greening, International Brigade

Greening was an observer attached to the British Battalion of the International Brigade. The letter is to the brother of a fallen brigade volunteer.

[Spain, late August 1938]

My Dear Dai Mark,

I regret having to write this, but Tom Howell was killed a few days ago (at 2.30 p.m., August 25 to be exact). We were together in an advanced position with the boys on some mountains called Sierra de Pandols, which overlook the town of Gandesa. I was in our company observation post, which was situated only 5 yards from where Tom was posted.

Every night Tom and I would have a little chat about home and other things, and that morning I had given him an Aberdare Leader the one in which Pen Davies' pilgrimage to the Aberdare Cemetery was reported, and he was very happy to receive it.

From early morning things had been very quiet on our sector. Then suddenly the enemy sent over some trench mortars; one of the shells made a direct hit on a machine gun post, nearly killing three men, a Spaniard and two Englishmen. I shouted to Tommy "All right there Tom?" and he shouted back, "O.K. Edwin."

Then this trench mortar landed near us. I called out again and receiving no answer, crawled to Tom's post, where I found him very badly wounded about the neck, chest and head. He was already unconscious and was passing away. I ran for the first aid man and we were there in two minutes, but Tom was, from the moment he was hit, beyond human aid and all we could do was raise him up a little and in two or three minutes, with his head resting on my knee, Tom passed away without regaining consciousness.

You can imagine how I felt because Tom and I had been very close to one another here. But I could do nothing.

That night Alun Williams of Rhondda, son of Huw Menai, and Lance Rogers of Merthyr, one of Tom's pals, carried his corpse to the little valley below, where he was to rest forever.

And there on that great mountain range, in a little grove of almond trees, we laid Tom Howell to rest. I said a few words of farewell but Tom is not alone there, all around him lie the graves of many Spanish and English boys.

Tom always made me promise to write you if anything like this

happened. You will have already heard about Tom a week or two
before you receive this letter.

His thoughts were to the last and always of his mother and the
people at home. He lived and died a good fellow.

If fifty years pass I shall not forget.

Miles Tomalin,
British Anti-Tank Battery, International Brigade

Tomalin writes to his young son in a series of letters illustrated
with pen and ink drawings.

Spain, January 12, 1938

Hullo Nicko

I hope you got the little engine and the map I put in my last
letter to you. Sometimes these things don't arrive, like the flag. But
never mind, we can get other things when I come home. Do you
know, I still haven't the faintest idea when that will be? Then
there'll be a fine home coming.

The other day I went into a huge house that used to belong to
the King of Spain when there was one. There isn't one now. He
wasn't any good so he was told to go. Well, there's his palace, a lot
of it just empty now. It was far too big a house for one man to
have—absurd it seems to me. In one of the rooms he had a throne,
which I suppose he used to sit on and try to look grand. (Kings
look pretty silly when they try to look grand—so does anybody, as
a matter of fact). The throne [was] not there, but you can see the
platform on which it used to be . . .

I had a funny Christmas day. Most of it I was driving along the
road. In the evening we reached a little town and slept there. It was
very old, and had a wall all round and a castle perched up on the
top of it. This sort of thing [drawing of castle]. The morning after
Christmas I climbed up to the castle. The path went round and
round the hill and it was a warm morning. I was very hot by the
time I got to the top. Although it was built all those years ago, the
men who built it had made a little swimming bath up there for
themselves. There was still some water in it.

On my way back to Madrid, it got colder and colder and colder,
until at last I was frightfully cold. Where I am now it is lovely and
warm I'm glad to say.

Goodbye and give my love to Mummy . . .

Daddy

[drawing of man pulling sack] < This sack is full of love for you. Me dragging!

Spain, February 28, 1938

Hello Nicko

Do you like underground places? I have just seen a fine one with a passage going down to it that turns corners in the dark. You stumble along and wonder where you are going to tread next. At last you arrive in the room which has lights, and find a lot of important officers there.

Spring is coming along. It comes sooner in Spain than in England. Winter is very cold, but not very long. Summer is very hot, so is Autumn.

[pen and ink drawings of people as the four seasons: "This is Winter, an ill-tempered old man, throwing snow on the ground"; "This is Spring, running over the ground and dropping flowers"; This is Summer, a man looking over a gate and not troubling to think very much about anything"; "This is Autumn, walking slowly along with her eyes on the ground because leaves and fruit and things fall there"]

The other day I took ammunition up to the other soldiers on the back of a mule. A mule isn't quite a horse and isn't quite a donkey, but something between the two. I didn't know anything about mules but fortunately for me this one did everything he was told and didn't seem to mind too much. Even when the rope slipped off my hand without my knowing it, he just stopped and ate grass until I came back [drawing of man with mule: "Me leading mule"]

At present I sleep on some straw each night. The straw is piled up on the floor. By now I am so sleepy that I am dozing off over this letter so I think I had better stop and go to bed. I haven't taken off all my clothes for a good many days days now. It would be too cold. Meanwhile I am bitten by little insects called lice. Lice are bigger than measles, but not very. Horrid little things. It isn't easy to get a bath and wash them off . . . Last night I dreamed you fell into water when I wasn't looking. However, it all came right in the end.

Goodnight,
Daddy

[Spain n.d]

Hullo Nicko

I have just had a letter from Grannie and she says you are very well now, which is fine. I expect by the time I come back you will have grown taller and instead of being this high [drawing of small boy] you will be this high [drawing of bigger boy]. I wonder if you have forgotten what I looked like? Sometimes when you try to remember what a person looks like, the harder you try, the more difficult it becomes to remember.

The people in Spain speak Spanish, which is different from English. I don't know how to speak Spanish, though I am trying to learn . . . By the way, I have met a little girl here called Carmen, who is nearly as old as you, but much smaller. Rather like this [drawing of girl]. I go and see her sometimes. She is the next best thing to you while I am all this long way away. I quite often have dreams about you, so that isn't so bad. Sometimes I dream we are playing games and the other night I dreamed we were by the seaside . . .

The comrades I live with are English or Scottish or Welsh. So I can speak to all of them easily enough. They have all come out to help do the same job of work that I came for. Spain ought to be a good sort of place by the time the job is finished. Perhaps one day I'll be able to bring you here on holiday . . .

> It is far, so far
> Goodbye from
> Daddy

Spain, Nov 17, 1938

Hullo Nicko.

I haven't written to you for a long time, and that is because I kept thinking I'd be leaving for home any day. I *still* think I'll be leaving any day, but here is a letter in case I've a week or more to wait.

It's all the fault of people who are friends of the fascists and not of us. They are what is called sabotaging our return home, that is to say managing to get it put off as long as they can. Otherwise I would have been home long ago.

Well, meanwhile I am waiting with the other English comrades in quite a nice little town in the mountains. We sleep in a theatre, all over the part where the seats usually are. Now the floor is covered just with mattresses and us. Sometimes we get a concert going on the stage [drawing of people on stage in play]

There is a lot of scenery about, so we chose what we want. Here you see a cardboard house on the left, a cardboard tree on the right, and a landscape with castles at the back, which is just the sort of mixture we might get. In front are two people, one pretending to be a woman with an umbrella. He's being funny at the other chap, who doesn't know what to say, so he stands about and does his best. Perhaps the next turn will be me [drawing of man with whistle] blowing tunes on my phoo, the little yellow one, which I haven't lost yet.

I still have a great many dreams about you, Nicko. Last night I dreamed you were reading from a book. Can you read yet?

It will be most exciting to see how much bigger you have grown since I last saw you.

If it isn't too difficult, ask mummy or grannie to bring you to Victoria station to meet me. It would be fun.

Very much love to you and everybody.

Daddy

(I think it *can't* be much longer now)

THE SECOND WORLD WAR
1939–1945

In retrospect the Spanish Civil War was a beginning not an end, a dress rehearsal for a larger clash between the forces of democracy and fascism. As the last of the 30s slid past, so Hitler pushed the boundaries of Germany outwards – the Anschluss *with Austria, the seizure of the Sudetenland. Almost everywhere he was appeased by capitalist democracies who considered him at worst a bulwark against the Stalinist regime to his East; at Munich in 1938, the British prime minister, Neville Chamberlain, extracted a peace pledge from Hitler, returning to Britain with a wave of paper and the advice to "Go home and get a nice quiet sleep." It was only following the seizure of Poland, a country whose independence Britain had guaranteed, that hostilities between Britain and Germany were declared on the late summer's day of 3rd September 1939. Nine months of "phoney war" followed, before the invasion of France and the Lowlands by Germany in May 1940. A British Expeditionary Force despatched to France traced almost exactly the footsteps of its 1914 predecessor, but ill-equipped and old-fashioned in philosophy it was sent hurtling backwards by the* blitzkrieg *('lightening war') of the Germans, in which their fast-moving army, led by a phalanx of tanks and backed by squadrons of planes as "flying artillery", smashed like an iron fist. (And behind* blitzkrieg *toiled a German economy already devoted to military ends, and a male population already dressed in field-grey. While other nations had talked of "everyman a soldier" the remilitarized Germany under Hitler had achieved it.) By 17 June 1940 the German invasion of France and the Lowlands was complete. The only consolation for Britain was the partial evacuation of its Expeditionary Force from the beaches of Dunkirk, a feat of "Tommy" courage which would inspire the nation in the days ahead.*

For a year Britain and her empire stood alone against Germany, but the war had raised forces which would not be constrained to

Western Europe. Already Britain and Germany were fighting over British possessions in North Africa, and then, in June 1941, Hitler invaded Russia. In December of that year Germany's ally, Japan, attacked the American fleet at Pearl Harbor. By reciprocal declarations of hostilities the world was at war.

Few nations would be uncommitted, while the advanced technology of warfare – bomber planes, the V1 and V2 rockets – meant that the war was brought home, literally, to the civilian populations of the participant nations. After the breaking of the initial mutual agreement not to direct aerial attacks against civilian targets, war rained down from the skies, epitomized by the "Blitz" on London from September 1940 to May 1941. Moreover, the vastness of the armies involved required conscription from the outset of hostilities. Warmaking had reached a totality undreamed of in the past. Perhaps 50,000,000 died during the war years of 1939–45.

With millions of families separated, the private letter assumed its greatest importance. Never before or again, would so many people keep in touch via the written word, or feel the need to commit their thoughts and experiences to a journal.

Sergeant Karl Fuchs, 25th Panzer Regiment, 7th Panzer Division

A schoolteacher, Fuchs was conscripted into the Wehrmacht in October 1939.

[Fall 1939]
Langwasser Training Camp

Dear Father,

A week has gone by and we're now settled in at the military installation. The entire compound is superb! We have had our psychological examinations and, based upon these tests, I was assigned as a tank gunner. Now, of course, we have to learn and train until we perfect all of our skills. Infantry training is almost behind us and in eight weeks we have to be fit for combat. You, as an old soldier, know best what this means. The intensity of training is tremendous and there is no rest for anyone. All of us are eager to make progress and no one complains, least of all your son. You won't ever have to be ashamed of me; you can depend on me.

Several days ago I had to report to the captain of our company and speak to him about my plans for officer training. Today for the first time we had to practice pistol shooting—five shots and five bull's-eyes for me! Next week we have training in shooting with rifles and machine guns. The recruits are looking forward to this training. All of us tank gunners need to be crack shots.

Next week we'll be able to climb into our tanks for the first time. Operating the vehicle will have to become second nature to us. Tanks are really awesome!

For the time being we will have no furlough, at least not until New Year's. Christmastime will be spent in our barracks. I hope that all is well at home. Please write to me if you are able to come and visit. One more request; please take care of Mädi so that she doesn't feel so alone.

That's all for today. Sieg Heil and on to old England!

Your loyal son, Karl

20 June 1940
Langwasser Training Camp

Dear Father,

You could be proud of your only son if he had been part of Germany's most magnificent victories [France was defeated by mid-June 1940.] Several weeks ago I told you that it was finally our turn to go to the front, but now nothing came of it. On 10 June our march unit went to the front but without us. Orders from head-quarters: All officer candidates have to remain here!! This time we weren't disappointed but enraged! We ran from officer to officer and finally to the commander, explaining to them that we would renounce all claims to becoming officers if we only got to go. All of our attempts were in vain. While we told them that we wanted to volunteer right away for the paratroopers, they asked us: "Gentle-men, aren't you proud of your tank unit?" Obviously, they were trying to call upon our loyalty. Apparently our division is in dire need of young officers, much more so than any other division. We have become pessimists and believe that we will never get to go to the front—not even to take revenge on England.

Oh Father, had I listened to you and gone into the Air Force, I would have been part of the action long ago. I am ashamed in front of you and all my comrades. You are a part of the action and I, the son of an old soldier, am banished to the hinterland. The war will be over and I won't have had a chance to do anything for our Führer or for our Fatherland. Perhaps my chance is yet to come.

Please write and console me.

Your sad son Karl

Letter to his wife.

Eastern Front
25 June 1941

Dearly beloved Mädi,

Today was a day of pride for us all! Victoriously we marched into Vilnius [Lithuania], cheered on by the jubilant citizens. Yesterday I knocked off a Russian tank, as I had done two days ago! If I get in another attack, I'll receive my first battle stripes. War is half as bad as it sounds and one thing is plain as day: The Russians are fleeing everywhere and we follow them. All of us believe in early victory!

Dear Mädi, just think of the time when I'll be able to be with you again. Don't worry about me; I will return. Now we must march on. I send my love to you. Kiss my dear son Horsti for me.

Your Papi

Eastern Front
25 June 1941

My dearest wife, my dear little Horsti,

After three days of heavy fighting we were finally granted a well-deserved day of rest. Unfortunately there is some maintenance work that has to be done.

How are you, my two loved ones? Since I received your postcard several days ago, I haven't heard from you. I suppose it's because of the postal delivery which, because of the huge distances now, only comes to us every three or four days. I myself am fine and healthy and today I received my first war decoration from our commander, namely, the tank assault medal. I wear it proudly and hope you are proud of me.

Up to now, all of the troops have had to accomplish quite a bit. The same goes for our machines and tanks. But, nevertheless, we're going to show those Bolshevik bums who's who around here! They fight like hired hands—not like soldiers, no matter if they are men, women or children on the front lines. They're all no better than a bunch of scoundrels. By now, half of Europe is mobilized. The entry of Spain and Hungary on our side against this Bolshevik archenemy of the world overjoyed us all. Yes, Europe stands under the leadership of our beloved Führer Adolph Hitler, and he'll reshape it for a better future. The entry of all these volunteer armies into this war will cause the war to be over soon.

The impressions that the battles have left on me will be with me forever . . .

Your Korri

[Eastern Front]
October 1941

. . . If you have an opportunity to buy woolen things for me, please go ahead and do it. I will be very happy to receive them.

In your letter of 13 October, you wrote again about our young son. I can't imagine that he is so big and strong already that he can sit by himself in the corner of the couch! Dear Mädi, what great fortune it is to have such a child. Just wait until I'm home! I will be able to rock him in my arms and won't give him back to you at all! Do you think he'll be astonished to see me in my black tank uniform?

I have to go outside now and make my rounds to make sure that everything is in order. Everytime I'm outside at night I look to the West, hoping that I can see you in the distance. Then I kiss and hug you and long for you.

Your Korri

Eastern Front
12 November 1941

My dear Mother,

Yesterday my son was five months old. You don't know how often I think of him. Soon he will babble his first word, "Mama," and maybe he'll say "Papa" as well, and I, his father, am farther away from home than ever. My plight today is similar to Father's in the Great War. We men out here on the front know what our duty is and act accordingly. All of us have become serious and mature in this struggle for the future of our people. If we won't see our homeland by the end of this year and maybe not right away next year either, then we simply have to endure the disappointment because we know that this sacrifice must be made.

Our thoughts, wishes and dreams fly to you at home and when we men gather out here around a small Christmas tree in a few weeks, our eyes will be bright because we'll know that our homeland and our loved ones can celebrate this feast in peace.

You at home must always keep in mind what would have happened if these hordes had overrun our Fatherland. The horror of this is unthinkable!

We know no fear. The cold is going to be a factor, but we shall endure that too. One of these days we will meet again and no one is looking forward to this more than I.

I send my greetings and remain forever

your loyal son, Karl

Karl Fuchs was killed in action on the Eastern Front a fortnight after writing this letter.

Sergeant L.D. Pexton, British Army

Pexton served with the British Expeditionary Force sent to France to counter a German invasion.

Diary 15 May 1940: [Cambrai, Northern France] Stood to at 3.30 a.m. Very quiet up to 4.15. German spotting plane came over pretty low. 6.30 a.m. First taste of bombers. 68 of them all trying to create hell upon earth together. What a day—just about blew us all out the ground. Got shelled all day too. Getting very warm round here now. Don't mind the bombs so much as the planes' machine-guns. They're wicked.

16 May. Stood to again at dawn. Quiet. Told they had come through Luxemburg with four armoured divisions, but that they could only last till Sunday with petrol. '*Must* hold them at all costs." Still more shelling. Cambrai must be in a mess by now. Got some more bombs today.

17 May. Dawn again. Lovely morning. Can't believe that war is anywhere near. Refugees still pouring out of Cambrai. I am only fifty yards from the main Cambrai-Arras road. Big steel bridge not far from my dug-out. Heard from Coy Commander today that Engineers will blow it up if he gets too near.

18 May. Stood to again. Pretty cold this morning. Spotter came over again at 4.30 a.m. Started getting a bit deeper into Mother Earth ready for his mates to come. They came all right. One hundred and seventeen bombers and fighters. Quite sticky while it lasted. The village that was in our rear just isn't now. Fighters began to machine-gun from the main road. What a mess. Be glad when night comes.

19 May. 2.45 a.m. Hell of a bang. They have blown the bridge up. He must be advancing again. Shells coming all over the place. Just in front of our position. Hope when he lifts he goes well over our heads. Lots of dud shells coming. Went to see the bridge at 9.30 a.m. Lots of dead there—must have gone up with it. Took a chance in between shells and dived in café. Got a bottle of Rum and two bottles of Vin Rouge. Didn't stay long. Good job, as café went west five minutes later. Direct hit. Shells are giving us some stick now, 12 noon. Afraid we shall have to retire soon. Can't hold tanks with rifles or bren-guns. 4 p.m. We HAVE to hold on till 8 p.m. and then retire. Roll on 8 p.m. It's been hell all day. Air battles have been worth looking at though. Got out at 8 p.m. and marched 6 kilometres and got some lorries. Arrived at small village at 3 a.m.

20 May. Slept till 8 a.m. Went out of barn to see what was happening and if possible scrounge some grub. Found that some grub was going on in one of the lorries but had to wait for the next party. Don't know where they are going. Refugees still coming through from somewhere. Saw two men running down the road. Refugees said they were Parachutists. Captain Martin and myself called on them to halt but they didn't. Not immediately. Dropped them. Both dead when we got to them. 10 a.m. Fun began. Germans came from nowhere. Properly surprised us. Got down to it in the open and fought for all we knew how. Getting wiped out this time all right. Got back out of the farm buildings, and he's sending everything he has at us. 11 a.m. Still holding out and there's a bit of a lull. Kid on my right will keep sticking his head up above the clover. He's sure to get his soon, I'm thinking. Can't really remember much about the next hour. Remember the order "Cease fire" and that the time was 12 o'clock. Stood up and put my hands up. My God, how few of us stood up. German officer came and spoke in English. Told to pick up the wounded and carry them to the road. There aren't many that need carrying. We have to leave our dead. Took us off the road into another field. I expected my last moments had come and lit a fag. Everyone expected to be shot there and then. Patched up our wounded as best we could and were taken back about two miles. Stayed the night in a Roman Catholic church. Learned that this village is called Ficheaux. Note: out of appr. 1,400 men only 425 spent the night in this church.

21 May. Roused out of it at 6 a.m. and put on road. I'm just beginning to realize that I'm a prisoner. We have had nothing to eat since Sunday and today is Tuesday. My water-bottle is empty now. Hope they give us something to eat soon. Got nothing to eat today.

22 May. Marched today to a village called Leincourt. They "promised" us some food but still we got none. My tummy is getting used to nothing now. We are just living on water.

23 May. Left Leincourt at 7 a.m. and marched to Frevent, the very village that we left to try and stop him. I'd had a few decent meals, and beer as well, in this place. Hell, but I could do with a meal now. Left here at 8 p.m. for Doullens and warned that if anyone tried to escape they would shoot the officers they had in the car with them. No one tried to escape. Got to Doullens at 3 a.m. Flaxmill. Rats galore.

24 May. What a night. Rats running all over the place. Left Doullens for Albert. Sent off with one packet of English biscuits and half a tin of bully. Did 21 miles today, and very hot. They keep us away from all water and it is hell. Got to Albert at 8 p.m., just about all in, and went to aircraft works. Slept on the landing-ground. He'd made a mess of things here. Airplanes smashed up and the works badly smashed as well. I realize I'm a prisoner now all right. Just about fed up with everything. Wouldn't taken much for me to make a break for it. It would be a quick way out anyway so long as he shot straight. Suppose I must not think that way and just carry on. It can't last for ever.

25 May. Had a very cold night at Albert and was glad to be on the road again. They gave us two packets of German biscuits and they taste awful. Black and bitter. Still they help to fill a terribly big hole. Lovely day but far too hot for marching, and in our condition too. Men are dropping out every mile now. Feet are in a terrible condition. I don't know how some of them march at all. Just the British spirit I expect. We're never beaten. Passed Delville Wood Cemetery today. Very big, and later passed Caterpillar Valley as well. Not as big but just as tidy. Cemeteries are all over this part of the country. Must have been some bother here in the last war all right. They look nice but I hope I don't end up in one. Arrived at the field and find this place is called Flers. Had a big thunderstorm just before arriving and got nice and wet. Everything wet to sleep on so I expect another lovely night.

26 May. The worst night yet. Left here for Cambrai and they gave us ONE biscuit on marching out. What a march. Will never understand how I did it, but here I am in the French barracks at last. There must be 30,000 of us on the road now. French mostly slept on the square although it was pouring with rain. We are that hungry we can't feel the wet. Germans say the war will be over in one month. I wonder.

27 May. Terrible night. Left for Le Cateaux. Long march and went right through, and got to a place called Cattilou. Got no eats all day. Sent letter home from here but don't think that it will get there. Still, I must chance anything that comes along.

28 May. Left for Avesne at 3.30 p.m. Raining heavy. They gave us a bit of black bread and a piece of cheese. Long and quick march. Gave us each a bale of angora wool to sleep on in the mill. Nothing to eat.

29 May. Left here at 10 a.m. and crossed into Belgium at a place called Sivry. Got one slice of bread and margarine before marching out. Have got an awful cold in the head. Head is buzzing like a top. No wonder, living this cowboy life. Very hot today for marching. Halted at place called Philippeville.

30 May. Very cold night. Left at 9.30 a.m. and marched to place called Marienbourg. Arrived at 5.30. Got soup, meat and bread. Heard we go by train to Cologne in the morning. Shall have to wait and see.

31 May. Many happy returns of the day, Ena. Suppose my good luck will begin today, on your birthday. Have had nothing but bad luck since my own—unless being alive is lucky. Left here at 9 a.m. and marched 20K to this village. Got ladle full of soup on arrival. Very weak. May get some later. Don't suppose we shall get any more food until tomorrow. Hope Ena has had news that I am a prisoner; would be a good birthday present for her. Place called Doische. No food.

1 June. Left Doische at 9 a.m. and marched to what looks like the railhead. Hope it is. I'm about fed up with tramping around France and Belgium. My boots are very bad. Got small ladle full of "coffee" to march out with. Nothing else. I'm as hungry as hell. If I didn't need what boots I have left to march in I'd eat them. Boys are trying to boil dandelions and nettles to make soup. Hope it works. Stayed the night here. Dandy went down all right but bitter. Sick afterwards. Place called Beauraing.

2 June. Stayed all day. Ate grass.

3 June. Left Beauraing at 9 a.m. and got a little soup and a small piece of black bread. Arrived at St Pierre about 3 p.m. Very hot. Not a long march but getting very weak in the legs. Had a drop of barley soup. No bread.

4 June. Looks like staying here at St Pierre all day. Stayed the night.

5 June. Left St Pierre at 5.30 a.m. Longest march yet. Got nothing on marching out to place called Bertrix. Marched about 43K. Lost three mates during the march.

6 June. Left Bertrix at 3 p.m. by Rail after the first really good dixie of soup. Arrived Luxemburg at 9.30 p.m. Only stayed half an hour and then went to a place called Trier. Climbed the big hill into Concentration Camp. We're just in Germany now, 3 a.m.

7 June. Left Trier at 10 p.m. after having some bread and jam. Passed through Germany via Hamburg and Posen to this place in Poland called Torun. I believe we have come to the end of the long trail at last. Just three weeks of it and I am all in. Shall be glad to stay anywhere for a bit. We spent 46 hours on the train from Trier.

9 June. Yes, this is our home camp. Getting treated a lot better now. Better and more food today.

10 June. Letting us rest for a day or two to get some of our strength back before going to work.

11 June. Got our numbers today. 8806 is my number. This camp is called Stalag XXA (17). We shall go to work soon.

12 June. Handed in our money today. 50 francs and 10d. in English is all I had. Got a receipt for it but don't suppose this will matter much. Heard today that Italy had declared war on Turkey and that Russia was helping Turkey. Wish it was all over and done with and I was on my way home again.

14 June. Told today that on Monday we could write home. This will be the first time. Hope it's true. Could do with a smoke but I reckon I'll have to wait a bit yet. Still hungry. Was told today that the Germans were in Paris but don't know how true it is.

15 June. Had a busy day. Went for a bath. First decent wash for five weeks. We are being issued with a blanket today. May sleep better tonight—Saturday night of all nights. Nearly heart-broken to think I should be having a pint and a game of darts. Never mind. It will have to end some day, I suppose.

16 June. Wrote home! Could have written a book of wants but space didn't allow. Hope it won't take too long for an answer. I'm not getting my strength back on this food. Can't get nearly enough to eat. Smokes are out of the question. Tried smoking the leaves off the trees but it didn't work. What an awful experience. Roll on peace and let's get home.

17 June. Monday and just a month a prisoner. Seems more like a year to me. Can't think how I've survived this length of time. Marching, fighting and hunger is a hell of a lot to face. I'm sure I couldn't do it again. Got some roasted spuds tonight on a little fire I made on the sly. Glad I wasn't caught.

18 June. Got caught boiling spuds after "dinner". Don't know what is going to happen.

19 June. Nothing happened about the spuds, thank God. Put my name down as a shoe repairer. Might get decent job for the winter.

21 June. No sign of work for Sergeants. We're not allowed to work yet. Men are getting work and extra food with it. Heard today that Hull had been bombed. Petrol dump had been set on fire. Hope everyone at home is OK.

18 July. Getting very monotonous now, more so when you're as hungry as hell. Wish we could get some sort of news through.

19 July. Heard today that Hitler had broadcast some peace terms and that Churchill had told him what to do with them. Don't know how true it is as the camp is always so full of rumours that you can't believe anything you hear. Hope they do patch some sort of terms up as everyone here wants it, and to get home. Still, I'm not being the soldier I thought I was, wanting peace terms.

23 July. Got a basinful of macaroni from German cook. Had been a prisoner in England during the last war. Very decent chap. Thinks war will soon be over now. France has given in. Hope he is right. He was as fed up as me with it.

24 July. Told that English mail would be issued on Friday. Hope I hear from home. Never thought I should miss a letter like this. Or a parcel.

There's constant and careful collecting
Of strongest brown paper and twine,
There's a special pen-nib for directing,
Free-flowing and not over-fine.
There's a far-sighted skill in the packing,
For the problem's increasingly great,
Not to leave out a thing that he's lacking,
And still keep an eye on the weight.
There's a soreness of feminine fingers,
For the knots must be terribly tight,
There's a look that half nervously lingers,
For fear the address is not right.
There's a trust that the waves will be tender,
That no submarine lurks near the coast,
And a wish in the soul of the sender,
That she might go too, parcel post.
All soldiers whose comforts are meagre,
When the corporal sings out your name,
When your hands are schoolboyishly eager
To seize and examine your claim,
Do you guess, as the paper you're tearing,
And the gifts in your pockets you shove,
That each parcel from Blighty is bearing
                              An ocean of love?

28 July. No mail yet. Got deloused today to move to farm tomorrow. No idea where but I think it will be in Germany.

31 July. Rotten camp this. Under canvas and very wet.

2 August. Heard today that the German army pay had a 25% cut. Could do with a nice fish and chips supper—or a hunk of bread, if it comes to that.

6 August. Red letter day. Left for farm at a place called Neuteich. Got bread and lard for supper from the farmer.

7 August. Went tying and stooking barely until dinner. Threshing all afternoon until 8 p.m. Never felt so tired in all my life. Am as weak as water. Bed at 9.30 and locked in by guard.

8 August. Threshing. Then it rained, so knocked off and worked inside until 7 o'clock. In bed by 8.30. More food now but very plain. Not much meat either. Just *waiting* for a letter from home. It wouldn't be so bad then.

9 August. Rained again today. Mixing meal all morning. Can't do much in this weather. Farmer sent us back to billet for half a day providing we work half day Sunday if it is fine. Don't give anything away, these Gerries.

12 August. Threshing today. Feet very bad. It's these terrible wooden Dutch clogs we have to wear. No socks, just toe-rags. The balls of my feet always seem red-hot. Roll on.

13 August. Just work. Had to go through village to field and got spat at and called names by a fellow. Don't know what he said but had a good guess. German pig.

16 August. Went 10K to work today with Poles. Girls as well. I love to hear them sing while they work, although what they find to sing about beats me. They're as badly off as us. Bed means straw, no blanket. Just lay down in what you work in, except taking these awful clogs off. We haven't a towel or soap, and only clothes to stand up in, shirt and thin drawers. All lousy. Even our uniform is full of them. Can't keep them down no how.

17 August. Saturday again. Wonderful. We got some soap from the boss, a small cake that I'm sure is pure sand. Been cutting beans with a sickle. Rotten job, but then I think these people like to make a job as rotten as they can for us.

18 August. Had a funny dream about getting discharged in Halifax on December 5th. Hope it comes true.

19 August. Beans again. One of the Pole girls has decided that I'm the only one to work with. She ties up behind me. Will insist I learn to speak Polish. If I'm here about ten years I might be able to say something in Polish. What a language! *Still* no news from home. Wonder if they think I'm dead.

20 August. Just the same as usual. I don't think I shall keep this diary up as it looks to me as if I shall not need it.

18 September. I pity the last war's prisoners having four years of it.

Pexton decided not to continue with his diary after this date.

Jack Toomey, 42nd Postal Unit, British Army

Toomey writes to his cousins, shortly after his evacuation from Dunkirk.

Darlington
Saturday
[June 1940]

Dear Folks,

Just a line to let you know that I am still knocking about, had a letter from Mum this morning and was glad to hear that Aunt Edie was a lot better.

Things up here aren't too bad, we are billeted in a British Legion Club—beer downstairs blankets upstairs. An air raid warning twice nightly but such things don't bother us veterans who have been bombed from dawn to dusk nearly every day for three weeks, well, not much anyway.

Would you like to hear all about the War straight from the horses mouth. You wouldn't, good 'cos you are going to.

Before the war started we were enjoying a pleasant tour of France. Landed at Cherbourg, went south to Laval, in Mayeuse, had one or two trips into Le Mans with mails. From there we went N.E. to Evreux, stayed the night then onto Amiens here we stayed a week or so and moved on to the Belgium border at a place called Vervique-Sud on the Lys, to the south-east of Lille, and about ten klms south of Armentiers, we were staying here when the war started, after that we moved so fast and often that I didn't have time to take any notice of names.

Well, it started and after two days and nights of constant "alert" and all clears, we drunk a bottle of rum and another of Cognac biscuit to get some sleep, the air raid siren was in a church tower opposite and about twenty feet from our window. We were determined to sleep somehow. I was still drunk when I woke next day. A day or so later we were in a chateau farmhouse affair when a dog fight developed about a thousand feet above us Messerschmidts, Hurricanes and Spitfires were having a hell of a good time. I don't know who won, I was too busy dodging planes, bullets, and AA. shrapnel. From that day onwards my tin hat stayed on my head—even in bed sometimes. Another day a twin Messerschmidt came into to M.G. an AA post near us only they got him first he hit the dirt at about 300 mph—very little was left of the plane, the pilot and observer was buried by the road with a prop: blade stuck over them. At another place they flew up and down the street, machine gunning as they went, nice quiet clean fun. At another place, the last before we made the Dunkirk dash, the dive bombers came over and bombed us in the afternoon. Never look a dive-bomber in the face, Bill, cos if you do you can bet your sweet life things are going to hum soon, but pray and pray hard and run, run like hell for the nearest ditches and dive into them. I got quite used to diving in the end, could make a flat dive from the middle of the road or a power dive from a lorry in one motion. Well, after the bombers had gone and we took stock of the wreckage and found we were all alive, they came back and threw out leaflets for our use.

Then came the order to move and a rumour had it that we were making for Dunkirk. Off we went, about half-a-mile in front of Jerry, after an hour we stopped and everyone went into the ditch, that is, except another bloke and myself who were jammed in the back of the lorry. We could hear M.G. fire and thought it was a quiet shoot up by Jerry planes but when tracer shells started coming through the roof of our lorry, I knew I was wrong. Two shells took a knapsack from the box next to my head and threw it out of the back looking like cotton waste another went past my ear so close that I felt the wind of it. All the time M.G. bullets were smacking and rickshetting off the struts. I just sat and gave up all hope of coming out of that lorry alive. However I heard a noise of a tank chugging past the lorry and the shooting stopped for us. The bloke driving the tank saw us in the lorry and calmly tossed a hand grenade under the tailboard! After it had gone off and we found we were still alive we came out of that lorry with our hands in the clouds. There are pleasanter ways of committing suicide than fighting five tanks, an armoured wireless car and a plane, with a rifle. Well, they took us prisoners and while we were looking after the wounded the French opened fire and we were between the two fires, so back into the ditch we went. The main body of prisoners were run off to a nearby village. We lay in the ditch in a thunderstorm for two hours and then went back to our own lines. So much for my "escape", more of a case of getting left behind. The engine of our wagon was so shot up that it fell out when we pressed the self starter. We managed to get a tow from our Ordnance and after ten hours we slung it into the ditch. We had got separated from our crowd and were alone in the middle of the night in France or was it Belgium, anyway we were lost, so we just ambled on until something came along—it did—one of our artillery crowds so we joined the arty for a spell. Then as dawn came up we found the main Dunkirk road and what a jam, after about ten hours of stopping and starting driving into ditches and back into lorries we got near Dunkirk, and here we had to dash thru' a barrage of shrapnel so we slammed the old bus into top and went flat-out down the road. When all was clear and we were on the outskirts of Dunkirk we stopped on a long raised road with the canal on either side and nice big trees sheltering us from the air. We got out and looked up—there were about seventy bombers (German make, naturally, we hadn't seen one of our planes for three weeks!!!) knocking hell out of the docks or what was left of them. From there to the beaches and they were black with troops waiting to go aboard only there were no boats. They gave us a raid that afternoon and evening and the following day they gave us a raid that lasted from dawn till dusk, about 17 hours. The fellows laid down on open beaches with the bombs falling alongside us lucky it was sand, it killed the effect of the bombs. At the end of the day there were about 8 fellows killed and injured out of about 100,000.

The following day dawn broke and we saw the most welcome sight of all about a dozen destroyers off the beaches and more coming up—boats of all shapes and sizes, barges, Skylarks, lifeboats and yachts. Fortunately the day was cloudy and misty, the bombers only came once and as they came low beneath the clouds the Navy let 'em have it. They slung up everything the guns, I never saw this action, I was scrounging for a drink, we hadn't had water for a fortnight it was too risky to drink and all we could get was champagne and wines. Spirits only made me thirstier. However on this morning I had a drink of vin blanc and had to sit down I was drunk as a lord, the last time I had anything to eat was about three days off, and on an empty stomach the wine had a devastating effect. That evening we went aboard after make dash after dash up the jetty to dodge shrapnel—Jerry had got close enough for his light artillery to shell us.

We got aboard and started, there were about 800 of us on one small destroyer. The Navy rallied round and dished out cocoa, tins of bully, and loaves of new bread. This was the first grub some of us had for nearly four days and the first bread we had for a fortnight.

When we were about an hours run off Dover and thought we were safe a bomber came down and slammed three bombs at us—missed us by six feet and put all the lights out downstairs. We got to Dover at 2 am and climbed aboard a train, we were still scared to light cigarettes, a light on the beaches meant a hail of bombs, and we just drowsed, at Reading we got out and shambled to the road outside it was about 8 am and people just going to work stopped and stared, we must have look a mob, none of us shaved or wash for a week, our uniform was ripped and torn, with blood and oil stains. I had no equipment bar a tin hat and gas mask, a revolver I picked up from somewhere stuck out of my map pocket. One or two old dears took one look at us and burst into tears. I dont blame them, I frightened myself when I looked into a mirror.

They had buses to run us to the barracks, we could just about shuffle to them, we were so done up. At the barracks breakfast was waiting and they apologised because it was tinned salmon and mashed potatoes, we, who had been on half or no rations for nearly three weeks were too busy eating. After grub we slept for a few hours and had dinner, got paid and changed our money to English, changed our uniform for a clean lot, had a shave, shampoo, haircut, and bath and breezed out for a drink of beer. We stayed here for a week and went to Bournemouth to be re-equipped. At Bournemouth, three Spitfires roared overhead one day just above the pier and over the beach. I was on the beach, laying flat on my face before you could say "Scarp". I just couldn't help it. Leaves a self preservation instinct or something.

From there we were sent up to here nothing much has happened, we work in the P.O. doing much the same as we do in civilian life. They, the army, did try to get us out of it into the country under canvas but we told them we couldn't work without a post office near us so they let us stay.

Thus ends my little bit of the epic of the battle of Northern France and Dunkirk.

The times were rather tough and altho' I was scared stiff for three weeks it was something I wouldn't want to have missed. My only regret was that one of our Rover Scouts was left behind.

Still, c'est la guerre.

Chin, chin,
Love to all,
Jack.

Pilot Officer D.H. Wissler, RAF

A Hurricane pilot, Wissler fought throughout the Battle of Britain, August–September 1940.

Diary 1 August 1940 [Martlesham Heath]
I did not get up until 8 this morning and then went down to flight. I did a convoy patrol this morning, acting as section leader. Then

in the afternoon there was a flap and took off. Joined Red section and went hunting. The aerodrome was bombed, several 1000lb bombs being dropped not doing too much damage. We didn't even get a chance to fire although F/1 Harper was shot down, but managed to jump, though wounded. In the evening we watched a raid over Harwich being machine-gunned and shelled. He[Heinkels] dropped one large bomb!

Monday, 19 August
I was recalled from leave today . . . The squadron is moving to TANGMERE. I flew "X", which was due for an inspection to Debden. "V", my own plane not ready so I spent the night in a comfortable bed for a change . . .

Tuesday, 20 August
I took off from Debden at about 10.15 and flew to Tangmere. I navigated my way ok but being on the coast this wasn't very hard. Tangmere is in a shocking state. The buildings being in an awful shambles, several 1000lb bombs having fallen. We were put to 30 mins at 1, and did nothing for the rest of the day. The dispersal hut is most cozy and puts ours at Debden to shame.

Wednesday, 21 August
We did five flying patrols today . . . but the Flight commander only saw one E/A [enemy aircraft] and then only for a second when it was between some clouds. The other section in our flight shot down a Ju88 as did yellow section in "A" flight. After it got dark we were sent up on patrol but having got to 7000 ft over the aerodrome we were recalled.

Friday, 22 August
I did not fly at all today, in fact it was very quiet. We were released at 1 p.m. and went up [to London] on train. I went home.

Saturday, 24 August
There was an air raid warning in Blackheath and thought I should miss my train. However, we caught it and arrived back ok. In the afternoon we went up on a flight and saw dozens of E/A going out to sea, however did not fire although the CO and P/O Stevens got an He111. We had one very short patrol after this, but nothing was seen.

Sunday, 25 August
This was a hard day being at 15 mins and readiness the day long.

At about half past seven we had a hell of a scrap over Portland in which 100 a/c were engaged. F/L Bayne made an attack below and astern quarter. The ME110 whipped up in a slow turn and I gave him a long burst while he was in a stalled condition, it fell over and went down. I then went on my own and made an Me111 break formation. I gave it another burst and it went towards the sea. F/L Bayne shot down but ok. F/L Williams lost wing. Shot off.

Saturday, 31 August
We did four patrols today ending up with one in which we intercepted about 30 Do.17s and 20–30 Me. 109s. I got on an Me 109s tail, after an ineffectual attack on the bombers, and got in several long bursts at about 300 yards, however nothing was observed in the way of damage. Another got on my tail and I had to break away. I succeeded in throwing him off in a steep turn but not before he had put a explosive bullet through my wing. Sgt Stewart was shot down, but was safe. I lost another tail wheel today.

Tuesday, 3 September
We did two patrols, in the first intercepted about 100 E/A (Do.215 and Me 110). F/Lt Bayne and I got on an Me 110's tail and firing together sent it down in flames. We then attacked a Do 215, [?] Leary finishing the attack and the bomber crashed in a field just North of the River Crouch. I collected a bullet in the radiator and got covered with glycol, force landing at Castle Crump. Collected a Hurricane off 111 Sqd., flew back to Debden . . . We did one more patrol over the Thames. Then in the night I was aerodrome Control Pilot.

Saturday, 7 September
I did two types again today, the one in the morning was uneventful, the second at 5.30, on which we used V.H.F. for the first time, we saw four huge enemy formations but as we were only 6 we did not engage. We had one short scrap with Me 109's, but I only had one short burst – with no effect. These raids created a lot of damage in London. The provisional casualty list say 400 dead, 15000 seriously injured: what compete swine these Jerries are.

Sunday, 8 September
Did not fly today and got afternoon off. Went on 4 days leave. Air raids have messed up London quite a bit.

Sunday, 15 September

I flew once today but missed the Big Blitz owing to my a/c being unservicable. Nothing was claimed by anyone because there were so many Jerries, over 200 in all. I am at 15 mins readiness tonight, and will be second off, if we have to fly. The RAF claimed 117 e/a destroyed, boy oh boy what a total. We had the station dance band in the mess tonight, and it turned into quite a party. Czernin is now DFC.

Tuesday, 17 September

We did a couple of patrols today but neither came to anything. I feel very depressed tonight. I don't know why, just a passing mood. Alf Bayne's engine cut taking off, and he had a glorious pile up, completely wrecking the Hurricane but only getting an odd bruise himself.

Wednesday, 18 September

We did four patrols today of over an hour each. On the first we saw lots of Huns way above us we could not engage, and anyway they were fighters. Nothing happened on any of the other patrols although there appear to have been lots of e/a about. We tried most unsuccessfully to play a game of snooker in the evening but the lights kept going out: switched out by the Control room when a hun is about, how they flap here!!

Friday, 20 September

I went to the Sergeants' Mess this evening for a party and got to know a sweet little W.A.A.F. named Margaret Cameron and we had quite a kissing session after the party was over.

Tuesday, 24 September

I had just one (patrol) and one blitz only (8.30). We were attacked by ME 109s and having made our attack on an Me 109 I was making a second . . . when I realized I should let it all go. I levelled off. Suddenly there was a bloody flash on my port wing and I felt a hell of a blow on my left arm, and the blood running down. I went into a hell of a dive and came back to Debden. A cannon shell had hit my wing and a bit of it had hit me just above the elbow and behind. The shell had blown away most of my port flap. So I tried to land without flaps and I could not stop and crashed into a pile of stones just off the field, hitting my face and cutting it in two places. I was taken to Saffron Walden General Hospital, they operated but had to leave small pieces in . . .

Thursday, 26 September
Hospital.

Sunday, 29 September
Did nothing during the day but there was the usual band in the
mess and when they packed up I completed the party at the
Sergeants' Mess. Met Edith Heap and fell in love with her at
sight. I rather cut Margaret Cameron and I am not as popular as I
was!!!

Monday 7 October
Returned to Debden, had grand party, and met Edith Heap, my
God it seems to be the real thing this time. She is so sweet and
seems to like me as much as I like her.

PO Wissler was reported missing in November 1940.

Flying Officer Michael Scott, RAF Bomber Command

Diary: 26 January 1941. I have got my wings, and am expecting my
commission through at any time now. I had a filthy journey yesterday, with a temperature and incipient 'flu, which has luckily died
away today. I passed out 13th at Grantham, Arthur being 14th! He
and I tied for our Navigation Test, which was very satisfactory.

24 February. The Course has started at last. Two hours' cockpit
drill on the Blenheim. Everything is so inaccessible that it is very
hard to place one's hand on the right knob at the right time. I seem
to have lost none of my old skill on the Link, in spite of being so out
of practice.

25 February. More cockpit drill and Link. Also Snooker, which I
enjoyed for three minutes, and then loathed more and more for the
rest of the game.

27 February. Twenty-five! But I don't feel any older than I did
yesterday. Thank God we have finished lectures and start flying
tomorrow, though the thought of flying a Blenheim terrifies me.

3 March. Over four hours in the air. Solo after 2¼ hours, which is
satisfactory. Blenheims are very nice to fly, though I find the

landings very tricky, holding off too high, I think, and getting the stick back too far. I went over Newbury yesterday and bust up a game of football. The boys were much impressed—by nothing, I'm afraid.

15 March. More flying at last. 1½ hours instrument finishing up by trying to land wheels up! I felt as if I had never flown a Blenheim and was completely ham-handed. Dirty-Dog Houlston put up the Hydraulic Selector Lever, which foxed me completely, BF that I was. Blast!

Yesterday Fl/Lt Hill wrote himself off shooting up the 'drome. He hit a tree on the boundary, probably not seeing it until too late. A sad end to a DFC. I expect I shall do plenty of low flying myself, but not with a crew on board.

18 March. Over three hours in the air. A cloudy day with wisps of mist below 3,000′. I went up to 11,000′ to look at the sea over Cromer way and then descended in spirals over Blocking Lake. A grand life.

21 March. ¾ hour IF (Blind take-offs). Quite successful. I seem to have no trouble with the instruments now. 100 mins. solo, a deplorable effort. I tried a one engine circuit without success, and made a very shaky landing. Then I went up above the clouds and lost myself. What an aviator! I am hoping that one day I shall not frighten myself too much, especially for the sake of the crew.

I hope to get back to Bicester soon, possibly before the end of term at Cheam. I want very much to see the boys again before the end of term.

25 March. The long nose is a delight to fly—much easier than the short, and freer in the controls. It is steadier and easier to keep at a constant A/S.

30 March. A trip with a staff-pilot to bomb. Julian did very well; average error 77 yards, much the best of the day. We had a trip together in the afternoon, with no success, as the bombsight was WS. A snappy landing at 45′ to the landing T finished a satisfactory day. We shall go to the OT [Officer Training] flight soon.

8 April. A bit too much flying. A 4½ hour trip in the morning, Kettering—Doncaster—York—Lincoln—Royston—Kettering—Bicester—Upwood—Henswell—York—Henswell—Melton—

Mowbray—Bicester. Then no lunch and an hour's map-reading in the afternoon which resolved itself into a trip to Aylesbury, and then to Newbury, where I shot up WJM and family, who were waving in his garden. We returned via Henley, and I was too tired to land properly, and had to go round again twice. Poor Julian. Photos of Lincoln Cathedral and Shefford Junction.

20 April. Low bombing level 250'. Not a bad effort. Average error 65–55 yards. Red landings in a cross wind.

21 April. More low level bombing. Much better. 35–30–34–18 yards average error. The last was the pilot's best so far (11 yards!). Landings good.

26 April. Operations loom on the horizon, but I have hardly realized their imminence yet. I would cloud-cover to low level at present, so I am praying for cloudy weather.

1 May. Wattisham. 1 van-load take-off with +9 boost. They are very heavy to land with such a weight, and I had to go round again once.

17 May. Got up at 2.30 to do a night cross country. Unfortunately we fouled the landing T on the way out to take-off, and so our early rising came to nought. Formation in the afternoon. This was quite good for a first effort, though I got rather close once or twice! On the battle order for tomorrow.

18 May (Sunday). A very heavy day, all formation flying. I found this very hard work at first, but it came a bit easier toward the end. We went over to Watton to join up with 21 and 89. Apparently we are to do a show on Tuesday morning with fighter escort. May the gods be with us! Formation flying is the most companionable of pursuits. Twelve dots in the sky linked by a spirit of fellowship and each dependent upon the rest. What more could a man ask! Today is the first day of Summer.

Scott took off for his first operational flight on 24 January 1942. He was killed in action that night. His sister, Flora, added footnote to his diary in her handwriting: 'First Operation Flight. Missing over North Sea. Never heard of again'. Among Michael Scott's effects was found a last letter, to be opened only in the event of his death.

Torquay, 21 June 1940

Dear Daddy,

As this letter will only be read after my death it may seem a somewhat macabre document, but I do not want you to look on it in that way. I have always had a feeling that our stay on earth, that thing which we call 'Life', is but a transitory stage in our development and that the dreaded monosyllable 'Death' ought not to indicate anything to be feared. I have had my fling and must now pass onto the next stage, the consummation of all earthly experience. So don't worry about me: I shall be alright.

I would like to pay tribute to the courage which you and mother have shown, and will continue to show in these trying times. It is easy to meet an enemy face to face . . . but the unseen enemies Hardship, Anxiety and Despair are a very different problem. You have held the family together as few could have done, and I take my hat off to you.

Now a bit about myself. You know I hated the idea of war, and that hate will remain with me for ever. What has kept me going is the spiritual force to be derived from music, its reflection in my own feelings, and the power it has to uplift a soul above earthly things. Mark has the same experience as I have, though his medium of encouragement is poetry. Now I am off to the source of music and can fulfill the vague longing of my soul in becoming part of the fountain whence all good comes. I have no belief in an omnipresent God, but I *do* believe most strongly in a spiritual force which was the source of our being, and which will be our ultimate good. If there is anything worth fighting for, it is the right to follow on our own paths to this good, and to prevent our children from having their souls sterilized by Nazi doctrines. The most terrible aspect of Nazism is its system of education, of driving in instead of leading out, and putting the state above all things spiritual. And so I have been fighting.

A few last words about the disposal of my scant possessions. I would like Mark to have my wireless and records in the belief that he will get out of them as much as I have done. I have nothing else of instrinsic value except my golf clubs, which you can distribute as you think fit. If I have any balance at the bank, which is extremely unlikely, could you arrange that Flora use it as she thinks fit, as she has been an ideal pair in our relation to each other.

All I can do now is to voice my faith that this war will end in victory and that you will have many years before you in which to resume a normal civil life. Good luck to you!

Frank Curry, Royal Canadian Navy

Curry was an Asdic operator on HMCS *Kamsack*, a corvette escorting convoys across the Atlantic.

Monday–January 19 [1942]
This morning spent doing a final check on the Asdic. We sailed at 1600, picking up oil from the Teakwood on the way out. Headed for the open Atlantic at dusk. Rounded up convoy of 78 ships and we took up our screening position on the port beam . . . here we go again.

Tuesday–January 20
Weather not too bad as we plunge ahead. Sea quite heavy and kicking us around a fair bit. We are operating Asdic 2 on and 4 off. No sign of an echo so far. Tough time holding onto the convoy in the pitch dark. Thinking a lot of home so far away.

Wednesday–January 21
We are steaming north-east with our large convoy. Heavy seas running, operating and watches down to a routine. So far not a sign of any trouble. Feeling pretty good—so far. Eating everything in sight—an enormous appetite. So it goes—where are we headed???

Thursday–January 22
Operating 2 on and 4 off. Visibility closed down to one half mile. Picked up a sub echo at 0530 and we gave it two solid patterns . . . resumed position at 0700.

Friday–January 23
Headed more easterly now—our convoy is steaming right along and for a change things are going very smoothly. Not a sign of trouble so far. Sighted two American destroyers and a patrol bomber off the port wing of the convoy . . . something to break the monotony.

Saturday–January 24
Seas are running much rougher and huge swells are rolling us 40 and 50 degrees at a roll. We are warned to be on the lookout for Hudson bomber down in the Atlantic in our vicinity. What a hope in all this water. No sign of subs since that echo of several days ago.

Sunday–January 25

Greek ship on the far side of our convoy was torpedoed at 0500 this morning, nothing doing on our wing. HMCS Rimouski picked up some survivors. Sure feel tense when I am operating Asdic, knowing that subs are close by. Split my knee going to action stations when I skidded on the icy decks. Depth charges going off all round the convoy. We haven't had a contact yet.

Monday–January 26

Looks as if we might be getting off lightly this time as we have not lost any more ships. Things quietened down considerably—perhaps it is the huge seas that are running. We are bouncing around like a top. My knee is driving me crazy with throbbing. Still heading east, ever east.

Tuesday–January 27

Well, we are still rolling—and I do mean rolling—due east. How vast this old Atlantic appears to be to an awed landlubber like myself when I gaze out in all directions day after day and see nothing but turbulent waters as far as I can see—never dreamt a few short years ago that this is what my future would bring.

Wednesday–January 28

Boy—are there ever huge seas running. I never expected to see them this big—ever. We are still keeping the port beam of our convoy covered and heading ever east. We run out of spuds today. Rice from now on. Double lookouts on watch for long-range German Junker aircraft which are spotting allied convoys.

Thursday–January 29

Huge seas still running. We ran out of bread today and it will be a diet of hardtack from here on in. British escort arrived at dusk as we are now off the north-west coast of Ireland. We five corvettes gladly turned over our convoy to them and we—the Kamsack, Rimouski, Trail, Trillium and Napanee headed on alone at full speed.

Friday–January 30

Great seas still pounding us. We are close to the coast of Ireland as I write this. What a wonderful feeling after two solid weeks at sea. German air activity in the Irish sea reported, and we got a red warning in our vicinity. Everyone highly enthused about getting near land. What a life.

Saturday–January 31

Today is a great day—a wonderful day. At dawn, even before darkness lifted, we could smell that wonderful smell of land, earth, long before we could see it. In the early dawn we slipped quietly into Loch Foyle. Immediately went alongside a British tanker where we filled our near-empty oil tanks brimming. Ireland looks beautiful. Guess any solid earth looks beautiful at a moment like this. We sailed twenty miles up Loch Foyle and at dusk tied up in Londonderry. Everyone busy buying fresh cream, live chickens for packages of cigarettes. I headed ashore for the first time in Ireland—went along with Yearsley, and we wandered around in the blackout and rain, finally finding a chip shop where we had a feed of chips. Returned early—drew two pound casual.

Tuesday–February 3

Morning spent lugging on board sacks and baskets of those huge Irish loaves of bread. We left Londonderry at 1300 and headed down Loch Foyle. Went alongside tanker at Moville. Rumor has it that we shall be boarded tonight.

Wednesday–February 4

Up anchor at 0400 (no boarding during the night) and sailed with St. Laurent and four other corvettes. Out of Loch Foyle and so off to sea facing us as a rather unpleasant prospect. Feeling pretty grim as we plunge our way out into the Atlantic. Headed north-west, where to, know not we. Heavy seas running, and already our little ship is a mess . . .

Thursday–February 5

A weird feeling to see it pitch dark at 0900 and a full moon shining down on us . . . we are heading to the north with our large westbound convoy, in the hope of eluding subs; operating steadily, with the seas having levelled off just a little, much to the relief of everyone on board.

Friday–February 6

Thick fog has settled down around us—rather a queer feeling to be escorting a convoy that is invisible—a huge convoy of 73 ships. Suddenly at 1500 we cleared the fog and it was an amazing sight to gaze on our convoy in the brilliant sunshine. Lots of time off watch spent behind the funnel, the gathering place for the Funnel Gang—off watchers.

Saturday–February 7
Sea smooth as silk—there has been trouble close by. We sighted several large pieces of wreckage and then we came upon two machine-gun-riddled life boats, two dead seamen in one—nothing we could do about it—a terrible sight and I feel it very deeply. Action stations in the noon hour and the Rimouski, our old winger, is going at it hot and heavy on the other side of the convoy with a sub contact. No contacts for us, but I feel pretty tense every minute I am operating on the old Asdic set.

Sunday–February 8
Beautiful sunrise as I operated on the 0400–0600 watch. Something to remember, just to sit high on the bridge and gaze out on such a magnificent scene, with a brilliant sun coming up in the east and our great convoy steaming quietly on its way, with little corvettes spotted out on all wings. Still smooth as anyone could wish for—everyone amazed and happy about it. We picked up a good sub echo on the Asdic at 1925 and threw four patterns of depth charges at it—crew pretty tense, not to mention one FC.

Monday–February 9
A bit rough today, but really nothing to moan about. We are ploughing right ahead with our large convoy and making good progress. We have certainly swung far to the north with this one, and are now well up between Iceland and Greenland . . . must be method in this madness . . .

Tuesday–February 10
Seas have flattened out again, and we are steaming right along, with nothing out of the ordinary for the last couple of days. Just a constant alertness for something to happen . . .

Wednesday–February 11
Still (I repeat still) smooth as smooth. Grand warm sun came out and poured down on us all this long day. If you were trying to convince anyone back home that winter in the north Atlantic was not exactly a picnic, you would have a tough time today. Seems more like a summer cruise in the Caribbean. But we are not complaining a bit . . .

Thursday–February 12
Does not take it long to change. This morning it is rather rough and much, much colder. Guess we have moved out of the Gulf

Stream and are now getting closer to the dear shores of New-foundland. Feeling in an awful mood, and thought I would go raving mad on the 2400–0400 watch. Staggered through it some-how.

Sergeant B.J. Kazazkow, United States Army

SOUTH WEST PACIFIC
March 21, 1942

Dear Mom:

We just enjoyed a very mild hurricane—the only damage done being the countryside made ideal for the growth of hordes of mosquitoes. I hate them so that when I manage to get one alive. I torture and maim him—then bury him alive. The war has made me hard and cruel!

Now for the local news—the sun beats down—as usual—and when it gets hot enough—a nice cool shower comes along. Between the incessant combination everything I own, either rusts, or turns green-moldy. Constant cleaning of equipment is, therefore, in order.

Sept. 22, 1942

Dear Mom:

Today a big vicious sea bass, mouth agape, sped like a bullet upon his prey, a small mallett. As he sped into range, I held my breath, squeezed, and then let fly. Stunned, he turned to go—and crash! I let him have another charge—and lo and behold we had fish steak—baked, garnished, and savory, for dinner. I tell you, this place is a fisherman's paradise. So what? It isn't the first fish dinner we blasted out of the sea, but never before a sea bass, the size and taste of that one.

Some days ago I spent a solid day up in the nearby hills, trying to chase a deer or two—being anxious for a taste of venison again. All day, mind you, and got not a scent. Yesterday morning, with breakfast on the fire, two of the elusive creatures popped up in a nearby pasture—grazing to their hearts content—so-o we sneaked up on them, and fell upon them, blazing away, and got not a hit—they led us a merry chase, finally we lost them, and went back to our French toast, cereal and coffee. No venison. Deah, Deah!

Sounds more like a rich man's holiday than a war—no? Feeling top-hole, hope you are too.

Love and kisses,
Benny

Jan. 8, 1943

Dear Mom:

So its come—1943, imagine being overseas for nearly a whole year—or at least it will be on January 23rd. On that day last winter we left New York—for parts unknown. We could have ended up in a much worse place, believe me. And time has flown, more rapidly than I ever thought possible, it seems like several weeks, instead of twelve months, since we landed.

And we landed looking for trouble, and we're still looking—and I don't think we'll ever find any here.

The past few nights I haven't been sleeping well, and I keep having dreams about you and home, and it's no good for my morale. I get very homesick, poor boy that I am.

. . . I suppose I'll visit you again, in my dreams tonight, and you might leave some milk and cake on the table for me.

Goodnight . . .

Your loving son,
Benny

Private First Class Wolfgang Knoblich, 7th Company, 2nd Battalion, 513th Infantry Regiment, Wehrmacht

Dedicated to My Dear Parents 25/3/42
"Conquer the heritage of your fathers
So that you may have the right to possess it."

I chose to prefix this epigraph to my diary because I realize that life at the front compels one to assess at their true value those good things in life which we failed to appreciate while they came to us easily.

31 March 1942
The front must be about forty miles away. The latest news from there contains little to comfort us . . . At such moments it dawns upon us what insignificant pawns we are in the big chess game that is now in progress. One order and we go thither, another order and we go thence. Yes sir! 'Ten-shun! About-turn; quick march! You cannot escape the eternal doom of fate . . .

1 April
Both in Kharkov and here in our quarters we, to our great surprise, have found books on mathematics, physics, English and ancient

history which attest to high mental culture. These are real cultural values. Evidently they did pay attention to public education.

2 April
The village where we are stationed is called Neopkrytoye. Comrades tell me that only about two weeks ago the Russians broke through as far as this place. At that time we had to blow up the guns sited in the forward section of our defence line. Many ran as fast as their legs would carry them, thinking only of saving their skins.

3 April
To-day it's a year since I joined the army. Just as I did a year ago, so to-day I feel greatly distressed, as if a stone were pressing on my heart. This feeling of embarrassment and maladjustment always weighs me down when I find myself in a new situation. Good for him who can adjust himself to a new environment with ease and without friction. So far my only enjoyment has been to recollect the past.

4 April
A host of new impressions, not always pleasant. They are still alluring because of their novelty and therefore interesting, but hardly for long. There is a baneful melancholy about the landscape and the service too will no doubt become in time intolerably dull.

5 April
. . . All Germany hopes and believes that this spring this horrible blood-letting war will at last take a decisive turn. We pray for victory and peace.

16 April
The sergeant who takes me through every possible course of instruction and wants to teach me gunnery possesses more conceit than knowledge.

22 April
The soldiers who have been in France and in the Balkans are anxious to get home, are impatiently waiting to be relieved. But their faith in our strength and their belief in victory are unlimited. This belief has its root in the consciousness of their superiority over the Russians.

12 May

To-day I can honestly state that I have experienced the horrors of the front. Nepokrytoye is the last fortified point on the line of defence before Kharkov. If it falls the road to Kharkov, which leads through open spaces, will be clear. It was still night when we were informed by our outpost at V. that Russian tanks were approaching. At daybreak eight of them actually loomed in sight. By that time I had a senior sergeant were already at our post in V. From early morning our batteries kept pouring a massed shell-fire into the array of enemy tanks. Results were not wanting. One tank was soon kaput. It remained immobile at its initial position. But the Russians were not slow to act. The height where post V. was stationed soon witnessed such a downpour of shells that we did not know where to betake ourselves. Besides, Russian bombers and fighters launched an attack to add to the frightfulness of the scene, but the worst was still to come.

The intense artillery bombardment had damaged both our lines and so we were cut off from all communications. Our actions could not be co-ordinated. The German artillery was silenced.

Then the Russian tanks launched an attack. Our infantry retreated. We made another frantic attempt to restore communications while our infantry was already stampeding to the rear. Then our turn came. We made a rather unseemly dash for safety, taking along only our field telephones and carbines. Bullets whizzed close by our ears. Now our gunners could sight the tanks and opened fire. It took the enemy some time to ascertain where our gun emplacements were. But now that he had spotted them their heavies shelled our guns almost without a miss and the air was filled with flying fragments of deadly iron and steel . . .

I helped to bring up ammunition, just to have something to do. After many hours of this sustained rifle and artillery effort our ammunition gave out. We had fired more than 800 rounds and were now compelled to take cover in our blockhouses. The Russians also ceased firing. Finally a truck drove up with new supplies of shells and the firing recommenced with new vigour on both sides.

The Russian marksmanship is devilishly accurate. Our first and third guns were knocked into a heap of scrap by two direct hits. But the crews were not touched. All the commissioned and non-commissioned officers assembled around the second gun, the only one that still kept up the fight. I felt ill at ease when I saw this assemblage of people and decided to change position. It was fortunate I did so, for immediately afterwards two shells crashed in among them. Eight were killed outright while six severely wounded lay on the ploughed-up ground. We bandaged their wounds as best we could and hastened our departure. Our troops were beginning to retreat. I helped to carry the wounded and therefore had to jettison even the little I had prepared to take with me. All my belongings can now find room in the bag I used to use for biscuits and things. But I did manage to salvage my shelter tent, carbine and cartridges out of the general wreckage.

As we left the village we were rallied and thrown into the fight as infantry. But the Russian artillery was up to our game and its shells rained thick and fast right in our midst. And this was capped by an air attack that also exacted a heavy toll.

Time passed by; it was already 4 p.m and not a single German plane in the air and not a single German tank acting in support of our land troops! We had been compelled, with heavy heart, to abandon all our artillery. In such distressing circumstances I think we did right to retreat fighting.

At last we have come to a hollow. It was a relief to find some shelter from the unceasing whistle of bullets. Behind a copse we have called a halt to get our breath. Thank the Lord, twilight was coming on or the Russians would have shot us like rabbits while crossing the wide plain that lies before Kharkov. There are exactly twelve men left in our battery.

21 May

I have been made a private first class. I can hardly believe it . . . I am exceedingly glad that I am rid now of those humdrum duties in the battery that simply stupefy your mind. I am sure that back there I would never have obtained my chevron.

27 May

We have again been transferred to a so-called reserve command. This command includes lads who are still quite young and require drilling. So we act as N.C.O.'s We do nothing all day except watch our "charges" clean the horses. Naturally, such a job is not to our taste.

5 June

Life is not a bed of roses here. All kinds of malicious and unjust complaints are made against us. The corporals and sergeants are particularly mean. The last few days have shown that we are fully able to cope with our duties.

17 June

Events come one after another with incredible rapidity. At 11
p.m. while I happened to be on duty, I was called to the
telephone. The conversation started with the fateful words:
"Well, Knoblich, to-morrow we go to the front." I was put
down as signaller. I shall have the doubtful pleasure of laying
cables. I'm called out in the middle of the night, and all because
I am unfortunate enough to be a "greenhorn" and can be
assigned to any nasty job. I am sick and tired of being kicked
about like a stepchild. After an hour's sleep we are to march for
several miles. I must admit the start was not very auspicious.
The same day we again changed position. I am fed up with this
by now. On the 12th we forced the Donets.

   Again and again we had to flop down in the muck. The
trench mortar and artillery fire was so intense that it gave one
the creeps. In the evening we returned to the battery. At dawn
we advanced eastwards. The fierce trench mortaring was too
much for our infantry. It was compelled to retreat to the height
where our post was located. Now Russian tanks appeared on the
battle scene. We abandoned our apparatus and hopped it. We
could not get away too soon or too fast from those iron-clad
monsters.

   . . . Here I am sitting in a filthy hole, all tired and broken up. I
have no change of socks, nor soap and towel for a wash. Only the
howling of mortars – that is now our constant companion. what a
dog's life we lead!

20 June

Very eventful days have come and gone. Life here hangs by a
thread. The war may be terrible and we may be cursing it, but
it has its good side, too. It constantly enriches the experience
of each one of us. We get new impressions or life and see its
seamy side, but much that is of value and will never be
repeated would be lost to us if we did not have to re-live it
day after day.

21 June

I dig too much into my soul and in general do much too much
thinking. I often catch myself trying to apprehend things that are
not subject to reason. Rationalist! Perhaps it is Russia that weighs
so heavily on my soul. I crave mental pabulum like a starving dog a
bone. How I long to engage in some scientific work! All I have at
hand to tide me over such moods is some *Münchener Lesebogen*, my

constant silent companions. They exhilarate and comfort me. In their pages I discover myself and at times find answers to my abstruse questions. They are my true friends day in day out, especially in hours of solitary introspection.

Both men and officers are in a sullen mood. They all feel disconsolate and genuine enthusiasm is actually non-existent. They are all consumed with one ardent desire: to get out of this holocaust, to be relieved, to go home, at least on furlough. The offensive spirit has long since gone from our ranks.

24 June

A night of horrors! The last few hours that we had to spend in this shabby little village unexpectedly proved frightful in the extreme. At 1 a.m. we were awakened by explosions of unusual violence. We jumped out of our beds and stretched out on the floor. This was the first news we had that Stalin's heavy guns had arrived here. In an instant we were out of the house and sheltered, after a fashion, in the nearest basement. It was raining hard. The muddy puddles made it difficult to pass. The village was soon on fire. Sinister flames lit up the houses, streets and soldiers.

6 July

Last week brought no good news. Our present mode of existence does not meet with my approval. We are back once more to barrack life. We had hardly returned from the front when they started to drill us again. That's the Prussian system for you!

9 July

To-day was enough to drive you crazy. They goose-stepped us worse than rookies in an absolutely unbearable heat. But influential circles maintain that in this merciless drill lies the secret of our victories.

. . . Perhaps I shall be promoted this time. I've earned it long ago. Although I frequently know more than any of those N.C.O.'s, they trust me, a private first class with a substantial and comprehensive education, less than they do them. Such are the difficulties that have to be overcome.

19 july

Our immediate superiors embitter our lives with their petty tyranny in the exercise of their self-imposed authority. For instance, we are forbidden to unbutton our collars on the march.

What martinets they are! They always overshoot the mark. There is no end to the reviews we have to pass and the duties we are assigned. The old Prussian drill sergeant regime in its pristine purity! And here it is even more strenuous than in the barracks.

25 July

I have cognized this whole mechanism and come to hate it. If I could only manage to escape from these dullards!

30 July

Sometimes I yield altogether to despair. For there is not a single person here to whom I can unbosom myself or who would really understand me. The people with whom I come in contact here are all so empty-headed, superficial and dull-witted. I have no choice but must needs remain alone with my thoughts. This is very difficult but I have become accustomed to it and shall get along somehow. I try to gain spiritual strength and comfort by solitary prayer. . . . I often picture to myself my return home. Great God, if that dream should ever come true! When that day arrives we shall return entirely different people, with entirely different conceptions of life, with a new appreciation of its blessings.

It sometimes seems to me that in many respects I am becoming a materialist. How often I catch myself engrossed in thought, not about philosophy, but some dainty morsel and other creature comforts. That of course does not mean that I am no longer the idealist I used to be. True, on witnessing some unjust, arbitrary act, I am often ready to fling my ideals to the winds, but then I would lose my sole support in the quiet hours of my solitude. It is in ideals alone that I found that perfection of which there is such dearth in a world full of envy and strife, injustice and tyranny, the innocent victims of which we so often are.

6 August

The Russians are attacking furiously. We return their fire measure for measure, not ceasing day or night. During short intervals we dig in. I am weary unto death. If this torture would only end soon.

12 August

My strength has been overtaxed and it literally takes my last ounce of energy to grind out these few lines. This terrible war cannot end too soon for me. I am nauseated with it all and wish I could get clear of the whole outfit, including those nice boys a bit higher up, those ordinary sergeants and sergeant-majors who do their utmost to make life sweeter for us. They fairly weigh us down with special jobs (foraging and the like) that really are a nuisance. They are enough to drive one to despair. I suffer acutely from all this. The life we are compelled to lead is without a ray of sunshine.

We are within a few miles of the Don and are told that we shall winter here.

31 August
. . . All our talk concerns two subjects: leave and women, yes women, even here in Russia. You often hear such talk from comrades as: "I consider myself married only in Germany . . ." One can readily imagine how these fellows spend their leisure time.

13 September
At last I can record the glad tidings that I was transferred back from my signaller's job in the trenches to my regular service at post V. Light of heart, I left on the tenth to enjoy this change from night to day. Shade and silence – what a treat!

26 September
We have again been relieved by Italians. Those wonderful, dream-like days at Post V. are a thing of the past. The order to prepare for immediate departure came to us like a bolt out of the blue. . . .

To-day we are stationed at a small town about 10 miles from Kaprin and about the same distance from Rossosh. No one knows what is to become of us, and we least of all. We can give free rein to our fancy.

I'm afraid we may be disillusioned in our new assignment! Everybody says that winter will find us fighting, though nobody is sure of it. On the other hand, everyone in the innermost recesses of his heart cherishes the dream of returning to Germany or at least to the occupied regions. Anywhere to get away from Russia.

Private Milton Adams, Company B,
240th Quarter Master's Battalion

Adams writes to Warren Hastie, the Unites States Government's advisor on "Colored Affairs".

> Pvt. Milton Adams
> Post Stockade
> Camp Livingston, La.
> May 13, 1942

Dear Mr. W. H. Hastie:

I am private Milton Adams of Co. B. 240th Q. M. Bn of Camp Livingston, La. I inlisted in the army Oct 17, 1942, in Chicago, Ill. And since I been in the Army, I never had any Trouble in the Army in or out of it in my life, until I came to Camp Livingston. I am asking for the help of the N.A.A.C.P. And the Crisis. I am not writing anything against the United States Army. But I am going to tell you what the White officers are doing to us races Soldiers down her in camp Livingston, La. Since they can't very well hang us, they take the next steps, which is court marital, and that is better know as rail-roading. Now you don't stand a chance, before them. They are just like a lynch mob with a neggro to hang. Well they do not want you down hear in the Army, and I did not ask to come down hear I was sent down hear. Well my trouble starter when they found out that I was from Chicago, and I have had a bad deal every since I been hear, I have tried to get away from hear, But it was the same old story. When we finde some places for you to go, we will let you go. Well my Commanding Officer did not like me because, I ask him not to use the word niggers, and he saide I was one of those smart nigger from up north. I was tried once for a offince, and given 30 days and a $12.00 fine. Now after I had finish my sentences, they saide they are going to try me over again. I wish you would look into my case. I thought they could not try any person a second time for the same offince. I really taken all the punishment I can take I could not get a three day pass or a furlo since I been in the army, until my mother pass away in April. They have just about rob me out of very pay day, for things I have never had. There are so many more case like this, a unfair chance. I don't know what to do now. I don't want do the wrong thing, so I am asking for help. But I am not going to take any more of these unfair trials, because I did three months in the stockade once for something I did not have any thing to do with. It was because I was from Chicago, and thats way every trial I ever had is base on the fact that I come from Chicago. So I whish you look into this case, because I can prove everything I am telling you. I will look forward to a answer from you in few days.

> Respectfully yours,
> Pvt. Milton Adams
> Post Stockade
> Camp Livingston, La.

Troop Sergeant Clive Branson, Royal Armoured Corps RAC

Before serving with the RAC in World War II, Branson had fought in the Spanish Civil War with the International Brigade.

> *Gulunche*
> *Nr Poona [India]*
> *20 June 1942*

You have little idea how badly we need the news of the second front—it is the difference between a body of good, stolid-humoured Britishers and an inspired army of warriors. This morning we went out on a scheme on foot in units representing tanks. We covered ten or twelve miles or more over ploughed fields. It was magnificent exercise and although I felt pretty tired I enjoyed it no end. That sort of thing will make real soldiers of us.

But tonight I had a terrible set-back. On parade this morning we were asked who had seen active service. I said I had. When we came back from the scheme I was told that I was to go on an inspection by the Duke of Gloucester in a few days' time. This parade is purely bullshit. It will take several days to polish boots, brasses, etc. It will take days and nights for some eight Indian tailors to alter, clean, press, etc. clothes for the white sahibs to wear like bloody waxworks. The Indians, of course, will not be on parade, the lucky fools. I have often been asked, "Have we got a fifth column here?" Yes, we have! For nothing could help the enemy more by undermining morale, destroying enthusiasm and making us incompetent fighters than this kind of tomfoolery. The farce develops. This morning we had an inspection. The Duke's show is in five days' time. On *the* day we get up at 5 a.m. Our clothes will be packed in boxes and taken by lorry to the scene of battle, where we will get into them. Sebastopol is falling and our CO is disappointed at the lack of polish on the topee chin straps.

Well, the Duke's show is over, at immense expenditure of precious petrol, wear and tear of vehicles, deadening bullshit. The Duke merely shook hands with unit commanders and squadron leaders—the men just didn't exist. Today a General paid us a visit. In one squadron they had many men change into PT kit, some ready to box, some to do PT, some to form two basket-ball teams, etc. They were kept sitting about doing nothing for ages until a scout saw the General's car. The scout signalled, and immediately everyone began boxing and playing basket-ball. As soon as the General disappeared the men were marched back to their tents. This is how things are going on here.

As a result of the rain the country has a lovely rich earth and green look about it; what enormous wealth could be produced if real irrigation was organized! I am feeling very tired and depressed, mainly because everything here is like a mad-house though apparently quite sane to the superior inmates.

16 January 1944
[Arakan Front, Burma]

From now on my letters will consist of scraps of paper written at odd moments during the coming campaign. We are only a few miles from the front line, and yet see very little sign of war—an occasional distant barrage, a few aeroplanes and, yesterday, AA puffs chasing a Jap machine. As to my own feelings, very rarely I feel a tinge of fear, plus regret. In the main I worry whether I shall command my tank as a Communist ought. I only hope I shall do the job efficiently. I am keeping very fit; in spite of being many years older than most of the fellows, I can still do everything they do, except run—there I am beat.

My gunner, Monte, has just got back from a trip to the forward area. What most impressed him is that while the British and Japs shell, mortar and bomb each other, cattle continue to graze on the battlefield, and peasants with children work on the road and farmsteads. He came across five graves of British soldiers, with the only mark a beer bottle—no cross, etc. The fellows, on hearing this, said it was a fine sign of good spirits, and just as good as any other tombstone.

26 January 1944 [Burma]

We are now only a few hundred yards away from glory. "There are those who would like to philosophize on the question of sacrificing space to gain time." You will remember the reference. But even so, it is still like a mad hatter's picnic. We make our beds down, we sit around and chat, we sunbathe (not so openly as before) and we sleep. While overhead scream mortars, etc. To this, and all other incidents of war, such as AA, Jap planes, or our own barrage, the lads react with "Ignore it" or "Quiet!", and just carry on sleeping or reading. But I must say one thought runs through my head continually—Spain. This morning a party is going to watch some strategic bombing. I am sending two others of my crew on the principle that the more each man knows of the landscape, the better in every way. The bombers are just coming over. We climbed up on our tanks to have a grand-stand view of twelve Liberators and dozens of Vengeance dive-bombers exterminating the Jap positions at Razabil cross-roads. Now that the bombers have gone there is a real barrage of small stuff. This may be the solution of the Burma problem. Now I am ever so excited to hear the reports of what was the effect. It may seem strange to you that in a sort of way I cannot help gloating over the affair. It is the reverse of Spain a hundredfold.

Branson was killed a month later during the fighting for the Ngankedank Pass.

Corporal John Green, Military Police

Green volunteered at the outbreak of World War II and served throughout its duration. Below is his diary of the battle of El Alamein, where he supervised track laying for British armour.

Diary: 23 Oct 1942. 1600 hrs take position, my position West of Quatara Track, which means I am in front of our own artillery. 1730 hrs L/C Newton reports to me track all ready & lit nothing to do now only wait.

App. 2140 hrs British Barrage goes over, it is like hell let loose, shells are screaming over my head by the thousand. I don't think anybody ever experienced any thing like this before. It is terrific. The push is on.

0000 hrs Tanks are using my track now hundreds of them nose to tail they are going in, it is going to be a terrific battle. I am choked with dust and deafened by the noise of the guns.

0200 Hrs 24th Oct. MT & tanks ease up on tracks to allow the stuff to get clear that went in front. Our bombers roaring overhead in one continuous stream & bombing Jerry's position. They are never going to stop. Barrage eased off about 0200 hrs. 0300 hrs. Traffic starts again Tanks, MT & Infantry going in 0400 hrs. Barrage bursts out again plastering Jerry with Shells. This continues until 0600 hrs All night our planes have been blasting Jerry's lines. 0730 I am relieved for breakfast & what a relief. Everybody is full of high spirits. The main topic is the barrage. Every one was impressed by the intensity of it, I should think the people most impressed are the Germans.

24 Oct., Go back to duty at 0930 hrs. We are right in the thick of it. German aircraft active today. 1730 back on the tracks, we are bombed. None of my gang hurt. A very similar night to last night, relieved at 0700 No sleep again tonight, duty again.

25.10.42 Resume duty at 0930 hrs, plenty of activity over the whole front dozens of dogfights. Our planes continue to bomb enemy without stopping day & night. We also get bombed quite frequently. At 15.30 I am relieved to go back to Alamein Station. I take on duties of visiting NCO to visit every post on all Tracks. This visiting job is sticky being in a truck, I cannot hear enemy aircraft. They are on you before you know. I go to bed at 7.30 pm for the first time since the night of the 22nd. I am tired to death. We are bombed at intervals during the night, but I am too tired I just snuggle in my hole and hope for the best. *26.10.42.* I continue visiting duty visiting each post on each track twice a day, these are very exciting days. On each journey I have to take cover and leave the truck at least a dozen times. We are bombed & straffed through the night. Bombs drop right across our laager, we are lucky again no one is injured. Reports say the battle is going in our favour.

27th. Same duty—visiting Tracks.

28th We move back a mile, it being too hot

29th All these days are nearly alike busy all day & getting as much sleep as Jerry allows at night. I am used to it by now. We hear Jerry is retreating—slowly but surely although the din he makes doesn't seem much like it, but things are going in our favour.

30th Oct. Bombed again during last night at frequent intervals. Detailed for a special job I take 6 L/Cpls with me. I have to go forward as far as the second German minefield and light the gaps for our armours to (go) through at night. This takes me right into the forward zone about 4 miles west of Quatara Rd. The Germans were here only a few hours ago. All my past experiences were nothing compared to this. We are right amongst it.

31st Oct. We had Bacon, beans & Stukas for Breakfast. 21 of them dive bombing. Lucky we have each got a good dug out. We are shelled for 2 hours. Our artillery are behind us & are replying. We are shelled again in the afternoon. Jerry seems to have taken a personal dislike to us.

We spend most of the day in our holes. At night our dug outs are one continuous boom, owing to the guns. After a while you get used to it & find you can sleep without difficulty. We light up the gap tonight. The N.Z's go through the gap "Good Luck to Them".

1st Nov. Plenty of air raids 1st night also Jerry dropped his shells around us. It is a hot spot here. L/cpl.S looks like cracking up. He takes hold of himself fairly well. All day is the same as yesterday. Lighting the gap again tonight.

Nov 2nd. 2 German planes are shot down quite near us. We see 7 shot down altogether. S. is definitely "Bomb Happy"—he has been much worse today I have taken him off duty tonight & do his duty myself—the gap lighting is pretty sticky when within range of enemy guns.

Nov 3rd
More air raids last night. We have had them every night since the push started we are shelled again at intervals Jerry is definitely being pushed back. More prisoners pass us today. Shelling is worse this afternoon. 3 pm DR brings message. I have to hand over to S. African Police at 4 pm. We are all pleased to leave this joint. We pack our kit and make ready to move—Jerry is shelling again (as we) pull out. My dug out has got hit. Lucky I got out.

We go back to Alamein & dig in once again.

Nov 4th. More bombing last night flares by the thousand. I am informed that the whole company is moving forward. We move west of Quartara Rd on the coast Rd at 9 am. At 11.30 I am detailed along with my section to lengthen Diamond Track, running it 2 miles nearer Jerry's lines, Jerry is shelling the track all the time. At 5.00 pm Hopkinson is killed & Power & Varley badly injured, both Varley's feet are blown off. At 5.15 Varley dies. Power has about 11 wounds. We get our job finished about 6 pm, from 12.00 to 7 pm we were shelled, straffed & Stuka-ed continuously. It has been a trying day. Young Hopkinson has only been out here three weeks & Varley has a baby he hasn't seen. It shook me a bit today to see my own blokes get wiped out.

Nov 5th. We had air raids again last night but I didn't hear them. I had a deep hole & I slept well. I am back with Coy at the new location. I am not put on duty today so I spend the day digging myself a good dugout.

It is bonfire night & all the boys are firing flares & shooting tracers into the air. It was quite a display but Jerry put a stop to it at 8 pm. He came over & dropped flares of his own, he wasn't long before he dropped something else. He hit 2 ammo trucks near us.

Nov 6th. There are signs that Jerry is flapping back, but is fighting strong rearguard action. One or two daylight raids. I got 2 bottles of beer today. At 6 pm we hear Darba has fallen.

Nov 7th. We move up to Darba at 9 am We see lots of German & Italian dead on the way & learn they are putting mines under their own dead. Our chaps refuse to bury them, they are afraid of being blown up in the process.

Coy make location at Darba. Dozens of knocked out Jerry tanks & MT & planes here.

The Darba airfield is littered with German planes. Fuka has fallen today.

Nov 8th. I am sent to Fuka, 25 miles west of Darba, this morning, with a detachment to take charge of water point. This job is a little quieter than the ones I have had lately. Jerry is flapping & only fighting rear guard action. Our troops are advancing & doing fine. The RE are busy all day & work through the night to get water.

Nov 9th. Start pumping water at 6.30 am. I learn that this is the only water point for miles. 14 Italian soldiers come in from across the desert & give themselves up.

Later nine Germans come & surrender. I keep filling batches of prisoners all day. They are all short of water & look hungry. They say they have been drinking water from pools left by the recent rains.

Nov 10th. O.C. visits me today & says we have to take it easy, the whole Company have been pulled out to rest. The Coy is 25 miles behind us.

Nov 11th. I go for a look round to-day & find dozens of enemy tanks knocked out on the desert. The bodies are still in some of them. There are about 30 German planes all knocked out on Fuka landing ground.

Prisoners still coming in. Enemy aircraft visit us during the night, & few shells from very long range guns.

Nov 12th.
Our rest doesn't last long, we are on a half hours notice to move. Jerry is going back faster now & we are to follow up. We move off at 11.30 hoping to make Mersa Matruh & if Jerry keeps running we shall be in Tobruk in a day or two.

Flight Lieutenant Laurence Stockwell, RAF

Stockwell served as a pilot with Bomber Command. The letter below is written to his wife, Gwenyth.

November 1942

My Darling,

When I was walking back from Heyford station yesterday, I realised how little I appreciated the beauty of the countryside, how little I seemed to take interest, and on realising that, I stopped on the road and looked about me, and for the first time noticed how lovely everything is about here.

Having found that out, I tried to fathom the question of why I hadn't noticed it before, why I wasn't taking my usual interest in the countryside, for although I'm not of poetic nature or anything like it, I feel that I've always taken quite a lot of interest in my surroundings. I loved the Isle of Wight and all places of natural beauty, especially St. Martha's which holds such wonderful memories for me.

And I came to these conclusions.

Firstly, this beastly war. War has no rightful place on this earth, besides destroying men and property, everything that is seen, it destroys those unseen things, ourselves, our sense of beauty, happiness, comradeship amongst all men, everything that is worth living for. Property is not essential, but happiness, a love of beauty, friendship between all peoples and individuals is life itself.

Secondly, you. I've put you second. I wonder if you feel that strange. But this affects everybody. I'd be very selfish if I put you first in this thought I'm trying to fathom out for myself. You are just everything to me. The unforgivable way I write would make another feel that you have been guilty of my loss in taking no notice in the surrounding beauty, but you understand, I'm sure, that it is only because I'm not constantly with you, that is the real factor. You, Darling, have made me able to see, to feel and to understand all the beauty that is in the world and life itself. Without you that understanding does not disappear, for you are with me constantly in my thoughts, but that understanding of life does seem to fade.

This war is keeping us apart, and therefore it is to blame in my loss, and that loss is not only mine but of every person in the world connected with this war.

I have never spoken to you of my feelings and thoughts about this war, and I hope will never speak of them again. Do you remember a small boy saying he would be a conscientious objector if war came? Things happened to change that small boy's views, talk of brutality, human suffering, atrocities, but these did not have any great effect on changing my views for I realise that we are all capable of doing these deeds of which we read so much nowadays.

It is the fact that a few people wish to take freedom from the peoples of the earth that changed my views. News of atrocities only breeds hate, and hate is contemptable in my eyes. I will never be capable I hope of hating anyone whatever they have done.

Why should I then fight in this war which only brings disgust into my thoughts?

It is so that I might live in happiness and peace all my days with you. You notice I put myself first, again it is a strange thing, but I am trying hard to be honest with myself and I find that I, and consequently everybody, am terribly selfish, it is human nature.

I am also fighting so that one day happiness will again rule the world, and with happiness that love of beauty, of life, contentment, fellowship among all men may return.

You may again have noticed that I have not mentioned fighting for one's country, for the Empire, that to me is just foolishness, for greatness in one nation will always breed hate and longing in another, and the whole of life will again be disrupted.

Mainly, however, I'm fighting for freedom of all men, and in that I am fighting just as much for the German as for the English people.

With freedom and the destruction of hate this world will enter into a period which I hope will be much in advance of anything it has ever known.

When peace returns, and may it be soon, the world must make sure that the men and women of the future are educated in the right way, a love of beauty not a love of war, and it is our own job to teach our children about all the lovliness of this world, to make them happy so that they can understand that love and happiness are the things really worth having.

Well Darling, I seem to have been rambling on for some time, really I must stop. I don't know whether I have made any sense out of my ramblings, I only hope so.

Todays news is very small. I saw "They flew alone" tonight, and I think I enjoyed it, I'm not quite sure.

"The Stars look down" although not a pleasant sort of book has held my interest and I'm reading solidly through it.

All my love Darling, you mean so very much to me,
Always,

Laurie

Laurence Stockwell was killed on a mission on the night of 17 January 1943.

Thomas Smithson, British Army

Smithson was captured by the Japanese and imprisoned as a POW in Taiwan. On a postcard issued by the Imperial Japanese Army, he writes to his wife.

MY DEAREST EILEEN
RECEIVED CARDS AND LETTER'S. HAPPY TO KNOW YOU WELL AND EVERYONE AT HOME. DEAREST I MISS YOU MORE EACH DAY. NEVER AGAIN SHALL WE SEPARATE. ALL I ASK OF THIS WORLD IS MY OWN LITTLE COTTAGE AND REMAINDER OF MY LIFE IN YOUR SWEET COMPANIONSHIP. GOD BLESS YOU, DEAR.
LOVE, EVER, YOURS TOM

Anon German Soldiers, Wehrmacht

The writers of the letters below were soldiers of the German Sixth Army, surrounded by the Russians at Stalingrad. The letters are from the last post from Stalingrad before the German surrender on 31 January 1943; they never reached the destinations, however, being impounded – on Hitler's order – along with several hundred others and analyzed as to what they betrayed about the state of Army morale. According to the subsequent Wehrmacht report, 2.1% of the letters approved of the conduct of the war, 3.4% were vengefully opposed to the war, 57.1% were sceptical and negative, and 4.4% were doubtful. Some 33.0% were indifferent.

... Once again I have held your picture in my hand. As I gaze at it my mind was filled with the memory of what we shared together on that glorious summer evening in the last year of peace, as we approached our house through the valley of flowers. The first time we found each other it was only the voice of our hearts that spoke; later came the voice of love and happiness. We talked of ourselves and the future that stretched out before us like a gaily coloured carpet.

That carpet is no more. The summer evening is no more; nor is the valley of flowers. And we are no longer together. Instead of the gaily coloured carpet there is an endless field of whiteness; there is no longer any summer, only winter, and there is no longer any future – not for me, at all events, and thus not for you either. All this time I have had a strange sensation which I could not explain, but today I know that it was fear for you. Over those many thousands of miles I was conscious that you felt the same about me. When you get this letter, listen very hard as you read it; perhaps you will hear my voice. We are told that we are fighting this battle for Germany, but only very few of us here believe that our senseless sacrifice can be of any avail to the homeland.

... So now you know that I am not coming back. Break it gently to Mother and Father. It has given me a terrible shock and the worst possible doubts about everything. Once I was strong and believed; now I am small and unbelieving. Much of what is going on here I shall never know about; but even the little bit I am in on is too much to stomach. Nobody can tell me that my comrades' died with words like "Germany" or "Heil Hitler!" on their lips. It cannot be denied that men are dying; but the last word a man speaks goes out to his mother or the person he loves most, or else it is merely a cry for help. I have already seen hundreds fall and die, and many, like myself, were in the Hitler Youth. But all those who could still do so shouted for help or called out the name of someone who could not really do anything for them.

The Führer has solemnly promised to get us out of here. This has been read out to us, and we all firmly believed it. I still believe it today, because I simply must believe in something. If it isn't true, what is there left for me to believe in? I would have no more use for the spring and the summer or any of the things that make life happy. Let me go on believing, dear Grete; all my life – or eight years of it, at least – I have believed in the Führer and taken him at his word. It's terrible the way people out here are doubting, and so humiliating to hear things one cannot contradict because the facts support them.

If what we were promised is not true, then Germany will be lost, for no other promises can kept after that. Oh, these doubts, these terrible doubts. If only they were already dispelled!

. . . I have now written you twenty-six letters from this accursed city, and you have sent me seventeen replies. Now I shall write just once again, and then no more. There, I have said it at last. I have long wondered how to word this fateful sentence in such a way as to tell you everything without its hurting too much.

I am bidding you farewell because the die has been cast since this morning. I shall entirely disregard the military side of things in this letter; that is purely a concern of the Russians. The only question now is how long we shall hold out: it may be a few days or a few hours. You and I have our life together to look back upon. We have respected and loved one another and waited two years. In a way it's a good thing this interval has elapsed, for though it has intensified our desire to be together again it has also greatly helped to estrange us. The passage of time is also bound to heal the wounds caused by my not returning.

In January you will be twenty-eight, which is still very young for such a pretty woman. I am glad I have been able to pay you this compliment so often. You will miss me a lot, but that is no reason why you should shut yourself off from other human beings. Allow a few months to pass, but no more than that. Gertrud and Claus need a father. Remember that you have to live for the children, and don't make too much song and dance about their father. Children forget quickly, particularly at that age. Take a good look at the man of your choice and pay special heed to his eyes and handshake, just as you did in our own case, and you will not be disappointed. Most of all, bring the children up to be upright men and women who can hold their heads high and look everyone straight in the face. I am writing these lines with a heavy heart – not that you would believe me if I said I found it easy – but don't worry, I am not afraid of what is to come. Always tell yourself – and the children, too, when they are older – that their father was never a coward and that they must never be cowards either.

. . . I was going to write you a long letter, but my thoughts keep disintegrating like those houses under gunfire. I have still ten hours left before this letter must be handed in. Ten hours are a long time when you are waiting; but they are short when you are in love. I am not at all nervous. In fact it has taken the East to make a really healthy man of me. I have long since stopped catching colds and chills; that's the one good thing the war has done. It has bestowed one other thing on me, though – the realization that I love you.

It's strange that one does not start to value things until one is about to lose them. There is a bridge from my heart to yours, spanning all the vastness of distance. Across that bridge I have been used to writing to you about our daily round and the world we live in out here. I wanted to tell you the truth when I came home, and then we would never have spoken of war again. Now you will learn the truth, the last truth, earlier than I intended. And now I can write no more.

There will always be bridges as long as there are shores; all we need is the courage to tread them. One of them now leads to you, the other into eternity – which for me is ultimately the same thing.

Tomorrow morning I shall set foot on the last bridge. That's a literary way of describing death, but you know I always liked to write things differently because of the pleasure words and their sounds gave me. Lend me your hand, so that the way is not too hard.

. . . What a calamity it is that the war had to come! All those beautiful villages laid waste and none of the fields tilled. And the most dreadful thing of all is how many people have died. Now they all lie buried in an enemy land. What a calamity, indeed! Be glad, all the same, that the war is being fought in a distant country and not in our beloved German homeland. That's a place it must never reach, or else the misery will be even worse. You must be really grateful for that and go down on your knees to thank your God. "On the banks of the Volga we stand on guard . . ." For all of you and for our homeland. If we were not here, the Russians would break through and wreck everything. They are very destructive and there are millions of them. They don't seem to care about the cold, but we feel it terribly.

I am lying in a hole in the snow and can only creep away to a cellar for a few hours at nightfall. You have no idea how much good that does me. We are at hand, so you have no need to be afraid. But our numbers get less and less, and if it goes on like this there will soon be no more of us. Germany has plenty of soldiers, though, and they are all fighting for the homeland. All of us want peace to come soon. The main thing is that we win. All keep your fingers crossed!

. . . I am finding this letter hard enough to write, but that is nothing like as hard as you are going to take it! The news it bears is not good news, I am afraid. Nor has it been improved by the ten days I waited. Our situation is now so bad that there is talk of our soon being entirely cut off from the outer world. A short while back we were assured that this post would go off quite safely, and if only I knew there would still be another opportunity to write I should wait a little longer. But that is just what I don't know, and for better or worse I must get this off my chest.

The war is over for me. I am in a field hospital in Gumrak waiting to be evacuated by air. Much as I long to get away, the deadline keeps being put off. My home-coming will be a great joy to us both, but the state in which I come will give you no cause for joy. It makes me quite desperate to think of lying before you as a cripple. But you must know sooner or later that both my legs have been shot off. I am going to be quite honest with you. My right leg is completely smashed and amputated below the knee; the left one has been taken off at the thigh. The medical officer thinks that with artificial limbs I should be able to run around like any normal person. The M.O. is a good man and means well. I hope he turns out to be right. Now you know it in advance. Dear Elise, if only I knew what you are thinking. I think of nothing else and have all day long to do it. And you are very much in my thoughts. Time and again I have wished I was dead, but that is a grave sin and does not bear mentioning.

. . . If there is a God, you told me in your last letter, He will bring me back to you safe and soon. And, you went on, God will always give His protection to a man like myself – a man who loves flowers and animals, has never done wrong to anybody, and is devoted to his wife and child.

I thank you for those words: I always carry the letter next to my heart. But, my dearest, if one weighs your words, and if you make God's existence dependent on them, you are faced with a terribly grave decision. I am a religious man, and you were always a believer. Now all that will have to change if we both draw the logical conclusions from our attitudes to date, for something has intervened which destroys everything we believed in. I am looking for the right words in which to say it. Or have you already guessed what I mean? There seemed to me to be such an odd tone about your last letter of 8th December. It's now the middle of January.

For a long time to come, perhaps for ever, this is to be my last letter. A comrade who has to go to the airfield is taking it along with him, as the last machine to leave the pocket is taking off tomorrow morning. The situation has become quite untenable. The Russians are only two miles from the last spot from which aircraft can operate, and when that's gone not even a mouse will get out, to say nothing of me. Admittedly several hundred thousand others won't escape either, but it's precious little consolation to share one's own destruction with other men . . .

Sergeant Carl Goldman,
United States Army Air Force (USAAF)

An aerial gunner on a B-17 Flying Fortress attached to the Eighth Air Force in England, Goldman wrote the following letter to his family. It was marked "To be opened in case of casualty only".

Feb. 16, 1943

Dear Mom, Pop, Frances, Edith,. Marion, Leon and Aaron:

Am going on a raid this afternoon or early in the morning. There is a possibility I won't return.

In any event, please do not worry too much about me as everyone has to leave this earth one way or another and this is the way I have selected.

I was not forced to go to gunnery school and even after I arrived overseas I could have gotten off combat had I chosen to do so.

If after this terrible war is over, the world emerges a saner place to live; if all nationalities are treated equal; pogroms and persecutions halted, then, I'm glad I gave my efforts with thousands of others for such a cause.

Wish I had time to write more, but sometimes the less said the better, so goodbye—and good luck—always.

Carl

Sergeant Goldman was lost in action over Western Europe.

Arnold Rahe, USAAF

England, September 1943

Dear Mother and Dad,

Strange thing about this letter; if I am alive a month from now you will not receive it, for its coming to you will mean that after my twenty-sixth birthday God has decided I've been on earth long enough and He wants me to come up and take the examination for permanent service with Him. It's hard to write a letter like this; there are a million and one things I want to say; there are so many I ought to say if this is the last letter that I can ever write to you. I'm telling you that I love you two so very much; not one better than the other but absolutely equally. Some things a man can never thank his parents enough for; they come to be taken for granted through the years; care when you are a child, and countless favors as he grows up. I am recalling now all your prayers, your watch-fulness—all the sacrifices that were made for me when sacrifice was a real thing and not just a word to be used in speeches. I know how you had to do without things to put me through school. You thought I didn't realize these things, but I did.

For any and all grief I caused you in this twenty-six years, I'm most heartily sorry. I know that I can never make up for those little hurts and real wounds, but maybe if God permits me to be with Him above, I can help out there. It's a funny thing about this mission, but I don't think I'll come back alive. Call it an Irish-man's hunch or a pre-sentiment or whatever you will. I believe it is Our Lord and His Blessed Mother giving me a tip to be prepared. In the event I am killed you can have the consolation of knowing that it was in the "line of duty" to my country. I am saddened because I shall not be with you in your life's later years, but until we meet I want you to know that I die as I tried to live, the way you taught me. Life has turned out different from the way we planned it, and at twenty-six I die with many things to live for, but the loss of the few remaining years unlived together is as nothing compared to the eternity to which we go, and it will be well worth while if I give my life to help cure a sickened world, and if you and I can help to spare other mothers and fathers and younger generations from the griefs of war.

As I prepare for this last mission, I am a bit homesick. I have been at other times when I thought of you, when I lost a friend, when I wondered when and how this war would end. But, the whole world is homesick! I have never written like this before, even though I have been through the "valley of the shadows" many times, but this night, Mother and Dad, you are very close to me and I long so to talk to you. I think of you and of home. America has asked much of our generation, but I am glad to give her all I have because she has given me so much.

Goodnight, dear Mother and Dad. God love you.

Your loving son,
(Bud) Arnold Rahe

Rahe was subsequently killed in action over France.

Tech Sergeant Harry Schloss,
17th Bomb Group, 34th Bomb Squadron, USAAF

Schloss was a waist gunner on a B-26 Marauder. The extract from his diary below covers the period from his enlistment to his twentieth mission. He survived the war.

Reported to Fort Jay, New York on Aug. 4, '43. It was a dreary, cold day and the 12 hour physical, which I passed, didn't help my spirits any. Got 14 days to clean up my business then report to draft board.

AUG. 18
Reported to Grand Central Station. Left for Camp Upton. Damp and cold. Only there 1½ days. Left for unknown destination. Rumors.

AUG. 23
Arrived in Miami Beach, was assigned to 574 Tech School Sq. Co. 841. Slept at Wm. Penn Hotel. Next day started basic training. PFC in charge. Holy terror, good actor. Passed I.Q. with 131. Very high. Given choice of schools. Took gunnery. Made two good friends, Manny Salters and Bernie Rosenthal. Left for unknown dest.

SEPT. 19

Arrived at Ft. Myers, Fla. Flexible Gunnery School. Met the swellest bunch of guys. Learned to fire and take apart and assemble 30 and 50 calibre machine guns. Shot skeet. Then flew in T-6. Not bad in air to air firing. Graduated as sergeant on Oct. 25. Memories. Tore up Morgan Hotel. Wally and his dice. Zeikus digging ditches. Left for unknown destination.

OCT. 30

Arrived Will Rogers Field, Oklahoma City. Attached to 38th Air Base Squadron. Awaited arrival of the 46th Bomb. Sq. Did nothing but eat and sleep. Finally given permission to send for Bea. The 46 arrived Nov. 21. Put into 53rd Bomb Sq. C.O. Major Huntington. Jerk.

NOV. 30

Transferred to 21 Observation Squad. Learned radio code. Took 7 to 8 words my first week.

JAN. 14

Transferred to hell hole called Shepard Field. Cold, dreary, gloomy. Men marching at all hours of the day and night. Told stripes don't count. Course is on air mechanics. Lasted for four dismal months, on B-26's and B-25. Passed as engineer. Average 86.

MAY 21

Transferred to Paradise. Barksdale Field. 2 days in A.C.R.C. Assigned to 335th Bomb Gp 475th Bomb. Squad. R.T.O. training until June 27. Got 11 day furlough. Bea gave birth to a son, Michael Robert, on Sept. 20. Put on crew with Lt. Gates, Zimmerly, Radin & Wingard. Later Schultz. Chas. McGonagle came in as radio man. He was in pretty bad breakup. OK now. Transferred to 477th to complete training.

NOV. 28

Left Barksdale for Hunter Field. Crew split up. Four to fly over. Wingar and I to go over by boat. Put in guardhouse for not saluting a major.

DEC. 5

Left Hunter for P of E. Arrived Camp Patrick Henry at Lee Hall, VA. Arr. Dec. 6. Got my first glimpse of Italian and German prisoners of war. Also different colors and styles of other allied uniforms. Dave still with me.

DEC. 16
Left camp Pat Henry for unknown destination. Sailed on "Empress of Scotland" formerly the "Empress of Japan".

DECEMBER 25
Christmas Day. Arrived safely in Casablanca, Africa. The trip across was dull. Thanks to the infantry officers in charge. Their main aim in life was to see how tough they could make it for the air corps men.

However, one noticed that after each meal (we got two a day, incidentally) it was the infantry men who beat a hasty retreat to the various latrines. We were hidden away in a cozy little trip on "D" deck. 2nd deck from the bottom of the ship. There was plenty of water. All the pipes leaked. Christmas Day lunch. Spam, bread and coffee. On debarking at Casablanca we were taken to Camp Marshall Lysantey about 16 miles north of the town. In town the natives were the dirtiest, poorest I've ever seen. They kept coming over to our truck and begging for bonbons or cigarettes. A sight I won't soon forget. At our arrival in Marshall Lysantey, we were put in one building. 78 of us with no beds and inadequate blankets. We slept on stone floors, all huddled up for warmth. I had always believed that Africa was a hot place. That's only two hours a day, during the winter months. The nights were cold. We also got our first taste of rationing. The people back home would kick if they were allowed one chocolate bar, 1 pack of gum and 8 packs of cigarettes a week. On our first day here, we were told we were not considered part of the Air Corps. We were infantry as long as we were at this camp. Hikes, drills, etc. Oh, unhappy day. However, we were saved from all this by the arrival of our crews at Cazes Air Field about 2 miles outside of Casa. I was never so glad to see anyone in my life. Did nothing for 10 days waiting for 50 hour inspection to be finished. Then was told our emergency air brake bottle was out. Another wait. Won $600 in black jack while waiting. Flew for first time in over a month on Jan. 5. Tested ships and guns. Expect to leave on Jan. 6 for Algiers. Took off for Algiers on Jan. 7. On arrival saw Col. Elliott Roosevelt. Looks like father. Algiers is nice city. Built on steps or hills. Beautiful boulevard in center of town. Spend one cold night here.

JAN. 8

Arrived in Sardinia. Attached to 17 Bomb Gp 34 Bomb Sq. A very famous outfit. Yano is only 12½ miles from here. Met a host of old friends. Flew on transition hops.

JAN. 13

First mission. Ship No. 13. Target. Air Drome. Got a piece of glass in my hand from turret. Flak came through, landed in Bill Schaffenaker's hand. Funny to be flying first mission with Bill. Old friend. Came on target too suddenly to be scared, was gone before I realized it. Heard flak. Big and black.

JAN. 19

Second mission. Milk run. Bombed hell out of an airport. Flew in lead ship. No excitement. Lost $200 of $600 I came here with. Went to visit Yano. Good to see him. Still the same great guy. Took me around and hugged me. The big lug was very depressed until I came along. Dave came here from the 319 on a visit. Bought coffee and sugar. I cooked 3 chickens. Unanimous in their praise of it.

JAN. 25

Third mission. The 1st objective was 40 minutes past Rome. Heavy overcast, could not get through, so flew to 2nd target. Too cloudy. Dry Run. Heavy flak but inaccurate. 7 slight holes in plane. First mission with crew intact. Brought back bombs. 1000 lbs. Flew to Naples for fuel. Right engine eats too much. Saw the famous Mt. Vesuvius. Naples bombed to shambles. I don't think there is 20 houses standing. Had a delicious sandwich of salmon and onions. First I've had in almost two years. Got my first letter from Bea in 11 weeks. Very happy. Got glimpse of invasion fleet, at least 100 ships were there. It looks great from the air.

JAN. 29

Fourth mission. Target–bridge. No flak, no fighters, it's a pleasure. Shot hell out of target. Germans laid smoke screen, but it did not reach target. Cooked 3 chickens last night. Boiled and made soup. Delicious. Dave came over for visit. Brought coffee, sugar and milk. He has 6 missions. Not bad, for the short time he's here. Still a good Joe. Got 8 letters. Hicky brought them back from Telergma. Don't know how it got there. Gates down there now as instructor. Owes me $100. He'll be back next month. Michael weighs 14 lbs. according to Bea. Boy, he's growing up. I miss Bea

& the kid terribly. Up to now, have refused to talk about women. Hard to believe I'm still a virgin in the army, but if you could see the faces and dirt on the women here, you'd never doubt it. Average of 10 v.d. cases a month. I'm thinking of Bea.

FEB. 5
Flew 5th mission. After 8 days of no flying, due to bad weather. I've been on spare for 9 days. Made the mission when 3 ships turned back. Supposed to be a tough target. Target. Marshalling yards. Blew it all to hell. 93 per cent accuracy. Lt. Fitzgerald could not use bomb sight as it was frozen. Toed the bombs out. Amount of accuracy is very amazing. Big write-up in "Stars & Gripes". Coldest day of my life. 23 below zero. Trouble with fuel transfer. Fuse blew. Reset button froze. Finally worked after 15 very anxious minutes. Only 30 gals. in each tank & 1½ hours of flying time. The ocean looked mighty cold. Saw Deanna Durbin in "His Butler's Sister". Best picture since I've been in Africa. She's terrific.

FEB. 7
Flew on 6th mission. Couldn't get to bomb target as the clouds were very heavy. Target—road junction where German replacements were. Ships the night before caught hell here. We made a 360 turn on coast of Italy near Anzio & came out. Dry run. Milk run. Sent Bea $400. Deposited $85 in soldiers deposit. Every night Wes Long, Mike Dearsdorff & sometimes Tip O'Neill & myself sing the old songs, cook eggs and have a bull session. It's the best part of the day for me. The weather cold & rainy. The rain sounds like someone is throwing rocks at our tent. Hicky and I bought a bottle of brandy for $8. Tonight I get drunk.

FEB. 15
Flew on 7th mission. Over land for half an hour. Target—Bridge at Marsciano. Missed it but hit railroad to it. Used 1000 lb. bomb. 20° below zero. No flak, no fighters. Next day get grounded for 4 days due to cold.

FEB. 20
Boy, today I hit the jackpot. Anzio Beachhead. Flak all over the sky. It was black. 9 holes in ship. Not bad. Dropped frags. Covered bridge area. On arrival back in camp Dave was waiting for me. Went to his camp for overnight stay. Also had chance to visit Yan.

Both going to different outfits. Next day did guard duty. Cold, but really cold.

FEB. 28
6 days trying to make number 9. Bad weather. Gates came back from Telergma today.

FEB. 29
Made number 9 today. Slight flak but very inaccurate. One ship cracked up on takeoff. 7 fellows burned to death. I almost cried. Then over the target at Viterbo two planes shot down, 11 chutes opened. Two of the boys flew right by my window. I prayed for them. On way out we fell out of formation to escort a ship in trouble. Escorted it to Corsica, where two spits took over. Hear he belly-landed. Hope & pray I never see another mission like this.

MARCH 2
Made first mission as crew since return of Gates, without Chuck, No. 10. Target—Anzio Beachhead. First two formations caught most of the flak, however, there was enough for us. Dropped frags. Good job.

MARCH 3
Flew on mission No. 11 over Rome marshalling yards. Every formation but ours dropped their bombs. 500 lbs. Gates damn good, so is Chuck. Saw some beautiful sights. Ruins of Colosseum, palaces, etc. Boy, those babies go in for beauty.

No. 12 on March 7 My 28th birthday. Target—Rome marshalling yards. Boy, they kicked hell out of it. 500 lb. bombs. Rome still more beautiful than on first mission.

Two days later went with Chuck and Long to Orestano to get bricks for house that Chuck, Magida, Gates & McGuire were building, on return found out McGuire shot down. Good Joe. Lots of boys heart-broken for whole crew.

MARCH 10
Went on mission no. 13. Bridge at Orvieto. Flew over land for 50 minutes, but did not drop bombs. Target all covered. Flak was light but accurate. One large whoom. Looked around for crew. All O.K. Very close. On way back R.P.M. gauge broke. Thought engine failure. Just gauge out.

MARCH 13
Flew on Mission 14. Target past Leghorn broke 4:45 time. Can low on fuel. Came home without formation. Not a milk run, lot of flak, but thank God it was inaccurate. I'd hate to go back there next month. Hit target. Bridge. 1000 lbs. Saw coast of France.

MARCH 14
Made mission 15. Target—Rome marshalling yards. 100 per cent concentration of bombs. Good job. Made 5.05 time. Cook's tour of Italy.

MARCH 15
Made Mission 16. Flying almost every day is tough. Target— Cassino Right on front line. We were only one of 16 Bomb Groups to hit the town. When we got over it, there was nothing left of Cassino. Only a hole in the ground. Loads & loads of trucks going to the front. It was a sight I'll never forget. The town was only dust. Captain Tate asked me to write up my impressions of the raid for the squadron book. I did so. Capt. Tate said I did swell. Tonight is my first broadcast on the group radio program. Made the broadcast. Quite successful except that I read the news too fast, but with a little experience might do right well.

MARCH 16
Flew spare. Saw two ships collide and explode. Chet Angell, V.E. Miller & Wise. My buddies all dead. Flew back to field. Sick. 13 good men dead. Can't stand it much more. Guess I'm a sissy.

MARCH 17
Went on Mission 17. Dropped 1000 lb. bombs on Orvatello marshalling yards. 34th did good job. On return we were given speech by Lt. General Baker. He can't get over our record. He says in England they say that if a B-26 does half as good as a 17 it's O.K. Here it's the reverse. He watched the Cassino run, says it amazed him. On mission today, piece of flak cracked window over Gates' head. If it had come through we'd all be in bad shape. Especially Gates. On primary target, couldn't make it. Overcast.

MARCH 21
Made mission 18 today. No flak, no fighters. We came in over Italy at 14,000 ft. Both my legs froze. They were paralyzed. I'll never forget the horrible thoughts that ran through my mind. We kicked the hell out of a viaduct at Avetta. Time 5:15. My combat hours are

piling up. O'Neill left for rest camp tonight. Boy, he needed it. Had to short Charlie. He has epileptic. We all miss him.

MARCH 23
Up all night with Wes. In the morning he was taken to Cagliari hospital. Malaria. Fine country for it. Got a beautiful write-up in "Stars & Gripes" by Stowall. About my announcing. Made 3rd broadcast last night.

MARCH 24
Made mission 19. Orvieto north bridge. Forgot baby booties for 1st & last time. Heavy flak, plenty of fighters. One of our escorting 47's shot down. Watched him all the way. Got 15 small holes in both engines. Flak still in them. One outfit hit target. 500 lbs. at 11,400 ft.

MARCH 27
Went on 20th mission. Poggaboni bridge. Hit both ends but not bridge itself. Dropped 2000 lbs. No flak, no fighters. Not very cold for a change. Next day General Anderson, British General in charge of operations, spoke highly of our bombing. Made awards.

Sergeant Sam Solomon, United States Marine Corps

Sept. 21, 1943

Dear Mom:

Permission has been given us to write home and say where we have been and some of the things we have done, so here goes.

Our ship was off the coast of Guadalcanal at dawn on August 7, 1942 in time to see the first shellings and the first troops go ashore, though it wasn't until the next morning that we went ashore, on Gavutu and Tonambago. I had a dose of dysentery and grew a nice long beard. It is forbidden to say anything of the fighting there, though you can read all about it in the magazines and newspapers. Guadalcanal Diary also gives a fairly accurate account of what happened.

After being on Gavutu about a month and a half we went to Guadalcanal in the middle of September, just when things were pretty hot over there, and it was there that I first got any mail from you.

Was it hot on Guadal! In the twenty mile trip across from Gavutu to Guadalcanal, we had three air raids; the third one came just after I left the ship and got into a small landing boat. One Zero tried to strafe our small boat, but was driven off by a pom-pom gun on shore. From the water we could see two battles going on in the jungle, from which the sound of artillery and machine gun fire never stopped.

While I think of it, buy the book Guadalcanal Diary. I was at the places and saw all the things that are shown in the pictures in the book.

A month and a half later we left Guadalcanal, or should I say one hundred and twenty-three [censored] to say nothing of naval shellings, land battles, artillery, and, worst of all, mosquitoes. From there, until we left the islands in the beginning of February, we stayed on Tulagi. That is, I was based on Tulagi, but most of the time I was on outpost duty and patrols all over Florida Island.

This is all for tonight, but I'll write real soon and tell you more about the islands.

With love, Your son,
Sam

Sept. 3, 1943

. . . We are allowed to say quite a bit now about where we have been and what we have done, but since I just wrote my mother a long letter about it, I won't say very much about it now. Instead, in each letter I will just put in a little bit at a time, just an incident or two to show you how things went.

There was only one thing in which I felt a very great deal of fear in all the while in the islands. It's funny, but it wasn't the idea of getting wounded or killed that worried me. Instead, I dreaded the prospect of being caught as the Japs were, with no navy to back them up, no reinforcements and absolutely no chance at all.

The time of my big fright came a week or two after we landed on Gavutu. I had dug myself a nice comfortable fox hole which actually was rain proof, mosquito proof, had a candle or two, and even a box to keep chow and water in, in case of attack. It was placed in what I figured was a safe place for a fox hole on the island and was close to our radio dugout. That night, a Sunday night, while on radio watch I copied a coded urgent message from Tulaga. There were forty thousand Jap troops on transports on their way in. Right then our commanding officer figured it was time to send a radio operator to Tanambago. Me!!! That is when that funny feeling hit my knees and the pit of my stomach! I had to leave my nice fox hole and go over where I had none. If I had to fight, I at least wanted a good place to fight from. In case of attack my position was in an old Jap pillbox which stuck up right out in the open like a sore thumb, and would have been blown sky high by a three inch shell. By dawn though, I felt better, for during the night while on guard I heard the rumble and saw the flashes of a battle way out at sea. And the Jap task force never came in!

Another time an unidentified ship was reported in the harbor; later it was identified as a Free French destroyer. It remained a Free French destroyer until about noon-time when it suddenly fired a few salvos in our direction and at the same time automatically became a Jap destroyer. Once I looked over a mound behind which I was crouching just in time to see a salvo go off right in my direction. The shells went directly over my head and landed in a group of small landing boats about five hundred yards beyond me, but only one sailor was injured. Later the Japs claimed that they had sunk a whole fleet of P.T. boats. They also shot one wing off a Catalina Flying Boat which was stranded in low water, and later claimed that they had destroyed eight of them.

Well, I have work to do, so for now—so long.

Yours,
SAM

May 5, 1944

Dear Mom:

Save this picture for me. It shows a group of dead Japs in a hole on Tarawa. The reason I want it is that I lived right next to this hole for two days and helped to bury them by throwing dirt into the hole when the stench became too strong to bear.

Originally there were also a few dead marines in the hole too. We took out the dead marines and covered them with a blanket. Then we threw some more Japs into the hole and covered it over.

The log in the background is in front of a little tunnel which led to another hole. The tunnel too was full of dead marines and Japs.

Sergeant Sidney Glassman, United States Army

Dec. 16, 1943

Dear Folks:

. . . The Army has initiated discussion periods to enable the men to discuss the problems of the world and the peace. They want to bring out to the men, or rather have the men bring out for themselves just exactly "why we fight." It's a very good idea. If you get these men thinking and they have sacrificed the most, perhaps they can, by judicious use of the power of the polls, prevent another catastrophe like the present. It all boils down to an apathy on the part of the people. I really believe that only a few know and care "why they are fighting." Most of them have caught the catchwords like "freedom" and "democracy". However, they use them to apply elsewhere and sometimes fail to apply to their own immediate friends and comrades. Such blindness may be helped by these discussions, but the talks are resented a little because they are on the men's time off. Sometimes it is to be wondered whether one will be better off afterwards. I know that our leaders today know, but they will not be in power forever. You cannot blame the men because they just want to get the damn war over with and get home. The democracy part and freedom are just concomitant parts of the victory and on the side, so to speak. They are here because they had no choice and they want to get home as quickly as possible. I do, too, but I hope to get home to a better world. It will be a better world, I know. It can't help but be after what everyone has been through. The men have had to absorb each other's ideas and manners, etc. They have seen the way other nations live and work and none of them will want to go through this again.

I have to lead a discussion tomorrow night and it's not an easy task, nor is it one I particularly relish.

Love to all,
SID

Lieutenant Joseph Feldman, USAAF

Feldman enlisted as a private and was later commissioned as a communications officer.

[Asiatic Zone]
January 8, 1944

Dear Folks:

Well, here it is almost a year since I left the States. I'm beginning to get the real veteran's feeling. I'm afraid I'm going to have this with me for a while over here. Communications officers are rare as hen's teeth in these parts—so count on me being an Asiatic fixture for at least as long as I've been over here already. From this end of the spy-glass, Folks, it looks like a long war. Here it is only five months short of the rains that paralyze action over here—and the Japs still squat in Burma. Those that die—die the hard way. There is no denying the Japs have courage and love of country. Don't believe the stories that have them running away. They don't. The boys out in the jungle who know, say they fight.

Lots of fresh faces around the Squadron these days—makes me feel old.

You know, I've lost some more of my men—my master sergeant was one. These things depress you terribly. You get to know these boys like your own kin and then—suddenly they're gone. But they were brave and so must we all be.

Enclosed you will find a clipping of an advertisement I'd like you to buy all five books listed and send them to me. I hope they'll help me. Since my graduation from Communications School a year ago equipment has changed and grown more complex. I have to extend my knowledge every day.

As far as the allotment goes, use your own judgment as to where the best place is to put it. I merely suggested that it would be useful for me to have some ready cash when I get leave.

How is Grandma? Is she still as young as ever? Wonder what kind of dog she has as pet now? Give her my love. Also all the family. Tell them not to worry about me. I'm as interested as anyone in taking good care of myself and I do, never fear.

Did I tell you about my two-week leave? It was grand. I danced, ate like a king, slept till noon everyday and wore my good uniforms for the first time since I left China. It was really the first leave I've had since entering the Army and I enjoyed it thoroughly.

Had a couple of letters from——She is very sweet to write me as she does and I love her for it.

Regards to everyone (the taxi drivers, too). Joe

Feldman was killed over Burma on 18 January 1944. He was posthumously awarded the Purple Heart.

Corporal Samuel Furash, United States Army

Furash writes to his daughter in Washington, DC.

SOMEWHERE IN ENGLAND
February 3, 1944

My dearest Toby:

Probably by the time you receive this, you will have reached your first birthday; and by the time you will be able to read and understand it, we will be together as father and daughter, living through the days being missed now. Then again, there is always the possibility that never shall we know the relationship which is so deserving of us, but that possibility is quite remote. However, whatever the future holds in store for us, now is the time for us to get acquainted. As difficult as it may be, your mother's words to me through letters are descriptive enough to offer a realization of your habits, characteristics, personality, and other traits of you in different stages of your young life, the scene still remains incomplete, of course, because we are still strangers to each other. However, Toby darling, I'm speaking to you now, because the words I say are my sincere beliefs and always will be, and some day you, too, shall share these thoughts with your mother and me.

You were born into a world which was experiencing the second stage of the "dark ages," a world filled with turmoil, suffering and grief, and a civilization on the verge of destruction and total chaos. By this statement you might easily assume that the responsibility for all this lies upon the shoulders of all mankind; and you would be right! I do not mean by this, that man is evil; to the contrary, man is good, *but* he has been lax and smug and because of this has allowed his basic principle of life, freedom, to be snatched from his hands by the long, murderous talons of fascistic tyranny through the rule of a small group of individuals. At this moment, this group of men have not succeeded in their attempts in this nation and a few others, but even though the people of these nations are in an all-out war against fascists and the principles of fascism, these men are still in important positions in our own set-up of government. And that is where you come in Toby, dear. You see, though we are fighting a war now, which we will undoubtedly win, the victory alone will not bring about the complete and happy change in our way of life. No! The struggle will then only begin and you and your generation will be the spearhead and main body of our fighting forces. We have begun the drive; you will finish it! Our victory will destroy tyranny; yours will establish freedom, freedom in every sense of the word; and that job constitutes the renovation of our whole system of society. Your mother and I are the fighters of the present; *you* are the builders of the future.

You are lucky, Toby, because your life will be full of love. It can be no other way; you see, you were born out of love. Never has there been a more perfect relationship than your mother's and mine, for when we are together, we are united as one individual, laughing as one, crying as one, thinking as one. We are melody, harmony and rhythm, together with courage, forming the most stirring symphony of love. Your mother is the "zenith" of kind-ness and understanding, and as you originated within her, and will learn from her now, you will be the same. You are under the watchful and loving eyes of four grandparents who cherish you as their own child; and you have a father, who as yet has offered you nothing materially, only a little help in the assurance of your free future.

You shall benefit by your parents' tutelage, and soon will be aiding us in the education of your younger brothers and sisters, for there will be more, and we shall be more than a family for we have a foundation which is stronger than the very earth that holds us, the belief in truth, righteousness, and the right of all men to live and work happily in a society of social and economic equality, and to receive all the fruits of his labors. You shall live to see this, for you shall believe as strongly as we, and shall fight to achieve such a glorious goal.

The things I am trying to say are difficult, but you will under-stand later for you will read the works of the great poets and authors, listen to the music of great composers, and their words and melodies shall fill your heart and mind with the understanding and spirit to carry on in the battle for freedom.

Though my body be miles away, my heart is with you and I remain forever, your father, whose heart is filled with love for you and your mother. You are the nearest stars in my heaven and each night I sing out my love and best wishes.

Cpl. Samuel Furash

Lieutenant–Commander Morris D. Coppersmith, USNR

Coppersmith was the commanding officer of USS LCI (Landing Craft Infantry) 432. He writes to his parents.

[South Pacific]
February 5, 1944

Dear Folks:

. . . We carried a shipload of Australian troops farther north, and then returned to our anchorage. I had tears in my eyes when they came aboard. You should have seen them. Conservatively, eighty percent of them wouldn't even have met the lowly standards of a 4-F back in the States. They slowly trudged aboard with huge packs on their backs. Most of them were veterans of the last war. Now aged, they show their weariness. Here is one with a patch over one eye, showing its loss. So many of them are completely gray. Some must have reached their sixtieth birthday—yet they come forward to do their bit. What a match for these treacherous, youthful Japs—and yet they come forward, voluntarily, for a job they know must be done. Their rations? A bit of hard tasteless hard tack and a tin of bully beef. Day after day—hard tack and bully beef. God, how sickening! How can you help but admire them and worship them? How can you long for the comforts of home or wish to be there, when you know you belong here? They play hell with your clean, well-painted decks with their hobnailed shoes, and they litter up your compartments with ants and dirt, but you don't mind. When you have seen the jungle they fight in, the quagmires of mud and filth they sleep in, when you picture the fire they face from ambush, and the nerve-wracking noise of bursting bombs— well, you know you belong here, and you know, too, that your lot is infinitely better and that you certainly have no case of complaint. We don't pray for an early return to the States—we pray for an early victory, so that when we do finally return to the States, we will know that we have not left others behind to stand our ground for us. Let's hope that day will be soon.

[South Pacific]
March 26, 1944

Dear Folks:
. . . It's hard to speak for the sentiment of the servicemen regarding their desire to vote. On a ship this size, you have too few men over the age of twenty-one, and those you do have think mostly of only one thing. That is, to get this war over with and to return to their loved ones and to their normal routine of living. I'm definitely convinced that MacArthur would gather but few votes from the men over whom he has command. Despite your publicity to the contrary, MacArthur is not popular with his men. He maintains a degree of discipline over them that sometimes runs to extreme proportions. As an example, he wants no beer or liquor anywhere in the vicinity of his command. Consequently, you will find very few officers' clubs that will serve more than orangeade. Now, I don't have to go into detail to convince you of the meaning of a glass of beer to the serviceman. I have spoken to many boys in the Army who would do most anything to spoil his chances of being elected to office. I know that there will be many servicemen who will resent not being given an opportunity to vote. Given the opportunity, most of them probably will do nothing about casting their ballot—but at least they want to know the right is theirs. I

also am of the personal opinion that Roosevelt would benefit greatly if the serviceman casts a ballot. The man in uniform does not blame the present administration for present world conditions, nor does he believe that a change of administration would be of any help. He does hate the Lewises and all the others like him, who are retarding the war effort, but again they do not blame Roosevelt for that condition. You might be able to convince a non-thinking public back home that the duration of the war would be shortened if there is a change of administration. It is my personal opinion that the serviceman knows better. He knows that there's a big job to be done and he is willing to stick by it until it is done.

[South Pacific]
August 1, 1944

Dear Folks:

. . . Most outstanding since the time of my last letter is the assault landing we participated in at Noemfoor. That's a small island about seventy miles from the beaching we made at Biak about a month previously. While it was not regarded as a large operation, I believe it is the most interesting one that we participated in to date. It is about fifty miles from Mankwari, a powerful Japanese stronghold on the Dutch New Guinea mainland. Not all of the troops we had aboard for that operation were new to us. We had ferried some of the troops to Toem not so long ago. It was interesting having them with us again, because they were able to relate their experiences since we last saw them. Their spirits were not too high. Many of their officers and men lie buried at Toem. Don't think for a minute that it doesn't have a profound effect on them to realize that their buddies are lost and that it might have been them. We too were sorry to hear of some of their losses, because we had made their acquaintanceship previously. So too, they seemed discouraged because they knew so little about where they were going. Some of our scouting parties had been able to get fairly close to the island—close enough to know that it would be not be easy pickings and that the beach itself was a very difficult one. We didn't know until we actually hit the beach, what its condition would be. We did know that there was a lot of coral and niggerheads around and that there was shoal water about four hundred fifty yards from the beach. It was believed that our boys would have to wade or swim through four hundred fifty yards of water before they hit the beach. Lots can happen to you if there are shells flying from the beach in the time that it would take to traverse that distance by foot. Nor did we know what the depth of water was on the other side of the shoal. Perhaps it would become so deep that it would be impossible to touch bottom. You can understand their anxiety when you realize that they are weighted down with their packs and their rifles. Should there be a sudden step off, they are loaded heavily enough to go straight down. Further, our intelligence reports disclosed a greater number of the enemy ashore than we were sending there, so that they began to feel that they were being sent as expendable. Our intelligence reports also disclosed that there are many enemy airplanes in the vicinity, some of which were serviceable. We didn't know whether we could expect air opposition or not. We didn't count too strongly upon it, because the Japs were having more than their hands full at the time with Saipan, which by now is in our hands. The fact that we had so little information made the adventure more exciting, because we really knew very little about what to expect.

We did know that our LCI would be in the first wave of LCIs that would make the beaching. That was a new experience for us. On previous occasions, our ship had been in the second wave of LCIs. It makes quite a difference in more than one respect. When you are in the second wave, you are able to watch the action of the first wave so that it isn't too difficult to tell the nature of the beach and how far out to drop your stern anchor.

We rendezvoused with the rest of the convoy on schedule. There was no moon and the way was pitch dark. No one was lost from the convoy, however, and the trip to our destination went off without a hitch. The soldiers aboard were seasoned fighters and know how to behave aboard. They had their ammunition with them and it was both plentiful and heavy. Day had not yet begun to break, when we reached the transport area. We stood by waiting for the light of day so that the targets could be seen. It wasn't a long wait. The destroyers and cruisers deployed into their stations. Then began the most significant barrage we have seen yet. The date was July 2nd so we watched the show as if it were an Independence Day fireworks display. What a demonstration of fire power it proved to be. For over an hour, shells of all sizes pounded into the beach and raised billows of smoke and fire. The tracers left almost a continuous path as if they were sky dockers. You could follow their trail. The din and fury seemed as if it would never end. At the time, I would estimate that we were within a half a mile of the shoreline where the busters were landing. Talk about your grandstand seats for the action. We had them. I permitted the troops to remain topside until the time we received orders to proceed into the beach. Imagine the relief the soldiers get when they see their

way being paved for them so beautifully. Every time a spray of fire
hit its mark, a big cheer would leave the throats of the troops. Then
came the bombers. We were so close in that we could see the
bombs drop from their bays. It's really a thrill to watch them. It
seems as if dozens of them drop from each plane. They fall out
about a foot apart and are excellently spaced. We could see them
reach the earth and explode. All that fire made so much noise, you
had to practically shout to be heard. If there were any movie
cameras around, they certainly had a field day. Now came the
rocket ships, and you could not only see their rockets leave their
bays, but you could also hear them swish going through the air.
Those rocket LCIs really throw the gunpowder.

Surely you would think that no enemy could survive that kind of
barrage. If they weren't struck directly, the concussion in and of
itself would shake hell into destruction. The barrage finally ceased
and the landings were to be commenced. Squadron after squadron
of planes had unloaded their cargo. The smoke that the exploding
shells and bombs had left seemed heavy enough to cut through
with a knife. You couldn't see through it, but hoped the ship ahead
of you would steer a straight course. Finally we got the word to
proceed into the beach.

We proceeded rather cautiously—slowly, barely feeling your
way through the smoke. You'd think you were going through a
heavy fog. The air smelled strongly of the burned gunpowder—
similar smell that you sense when you let a large firecracker go off.
It wasn't far to go into the beach—as I've already said we were
lying in fairly close, by this time less than a quarter of a mile away.
It was most fortunate that there were no enemy planes. Because of
the indefiniteness of the beaches, etc., and also because we had to
wait almost until the last minute before they knew which ships to
unload first, all the ships in the convoy were mighty close together.
You had to run a zigzag course to get into the beach. An enemy
flyer would have had no trouble at all making a direct hit and if he
made a near miss, he probably would have damaged at least two
ships with one bomb. You just had to make a wild guess as to
where to drop the stern anchor.

The beach itself was really something to remember. It wasn't
sand. It was coral, and at the brim of it the water seemed to go
straight down. The niggerheads were the worst we have seen. We
thought we saw a lot of niggerheads at Kiriwina. The latter was a
smooth plantation in comparison. The shoreline was very jagged.
It didn't seem to run straight continuously for more than a foot at a
time. Our ships are not wide. Our beam is less than twenty-five

feet. And yet, you couldn't find a spot on the beach where you could put both ramps down at the same time. That meant that the plans of unloading would have to be changed. Instead of systematically running down both ramps, they had to use only one. The unloading process was a nightmare, and you can gather that when you realize that it took us forty-five minutes to unload, when normally we unload in less than three or four minutes on an assault beaching. I kept hollering my head off, trying to hasten the disembarkation. It didn't do any good. Poor bastards—they were afraid of drowning and you couldn't help it. That pack is secured to their backs, and it wouldn't be easy to shed it in just a second or two.

We put the ramp on a niggerhead on the port side of the ship. It was hard to hold the ship in one place. There was a very strong current which would set you off, and in addition, the pounding surf kept jiggling the ship around. As a consequence, part of the time the ramp was on the niggerhead and part of the time it just went off to the side where a step from the ramp led directly into the water. It was a wet landing anyway you look at it. The troops had to start off in four and one-half feet of water until the water gradually became more shallow. It wasn't smooth walking. That coral is rough and sharp. You didn't see any troops carry their shoes to keep them from getting wet. If they had done so, their feet would have been cut to shreds. In a way, it was almost laughable, and yet it was a tragic picture to see those fellows grope their way off the ramps. A couple of them got on to the niggerhead, and their next step took them straight down. Luckily, someone behind them grabbed them and pulled them to safety. The ammunition was heavy and cumbersome. Delayed matters a lot, yet it couldn't be left behind. They would need the mortars for their field pieces. The firing from the larger ships had not ceased. As we were going in, we received the report from the beachmaster: "Heavy opposition being encountered ashore." I believe the troops could sense that without being told. Planes circling overhead kept the destroyers informed on where the fire was coming from and salvos followed them up. That's one of the fantastic things about those fanatical Japs. Why, with all that preliminary bombardment, you'd think the island itself would be blown out of existence, let alone the human beings on it. Yet there those little bastards returned their fire.

After sitting on the beach for about fifteen or thirty minutes discharging the troops, their mortars began to drop in front of our bow. Fortunately again there were not Jap planes around that could spot where the mortars were dropping. If there had been, it wouldn't have been many minutes before they would have found their range and hit the ship. As it was, the mortars kept dropping in the same area in front of the bow of the ship about fifty or seventy-five feet, or perhaps a bit more. The mortars dropped into the water before they exploded so that there was no damage occasioned by flying shrapnel. I will say that some of the mortars hit so darn close to some of the men that were going ashore that some of them undoubtedly were hit.

We had hoped that DUKWs would be able to draw up alongside our LCI and take the troops off and onto the shore. Those babies are designed just for that purpose.

But the DUKWs and Buffaloes were busy with other cargo . . .

I believe most of the fire power did get ashore. So far as I know, none of the LCTs were hit, nor did I hear of any of them being stranded. When they unloaded their own cargo, they assisted with the cargo of the LSTs. We of course did not stick around to find out. When our job is done, we get the hell out of the place and in this instance it was none too soon. The Japs apparently did expect us to land somewhere in that particular area and probably had their guns set for the beach. Had we been able to go in as far as we had hoped, we undoubtedly would have suffered considerable damage.

Even at that, the LCI that went into our spot just after we did got a very near miss. A mortar shell dropped just alongside her port side, forward of the deckhouse. One soldier standing between two sailors on the rampway got hit with shrapnel. He went down, but was revived and given medical attention and sulfa. He was taken in one of the compartments of that particular ship and went back with it. He'll recover. The sailors were unhurt.

I wasn't scared or in fear at any time. I did get aggravated with the unconcern of the soldiers in getting off at the earliest possible time, but when you think it over, you can't exactly blame them. The way before them was mighty treacherous. Funny how you don't seem to get bothered even with the shells bursting around you. You don't see them being fired at you. They aren't even discernible as they fly through the air. The first time you are conscious of them is when you see them hit the water and shoot up their spray as they burst.

Petty Officer Milton Seltzer, United States Navy

Seltzer writes to his brother's children.

Feb. 28, 1944

Hello Kids:

. . . I'm a qualified submarine man now and can wear my
dolphins. You see, it takes about two runs to understand what
makes these babies tick—and they do tick like a fine Swiss watch.
They're really something to be proud of. You've no doubt seen
pictures of the many dials, valves, gauges and instruments that
they contain but you really haven't seen the half of it. In order to
qualify you have to go through with a qualified officer—it took
about five days in my case—and name, operate and explain everything. The men and officers of my boat are regular fellows. My
skipper is really a swell guy. He and I knock it off swell. My work
brings me in close contact with him and many a quiet evening, in
the conning tower, we talk of cabbages and kings, and his interest
in our background and welfare is really sincere. In tight spots the
officers really pitch in with the rest of us. Ratings and gold braid
are left on the dock in this branch of service. There is a nickname
for everyone (mine is Alkie), even the officers. The skipper is
"Slug," some of the officers are "Junior," "Weeping Willie,"
"The Green Hornet," "Napoleon"; some of the men—"Radar
Pete," "Shaky," "Husky," "Horrible Hadley," "Blackie" and
"Tandelego," oh yes, and "Hackensack." The cooks are
"Stew-Burner," "Bellyrobber," and "Ptomaine." The pharma-
cist's mate is always "Doc," the navigator, "Star Gazer."

We had a lot of fun with rivalling Frank Sinatra and Bing
Crosby clubs. The old man hates the sight of "our Frankie"
and he'd always find his pictures and poems about him in his
stateroom. The fellows made up club badges, secret handshakes.

Crews of subs are never the same. After each run lots of fellows
are transferred for new construction or to other boats and new men
are taken on. I'm getting to be a "plankie" (old timer) on my boat.

I've tried to give you a few of the highlights of this life, but I
know I've only skimmed the surface. It would take lots of pages to
cover the subject adequately. Well, perhaps some day if my luck
holds out, I'll be able to give you all the dope. Many times it takes
luck, faith and a strong back, but then again, war is no picnic. I've
already helped take my share of the toll inflicted on the enemy. But
there is really no set quota. After this gadget is over we'll sit back
and compare notes. I'm really proud to be doing my share. The

brave boys of Spain, North Africa and Stalingrad and South Pacific are being avenged every time a ship bearing the Rising Sun goes down.

Loads of love,
Milt

Corporal G.E. Hughes,
1st Battalion, Royal Hampshire Regiment

In this extract from his diary, Hughes details the Allied invasion of Normandy on 6 June 1944, and the first days of the Battle of Normandy.

Diary, 6 June 1944
06.00 Get in LCA. Sea very rough. Hit the beach at 7.20 hours. Murderous fire, losses high. I was lucky T[hank] God. Cleared three villages. Terrible fighting and ghastly sights.

June 7. Still going. Dug in at 02:00 hrs. Away again at 05.30. NO FOOD. Writing few notes before we go into another village. CO out of action, adjutant killed. P Sgt lost. I do P Sgt['s job]. More later.

June 8. 07.30, fire coming from village. Village cleared. Prisoners taken. Night quite good but German snipers lurking in wood. Had 2 hrs' sleep. Second rest since the 6th.

June 9. 06.30 hrs went on wood clearing. Germans had flown. Only one killed for our morning's work. We are now about 8 to 10 miles inland. Promoted to Sgt.

June 10. Joan darling, I have not had you out of my thoughts. T[hank] God I have come so far. We have lost some good men. Our brigade was only one to gain objectives on D-Day.
The French people give us a good welcome. Had wine.

June 11. Contact with enemy. Lost three of my platoon. Very lucky T[hank] God. Only had 5 hours sleep in 3 days.

June 12. This day undescrible [sic] mortar fire and wood fighting. Many casualties. T[hank] God I survived another day.

June 13. Just had my first meal since Monday morning. Up all night. Everyone in a terrible state. I keep thinking of u.

June 14. Counter-attack by Jerry from woods. Mortar fire. 13 of my platoon killed or missing. After heavy fighting yesterday CSM also wounded, also Joe. O[fficer] C[ommanding] killed. I am one mass of scratches. Advanced under creeping barrage for 3 miles. Drove Jerry back. It is hell. 3 Tiger tanks came here, up to lines during night.

June 16. [resting] Received letter from home. Wrote to Joan and Mum.

June 17. [resting]

June 18. Day of Hell. Counter-attack.

June 19. Day of Hell. Counter-attack.

June 20. Day of Hell. Advanced. Counter-attacked.

June 21. Quiet day. We have been fighting near Tilley [Tilly]. Bayonet charge. Shelled all day. Letters from home.

June 22. Out on patrol. Got within 35 yards of Tiger before spotting it. Got back safely T[hank] God. Shelled to blazes. Feeling tired out.

June 23. No sleep last night. Exchanged fire, out on patrols all day, went on OP for 4 hours. Stand-to all night. Casualties.
   Just about had enough.

June 24. Had to go back to CCS [Casualty Clearing Station]. Malaria.

Sergeant Hughes was hospitalized with malaria for most of the rest of the Normandy campaign.

Anon GI, United States Army

18 June [1944]
[Normandy]

Dear Mom,

We get milk and cider off these French people. It looks like they are very glad to see us yanks. They should be these dirty Germans tried to make slaves out of them. I met a little boy I used to go to school with on the boat crossing the channell.

There is lots of things I would like to tell you but maybe later I will be able to.

I still have my little prayer book and I have used it. I am sure it has done me lots of good, you know what I mean . . . Take care of yourself,

love,
Son.

Colonel G. Tilly, 5th Dorsets

Tilly writes to his wife.

France 29 June [1944]

Dear Dorothy

Had a drop of "Homemade French Champagne Brandy" last night—whoosh nearly lifted my head off.

We have got a cow—poor dear mooing its head off full of milk and shrapnel—and then it gets milked about every half-hour—still, makes the good old cup of tea taste good.

Do you remember Jack Atherton? He and his wife had dinner with us in the Fleur de Lis in Sandwich about two years ago . . . he was a bit unlucky the night before last and was killed.

I am very well Dot so there is no need for you to worry at all—only thing is I really would like a good bath.

Anon Soldier, Canadian Third Division

[Normandy] *10 July 1944*

Dear Mother

I feel like a heel for not writing regularly to you and I know how anxious I would feel if I didn't hear from you. Please never stop writing dear.

I cannot tell you much about what is going on over here, as we haven't been very far inland and cannot tell about the people or the country either. I can say this though: it is a gigantic business and we are fighting a tough enemy.

Mother, before I close for a while, I am a bit mixed up about things but am straight on this: Dad and you are my ideal couple. If I can be half the man Dad is and have the outlook you have on life, I won't ever have to worry. I have been scared and I guess there will be plenty of times in the future when I will be scared, but as long as I don't let you, Dad, Dot, Rich and David down, I shall be happy, no matter the outcome of this do, in so far as it affects my personal future behaviour. Will say cheerio for now, sweetheart.

All best love,
Art

Friedrich Gadecke, Wehrmacht

27 August 1944
France

Dear Parents,

A time of uncertainty, apprehension and fear is now beginning for you as well. I pray sincerely that God gives you courage each day, and that you don't sink into worry but hold onto the certainty that your prayers will be heard. Rest assured and be happy! That is my wish and my plea to you. Don't be afraid, even during the days when you hear nothing and can know nothing about how things are for me. Everything that I experience and am permitted to live through in these times reassures me that I will be kept safe for you, for God does nothing by halves. I shall come through these dangers. God granted me life through you. For that I am always grateful to you.

Your son,
Friedrich

Gadecke was killed in action on 13 September 1944.

Private Bernard Sasnowitz, United States Army

NETHERLANDS EAST INDIES *Nov. 10, 1944*

Dear Mother:

I found that I had time on my hands and I also remembered that I hadn't written to you in a long while so here it is.

I've had quite a bit of action since I've been at this new A.P.O. The first night we camped we thought there were Japs in every bush and we did a heck of a lot of firing. The next morning we sheepishly found out that we were just plain nervous and trigger happy. After that, we didn't do anymore firing on the ground. The next bit of action you already know. We shot down a Jap bomber, so we painted a flag on our gun. We had some quiet after that for a few days, and then we had a number of raids which caused a bit of excitement, naturally. Then some strafers came over low. We were on the ball, and we fired at it as soon as we spotted it. So did a couple of other gun crews. We saw a slight burst of flame on the plane, and then smoke started to pour out of the plane. It crashed, and its pretty nice to see a Jap plane crash. Later we heard that the pilot was very young, no more than a kid. Since there was some argument between the sections as to who should be given credit for bringing the plane down, it was decided that all of the sections would get credit for it. So we have two flags painted on our gun. We had some more raids after that but we didn't bring down any more planes. Some other outfits succeeded in doing so.

I haven't seen many natives on this island. Those I have seen are tall and well built, unlike the natives of New Guinea.

We cook our own meals. Some are good and others are so-so. It's according to what we have. Sometimes the cook can really make up a nice combination from a variety of things. Enough of that.

Good luck to all of you.

Bernard

Jack Clark, 143 Field Regiment, Royal Artillery

8 May 1945

> *2058212 Clark J*
> *B Troop 190 Bty*
> *143 Field Reg. RA*
> *B.L.A.*

My Own Darling Olive,

Wasn't it wonderful news darling? In fact it seems all too good to be true. Today—VE Day is the day we have been waiting for as many years but even so it doesn't seem possible somehow that we have at last won our War. I suppose you were tremendously excited and happy when you heard the news at home but its hard to explain really and it may sound funny but it didn't somehow make much impression on us when we first heard the capitulation. That was at twenty to eight on Friday the 4th of May and only concerned our part of the front—Holland and Northern Germany. It didn't seem to make a lot of difference at first. We had just come in from the O.P. and were due to go out on a practice scheme in the morning as we were pretty browned off. It was an English speaking civilian who came and told us and he must have thought us a pretty poor lot because, we didn't take much notice but just went on cleaning our Carrier! Later on in the evening we went over to the Gun Position and did a bit of celebrating. For this purpose we dug out our Rum Bottle and drank the contents between the four of us and a double ration which was issued to mark the occasion as well! Outside all around and as far as you could see the sky was full of lights, parachute flares, and illuminating flares of all colours. There were lines of tracer bullets and bofors shells streaming across the sky and in fact it was a real Guy Fawkes night. That was when I wrote that letter form to you and it is signed by our carrier crew—the driver, the other driver op, the officer and his assistant.

After this we had to spit and polish everything in preparation for the big march forward. Whilst we were waiting yesterday morning to move off dressed in our Sunday best with all the vehicles shining and our webbing scrubbed white we received the news from Regimental Headquarters that all resistance everywhere had ceased. This was before it was broadcast on the wireless. Our job is to go on into Holland and round up and disarm the Germans mostly S.S. troops and send them back to Germany. We started yesterday midday and came into the German lines about 25 miles. All along the roads the civilians were lined up cheering and waving flags and wearing orange shirts and ties and the girls orange dresses and ribbons and painted on the trees and walls were big slogans "Welcome" and "We Thank You". We have come as far as DOORN where you remember the Kaiser was held captive since the last war. You will find this place on the map quite easily and I will be able to let you know exactly where we are in future as we have been told we can now do this. We expect to be here for about a week then are going on into Germany as Occupation troops.

It's funny here really for there are Jerries all over the place and all of them fully armed. We came into our Billet about seven o'clock yesterday evening and it was occupied by Jerries up to an hour of us arriving. Our advance party came along and told them to clear out so they just packed up and moved about 200 yards away and there they are. They ride around on bikes with rifles on their backs and some of them actually had the nerve to come and ask us for cigarettes today! You don't need a very vivid imagination to guess what our answer was. It seems so strange that everything could have altered so much in 24 hours just by the signing of a piece of paper.

On the wireless this morning we heard the official announcement of VE Day and that everyone, all over the world was celebrating it. We had no opportunity of celebrating at all and nothing to celebrate with literally not even water because the water supply has been off all day and only just come on again. Out here we always said that when Victory came the only people who would have the opportunity of celebrating would be those who did no fighting but I suppose that's just hard luck and we don't begrudge anyone who feels happy and has a good time these days.

We have a fine billet here, a large detached house in the middle of a pine forest just outside Doorn. It's been a lovely day and wonderfully peaceful and quiet. Now it is evening and the sun is just going down—Darling this would be such a wonderful place to go walking with you just you and I together with no more worries and fears for each other.

I have your three lovely letters nos. 72, 73 and 74 which has just arrived. Although I love reading your sweet words so much Darling it will be wonderful when we no longer have to write letters to each other but can speak our words of Love and Adoration to each other.

I am on duty from midnight until four o'clock as I'm going to bed now and will join you again in four hours time. You will be sleeping whilst I am writing so Sleep Well Darling and God Bless you and bring quickly the moment when we shall be lying together in each others arms once again for I love you and long for your Love to the very depths of my heart.

Sergeant CFN Louis Rose, REME

Rose writes to his wife, Celia

[North Africa]
9 May 1945

My darling,

It is VE day here. You probably all went crazy there, but I can assure you no crazier than us here. Last night we had a free do in the canteen and I was completely sozzled, and finished up in the Sergeants' Mess with my Sergeant Major. The boys got up to some rare antics last night and my friend the Sergeant Major lost his beautiful military moustache. The boys mutilated it terribly. They then got hold of another HQMS who was sozzled, put him in a barrel and rolled him up and down the workshops. Well, darling, sozzled though I was, you and the cherubs were still in my thoughts.

Lou

THE KOREAN WAR 1950–1953

After the Soviet Union declared war on Japan in 1945, its troops moved to occupy the north of Japan's former colony of Korea. Shortly afterwards, US forces moved into south Korea, with the 38th parallel chosen as the dividing line between the two zones. In the north, the Soviet Union installed Communists under Kim il-Sung in power and in June 1950 Kim launched an invasion of the south in an attempt to forcibly reunite Korea. South Korea called upon the UN for support, which was accorded. Sixteen member nations sent troops, among them Britain and, especially, the US, which committed 2 million servicemen. A counter-attack by MacArthur (at Inchon) pushed the Communists back, which in turn provoked Communist China into sending 200,000 "volunteers" to North Korea. Forbidden the use of A-bombs, the UN forces fought a trench-warfare campaign similar to that in World War I. Eventually the conflict bogged down in stalemate, and an armistice was signed at Panmunjon in July 1953.

Major Patrick Angier, 1st Battalion, Royal Gloucestershire Regiment

Angier writes to his wife and family.

> *Korea, 23 November 1950*
>
> We are in action at last and have found something to fire at. We are all pleased as we want to get on with it. "A" Company are in reserve.
>
> Had a letter from you just now and cannot reply but will get this straight off on the convoy. Don't worry if letters are scarce. I am either busy or it is night and no lights permitted or too cold to hold a pencil.

> *26 November*
>
> I got a letter from you last night in the dark and, therefore, could not read it until after stand down this morning (no lights per-

mitted). However, it was very nice to look forward to and very heart warming to read even in 18 degrees of frost, which was the prevailing temperature when the sun rose this morning.

I find it unbelievable to think of you and of our life together in these very hard surroundings. Heve it is all claws and teeth, nature stripped cruel and bare, and the survival of the fittest, the law of the jungle. Raw noses, dripping noses, and splitting bandaged fingers. However, let us remember these days when we are together again and we shall then be thankful that we should appreciate to the full the joys of home life.

I am becoming more and more determined to break free from military life on my return. The more I see of the state of other regular soldiers, some ten years senior, and with very adequate careers, the more I am not impressed that the gamble of soldiering on is worth the sacrifice demanded. In short, I hope this will be my last campaign in peace time.

I shall have more grey hairs and look a bit worn after this. I have no Elizabeth Arden to keep me young!

I am keeping notes in my Diary and I shall send them to you at the end of the year.

It is impossible to wash clothes here, they freeze in the sun and so you can't dry them except round a fire. We have made shelves in the dug-out today and placed straw on the floor to keep our feet warm when standing too.

I hope you have heard from me by now from Korea. The mail is very good, ten days your letters take for a 10,000 mile trip to this inaccessible place just north of the 38th Parallel.

It is very difficult to read at all here. I read poems because they can be taken up and put down at short notice. There are too many interruptions to read a novel.

I am writing this by our own electric light made from a 12-volt battery (brought by Ron who was former M.T.O.) and resting on a nice polished table. The height of the table is only 9″ as the Koreans do not sit on chairs. We, therefore, are obliged to adjust our ways and live likewise at floor level.

The room has a large built-in cupboard with sliding doors painted in Japanese style. The walls are papered also in Japanese birds design and, at the opposite end of the room, is a mahogany chest of drawers. The slow tick of the large wall clock gives a homely, rather English finish to the atmosphere of what is, until the next bugle drags us out, a home from home. When I got back I was greeted by a letter from you.

The only thing I would like is A.E.Housman's "Shropshire

Lad". I like Housman and I want to learn one or two poems.

I enclose a picture for the children from Brenda (Godbold's little girl). In return one of Rosalind's pictures has gone to her.

Breakfast is up and so I will close. I have planned a small cocktail party (on half a bottle of gin) for the Company Officers. The guests will be Tony Farrar-Hockley and Lackery Wood. We do not drink a great deal but I think it is good for morale to have these little social occasions.

15 February 1951

My letter writing has gone awry as the rate of military business has increased rather rapidly.

I am on the top of a hill now smoking a cigar and watching the landscape around. I am in command of the position which is, of course, a bit isolated and this responsibility has caused me to pray as earnestly as if I was on the end of an unopened parachute.

We were engaged in a fight two nights ago in which Tony Preston was wounded in the upper arm and the back of the head. Neither are likely to prove serious in the long run and I am almost relieved as I am very fond of him and could not have borne his loss.

Now I would be very pleased darling if you would go as soon as possible to visit his parents at Prestbury and reassure them that he will be all right and that his Platoon did very gallantly.

In the engagement we killed eleven Chinese and wounded two (more probably wounded) and lost two killed and six wounded ourselves. It was between 3 and 7 in the morning and I was somewhat concerned at the outcome until light revealed that the enemy were retiring. We have learnt some tips from this our first battle and they should help us later on.

At this moment an Air Strike is in progress with Jets; very spectacular and noisy.

First hand experience has not altered my political views. It will take years to reach a military solution in this mountain country where our superior air and fire power cannot be fully applied. The politicians must think again and think practically this time. If they want us to win this war for them they must be prepared to commit many more divisions than they have here now and this is impossible in view of the threat to all important Europe. I still regard this affair as a trap set by Russia and she will I think stir the pot ad infinitum. Do please impress this practical side to people who are interested.

I am sorry to dwell on this so much but I live with this seven days a week, and therefore, am apt to think about it!

Thank you for your beautiful letters; have hope and faith. I feel sustained, serene, and calm in the midst of all this horror and confusion.

21 February

This is a personal letter to you. I seem to write so much about politics and warfare.

There is little to recount today except that it is raining and rather miserable—a day that makes me think like the Prodigal Son of the condition of the servants in his father's house. I think of the Bath! and the armchair in my own home and wonder what it is that keeps me away from them! I think of the garden and the new car, but mostly of you and our children. I think of life's hours passing and youth's days expiring; of children growing up without their father; of separation's strain and of the warm heart tired by the long hours of loneliness. And when I think of these things and sadden, my sadness turns to joy—a joy that this has been and may yet be. A great inward glow of hope for the days to come and of thanksgiving for having thus lived so fully.

I am so glad the children are better now. It is sweet of you to struggle with the garden. Don't do too much. You know I should never be angry whatever happened to it.

I am going to write to Stan Cargill in Japan to ask him to send me a book on the local wild flowers to keep me interested in something other than the Army.

Lots of love to our dear children; do tell them how much Daddy loves them and misses them and will come back as soon as he has finished his work.

16 April

I am now settled down to trench life after leave and am busy to catch up with all the letters from you. I have sent two small parcels today. Some wooden mats for glasses purely souvenirs and two little wooden dolls for Philip. Be careful he does not swallow the very small doll inside the inside! I will be sending you about ten silk handkerchiefs all of which show scenes from Mywakuni Island. Now that I have lived in the East I can understand Chinese and Japanese traditional art. It is most descriptive.

I have now plenty of writing instruments and ink thank you; all I need is the time and energy to use them.

I am in the trench again tonight and so it is difficult to write.

I am reading your letters through. I have seen lots of Kerria Japonica in its wild state out here.

21 April 1951

Well I give up! I can't understand this war. After attempting at length to try to give you some ideas on it in my last letter, I have since been on a Patrol twelve miles into enemy territory and found almost nothing. They tell us that the enemy has an Army Group in front of us (they must have drawn a long way back) but our Patrol consisting of forty tanks achieved the death of one Chinaman and the capture of one more. It was a most spectacular affair and must have cost a fortune. Perhaps £25,000 to £50,000.

We crossed the ford some two hundred yards long across the Imjim River and went into close laager for the night. The forty tanks (Centurions) and all the ancillary vehicles made a display like a car park at a race meeting. The Task Force was commanded by Col. Lowther. a relative of the late Lord Lonsdale. It was a very Cavalry occasion and the start across the Paddy and banks in the morning was just like the hunting field; tanks roaring, galloping, jumping and bogging everywhere. I was mounted in an Oxford carrier which is a new and larger edition of the Bren Gun carrier, you know. It has an amazing performance and could more than hold its own with the Centurions. Mud and dust together were thrown up as we charged forward in the early light.

Well the enemy had withdrawn and for my part, I spent the day picnicking on the top of a hill where they might have been. The Azaleas were splendid and made the journey worthwhile to me at any rate.

We saw a pilot bale out and be rescued by a helicopter within less than an hour of descending. The freemasonry among pilots must be good. Within ten minutes there were twelve fighters swooping down round him to make sure the enemy did not molest him.

A tank broke down and preparations were made for my Company to stay the night forward but they got it back all right. I slept well last night after all the bumping and tossing about.

It's been a quiet day today and I finished the painting and posted it to you. It takes a long time under trench conditions but it is very diverting and gives me an interest. I am fortunate to have plenty of advisers among the Company Officers.

Major Angier was killed in the Battle of Imjin River two days after writing this letter.

Gunner Eric Stowe,
116/41 Field Regiment, Royal Artillery

Stowe writes to his wife.

[Korea] *22/2/51*

My Dear Jean,

. . . Regarding leave to Japan, providing they don't change [things] I'm now number 5 on the list and nos 1 and 2 have gone so I should be going the second week in March, but . . . it would be far nicer to come home. But I wouldn't like to come home and then have to come back here, I don't think I could stand that, it must be for good when I come home . . . Life for me varies from week to week and it must puzzle you reading my letters . . . you see I'm either right in the thick of it or right out of it. I hope my news doesn't depress you darling all my love Eric

[Korea] *12/4/52*

My Dear Jean

. . . Apart from a bit of trouble with my feet, I'm on top of the world . . . the weather moderately good and everything is quite and peaceful . . . only the odd bang in the distance to remind that there is still a war on. If you look at a map of the war front, we are in the part of the line that is between the 38th = . Someone I hope will soon realise we have been in action since xmas, with the exception of two days, without a break and in all that time only supported our own infantry twice . . . We all are wishing it would come soon to an agreement because it is a meaningless war, and the majority of us think it was a real deal to bring us here in the first place . . .

Second Lieutenant Julian Potter, 43rd Light
Anti-Aircraft Searchlight Regiment, Royal Artillery

Potter was a conscripted National Service soldier.

26th March [1951]—*on the move*

Dear Mum and Dad

I am sorry this letter is a day late, but yesterday (Easter Sunday) I didn't get a spare moment. Ever since I joined this troop it has been on the hop trying to keep up with the 45 Field Regt. who themselves have been trying to keep the Chinese in range. Whenever there is a move, two of our three officers go forward with an advance party to decide exactly where each gun is going to be placed. The season of "small rains" ("big rains" come in July) has just begun, and the roads, which are mostly built on embankments running through flooded paddy fields, have a very nasty habit of crumbling in, although the wheels of the vehicles be 18″ from the precarious edge. So if you choose a position with a precarious route in, not only will the adjacent paddy fields be strewn with upturned gun tractors etc, but you have the loss of the whole battery of guns on your conscience.

. . . We have moved four time during the last six days, which is a great strain on the gunners, as every time they come to a new position they have to dig a huge pit for the LAA gun, as well as camouflaging it, digging latrines and erecting bivys etc. During the first two moves the officers slept in the back of a Bedford 3-tonner, which had been converted into a caravan. But then its front axle broke, so we have to pitch our tents either in a paddy field, or else in the ruins of some village. All the villages around here are on the average of 95% flattened . . .

1st April—on the move

Dear Mum and Dad,

We are still moving nearly once a day, but this does not worry us as much as it did as our "caravan" has had a new front axle put on it and it provides the officers with a much more mobile command post cum bedroom than did a tent. In spite of all the moves, the field guns have rarely been in range [of the Chinese]. To let off some of their suppressed energy, the OP called down a barrage from the whole regiment onto one enemy gun—but failed to put it out of action. The next morning it was discovered by some brass hat that there was no friendly infantry between us and the Chinese front defence lines—so the regiment was withdrawn five miles, without a rifle being fired!

The Koreans themselves seem to be imperturable and concentrate all their energies on keeping alive. I stopped my jeep in the middle of Seoul main street, which I had thought to be deserted, and brought out a loaf and some corned beef onto the bonnet for my lunch. I was immediately surrounded by about ten Koreans and I had no alternative but to share the bread with them . . . love Julian

29 April 51

Dear Mum and Dad

In case you did not get my last letter, my release has come through: I am to be demobbed October 1st and in "J" RHU by July 1st. With the Chinese Communist offensive in full swing, however, one cannot be *certain* that things will work out just like that . . . there is a rumour that all leave to Japan has been stopped. If the Chinese advance is stemmed north of Seoul we will presumably carry on in our safe role of protecting the bridges, in which case nothing should go awry. Since the offensive began 11 Bty has only had one sergeant injured in the way of casulaties, which shows the comparative safety of our job: the infantry battalion of 29 Brigade suffered an appalling proportion of killed, wounded and missing—I don't know if the papers published the figures.

Although I try very hard I am not getting on with our BC, which is a good thing as far as my release is concerned. The other day he was outraged to discover that I did not know where the latrine on Sgt Mason's gun site was. He also passed me driving a jeep without a "co-driver", which is against the rules.

At the moment there is a general air of anticipation and excitement and everyone is digging in for the defence of Seoul. All the gun detachments are scrounging and pilfering from the American's supply of sandbags in order to increase the width and height of the gunpits. The airstrip is in continuous use, as sortie after sortie of our planes take off loaded with napalm bombs, rockets etc. UN gunfire has now been rumbling in the distance for 24 hours non-stop. No more refugees are allowed to use the river, for fear of letting through enemy in disguise. Today one of the more nervy gun detachments complained that they had spotted Koreans digging trenches on the other side of a gulley in front of the gun. On investigation I found that the holes they had dug and been filled in. Fearing the civilians might be hiding arms for the eventual use of the Communists I made them dig the holes out again, only to find that they had been protecting their food and clothing from any bombs or shells that might come down.

I haven't had this week's letters from you yet, but there is another batch due in the evening.

Love from Julian

Lieutenant Frederick P. Pelser, USAAF

Pelser was shot down over North Korea on 17 September 1951, and subsequently made a POW.

Dear Mother and all the family,

Today it seems that we are permitted to write a letter home. In case you do not already know, I am a POW of the Chinese People's Volunteers. I was allowed to write you late in September, but it is quite possible the letter became lost en route. Fortunately I am in quite good health so you need not worry about me in that respect. Our basic needs are supplied and of course we receive the usual two meals daily. Please give my best regards to Marvin and Roselyn, Walter and Mildred. I am looking forward to seeing you all again before long.

Love, Fred.

Private James Cardinal, United States Army

Korea [nd]

It's late in the afternoon here in North Korea. I'm on a road-block with my squad about 11 miles south of Sunchon. The entire army is retreating south. Just how far no one knows, but they're all headed away from the Chinese, who are only about 10 miles away now. Anyway, no matter what happens I'll take damn good care of myself. They're certainly not going to take me prisoner.

I feel terribly sorry for the refugees. They seem so miserable and all are hungry and cold. Six little girls, none over seven years old, just came down the road. Three had no shoes or socks, and they were all homeless orphans. We're letting them sit by the fire and are feeding them. I guess it's all part of the horrors of war. They'll probably wander along till they freeze or starve to death. Joan should see them and then she would appreciate her home, her parents and her school life more than she does.

Lance Corporal D.G. Kaye, 1st Battalion, Royal Gloucestershire Regiment

Kaye writes to his family from a North Korean POW camp.

> *POW Camp No 3*
> *Democratic Peoples Republic of Korea*
> *c/o Committee of Chinese Congress*
> *Defenders of World Peace*
> *24th December 1951*

Dear Mother Dad and Family

. . . Season's greetings and all that! Yes, it's me again, just to let you know what sort of Christmas we are having here with the CPUs. To start with they have given us a present of a packet of cigarettes, a bar of scented soap and a pair of socks and a handerchief. As for food—tonight we've got steamed bread, fresh fruit, pork and beef, [for] tomorrow's breakfast, 2 boiled eggs, chicken and pork and beef, mushrooms and turnips. Not only this but also sweets, wine, biscuits, cakes and peanuts. Can you beat that? We've got a full programme of sport, concerts, services, and even Father Christmas is coming round tonight.

I've still had no word from you but I keep hoping. Anyway as long you know that I am alright that is all that really matters.

The weather has turned cold these last two days, but up to now it has been really warm. Very queer weather altogether.

Well, that's all for now. Hope you are all keeping as well as I am . . .

love David

> *POW Camp No 3*
> *Democratic Peoples Republic of Korea*
> *c/o Chinese People's Committee of*
> *Defenders of World Peace*
> *Peking China*
> *April 6th 1952*

Dear Mother, Dad and Family,

We are now on the Summer routine. Get up six thirty, walk and PT from seven to eight, milk at eight, breakfast at nine, dinner at twelve thirty and tea at five. In between we have games, PT, study and other odds and ends to keep our time occupied. Once a week for tea we now get meat pasties, very nice too.

You will never guess what game is the lastest fashion here, I'll tell you—it's bridge. We've been playing it for some time. It's easily the most interesting game I've played. They don't call me "Grand Slam Kaye" for nothing you know. At one time it was all crib, then rummy, then whist and now its bridge night and day.

Pleased to hear that Jim is doing well. I can just imagine how Auntie Doll feels about him wanting to be a test pilot! . . . I tried to stop smoking last week when I had a sore mouth. I did manage to to cut down to three cigarettes a day but now that the doctor has cured it I'm smoking just as much as I used to.

I have still been keeping up with my reading, thanks to the library . . . also we keep getting the Daily Worker in regularly which keeps us in touch with what's happening in England. I was sorry to hear about the death of the King. I suppose we are now soldiers of the Queen.

Well . . . that is about all my news for now. I hope this letter reaches you because you must be worrying about me. Quite unneccessariily I assure you because I'm perfectly OK and in the best of health and spirits.

The talks seem to be making slow and steady progress so it shouldn't be too long now before we hear the news that we have all been waiting for. Let's hope so anyway.

Love from David

> POW Camp No 3
> Democratic Peoples Republic of Korea
> c/o Chinese People's Committee of
> Defenders of World Peace
> 1st July [1952]

Dear Mother, Dad and Family
 . . . Have received four letters from you and three from Ursula. We now only have rice for breakfast . . . biscuits for dinner and bread at night . . . We should shortly be starting the rainy season here, just about when you are going on your holidays. By the way, where are you going this year? I don't think that I'll be going on one myself, but I'll make up for that when I get home, believe me . . .

Cheerio, from David

> POW Camp No 3
> Democratic Peoples Republic of Korea
> c/o Chinese People's Committee of
> Defenders of World Peace
> 22nd September [1952]

Dear Mother, Dad and Family
Once again I start my forthnightly letter to you. I have just received nine letters from you, the last one written in July, so you

can see that it is a long time since I have heard from you. What irritates me is the fact that I keep writing to you regularly—yet you have heard nothing from me since last Christmas. I know that this must worry you, but there is absolutely nothing I can do about it but keeping writing and hoping for the best . . .

love David

THE VIETNAM WAR, 1965–73

The beginnings of the Vietnam War long preceded US involvement. With the defeat of Japan in South East Asia in 1945, France tried to reimpose colonial control on Vietnam but encountered fierce resistance from Communist guerrillas in the north of the country. The struggle lasted for eight years with the guerrillas fighting a "protracted war" campaign of hit-and-run which wore down the will-to-win of the French. In 1954 the guerrillas, under Giap, defeated elite French forces at Dien Bien Phu. France conceded power to the Communist Viet Minh in the north, and the country was divided along the 17th parallel.

In the early 1960s, the North Vietnamese began sending Communist guerrillas, Viet Cong, below the 17th parallel with the intention of overthrowing the pro-Western government there. The US in response sent in 2000 "military advisors" to the South. By 1965 the USA was becoming increasingly embroiled in what had become a major civil war. More and more troops were committed (peaking at 542,000 in 1969), with their ranks raised by a draft of eligible males. The numbers were never enough, however. As the war dragged on in jungle skirmish after skirmish (a type of warfare ideally suited to the guerrillas), its popularity at home began to decline. There were widespread protests. Eventually, in 1973, the US withdrew from its longest war. Thirty six thousand American men had been killed.

Sergeant John J. Woods, US Army

Yam-Ky, Vietnam
23 November 64

My dearest daughter,

This letter is just for you. I'm writing it because I don't want you to worry about me.

Over here many people are dying because there are people who think that they should rule the whole earth. There is a road—not one that you can see. This road is one that they are building. It's a road that is built on communism at the cost of many people's freedom. This country of Vietnam is in the way but the people don't want this road, so that is why they are fighting here.

Your daddy, just like other daddies, is trying to help them with this fight so we can stop this road. If we don't it may someday reach America. Freedom is something you should never take for granted. The freedom that you enjoy today cost many lives, and so will this country, too.

If for any reason Daddy goes away, remember I will not be sorry. Because Daddy believes in freedom for all people, and especially for you and Mommy.

I love you and miss you. I'm taking care to see that I do come home and help Mommy raise you to be above all a good American.

Love,
Daddy

Joe Pais, USMC

August 30, 1965

Dear Mom,

. . . Mom, I know I will never be the same Joe. Last night I lost one of my best buddies. It wasn't Bob, but he used to run around with us. Somehow the V.C. got through our lines and threw a grenade into where my buddy was sleeping. One of my other buddies was wounded seriously and he's expected to die any time. You know, Mom, things didn't really bother me until we got out here in the bad part of Da-Nang. And now I lose two of my buddies. It's hard, Mom, to get over something like this, that's why I say it's gonna be different.

I can't even smile anymore, nothing seems funny to me, everything is serious now. Once I get out of here I never want to hear another word about Vietnam or wars. You read in the papers about demonstrators and all this other bull . . . they ask why we are over here. Well we're stopping communism over here instead of in the people's backyard back home in the U.S.A. And we're doing a damn good job over here and we'll keep on doing a good job. Our Marine Corps saying "Death Before Dishonor."

Well the rainy season has finally moved in. It rains just about every day now. Sometimes all day and all night.

I've moved to a new position now, I'm squad leader. I'm in charge of six men. Of course I'm still in heavy machine guns, our job is real dangerous, our life expectancy in combat is 7 seconds. I'll be home though, I won't let anything stop me.

I sure would like to see my family, especially my little niece. It's gonna be like a new world when I get home. Everything is gonna be so different. You know I haven't slept in a good old bed since Jan. 2. Out here we sleep on a shelter half or a poncho with one blanket. The hard ground doesn't even bother me anymore. Hot chow, we very seldom get that. We've been eating C rations ever since we got here. I'm gonna have a straight back and an iron stomach. No more food poison for me. It wouldn't even bother me . . .

Well, Mom, I'm gonna have to rush off now. I'll write more later. God bless you.

I love you,
Joe

Private John O'Halloran, United States Army

18 July 1965

Dear Dad:

. . . Well guess what, I am in *Vietnam*. Today is Sunday, July 18 and I've been here since Wed., 14 July. That makes a total of four days so far spent in hell. Since I've been here I've been in one killing, and almost killed myself. Last Friday, July 16, we went on a fire mission into war zone "D" (that's where there is nothing else but Viet Cong), and were under heavy mortar fire. Believe me, I was never so scared in all my life, seeing everything around me being blown up. Two guys were killed and seven more wounded. The Captain ordered a quick retreat, and those words sounded so good I could have kissed him.

Saturday was the worst day of all. I was one of the guys picked to go out on a patrol . . . That was the most sickening day of my life. We were walking down a road, and coming from the opposite direction was a woman and a little baby in her arms. The Sergeant told us to watch out for a trap, because the V.C. use women all the time. We were maybe fifteen feet from her and she started crying like a baby. I didn't know what was going on, and the next thing I knew the Sergeant shot the hell out of the both of them. She had a grenade under the baby's blanket which was noticeable, but she was afraid to sacrifice her kid to kill us, so she started crying. The Sergeant said it's a dirty war, but it's kill or be killed.

This coming Wed., we are going on a six-day field mission into "D" war zone that should be a wild battle. I am in Bien-Hoa, five miles from the "D" zone. The temperature out here ranges from 100 to 133 degrees. Today the temperature is 117, and it's hot. I pull guard duty every night for two hours, so you don't get much sleep. The other night some V.C. tried to capture one of the Australians from their camp. They tried to drag him away but he blew the hell out of two of them and the others took off. We sleep in sandbag bunkers built next to our howitzers.

Well I guess that's about all for now, write soon . . . I intend to buy a camera, so that I can take some pictures and show you what this jungle looks like. To prove to you how scared I am, I went to mass and confession today.

Hope to see you soon.
Love,
John

Kenneth W. Bagby, 1st Battalion, 7th Cavalry

Bagby writes to his parents describing the battle of Ia-Drang.

Plei-Ku, Vietnam
Nov. 17, 1965

Dear Folks,

I met a boy on the ship coming over to Vietnam. He was a good guy from the State of Missouri. He was my friend. We lived in the same tent together, went into An-Khe together, and spent most of our free time together. I got to know this boy well, and he was my best friend. His name was Dan Davis.

On Monday morning, the 15th of November, he died in my arms of two bullet wounds in the chest. He said, "Ken, I can't breathe." There was nothing I could do.

To the right of me another friend, whose last name was Balango, died of a wound in the throat. Up front Sergeant Brown, my squad leader, was hit in the chest and leg. To my left Sp-4 A. Learn was hit in the ankle.

We were crossing a field and were pinned down by automatic weapons fire from the enemy. We were pinned down for about 45 minutes before the rest of the platoon could get to us, and save the rest of us.

So went the biggest and worst battle that any American force has had in Vietnam. We outdone the Marines and Airborne by a long shot. Estimated V.C. killed, 2,000. Our casualties, I cannot give the information out. The battle took place on the Cambodian border.

In another line of attack my platoon leader Lieutenant Marm was shot in the neck right beside me, about ten feet to my right. Me and Sp-4 Ahewan took him back through the lines to the aid station.

Another situation, me, Daily, and Sergeant Riley captured two V.C. and were bringing them back through the lines when we were pinned down again, as one of them spotted a buddy and tried to signal him. I was going to kill both of them but Sergeant Riley stopped me.

Our battalion, the 1st BN 7th Cav., is completely inactive due to the killed and wounded of its men. My squad which consists of nine men, three came out, myself, Sergeant Scott, and a boy named Stidell.

Folks, by all rights I should be dead. The good Lord evidently saw fit to spare me, for some reason. I prayed, and prayed and prayed some more, the three days we were in battle.

The many men that died, I will never forget. The odor of blood and decayed bodies, I will never forget. I am all right. I will never be the same though, never, never, never. If I have to go into battle again, if I am not killed, I will come out insane. I cannot see and go through it again. I know I can't. The friends I lost and the many bodies I carried back to the helicopters to be lifted out, I will never forget.

The pen that I am writing this letter with belongs to Stash Arrows, the boy that rode up to Winchester with me, on my emergency leave. Pop, remember him. He was hit three times in the back. I don't know if he is still alive or not. I hope and pray he is. God, I hope so.

Folks, don't let these men die in vain. Appreciate what they are doing over here in Vietnam. They died protecting you all, and all the people in the United States. We just cannot have the enemy get to the folks back home. We have got to stop them here, before that happens. If it is God's will, we will do it. Tell the people back home to pray for us, as we need their prayers . . .

We raised the American flag on the grounds. We were fighting on Tuesday, the 16th of November. It waved proudly for the Armed Forces and the people of America, as it did in so many battles won in World War II and Korea. I sat beside a tree and looked at it, and hoped I would never see the day it would be torn down and destroyed.

Folks, I am glad Eddy is not here and my son Kenny is not here. I hope they never have to see or experience the horrors of war. I will give my life to see that they don't . . .

As always,
Your son,
Kenneth

PFC Richard E. Marks, Company C, 1st Battalion, 3rd Regiment, 3rd Marine Division

Last Will & Testament
of PFC Richard E. Marks
December 12, 1965

Dear Mom,

I am writing this in the event that I am killed during my remaining tour of duty in Vietnam.

First of all I want to say that I am here as a result of my own desire—I was offered the chance to go to 2nd Marine Division when I was first assigned to the 4th Marines, but I turned it down. I am here because I have always wanted to be a Marine and because I always wanted to see combat.

I don't like being over here, but I am doing a job that must be done—I am fighting an *inevitable* enemy that must be fought—now or later.

I am fighting to protect and maintain what I believe in and what I want to live in—a democratic society. If I am killed while carrying out this mission, I want no one to cry or mourn for me. I want people to hold their heads high and be proud of me for the job I did.

There are some details I want taken care of. First of all, any money that you receive as a result of my death I want distributed in the following fashion.

If you are single, I want you and Sue to split it down the middle. But if you are married and your husband can support you, I want Sue and Lennie to get 75% of the money, and I want you to keep only 25%—I feel Sue and Lennie will need the money a lot more.

I also want to be buried in my Marine Corps uniform with all the decorations, medals, and badges I rate. I also want Rabbi Hirschberg to officiate, and I want to be buried in the same cemetery as Dad and Gramps, but I do not want to be buried in the plot next to Dad that I bought in mind of you.

That is about all, except I hope I never have to use this letter—I love you, Mom, and Sue, and Nan, and I want you all to carry on and be very happy, and above all be proud—

> Love & much more love,
> Rick

Private Marks was killed on 14 February 1966. He was nineteen years old.

Staff Sergeant Nolan Drewry, United States Army

Drewry writes to his sister, Mary.

> *Vietnam, February 1966*
>
> I had to leave for Saigon at the drop of a hat. Some equipment came in and I had to fly down and bring it back. The 17th we lost men going out on convoy. Two of them were old buddies of mine I had known for some time. I try and not get too attached to my men as I feel bad more so than usual when one is lost. Not much to write about here except the usual unpleasant things, no more of that. I hope you can read this. My nerves are getting a little shaky. Write when you can.
>
> Love, N.

Nolan Drewry was killed in action near Bon Long on 8 March, 1966.

Captain Rodney R. Chastant, 1st Marine Air Wing

> *Vietnam, 19 October 67*

Mom and Dad—

Your oldest son is now a captain in the United States Marine Corps. I was promoted yesterday. Of all the men selected for captain, 1,640 men, only about 50 men have been promoted to date. I was one of the 50, to my surprise and pleasure. My effective date of rank is 1 July 1967, which means I have technically been a captain for 3½ months. I am thus due back pay for 3½ months. With this promotion, my annual income is $9,000.00 a year. I'm single, 24 years old, college-educated, a captain in the Marine Corps, and I have $11,000.00 worth of securities. That is not a bad start in life, is it?

As I understand, Dad, you were married about this point in life. There was a war going on then too. I really know very little about those years in my parents' lives. Sometime you will have to tell me about them—what you were doing, what you were thinking, what you were planning, what you were hoping.

Mom, I appreciate all your letters. I appreciate your concern that some of the things you write about are trivial, but they aren't trivial to me. I'm eager to read anything about what you are doing or the family is doing. You can't understand the importance these "trivial" events take on out here. It helps keep me civilized. For a while, as I read your letters, I am a normal person. I'm not killing people, or worried about being killed. While I read your letters, I'm not carrying guns and grenades. Instead I am going ice skating with David or walking through a department store to exchange a lamp shade. It is great to know your family's safe, living in a secure country; a country made secure by thousands upon thousands of men who have died for that country.

In the Philippines I took a bus ride along the infamous route of the death march in Bataan. I passed graveyards that were marked with row after row after row of plain white crosses. Thousands upon thousands. These were American graves—American graves in the Philippines. And I thought about the American graves in Okinawa, Korea, France, England, North Africa—around the world. And I was proud to be an American, proud to be a Marine, proud to be fighting in Asia. I have a commitment to the men who have gone before me, American men who made the sacrifices that were required to make the world safe for ice skating, department stores and lamp shades.

No, Mom, these things aren't trivial to me. They are vitally important to me. Those are the truly important things, not what I'm doing. I hope you will continue to write about those "trivial" things because that is what I enjoy learning about the most.

Your son,
Rod

Captain Chastant was killed in action on 22 October 1968.

Lieutenant James Simmen,
5th Battalion, 60th Infantry (Mechanized)

Simmen writes to his brother.

13 March [1968]

Hi Vern,

The shit has been hitting the fan, but I've managed to miss the spray. One guy was shooting at my ambush last night. I reported it as heavý contact and got eight barrels of artillery to shoot white phosphorus and high explosives in the wood line. We found a body this morning so the colonel was happy.

A company ambushed my platoon, and I only lost one man. A rocket ricocheted off my truck, and the VC charged it. Your prayers must have been talking up a storm to God then. No kidding. I believe!

You'd be surprised how similar killing is to hunting. I know I'm after souls, but I get all excited when I see a VC, just like when I see a deer. I go ape firing at him. It isn't that I'm so crazy. I think a man who freezes killing a man would freeze killing a deer. I'm not perverted, crazy, or anything else. Civilians think such thinking is crazy, but it's no big deal. He runs, you fire. You hunt so I think you'd feel the same way. It isn't all that horrifying.

When you see a man laughing about it, remember he talks the same about killing a deer. Of course, revenge has a part in wanting him just like you want a deer for a trophy and meat. I know I'm not nuts. If I killed a man in the U.S., everyone would stare. Last night I killed and everyone has been patting me on the back, including the battalion commander. What do you think?

A friend got killed on an ambush last week. [The colonel] told him to move in the middle of the night. As he drew in all his claymores, Charlie hit. Last night they told me to move twice. It'll be a cold day in hell when I move. Thirty minutes later I reported "Moved." The colonel isn't about to come out to see where I am. I'm chicken but not stupid!

It isn't all that horrifying. It's rough living in the field, but big deal. They sell mohair tailored sports coats for $35 here and sharkskin suits for $60. I'll buy a few before I leave. What a deal! . . .

Lieutenant Joseph Abodeely, 2nd Battalion, 7th Cavalry, 1st Air Cavalry Division

Abodeely maintained a regular correspondence with his family throughout his entire tour of Vietnam, and in addition kept a diary detailing events. In the letter and diary extract below, Abodeely describes his part in the relief of the Khe Sanh firebase, besieged by the North Vietnamese during their Tet Offensive.

Vietnam 21 March 1968 (1440)

Dear Mom and Dad,

This time it is a legitimate greeting as I received both leters [*sic*] (from both of you) yesterday. Thank you both for writing. Today is the first day of Spring and it's very hot. It's been getting hotter (both day and night) and we still get occasional [*sic*] showers in the evenings. I'm sitting on an air mattress on the ground. I rigged up a little sun shelter composed of 4 stakes in the ground to which I tied my poncho liner [quilt-like cover]. At night 6 of us (my headquarters) sleep in a 3 sided sand bag fortification because the VC frequently rocket and mortar Camp Evans. In case you're wondering what Camp Evans is – it's going to be the 1st Cav's HQ up north as An Khe used to be. My back is to the perimeter wire now so I'm looking into the center where there are many tent structures. There are loads of trucks and jeeps and, of course, choppers. There are underground fueling points where the choppers refuel and can be airborne immediately. My company, D company, is manning the southern sector of the Camp's perimeter. If we go to the field on an operation [sweep of villages or search and destroy], then other units are substituted to cover the perimeter. So far we've been here a few days now. Each night and sometimes during the day, the company sends out patrols. Last night, my platoon went one way and 3d platoon went another. We've been receiving our missions pretty late in the evening so last night we moved out just before dark. We moved about 1000 meters to a hill where I put my platoon in a perimeter defense. Because it was dark and I could not see the surrounding hills to shoot an asimuth on my compass, I called for artillery to shoot two air bursts of white phosphorus from which I took readings in the dark and knew exactly where my platoon was located on the map. When we set up night "goats" [ambushes], we dig in [usually on trails or well traveled paths] and set up trip flares and claymore mines to give warning of enemy approaching. Last night nothing happened and we walked back to this perimeter this morning.

One night when we were sweeping villages along the coast, my platoon set us right on a river to catch any escaping VC moving down the river. I was sitting in my foxhole with baboo [sic] thickets between the river and me when I heard a lot of automatic weapons fire about 30 meters away. I jumped down and got my weapon and then I checked the situation out as I discovered I wasn't being shot at. One of my positions, about 30 meters away along the river, opened up on people getting out of a san pan [boat]. They were VC. One man got away; we captured one man and woman, and killed two women. I had no remorse about seeing the wounded man and woman or the two dead women as we found a Chineese [sic] – Communist grenade and 2 rifles in the boat. One of the dead women had a VC insignia on her clothing. As I stared at her head split open by an M-16 bullet and saw her brains hanging out, I felt no remorse at all. Five of my men were wounded on 27 Feb and my men and I have been shot at too damn many times for me to feel sorry if a young boy or woman dies who sides with or personally participates with those trying to kill my men or men. This incident is just to give some insight into the horror of this war, but none the less, it is war. I read the articles you both sent me and I want the war to end, too; but, I believe we have commitments – to ourselves and to others. We are fighting a worthwhile war but we're not going all out. I believe the government (U.S.) and the people should go all out – send troops – gear the economy, etc. to win the war rather than prolong it. People who want to pull out or stay half-ass either don't realize the military and political repercussions which are bad or they have other interests which they are putting first. No one is brain washing me on this stuff; I just hate to see these times exist.

I must admit though, there are some light moments and good times. I have a good platoon as you would expect because I constantly check on them. There is a water hole right outside the perimeter where the camp purifies its water, and some of my men and I went swimming bare-assed in the water hole. We also washed out fatigues there as there is no laundry set up yet. I wear the same clothes weeks at a time. I haven't had a good bath in months except in water holes or even some murky water holes filled with leaches [sic].

Yesterday, my platoon was on a wire laying detail on the other side of the perimeter. It was hot and the men were tired. Because I'm the platoon leader, I didn't lay wire so I bummed a truck and went to the PX. Beer and coke can only be bought at batallion [sic] level, but I talked a sergeant into selling me 4 cases, of beer for my platoon. I took it back to the perimeter where they were laying wire and we drank beer until we had to come back to our sector of the perimeter. We've been getting a lot of replacements lately so now I have 38 people in my platoon. I was down to 27 at one time.

I don't know how long I'll be here at Evans (between Quang Tri and Hue). We may just work out of Camp Evans for awhile and conduct patrols nearby or maybe they'll send us back along the coast to sweep villages there. There is rumor that we may go to Khe Sanh where the marines are getting rocketed and mortared just about every day. I suspect that if we don't go there, we'll stay here just in case the VC and NVA make another bid for Hue. We're close enough that we can support a defense there.

Ma, I believe I told you before that I got the radio and flashlight batteries. Thanks. I use both. I have my radio in this bunker. We listen to it at night when reception is best. Dad, thanks for the letter and the statistics money-wise, etc. I'm not worried about my money. Don't you worry about me – hang on to what you get through liquidation. I'll have the GI Bill when I get out. I still want to finish law school but I'm seriously considering extending in the Army for 6 months *only* if I get the job I want. That way I'd make captain, get the money, and enjoy myself if I get a job like officer in charge of an R&R center. I'll have to wait and see what happens. Meanwhile, I live day to day hoping I get through it to the next day. I just hope everything turns out all right. I'm glad to hear Bob is doing well in school. I think he'll like teaching. It'll give him the time he needs for extra curricular activities such as hunting and scuba-diving. Tell Bob I can show if [sic] a few tricks about living in the boonies under *very* adverse conditions.

Well, I'll close for now. All is well. Give my regards to everyone – Aunt T, Aunt Emily, Grandma, Uncle Kenny, Rose G., and anyone else who asks about me.

Diary: Friday, March 22 1968. 1507. It's hot. I'm sitting under a poncho liner tied to four stakes for a sun shelter. Tonight my platoon is to go out to set up a goat on Highway 1 to catch any VC setting up mines on the road. We're supposed to be air assaulted but we could go by truck or walk. We turned in one of our M-60 MGs today to get a new one. Rumor still is that we'll go to Khe Sanh. During the evenings, it's been raining.

Saturday, March 23. 0637. My platoon and I are sitting on top of a hill overlooking Highway 1. It's dawn now and I just went to my positions to check if the men were awake. As we moved in last night, three of my men saw two people across the highway on the other side. I thought for sure we'd be sniped at, but we weren't. Today, we'll probably act as a blocking force.

2310. We hit some NVA today. Several of 1st plt. got wounded; one medic killed. My plt. and I moved under fire to get the wounded out. Tomorrow we go back to recover the dead body.

Sunday, March 24. 1635. We air assaulted to find the body. The medic had been shot in the eye. Tonight we go out on a goat here from Camp Evans.

Monday, March 25. 1700. Last night on our goat, it rained. VC started mortaring Camp Evans, but I called artillery in on the mortar positions in the dark. Today, my platoon found the mortar site and brought back mortar rounds and other equipment. The battalion commander and CO were pleased. Now we are at a bridge in an old French bunker. An ARVN Sgt. is in here; we made friends as I talked to him from my translation book.

Tuesday, March 26. 1655. Today I coordinated with a Major at the ARVN compound down the road. On the way back, Sgt. Blank, Pvt. Osman and I stopped and had a beer in the village. We got in trouble with some MPs who passed by and said we were "off limits." A "mamason" who sells stuff nearby came to the bunker. I got "laid" today. My men are filling sandbags now. Some ARVNs are helping them. We are setting claymores and trip flares all around our positions—more than usual. Last night, a VC turned two claymores around. It was good we did not set them off.

Wednesday, March 27. 1115. Last night we spotted some VC moving around and shot at them. I called some artillery illuminations. The "mamason" came today and we bought fourteen more hats. She left some "pot" with me for safe keeping because the ARVNs will kill her if they find out she has it. Since I don't even smoke cigarettes, much less pot, I buried the marijuana by the bunker just in case "mamason" was trying to set me up.

Thursday, March 28. 1130. Some of my men and I are here at the river. I'm sitting here nude on the grassy bank. Some Vietnamese children are washing my pants and socks. We got the word yesterday—we move north. Some of the children are sitting next to me. My men are swimming. We will probably leave the bridge today or tomorrow.

THE VIETNAM WAR, 1965–73

Friday, March 29. 0940. The sun is getting bright now. I'm in the tower bunker. There are a lot of flies. The ARVNs got in a firefight this morning to our south. We could hear the shooting. I've been practicing speaking Vietnamese and I can get by O.K. now. One of the ARVNs told me this morning that four VC slept in the village last night and left in the early morning. My company will probably go back to Camp Evans today.

Saturday, March 30. 1435. My half of the platoon moved to the company site along the road between the bridges. It was relaxing being at the bridge. The kids who sold the cokes and beer were cute. Now, we'll go to Camp Evans to move north near Khe Sanh.

Tuesday, April 2. 0645. We air assaulted to the top of this mountain surrounded by a river on three sides. It's jungle and grassy. I jumped from the chopper and hurt my arm. I could see bomb strikes off in the distance as the sky lit up and the ground shook.

1000. The sun is out. We're on a high mountain top. Today my company is to air assault to a new location to set up there. We just got a log ship with food and water. It was nice sleeping last night.

1720. D Company led the air assault to where we are now. My platoon led a ground movement. We found an NVA site for a 50-caliber anti-aircraft gun. Also some of my plt. found some ammo and grenades. Now we are waiting to see where we'll set up. We're hot and tired.

Wednesday, April 3. 0953. We are sitting in the jungle right now. 3d plt. hit some NVA a little while ago. They got one of their men KIA. The S-3 carried him back on his shoulders and then three of my men took the KIA to the rear. We're waiting for artillery to come in. There are huge bomb craters all around. I can hear the choppers circling the area now. There are trees, high grass, and ferns all around.

1808. We moved to Hill 242. The NVA mortared us; we had ten or eleven wounded. NVA have us surrounded now. One platoon from another company tried to bring us food and water, but got pinned down. I hope we make it through the night. We dug in and made overhead cover.

Thursday, April 4. 1540. Last night we received more mortar and artillery fire. We are now back at the guns. I have my platoon in position on the perimeter. As we came back today, we picked up a couple of the dead and wounded who tried to get us supplies yesterday. When we got back here we saw more dead and wounded. The 2d plt. ldr. of C Company was killed. One medevac chopper was shot up. The NVA here are dangerous. I don't like this area. I hope we all get out alive. I got a card from Colleen today which cheered me up. We didn't have any food or water all day yesterday and for most of today. Everyone is tired.

Friday, April 5. 1550. I got the word today that our battalion may walk to Khe Sanh tomorrow. This could be disastrous. We've incurred a lot of dead and wounded since we've been here. I hope to God we make it alive. I've had a lot of close calls and I'm getting scared again. Everyone is scared of this area. The NVA are near us and good fighters. We're digging in again for tonight.

Jets keep circling the hill. There are also a lot of choppers in the air. Artillery keeps pounding the surrounding areas also. I hope the NVA move out. They ambush a lot here.

Saturday, April 6. 1400. Well, we tried to walk from this LZ to Khe Sanh, but we had to come back as the two forward companies received effective fire. Now our company is supposed to air assault to five hundred meters east of Khe Sanh. I hope we make it; we have many reporters with us.

Sunday, April 7. 1045. We air assaulted to an open area on a mountain top and received light sniper fire. We found an NVA complex with rockets, mortar-tubes and ammo, AK-47s, and all sorts of material. I have a sharp AK-47 which I hope to keep. We are to go to Khe Sanh.

1700. We are at Khe Sanh camped outside the east entrance on Highway 9.

Monday, April 8. 1130. Today, D Company was the first to walk into Khe Sanh on Highway 9 in over two months. The marines had been pinned in, but now they can move. My platoon was the first in. This place is bunkers and trenches. The incoming artillery is deadly. I sent my AK-47 in with Sp. 4 Sanders who I hope will take care of it for me. My men sent in their captured weapons yesterday and they've been distributed out as trading material. This pisses me off, but I talked to the CO and maybe we can do something about it.

2345. I'm writing by moonlight. I'm sitting on guard at a bunker. I can see to the west (Laos) where flares are shot over the mountains. A plane is shooting red streams of tracer bullets into the mountains.

Tuesday, April 9. 1055. Our company is waiting along the air strips to get air lifted back to LZ Mark (named after CO's son—also called LZ Thor) to the fire base there. I've still got a VC bugle that I blow for the company. I blew it when we came to Khe Sanh. There is rumor we'll go back to Evans soon. I hope so.

Thursday, April 11. 0730. Yesterday afternoon my plt. took a bulldozer west down Highway 9 to fill in bomb holes and clear away trees. We found two dead NVA. They smelled and flies and maggots covered the distorted bodies.

Today we moved from LZ Thor to a mountain top overlooking a bridge below. The rest of the company is at another bridge. I'm pissed off because we didn't get food and water because we weren't on the right radio frequency to call the log ship in. The CO didn't even act concerned.

Friday, April 12. 1405. Today my plt. hitched a ride with a Marine convoy (trucks and tanks) to LZ Thor. We're waiting here to go to Khe Sanh and later to Camp Evans. It appears that our work is done here. I hope so. Last night it was cold on the mountain top. The sky looks like rain.

Tim Driscoll, United States Army

Vietnam, March 4, 1968

Well Mom,

There really is a war going on over here. We made contact in daylight yesterday for the first time since I've been here. You know how they say war is not like the movies show it. Well, they're wrong. It's exactly like the movies.

We were on a Company-size patrol when they hit us. 1st plt was in the front, we were next, and 2nd plt was in the rear. Wayne was working with the 2nd plt on the machine guns.

They hit the first plt, and everyone got down. Then first moved up 50 meters, and we moved out to the left. As soon as we moved behind a hedgeline, an automatic weapon opened on us. We just kept moving.

We finally got out of range about 100 meters down the trail. Then we got on line and assaulted a hedgeline 50 meters in front of us. We didn't meet any resistance; so, after we got on the other side, we got down and waited. Then we got the word the 1st plt was in bad shape and needed us. So, we were going to move out on line about 50 meters and then swing to our right and get the gooks in the middle of us and 1st.

We started out on line, keeping low and moving slow. It was a clear, open field we were going across. We were halfway across when fire opened up from our right. Everyone got down, and the St/Sgt started yelling at us to keep moving; so, we being young, brave Marines got back on line and kept moving.

But then the bullets started zipping around our legs and raising dust. We knew for sure they were shooting at us then. We weren't about to stay on line after that. We bolted to the right, ran about 25 meters, and took cover behind dirt piled up all along this road.

We waited there, just the 1st squad (2nd and 3rd squad were behind us), for about five minutes. They weren't shooting anymore; so, we start sticking our fool necks up to see what was happening. And they started shooting again. Now we knew where they were, tho. They were dug in right behind a thick bamboo patch, about 2 squads. At least now we could shoot back. We were doing pretty good—holding our own. Four of them started to run, and we cut them down.

THEN! we started receiving fire from our rear. I started getting scared, then, because we had no protection to the rear. They had us pinned down for ½ hour. We couldn't even raise our heads to see where they were. Finally the 2nd and 3rd squads moved up and cleared up our rear. We continued the fire fight to our front.

By this time, we had taken a few casualties, including our St/Sgt—shot through the neck close to the collarbone. A medevac chopper landed right behind us as we set up a hard base of fire, turning our M-16s on automatic. Our St/Sgt wouldn't leave tho; and he kept running around yelling orders, his neck all patched up. (He thinks he's John Wayne.)

After awhile, we thought we had wiped them out because they kept running and we kept cutting them down. After awhile, the fire stopped; and the St/Sgt wanted a frontal assault on the positions. We didn't like that idea because, if there was one automatic weapon left, it could tear our whole squad to pieces.

We finally made him see the light. We threw a few grenades; and, sure enough, they started shooting again. We just exchanged fire for another hour, and then the TANKS!!! came.

Three tanks with the 2nd plt swept through the position from our right. I saw Wayne with the M-60. There were 3 gooks left. The tanks opened fire when they saw them. Killed two and took one prisoner.

All that took a little over five hours. One of our Corpsmen was put up for a medal.

Wayne told me later that he was feeding the machine gun, and the A gunner was shooting, when a chicom landed right next to the A gunner. He toppled over Wayne, and Wayne had to take charge of the gun. That plt had one killed.

Mike sent me a letter and told me not to tell you he is coming to Nam. I'll write him and tell him how lousy everything is around here. We got mail three times last week, and I got a whole mess of letters from you. I got a letter from Sonny, and he says Dan will be OK. I hope so.

Where do you think I should go for R&R (in 5 months)? Tokyo, Hong Kong, Bangkok, Taipei, Australia, Hawaii, P.I. or Oki?

I'll write soon . . . Tim

Second-Lieutenant Robert ("Mike") Ransom Jr, 4th Battalion, 3rd Infantry

April 1968

Dear Mom and Dad,

Well, I've had my baptism by fire, and it's changed me I think. Two days ago my platoon was on a mission to clear three suspected minefields. We were working with a mechanized platoon with four tracks, and our tactic was to put the tracks on line and just roar through the minefields, hoping to blow them. Since the majority of the VC mines are antipersonnel, the tracks could absorb the explosions with no damage done to them or the people inside. My platoon rode along just as security in case we were attacked. We spent the whole day clearing the three fields and came up with a big zero.

The tracks were then returning us to where we would stay overnight. When we reached our spot we jumped off the tracks, and one of my men jumped right onto a mine. Both his feet were blown off, both legs were torn to shreds—his entire groin area was completely blown away. It was the most horrible sight I've ever seen. Fortunately he never knew what hit him. I tried to revive him with mouth-to-mouth resuscitation, but it was hopeless to begin with.

In addition, the explosion wounded seven other people (four seriously) who were dusted off by medevac, and three others lightly, who were not dusted off. Of the four seriously wounded, one received a piece of shrapnel in the heart and may not survive. The other three were almost completely riddled with shrapnel, and while they will be completely all right, it will be a slow and painful recovery.

I was one of the slightly wounded. I got three pieces in my left arm, one in my right knee, and about twenty in both legs. I am completely all right. In fact I thought I had only gotten one in the arm and one in the knee. It was not until last night when I took off my clothes to take a shower that I noticed the other spots where I had been hit.

I came back to Chu Lai yesterday because my knee is now quite stiff and swollen, and will probably be here a couple of days, what with x-rays and what not. Believe it or not, I am extremely anxious to get back to platoon. Having been through this, I am now a bonafide member of the platoon. They have always followed my orders, but I was an outsider. Now I'm a member of the team, and it feels good.

I want to assure you that I am perfectly all right. You will probably get some sort of notification that I was lightly wounded, and I just don't want you to worry about it at all. I will receive a Purple Heart for it. People over here talk about the Million-Dollar Wound. It is one which is serious enough to warrant evacuation to the States but which will heal entirely. Therefore, you might call mine a Half-Million-Dollar Wound. My RTO, who was on my track sitting right next to me, caught a piece of shrapnel in his tail, and since he had caught a piece in his arm about two months ago, he'll get out of the field with wounds about as serious as a couple of mosquito bites.

I said earlier that the incident changed me. I am now filled with both respect and hate for the VC and the Vietnamese. Respect because the enemy knows that he can't stand up to us in a fire fight due to our superior training, equipment and our vast arsenal of weapons. Yet he is able. Via his mines and booby traps, he can whittle our ranks down piecemeal until we cannot muster an effective fighting force.

In the month that I have been with the company, we have lost 4 killed and about 30 wounded. We have not seen a single verified dink the whole time, nor have we even shot a single round at anything. I've developed hate for the Vietnamese because they come around selling Cokes and beer to us and then run back and tell the VC how many we are, where our positions are, and where the leaders position themselves. In the place where we got hit, we discovered four other mines, all of them placed in the spots where I, my platoon sergeant, and two squad leaders had been sitting. I talked to the mechanized platoon leader who is with us and he said that as he left the area to return to his fire base, the people in the village he went through were laughing at him because they knew we had been hit. I felt like turning my machine guns on the village to kill every man, woman and child in it.

Sorry this has been an unpleasant letter, but I'm in a rather unpleasant mood.

All love,
Mike

Ransom died of wounds on 11 May 1968.

PFC David Bowman,
Company B, 1st Battalion, 8th Cavalry

n.d. [1968]

Dear Civilians, Friends, Draft Dodgers, etc:

In the very near future, the undersigned will once more be in your midst, dehydrated and demoralized, to take his place again as a human being with the well-known forms of freedom and justice for all; engage in life, liberty and the somewhat delayed pursuit of happiness. In making your joyous preparations to welcome him back into organized society you might take certain steps to make allowances for the past twelve months. In other words, he might be a little Asiatic from Vietnamesitis and Overseasitis, and should be handled with care. Don't be alarmed if he is infected with all forms of rare tropical disease. A little time in the "Land of the Big PX" will cure this malady.

Therefore, show no alarm if he insists on carrying a weapon to the dinner table, looks around for his steel pot when offered a chair, or wakes you up in the middle of the night for guard duty. Keep cool when he pours gravy on his dessert at dinner of mixed peaches with his Seagrams VO. Pretend not to notice if he acts dazed, eats with his fingers instead of silverware and prefers C-rations to steak. Take it with a smile when he insists on digging up the garden to fill sandbags for the bunker he is building. Be tolerant when he takes his blanket and sheet off the bed and puts them on the floor to sleep on.

Abstain from saying anything about powdered eggs, dehydrated potatoes, fried rice, fresh milk or ice cream. Do not be alarmed if he should jump up from the dinner table and rush to the garbage can to wash his dish with a toilet brush. After all, this has been his standard. Also, if it should start raining, pay no attention to him if he pulls off his clothes, grabs a bar of soap and a towel and runs outdoors for a shower.

When in his daily conversation he utters such things as "Xin loi" and "Choi oi" just be patient, and simply leave quickly and calmly if by some chance he utters "didi" with an irritated look on his face because it means no less than "Get the h— out of here." Do not let it shake you up if he picks up the phone and yells "Sky King forward, Sir" or says "Roger out" for good-by or simply shouts "Working."

Never ask why the Jones' son held a higher rank than he did, and by no means mention the word "extend." Pretend not to notice if at a restaurant he calls the waitress "Numbuh I girl" and uses his hat as an ashtray. He will probably keep listening for "Homeward Bound" to sound off over AFRS. If he does, comfort him, for he is still reminiscing. Be especially watchful when he is in the presence of women—*especially* a beautiful woman.

Above all, keep in mind that beneath that tanned and rugged exterior there is a heart of gold (the only thing of value he has left). Treat him with kindness, tolerance, and an occasional fifth of good liquor and you will be able to rehabilitate that which was once (and now a hollow shell) the happy-go-lucky guy you once knew and loved.

Last, but not least, send no more mail to the APO, fill the ice box with beer, get the civvies out of mothballs, fill the car with gas, and get the women and children off the streets—BECAUSE THE KID IS COMING HOME!!!!!

Love,
Dave

Sergeant Stanley Homiski, 3/4 Cavalry, 25th Infantry Division

Homiski writes to his wife.

Vietnam, 25 May, 1968

Dear Roberta,

Today is probably the worst day I have ever lived in my entire, short life. Once again we were in contact with Charlie, and once again we suffered losses. The losses we had today hit home, as my best friend in this shit hole was killed. He was only 22 years old and was going on R&R on the first of June to meet his wife in Hawaii. I feel that if I was only a half second sooner in pulling the trigger, he would still be alive.

Strange how short a time a half of a second is—the difference between life and death. This morning we were talking about how we were only two years different in age and how we both had gotten married before coming to this place. You know, I can still feel his presence as I write this letter and hope that I am able to survive and leave this far behind me.

If there is a place called Hell this surely must be it, and we must be the Devil's disciples doing all his dirty work. I keep asking myself if there is a God, then how the hell come young men with so much to live for have to die. I just hope that his death is not in vain.

I look forward to the day when I will take my R&R. If I play my cards right, I should be able to get it for Hawaii so our anniversary will be in that time frame. The reason I say this is by Sept., I will have more than enough time in country to get my pick of places and dates. I promise I will do everything necessary to insure that I make that date, and I hope that tomorrow is quiet.

We will be going into base camp soon for our three-day stand down. I will try to write you a longer letter at that time. Please don't worry too much about me, as if you won't, for I will take care of myself and look forward to the day I am able to be with you again.

Love,
Stan

Larry Jackson, 129 AHC

Vietnam, 11 September 1969

Dear Mom and Dad,

Getting short, Mom, coming home pretty soon. Going to quit flying soon, too much for me now. I went in front of a board for sp/5 will know soon if i made it. I have now 20 oak leaf clusters and some more paper for you. I have flown 1500 hours now, and in those hours I could tell you a lifetime story. I have been put in for a medal again, but this time I have seen far beyond of what ever you will see. That is why I'm going to quit flying. I dream of Valerie's hand touching mine telling me to come home; but I wake up, and it's some sergeant telling me I have to fly. Today I am 21, far away but coming home older.

Love,
Larry

This was Jackson's last letter home. He was killed in action on the following day.

Sergeant Joseph Morrissey, Company C, 1st Battalion, 12th Cavalry, 1st Cavalry Division (Airmobile)

Oct. 1969

Hello Brother,

How are you treating life these days? Have you gotten a grip on those Merrimack students yet? . . .

This place is sort of getting to me. I've been seeing too many guys getting messed up, and I still can't understand it. It's not that I can't understand this war. It's just that I can't understand *war* period.

If you do not get to go to that big peace demonstration [on] October 15th I hope you do protest against war or sing for peace— I would. I just can't believe half of the shit I've seen over here so far . . .

Do you know if there's anything wrong at home? I haven't heard from anyone in about two weeks, and normally I get 10 letters a week. You mentioned in your last letters that you haven't heard from them for a while either. I couldn't take sitting over [in] this place if I thought there was anything wrong at home.

Well, brother, I hope you can get to your students and start them thinking about life. Have you tried any marijuana lectures lately? I know they dig that current stuff.

I gotta go now. Stay loose, Paul, sing a simple song of freedom and I'll be seeing you come summer.

Feb. 9, 1970

Hello Brother,

How is America acting these days? Are the youth still planning new ways to change our world? I think the 70s will see a lot of things changed for the better.

I'm still trying to survive over here but the NVA aren't making it too easy lately. We've just been in contact with them for three days and things aren't looking too bright. When you have bullets cracking right over your head for a couple days in a row, your nerves begin to fizzle. When you're getting shot at, all you can think about is—try to stay alive, keep your head down and keep shooting back.

When the shooting stops, though, you sort of sit back and ask yourself, Why? What the hell is this going to prove? And man, I'm still looking for the answer. It's a real bitch.

Thanks for that *Playboy* you sent me. I sort of forgot what girls looked like. I think the real personality of Jesus has been sort of hidden from us. Either that or no one's wanted to look for it before. If he were alive today he'd probably be living in Haight-Ashbury and getting followed by the FBI who'd have him labeled as a communist revolutionary. He'd definitely be shaking some people up . . .

Well, it's time to make my delicious C-ration lunch. Stay loose and stay young . . .

The beat goes on,
Joe

Thomas Pellaton, 101st Ambulance Division

6 September '70

Dear John,

. . . Saigon [is] completely different from I Corps—almost luxurious. The MACV [Military Assistance Command/Vietnam] complex, where so many of my friends work, has a golf course, Olympic-size swimming pool, etc. But with all the surface glitter and bustle of Saigon, I came away with a very gloomy feeling. The people are frantically trying to make every last cent they can from the Americans before [the soldiers] leave. The war has brought out all the venality imaginable in these people . . .

My friends are somewhat depressed. It now seems they have to rewrite all their reports because the truth they are putting out is too pessimistic. The higher echelons, for their career's sake and the plans of Nixon's Vietnamization, will not allow a bad situation to exist—no matter how true it may be! I saw myself some of the different drafts of some reports that were to go to [General Creighton] Abrams [commander of American forces in Vietnam]—and how they had to be changed to get to him. What a disgrace—and still people are dying every day!

To top this all off, we got hit again last week—twice in one night. The second phase was while we were all watching a Korean floor show. It was mass hysteria when those rockets started coming in! Chairs flying, people running to bunkers! Boy, do I hate those things. I'm going to be a nervous wreck when I get out of here! Then, there has begun a witch hunt for pot smokers. We have a group of self-appointed vigilantes (most of whom are Southern beer-drinking, obnoxious alcoholics! You can see my prejudices in that statement!) who go around spreading untrue rumors about those they do not like. It's at such a point that open warfare might break out in the company. I'm so worked up now because one of the vigilantes is my own boss. It just makes me sick! My own impressions are that the supposed "pot heads" are much easier to work with, more pleasant, never bothersome, and more intelligent than the redneck faction of boozers! Yet that counts for nothing in the Army . . .

John, Peace—my warmest regards—and thanks for letting me ramble on and take out my frustrations.

Tom

THE FALKLANDS WAR 1982

A small archipelago in the South Atlantic, the Falklands Islands became a British colony in 1830. Argentina long disputed their sovereignty and on 2 April 1982, launched an invasion. A Task Force was despatched from Britain which, as it neared the Islands, was attacked by Argentinian fighter planes. HMS Sheffield, Antelope, Ardent, Sir Galahad *and the supply vessel* Atlantic Conveyor *were all lost to air and missile attacks. The British troops when landed had to "yomp" over rough terrain, sometimes carrying their own bodyweight in loads. Although the Argentine army was largely conscripted, it put up fierce battles at Goose Green and Mount Longdon before surrendering on 13 June 1982.*

Sergeant Ian McKay, 3rd Battalion, Parachute Regiment

McKay joined the Parachute Regiment in 1970, aged 17. He writes to his parents in Sheffield.

26 May [aboard] *Canberra*

Dear Mum and Dad

. . . We were all shattered by the loss of the *Sheffield* and I felt the loss more so than most because of the home tie. We are within a few days of meeting up with the main fleet and will certainly be with them when you get this letter. I don't suppose we will hang about as we will be extremely vulnerable at that time and in all honesty we should be safer on the Island. The Canberra is a large target and must be high on the list of Argentinian attack plans. After all the waiting and the seas starting to get up it will be a relief to get off the ship and stretch out. We will probably find ourselves rocking about for a bit until we get our land legs back again having spent so long rolling in time to the ship.

I have some pictures on my wall that Melanie drew for me and even some writing she put on a letter Marica sent. I must admit I have missed them terribly, especially [at missing] another landmark in Melanie's life, that of starting school. Donny wrote me a letter, probably his first ever, mostly about his work with the cadets. He seems to enjoy creeping about in the woods and hills much the same as I did. I think Marica is making the best of her new found freedom, especially as Melanie is off her hands for longer during the day . . . I understand my flowers are blooming and plants coming on. I hope Dad didn't do any damage when he was there. Mind you I don't expect my beloved has done much to improve its [the garden's] looks. I hope the Guards and Ghurkas relieve us when they arrive so we can return and get some leave. We will be up to see you as soon as we can. All my love for ever, Ian

[Falkland Islands n.d.]

Sorry this is a bit scruffy but the bottom of my hole in the ground might not be the cleanest part of the island, but it is the safest.

Some clown has put one of our artillery batteries just behind our postion and as the Argentinian guns try to range in on them they sometimes drop one in [and] around our position, so life isn't dull all the time.

Mail is taking the best part of 3 weeks to get here so I assume the same applies vice versa. It is quite possible we will be on the way home before this gets to you.

Personally I can't wait to get back on board. I have never known a more bleak, windswept and wet place in my life. We spend our life with wet feet trying to dry out and keep warm.

The wind blows constantly but is cooling rather than drying. You cannot walk 50 paces anywhere, even on the mountainside, without walking in a bog.

I thought the Brecon Beacons was bad, but this takes the biscuit.

One of the officers I knew in the depot was shot while standing under a white flag when 2 Para took Goose Green so feelings are quite high in both 2 and 3 Para.

Also the papers we get, again all well out of date, mention only Marines and Guards so if we aren't officially here we might as well come home.

Apart from that bit of grousing things aren't too bad and things should be over one way or another in a week, so you will probably be [seeing] this with hindsight.

We will be home hopefully about two weeks afterwards.

All my love,
Ian

This is the last letter McKay wrote. He was killed at Mount Longdon on the night of 11 June 1982. He was posthumously awarded the VC for bravery.

Murray Duffin, Royal Navy, HMS *Arrow*

Duffin writes to his family.

4 Mess
HMS Arrow
6/6/82

Dear All

I got mailys from you today dated 16–20 April. Thanks very much, they cheered me up no end and believe me I needed it as yesterday was pretty terrible.

At 1400 we went to action stations due to an air threat and straight after [wards] Sheffield was hit by an Exocet fired from an aircraft. As I've told you, this is a devastating missile and one alone can sink a ship. We were the nearest and we went to her aid. As we closed in a sub fired two torpdoes at us. We managed to avoid them both by some skillful manouvering. We went in and after some valiant efforts to save the ship she had to be abandoned as they thought the Sea-Dart mag was going to blow and that would have taken us as well.

I was busy with the torpedoes as we were attacking the sub. Some debris was spotted but we're unsure as to whether it was sunk or not.

When I was not prepping torps I was helping with the casualties which were in the hanger. It wasn't very nice and there are some things I pray I'll never see again.

We took off about 220 and kept them overnight, we all gave up our pits but I only had 0200 to 0600 off during the whole day anyway so I slept on station as it wasn't worth leaving.

I know this isn't much of an account but I don't really want to write it all out . . . The death toll is estimated at 20–30 but I haven't heard any definite reports.

One side of our ship is all battered where we were bouncing off the Sheffield. In fact Arrow's looking pretty sorry for herself altogether what with the punishment we've been taking. I expect once we turn for home we'll work harder than ever painting and cleaning so she looks good for when we get in. Me and Debbie [a crewman] were both told that they were very pleased with the way we worked and it was noted that we were always there to lend a hand—It's nice to be appreciated for a change.

Anyway let's hope that's the first and last time that happens . . . I think it's a good idea, transferring my money into a Deposit

Account so ta very much. As to me needing anything—actually there isn't.

I got four letters from the girl in Guzz—her name's Kerry and she sent me her gold cross and chain to wear as she thought it would protect me and remind me of her. She's being great with letters and stuff so that's nice . . . Anyway folks that's about all. I'm well and in good spirits and the morale aboard is high, especially now that we've had a mail drop. I don't think it could have come at a better time—ie the day after Sheffield got hit.

I've just heard that she's still floating; when we left her she was engulfed in flames and the intention was to sink her with gunfire but then another air attack came and we left rather smartish so I don't know what will happen to her now.

I'm glad everythings ok at home and the pennies are rolling in Don't worry about me. I'll be ok

lots of love
Murray

Anon Argentine Soldier, Argentine Infantry

Falkland Province, Argentina
10 June 1982

My dear family

God willing, when you receive this letter you will all be well. I, despite everything, am well, thanks to God and the Virgin Mary. Children: I don't think it is necessary for me to tell you what is happening here. You will have learned through the television and radio . . . [so] I'll tell you about myself. Well, I am in the front line with the 4th Regiment and the Reserve of the 12th Regiment. We have confrontations every night with the enemy, who are just in front of us.

I fulfill the role of medic and marksman. I have had to attend to various wounded besides, in my company, there are many sick with bronchitis, flu, fever and the beginning of frostbite. I am bearing it and am going to take as much as I can. I am tired, cold, unhappy . . . I want to leave and can no longer see the time of my departure and my being back with *you*. Even though this is my duty, as a man and a soldier of the Fatherland that I am; besides I *swore* to defend my *Fatherland* until death if necessary.

We are about 18 to 20 kilometres from Puerto Argentina [Port Stanley] and some 6 km from Fitzroy, where two enemy fighters we shot down by our airforce (we saw it clearly, because we are on a

position on the ridge called Harrier [Harriet]) We also saw them
bring down another enemy aircraft—a Sea Harrier. I have a cave
between the rocks together with a soldier called Toledo, Ricardo
s/c 62, who is like bread from Heaven. He is my best friend here;
we share our sickness, necessities and fear. Don't call it cowardice,
but a wish to live. Children, I am aware that this letter is very sad
and that it is going to worry you. Be strong. I will be with you soon
. . . I won't you know that you are always in my thoughts and that
I love you. I love you with all my heart and with all my soul. Kisses
and more kisses to you. Love from an Argentine soldier,
     Pichon

Lance Corporal Andrew Mortimore, 1st Battalion, Welsh Guards

Mortimore writes to a fellow soldier in Britain.

23 June [1982] Town Hall Port Stanley

Dear Kay
     Many thanks for the postcard . . . Two weeks ago, as I'm sure
you know, we were hit badly as we waited to go ashore from "Sir
Galahad". By not being where I should be I escaped with singed
hair and a large burn hole in my waterproof. Had I been where I
should have been I wouldn't be writing this. Thanks to your first
aid lessons at least one soldier got away alive who wouldn't had I
not known what I was doing—only two medics got out. The whole
thing was a mess—a mess that got 25 of my mates killed. We were
left in daylight for eight hours without air cover! There was hardly
any warning, just someone screaming AIR RAID WARNING
RED AIR RAID—He never finished it. A 500 lb bomb came
thro'the wall about 15 feet away from me and carried on thro' two
more walls and a floor where it exploded. The guy stood behind
me was killed. I didn't have time to panic or be scared. Even after I
got out I had to go back again to bring some others out. The smoke
was so thick you could walk on it.
     Luckily every other man was carrying a 1 litre Hartmans drip—
these saved a lot of guys with burns. Later on today we're going
back to "Bluff Cove" by chopper for a memorial service. Then the
wreck of the ship will be towed out to sea and sunk as an official
war grave.
     I lost nearly all my kit—I got away in what I was wearing. The
lads from 2 Para who put us up for the night in their sheep shed

were fantastic. Some of them stayed up all night making tea. Next day we were choppered out to HMS Intrepid where we rested and [were] issued with new kit.

Don't know how long before we get home but in the meantime we are doing a Northern Ireland type job in Stanley—patrolling—chatting up the locals, checking possible booby traps etc. Mines are still a big problem—they won't let us use an Argie to find them! Looking after the POWS was a bit like giving treatment to the people in Cusichach who had stolen from us—crazy!

Still thats life—thats war, and I've had enough of this one for the moment . . . love and best wishes

Andy.

THE GULF WAR, 1991

Iraq invaded the adjacent state of Kuwait on 2 August 1990. After diplomatic methods failed to produce a withdrawal, the United Nations launched Operation Desert Storm, the largest concerted military action since World War II.

The Iraqi war machine of Saddam Hussein seemed formidable: a million-strong, hardened in a long war with Iran and possessing enormous firepower. To soften Iraqi resistance the United Nations' Coalition launched a two-week aerial Armageddon of 110,000 sorties against Iraqi targets. The bombardment broke the morale of the Iraqi Army—largely composed of fatigued conscripts with little desire to die for a dictator's cause—and when the Coalition launched its ground invasion on 23 February 1991 it swept through Iraqi positions everywhere. Some 86,000 Iraqis surrendered and within 100 hours the "Mother of All Battles" was over. There were around 8000 Iraqi casualties. Coalition losses were 150 killed in action, a quarter of these, victims of "friendly fire" incidents.

Anon Lieutenant, Iraqi Army

Diary: Tuesday 15 January 1991
Leave was suspended today for officers and men because of the end of the period (granted) by the Security Council for Iraq to withdraw from Kuwait. We are there and it is a historic right that was stolen from us when we could do nothing. The army is in a state of total alert to prepare itself against allied and American aggression expected against our well-loved territory. I am very worried for my parents because I know what these conditions represent for them. But God is good. We wish the war had not happened, but it has, so combat would be welcome.

Tuesday 17 January 1991
"Say this: all that happens is what God has decided for us." [A verse from the Qur' an]. God has spoken truly. This morning at 2:45 a.m. I heard military aircraft. A few seconds later, the guard

came in and told me in a voice tinged with caution, fear and consternation, "Lieutenant, lieutenant, there may be bombing." I dressed quickly and then realized that the American and Atlantic attack against our country was starting and that the war had begun. This is war, with all that the word implies. Afterwards, the enemy planes began their intensive bombing on the airfield that we have been assigned to defend, at As-Salman in Al-Matna province.

I am very worried. Rather I am very worried for my relatives. They are alone out there. And I know how afraid they are.
O God! Protect.
O God! Patience.
O God! Save us all.

Friday 18 January 1991
Heavy enemy bombing continues. The bombing and raids kept up all last night.

Saturday 19 January 1991
Few enemy air raids today because of the bad weather, and our missiles have been fired at Israel for the second time. I am very worried for my relatives.

Sunday 21 January 1991
The bombing and enemy raids began very early today. Air-to-ground missiles began to explode at 3:30 a.m. this morning. I am very worried for my relatives.
O God! Protect.
O God! Save us all.

Monday 21 January 1991
Few enemy raids today. Our military communiques say that the enemy has bombed most of the regions and provinces of Iraq with planes and missiles. I am constantly gripped by anxiety.

Tuesday 22 January 1991
Thanks be to God. Many thanks be given him. Dawn has come and no raids have taken place, at least not so far . . . Now heavy raids have begun again. God protect us! I went to the . . . of the . . . brigade at the bunker to move them to another place because of the raids and heavy bombing at the emplacement. When I got there, I found four bombs. The situation was very difficult, because we had to pass close by them. But God protects. What

an awful sight: one of the soldiers [disturbed] one of the bombs and suddenly it exploded and the soldier disappeared and I saw two pieces of his flesh on the second storey of the bunker. Allah aqbar. What a horrible thing to see. I went back to the regiment and found the first section at another place. They had moved to safety.

Wednesday 23 January 1991
Threatening weather. Time drags. We wait and watch. I am very afraid for my brothers. . . . is in Kuwait. . . . is in Fao and the nearby area. I am most afraid for . . . in the name of God the compassionate and merciful . . . "We have built bulwarks around and behind them and they see nothing." [a verse from the Qur'an] O God, protect! O God, save us! The planes came back to bomb again. They were close and we could see them. "If only I had wings."

Thursday 24 January 1991
The raids began early. They began at about 2:30 a.m. today and have continued heavily without a let-up. I heard news that Bassorah has been bombed heavily. May God have come to help my relatives; I am very worried about them. How I want to see them and find out how they are! God is beneficent. Where are they now? God only knows. Ahhhhhhhhh!

Friday 25 January 1991
The raids stopped today and then started up again after sunset. Leaves had been suspended but were granted again. But that doesn't help me because only 5 percent are given leave. The important thing is that they've begun again. I sent a letter to my relatives and was so worried I forgot to ask about my children and about . . . and . . . and my sister, but I said hello to everybody. I ask God to protect them all.

Saturday 26 January 1991
Enemy air strikes continue, and I'm very worried, depressed and bored. I think about my children.

Sunday 27 January 1991
The air strikes began this morning. I learned before noon today that I have been promoted to the rank of lieutenant and that the decision reached Brigade headquarters after a delay of . . . weeks. This afternoon I got back the letter I had sent to my relatives. It was returned to me because the soldier who was going to mail it

didn't go on leave. I was very upset by this turn of events. My mind and heart are with my relatives, and only my body is with the army. I very much need to see my relatives. I had a dream yesterday and it was not a good omen at all.

Monday 28 January 1991
The enemy air raids continue and I am in a (shelter). The top of it is only tent canvas. God protect us all. After sunset, a flock of sheep came up to us. Apparently the owner of the flock had been killed in the air raids. The enemy with his modern planes has launched air strikes on a shepherd. Maybe the enemy took the sheep for nuclear or chemical or petroleum sheep. For shame.

Tuesday 29 January 1991
This evening, after a series of enemy air strikes and watching their in-flight refueling over our territory, I decided to go to Company . . . in the tank battalion that belongs to the armored brigade. I went to sleep without eating. All the food I had was a little gruel and tea.

Wednesday 30 January 1991
The air strikes began heavily today and I am still alive. I could be killed at any moment. I am more afraid for my relatives than I am afraid to die. The air raids are nothing new to me, but I am very worried.

Thursday 31 January 1991
The attacks continue. Only one officer went on leave. It was . . . It was agreed that I would go on leave if war breaks out between Iraq on one side and 29 countries on the other. That is just not fair.

2 February 1991
I was awakened this morning by the noise of an enemy air raid. I ran and hid in the nearby trench. I had breakfast and afterwards something indescribable happened. Two enemy planes came toward us and began firing at us, in turn, with missiles, machine guns and rockets. I was almost killed. Death was a yard away from me. The missiles, machine guns and rockets didn't let up. One of the rockets hit and pierced our shelter, which was penetrated by shrapnel. Over and over we said, "Allah, Allah, Allah." One tank burned and three other tanks belonging to 3rd Company, which we were with, were destroyed. That was a very bad experience.

Time passed and we waited to die. The munitions dump of the 68th Tank Battalion exploded. A cannon shell fell on one of the soldiers' positions, but, thank God, no one was there. The soldiers were somewhere else. The attack lasted about 15 minutes, but it seemed like a year to me. I read chapters in the Qur'an. How hard it is to be killed by someone you don't know, you've never seen and can't confront. He is in the sky and you're on the ground. Our ground resistance is magnificent. After the air raid, I gave great thanks to God and joined some soldiers to ask how each of them was. While I was doing that, another air attack began. 2 February at 2000 hours.

3 February 1991
Few air raids today. The pain I've been having all the past 6 months has returned. I am sad. In the last 5 days I've eaten only a few dates and boiled lentils. What have we done to God to endure than? I have no news of my relatives. How can I, since I don't know what is happening to me.

What will become of me? What is happening to them? I don't know. I don't know. God protect them. How I miss my children. I know that [woman's first name] is very, very frightened. What happens to her when she hears the planes and missiles? I don't know. P.S.: 3 February 1991 at 2100 hours. While I was writing these lines, another air raid occurred.

Monday 4 February 1991
Few air raids today. I stayed alone in the shelter. Worried about the bombing.. worried about hunger . . . worried about water . . .

Tuesday 5 February 1991
I woke up this morning to the sound of enemy air raids. I quickly put on my uniform and ran to the trench. I had my helmet on. Thank God, the raid ended. In the afternoon I went to wash up inside an armored troop carrier. I washed quickly because these vehicles are usually targets for aircraft.

Wednesday 6 February
I awakened to the noise of air raids. I dressed quickly and put on my helmet. Afterwards, I had breakfast. Then there was another air attack. I ran to the trench. It was small, but it held all three of us: myself, the lieutenant in charge of the 2nd Section of the 3rd Company of the Tank Battalion and a communications man. The

planes dropped a lot of bombs before returning to Saudi Arabia. We were covered with dirt. We were buried alive. God is good.

Thursday 7 February 1991
Not many air strikes on us. I thought of my relatives. My illness is getting worse and I feel tired. The planes come and go, and the shelter holds many a comrade.

Friday 8 February 1991
Few air raids today. At about 2000 hours, while I was talking with a guard, a plane flew over us, very very low.

Saturday 9 February 1991
I woke up along with Lieutenant[-] head of the 1st section of my 3rd Tank Company, who was in the same shelter with me, when planes began to attack. We went to the bay trench. The planes left without firing at us. The air raids began, and with them began my descent into the grave.

Monday 11 February 1991
Enemy planes have come back and bombed heavily. We went to the trenches or, rather, the graves. I was very upset when I heard that people born in 1973 are being drafted. That means that my brother . . . will have to go into the army. He is naive. He can't manage by himself. He'll make a fool of himself. He's too picky about his food. Where will he find room for that in the army? And especially this army! How I wish I were with him so I could help him.

Tuesday 12 February 1991
I have been here for more than 35 days because leaves were canceled. I am bored and sad. This morning, I learned that 26 soldiers from our division were condemned to death for deserting the front. They were apprehended near Samawa and executed at 2nd Division headquarters. Two of them were from the 68th Tank Battalion that we were with. They were unlucky. Their shame is very great. God is good. God protects.

Thursday 14 February 1991
I woke up at 8 a.m. this morning and said my prayers. I couldn't make my ablutions with water before praying, so I had to use the sand that had fallen on me and covered me from head to foot in an enemy air raid that had been going on continuously since midnight.

The planes launched missiles at our positions and the tanks that
were with us, believing that the tanks were missile-launching sites.
Smoke and dust rose into the sky and mingled with the smell of
powder. None of us thought we could get out of this bombardment
safely. But thanks be to God. I stood because I couldn't get into
the trench on account of my illness. But, thank God, I wasn't hit.

Friday 15 February 1991
I went to field hospital number . . . because I was very ill. I heard
that Iraq has decided to withdraw from Kuwait.

Saturday 16 February 1991
I feel so fatigued that I can't breathe, and I think I am going to
faint at any moment from my illness. The only thing that you can
find everywhere in the world is air, and yet I can't breathe it. I
can't breathe, eat, drink or talk. I have been here for 39 days and
have not yet gone on leave. The planes came and bombed Battalion
headquarters. Most of the positions were destroyed and three
soldiers were killed. When the planes came to bomb us, I remained
standing because I can't go into the trench.

Sunday 17 February 1991
My illness is getting worse. I am short of breath. I hurt. I have
begun taking medicine; I don't know what it is for, but the main
thing is to take it because I know the medicine can't cause me any
more pain than I'm already enduring. The air raids have started up
again.

[Last entry]

SOURCES AND ACKNOWLEDGEMENTS

The editor has made every effort to locate all persons having any rights in the selections appearing in this anthology and to secure permission from the holders of such rights. Any queries regarding the use of material should be addressed to The Editor, c/o Robinson Publishing.

Lt. James Waller (1775 letter), *Historical Records of the Royal Marines Forces*, ed. Paul Harris Nicolas, 1844; Capt. W.G. Evelyn (1775 letter), *The Evelyns in America: Compiled from Family Pages and Other Sources 1608–1805*, ed. G.D. Scott, 1881; Abner Stocking (1775 diary), 'The Journal of Abner Stocking as Kept by Himself During His Long and Tedious March Through the Wilderness to Quebec', *The Magazine of History*, 1911; Albigence Waldo (1777 diary), 'Journal of Valley Forge', A. Waldo, *Pennyslvania Magazine of History and Biography*, 1896; Solomon Downe (1780 diary), *Journal of a Cruise in the Fall of 1780 in the Private Sloop of War, Hope*, 1872; Corporal George Robertson (1793 letters), *Everyone a Witness*, A.F. Scott, 1970; J. Wilkinson (1794 letter), ref DDWD 105/1, North Archives Office, U.K., first printed in *The Age of Napoleon* ed. Keith Rayner; Midshipman R.F. Roberts (1805 letter), *Letters of English Seamen*, ed. E. Moorhouse, 1910; Adam Neale (1809 letters), *Letters from Portugal and Spain*, A. Neale, 1809; Private William Wheeler (1811 letters), *The Letters of Private Wheeler*, ed. Basil Liddell-Hart, 1951; Ensign John Mills (1812 letters and diary), *For King and Country: The Letters and Diaries of John Mills, Coldstream Guards, 1811–1814*, ed. Ian Fletcher, 1995; Private Charles Stanley (1815 letter), red DD191/1, Nottinghamshire Archives Office, U.K., first published in *The Age of Napoleon*, ed. Keith Rayner; John Marshall (1815 letter), *Additional Particulars to the Battle of Waterloo, 1815*, J. Booth, 1817; Lieut. William Turner (1815 letter), *History of the XIII Hussars*, C.R.B. Barrett, 1911; Samuel Stubbs (1812 letter), *The Magazine*

of History, 1929; James Miller (1812 letter), Special Collections,
US Military Academy Library, West Point, NY; Ensign Thomas
Warner (1812, 1813 letters), 1812 Re-enactors Home Page,
www.haemo-sul.cum/thomas/thomas.html; Lieut Napoleon
Dana (1845, 1846 letters); *Monterrey is Ours!: The Mexican
War Letters of Lieutenant Dana, 1845–1847*, ed. Robert H.
Ferrell, 1990. Copyright © 1990 University Press of Kentucky;
Private Carr White (1846 letter), The Ohio Historical Society,
Columbus, Ohio; Captain Edmund B. Alexander, Special Col-
lections, US Military Academy Library, West Point, NY; Wil-
liam A. Montgomery (1861 letter) 33rd Va. Vol. Inf. Company A
web page; John Ervine, VMI Archives; George Sargent (1861
letter), New Hampshire Historical Society, Concord, first pub-
lished in *Yankee Correspondence: Civil War Letters between New
England Soldiers and the Home Front*, ed. Nina Silber and Mary
B. Sievens, 1996; Isaac Brooks (1861 letter), Boston Public
Library, Rare Books and Manuscripts, MS.Am 1546, first published in *Yankee Correspondence*; *op.cit.*; Charles Wodward Hut-
son (1861 letter), The Hutson Papers, #362, Southern Historical
Collection, University of North Carolina at Chapel Hill; Capt
Albion Martin, 33rd Va. Vol. Inf, Company Web page, copyright
© Carolyn Martin Rutherford and David Rutherford; Wilbur
Fisk (1861 letters), *Anti: Rebel: The Civil War Letters of Wilbur
Fisk*, ed. Eric Rosenblatt, 1983, copyright © 1983 Eric Rosenblatt; Austin Perkins (1861, 1862 letters), copyright © Jana
Alexander; Francis William Kimble (1862, 1863 letters), copy-
right © 1996, 1997, 1998 DCD; Lieut. Dana Green (1862 letter),
US Postal Services web site; Lieut-Col. William M. Bentley
(1862 letter), MS 117, VMI Archives; Henry C. Clines (1862
letter), Yale University Library, Civil War Manuscripts Collec-
tion, first printed in *Yankee Correspondence*, *op.cit*; William
Cooley (1862 letter); The Cooley Papers #3678, Southern Historical Collection of the University of North Carolina at Chapel
Hill; Marshall Phillips (1862 letter), Maine Historical Society,
Portland; William Willoughby (1862 letter), American Antiquar-
ian Society, Worcester, Mass. W.A. Willoughby Papers; Lieutenant Edwin I. Kursheedt (1862 letters), Manuscripts
Department, CB 3926 Wilson Library, University of North
Carolina at Chapel Hill; Dennis Ford (1862), Life in the 28th
Massachusetts: Letters by the Soldiers web page; Oliver Giberson (1862 letter), Letters to and from Civil War Participants web
page, transcribed by Thomas Hansen; Sergeant Ambrose Doss
(1862 letter and notification of death), Selected Letters of Ser-

geant Ambrose Doss, 19th Alabama web page, copyright © 1995; Sergeant Charles Wickesberg (1862, 1863 letters), translated Ingeborg Wolferstetler, compiled by Alfred Wickesberg, 1961; Galutia York (1862, 1863 letters), copyright © Colgate University Libraries; Corporal Adam Muenzenberger (1862 letters), The Civil War Letters of Corporal Adam Muenzenbergcr Web page, copyright © Professor M. Lamers and Clara M. Lamers; William H. Jackson (1862 letter), Letters of William H. Jackson Web page, copyright © Judith Carver Fieldhouse; Captain Michael Shuler (1862 diary), 33rd Va. Vol. Inf. Company A web page; David Humphrey Blair (1862, 1864 letters), Civil War Diary and Letters of David Humphrey Blair web page, edited by Raymond R. Parker, copyright © 1989 Raymond R. Parker; John Garibaldi (1863 letters), VMI Archives; Reuben Thornton (1863 letter), Public Library, Providence, RI., C. Fiske Harris Collection on the Civil War, first published in *Yankee Correspondence*, *op.cit*; Samuel Cormany (1863 diary), *The Cormany Diaries: A Northern Family in the Civil War*, ed. James Molr, 1982; Corporal George Bolton (1863 letter), www.cwc.isu.edu; Private Edmond Hardy Jones (1863 letters), copyright © Charles Jordan, reprinted by permission of C.L. Jordan with acknowledgement to Addie Lee Jones; Private John F. Brobst (1864 letter), *Well, Mary: Civil War Letters of a Wisconsin Volunteer*, ed. Margaret Brobst Roth, 1964; Anon (1864), *A Grand Army of Black Men*, ed. Edwin S. Redkey, 1992; Lewis Warlick (1864 letter), McGimsey Papers, 2680, Southern Historical Collections, University of North Carolina at Chapel Hill; Private Frederick Buerstatte (1864 diary), *Manitowoc Country Historical Society Newsletter*, March 1975, vol 9, no. 2 translation and copyright © 1974 George Ermne; James Harden (1864 letter), *A Grand Army of Black Men*, *op.cit*; William A. Gray (1865 diary), The Iowa Civil War web page; Abram Fulkerson. MS#0363, VMI Archives; Lieut Albert Barnitz (1868 letter), *Life in Custer's Cavalry: Diaries and Letters of Albert and Jennie Barnitz, 1867–1868*, ed. Robert M. Utley, 1967; Second Lieut. Charles W. Larned, (1873 letters), edited by George Frederick Howe, *Mississippi Valley Historical Review*, No 39, December 1952; Lieut. T.W. Holdsworth, *Campaigns of the Indus*, ed. A. Holdsworth, 1840; John Hopkins (1854, 1855 letters), *Letters Received During the Crimean War from John Hopkins*, n.d.; Douglas A. Reid (1855 letters), *Soldier-Surgeon: The Crimean War Letters of Douglas A. Reid*, ed. Joseph O. Bayler and Alan Conway, 1968; Henry Moses (1879 letter), *Red Soldier*, F.

496 Acknowledgements

Emery, 1976; William Meredith (1879 letter), *Red Soldier op.cit*;
Richard Stevens (1879 letter), *Red Soldier, op.cit*; Gunner Osman
Green (1900, 1901 letters), *My Reminiscences of the Latter Part of
the Boer War and the Guerilla War from 1900 to 1902*, Osman
Green, n.d. reprinted by permission of the Portman and Colling-
wood families, copyright © 1998 the descendants of Osman
Green; Lieut. David Miller (1901 letter), *The Great Boer
War*, B. Farwell, 1972; Lieut. Frank Isherwood, *Kathleen and
Frank*, C. Isherwood, 1971; Walter Limmer (1914 letter), *Ger-
man Students War Letters* Philip Witkopp, 1929; B. J. Fielder
(1914, 1915 letters), Imperial War Museum; Lothar Dietz (1914
letter), *German Students War Letters, op.cit*; Fritz Meese, *German
Students War Letters, op.cit*; Werner Liebert, *German Students
War Letters, op.cit*; Second Lieut. A.D. Gillespie (1915 letter),
Letters from the Front, John Laffin; Major Oliver Hogue (1915
letter), *Letters from the Front, op.cit*; Private Horace Bruckshaw
(1915 diary), *The Diaries of Private Horace Bruckshaw, Royal
Marines Light Infantry, 1915–1916*, ed. Martin Middlebrook,
1979; Sergeant S.V. Britten (1915 diary), *Voices and Images of the
Great War*, Lyn Macdonald, 1988; Montague Goodbar (1915
diary), Imperial War Museum; Second Lieut. Graham Greenwell (1915 letters), *An Infant in Arms*, Graham H. Greenwell
MC, 1972; Capt Rowland Fielding, *War Letters to a Wife*,
Rowland Fielding, 1929; Capt. Norman D. Down, *Temporary
Heroes*, 1917; Hugo Muller (1915 letter), *German Students War
letters, op.cit*; Athanse Poirier, *L'Evangeline*, 26, 11 1916, pub-
lished on the Internet as *Lettres du front d'Athanse Poirier*, C.
Leger, English trans. Joyce Lewis; Francis James Mack (1917
letter), *Trenches on the Web* Internet site, reprinted by permission
of Frank Mack; Capt. Bill Bland (1916 letter), Imperial War
Museum; Lance Corp. Thomas Part (1916 diary), The Diary of
Thomas Reginald Part web page, transcribed by Pauline Carter
and David Jones, copyright © 1997 Pauline Carter; Lieut. E.
Russell-Jones (1916 diary), Imperial War Museum; Private
Arthur Hubbard (1916 letter), Imperial War Museum; Fredrich
Steinbretcher (1916 letter), *German Students War Letters, op.cit*;
Lieut Brian Lawrence (1916 letter), *Letters from the Front*, ed.
Ian Fletcher, 1991; George Cracknell (1916 letter), Imperial War
Museum; Adolf Sturmer (1916 letter), *German Students War
Letters, op.cit.*; Helmut Zschuppe (1916, 1917 letters), *German
Students War Letters, op.cit.*; Lieutenant Eric Marchant (1917
letter), Imperial War Museum; Rifleman B. P. Eccles, *Voices and
Images of the Great War. op.cit.*; Captain John Coull (1917 letter),

Imperial War Museum; Lieut. Henri Desagneaux (1916 diary), *A French Soldier's Diary*, Emfield Press, 1975; Rudolf Kruger (1917 letter), *German Students War Letters, op.cit.*; George W. Lee (1917 letter), US Postal Services web site; Private George Barlow (1917 letter), US Postal Services web site; Lieut. Lambert Wood (1917 letter), *Letters*, Lambert Wood 1936; Rudolph Bowman (1918 letter), file 180920, World War I Document Archives web site; Lieut. A. J. Robinson (1919 letter), Imperial War Museum; Private Charles Bottomley (1918 diary), Veterans Affairs Canada web site; Bosco Jones (1937, 1938 letters), Imperial War Museum; Will Lloyd (1937 letter), *Miners Against Fascism*, Hywell Francis, 1984; Jim Brewer (1937 letter), *Miners Against Fascism. op.cit.*; Jim Strangward (1938 letter), *Miners Against Fascism, op.cit.*; Edwin Greening, *Miners Against Fascism, op.cit.*; Miles Tomalin (1938 letters), Imperial War Museum, reprinted by permission of Claire Tomalin; Sergeant Karl Fuchs (1939, 1940, 1941 letters), *Sieg Heil!: The Letters of Tank Gunner Karl Fuchs*, ed. Horst Fuchs Richardson, 1987; Jack Toomey (1940 letter), Imperial War Museum; Sergeant L. D. Pexton (1940 diary), Imperial War Museum; D. Wissler (1940 diary), Imperial War Museum; Flying Officer Michael Scott (1941 diary), Imperial War Museum; Pilot Officer Victor Bagley 1940 letter), Imperial War Museum; Flight Lieut. Laurence Stockwell (1942 letter), Imperial War Museum; Wolfgang Knoblich (1942 diary), *True to Type*, Hutchinson, 1946; Corp. John Green (1942 diary), reprinted by permission of R. K. Green, copyright © 1998 family of John Green; Frank Curry (1942 diary), Veterans Affairs Canada web site; Private Milton Adams (1942 letter), *Taps for a Jim Crow Army*, ed. Phillip McGuire, 1983; Troop Sgt Clive Branson (1942, 1944 letters), *British Soldier in India: The Letters of Clive Branson* 1944; Anon German Soldiers (1943 letters); *Last Letters from Stalingrad*, 1956; Sgt Harry Schloss (1943 diary), *American Diaries of World War II*, ed. Don Vining 1986, The Pepys Press, NY; Sgt Sidney Glassman (1943 letter), *Jewish Youth: Letters from American Soldiers*, J. Rontch, 1945; Sgt Carl Goldman (1943 letter), *Jewish Youth op, cit.*; Sgt Sam Solomon (1943, 1944 letter), *Jewish Youth*; Lieut.-Commander Morris D. Coppersmith (1944 letters), *When Victory is Ours: Letters Home from the South Pacific*, 1943–45 web page, ed. Galia Berry, copyright © 1996 Galia Berry; Arnold Rahe (1943 letter), US Postal Services web site; Lieut. Joseph Feldman (1944 letter), *Jewish Youth: Letters from American Soldiers*, J. Rontch, 1945; Corp. Samuel Furash, *Jewish*

Youth, op. cit.; Private Bernard Sasnowitz (1944 letter), *Jewish Youth. op. cit.*; Petty Officer Milton Seltzer (1944 letter), *Jewish Youth, op. cit.*; Corp. G.E. Hughes, Imperial War Museum; Col. G. Tilly (1944 letter, Imperial War Museum; Jack Clark (1945 letter), *Last Letters Home*, Tamasin Day-Lewis, 1994; Louis Rose (1945 letter), Imperial War Musuem; Major Patrick Angier (1950, 1951 letters), Imperial War Museum; Lance Corp. D.G. Kaye (1951, 1952 letters), Imperial War Museum; Lieut. Frederick P. Pelser (1951 letter), US Postal Services web site; Private James Cardinal (letter), US Postal Services web site; James Lutze (letter), Korean War web site copyright © David J. Lutze; Gunner Eric Stowe (1951, 1952 letters), Imperial War Museum; Second Lieut. Julian J. Potter (1951 letters), Imperial War Museum; Sgt John Woods (1964 letter), *Letters from Vietnam*, ed. Bill Adler, 1967; Joe Pais (1965 letter), *Letters from Vietnam, op. cit.*; Private John O'Halloran (1965 letter), *Letters from Vietnam, op. cit.* Kenneth W. Bagby (1965 letter), *Letters from Vietnam, op. cit.*; P.F.C. Richard E. Marks (1965), *The Letters of Richard E. Marks USMC*, 1967, copyright © 1967 Gloria D. Kramer, executrix of the estate of Richard E. Marks; Staff Sgt Nolan Drewery (1966 letter), US Postal Services web site; Capt. Rodney R. Chashant (1967 letter), *Dear America: Letters Home from Vietnam*, ed. Bernard Edelman, 1985, copyright © 1985 The New York Vietnam Veterans Memorial Commission; Second Lieut. Mike Ransom (1968 letter), *Dear America, op.cit.*; Sgt Stanley Homiski (1968 letter), copyright © 1997 Stanley Homiski; Lieut. Joseph Abodeely (1968 letters and diary), reprinted by permission of Joseph Abodeely in recognition of 'all the splendid soldiers who served with me in the first Air Cavalry Division'; Lieut. James Simmen (1968 letter), *Dear America, op.cit.*; Tim Driscoll (1968 letter), Vietnam Veterans Homepage, copyright © 1997 Tim Driscoll; Pfc David Bowman (1968 letter), *Dear America, op.cit.*; Sgt Joseph Morrissey (1969, 1970 letters), *Dear America; op.cit.* Larry Jackson (1969 letter), copyright © Mark Jackson; Thomas Pellaton (1970 letter), *Dear America, op.cit.*; Lance Corp. Andrew Mortimore (1982 letter), Imperial War Museum; Anon. Argentine Soldier (1982 letter), Imperial War Museum; M. Duffin (1982 letter), Imperial War Museum; Sgt. Ian McKay VC (1982 letters), Imperial War Museum; Anon. Iraq Lieut. (1991 diary), discovered by Jacques Godelfrein, trans. from French by Sheryl Blackstone and Donald Webb, Historical Text Archive, Mississippi State University, www.msstate.edu.